Management

meeting and exceeding customer expectations

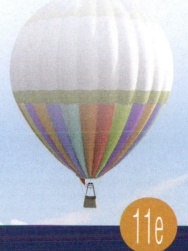

11e

Management

meeting and exceeding customer expectations

Warren R. Plunkett

Emeritus, Wright College

Gemmy S. Allen

North Lake College

Wessex Press, Inc.
www.wessexlearning.com

Wessex Press, Inc.

www.wessexlearning.com

Founded in 2007 by Prof. Noel Capon (R. C. Kopf Professor of International Marketing; Chair of the Managerial Marketing Division at Columbia University Business School), Wessex Press, Inc. is a small publisher of marketing, account management, sales, and other higher education and continued learning textbooks. The company's goal is to provide high quality learning tools without charging prohibitive prices. Publishing under the brands Wessex Press and AxcessCapon, Wessex Press, Inc. offers titles in multiple formats: print (hard cover, paperback), PDF, and ePub.

Management: Meeting and Exceeding Customer Expectations — 11th edition
Walter R. Plunkett, Gemmy S. Allen

Editor
Lyn Maize

Copy Editor
Janet Garraty

Book / Cover Design / Production
Anna Botelho

Indexer
Judi Gibbs

ISBN: 978-0-9967578-1-2 (hard cover / color interior)
     978-0-9967578-2-9 (soft cover / black interior)
     978-0-9967578-3-6 (Active Learning Edition)
     978-0-9967578-4-3 (ePub – Kindle)
     978-0-9967578-5-0 (ePub – iTunes)

We dedicate this book to our past and present students, who have taught us how to be better managers.

Brief Table of Contents

Table of Contents

Appendices

This eleventh edition of *Management: Meeting and Exceeding Customer Expectations* is a comprehensive survey of the functions of management as they are currently being applied in the United States and around the world. The content and features are structured to reinforce three continuing themes that are woven into the chapters' narratives: (1) the never-ending effort by managers and organizations to meet or exceed customers' needs, (2) the need organizations and their people have to be guided by effective leadership, and (3) the growing use of technology, including social media.

The authors have made every effort to keep this text objective, timely, and interesting to both the student and the instructor. All case problems, examples, and features portray actual companies and managers in action. Companies have been selected to provide balance between large and small organizations representing service, manufacturing, and retailing industries. Successes as well as failures are included to lend perspective and aid in understanding.

PUTTING THIS BOOK IN CONTEXT

Your study of management should not be and does not need to be purely theoretical, abstract, and distant. Throughout your study of this text, try to relate what you read and discuss to your own real experiences at work, in the classroom, on the athletic field, and at home. You have already been practicing—and perhaps violating—many of the principles of management. What you are about to learn is an extension and refinement of what you already know—a blending of it with the experiences of others.

Although you will be reading each chapter as a separate area of study, try to relate it to what you have experienced and read previously. By linking the content of each chapter to that which has preceded it, you will begin to appreciate that management is a tapestry with many threads that run parallel to and across one another. For example, planning relates to all the management functions; it is part of every management activity in much the same way as is communicating. Periodically step back from your study to see the "big picture" of which each chapter is but a part.

Upon completion of this text and course, you will have developed your own philosophy of management and be armed with the essentials necessary for improving your career. You will become a better manager of your own concerns as well as the work of others.

FEATURES OF THE ELEVENTH EDITION

This text is designed to introduce you to terminology, theories, and principles at the core of business management, and to show you how management is practiced in the real world of business. The book is divided into six comprehensive parts, comprising a variety of examples, applications, exercises, and devices. Each chapter contains the following components:

- A list of specific **Learning Objectives**—concepts to be mastered through chapter content—at the beginning of each chapter. Each Learning Objective is also highlighted in the page margin to identify where the content addresses the objective.

- A chapter-opening **Management in Action** quiz that helps students relate chapter concepts to their own lives in a fun and engaging manner.

- **Key Terms** defined within the chapter's narrative are also highlighted in the page margin and listed at the end of each chapter with page numbers where you can locate the Key Term. Key Terms with definitions are also presented in the *Glossary* at the back of this book.

- Figures designed to illustrate and summarize essential concepts; also available as images in PowerPoint and the *Active Learning Edition*.

In This Edition

- **Quality Management** feature in each chapter that explores techniques for continuous improvement in the high-performance workplace.

- **Managing Social Media** feature highlighting modern technologies, such as social networking and blogging that can make the manager more productive and the business more successful.

- **Global Applications** feature demonstrating the successful application of one or more of a chapter's concepts to the practice of management in other countries. At least one critical thinking question is found at the end of this feature.

- **Ethical Management** feature reporting on managers facing decisions that contain a variety of issues and consequences for themselves and others. At least one critical thinking question is found at the end of this feature.

- **Valuing Diversity and Inclusion** feature depicts unique ways in which organizations show appreciation for their diverse employees. At least one critical thinking question is found at the end of this feature.

Following each chapter's content is a review section called **Review What You've Learned**, which includes:

- **Chapter/Appendix Summary** providing a narrative explanation for each of the chapter's learning objectives.

- **Key Terms** list with page references for quick study and test preparation.

- **Review Questions** designed to assist in mastery of the chapter's key concepts and terms.

- **Discussion Questions for Critical Thinking** intended to provide an opportunity to analyze and apply the chapter's concepts to practical situations.

Following each chapter's review is an application section called **Apply What You Know**, which includes:

- **Managing Social Media Exercises** designed to use current technology, especially social media, to apply one or more of the chapter's key concepts.

- **Experiential Learning Exercises** presenting managers and organizations and their attempt to cope with the major issues raised in that chapter.

A video case for each chapter is found online at the book's companion website!

HIGHLIGHTS OF THE CONTENT

Included in this edition are references to and explanations of many of the most important current trends, issues, topics, data, events, and theories in business today. Much of this information is provided in the form of examples, and these examples reflect the global nature of enterprise in the twenty-first-century. Some highlights include:

- Business organizations that range from global giants to smaller domestic firms, such as PepsiCo, Groupon, Samsung, Siemens, Facebook, Nokia, Facebook, Motorola, Toyota, Tenet Healthcare, Semco, Deloitte, Risk International, Datatec, General Motors, Coca-Cola, Barnes & Noble, Merlin Metalworks, Alcoa, Toshiba, the Container Store, Building Blocks International, VF Corporation, GB Tech, and many more.

- Topics specific to the issue of diversity and inclusion such as the benefits of collaboration, mature workers, workplace diversity audits, cultural heritage in business, and the emergence of chief diversity officers.

- Ethical issues surrounding such topics as public mistrust of business, unannounced layoffs, database marketing, peer reviews, employing illegal immigrants, payoffs and kickbacks, downsizing, and the production of knockoffs.

- The latest information on quality management topics, including flowcharting, just-in-time production, the Socratic Method, *kaizen*, the Scientific Method, and the PDCA Cycle.

- Social Media technologies and topics, such as mobile sites, learning communities, crowdsourcing, workplace wikis, monitoring a corporate image online, geolocation-based social networking, social bookmarking, customer communications on the web, metrics for social media, and enterprise social networks.

- And finally, emerging thinking on management-related topics such as interpreneurship, open leadership, managing varying age groups from millennials to Baby Boomers, enterprise 2.0, rightsizing, technology-based communications, and twenty-first-century career skills.

ORGANIZATION OF THE CONTENT

Part 1: Management Concepts

Chapter 1 explores what management is about, why it is necessary, the needs managers must address, management functions, management roles, management skills, and management myths and realities.

Chapter 2 takes you on a journey through the past, examining the evolution of management theory from the classical schools through today. It assesses the contributions made by each and explains the links among them.

Chapter 3 lists and defines the internal and external environments that affect and challenge the practice of management. Business as an open system and the demands of stakeholders are the major focus.

Part 2: Planning

Chapter 4 explains the importance of planning, the framework for plans, types and uses of plans, and the planning process.

Chapter 5 guides the student through the steps for rational decisions, decision-making climates, quantitative methods, and the various influences on the manager's problem-solving efforts.

Chapter 6 examines ethical issues and the need to be proactive when managing for social responsibility. After defining both concepts, the chapter explores ethical tests, approaches to social responsibility, and the links between them and applicable legal requirements. It also deals with the issues of responsibilities to stakeholders and of government regulation of business activities as well.

Part 3: Organizing

Chapter 7 looks at the formal organization, the organizing process, its key principles and concepts, and the informal organization.

Chapter 8 covers organizational design, the range of organizational-design outcomes, organizational culture, and handling change.

Part 4: Staffing

Chapter 9 surveys staffing from human resource planning to employee separations. It addresses sociocultural and legal influences, along with such activities as job analysis, job evaluation, training and development, and the practice of staffing in a union environment.

Chapter 10 focuses on communication—organizational and interpersonal—and demonstrates the communication process and barriers to it, along with how managers can improve their communication efforts.

Part 5: Influencing

Chapter 11 explores motivation and the applications of the most relevant theories. It gives special consideration to how managers can use their insights and principles to get the most from themselves and team members.

Chapter 12 looks at leadership and details its importance and associations with power and authority. It reviews the roles leaders must play with their followers, along with the theories that govern the practice of leadership and the styles that leaders may adopt.

Chapter 13 examines team management and conflict, including the nature and types of teams, philosophical approaches to team management, and how to establish team-based organizations. It defines conflict and discusses the causes and methods for managing it.

Part 6: Controlling

Chapter 14 focuses on information flow and how it can be managed in organizations and discusses in detail management information systems and decision support systems.

Chapter 15 focuses on the nature of control, the control process, types of controls, and characteristics of effective controls, and gives special attention to the art of making controls effective.

Appendices

Appendix A focuses on management's commitment to continuous improvement. It explains the link between quality, productivity, and profitability. Factors that affect productivity, along with the commitments necessary by top, middle, and first-line management to improve quality and productivity, are explained.

Appendix B looks at operations management—its nature; its link to planning, processes, and facilities; and how to manage operations, and includes information on how to control operations for both quality and productivity.

Appendix C explores the recent trends affecting businesses in global markets, the nature of the international business environment, and the nature of multinational corporations. It discusses each function of management as it applies to an international operation and environment.

Appendix D is concerned with career management. It analyzes stages in career development and steps in career planning, and follows the analyses with several strategies managers can take to advance their careers.

SUPPORT MATERIALS

A full set of supplements is available for both students and adopting instructors, all designed to facilitate ease of learning, teaching, and testing.

- For students there is a frequently updated website and social media presence along with supplemental quizzing and interactive exercises in the *Active Learning Edition*.
- For instructors there is a revised test bank with revised multiple choice, matching and true false questions, with all new essay and short answer questions. Also available PowerPoint slides, and an Instructor Manual with new teaching notes aligned to video cases.

Management 11e includes the *Active Learning Edition*, supported by Café Learn. This is not a static digital study guide or a companion presentation tool. The *Active Learning Edition* of *Management 11e* is built around a dynamic outcomes based course design based on the core topics and competencies from the textbook. It includes the integrated 11e eBook with all the extra content, media, social tools and adaptive quizzes needed to help instructors turn an existing syllabus, lectures and assignments into active, collaborative and engaging course experiences for students—in and out of class.

It is easy to use and customizable for each instructor's syllabus! Café Learn, our learning partner, has created a teaching and learning platform that is so easy, it gets you up and running in a couple of hours. Dedicated engagement specialists help *Management 11e* instructors "recast" and personalize their existing syllabus with the ability to "curate" new content and exactly which portions of the textbook you wish to assign; along with adding other media, active learning assignments and adaptive low stakes quizzes.

Café Learn works seamlessly with campus technology and the LMS, and is compliant with Accessibility Standards. Wessex and Café Learn will provide support services, before and after adoption, to both faculty and students throughout the term of use.

ACKNOWLEDGMENTS

We extend heartfelt thanks to the following reviewers who have been so helpful in preparing this tenth edition:

Felipe H. Chia, Harrisburg Area Community College

Linda Hefferin, Elgin Community College

Deborah Hopkins, Broward College

Eddy P. Miracle, Southeast Kentucky Community and Technical College

David L. Nagy, University of California, Irvine

Dr. Michael J. Renahan, College of Saint Elizabeth

With thanks,

Warren Plunkett
Emeritus, Wright College

Gemmy Allen
North Lake College

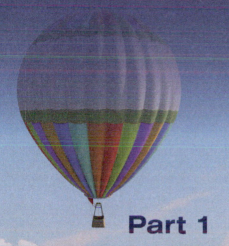

Part 1

Management Concepts

Chapter 1

Management: An Overview

LEARNING OBJECTIVES

After studying this chapter, you should be able to:

1 Explain why organizations need managers

2 Determine the needs that affect a manager's universe

3 Identify three levels of management

4 Describe five management functions

5 Apply management functions to each level of management

6 Summarize ten management roles

7 Analyze three management skills

8 Contrast the myths with the realities of a manager's job

9 Discuss the criteria used to evaluate a manager's performance

Skills for the 21st Century

What skills do employees need to compete in the workplace? The American Management Association surveyed 2,768 U.S. managers and executives about the importance of critical skills to their organization today and in the future. Executives said they need a workforce fully equipped with skills beyond just the basics of reading, writing and mathematics in order to grow their businesses. Skills such as critical thinking and problem solving, communication, collaboration, creativity and innovation (the four C's) will become even more important to organizations in the future.

Four C's Defined

- Critical thinking and problem solving—the ability to make decisions, solve problems and take action as appropriate.
- Effective communication—the ability to synthesize and transmit your ideas both in written and oral formats.
- Collaboration and team building—the ability to work effectively with others, including those from diverse groups and with opposing points of view.
- Creativity and innovation—the ability to see what's NOT there and make something happen.

Are you ready for the 21st century workplace? For each of the following statements, circle the number which indicates your level of agreement. Rate your agreement as it is, not what you think it should be. Objectivity will enable you to determine your management skill strengths and weaknesses.

Compute your score by adding the circled numbers. The highest score is 50; the lowest score is 10. A higher score implies you are more likely to be skilled for the workplace. A lower score implies a lesser degree of readiness. But, a low score can be increased. Reading and studying this chapter will help improve your understanding.

How will you prepare yourself for the future workplace?

	Almost Always	Often	Sometimes	Rarely	Almost Never
I understand written sentences and paragraphs in work related documents.	5	4	3	2	1
I communicate effectively in writing as appropriate for the needs of the audience.	5	4	3	2	1
I use mathematics to solve problems.	5	4	3	2	1
I use logic and reasoning to identify the strengths and weaknesses of alternative solutions, conclusions or approaches to problems.	5	4	3	2	1
I make decisions, solve problems, and take action as appropriate.	5	4	3	2	1
I synthesize and transmit my ideas both in written and oral formats.	5	4	3	2	1
I work effectively with others, including those from diverse groups and with opposing points of view.	5	4	3	2	1
I motivate, develop and direct people as they work, identifying the best people for the job.	5	4	3	2	1
I understand the implications of new information for both current and future problem solving and decision making.	5	4	3	2	1
I see what's NOT there and make something happen.	5	4	3	2	1

Source: 2012 Critical Skills Survey, AMA, December 2012.
Retrieved from *http://playbook.amanet.org/wp-content/uploads/2013/03/2012-Critical-Skills-Survey-pdf.pdf.*

INTRODUCTION

Key people—managers—create, oversee and expand the operations of a business organization by coordinating various resources, skills and activities. In addition to profit-seeking enterprises, key people initiate, oversee and expand other types of organizations such as not-for-profit enterprises, including charities, private schools and governmental agencies in every country in the world.

Peter F. Drucker—the late, preeminent management thinker—asserted that, "management is *not* business management."

> *There are, of course, differences in management between different organizations— mission defines strategy, after all, and strategy defines structure. But the differences between managing a chain of retail stores and managing a Roman Catholic diocese are amazingly fewer than either retail executives or bishops realize. The differences are mainly in application rather than in principles.*[1]

The paragraphs that follow provide a brief introduction and overview of the ongoing features and themes of this text. They explain what management is and why it is needed and describe the functions, roles and skills executed by all managers. The following chapters examine the details of what managers do and how they do it.

Each chapter contains seven features designed to help you understand and apply its contents.

- **Management in Action:** Introductory self-assessments providing insight into management talents and skills.
- **Quality Management:** Continuous improvement of the high performance workplace.
- **Global Applications:** Successful application of one or more of a chapter's concepts from the practice of management in other countries.
- **Ethical Management:** Managers making or facing decisions that contain a variety of issues and consequences for themselves and others.
- **Valuing Diversity and Inclusion:** Unique ways in which organizations show appreciation for their diverse employees.
- **Managing Social Media:** Ways in which organizations use the internet, digital communities and applications to engage their employees and customers.
- **Experiential Learning:** Positioned at the end of each chapter, these exercises provide application of managers' and organizations' attempts to cope with each chapter's major issues.

Each of these features serves to reinforce two continuing themes that are woven into the chapters' narratives: (1) the continual effort by managers and organizations to meet or exceed their customers' needs and expectations; and (2) the need organizations and their people have to be guided by effective management.

MANAGEMENT AND MANAGERS

Great companies have great **managers:** people who allocate and oversee the use of resources. Collectively, a company's managers constitute its **management:** one or more managers individually and collectively setting and achieving goals by exercising related

managers
People who allocate and oversee the use of resources

management
One or more managers individually and collectively setting and achieving goals by exercising related functions (planning, organizing, staffing, leading and controlling) and coordinating various resources (information, materials, money and people)

functions (planning, organizing, staffing, influencing and controlling) and coordinating various resources (information, materials, money and people). A small organization's management may consist of only one person; such is often the case in sole proprietorships. The owner is the manager. Each management function listed above is briefly defined later in this chapter and examined in great detail in Parts II through VI of the text.

goal
An outcome to be achieved or a destination to be reached over a period of time through the exercise of management functions and the expenditure of resources

A **goal** is an outcome to be achieved or a destination to be reached over a period of time through the exercise of management functions and the expenditure of resources. For example, long-term goals for many companies include profit and customer satisfaction. All of a company's managers must coordinate their efforts with each other to achieve these goals.

A specific kind of goal is called an *objective*. A goal is general and long term. An objective is short-term, rather than long, usually achieved in less than a year. Since employees cannot, "do a goal," objectives are set to help them realize their accomplishments. An objective is written to be specific, measurable, attainable, result-oriented and time limited. For many managers, *selecting highly talented employees for the right jobs* is a continuing short-term goal (objective). This chapter's Management in Action allows students to identify areas of strength and areas for improvement in critical skills for the 21st century workplace for themselves.

As you have noticed, student learning objectives appear at the beginning of this chapter. These and the ones listed in following chapters can be achieved over the span of this course.

1 Explain why organizations need managers

organization
An entity managed by one or more persons to achieve stated goals

ORGANIZATIONAL NEED FOR MANAGERS

Basically, an **organization** is an entity managed by one or more persons to achieve stated goals. Renowned management author, professor, and consultant Peter Drucker wrote that managers have two basic tasks: "One, running a business, and two, building an organization."[2] To do both, managers in charge of activities must coordinate what they do with each other while simultaneously accepting, "the values [and] the goals of the organization."[3]

Values constitute beliefs and basic tenets that are important and meaningful to those individuals and organizations that hold them.[4] They must be harmonious and support one another. All employees contribute in various ways to making the company's values an everyday reality for its customers.

Best Buy is a company which lacks the advantages that come with product innovation, but is a leading consumer technology and entertainment products and services retailer. In fact, it is number 11 in the *Stores* ranking of retailers.[5] The values are listed below.

Best Buy's Values

- Have fun while being the best
- Learn from challenge and change
- Show respect, humility and integrity
- Unleash the power of our people

Source: Best Buy Code of Business Ethics.
Retrieved from *https://corporate.bestbuy.com/wp-content/uploads/2015/02/best-buy-code-of-ethics.pdf*

James C. Collins, business consultant and coauthor of the best-selling book *Built to Last,* reports that companies achieve long-term success by sticking passionately to a set of values and creating systems that encourage employees to act in parallel with those values.[6] The systematic ways in which a company's management selects, trains, evaluates and rewards its employees demonstrate the values that managers want to promote and their commitment to them.

Organizations exist everywhere and provide the means for individuals, groups, and societies to meet their needs. Managers create organizations. Once created, organizations need one or more managers to oversee their operations and change or update them as needed. Thus, whether a new organization or an old, there is a universal need for managers.

THE MANAGER'S UNIVERSE

2 Determine the needs that affect a manager's universe

Change is often said to be the only constant in business. Therefore, as we shall note in discussions throughout this text, managers must be able to sense the need for change in themselves, the need for change in their areas of influence and in their organizations, and the need to become the driving force for achieving change.

This section begins the development of the six continuing and evolving themes that are reinforced by each chapter's features:

1 Managers and their organizations need to please customers by meeting or exceeding their needs and expectations.

2 Organizations must continuously improve their products and services.

3 Managers should provide leadership.

4 Managers and organizations must act ethically.

5 Organizations should value diversity in their employees.

6 Managers and organizations must learn to cope with global challenges.

How each need is met is largely affected by each manager's and organization's values, how well each manager executes the five management functions, and the availability of needed resources. We examine each of these needs, beginning with the need to please customers.

The Need to Please Customers

Managers know that the survival and profitability of their organization are directly linked to meeting or exceeding customers' needs and expectations. They can satisfy customers by guaranteeing that all individual efforts and their results possess **quality**: "The totality of features and characteristics of a product or service that bear on its ability to satisfy stated or implied [requirements of those who use or consume them]."[7] Quality translates into the ability of some person's, groups, or organization's output to meet or exceed some other person's, group's, or organization's (i.e., a customer's) needs. Satisfying customers involves engaging all employees, every day, in solving problems, which turns into innovation and leads to better products and services. Managers encourage continuous improvement by using the Socratic Method discussed in this chapter's Quality Management highlight.

Throughout this text, a **customer** includes any person or group, both inside and outside an organization, who uses or consumes outputs from an organization or its

quality
The features and characteristics of a product or service that allow it to satisfy requirements of those who use or consume them

customer
Any person or group, both inside and outside an organization, who uses or consumes outputs from an organization or its members

The Socratic Method

Quality management is about creating a system to make employees think. The quality manager's goal is for every employee to understand his or her job. In this way, every employee solves problems every day, which leads to better products, as well as more value for customers. Thus, quality products and services, resulting in customer satisfaction, are created by all employees.

The ultimate measure of a manager's success is the employee's development over and above what they could otherwise achieve by simply learning on their own. Many problems encountered by employees cannot be predicted. Therefore, each employee must become a capable, independent problem solver.

Quality managers employ the Socratic Method to develop problem solvers. (Socrates was a classical Greek philosopher renowned for using questions to encourage critical thinking.) People are natural problem solvers, and the Socratic Method is a way of engaging employees by helping them discover the answers to problems. The manager using this method avoids giving away answers to problems and focuses on helping the employee systematically think through situations to arrive at appropriate answers.

Instead of telling employees the answers, the quality manager asks neutral questions that encourage independent thought. The questions probe the implications and consequences of changing the conditions of the original problem. The employee is required to understand the problem in its entirety rather than just memorizing the approach used for specific situations. Examples of neutral questions follow; *"What do you think?" "Why do you think that?" "Have you considered . . .?' "How would you approach…."* The manager discusses the situation with the employee, summarizes what the employee says and checks for understanding. Since the employee is engaged in solving the problem, he or she will not forget the lesson. Learning has taken place.

➤ **It's so easy to solve others' problems by giving quick solutions, but that makes people dependent on you. The next time someone asks you what to do, what will you say?**

members. The *internal* customer is any person or group inside the organization who receives what is needed from others in the organization. Examples include:

- Managers at headquarters receiving reports on time from their regional managers.
- An employee receiving her office supplies on time and in the right amount from the company's office inventory clerk.
- Each of the company's sales persons receiving properly prepared shipping reports in a reasonable time from shipping/receiving.

External customers are persons or groups outside the organization who expect the organization's outputs to meet their needs and include:

- The customer receiving what he ordered in a reasonable period of time and with friendly service
- An outside supplier receiving quality specifications for a service it must provide.
- A building contractor receiving payments on time and in the proper amounts for services and materials provided.

Management must understand that companies are evaluated in the marketplace by both customers and investors on how well they meet all their customers' needs and manage customer relationships. Quality is defined by both internal and external customers' needs, but those needs and expectations are like moving targets—always changing. Customers continue to want things faster, better and cheaper. Today's external customers can choose from the best that producers anywhere in the world have to offer. This expectation puts pressure on managers to make the quality of their activities and outputs "world class," a set of standards that can be used to measure and compare performance. To guarantee that its employees deliver quality outputs, employees are expected to focus on the needs of customers. We will examine quality in more detail throughout the book with additional detail in Appendix X.

A website is a company's lifeline with its customers. Yet, to satisfy customers, websites must evolve. The first websites were static brochures providing information to prospective customers and other interested parties. In other words, companies controlled what people could read on their websites. Next, websites became e-commerce enabled, allowing customers to make purchases or conduct transitions online

The internet fundamentally changes the economics of transactions in ways that greatly benefit both consumers and producers. It reduces the transaction costs, the costs involved in bringing a product to market. In 1991, Ronald H. Coase won the Nobel Prize in economics in large part for his insight that businesses exist to eliminate transaction costs between entrepreneurs. According to the theory, without transaction costs everyone would be an independent contractor. In other words, organizations exist because it takes a lot of time and costs a lot of money to coordinate people outside the organization. But given the internet, it gets cheaper and easier all the time to coordinate with people outside the company.

Today, the most customer friendly websites use applications, such as live chat, blogs, wikis, and social networking. Companies share information, rather than control; and people read, as well as write on sites that are attractive to the consumer. Social media allows people to be engaged, build social and professional connections, share information, express likes and dislikes and collaborate on projects online.

> *There has been a fundamental shift in the paradigm of how we think about and use the web. Instead of reading static web pages, users are now cataloging their personal libraries, organizing their favorite bookmarks, writing online documents, and sharing their information with others through new generation social software. What began with blogs and wikis has blossomed into an all-encompassing and standard phenomenon of sharing, collaboration and user involvement.*[8]

This chapter's Managing Social Media sections discusses customer relationship management (CRM) and online tools to encourage customers to join the conversation to help companies improve their products and services.

Customer relationship management (CRM) allows organizations to track and analyze shifting customer needs, link marketing campaigns to sales results and monitor sales activities for improved forecasting accuracy. It does this by bringing together many pieces of information from customer profiles, sales, effectiveness of advertising campaigns and responsiveness to market trends. Management, salespeople, customer service and the customer can directly access information. For example, other products a customer has purchased can be accessed and matched with satisfying product offerings. In addition, customers can be reminded of service requirements. CRM provides the organization with a complete, dependable and integrated view of its customer base.

All employees are simultaneously customers and the means to satisfy customers. As customers, they must make those who exist to serve them aware of what they need. As the means to satisfy customers, they must determine who their customers are and what they require. Finally, employees must make it both a personal commitment and a primary duty to meet customer needs.

customer relationship management (CRM)
A long-term management approach to customer relations that attempts to strengthen the bond between the customer and the organization

Customer Relationship Management

Understanding customers' wants and needs are crucial elements for success in business. Who are our customers? What do they like to buy? How much do they spend? What motivates them? Where do they live?

Organizations get to know their customers through customer relationship management (CRM), a team relationship among sales, marketing, support and between the team and its clients. CRM software organizes contact information for current and prospective customers, and allows multiple users to track customers' buying habits. For example, when engineering has a product update, it sends a notification to sales and support. Messages and screens of data pop between managers, based on rules established by the users in the software. Engineering, sales and support collaborate concerning customers with that product need.

Social Media technologies take CRM a step further. Customers can give direct feedback to the business by rating products, writing reviews, uploading images, videos, audio clips and quotes. Thus, organizations are able to use CRM and the power of the internet to more effectively and efficiently respond to customer demands.

Each time the customer contacts the business—whether in the store, by phone, by direct mail or on the internet—information can be collected. With each piece of information collected, the business becomes more familiar with the customers and can tailor messages to a customer's specific needs, as seen in the graphic below.

➡ **Customer driven CRM means that organizations must first understand the *customer*. Recall a recent shopping experience where your expectations were not met. What recommendations to the management could you make so that it can see its business from the customer's perspective, rather than from its own?**

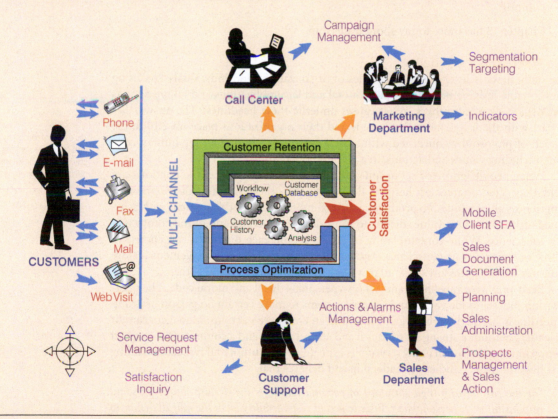

Source: Amilog, Customer Relationships Management,
http://www.amigolog.com/NewSite/index.php/en/conseils-et-services/gestion-de-la-relation-client

The Need to Provide Leadership

"Without leaders who can attract and retain talent, manage knowledge, and unblock people's capacity to adapt and innovate, an organization's future is in jeopardy."[9] **Leadership** practitioners (leaders) accomplish this in part by exhibiting sets of values, skills, abilities and traits that are needed by and are an inspiration to others. Leadership involves gaining commitments from organizational members to achieve management's goals and properly equipping them to do so.

According to professor and author John Kotter of Harvard University, leaders initiate and facilitate change.[10] They face two basic tasks: "First, to develop and articulate exactly what the [organization] is trying to accomplish, and second, to create an environment in which employees can figure out what needs to be done and then do it well."[11] To be successful, companies must have leaders at every level and in every unit, creating and maintaining supportive environments.

Warren Bennis, distinguished professor of business administration and founding chairman of the Leadership Institute at the University of Southern California's Marshall School of Business, provides further insight.

> *"The truth is that no one factor makes a company admirable," wrote Thomas Stewart, "but if you were forced to pick the one that makes the most difference, you'd pick leadership. In Warren Buffett's phrase, 'People are voting for the artist and not the painting.' "*[12]

Chapter 13 has more to say about leadership.

leadership
The ability to get people to follow voluntarily

The Need to Act Ethically

The daily news is littered with examples of organizations and individuals exercising questionable judgment, ignoring their moral and legal obligations and taking actions that negatively affect others. What causes underlie these headlines? The answer lies in part with the importance that people and their organizations place on **ethics**: the branch of philosophy concerned with what constitutes right and wrong human conduct, including values and actions, in a given set of circumstances.

When people ignore or act in spite of the negative consequences their actions can yield, they often do needless harm to themselves and others. An individual's previous experiences all combine, "to produce a personal moral code of ethical values with associated attitudes."[13] Our values dictate to some degree our ethics and moral compass—our conscience. While contemplating or taking action, each one of us can choose to follow or suppress our conscience. And, as this chapter's Ethical Management feature indicates, various pressures exist to drive individuals from an ethical path.

Each employee must have and act on a personal ethical and moral code. The organization must provide values and support systems to make certain no person or group is needlessly harmed by the organization's or an employee's actions. Managers cannot be leaders without a strong set of moral and ethical values and a commitment to avoid compromising them. Certainly customers expect no less. Author and researcher Danny Cox has conducted studies on leadership and believes that

ethics
The branch of philosophy concerned with what constitutes right and wrong human conduct, including values and actions, in a given set of circumstances

> *"at the core of any high standard of personal ethics is the declaration of personal responsibility. A person who refuses to accept responsibility lacks the ethical armor to stand against temptation."*[14]

Chapter 6 explores ethical concepts in more depth.

Unsolicited Electronic Mail

Many legitimate companies sell their products and services through electronic mail (e-mail), because it is productive and efficient. E-mail efforts sell everything from used books to home repairs and exist at the manufacturing, wholesale and retail levels in every major industry. Even charitable organizations use e-mail to raise money. E-mail generates more sales than its direct-mail counterpart and costs far less than putting salespeople on the streets.

There is a dark side, however. Some consumers find unsolicited e-mail, known as "spam," to be bothersome. Others have lost money by responding to spam. In the US, almost 50 percent of e-mail is spam (Symantec).

Typically, an e-mail spammer buys a list of e-mail addresses from a list broker, who compiles it by "harvesting" addresses from the internet. If your e-mail address appears in a newsgroup posting, on a website, in a chat room, or in an online service's membership directory, it may find its way onto these lists. The marketer then uses special software that can send hundreds of thousands—even millions—of e-mail messages to the addresses at the click of a mouse (FTC Facts for Consumers).

Every state's attorney general can testify to the abuses deceptive e-mail marketing efforts bring. Fraud by e-mail marketers includes asking consumers to send money to claim a prize or for a free gift. Other scams include work-at-home schemes, weight-loss claims, credit repair offers, advance fee loans and adult entertainment.

In response to complaints against spammers, the federal government passed the CAN-SPAM (Controlling the Assault of Non-Solicited Pornography and Marketing) Act. The law sets the rules for commercial e-mail, establishes requirements for commercial messages, gives recipients the right to have businesses stop e-mailing them and spells out tough penalties for violations.

➡ **Almost 200 million people have placed their telephone number on the national Do-Not-Call Registry to stop telemarketers from calling. Should a similar list be put in place for e-mail? Defend your answer.**

Sources: Symantec Intelligence Report June 2015, *https://www.symantec.com/content/en/us/enterprise/other_resources/intelligence-report-06-2015.en-us.pdf*; FTC Facts for Consumers, "You've Got Spam: How to Can Unwanted Email," *http://www.ftc.gov/bcp/edu/pubs/consumer/tech/tec02.pdf*

The Need to Value Diversity and Inclusion in Their Employees

Managers no longer manage a homogeneous workforce. Organizations are composed of a heterogeneous mix of people that reflects our nation's population. Data from the U.S. Department of Labor show," the future racial and ethnic makeup of America will be considerably different than it is today. Trends show that whites will be a declining share of the future total population, while the Hispanic share will grow faster than that of non-Hispanic blacks. By 2050, minorities are projected to rise from one in every four Americans to almost one in every two. The Asian and Pacific Islander population is also expected to increase. Growth rates of both the Hispanic-origin and the Asian and Pacific Islander populations may exceed two percent per year until 2030."

America's **diversity** includes people from differing age groups, genders, ethnic and racial backgrounds, cultural and national origins and mental and physical capabilities. Our nation's diversity represents three challenges for managers:

diversity
Includes people from differing age groups, genders, ethnic and racial backgrounds, cultural and national origins and mental and physical capabilities

1 Integrate the diversity that exists in their communities and in their external customers into their workforces.

2 Learn about and understand their employees' differences.

3 Find ways for themselves, their employees and their organizations to utilize and celebrate these differences.

America's equal employment opportunity laws help guarantee access to organizations for all its citizens. The key issues then become how these differing individuals and

Chief Diversity Officer (CDO)

To meet the needs of an increasingly diverse workforce, many organizations have developed the position of chief diversity officer (CDO) to guide their diversity and multicultural agendas. CDOs cultivate diversity as an organizational resource. Duties include affirmative action and equal employment opportunity for minorities, women and other bounded social identity groups. Maria Castañón Moats, chief diversity officer at PwC (formerly PricewaterhouseCoopers), states on the company's website, "At PwC, we believe in confronting the hard realities—and then doing something about it." She writes in *Fastcompany*, "Business leaders need to dream big for their employees, especially for minorities, women, and those from low-income backgrounds who may have been the first in their family to go to college."

PwC, a provider of audit and advisory services, is recognized as best places to work in diversity/inclusion. Below are some of its awards.

- Vault Accounting firm rankings for 2016: #1 in Overall Diversity
- Ranked in the Top 10 on four 2015 DiversityInc specialty lists: #1 – Recruitment; #3 – Employee resource groups; #4 – Mentoring and #10 for LGBT employee

- Ranked among Working Mother's "Best Companies for Multicultural Women" in 2005-2015
- Ranked among the, "Top 10 Companies for Working Mothers" by Working Mother magazine, 2002-2015
- Ranked among the "Best Adoption-Friendly Workplaces" by the Dave Thomas Adoption Foundation, 2011–2015
- Recipient of the 2012 NABA Corporate Partner of the Year Award
- Winner of the 2009 **Point Inspiration Award** for GLBT inclusion

➡ **What is the significance of making diversity the responsibility of a chief officer?**

Sources: PwC, About the Office of Diversity, *http://www.pwc.com/us/en/about-us/diversity/pwc-diversity-office.html* PwC, Our Awards, *http://www.pwc.com/us/en/about-us/pwc-awards.html* Maria Castañón Moats, June 30, 2014, "How Far Corporations Still Need to Go to Actually Reflect America's Diversity," *FastCompany*, retrieved from *http://www.fastcompany.com/3032433/the-future-of-work/how-far-corporations-still-need-to-go-to-actually-reflect-americas-divers*

groups will be welcomed and managed once inside. Women in the Workplace 2015, a comprehensive study of the state of women in corporate America by LeanIn.Org and McKinsey & Company found that prejudice in management still exists. Results of their study revealed that women are underrepresented at every corporate level. This chapter's Valuing Diversity and Inclusion feature highlights how PwC, a large professional services firm is working to value the diversity of its employees.

The Need to Cope with Global Challenges

Conducting business internationally is a way of life for many businesses. According to the Trade Promotion Coordinating Committee's *2012 National Export Strategy*, "Virtually all (97.7 percent) exporters in 2012 were small- and medium-sized companies (i.e. firms with fewer than 500 employees), though large firms accounted for roughly two-thirds of the value of exports in 2012." It's become a necessity for any business to export because 96 percent of the world's customers reside outside of the U.S. Thus, increasing sales abroad is the future of business.

Most of America's 1000 largest companies, such as the giant commercial aircraft producer Boeing, make more than half their sales dollars from foreign customers. Even the smallest of businesses that call their customers neighbors cannot escape influences from abroad. Many of their raw materials, supplies and retail inventories come from growers, producers and service providers around the world. For example, nearly all the coffee processed and sold in the United States comes from sources outside its borders.

College Graduates

It is hard to accept the fact that the United States (U.S.) no longer leads the world in college completion. The U.S. is known all around the world for innovation in technology and increases in productivity. This success in the global marketplace is attributable to a highly skilled population.

Now, the competitiveness of the U.S. is threatened because of a decline in its share of college graduates. The percentage of American adults with an Associate degree or higher is not keeping pace with other industrialized nations.

According to the annual report of the Paris-based Organization for Economic Cooperation and Development (OECD), "Education at a Glance 2015," 43 percent of Americans (ages 25-64) have a university-level education; 44 percent of U.S. 25-34 year-olds have a college degree; 42 percent of U.S. 55-64 year-olds have a college degree. College graduation rates in the United States rank 19th out of 28 countries studied by the OECD.

➥ **How do you think the U.S. can increase its college completion rate?**

Source: http://www.oecd.org/edu/education-at-a-glance-19991487. htm.

In a global economy, national borders become insignificant. Companies in every industry must locate operations wherever they can serve their customers best and procure needed resources. Organizations including Germany's BMW, England's BP, France's Michelin and Japan's Toyota have built production facilities in the United States and in dozens of other nations in order to better serve their customers and lower their production costs. They also obtain needed resources and market their production output in the countries where they have built facilities as well as many other countries.

According to David Fagiano, former president and CEO of the American Management Association—a worldwide professional development organization with branches in 30 countries—American managers can learn much from the practice of management by foreigners wherever they do business. "We must stop thinking that the United States has cornered the market on intelligence and realize that innovations in management are happening everywhere."[15] This chapter's Global Application reinforces this point by comparing college completion rates of industrialized nations.

Clearly, integrating the preceding idea into each manager's philosophy and, therefore, into management's approaches to solving problems and making decisions makes the practice of management an awesome challenge. In addition to the above-mentioned needs, however, the manager's universe is made even more complex by several additional factors:

- Technological advances that lead to breakthroughs in such areas as virtual reality, telecommunications, robotics and computer applications require managers to learn new skills, design new training programs and reexamine operations and processes.

- Economic changes in levels of interest rates, inflation, taxation and the onset of a recession in one or more markets require managers to revisit their plans and make adjustments in a variety of areas, including the size of workforces and the spending for resources.

- Natural disasters, such as the 2014 Mount Everest avalanche and the 2005 hurricanes of Katrina and Rita in the Gulf Coast area of the United States require managers in insurance companies, farm cooperatives, utilities, and transportation companies to act immediately and decisively; they must adjust their goals and their timetables.

- Crises, such as the leaking BP well in the Gulf of Mexico in 2010, September 11, 2001 (9/11) and the bombing of the Alfred P. Murrah Federal Building in Oklahoma City in 1995, activate chains of management decisions in dealing with rescue teams, aid agencies and the media.

- Social and political changes (e.g., widespread drug use discovered in a company's workforce and changes in both laws and population mixes where a company's operations are located) require managers to rethink practices, adjust spending priorities and implement new training programs.

In a global economy, managers must adapt their execution of basic functions to unfamiliar cultures, commercial regulations, economic conditions and climates. Customer demands and preferences, as well as the values and customs of indigenous workforces must be respected and accommodated. Wipro, headquartered in Bangalore, India, hires local nationals wherever it does business. Azim H. Premji, Wipro chairman and managing director, relates, "A true global company appears to be local wherever it does business."[16] One of Wipro's goals is to have local nationals as three-quarters of its employees.

All the preceding factors combine to make the real world of management complex, ever-changing, exciting and filled with pressure. As Roger Penske, famous automobile racer and Chairman of Penske Corporation puts it, "The challenges are there every day and stress is a persistent adversary."[17] Appendix B examines the conduct of business in an international arena in more detail.

LEVELS OF MANAGEMENT

3 Identify three levels of management

Although all managers perform the same set of functions, they actually do so on only three organizational levels. Generically speaking, managers are found at the top, middle and first-line—sometimes called the supervisory, front-line, or operating—levels of management. Collectively, these levels constitute the **management hierarchy**, as shown in Figure 1.1.

Shown at the left in Figure 1.1 is a pyramid representing management in a medium- or larger-sized sole proprietorship and partnership. On the right is the model of a traditional management structure in a similar-sized corporation. The latter model includes a board of directors consisting of members elected by stockholders (the owners of a corporate enterprise) who, in turn, appoint key members of a corporation's top management.

management hierarchy
The top, middle and first-line levels of management

Top Management

The tip of the pyramid consists of the organization's **top management**: The chief executive officer (CEO) and/or president and his, her, or their immediate subordinates, usually called vice presidents. Top management is responsible for overseeing the entire organization. It establishes long-term, company-wide goals and oversees the work of middle managers. Top management also creates and coordinates alliances and partnerships with outsiders. For example, Ford and Nissan formed an alliance to develop and produce a front-wheel drive minivan to counter Chrysler's models. Both have benefited from the partnership through lower product-development costs and higher profits.

top management
The chief executive officer (CEO) and/or president and his, her, or their immediate subordinates, usually called vice presidents

Figure 1.1	Levels of the Management Hierarchy

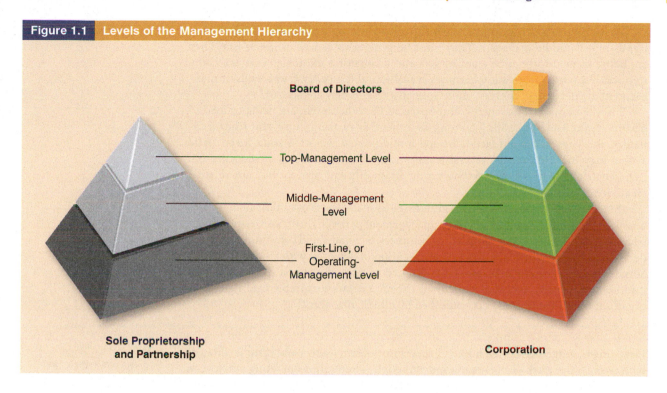

Best Buy, Inc. is a company that owns and operates stores in the United States as well as Canada, Mexico and Asia. Its operations include: Best Buy, Future Shop, Geek Squad and Magnolia Audio Video. Hubert Joly is chairman and chief executive officer of Best Buy; Shari Ballard is president, U.S. Retail and chief human resources officer; Mary Lou Kelley is President, e-commerce; Sharon McCollam is chief administrative officer and chief financial officer; Matt Furman is chief communications and public affairs officer; Mike Mohan is chief merchandising officer; and Greg Revelle is chief marketing officer. They compose the organization's top management. Expanding the company and keeping it competitive are their primary concerns.

Middle Management

middle management
Includes managers below the rank of vice president but above the supervisory level

Middle management includes, "any managers two levels below the CEO and one level above line workers and professionals."[18] The smallest organizations have no middle managers; larger ones have several layers of them. Along with setting their own goals, middle managers typically translate top management's long-term goals into shorter-term objectives that the middle managers will be responsible for achieving. They oversee the work of other middle managers and those on the operating level. Such is the case with Best Buy's regional managers. Their primary job is to add new stores and oversee the performances of their subordinate managers, including the store managers in their regions.

Middle managers must communicate with and satisfy their managers, respond to end users and energize and nurture their employees. Then there are budgets, meetings and reports to tend to. They must hire new workers, juggle limited resources, stay on top of ever-evolving technology and anticipate future directions.[19]

According to a variety of management consultants and industry experts, several trends affect middle managers. They must be generalists as well as specialists. They are being trained to become team leaders and facilitators, and their ranks are being thinned. "As more information becomes available and less costly, fewer levels of management are needed. In contrast, more specialist task leaders are needed."[20]

Middle managers, like their counterparts at the other levels, are being trained to become team leaders—leading a group as a member of the group—and team facilitators. Bic Vogel is a team facilitator and a middle manager of Atlanta-based Delta Technology Inc. He oversees several teams and describes his job as a balancing act: "The challenge is to deliver effective results in an efficient manner but not to stifle creativity."[21]

In the 1990s, corporate America eliminated as many layers of middle managers as possible (thus reducing the height of the management pyramid) in order to reduce costs, become more flexible and responsive to customers, facilitate rapid communication and decision making and replace the vertical execution of activities with a horizontal one. Some concluded middle managers were doomed to extinction. But a six-year study of middle managers by Quy Nguyen Huy of INSEAD shows that implementing radical organizational change is best accomplished by middle managers.[22]

First-Line Management

First-line management is the home of supervisors, team leaders and team facilitators who oversee the work of non-management people, often called operating employees, associates or team members.[23] These managers convert middle managers' goals and objectives into their own sets of objectives. Of all the levels, the first-line is most concerned with the day-to-day execution of ongoing operations. It executes the tasks that directly affect most of an organization's external customers each day.

At Best Buy, the store managers and their assistant managers are its first-line management. They directly interface with customers each day, thus affecting, more directly than any other level of management, the company's image and the quality of service experienced by external customers.

Functional Managers

Managers may also be identified by the kind of business functions for which they are responsible. Like the functions of management, business functions are universal and apply to every type of business. The most essential business functions are marketing, operations (production of goods and services), finance, and human resource management. Managers whose expertise lies primarily in one or another of the specialty areas are known as **functional managers**. All other managers are usually referred to as general managers.

Many businesses, such as Best Buy, are organized around these functions and execute the varied activities of each function through both individuals and teams, horizontally or vertically and at all three management levels. Figure 1.2 illustrates the three levels of management organized to execute the basic business functions. Note that only the marketing department is shown in the middle and operating levels of management.

Marketing Managers The marketing function involves identifying current and potential customers' needs and preferences, along with developing goods and services that will satisfy them. Working with the other functional managers, marketing managers determine the physical and performance characteristics for products. In addition, they

first-line management
Supervisors, team leaders, and team facilitators who oversee the work of non-management people, often called operating employees, associates, or team members

functional managers
Managers whose expertise lies primarily in one or another of the specialty areas

Figure 1.2   Typical Titles in the Three Levels of Management

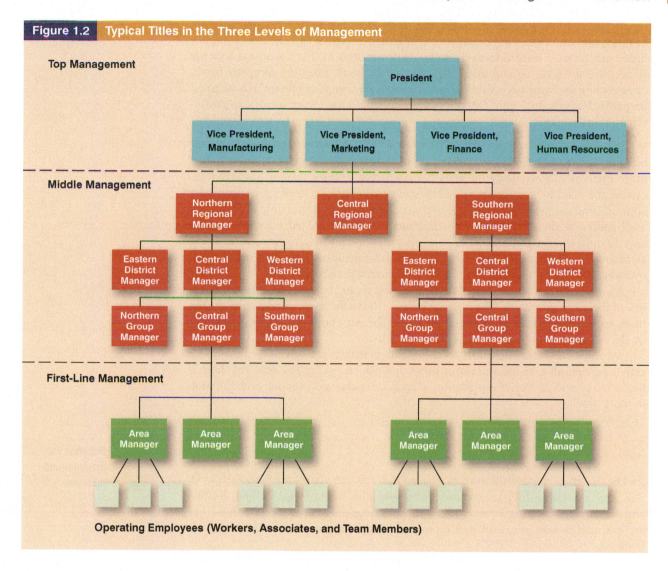

Top Management

President

Vice President, Manufacturing

Vice President, Marketing

Vice President, Finance

Vice President, Human Resources

Middle Management

Northern Regional Manager

Central Regional Manager

Southern Regional Manager

Eastern District Manager

Central District Manager

Western District Manager

Eastern District Manager

Central District Manager

Western District Manager

Northern Group Manager

Central Group Manager

Southern Group Manager

Northern Group Manager

Central Group Manager

Southern Group Manager

First-Line Management

Area Manager

Area Manager

Area Manager

Area Manager

Area Manager

Area Manager

Operating Employees (Workers, Associates, and Team Members)

focus on ways to properly price, promote, sell and distribute an organization's goods and services. In Figure 1.2, the vice president of marketing is the member of top management in charge of this function.

Operations Managers Managers in operations perform the activities needed to manufacture an item or provide a service. In manufacturing companies, operations managers are concerned about controlling inventory levels and deliveries, determining factory layout, scheduling production, maintaining equipment and meeting quality requirements for all production activities. Best Buy's store managers are concerned with delivering both products and services. They focus on maintaining efficiency and meeting quality requirements in the conduct of selling, delivery and installation activities. In Figure 1.2, the vice president of manufacturing is the member of top management in charge of operations.

Finance Managers Finance managers are most concerned with managing the flow of funds into and out of the organization, and they help to determine how company funds can be used most effectively. Individual managers in this functional area are responsible for granting and using their company's credit, investing company funds, safeguarding the company's assets, keeping track of the company's financial health and preparing budgets. In Figure 1.2, the vice president of finance oversees the organization's financial activities.

Human Resource Managers Human resource (HR) managers are responsible for building and maintaining a competent and stable workforce. They perform and assist other managers in executing the activities connected to these tasks to include forecasting the need for recruiting, selecting, and training people; creating performance appraisal and compensation systems; overseeing relations with the company's unions; and handling all these activities within the limits and demands of federal, state and local laws. In most small organizations, HR activities must usually be performed without the assistance of full-time HR managers. In Figure 1.2, the top-management person who oversees these activities is the vice president of human resources.

Most middle managers and all those at the top should be familiar with more than one of these specialty areas. The higher a person rises in the levels of management, the more knowledge about each of these areas he or she must possess. Chapter 10 focuses on the execution of human resource (staffing) activities.

We now turn our attention to the major management functions (groups of activities) that all managers perform to set and achieve goals. The objective here is limited to providing a brief explanation of each. Later chapters examine each function in more depth.

MANAGEMENT FUNCTIONS

4 Describe five management functions

Part of this chapter's definition of management states that goals are set and achieved, "by [the] exercising [of] related functions—planning, organizing, staffing, leading and controlling." Managers everywhere perform management functions, but how they are executed is determined in part by organizational influences and the individuals involved.

Although we discuss these functions separately, they are interdependent and must be considered simultaneously. Managers do not plan in the morning, organize before noon, staff between 1:00 P.M. and 2:00 P.M. and control from 2:30 P.M. until the end of the day. Acquiring human resources (staffing), for example, requires planning; the changes that will occur to established work groups must be implemented (organizing); subordinates must be guided as they execute staffing functions (leading); and the progress toward staffing goals and the expenditure of resources in doing so must be monitored and measured (controlling).

Planning

Planning is often called the first function because it lays the groundwork for all other functions and is the first step taken when performing them. When planning, managers begin by identifying goals and alternative ways of achieving them. Managers assign priorities to each goal and determine the resources required to reach each one. Planning determines actions that commit individuals, departments and the entire organization for days, months, or years to come.

Duration and Scope of Planning The length of time covered by a manager's plan—its duration—depends on his or her position in management. In general, top managers plan beyond one year and frequently focus on five or more years into the future. Such plans must be continually updated in light of changing circumstances. Top management's plans affect middle management's. Middle managers focus on what they must accomplish each year to guarantee that long-term, company-wide goals will be achieved. At first-line levels, planning is affected by middle managers' plans and spans a day, week, or month.

The scope of plans at each level varies as well. Top management is concerned with the entire organization. Middle managers' plans might be focused on executing and improving a business function like marketing or a process such as purchasing. First-line managers are most concerned with planning their departments' activities and the work of their individual employees and teams.

Influences on Planning Both internal and external forces influence plans. The most immediate internal influences come from the plans created at higher management levels and the resources they will make available. All managers' plans must adhere to these constraints in order to be both compatible with and supportive of one another. This influence of higher levels on lower ones is known as a vertical influence.

Each planner must also consider the impact of a plan on others. Unit managers occupying the same levels must coordinate their plans and planning efforts to prevent confusion and the wasting of resources.

In addition, every manager's plans are continually affected by influences outside the organization (the environmental forces in a manager's universe discussed earlier)—social, legal/political, technological and so forth. Changes in numerous areas beyond managers' and their organization's abilities to control affect every management and business function. Managers at all levels must continually monitor these external influences to identify trends and changes and adjust their plans as necessary. Chapter 3 examines the manager's environment in greater detail.

Flexibility in Planning Because of the preceding factors, planning is not a one-time activity. Plans cannot be carved in stone. As time passes and circumstances change, plans that have not been executed must be reviewed and updated. Also, because many plans do not yield the precise outcomes expected, managers must prepare and be ready to use alternative plans to deal with any deficiencies in their original ones. Chapter 4 explores planning in greater detail.

Organizing

Organizing creates a structure to facilitate the accomplishment of goals—the management hierarchy—and all the non-management positions that support it. In executing the organizing function, managers determine the tasks that must be accomplished, group these tasks to form positions to be occupied by full- or part-time employees and decide on the relationships the positions will have to one another.

Organizations are usually a mix of divisions, departments, regions and individuals or teams within each. Automobile manufacturers may choose to organize by product groups, such as General Motors' Buick, Cadillac, Chevrolet, GMC and Pontiac divisions. Each of these, in turn, can be organized to execute functions either nationwide or by region. FedEx, the international package carrier, is organized to conduct both ground and air delivery services by regions and nations served.

Like the other functions, organizing is a continuing concern. As a company's situation changes, so, too will its goals and objectives. This often results in a change to its management structure. As Best Buy expands into new territories, it must add new regional managers. New store managers must be integrated into each region's management structure. Chapter 7 explores the organizing function.

Staffing

Staffing—the acquiring and placing of people—breathes life into an organization. Sometimes executed as the final stage of the organizing function, staffing executes the human resource management activities—recruiting, hiring, training and so on. Planning to staff an organization includes determining what skills and experiences people must possess to hold each position and how many persons will be needed to meet both short- and long-term requirements.

At Best Buy, staffing is a primary concern of regional and store managers. As new sites are chosen, new first-line managers are hired to run the new facilities. The first-line managers must then hire, train and help motivate each store worker and assistant manager. Staffing is the primary focus of Chapter 10.

Leading

Everything stated in this chapter about leadership and leaders applies here as well. Through leadership, managers help their organizations and their employees achieve their goals. They serve as models for expected behaviors. They coach, counsel, inspire and encourage both individuals and groups. Leaders build and maintain work environments that encourage motivation and construct working relationships based on mutual respect and trust. These activities place a premium on a manager's ability to work with and through people.

To build and maintain a supportive environment, a manager must use two-way communication channels to convey values, goals and expectations; listen to employees; respond to their concerns; and resolve disputes. Chapters 10 through 13 deal with communication and influencing.

Controlling

Managers know that the other functions may result in wasted effort unless a mechanism is provided to ensure things go according to plan. That mechanism is controlling. Basically, controlling attempts to prevent, identify and correct deviations from guidelines set to evaluate both people and processes. Locks, timing devices and security guards are examples of prevention controls. Observing ongoing operations and measuring them against maximum and minimum guidelines for acceptable levels of output help workers and managers identify unacceptable deviations. Finally, identifying and correcting the causes of such deviations must be accomplished to eliminate waste. Chapters 14 and 15 examine controlling.

FUNCTIONS AND THE LEVELS OF MANAGEMENT

Apply management functions to each level of management

Regardless of title, position, or management level, all managers execute these five management functions and work through and with others to set and achieve the organization's goals. Figure 1.3 shows the relative amounts of time spent by each management level on each function. Note that although all managers perform the same functions, managers at the various management levels require different amounts of time for each function. The points of emphasis in each function also differ. As you read the following paragraphs, note the differences at each level of management.

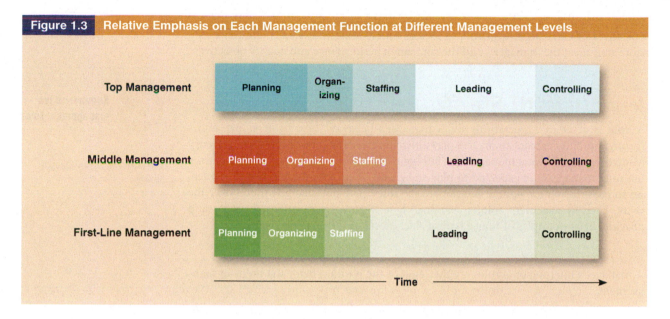

Figure 1.3 Relative Emphasis on Each Management Function at Different Management Levels

Top Management

Top managers plan for the entire organization and the acquisition of needed resources. They develop the organization's values, purpose, long-term goals and partnerships with outsiders. Their organizing efforts focus on creating and adapting the overall organizational structure to cope with varying challenges and opportunities. Staffing at the top is concerned with determining long-term human resource needs and creating guidelines to govern the staffing practices of managers at all levels. Top management's leadership concerns consist of creating a company-wide management philosophy and putting systems in place to support the development and practice of leadership at all levels. Controlling efforts set guidelines for evaluating overall company performance and determine how efficiently key resources are used and company-wide goals are achieved.

Middle Management

Middle managers develop objectives to implement top-management goals. Organizing and staffing efforts modify the company structure, increase or decrease the number of positions and people, in line with top-management guidelines, at both the middle- and operating-management levels. Leading focuses on facilitating the work of individual managers and their teams in the middle and operating levels. Controlling consists of monitoring the results of plans and making adjustments as required to ensure the organization's goals and objectives are achieved.

First-Line Management

First-line managers plan primarily for the short term. For Best Buy's store manager, planning involves scheduling employees and establishing detailed procedures to perform worker tasks. Organizing may consist of adding additional persons to a shift to handle an unusually large group of shoppers and reassigning tasks to cover for an absent employee. First-line staffing consists of building an initial staff, training each new hire and replacing employees as needed. Leading includes gaining the commitments of employees to the values and goals of Best Buy as well as to the methods and objectives of each store. Controlling focuses on ensuring individuals and the entire store staff meet the manager's and the company's performance and quality objectives.

MANAGEMENT ROLES

6 Summarize ten management roles

A **role** is a set of expectations for a manager's behavior. Like professional actors throughout their careers, managers play different roles as circumstances dictate. Henry Mintzberg studied what managers do. His book *The Nature of Managerial Work* defines ten roles managers are expected to play and groups them into three categories: interpersonal, informational, and decisional. The roles have not changed much over the years. Each management role is examined here. Figure 1.4 describes the roles and provides brief examples of how a typical chief executive officer plays them.

role
A set of expectations for a manager's behavior

Interpersonal Roles

A manager's interpersonal roles are the result of the position he or she holds in management.

- **Figurehead.** As head of a work unit (division, department, or section), a manager routinely performs certain ceremonial duties. Examples of ceremonial duties include entertaining visitors, attending a subordinate's wedding and officiating at a group luncheon.

- **Leader.** As a leader, a manager creates the environment, works to improve employees' performances and reduce conflict, provides feedback and encourages individual growth.

- **Liaison.** In addition to superiors and subordinates, managers interact with others—peer-level managers in other departments, staff specialists, other departments' employees and suppliers and clients. In this role, the manager builds contacts.

Informational Roles

Partly as a result of contacts inside and outside the organization, a manager normally has more information than other members of the staff have. Three key roles derive from the use and dissemination of information.

- **Monitor.** While constantly monitoring the environment to determine what is going on, the manager collects information both directly (by asking questions) and indirectly (by receiving unsolicited information).

- **Disseminator.** As a disseminator, a manager passes on to subordinates some information that would not ordinarily be accessible to them.

- **Spokesperson.** A manager speaks for the work unit to people outside the work unit. Sometimes a spokesperson informs superiors; sometimes he or she communicates with people outside the organization.

Decisional Roles

In playing the four decisional roles, managers make choices, alone or with others, or influence the choices of others.

- **Entrepreneur.** In sharing and initiating new ideas or methods that may improve the work unit's operations, a manager assumes the entrepreneur's role.

Figure 1.4 | Mintzberg's Ten Management Roles

Role	Description	Identifiable Activities from Study of Chief Executives
INTERPERSONAL		
Figurehead	Performs symbolic routine duties of legal or social nature	Attending ceremonies or other public, legal, or social functions; officiating
Leader	Motivates subordinates, ensures hiring and training of staff	Interacting with subordinates
Liaison	Maintains self-developed network of contacts and informers who provide favors and information	Acknowledging mail and interacting with outsiders
INFORMATIONAL		
Monitor	Seeks and receives wide variety of special information to develop thorough understanding of the organization and environment	Handling all mail and contacts concerned primarily with receiving information
Disseminator	Transmits information received from outsiders or subordinates to members of the organization (some information is factual, some involves interpretation and integration)	Forwarding mail into the organization for informational purposes, maintaining verbal contacts involving flow to subordinates
Spokesperson	Transmits to outsiders information about organization's plans, policies, actions, results, and so forth; serves as expert on organization's industry	Attending board meetings, handling mail and contacts involving transmission of information to outsiders
DECISIONAL		
Entrepreneur	Searches organization and its environment for opportunities and initiates projects to bring about change	Implementing strategy and review sessions involving improvement
Disturbance Handler	Initiates corrective action when organization faces important, unexpected disturbances	Implementing strategy to resolve disturbances and crises
Resource Allocator	Fulfills responsibility for the allocation of organizational resources of all kinds—in effect, makes or approves all significant decisions	Scheduling, requesting authorization, budgeting, programming of subordinates' work
Negotiator	Represents the organization in major negotiations	Negotiating

Source: Chart from *The Nature of Managerial Work*, by Henry Mintzberg. Copyright © 1973 by Henry Mintzberg. Reprinted by permission of the author.

- **Disturbance handler.** As a disturbance handler, a manager deals with schedule problems, equipment failure, strikes, broken contracts and any other feature of the work environment that decreases productivity.

- **Resource allocator.** A manager determines who in the work unit gets what resources—money, facilities, equipment and access to the manager.

- **Negotiator.** A manager must spend a significant portion of time negotiating, because only a manager has the information and authority required to do so. Items to be negotiated include contracts with suppliers, trade-offs for resources inside the organization and agreements with labor organizations.

Roles and Managerial Functions

By effectively discharging these multiple roles, managers accomplish their managerial functions. In planning and organizing, a manager performs the resource allocator role. In staffing, managers play the leadership role by providing subordinates with feedback on performance. In leading, managers perform as disseminators, entrepreneurs and disturbance handlers; in controlling, they perform as monitors.

Roles and the Expectations of Others

Simultaneously, managers may be expected to play several roles by several different individuals and groups. Figure 1.5 shows the potentially conflicting role demands on a manager. The ability to meet these multiple role demands makes the difference between a successful manager and an unsuccessful one.[24] Any manager who has a problem adjusting to such conflicts will have a work unit that suffers to some extent.

Figure 1.5	Conflicting Role Demands on a Manager

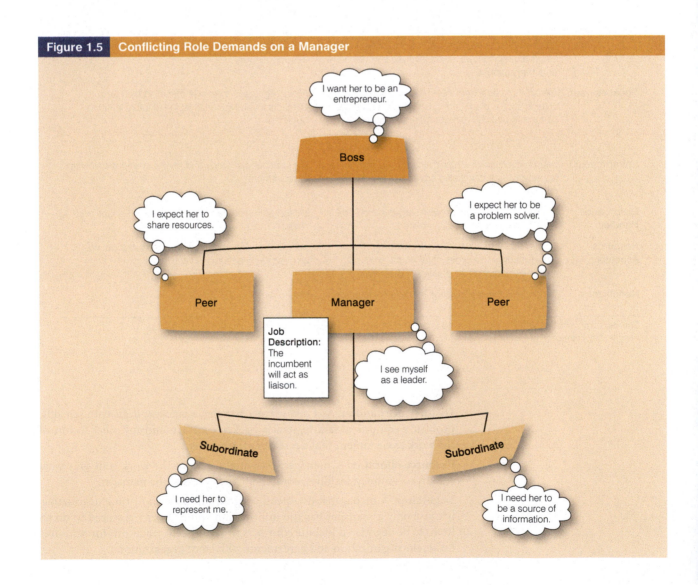

Analyze three management skills

MANAGEMENT SKILLS

Skills allow individuals to perform activities and to function in society. For instance, everyone needs basic reading, writing and oral communication skills to grow intellectually and share ideas with others. Communication (the subject of Chapter 10) is at the heart of every human interaction not just those of managers.

Our focus here is on the three basic sets of skills required of and routinely exercised by managers—technical, human, and conceptual—as identified and described by author and researcher Robert Katz.[25] All are needed to properly execute the five management functions and play the interpersonal, informational and decisional roles just discussed.

Technical Skills

technical skills
The abilities to use the processes, practices, techniques and tools of the specialty area a manager supervises

Technical skills are the abilities to use the processes, practices, techniques and tools of the specialty area a manager supervises. The manager supervising accountants, for example, must know accounting. Although he or she need not be an expert, the manager must have enough technical knowledge and skill to intelligently direct employees, organize tasks, communicate the work group's needs to others and solve problems.

technology
The practical application of knowledge

Successful companies have always used **technology**, the practical application of knowledge, to aid in the conduct of business. Technology used in most companies is the computer. To be considered computer literate, managers must have a basic knowledge of computer terminology and hardware and software components; they must also be able to perform basic tasks or analysis using common computer applications. Managers must be able to leverage the internet (referred to as internet literacy) to search for information, evaluate content and present information. For example, managers should visit their own company's website(s), compare them to competitors' websites, and analyze them from a customer's point of view. Technology-savvy managers can access, store and move digital information, including voice, sound, text, graphics and numbers.

Technical skills are most essential at the first-line level of management and least important at the top. An example of technical skills being least important at the top is Louis V. Gerstner Jr., the former chairman and chief executive officer of International Business Machines Corporation (IBM). He did not have a background in technology or computers, but he possessed enough technical knowledge to communicate effectively with those among his operating employees who were knowledgeable. Their job was to help corporate customers decide which computers and software to buy to meet their needs. Gerstner's job was to help them to do so by providing needed resources and support.

Human Skills

human skills
The abilities to interact and communicate successfully with other persons

Human skills (sometimes called *human relations*) consist of the abilities to interact and communicate successfully with other persons. These skills include leadership of subordinates and facility in intergroup relationships. A manager must be able to understand, work with, and relate to both individuals and groups to build a team environment. The manager's ability to work effectively as a group member and to build cooperative effort within the group depends on human skills.[26]

As managers move into the international environment and function within a global enterprise, human skills will become even more important. The ability to communicate with and be sensitive to different cultures will be at a premium.[27]

Conceptual Skills

Conceptual skills—the mental capacity to conceive and manipulate ideas and abstract relationships—allow the manager to view an organization as a whole and to see how its parts relate to and depend on one another. The conceptually skilled manager can visualize how work units and individuals interrelate, understand the effect of any action throughout the organization and imaginatively execute the five basic management functions.

Well-developed conceptual skills equip the manager to identify a problem, develop alternative solutions, select the best alternative and implement the solution. According to one of the American Management Association's AMA Fast-Response Survey, "the gap between what companies need and what managers can contribute is widest in the area of conceptual skills, including the ability to identify opportunities for innovation; and to recognize problem areas and implement solutions."[28]

Skills and Levels of Management

Figure 1.6 shows the importance of each management skill at each of the three levels of management. Note that human skills are required to the same degree by all three levels. One reason for this is contained in a quote from Herb Kelleher, former chairman and CEO of the superefficient and highly profitable Southwest Airlines.

> *[Recognize] that your own people are absolutely the key to your success.... If you serve your own people well, then they will serve the public well. Everybody, be they a producer of products or a producer of services, is in the Customer Satisfaction business.*[29]

As one progresses upward in the management ranks, technical skills become less important and conceptual skills become more important. Middle managers need to work within and visualize a larger piece of the organizational "pie" than do first-level managers. Top management must be concerned with the whole pie—its basic ingredients and making it larger.

conceptual skills
The mental capacity to conceive and manipulate ideas and abstract relationships

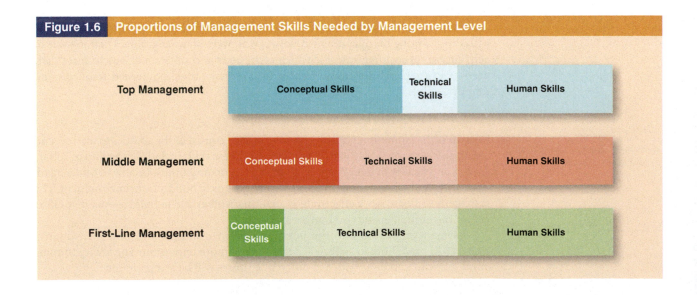

Figure 1.6   Proportions of Management Skills Needed by Management Level

Top Management	Conceptual Skills	Technical Skills	Human Skills
Middle Management	Conceptual Skills	Technical Skills	Human Skills
First-Line Management	Conceptual Skills	Technical Skills	Human Skills

Contrast the myths with the realities of a manager's job

MANAGEMENT MYTHS AND REALITIES

People who have not held management jobs and have not studied management often hold perceptions disconnected from reality—that is, myths—about managers' needs and functions. The following six myths and their corresponding realities have been uncovered by the research of several management experts.

As previously mentioned, Henry Mintzberg studied how managers actually work. He published an article examining the effect of multiple demands on managers. "The Manager's Job: Folklore and Fact," was chosen by *Harvard Business Review* as a "classic" article for its enduring value. His research is still relevant today. He identified commonly held beliefs about managers and countered them with the reality of a manager's regular existence:

Myth #1. *Managers are reflective, methodical planners with time to systematically plan and work through a day.*
Reality: Typical managers take on so much and encounter such constant interruption that little time remains for reflection. Events range from trivialities to crises; the average time spent on one activity is nine minutes.

Myth #2. *Effective managers have no regular duties to perform. They establish others' responsibilities in advance and then relax to watch others do the work.*
Reality: Although their days may be interrupted by crises, managers have regular duties to perform. They must attend meetings, see visitors from the community and other parts of the organization and continuously process and report on information related to the performance of their business. To perform all their duties, managers often extend the day into the night.

Myth #3. *The manager's job is a science; managers work systematically and analytically to determine programs and procedures.*
Reality: The manager's job is less a science than an art. Rather than systematic procedures and programs, managers rely heavily on intuition and judgment.

Authors and researchers Clinton Longenecker and Dennis Gioia[30] have added the following three myths and realities of a manager to Mintzberg's list:

Myth #4. *Managers are self-starting, self-directing, and autonomous, or they would not be managers.*
Reality: Good managers are self-managing, often to an extraordinary degree. They want, appreciate and accept autonomy, but they also want input, attention and guidance that only their superiors can provide.

Myth #5. *Good managers seek out the information they need.*
Reality: Good managers are [active] information seekers. Yet they often do not have access to the information that their bosses have. Their [efforts are] thus wasted on unnecessary work that their superiors could eliminate with better information flow.

Myth #6. *Competition among managers is good for ... business.*
Reality: Competition is effective among businesses but not necessarily within a business. Collaboration and cooperation within the organization are ... better ... for improving competitiveness in the business arena.

As you read further in this text, you will discover additional research, principles and real-world examples that influence the practice of management. They will help you to identify and abandon some of your own myths about management.

EVALUATING A MANAGER'S PERFORMANCE

Discuss the criteria used to evaluate a manager's performance

Managers are evaluated by using a variety of factors:

- How effectively they play the three sets of management roles listed in this chapter.
- Whether they possess and properly apply needed management skills.
- How effective they are in setting objectives and achieving goals.
- How efficiently they use their talents and resources.
- How well they demonstrate leadership.
- Whether they act ethically.
- How effectively they make use of the diversity of their people.
- How effectively they and their people please customers.

In short, managers are evaluated in how well they demonstrate through everyday actions the essential ideas in this chapter.

Noted Leadership expert Ram Charan found that 38 derailed chief executive officers, "just weren't worrying enough about the right things: execution, decisiveness, follow-through, delivering on commitments."[31]

In addition to the preceding factors, consider the findings of an alliance of consulting firms—Manchester Partners International. "About 40 percent of managers and executives who take new positions fail within 18 months."[32] The primary reasons for the failures include the following:

- Being uncertain about the expectations of their bosses.
- Being unable to make tough decisions.
- Taking too long to learn the job.
- Being unable to build partnerships with subordinates and peers.
- Lacking political savvy.

Do you see the link between and among these reasons for failing and the skills, roles and functions discussed in this chapter? Managers' uncertainty about their boss's expectations may be based on poor communication skills and ignorance of the criteria being used in their organization to evaluate managers. Tough decisions often involve ethical issues and effective and efficient use of resources. Building partnerships requires all the skills and leadership concepts discussed. Political savvy requires partnerships and the practice of human skills.

Chapter Summary

1 Explain why organizations need managers.

Managers—people who set and achieve goals with and through others—are needed to create organizations and oversee their operations and growth. By playing various roles, exercising a variety of skills, and performing five basic functions, they provide the leadership and coordination needed to meet the objectives of every organization.

2 Determine the needs that affect a manager's universe.

Management's universe is complex, ever-changing, exacting, exciting and filled with pressure. Managers and their organizations must simultaneously focus on meeting customers' needs, providing leadership, acting ethically, valuing diversity and coping with international challenges. The manager's universe is shaped by external environmental forces including competition, technological advances, natural phenomena, emergencies, as well as social, cultural and political factors.

3 Identify three levels of management.

Most organizations contain the three traditional levels of management: top, middle and first-line or operating. Top management consists of the chief executive officer and/or president and his or her immediate subordinates—vice presidents. Middle management includes all managers below the rank of vice president but above the first-line level. First-line managers manage workers. Like their counterparts in middle management, they are rapidly being transformed into team leaders and team facilitators.

4 Describe five management functions.

The five management functions are planning, organizing, staffing, leading and controlling. Planning involves identifying goals, alternative ways of achieving them and the resources required. Organizing includes defining the tasks required to meet goals, grouping these into positions, and creating the management hierarchy. Staffing includes determining the organization's need for people and then recruiting, hiring, training, appraising and compensating the personnel. Leading involves providing guidance and inspiration to individuals and groups, providing a climate in which individuals can deliver motivated behaviors and communicating and winning commitments to organizational values and goals from employees. Controlling attempts to prevent, identify and correct deviations from guidelines established to evaluate performances and outputs of both people and processes.

5 Apply management functions to each level of management.

Managers at every level perform the same functions. They differ in the time spent on each function and the depth of their involvement with each. Top management is most concerned about the long term and the entire organization. Middle managers focus on translating top management's goals into objectives for the execution of both business and management functions. First-line managers take a narrower view. They focus on converting middle managers' objectives into ones of their own, and they concentrate on the execution of operations and functions that directly interact with external customers.

6 Summarize ten management roles.

To carry out their jobs, managers must be able to perform certain roles. The roles are influenced by a manager's job description and the expectations held by a manager's superiors, subordinates and peers. The ten management roles are grouped into three categories: interpersonal roles (figurehead, leader, liaison), informational roles (monitor, disseminator, spokesperson), and decisional roles (entrepreneur, disturbance handler, resource allocator, negotiator).

Interpersonal roles require interactions with others on a regular basis. Informational roles require managers to gather information from many sources, share what they discover with the appropriate people and represent their units to others inside the organization. Decisional roles require managers to acquire, distribute and safeguard needed resources. Managers must also negotiate with and between competing forces and handle disruptions to their operations.

7 Analyze three management skills.

Managers need three basic skills: technical, human and conceptual. Technical skills grant the ability to use the processes, practices, techniques and tools of a specialty area. Human skills consist of the ability to interact and communicate with other persons successfully. Conceptual skills are the ability to: (1) view an organization as a whole and see how its parts relate and depend on one another, (2) deal with ideas and abstractions and (3), diagnose and solve a problem.

8 Contrast the myths with the realities of a manager's job.

Six myths are associated with a manager's job and the realities:

1 *The myth:* Managers are reflective, systematic planners. *The reality:* The typical manager is so busy there is little time for reflection.

2 *The myth:* Effective managers have no regular duties to perform. *The reality:* Managers, although interrupted by crises, have a job description containing regular duties to perform.

3 *The myth:* The manager's job is a science. *The reality:* The manager's job is less a science than an art.

4 *The myth:* Managers are self-starting, self-directing and autonomous. *The reality:* Good managers appreciate autonomy, but also want input, attention and guidance from superiors.

5 *The myth:* Good managers seek out needed information. *The reality:* Effective managers are proactive information seekers, but too often managers do not have access to information they need and their bosses possess.

6 *The myth:* Competition among managers is good for managers and the business. *The reality:* Competition is not effective within a business. Collaboration and cooperation within the organization and among managers is a better approach.

9 Discuss the criteria used to evaluate a manager's performance.

Managers are evaluated through the use of many criteria including how well they play their roles, exercise their skills, execute the management functions, set and achieve goals, please customers, provide leadership, act ethically and value diversity, as well as how effectively and efficiently they use their resources.

KEY TERMS

conceptual skills   **26**

customer   **6**

customer relationship management (CRM)   **8**

diversity   **11**

ethics   **10**

first-line management   **16**

functional managers   **16**

goal   **5**

human skills   **25**

leadership   **10**

management   **4**

management hierarchy   **14**

managers   **4**

middle management   **15**

organization   **5**

quality   **6**

role   **22**

technical skills   **25**

technology   **25**

top management   **14**

REVIEW QUESTIONS

1. How do managers assist an organization to achieve its goals and objectives?

2. What factors make the manager's universe complex?

3. Where are managers located within an organization's management hierarchy? How are the different levels similar? How are they different?

4. What are the regular activities that all managers perform? Which of these activities is called the "first" function? Why?

5. How do the functions in question 4 apply to the three levels of management found in most organizations? In what ways are the execution of controlling activities similar on each of the three levels of management? How are they different?

6. What is a management role? Do all managers perform the same roles? Why or why not?

7. What management skills are most essential for a CEO? Why? What skills are required by all managers? Why?

8. Why do people hold the different myths mentioned in this chapter? How do you think people create these myths?

9. If you were a CEO of a small company, what criteria would you use to evaluate your managers' performances? Which criterion do you believe is most essential? Why?

DISCUSSION QUESTIONS FOR CRITICAL THINKING

1. Denzel Jones now holds the job of data entry clerk and is being considered for a promotion into a first-line management position over his coworkers. What additional skills will he need? What types of training should the organization provide to help Jones make the transition to manager? What would you recommend Jones study if the organization doesn't provide management training?

2. What did you think about management before you read this chapter? Did any of those thoughts match the myths about management mentioned in the chapter? How did that view of management change now that you've read the chapter?

3. How are the three types of skills related to the execution of the ten management roles and the five management functions?

Social Media Management Exercises

1 Prepare to Blog

Some managers have websites, called web logs or blogs, where they journal their thoughts and post them on the web. Thus, a blog is an online journal. Keep a journal about the discoveries you make about your management class experience. Complete at least one entry per chapter. Use the starter guides below.

- Something important I learned in this chapter is. . .
- A few things I liked about this chapter are . . .
- Something that threw me for a loop in this chapter was . . .
- I agree with . . .
- I'm confused by . . .
- I disagree with . . .
- I'd like to learn more about . . .
- I was successful in using the following ideas . . .

2 Blog Links

Most corporate websites are informative, but lack customer interaction. Thus, a blog is the best way for a business to put its voice out there on a regular basis. The idea is to attract people to the blog, not to promote the business.

1. Identify one of your favorite products. (For example, you might choose Nike athletic shoes.)
2. Identify the company's blog. (For example, search for "Nike blog.")
3. What is the name of the blog?
4. What is the web address (URL – Uniform Resource Locator)?
5. Note whether or not the blog allows customer interaction. (How can customers interact without commenting? Does the blog allow pictures to be uploaded? How can customers interact with the brand?)
6. Who writes the blog? (Identify the name and position, etc. about this person.)
7. What have you learned from visiting this blog?
8. How does this blog inform your thinking about management?

Experiential Learning

Great Managers

Marcus Buckingham—author of *The One Thing You Need to Know ... About Great Managing, Great Leading, and Sustained Individual Success* (Free Press)— spent 17 years researching the world's best managers for the Gallup Organization. The Gallup Organization studied one million employees and 80,000 managers in all kinds of organizations, at all levels, in most industries, and in many countries. Marcus Buckingham and Curt Coffman of the Gallup Organization presented the findings of Gallup's in-depth study of great managers in their book *First, Break All the Rules* (Simon & Schuster). They found that "great managers share one common trait: They do not hesitate to break virtually every rule held sacred by conventional wisdom."

From this research, Gallup identified 12 questions that measure dimensions that managers can influence.

Employee satisfaction on Gallup's 12 questions distinguishes the greatest managers from all the rest. (For more on the Gallup Organization, read About Us at *http://www.gallup.com*. For more on what the world's greatest managers do differently, read Marcus Buckingham and Curt Coffman, *First, Break All the Rules* (Simon & Schuster, 1999) and *Now, Discover Your Strengths* (Free Press, 2001).

Interview a full-time employee. Identify the organization, the job title of the employee and the job title of the employee's manager. Ask the questions below. After the interview, report your findings. Does this employee have a great manager? If not, what would you recommend the manager change?

1. Do you know what is expected of you at work?
2. Do you have the materials and equipment you need to do your work right?

3. At work, do you have the opportunity to do what you do best every day?

4. In the last seven days, have you received recognition or praise for doing good work?

5. Does your supervisor, or someone at work, seem to care about you as a person?

6. Is there someone at work who encourages your development?

7. At work, do your opinions seem to count?

8. Does the mission/purpose of your company make you feel your job is important?

9. Are your associates (fellow employees) committed to doing quality work?

10. Do you have a best friend at work?

11. In the last six months, has someone at work talked to you about your progress?

12. In the last year, have you had opportunities at work to learn and grow?

Chapter 2

Management Thought: Past and Present

LEARNING OBJECTIVES

After studying this chapter, you should be able to:

1 Discuss why knowledge of the evolution of management theories is important to managers

2 Explain the contributions of the following:

    a. Classical schools of management thought

    b. Behavioral school of management thought

    c. Quantitative school of management thought

    d. Systems school of management thought

    e. Contingency school of management thought

    f. Quality school of management thought

Openness to Change

Many industries—such as travel, music, publishing and financial services—look very different today than they did in the past. Furthermore, these industries, as well as others, may look different in the future. Change is a constant in business, and the most successful companies recognize when they must change. They transform themselves faster than their competitors.

An important step in becoming a successful employee is to assess your openness to the changes that work demands. Are you open to change? Assess your readiness for changes at work. For each of the following statements, circle the number that indicates your level of agreement. Rate your agreement as it is, not what you think it should be. Objectivity will enable you to determine your management skill strengths and weaknesses.

	Almost Always	Often	Sometimes	Rarely	Almost Never
I am confident about my abilities to succeed at work.	5	4	3	2	1
I am open to change some of my personal behaviors and follow company policies.	5	4	3	2	1
I get personal satisfaction from completing my goals.	5	4	3	2	1
I assist others when I see they need help.	5	4	3	2	1
I engage in difficult projects without giving up too easily.	5	4	3	2	1
I enjoy learning something new.	5	4	3	2	1
My paycheck is (will be) a good indicator of my abilities.	5	4	3	2	1
I try to think openly about issues even if they conflict with my ideas.	5	4	3	2	1
I use different techniques for solving different problems.	5	4	3	2	1
I am hopeful about my success at work.	5	4	3	2	1

Compute your score by adding the circled numbers. The highest score is 50; the lowest score is 10. A higher score implies you are more likely to be open to necessary changes in the workplace. A lower score implies a lesser degree of readiness, but a low score can be increased. Reading and studying this chapter will help improve your understanding of change.

➡ Do you embrace change? Are you open to new ideas? Are you able to react and adapt quickly? If not, which dysfunctional behaviors, practices and beliefs will you discard?

➡ How can you change faster than your rivals?

Adapted from De Sellers, Carol W. Dochen, and Russ Hodges, *Academic Transformation: The Road to College Success*, Third Edition (Pearson, 2015) p. 16

INTRODUCTION

For many generations people believed that the Earth was flat and the center of the universe. No educated person believes this today. Throughout history, one generation's "fact" has become, in part or in total, the next generation's fiction. The conventional wisdom of every era evolves as its cherished beliefs are challenged by the new, leaving behind only those elements that have survived the test of time. So it is with the various schools of thought about the ways in which organizations, their resources and their processes should be managed.

Since the Industrial Revolution began in the late 1700s, those in charge of organizations have been alternately creating, testing, embracing and rejecting multiple theories of management. All have contributed in various ways to how managers currently practice their art. This chapter examines the six major theories or schools of management that have evolved over the past 200 years and assesses them for their relevance to the twenty-first century.

HISTORY AND THEORY OF MANAGEMENT

Each generation of managers needs to understand the lessons learned by its predecessors and build on them. This is how organizations continuously improve. As you shall see throughout this text, preceding generations of managers have much to teach.

Value of History

People who ignore the past are destined to relive it. A person unaware of mistakes made by others is likely to repeat them. The wise person studies the past to avoid its pitfalls and benefit from its achievements.

Ancient History

Graphic records from ancient times—the Bible, Egyptian tomb paintings, Babylonian clay tablets and rock drawings from Bhimbetka, India—record how early civilizations thought about management and how they managed their affairs. Management began when the earliest humans banded together in clans and tribes. Their survival depended on effective hunting and gathering. Such activities needed both skilled individuals and cooperative efforts. In time, strong individuals with the ability to manage emerged within each community to take over the management of specialized tasks and of the community as a whole.

Value of Theory

A **theory** is a part of an art or science that attempts to explain the relationships between and among its underlying principles. Theories give people a reason for doing things one way rather than another. Various management theories have arisen over past decades; some aspects of each have failed the test of time, others have survived it and are used by managers today.

To summarize the evolution of the six major theories or schools of thought about management, see Figure 2.1. It provides a time line showing when each emerged. Notice that all the theories continue into the present, indicating that parts of each are still affecting the ways in which managers practice their art.

1 Discuss why knowledge of the evolution of management theories is important to managers

theory
Part of an art or science that attempts to explain the relationships between and among its underlying principles

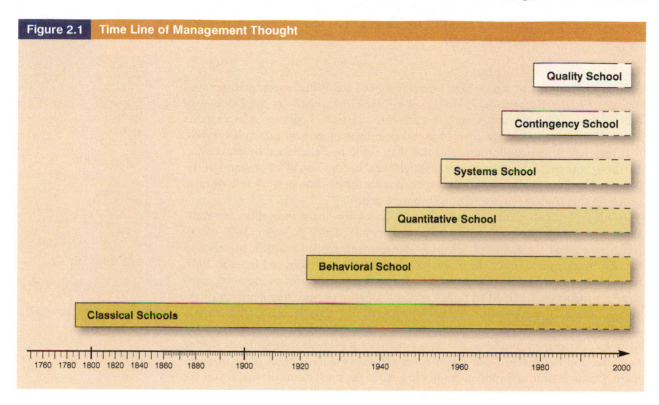

Figure 2.1   **Time Line of Management Thought**

2a Explain the contributions of the classical schools of management thought

classical management theory
A theory that focused on finding the "one best way" to perform and manage tasks

classical scientific school
Focused on the manufacturing environment and getting work done on the factory floor

classical administrative school
Emphasized the flow of information and how organizations should operate

CLASSICAL MANAGEMENT THEORY

The **classical management theory** originated during England's Industrial Revolution, which began in the late 1700s with the invention of reliable steam-powered machinery. Steam power freed manufacturers from dependence on running water and wind. For the first time, manufacturers could mass-produce goods in factories that operated year-round. The textile industry was among the first to capitalize on the new technology. Before steam power, an individual working on a home loom wove cotton or woolen cloth. After the Industrial Revolution, weaving was done in urban areas by large groups of semiskilled workers using reliable machines under one roof. The Industrial Revolution allowed manufacturers to make standardized goods for domestic and overseas mass markets.

Early factories depended on a constant flow of labor and materials. Owners needed to plan, organize, lead, control and staff many different kinds of operations. Writing of the new managerial skills required of successful industrialists, economic historian P. L. Payne observed, "In many cases, better organization contributed almost as much to increased production as the use of the machines themselves."[1]

The classical management theory focused on finding the "one best way" to perform and manage tasks. As the Industrial Revolution continued, the environment of the early factory gave rise to two separate doctrines of management—two schools of thought linked under the label "classical."

First came the **classical scientific school**, which focused on the manufacturing environment and getting work done on the factory floor. Then came the **classical administrative school**, which emphasized the flow of information and how organizations should operate. Both schools articulated principles and functions of management discussed throughout this text.

Classical Scientific School

Among the pioneers of the classical scientific school was British mathematician and inventor Charles Babbage (1792–1871), who in 1832 published *On the Economy of Machinery and Manufactures*, a study that presented the fruit of Babbage's observations of the factory floor. Babbage concluded that definite management principles existed, that they had broad applications and that they could be determined by experience. He thought that the most important principle was "the division of labor amongst the persons who perform the work." Babbage called for the division of work into discrete processes that could be mastered quickly by one person.

Other pioneers of the classical scientific school also made theoretical contributions that increased labor efficiency and productivity. Frederick W. Taylor (1856–1915), sometimes called the Father of Scientific Management, applied scientific methods to factory problems and urged the proper use of human labor, tools, and time. In 1909, he published *Principles of Scientific Management*. During a career as executive, consultant, production specialist and efficiency expert, Taylor pursued four key goals (principles of scientific management): to develop a science of management, to select workers scientifically, to educate and train workers scientifically, and to create cooperation between management and labor. From his experience at Midvale Steel, Simonds Rolling Machine, and Bethlehem Steel, Taylor developed the core ideas of scientific management. Devising time and motion studies to analyze the movements of workers on the job, he determined the output that individual workers should be able to achieve with specific materials and equipment. From such data he determined the quickest ways to perform tasks. Taylor introduced work breaks and the piece-rate system for worker pay.[2]

Frank Gilbreth (1868–1924) and Lillian Gilbreth (1878–1972) added to Taylor's findings. The Gilbreths used time and motion studies to analyze workers' activities and remove unnecessary movements and causes of fatigue. One of Frank's first studies involved bricklaying. Frank reduced a ten-step process to five steps, thus doubling productivity. His study of hospital operating-room functions saved resources and shortened the time patients spent on operating tables. Lillian assisted her husband and expanded on his work after his death.

Henry Metcalf, another thinker of the classical scientific school, emphasized the need for scientific administration. The management system he advocated relied on fixed responsibilities for cost control and an effective flow of information. He urged managers to record their experiences for the benefit of others.

Henry Gantt's idea represented a move away from authoritarian management. He advocated a bonus system to reward workers for acceptable and superior work, and he invented the Gantt chart, a graphic means of representing and planning production activities and time frames (still used today).

Assessment The theories and principles developed by the early classical scientific thinkers are with us today, although experience and accumulated data have modified the ideas significantly. One of the methods used by the early thinkers, the time and motion study, is still in common use.

Authors, professors and researchers Christopher A. Bartlett and Sumantra Ghoshal provide this tight summary of classical thinking:

> *Early in this century, [Frederick] Taylor wrote that management's role was to ensure that workers' tasks were well defined, measured, and controlled. With the objective of*

making people as consistent, reliable, and efficient as the machines they supported, managers came to regard their subordinates as little more than another factor of production. In that context, managers designed systems, procedures, and policies that would ensure that all employees conformed to the company way. The goal was to make the middle managers' and workers' activities more predictable and thus more controllable…. The systems that insured control and conformity also inhibited creativity and initiative…. At best, the resulting organizational culture grew passive; with amused resignation employees implemented corporate-led initiatives that they knew would fail. At worst, the tightly controlled environment triggered antagonism and even subversion; people deep in the organization found ways to undermine the system that constrained them.[3]

The classical school failed to welcome or tap into the great diversity that existed in organizations. Employees with beliefs, values, and customs different from those held by the people in charge—owners and their managers—were told to suppress them and

Valuing Diversity and Inclusion

From Equal Opportunity to Valuing Diversity

Since its very first people arrived, the United States has been populated by diverse groups of immigrants and their descendants. But as history points out, they have not always tolerated one another's existence.

Since the 1964 Civil Rights Act, various federal, state and local laws have been passed to promote equal employment opportunities for a variety of protected groups: most notably, women and minorities such as African Americans, Hispanic-surnamed Americans, American and Alaskan natives, Asian Americans, the physically and mentally challenged, and people age 40 and over. Although equal opportunity laws and the agencies designated to enforce them can help to promote entrance of the above-mentioned groups into organizations, they cannot guarantee their acceptance, inclusion and effective utilization.

Once diversity is created in an organization's ranks, diverse individuals and groups are often received with some hostility and a little tolerance (but usually not acceptance and respect) from preexisting personnel. Separateness exists rather than inclusion. To move from these conditions, carefully planned and executed training programs—usually conducted with the aid of outside consultants—are necessary. For these programs to be effective, most organizations must pass through two distinct phases, both of which call for commitment and leadership from top to bottom and for the elimination of biases and stereotypes.

The first phase is an inclusion phase. As diverse individuals and groups are allowed to display their uniqueness, support groups form, often spontaneously, whether encouraged or not by the organization's leadership. The diverse groups and individuals begin to interact, demonstrate their talents, and build respect and appreciation for each other's values, customs, traditions and contributions.

In the second phase, all organizational members learn to appreciate and value both the need for and the contributions of diverse individuals and groups. Through a variety of company-sponsored programs and activities, employees become active, committed, contributing members, accepted and respected by those who differ from them. All members become full participants individually and in teams. Only in this second phase can the true potential in every employee be developed and effectively utilized. Imagine a company with thousands of employees, most of whom differ from each other in many ways. Imagine further that these people are willing to contribute their talents and energy to help each other and solve both the organization's and its customers' problems. You are imagining a reality in many of America's most successful large and small organizations.

➡ **What examples from your own experience can you give that demonstrate your valuing diversity?**

conform to the organization's beliefs, values and customs. See this chapter's Valuing Diversity and Inclusion feature for the evolution of how diversity has been handled in America. Leadership was expected at the top but suppressed everywhere else; management's primary concern was to meet the organization's needs. People doing the work were taught a precise set of motions for doing it and were not asked about or allowed to deviate from the ways they were taught.

In most industries, U.S. companies had little competition from abroad. Whatever they built, they could sell. Quality, where concern for it did exist, was the responsibility of a quality-control department and depended in large measure on final inspections of finished goods. When defects were spotted, items were reworked or scrapped.

The classical school grew and prospered in a sellers' market with few laws to constrain the conduct of business. The prevailing ethical view among business leaders was that if it was good for business, it was good for the country. Most consumers soon learned to govern their behavior by the motto, "Buyer beware!"

The classical scientific thinkers taught managers to analyze everything, teach effective methods to others, constantly monitor workers, plan responsibly, and organize and control the work and the workers. Their successors—today's managers—realize that, without committed men and women empowered to examine their own output and take responsibility for it, neither productivity nor quality can improve. The idea of specialization, prized in the classical scientific school, has been modified. The aim today is to avoid the physical and psychological hazards of boring, repetitive work, for example. Modern managers emphasize cross training, which allows workers to perform a variety of tasks, many of which require high literacy and computational skills. Successful modern factories depend on innovation, imagination and creativity from dedicated workers who are backed by managers. These managers act not as commanders, but as teachers, coaches and servants.

Classical Administrative School

As the complexity of organizations grew, managers needed a new theory to help them meet their new challenges. To meet this demand, the classical administrative school grew from classical scientific roots. The administrative branch emphasized efficiency and productivity in running factories and businesses. It provided a theoretical basis for all managers, no matter their area of expertise.

Early Contributors Frenchman Henri Fayol (1841–1925) believed that management ability was not a personal talent that some had by birth and others did not. From practical experience, he knew that management required specific skills that could be learned and taught. As mentioned in Chapter 1, the roots of today's management functions—planning, organizing, staffing, leading and controlling—can be found in Fayol's universal management functions: planning, organizing, commanding, coordinating and controlling. (It should be noted here that some authors and managers view staffing as a part of either leading or organizing. Also, coordinating is usually done by all managers while they are executing the other functions.) Fayol also developed 14 principles (summarized in Figure 2.2) that form the foundation for modern management practice and sound administrative structure.[4]

Another contributor to the administrative school was American political scientist Mary Parker Follett. Her work in the 1920s focused on how organizations cope with conflict and the importance of goal sharing among managers. She emphasized the human element in organizations and the need to discover and enlist individual and group motivation. Believing that the first principle for both individual and group success is the "capacity for organized thinking," Follett urged managers to prepare

Figure 2.2	Henri Fayol's General Principles of Management
1. Division of Work	Specialization allows workers and managers to acquire an ability, sureness, and accuracy that will increase output. More and better work will be produced with the same effort.
2. Authority	The right to give orders and the power to exact obedience are the essence of authority. Its roots are in the person and the position. It cannot be conceived apart from responsibility.
3. Discipline	Discipline comprises obedience, application, energy, behavior and outward marks of respect between employers and employees. It is essential to any business. Without it, no enterprise can prosper.
4. Unity of Command	For any action whatsoever, an employee should receive orders from one superior only. One person, one boss. In no case can a social organization adapt to a duality of command.
5. Unity of Direction	One head and one plan should lead a group of activities having the same objective.
6. Subordination of the Individual to the General Interest	The interest of one person or group in a business should not prevail over that of the organization.
7. Remuneration of Personnel	The price of services rendered should be fair and satisfactory to both employees and employer. A level of pay depends on an employee's value to the organization and on factors independent of an employee's worth—cost of living, availability of personnel, and general business conditions, for example.
8. Centralization	Everything that serves to reduce the importance of an individual subordinate's role is centralization. Everything that increases the subordinate's importance is decentralization. All situations call for a balance between these two positions.
9. Scalar Chain	The chain formed by managers from the highest to the lowest is called a scalar chain, or chain of command. Managers are the links in the chain. They should communicate to and through the links as they occur in their chains. Links may be skipped only when superiors approve and when a real need exists to do so.
10. Order	There should be a place for everyone, and everyone in his or her place; a place for everything, and everything in its place. The objective of order is to avoid loss and waste.
11. Equity	Kindliness and justice should be practiced by persons in authority to extract the best that their subordinates have to give.
12. Stability of Tenure of Personnel	Reducing the turnover of personnel will result in more efficiency and fewer expenses.
13. Initiative	People should be allowed the freedom to propose and execute ideas at all levels of an enterprise. A manager able to permit the exercise of initiative by subordinates is far superior to one unable to do so.
14. Esprit de Corps	In unity there is strength. Managers have the duty to promote harmony and to discourage and avoid those things that disturb harmony.

Source: Adapted from *General Principles of Management* by Henri Fayol.
Copyright 1949 by Pitman Learning, Inc., 6 Davis Drive, Belmont, CA 94002.

themselves for their profession as seriously as candidates for any of the traditional learned professions.[5]

Another American theorist of the administrative school was Chester Barnard, who was president of New Jersey Bell Telephone Company. In his 1938 work, *The Functions of the Executive,* Barnard argued that managers must gain acceptance for their authority. He advocated the use of basic management principles, and he cautioned managers to issue no order that could not or would not be obeyed. To do so, he believed, destroyed authority, discipline and morale.[6]

The German theorist Max Weber (1864–1920) was a professor of law and economics who wrote about social, political and economic issues. Weber was the first to describe the principles of **bureaucracies**—rational organizations based on the control of knowledge. Although Weber's milestone work, *The Theory of Social and Economic Organizations,* appeared in Germany early in the twentieth century, it was not translated into English until 1947. The book describes how bureaucratic organizations operate and how they lend themselves to the administration of ongoing work and functions.

Weber argued that the bureaucratic organization developed in parallel with the evolving capitalist system. He saw the bureaucratic organization as a superior mechanism for administering businesses, governments, religious orders, universities and the military. He based his conclusion on his view that technically competent individuals who provide stable, strict, intensive and continuous administration are the people who control bureaucracies. In the typical bureaucratic hierarchy, he said, clearly defined offices (positions) are occupied by qualified career people selected on the basis of their expertise and experience (often on the basis of standardized examinations). By and large, these workers are promoted according to the judgments of superiors, and the workers are subject to the disciplinary system of the organization. A fine example of a classic bureaucracy is the federal government of the United States. Career professionals who hold their positions until retirement age, regardless of political administration, generally are the staff at the Agriculture Department, the Federal Bureau of Investigation, the Bureau of Land Management, the Internal Revenue Service and many other federal departments.

Assessment By 1900, industrial leaders began to recognize that a manager did not have to be the one who owned the business. The flow of authority and paperwork could be governed by scientific principles, and people could be trained to be effective managers. Industrial leaders realized that successful organizations needed unity of purpose, command and direction. An ordered environment; subordination of individual interests to the survival of the organization; and harmony, equity, and stability of tenure for key personnel all became hallmarks of effective organizations.

Management according to the classical administrative school has limitations, however. The monumental difficulties experienced by the former Soviet Union—possibly the most rigidly bureaucratic system yet attempted—illustrate the downside. Rigid and unresponsive decision making and a lack of commitment among workers given no autonomy led to a strangled economic system.

Within the classical administrative school, the work of Mary Parker Follett most directly discussed the disadvantages of bureaucratic theory. She emphasized for the first time the importance of the individual—both manager and worker. As we briefly discussed previously, Follett believed that scientific methods could be applied to human relationships, and she believed that people could reach their potentials only through groups.[7] Follett and others defined the social context of work and emphasized reliance on skilled, principled and professional managers.

The classical administrative school opened the door for the next important school: the behavioral, or human relations, school.

BEHAVIORAL MANAGEMENT THEORY

The **behavioral school** took management thinking one step further. Its proponents recognized employees as individuals with concrete human needs, as parts of work groups, and as members of a larger society. Enlightened managers were to view their

bureaucracies
Rational organizations based on the control of knowledge

Explain the contributions of the behavioral school of management thought

behavioral school
Recognized employees as individuals with concrete, human needs, as parts of work groups and as members of a larger society

subordinates as assets to be developed, not as nameless robots expected to follow orders blindly.

Behavioral School Proponents

The first modern author to address the concern for people in the work environment was Robert Owen, considered by many the father of modern personnel management. In 1813, with the publication of "An Address to the Superintendents of Manufactories," Owen asserted that the quality and quantity of workers' output were influenced by conditions both on and off the job. Owen demonstrated, by referring to the textile mills he managed in Scotland, that devoting attention to the "vital machine" (people) made as much sense as devoting attention to inanimate machines.[8] Owen was far ahead of his time, and not until the work of Mary Parker Follett in the 1920s did the individual worker again receive scholarly attention.

Like Follett, psychologist Elton Mayo emphasized the behavioral aspects of workers. Beginning in 1924 Mayo and the National Academy of Sciences conducted five studies. Each focused on the Western Electric plant in Cicero, Illinois. The studies heightened management's awareness of the social needs of workers and showed how an organization's social environment influenced productivity. He discovered that when employees were treated with dignity, in a way that showed concern for their welfare and individuality, commitment and productivity increased.

Mayo's studies on the effects of piece rates on production led to the discovery that social pressures exerted by coworkers were a significant influence on performance. In the bank-wiring study at Western Electric, workers in teams developed their own production quotas. Mayo found that, rather than release finished pieces, workers kept pieces to help the group meet future quotas, and they pressured coworkers to keep production within the bounds of established quotas.[9]

Abraham Maslow—a humanistic psychologist, teacher, and practicing manager— developed a needs-based theory of motivation. Maslow's theory is now considered central to understanding human motivations and behavior. His work paralleled many of the findings of psychology and sociology, social sciences that were then emerging. These sciences affirmed what artists and historians had always known—that people are extraordinarily complex creatures with many motives for behaviors on and off the job. Maslow's seminal work on human behavior in the workplace, *Eupsychian Management,* published in 1963, was updated with Deborah C. Stephens and Gary Heil in 1998 and entitled *Maslow on Management.*

In a 1943 article for *Psychological Review* titled "A Theory of Human Motivation," Maslow identified and analyzed five basic needs, which he believed are fundamental to all human behavior. These needs related to physiology (food, water, air, and sex), security (safety, the absence of illness), society or affiliation (friendship, interaction, love), esteem (respect and recognition) and self-actualization (the ability to reach one's potential).

Maslow's list of needs provided a radically different perspective for managers. Before Maslow, most managers assumed that people were primarily motivated by money. Maslow's work caused many managers to evaluate their own actions, their companies' conduct, and their individual philosophies about people. Chapter 11 will discuss Maslow's hierarchy of needs at length.

In 1960, Douglas McGregor expanded the ideas of his predecessors in management theory by publishing *The Human Side of Enterprise.* In it, McGregor explained his view that all managers operated from one or two basic assumptions about human behavior: Theory X and Theory Y. The first theory, the view traditionally held about labor, portrayed workers in industry as being lazy and needing to be coerced, controlled, and directed. The second described people as McGregor thought them to be: responsible; willing to learn; and, given the proper incentives, inherently motivated to exercise ingenuity and creativity. McGregor believed that the traditional way of treating people—regarding them as unthinking, uncaring robots—must change. Indeed, McGregor stressed that only by changing these assumptions could managers tap into workers' vast talents. What mattered, he emphasized, was how people were treated and valued in their work settings. McGregor told managers that if they gave employees a chance to contribute and to take control and responsibility, they would do so.[10]

Assessment The behavioral management school brought the human dimension of work firmly into the mainstream of management thought. The results continue today. Many managers work hard to discover what employees want from work; how to enlist their cooperation and commitment; and how to unleash their talents, energy, and creativity. The behaviorists integrated, for the first time, ideas from sociology, anthropology, and psychology with management theory.

One result of the behavioral school was the creation of positions for professional human resource managers. Behavioral management theory effectively paved the way for modern-day employee-assistance programs, such as substance-abuse intervention and day care for children, and innovations in communication involving subordinates and peers, individually and collectively.

The major limitation of behavioral management theory is its complexity. It does not yield quick or simple conclusions, and it does not conclusively explain or predict the actions of individuals or groups. Most managers, not being trained social scientists, have a difficult time using the vast amount of information provided by the social sciences, as the behavioral school says managers should do. Behavioral theory becomes even more complicated in light of the facts that people are motivated by more than one need at any given time and that they must constantly reconcile conflicting demands. No simple formulas can always motivate all individuals in the workplace. What's more, people's needs change with time, making the same person tough to manage one day and a delight the next. Nevertheless, by considering psychology, managers can prepare themselves to effectively manage their most important and complex resource: people.

The primary difference between one company and another is its people. "To compete in today's market, large corporations need to provide workers an environment in which they can make their own decisions and create their own visions. That means letting go of the old command-and-control model in favor of a looser approach."[11] This could describe openness to change, the subject of this chapter's Self-Management assessment.

QUANTITATIVE MANAGEMENT THEORY

2c

Explain the contributions of the quantitative school of management thought

The next wave of management thought moved from concern for people to the use of quantitative tools to help plan and control nearly everything in the organization. The emphasis in this new school, the **quantitative school** of management theory, was on mathematical approaches to management problems. This approach was born during World War II with research teams that developed radar, guidance systems, jet engines, information theory and the atomic bomb. Since then, quantitative tools have been applied to every aspect of business.[12]

quantitative school
Emphasized mathematical approaches to management problems

management science
The study of complex systems of people, money, equipment, and procedures, with the goal of understanding them and improving their effectiveness

Management science is the study of complex systems of people, money, equipment, and procedures, with the goal of understanding them and improving their effectiveness.[13] Management science is a facet of quantitative management theory. Historians Lester Bittel and Jackson Ramsey presented the following explanation of the management science approach:

Such studies are conducted through the use of the scientific method, utilizing tools and knowledge from the physical, mathematical, and behavioral sciences. Its ultimate purpose is to provide the manager with a sound, scientific, and quantitative basis for decision making.

Management science enables managers to design specific measures, such as a computer program, to test or evaluate the effects and effectiveness of a process or intended action. Airlines use management science to schedule flights, to schedule maintenance, and to book passenger reservations. An area of management science called **operations research** commonly uses models, simulations, and games. For example, sophisticated computer models and simulations of the interactions between and among atmospheric forces forecast the weather. For another example, through the use of several commercially available software programs, we can predict and understand in advance the impact throughout a business of an expected price increase for vital raw materials.

operations research
An area of management science that commonly uses models, simulations, and games

The techniques and tools of management science are frequently used to plan, organize, staff, lead and control production operations; this aspect of management science is known as operations management. The management science approach is also used to direct facilities, purchasing, investments, marketing, personnel, and research and development. Management science depends on the participation of a variety of experienced researchers and practitioners to gather and process information, analyze operations, and develop and use the appropriate tools and techniques. Regardless of the methods, tools, and personnel used, however, the ultimate test of management science is whether better decisions are made and more effective processes are developed.[14]

Operations Management

operations management
The branch of management science that applies to manufacturing or service industries

The branch of management science that applies to manufacturing or service industries is **operations management**. Some of the most common tools of operations management include:

- Inventory models that determine optimum storage levels and reorder points
- Break-even analyses to determine levels of production and sales at which the organization recaptures the total costs of development and manufacturing
- Production scheduling, which determines when operations begin and end
- Production routing, which directs the path followed by parts and products during assembly

You can find more about operations management in Appendix A.

Management Information Systems

A key ingredient in management science is the timely and efficient delivery of up-to-date information. Most organizations utilize information technology to implement, maintain, and oversee their use of computers. A management information system (MIS) is a computer-based system that gives managers the information they need to make decisions. Specialists who know what the users of system output need maintain an MIS. The Walmart chain of retail stores implemented a management information system by using computer links to connect headquarters, suppliers (such as Procter & Gamble) and outlets. The system allowed Walmart to minimize expenses and the time needed to gather and process information about sales and inventory.

Companies that depend on domestic and foreign suppliers and outlets for their goods and services must know promptly and precisely what is happening in all vital operations. Without such information, managers cannot make timely and appropriate decisions. Chapter 14 will examine information technology and management information systems in detail.

Assessment From the 1950s well into the 1980s, large numbers of American managers became preoccupied with quantitative measurement. The management of business after business was given over to engineers and financial managers dedicated to achieving the lowest possible cost and the highest short-term profits. Symbolic of this view were the substantial bonuses paid to managers according to financial performance in each quarter or year. A decision not based on a quantitative tool or technique was considered a poor decision.

This prolonged, intense focus on immediate results generated significant difficulties. Long-term investment was neglected—especially investment in research and development. Companies ignored trends developing overseas and, as a result, lost market share to innovative competitors. Organizations forgot the humanism of the behavioral approach and the lessons learned from behavioral management theory. Companies produced what they wanted to produce in the way they wanted to produce it; they forgot about quality and their customers. The result was disastrous for many firms and whole industries. Perhaps the most dramatic examples of such industries are the American steel and auto manufacturers. However, examples exist in every industry. The losers run the gamut, from the makers of small appliances and footwear to the manufacturers of textiles and tires.

In hindsight, the lesson of overemphasizing the quantitative management approach is clear. It is not the tools that are important but the results they bring to the organization and the community. Management science can help managers analyze, develop and improve operations, but management science techniques cannot substitute for sound, balanced judgment and management experience.

The wise manager draws upon the best aspects of each management theory and integrates them with insight and imagination.

SYSTEMS MANAGEMENT THEORY

Explain the contributions of the systems school of management thought

A **system** is a set of interrelated parts that work together to achieve stated goals or to function according to a plan or design. Figure 2.3 shows an organization as a system, with inputs being processed, through operations, into outputs. Outputs go to users who are either inside or outside the organization. An internal user is the person down the line who receives a part or a project when another worker finishes with it. Anyone in the organization who uses or depends on the output of others in the organization is an internal user, or internal customer. Information, products, or services sent outside go to external users (suppliers, customers, or government agencies).

system
A set of interrelated parts that work together to achieve stated goals or to function according to a plan or design

Systems School

The **systems school** holds that an organization comprises various parts (subsystems) that must perform tasks necessary for the survival and proper functioning of the

systems school
The theory that an organization comprises various parts (subsystems) that must perform tasks necessary for the survival and proper functioning of the system as a whole

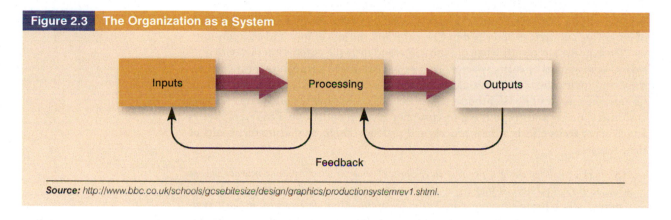

Figure 2.3   The Organization as a System

Inputs → Processing → Outputs

Feedback

Source: http://www.bbc.co.uk/schools/gcsebitesize/design/graphics/productionsystemrev1.shtml.

system as a whole. The functional areas of a business—marketing, finance and human resources management—are subsystems. So, too, are various processes such as billing and order processing when managed by teams. All managers should understand how each subsystem works, how each interacts with others, and what each contributes to the whole. Changes in any one subsystem usually affect other subsystems and, therefore, the entire system.

When managers adopt a systems approach, they determine how planned changes will affect others and their operations before they implement them. By keeping the entire system and its subsystems in mind, they hope to ensure that a positive move in one area does not negatively affect another.

A malfunctioning subsystem causes ripple effects that have an impact on other systems. Consider, for example, a United Airlines 777 twin-engine jet carrying 200 passengers from Los Angeles to Chicago. Once serviced and refueled in Chicago, the plane will continue on to New York. Some Los Angeles passengers must make connections in Chicago or New York for other flights, and some passengers boarding in Chicago must make connections in New York. United baggage handlers in Los Angeles fail to properly secure the 777's cargo door. As the plane moves to its takeoff position, a crew member discovers the problem. The plane returns to the loading gate so the door can be secured, thus losing its takeoff position and causing a 30-minute delay. Several Chicago-bound passengers will now miss their connecting flights; many heading for New York are similarly inconvenienced. The delayed departure means a delay in finding an available gate in Chicago. In addition, passengers' families are frustrated and business schedules are affected.

Cumulative Energy of Synergy

Systems and Synergy **Synergy** is the increased effectiveness that results from combined action or cooperation. It is sometimes described as the 2 + 2 = 5 effect, because the result of a synergistic partnership is actually more than the sum of the production of each partner alone. A corporate merger often provides an illustration of a synergistic "win." When Procter and Gamble (P&G) merged with Gillette to form the world's biggest consumer-products enterprise in 2005, many experts saw enormous synergistic potential. The combined organization, they believed, offered powerful product and marketing potential unavailable to the separate firms. In such mergers, old identities are lost and a new, stronger combination may be formed. Some combinations produce

synergy
The increased effectiveness that results from combined action or cooperation

negative effects, however. Possible threats to a merger of two companies include a clash of corporate cultures, as described in Chapter 8 and the loss of jobs and competition.

Synergy usually occurs when organizations and their subsystems interact with outsiders—subsystems or entire systems. This is one reason why companies form partnerships and invite outsiders to evaluate their operations or products and services. Since its founding, many of P&G's products have been the result of astute salespeople sensing customers' needs and responding to customer recommendations. P&G's employees add synergy to its efforts at new process and product design by sharing the results of their research.

> *At P&G, package design, product development, manufacturing, and marketing are like fingers of a hand. If they're not in sync, the task won't get done smoothly. For example, take a Pringles potato chip. The shape of the chip is determined, in part, by its cylindrical container, which has to be designed so the snack won't break between when it's made and when the can is opened by the hungry consumer. In addition, package designers need to incorporate in the artwork color, shapes, logo, and other elements preferred by customers based on marketing surveys. Manufacturing has to stay on top of all development work, since it will have to make the chip and the packaging.*[15]

Assessment According to systems theory, the components of an enterprise interact to create synergy that can benefit each component and the whole. The systems approach encourages managers to view their organizations holistically—to envision workers, groups, and tasks as interrelated parts of an organic whole. This integrated approach requires information systems that can provide managers at every level with enough accurate and timely input to facilitate sound decisions. Such a situation brings Henri Fayol's principles—unity of command, unity of direction and harmony—to mind. Keeping people focused on the objectives to be achieved is the manager's most important task. When everyone works together toward a goal to which they are all committed, synergy results.

The systems view has led managers to think about quality (defined in Chapter 1) as a concept affected by each action of every employee and every unit. The result has been a commitment by all employees of an organization, beginning at the top, to focus their energies on meeting or exceeding the organization's internal and external customers' needs. Fear can beset managers when they consider just how complex and connected their organizations' subsystems are. This fear can lead to paralysis. Managers may become overly cautious and refuse to act until they have contacted every possible source, conducted exhaustive analysis and asked for reviews from upper management. The time constraints and conditions of business seldom allow such luxuries.

CONTINGENCY MANAGEMENT THEORY

2e Explain the contributions of the contingency school of management thought

The **contingency school** is based on the premise that managers' preferred actions or approaches depend on the variables of the situations they face. Adherents of the school seek the most effective way to deal with any situation or problem, recognizing that each situation encountered, although possibly similar to others in the past, possesses unique characteristics.

Managers holding the contingency view feel free to draw on all past theories in attempting to analyze and solve problems. The true contingency approach is integrative. During a typical day, a manager may have to use behavioral approaches to soothe

contingency school
A theory based on the premise that managers' preferred actions or approaches depend on the variables of the situations they face

a subordinate's hurt feelings, apply management science to program production for a new assembly and use classical scientific tools to study an assembly operation to determine where it can be improved.

Adherents of the contingency school recognize that a human resource manager at Citibank may need to analyze a job applicant's interview and test results differently than would a human resource manager at First National of Chicago. Both managers have differing systems, needs and experiences; the contingency school maintains that their choices should reflect those differences as well as the unique characteristics and histories of the job applicants.

The contingency theory can be summarized as an "it all depends" device. Right and proper conduct under one set of circumstances may fail utterly under another set. Since no two problems possess identical details and circumstances, neither should any two solutions. Several solutions and approaches may be possible and might yield equally good results. Supporters of the contingency theory would acknowledge that many roads lead to a city from several directions; they would also stress that the route that appears the shortest might not be the best choice if it is undergoing repairs.

The contingency theory tells managers to look to their experiences and the past and to consider many options before choosing the course of action. It encourages managers to stay flexible and to consider alternatives and fallback positions when defining and attacking problems. The theory also tells them that intelligent choices come only from adequate preliminary research.

Assessment The contingency theory applies to any organization and to managers who face change. The purchase of one company by another is an example of significant change. By using the contingency approach, top managers of the purchasing company may discover that they need to learn or embrace the methods of the purchased company. If the theory works as its supporters predict, they will make the discovery before imposing inappropriate methods on the acquired firm.

The contingency theory requires managers to know the history of management thought. Managers must be familiar with the tried and true principles and practices that have provided benefits in the past but not be bound to mindlessly repeat them. Contingency thinking tells managers to try the new, to experiment—to think "outside the box" of the past—until they find the right means. It also encourages managers to stay flexible; to consider alternatives and fallback positions when attempting to solve problems, meet challenges, or take advantage of opportunities (regardless of where in the world they arise) within a framework of both the law and ethics. The diversity in most of today's organizations helps to guarantee that additional and unique perspectives will be brought to bear on problem solving when it is truly valued. Contingency theory, along with those theories previously discussed, has led managers to the most recent theory of management thought: quality management.

QUALITY MANAGEMENT THEORY

2f Explain the contributions of the quality school of management thought

After World War I, the United States emerged as the leading industrial power. During the first 50 years of the last century, American companies in such major industries as electronics, textiles, automobiles and steel supplied most of the world's consumer and industrial products. If it wasn't produced by U.S. manufacturers, it either wasn't available or it wasn't as good.

One of the reasons for the success of U.S. manufacturing was the War Manpower Commission (WMC), formed by the U.S. government in 1942 to help industry train defense plant workers for World War II. The training program for industry was based on Charles Allen's 4-point method: Preparation, Presentation, Application and Testing. The training within industry program covered the Five Needs of the Supervisor: Knowledge of the Work, Knowledge of Responsibility, Skill in Instructing (Job Instruction), Skill in Improving Methods (Job Methods) and Skill in Leading (Job Relations). After World War II, the WMC was abolished in 1945. But from 1942 to 1945, training within industry certified over a million and a half workers and resulted in cost savings and improvements in safety, quality and deliveries. (See the official archives of the WMC at *http://www.archives.gov/research/guide-fed-records/groups/211.html*).

Throughout the 1940s and into the 1950s, our major competitors and trading partners today—United Kingdom, Germany, France, Italy, Japan and most of its Asian neighbors—were engaged in recovering from the devastation of World War II. With little or no competition, many manufacturers did not see the need to continue to improve. Most forgot the training within industry lessons. U.S. industries were dominant largely because they had no serious foreign competition and were untouched by both world wars.

But challenges came swiftly to most U.S. industries by the 1960s, and their impacts were magnified with the oil shortages caused by the major oil-producing nations in the early 1970s. American consumers, along with those in other nations, had discovered alternative products from several foreign nations that better met their needs.

As Chapter 1 pointed out, quality is defined as the ability of a product or service to satisfy the stated or implied goals or requirements of users or customers of that product or service. How managers and organizations can create and nurture this ability is a continuing theme in this book, as its title suggests. You will recall that users/customers exist both inside and outside organizations. Users/customers receive the output generated by people, machines and processes. The essence of the quality of any output is its ability to meet the needs of the person or group requiring it. This is the heart of the **quality school** of management thought. Quality management is often referred to as total quality management (TQM), continuous improvement, Lean Manufacturing, or just Lean concepts or work processes.

quality school
The essence of the quality of any output is its ability to meet the needs of the person or group

Kaizen Approach

Training within industry developed in the U.S. for U.S. industry was embraced by the Japanese during the occupation of Japan after World War II, and became the basis of the *kaizen* culture. ***Kaizen*** is a Japanese term used in business to mean small, incremental, continuous improvement for people, products and processes. In order to ensure that every person's creativity is being fully utilized, *kaizen* has three rules: spend no money; add no people; add no space. The *kaizen* approach to quality means that an individual or organization cannot rest after any achievement. No matter how well things are going, the individual or organization can do better. When defect rates drop from 5 percent to 2 percent, the goal is to continue to drop until no defects occur. Once adopted, the *kaizen* philosophy commits organizations, their leaders and their employees to a never-ending journey: to continually strive to improve, learn and grow. This chapter's Quality Management feature compares the basic 4-step *kaizen* training to those of Charles Allen and Training Within Industry (TWI).

Increasing sales revenue through better-quality products and services that attract more customers and realize better prices can improve profits. However, quality has to

kaizen
A Japanese term used in business to mean incremental, continuous improvement for people, products, and processes

Kaizen's American Roots

In the kaizen spirit, management means improving. Some of the basic philosophies of Japanese management and kaizen evolved from training used in the early 1900s in the United States of America. Charles Allen developed his 4-Point method of training prior to World War I for use in shipbuilding. His book, *The Instructor, The Man, and The Job*, was published in 1919 in Philadelphia and London by the J.B. Lippincott Company. This book became the basis for training within industry in the U.S. during World War II and then after the war in occupied Japan. Kaizen has developed to be one of the most successful management techniques used in industry today. See the table below for a comparison of steps used by Charles Allen, TWI and kaizen.

➡ When you have a problem, do you divide the problem into small manageable pieces? Do you try to fix the problem by making little improvements along the way? Do you think of alternative methods for getting work done? If you answered "yes" to the above questions, you practice kaizen. Keep improving.

➡ If you answered "no" to the above questions, focus on small changes. Small improvements can make your life easier. What is one small improvement you will make?

			COMPARISON OF STEPS		
Steps	Charles Allen	Job Instruction	TWI Job Methods	Job Relations	Kaizen
1	Preparation	Prepare	Breakdown	Get the facts	Observe and time current process
2	Presentation	Present	Question	Weigh and decide	Analyze current process
3	Application	Try out	Develop	Take action	Implement and test new process
4	Testing	Follow up	Apply	Check results	Document new standard

Source: Jim Huntzinger, "The Roots of Lean: Training Within Industry: The Origin of Japanese Management and Kaizen," TWI Summit, May 2007.

be focused on the customers' needs first. This chapter's Ethical Management feature focuses on what can go wrong when a company becomes obsessed with producing quality products.

Business Process Improvement

It has been said that the only constant in business is change. Perhaps the greatest challenges facing managers at every level are to sense the need for change, see change coming and react quickly and effectively to it when it comes. It is precisely for these reasons that a *kaizen* approach—implementing process changes in small increments— to managing change has been challenged.

Rapid radical and even revolutionary changes may be necessary. In the 1990s, Michael Hammer and James Champy called for such an approach to managing change and efforts to improve quality of products and operations. They called their approach **reengineering** and defined it as "the fundamental rethinking and radical redesign of business processes to achieve dramatic improvements in critical, contemporary measures of performance, such as cost, quality, service, and speed."[16] Companies adopting a reengineering approach quickly learned to question everything they did

reengineering
Business processes are redesigned to achieve improvements in performance

Lean Doesn't Have to be Mean

Toyota and other Japanese manufacturers pioneered the Lean Manufacturing system, which is built around single piece flow (Flow), waste elimination, just-in-time (JIT) production and delivery. The goal is continuous improvement. *Kaizen* events help traditional manufacturers implement lean production. Cross-functional teams spend several days focusing on a defined area of the plant, analyzing, implementing changes, and measuring effects of the new system.

Lisa Bergson is President and CEO of MEECO Inc., a manufacturer of trace analyzers for the gas, chemicals and semiconductor industries. She chose Lean Manufacturing to implement change in her factory. Bergson says, "Lean is a commonsense approach to mapping out a work process for identifying bottlenecks and implementing solutions. Done well, a more efficient, cleaner, more compact, cross-trained, and profitable organization results" (Bergson).

Lean production reduces the cost of quality if it is part of the company's culture. Bergson found that lean conversion cannot progress without the support from employees. MEECO's fanatical obsession with product quality began to alienate its employees. Donna Callahan, MEECO's Sales & Service Coordinator, helped Bergson understand why her employees attended the meetings conducted by Frank Garcia, a consultant for the Delaware Valley Industrial Resource Center (DVIRC), but did little to implement the training. "Callahan concluded that instead of converting to a lean machine, MEECO's production floor became a mean machine. The employees blamed Lean for problems it either didn't address, like personality clashes, or for problem areas where MEECO had yet to implement the concept, such as purchasing and inventory control" (Bergson).

Bergson realized that "our mismanagement, compounded by the factory floor's misunderstanding, got Lean off to a bad start at MEECO" (Bergson). However, MEECO is committed to Lean. Employees must understand and embrace the importance of the changes. Bergson accepts "enlightening and inspiring" employees as part of her top management job. The irony of MEECO's commitment to quality was that it did not extend to meeting or exceeding its customers' needs. It had lost sight of the ultimate measure of quality—happy customers, be they internal or external.

➡ **What harm can come from changes when employees don't embrace those changes?**

➡ **What additional ethical issues do you note in this feature?**

Sources: Lisa Bergson, "Lean Manufacturing? Fat Chance!" *BusinessWeek*, May 24, 2002, http://www.businessweek.com/smallbiz/content/may2002/sb20020524_4859.htm; MEECO, http://www.meeco.com.

and why they did it. "Reengineering first determines what a company must do, then how to do it. Reengineering takes nothing for granted. It ignores what is and concentrates on what should be."[17] Reengineering had counterproductive results in many companies trying to implement Hammer and Champy's ideas. The companies did not implement change management discussed in Chapter 8 So, the term "reengineering" became tarnished and has been replaced by such terms as business process redesign, internal business improvement or process innovation.

A key concept in examining business processes is to determine what a company should be doing, based on its core competencies and experience—that is, what it can do best. The company can then determine if what needs to be done is best done in-house or by some other entity. This approach has led companies to downsize and outsource. Organization owners and managers must continually ask two questions: "What are we doing?" And, "What should we be doing?"

> *The most profound lesson of business process reengineering was never reengineering, but business processes. Processes are how we work. Any company that ignores its business processes or fails to improve them risks its future.... For technologists, the lesson from reengineering is a reminder of an old truth: information technology is only useful if it helps people do their work better and differently.*[18]

cloud computing
A concept used in information technology (IT) to depict sharing computer resources remotely rather than storing software or data on a local server or computer. This allows companies to store data—such as customer contacts, inventory lists and documents—on servers owned by others and access that data via the internet.

Today, many companies are achieving impressive savings by redesigning business processes around **cloud computing**.

They will leverage so called cloud technology, which lets users tap into computing power available via the internet, rather than on a desktop or computer server housed locally. The appeal is scale, flexibility, and efficiency: Thousands of server computers can attack a task more quickly—and cheaply—or handle a patchwork quilt of different technologies that companies use to run their businesses. This approach will let businesses outsource entire tasks such as the tracking of inventory, paying only for the information accessed or used. That's where the cloud comes in. It shifts the center

Managing Social Media

The Networked Enterprise

According to the results of a McKinsey Global Survey, the use of social media tools and techniques in companies is high. Social, browser-based technologies, such as solution blogs, wikis and group messaging software are used to enhance information flow, as well as to encourage employee, partner and customer collaboration, engagement and problem solving.

Restrictive, linear work-flow technologies would include document, postal, and telephone communications. Old communication is controlled by companies to con-sumers and is one-way.

No one controls the social world. Communication is multi-way, two-way and any-way. The goal of the networked enterprise is to get the best ideas from employees, partners, and customers and then to share those ideas throughout the organization. To do this, organizations must move from closed, linear processes to a more consciously collaborative design, as seen in the graphic below.

➥ **How do closed, linear processes restrict work flow? Why is the networked en-terprise better for work flow?**

Moving from closed, linear processes...   to a more consciously collaborative design

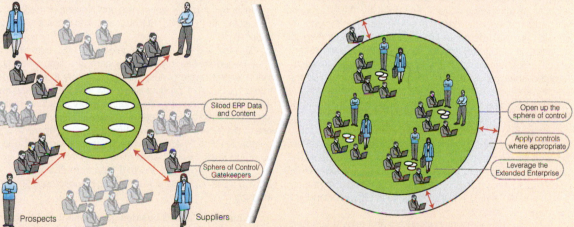

Siloed ERP Data and Content

Sphere of Control/ Gatekeepers

Prospects

Suppliers

Open up the sphere of control

Apply controls where appropriate

Leverage the Extended Enterprise

Sources: McKinsey & Company, Evolution of the Networked Enterprise: McKinsey Global Survey Results, March 2013, Retrieved from http://www.mckinsey.com/insights/business_technology/evolution_of_the_networked_enterprise_mckinsey_global_survey_results; Oliver Marks & Sameer Patel, Sovos Group, "Accelerating Business Performance," *Enterprise 2.0 Conference*, Spring 2010 http://www.e2conf.com/downloads/whitepapers/ent2-10_TWwhitepaper.pdf

of gravity in outsourcing from physical ownership of assets and process expertise. It focuses on the skills necessary to efficiently manage computing operations that can scale and at the same time are flexible enough to handle scores of different tasks.[19]

Enterprise (business or commercial) resource planning software is used to integrate all departments and functions across a company (such as accounting, human resources and manufacturing applications) onto a single computer system that can serve all those departments' particular needs. For example, software for electronic commerce consolidates online purchasing, supply chain and sourcing. Enterprise systems and use of cloud based tools in organizations, ties both data and collaboration together to support business activity.

Major Contributors to Quality Management

Beginning in the 1950s, foreign-made goods within several industries began to meet or exceed the requirements of the world's consumers better than did American-made goods. One measure of that is in the chronic, continuing deficit in America's balance of trade with the world. On average, the United States imports about 50 percent more goods and services than it sells abroad.

Global Applications

Government and Industry Cooperation in Japan

With the end of World War II, Japanese policy makers chose to allow government and business to work together to rebuild their nation and its economy. The Japanese created the Ministry of International Trade and Industry (MITI) to work with industrial leaders to determine what direction the country should take. MITI began the re-building by concentrating on the creation of a strong infrastructure and the reestablishment of core industries, particularly iron and steel. Next, the ministry targeted shipbuilding as the principal industry in which the country should excel. By the 1960s, Japan led the world in building seagoing vessels of nearly every type, including oil tankers and bulk freighters.

Through MITI, Japan's industrial community cooperates and shares resources. National and industry-wide goals are set, and strong commitments are made to achieve them. The Japanese government protects the industries it determines to be vital to the national interest (farming, steel, communications), and industrial trade associations act to protect individual corporate interests.

A strong network of manufacturers and related suppliers dedicated to the survival of the whole is but one reason why foreign corporations find it difficult to do business in Japan. Industries are targeted by Japanese manufacturers, which make long-term efforts to capture market share. America's consumer electronics industry yielded to Japanese competition by bits and pieces. Zenith remained as the only American producer of consumer electronics until November 1995, when LG Electronics Inc. (LGE) of Korea acquired a majority interest in Zenith.

Similarly, the Japanese targeted the U.S. auto market. They began by offering economy cars at a time when U.S. manufacturers were neither willing nor ready to modify their traditional full-size product lines. By the 1980s, Japanese automakers moved upscale, offering luxury cars for a market long dominated by European manufacturers. By 1990, about one in three new cars sold were produced by Japanese auto companies. Ford's and General Motors's share of the U.S. auto and truck market has continued to decline—Ford from 24.1% in 2000 to 15.6% in 2016; GM from 28.3% to 16.9% in 2016. (See *http://online.wsj.com/mdc/public/page/2_3022-autosales.html*).

➡ **What other factors besides government and industry cooperation have helped Japan advance with extraordinary speed to become one of the largest econo-mies in the world?**

As an example, the American auto industry experienced its first serious threat from Volkswagen's Beetle. "Volkswagen sold 330 Beetles in 1950, 32,662 in 1955, and 61,507 in 1959, by which time the Big Three auto marketers were fretting: Who is this contrarian new consumer?"[20] By the 1960s, Japanese cars were gaining a foothold by offering fuel-efficient, low-cost, and high-quality subcompact and compact cars. Their sales really took off with the oil embargo of the 1970s, as Detroit carmakers had few fuel-efficient quality products to meet the domestic demand. By the 1980s, import cars had taken more than one-third of the American car market. This trend continues today. Slightly more than one-half of new auto sales in the U.S. are from foreign companies. See this chapter's Global Applications feature for more information on how the Japanese penetrated the U.S. market for cars.

Producers in several nations had discovered the importance of quality. In contrast, most U.S. companies had not, and they waited until the early 1980s to embark on serious efforts to improve the quality of their goods and services. By that time many domestic markets had fallen entirely or in large part to the dominant foreign producers. The real irony of America's late recognition of the importance of quality is that much of the training was developed by Americans and nearly all of quality's strongest proponents are Americans. Figure 2.4 profiles the major contributors to the evolution of quality management theory. Two of the listed individuals—W. Edwards Deming and Joseph M. Juran—taught Japanese manufacturers most of the major quality concepts and principles the Japanese companies operate under to this day.

Assessment The quality school of management thought has its roots most directly in the behavioral, quantitative, systems and contingency schools of management theory. People are the key to both commitments and performance. What is done must be measured and evaluated quantitatively and qualitatively. Systems interact and execute the vast majority of processes. What needs to be done at any given time must be done in the most appropriate manner. Past practices and traditions have many current applications to today's management problems.

The quality school is the most current and is embraced worldwide, to varying degrees, by managers and their organizations in every industry. Some adopt a total commitment; others engage in a short-term quest to make substantial improvements in their quality. Once improvements are made, efforts cease. The former is exemplified by companies like Motorola, Xerox and Ford, and all of their suppliers, both large and small. The latter approach is quite common among smaller enterprises with fewer resources and less enlightened leadership. A company committed to total quality will choose only suppliers and partners who make the same commitment.

The price for not striving for quality and for failing to make a total commitment to the quest is to risk being surpassed and overwhelmed by the competition and to provide products and services that do not meet or exceed customer expectations. In the final analysis, a company exists to help its members and its external customers meet their needs. The company that can do this best will survive and prosper in its industry. Appendix 1 extends our investigation of quality.

Figure 2.4	**Major Contributors to Quality Management Theory**
G. S. Radford	In 1922, Radford published *The Control of Quality in Manufacturing*, in which he advocated inspection as the cornerstone of industrial quality control. In his view, "it was the inspector's job to examine, weigh, and measure every item prior to its being loaded on a truck for shipment" (Hart and Bogan, 1992). Radford believed that maintaining quality was a management responsibility and that quality should be considered during the design stages of a product (Garvin, 1988).
Walter A. Shewhart	Shewhart advocated the control of quality through scientific methods and quantitative measures. He and his colleagues at Bell Laboratories, then a division of AT&T, created what is now called statistical quality controls and statistical process controls. Through the use of these tools, any process can be determined to be in control (predictable) or out of control (unpredictable). W. Edwards Deming and Joseph M. Juran, both of whom worked with Shewhart at Bell Labs, adopted and developed Shewhart's ideas (Gabor, 1990).
W. Edwards Deming	Deming taught the value of quantitative tools for measuring processes and controlling quality. Following World War II, the Union of Japanese Scientists and Engineers, organized to help in the rebuilding of Japanese industry, contacted Deming and asked for his assistance. Deming, along with Joseph Juran, helped to make Japanese product quality a standard for the world's producers. Japan's most esteemed awards for quality bear Deming's name. In the 1980s, he helped Ford and other U.S. companies launch their never-ending journey towards quality improvement.
Joseph M. Juran	Juran argued that quality should not be considered merely an expense. It should be viewed, instead, as an investment in a firm's profitability. Juran held that managers must design quality into products, services and processes during the planning phase. He urged a systems approach to managing quality, combining three subsystems: quality planning, quality control and quality improvements. Using Deming's and Juran's teachings, the Japanese developed the *kaizen* concept.
Armand V. Feigenbaum	Following up on Juran's contributions was Armand Feigenbaum, manager of quality control for General Electric headquarters in the 1950s. Feigenbaum believed that "quality was too central to a company's identity to be entrusted to an isolated corps of inspectors. For a total response, every single employee and vendor had to be brought into the process" (Hart and Bogan, 1992; Feigenbaum, 1956). Although quality involved everyone, Feigenbaum believed that managers who were specialists in quality control should take charge of the quality effort. Today the approach differs. Top managers want all employees to be quality control experts and committed to quality in all their undertakings.
Philip B. Crosby	Crosby was a 40-year employee of AT&T, a company that has contributed much to management know-how and technological breakthroughs. He was a vice president of ITT for 14 years. In his books, Crosby asserted that everyone needs to be trained by quality experts in quality control, quality assurance and total quality management. Crosby popularized quality through his down-to-earth language and approaches. He and Thomas J. Peters have accelerated national awareness of the importance of quality to our lives, our economy and the perpetuation of our standard of living.
Thomas J. Peters	Author, lecturer, consultant, and professor, Tom Peters has given us a look at companies doing the right things. Peters has sounded alarms and taught average Americans about the need to get better at everything we do, and to become more like our competitors by imitating them, learning from them, and trying to stay ahead of the trends.
Michael Hammer	Hammer, author, president of his own consulting firm, and former professor, has added reengineering as a concept related to quality. He calls for giant leaps forward and a continual questioning of what is done, why it is done, and how it is done. Change must sometimes be radical. Managers can tinker with existing systems just so long before they must be replaced or eliminated. Only through a constant rethinking of everything can organizations and their people compete effectively.
James Champy	Chairman of a consulting company, Champy, along with his coauthor Michael Hammer, has popularized the reengineering approach in corporate America. Their book, *Reengineering the Corporation* (1993), created a revolution. Their hands-on experiences as consultants allow them to show companies how a horizontal process focus can lead to higher levels of customer satisfaction, greater speed in cycle times, and huge improvements in cutting costs and increasing profits. He rejects gradual (*kaizen*) improvement in favor of creating new structures and processes.

Chapter Summary

1 **Discuss why knowledge of the evolution of management theories is important to managers.**

People ignorant of the past are destined to repeat it. Knowing what has gone before allows us to avoid mistakes and repeat successes. In order to understand the present you must see its connections to the past. All the theories and schools that make up the history of management thought have some value for today's managers. A manager should use the best and reject the obsolete contributions of each theory.

2 **Explain the contributions of the following:**

a **Classical schools of management thought.**

Classical management thinkers looked for the "one best way" to do something. Skilled, principled, professional managers continue to search for better ways to do everything, knowing that today's best way will not be tomorrow's. They used time and motion studies and a scientific approach to study work and work flow and to solve problems. Many of these tools are used today. Nearly all of Fayol's general principles of management exist in modified form and govern management behavior in today's organizations. Although the following concepts persist, many have fallen from favor: narrow job descriptions; the concept of the one best way; top-down decision making; bureaucratic structures in highly competitive, fast-changing industries; discouraging leadership at lower levels of an organization; and the suppression of diverse groups.

b **Behavioral school of management thought.**

Managers now realize that their most important and complex resource is people. Employees and their contributions are the primary differences between one organization and another. Motivated, satisfied employees perform outstanding work, which leads to satisfying user/customer needs—the central purpose behind any organization. People are viewed as assets, not expenses. Money invested to train and develop talent returns to the business many times over. Only by enlisting the creativity and diverse contributions of all employees can an organization expect to achieve its goals.

c **Quantitative school of management thought.**

Quantitative tools used in decision making proliferate and are made more effective and efficient through a variety of computer software applications and hardware interfaces. They continue to be valuable aids to decision making but are not substitutes for sound, balanced judgment and experience. They also continue to be part of problem solving, but they do not rule the process. Without a continuing focus on ethics and customers' needs, even the best of scientifically based, quantitative decisions can lead to disaster. In the diversity of today's organizations, many alternative problem-solving methods and models exist. In the final analysis, a decision is evaluated on the results it achieves, not on the way it is made.

d **Systems school of management thought.**

A systems approach encourages managers to view their organizations holistically—to envision workers, groups, and tasks as interrelated parts of an organic whole. Systems are affected by both internal and external forces, not the least of which are customer demands. Changes in any subsystem can affect other subsystems and the operations of the whole. The systems view has led managers to think about quality as a concept affected by each action of every employee and unit and as customer driven. The result has been a commitment within organizations by all its employees to concentrate their energies on meeting or exceeding all their customers' expectations. The basic tenets of the systems school are very much a part of the contingency and quality schools of management thought.

e **Contingency school of management thought.**

The contingency theory tells managers to experiment and be creative—to try the new and different, to think "outside the box." Although using the best from the past, they are not bound to repeat it in a mindless way. For innovation and creative urges to succeed, managers must develop innovative techniques. This theory also tells managers to stay flexible and to consider alternatives and fallback positions when attempting to solve problems, meet challenges, and take advantage of opportunities. Through contingency thinking, diversity becomes a clear advantage to organizations. Diverse individuals and groups bring differing perspectives and perceptions to bear on every issue. Considering that no two problems exist in identical circumstances, different approaches allow for tailored solutions.

f Quality school of management thought.

The behavioral, quantitative, systems, and contingency schools converge in the quality school of management thought. To determine the quality of products and services, quantitative and qualitative measurements must be used. People are the key, and highly motivated and committed people make quality decisions and deliver quality outputs. Quality depends on everyone's commitment to meet and exceed customers' expectations. The quality commitment must extend beyond an organization's borders to encompass its suppliers' and partners' personnel. Without quality inputs, quality outputs are not possible. Since one size of anything will not fit all, companies must innovate to meet the needs of their customers. Companies must develop and utilize the leadership potential that exists within their employees.

KEY TERMS

behavioral school   43

bureaucracies   42

classical administrative school   37

classical management theory   37

classical scientific school   37

cloud computing   53

contingency school   48

kaizen   50

management science   45

operations management   45

operations research   45

quality school   50

quantitative school   44

reengineering   51

synergy   47

system   46

systems school   46

theory   36

REVIEW QUESTIONS

1. How can knowledge of past schools of management thought benefit today's managers?

2. What are the major contributions of the two schools of classical management thought?

3. How are the contributions of the behavioral school of management thought exhibited where you attend school? Where you work?

4. What areas of business activity can benefit most from the contributions of the quantitative school of management thought? Are there any areas that cannot benefit? Why or why not?

5. In your experience, how have the concepts introduced in the systems school of management thought been illustrated?

6. What are the major contributions of the contingency school of management thought?

7. Why is the quality school of management thought so popular?

DISCUSSION QUESTIONS FOR CRITICAL THINKING

1. What evidence can you cite from your experiences to prove the existence of classical school thinking in some of today's organizations?

2. In what specific ways has each of the following contributed to the quality school of management thought?

   a. Behavioral school
   b. Quantitative school
   c. Systems school
   d. Contingency school

3. Choose a company. How does it exhibit elements from the behavioral school? The systems school? The quality school?

4. What specific examples can you give that demonstrate an application of the *kaizen* approach to managing organizations? The business process improvement approach?

Social Media Management Exercises

1 Wiki at Work

You've just been hired as a management intern. You are working for a manager with 28 years of experience. He returns from a meeting with the following notes. "Our company is a digital enterprise. Communication behaviors and patterns have changed. My task is to increase participation in and contribution to these tools. This is hard because most of our employees want to read blogs and wikis, but they don't want to write them. Get employees to stop using e-mail and start using a wiki for collaboration."

- Your manager asks you to write him a short report answering the following questions. What is a wiki? How is it used in business for collaboration? Why would employees want to use a wiki?

2 Choose Blog Software

You want to start your own company and have heard that it is a necessity to have a blog. Furthermore, you would like to raise your profile as an industry expert. Before you start writing, you need to choose blog software.

- Visit the Top Ten Reviews and read about blog software. Which blog software would you choose and why? *http://blog-software-review.toptenreviews.com*

Experiential Learning

Ford and Toyota

Born during the classical school of management thought, Ford Motor Company was founded in Dearborn, Michigan, in 1903 by Henry Ford, the son of a farmer. Ford's most famous car, the Model T, was sold from October 1908 to 1927, with little change in design and functioning. The Model T set production and sales records. In 1913, Ford used the moving assembly line to speed up production. By 1920, the Highland Park plant was producing one car per minute. A black enamel paint was the only one that could keep up with this speed. Henry Ford's famous statement, "You can have any color as long as it's black," stemmed from his desire to speed automation. Faster assembly resulted in lower prices and more people being able to afford a Model T. By the early 1920s, more than half of all the cars in the world were Model Ts. In 1927, Ford sensed the need to initiate change. Model T production was shut down for several months while the company retooled. (See Ford Motor Company, *http://www.ford.com/about-ford/heritage*).

Beginning in the 1940s and into the 1960s, the quantitative and systems schools of management thought were warmly embraced by a number of large and small U.S. firms, Ford among them. The company adopted a variety of quantitative methods, including computer modeling, to focus on the best ways to design its cars. During this time, after World War II in the 1950s, Eiji Toyoda, as a guest of Henry Ford II, studied engineering and manufacturing at Ford's Rouge plant in Detroit. Toyoda was a Japanese engineer and worked for his family's Toyota Motor Company, which had been founded in 1937. At that time, the Toyota plant produced about one third of the automobiles per day that the Ford plant produced per day.

After visiting Ford, Taiichi Ohno, hired by Toyoda to improve efficiency of Toyota operations, concluded with Toyoda that mass production would not work in Japan, but Toyota's production system could be improved. It took Toyota 30 years to develop the Toyota Production System (TPS). Innovations include developing flexible, right-sized machinery and quick changeovers to produce smaller batches which improved quality. This resulted in cost savings because defects could be detected more quickly and lead times reduced because there was less work-in-process. (See "Eiji Toyoda on the Roots of TPS" *http://artoflean.com/files/Eiji_Toyoda_On_The_Roots_of_TPS.pdf*.)

In the 1970s, Ford embraced the quality movement and adopted the motto, "Quality is Job 1." But, it wasn't until 2008 that Ford caught up with Toyota's total quality. The companies tied for leading in the most segments on Strategic Vision's Total Quality Index™ (TQI), a measure of new vehicle owner satisfaction. Alexander Edwards, president of Strategic Vision's automotive division, comments on quality.

Over the past quarter century in the US, customer perceptions of quality of domestic and Asian manufacturers underwent large swings. Today, it doesn't matter if you are a Toyota or a Ford,. . ., each manufacturer has the opportunity and mandate to produce a product with the right Cues of Quality—those product attributes that signal quality and create customer Trust—and present vehicles that have a greater impact on the purchase decision. (Strategic Vision, PR Release, "The 2008 Total Quality Awards," May 28, 2008 *http://www.strategicvision. com/press_release.php?pr=31*).

Questions

1. Which schools of management thought are illustrated in this case?

2. Customers' perception of quality includes performance, reliability, durability, serviceability and aesthetics. What else do car customers want? Add to the perception of quality and create a list of the most-desired quality characteristics in a car.

3. Rate Toyota and Ford using the list from the previous question. How do they compare? Report on your findings.

Chapter 3

The Manager's Environment

LEARNING OBJECTIVES

After studying this chapter, you should be able to:

1 Discuss why organizations are open systems

2 Identify the elements in an organization's internal environment

3 Describe the directly interactive forces in an organization's external environment

4 Determine the indirectly interactive forces in an organization's external environment

5 Discuss the means available to managers for boundary spanning

6 Explain how managers can influence their external environments

7 Describe the obligations that organizations have to their stakeholders

Learning Style

Successful organizations recognize that they must learn quickly to satisfy customers faster than their competitors. The term **learning organization** describes the process whereby groups and individuals within the organization challenge existing models of behavior and learn to rapidly and creatively adapt to a changing environment (Senge). Herbert Spencer, the creator of Social Darwinism, referred to this process of adaptation as "survival of the fittest." In other words, the firm that is most successful in modifying its strategy to adapt to changing conditions in the environment is the firm that is most likely to survive its competitors and thrive in the future. A competitive advantage may be gained by effectively adapting to novel and unpredictable situations faster than the competition.

Understanding learning styles can make it easier for employees to transform themselves and their organizations. Most people have a clear preference for one learning style. How do you prefer to learn? Are you a visual learner? Auditory learner? Tactile learner? Assess your learning style. For each of the following statements, circle the number next to the ones with which you agree.

1. I would rather read directions than hear them read to me.

2. I remember more about a subject through the lecture method with information, explanations and discussion.

3. I enjoy working with my hands or making things.

4. I play with coins or keys in my pockets.

5. I remember things better if I write them down.

6. I learn to spell better by repeating the word out loud than by writing the word on paper.

7. I can read most graphs and charts without too much trouble.

8. I chew gum or snack when I study.

9. I prefer to listen to the news on the radio rather than read about it in the news-paper.

10. I feel the best way to remember is to picture it in my head.

11. It's easy for me to remember jokes.

12. I feel very comfortable touching others, hugging, hand-shaking, etc.

Note the statements that you circled. Statements 2, 6, 9, 11 identify an auditory learner, who prefers to learn by hearing. The auditory learner progresses by listening, taking notes while others are speaking and reciting study notes out loud. Statements 3, 4, 8, 12 identify a tactile learner, who prefers to learn by feeling and touching. The tactile learner progresses by writing down facts, making study notes and actually per-forming a procedure or activity. Statements 1, 5, 7, 10 identify a visual learner, who prefers to learn by seeing. The visual learner progresses by using videos, charts, maps, posters, slides and flash cards. He or she visualizes with pictures what is being read.

➡ Identify your preferred learning style. How can understanding your preferred learning style help you at school and work?

Peter M. Senge, *The Fifth Discipline: The Art and Practice of the Learning Organization* (Currency/Doubleday, 1994); Assessment adapted from Deborah L. Nelson and James Campbell Quick, "Learning Style Inventory," *Organizational Behavior: Science, the Real World, and You*, 6th Edition (South-Western/Cengage, 2009), p. 21 and School Family "Learning Styles Quiz," http://www.schoolfamily.com/school-family-articles/article/ 836-learning-styles-quiz.

INTRODUCTION

In this chapter we examine the major influences and answer two questions: (1) How do both internal and external influences affect organizational activities (other than those affecting quality and productivity)? (2) What can managers do to sense and cope with them?

THE ORGANIZATION AS A SYSTEM

Chapter 2 introduced the systems school of management thinking. A systems perspective of organizations provides a useful framework for examining the relationship between an organization and its environment. It is the element that integrates the other disciplines together in the **learning organization**.[1] Managers think of their organization as systems: interrelated subsystems that process various inputs to generate various outputs, pleasing users and customers as they do so.

Systems consist of sets of subsystems (interrelated parts) that act as a whole to generate outputs and function according to a plan or design. Any change in a subsystem can mean change to other subsystems and to the system as a whole. In this context, all of an organization's units and personnel affect and are affected by all others to some extent.

An organization must be concerned not only with what happens within and among its subsystems and people, but also with what happens outside of itself. No organization exists or operates in a vacuum. Management decisions must fit within the surrounding environment, which is divided into two components: internal and external. These forces influence conditions of every organization; however, the most influential force in one organization may have little impact on other organizations. Managers must continually scan and monitor the environment.

Environmental scanning is the process of collecting information about the external environment to identify and analyze trends. This allows managers to determine their organization's best response to an environmental change. Organizational adaptability is a function of the ability to learn and to perform according to changes in the environment. Scanning identifies signals of change and monitoring follows these signals.

L. von Bertalanffy, a biologist, was the first to call systems, which interact with their environments, *open systems*.[2] These systems take in inputs from their environments, process them, and return outputs back into the environment. Open systems depend on their environments to survive. Even modest environmental shifts can alter the results of management decisions. Figure 3.1 depicts an organization as an **open system**—one that regularly affects and is affected by various and constantly changing forces (elements and components) outside itself. Open systems remain efficient and effective by adapting to shifts in their environments. In contrast, a closed system does not interact with its environment.

At the center of Figure 3.1 is an organization consisting of an **internal environment** shown as the basic system with inputs–processing–outputs introduced in Chapter 2. Every organization's internal environment is composed of resources within its borders that managers create, acquire and utilize. These resources include the organization's people, information, facilities, equipment, machinery, materials, supplies, finances and infrastructure. For example, the inputs for a college would be the faculty, administra-

Discuss why organizations are open systems

learning organization
A process whereby groups and individuals within the organization challenge existing models of behavior and learn to rapidly and creatively adapt to a changing environment

environmental scanning
The process of collecting information about the external environment to identify and analyze trends

open system
A system that regularly affects and is affected by various and constantly changing forces (elements and components) outside itself

internal environment
Composed of elements within an organization's borders that managers create, acquire, and utilize, including the organization's mission, vision, core values, core competencies, leadership, culture, climate, structure, and available resources

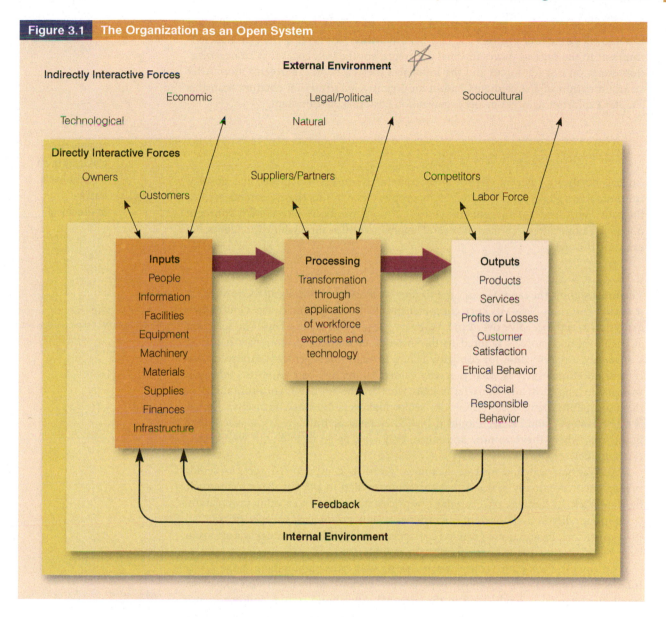

Figure 3.1   The Organization as an Open System

External Environment

Indirectly Interactive Forces

Economic   Legal/Political   Sociocultural

Technological   Natural

Directly Interactive Forces

Owners   Suppliers/Partners   Competitors

Customers   Labor Force

Inputs
People
Information
Facilities
Equipment
Machinery
Materials
Supplies
Finances
Infrastructure

Processing
Transformation through applications of workforce expertise and technology

Outputs
Products
Services
Profits or Losses
Customer Satisfaction
Ethical Behavior
Social Responsible Behavior

Feedback

Internal Environment

tion and staff, students and their information, buildings, computers and money. Processing would be the teaching and learning that takes place in the college. The outputs would be the graduates of the college. The internal environment is a subsystem of the larger, external environment, which exerts substantial influence on the organization.

Notice the two colored bands surrounding the organization. Together these represent any organization's **external environment** and include all the forces outside its borders that interact directly or indirectly with it. Originally, W. Churchman defined external environment as those factors that not only are outside the system's control but that determine in part how the system performs.[3] In any organization external forces may have a significant impact on the organization but are outside the control of the

external environment
Includes all the forces outside an organization's borders that interact directly or indirectly with it

manager. The boundary that separates the organization from its external environment is not always clear and precise. The two-headed arrows, connecting the external environment to the organization's internal one, represent the influences that an organization exerts on outside forces and the influences they exert on the organization. After an examination of the elements within an organization's internal environment, this chapter explores the forces in any organization's external environment.

INTERNAL ENVIRONMENT

An organization's internal environment contains resources it acquires and absorbs from outside and resources created by its people. Once inside, these elements are, for the most part, under management's control. An organization's internal environment makes it unique and is revealed by several tangible as well as intangible expressions. We examine this next.

Identify the elements in an organization's internal environment

Core Competencies

The most significant cause for an organization's success is a continuing focus on what it knows and does best—its **core competencies**. Core competencies are a company's expertise, and they evolve over time. Walmart knows what it does best. The selection at each Walmart store is tailored to the interests of the local community it serves. Conversely, a major cause for company failure is senior management's failure "to ask central questions, such as what precisely is their company's core expertise, what are reasonable long-term and short-term goals, what are the key drivers of profitability in their competitive situation?"[4] Every day senior managers must ask themselves, "What is our business?" and "What should it be?" They must continually assess where they have been, where they are now and where they wish to go in line with where their expertise lies.

core competencies
What an organization knows and does best

As Walmart watched upscale customers go to its competitor, Target, its senior management eventually realized that the company had to refocus. Now Walmart is fighting back. Its heritage of "everyday low prices" has evolved to a value proposition, "save money, live better," where it offers better quality products at cheaper prices than its competitors. Products are grouped by experiences in Walmart stores—vacations in back yards, meals eaten at home, family game nights, etc.

An organization's core competencies, along with other intangibles, make up its **intellectual capital**—its collective experiences, wisdom, knowledge and expertise. Intellectual capital is "embedded in the personal skills, brain power, and experience of a company's employees. It's in a company's libraries, its filing cabinets, electronic data bases and patents, copyrights, trademarks, [and] skills."[5] Along with its tangible assets, intellectual capital constitutes the current worth of a company and its future prospects. All organizational members must effectively utilize the intellectual capital if it is to yield the greatest benefits and advantages. One method of capturing intellectual capital is knowledge management (KM), the topic of this chapter's Managing Social Media. This system allows individuals and groups across an organization to leverage their information resources into organization value.

intellectual capital
An organization's collective experiences, wisdom, knowledge, and expertise

Organizational Culture

All organizations are dynamic systems of shared values, beliefs, philosophies, experiences, customs and norms of behavior. The combination of these elements gives an organization a distinctive character called **organizational culture**. Top management

organizational culture
Dynamic system of shared values, beliefs, philosophies, experiences, customs, and norms of behavior that give an organization its distinctive character

Knowledge Management (KM)

Peter Drucker coined the term "knowledge worker" to describe an individual who develops and applies knowledge and information in the workplace. Today, in the United States, most employees are knowledge workers. Employees have a great deal of knowledge, and organizations want to collect it. Knowledge Management (KM) goes beyond information or data management by capturing the experience of the individual. The organization captures, organizes, maintains, distributes and builds on this knowledge to increase productivity. Idea sharing, collaboration and teamwork create a culture of innovation for competitive advantage. Social media and networking tools within the enterprise (E 2.0 in graph)—tags, blogs, wikis and social networking—make it easier for employees to collaborate and for the company to gather collective intelligence from the minds of many. Each tool's impact on collaboration can be seen in the model below.

Social tools are designed to help employees create content, rather than just to consume it. They encourage knowledge transfer through employee interactions.

➡ During an interview for your "dream job," you discover that Microsoft Word is not available on company computers. To communicate with three or more people, employees are required to use blogs for conversations and wikis or document sharing drives for collaboration. The explanation given is that blogs, wikis and shared drives look better and the information is more useful to employees because it can be searched, tagged, versioned and linked. Will you accept the job and give up Word? Explain your decision.

E20 Effects \ E20 Activites	Tagging	Blogging	"Wiki"-ing	"Social Network"-ing
Input	Costs of implementation	Costs of implementation; costs of blogging activity	Costs of implementation; costs of input time per user; costs of "wiki gardening"	Costs of implementation; costs of socializing per user; costs of administration
Output	No. of tags defined per time unit or object	No. of blog posts per time unit	No. of content objects edited per time unit	No. of established relationships/scope of social graph
Outgrowth	Usage of tags to find information	No. of views per blog posts; no. of comments per blog posts	No. of content objectives viewed per time unit; no. of discussions on editing	No. of comments on user statusses; no. of comments on discussion boards
Oucome	Understanding of information context for used information	Understanding of blog context (e.g. corporate vision in case of a CEO blog)	Understanding of products, projects and processes	Perceived proximity to coworkers; understanding of business context
Outflow	New processes & products; cross-departmental collaboration	Higher contentedness & identification of coworkers with corporate mission	Product quality; process efficiency	Higher identification; cross-departmental collaboration

Source: Bjoern Negelmann, "Ideas for the measurement of Enterprise 2.0 effects," Enterprise2Open, http://blog.enterprise-digital.net/2009/06/ideas-for-the-measurement-of-enterprise-20-effects/.

The Scientific Method

Culture is simply the sum of how those in an organization would describe "the way we do things here" (Mann). The key to a culture of organizational learning is to systematically discover problems and to systematically solve problems. In a lean enterprise, culture is described as the sum of daily habits, which include safety, standardization, simplification, scientific method and self-discipline.

The application of the scientific method to work forces an orderly problem-solving process. Managers and employees analyze and interpret empirical evidence (facts from observation or experimentation) to confirm or disprove prior conceptions.

Steps in the Scientific Method Applied to Work

1. **State the problem.** (Systematically recognize problems.)
2. **Form a hypothesis.** (Attack problems through detailed observation.)
3. **Test the hypothesis.** (Investigate options.)
4. **Draw conclusions.** (Resolve problems one after the other.)

State the problem. Systematically recognize problems. It has been said, "A problem well defined is half-solved." The problem must be clearly defined and the objectives precisely stated to properly guide the rest of the research process. Yet, defining the problem can be one of the most difficult parts of the research. An incorrectly defined problem can lead to incorrect research objectives and consequently a poor decision. Not only is it important for the right problem to be identified, but the definition should be specific. Many people define symptoms of the problem as the problem (for example, declining sales) instead of the defining the real problem (for example, declining quality).

Form a hypothesis. Attack problems through detailed observation. Quality managers go to where the work is done and see the problem for themselves. Data about the problem must be gathered before a possible solution to the problem can be formed.

Test the hypothesis. Investigate options. Research is implemented to determine if the hypothesis solves the problem or not. The data must be collected, processed, analyzed and interpreted. Observation is often used for exploratory research. For causal research, the best approach is experimental research. After analyzing the data from the research, conclusions can be drawn. Relationships, trends and patterns can be identified. In its simplest form, the conclusion will be "yes" the hypothesis was correct, or "no" the hypothesis was not correct.

Draw conclusions. Resolve problems one after the other. Confirm or negate the hypothesis.

In Chapter 2, the major contributors to quality management theory were introduced. Two of those contributors, Walter A. Shewhart and W. Edwards Deming, advocated quality control through the scientific method. Shewhart originally proposed the use of the Plan-Do-Study-Act (PDSA) Cycle for any process changes. Deming popularized the Shewhart Cycle and referred to it as the Plan-Do-Check-Act (PDCA)) Cycle.

Plan-Do-Check-Act (PDCA) Cycle

Plan – Form a hypothesis. Identify the current situation and compare it to the desired situation. Determine changes in the process.

Do – Test the hypothesis. Make the changes or improvements.

Check – Verify the results. Study the effect of the changes. Is it the same, better or worse?

Act – Standardize the method. If satisfied, standardize the improvements and plan for more improvements. If dissatisfied, plan for further actions.

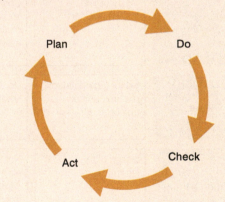

➡ How does the PDCA Cycle relate the Scientific Method?

Source: David Mann, "The Missing Link: Lean Leadership," Frontiers of Health Services Management, Fall 2009 (26: 1), pp. 15–26, *http://www.dmannlean.com/pdfs/The%20Missing%20Link_Lean%20 Leadership_DWMann.pdf*

provides a primary framework for an organization's culture. Management establishes and articulates the company's values and norms of behavior. Especially in large companies, top management may invest substantially to familiarize employees with these values. McDonald's Hamburger University is an example of such an investment, as are the ritual celebrations for top sellers sponsored by Mary Kay Cosmetics and Avon Corporation. The scientific method, discussed in this chapter's Quality Management, is part of the culture of the lean enterprise.

A firm's culture is also shaped by employees. They shape the culture by bringing their own values and norms to the organization and by the extent to which they accept the management-defined culture. Southwest Airlines' culture thrives on the many and often-told stories about coworkers who go to extraordinary lengths to care for customers. Newsletters, in-flight magazines and advertising emphasize the airline's people, and all these communications reinforce the attitude that management and employees prize.

Moreover, within a company's formal and social subsystems, distinctive mini-cultures usually flourish. Such subcultures develop spontaneously, and management encourages some. The marketing department may have a unique culture (formed in part by past successes as well as failures), separate from and parallel to the organization's culture. Such a subculture influences the corporate culture.

Members of ethnic groups bring their cultures with them and often create, within the workplace, subcultures based on their languages, customs, traditions, values and beliefs. These subcultures contribute to the corporate culture. Sometimes they blend,

Valuing Diversity and Inclusion

Cultural Heritages at Frito-Lay

All of Frito-Lay's employees are encouraged to form organizations based on their cultural heritages and to participate. Resource groups include Mosaic (African-American network), (PAN) Asian Network, Adelante (Hispanic network), RISE (Native American Network), EnAble (people with different abilities) and WIN (Women's Initiative Network) (Source: Snack Chat). Charles Nicolas, a spokesman for Frito-Lay, says, "It's reflective of America today. There are a lot of different cultures out there, a lot of different ideas. They bring the richness of their culture to the business" (Source: Souder).

Resource group activities reinforce Frito-Lay's commitment to diversity and inclusion. For example, Frito-Lay's Black Professional Association organizes the events to celebrate Martin Luther King Jr. Day, which includes a diversity network fair and cultural showcase (Source: Souder). Martin Luther King Jr. Day is a federal holiday celebrated on the third Monday in January, honoring the late civil rights leader by remembering his dream for equality of all races and peoples.

Richness of culture has enriched Frito-Lay. The organizations came up with two recent products: guacamole-flavored Doritos and wasabi-flavored Funyuns.

➡ **Why is it important for employees to share knowledge and viewpoints about their cultural traditions?**

➡ **What cultural traditions could you share at work?**

Sources: Snack Chat, "Frito-Lay Celebrates Asian Pacific American Heritage Month," May 26, 2010, *http://www.snacks.com/good_fun_ fritolay/2010/05/fritolay-celebrates-asian-pacific-american-heritage-month.html*; Elizabeth Souder, "Frito-Lay Builds on MLK Day," *The Dallas Morning News*, January 16, 2006, *http://www.dallasnews. com/sharedcontent/dws/bus/stories/DN-mlk_16bus.ART.State. Edition2.911f300.html.*
http://www.fritolay.com/blog/snack-chat/2015/03/31/nine-women-who-exemplify-greatness-at-frito-lay
http://www.fritolay.com/blog/snack-chat/2013/11/05/frito-lay-wraps-up-hispanic-heritage-month-festivities

sometimes they remain distinct. If management values diversity, it will do more than respect such subcultures; management will seek to derive from them benefits for the entire organization. Frito-Lay, the snack-maker unit of PepsiCo, knows how to provide a nurturing environment to employees. This chapter's Valuing Diversity and Inclusion feature takes you inside one of its celebrations and indicates some of the accomplishments diverse groups can achieve.

Organizational Climate

An outgrowth of a corporation's culture is its **organizational climate**—how employees feel about working there. Successful organizations often have climates that feel open—they foster the individual's creative energies and take advantage of employees' eagerness to participate. Employees are empowered through the practice of open-book management and other means and have the freedom to fail.

Open-book management commits organizations and their people to continual learning and requires that well-trained people be allowed to apply, without fear, what they learn. Through information-sharing techniques and training sessions, employees learn the calculation methods and meanings of the critical numbers used to measure a company's processes and guarantee its success. An open-book organization fosters continual learning and helps to create committed individuals who, both in and out of teams, perceive themselves to be partners working toward a common purpose. The technique of **scoreboarding** routinely keeps employees aware of changes in these numbers as operations progress. Employees are kept informed through meetings, the posting of these numbers in strategic places, and the networking of individuals and groups via computers and other means.

Empowerment, the sharing of information and decision making, gives employees ownership of their tasks and the freedom to experiment and even fail, without fear of reprisals. Empowerment requires managers to develop relationships built on mutual trust and respect, provide needed training and resources, listen to their people, and act on the recommendations they receive. Empowered individuals and teams give enormous flexibility to organizations. Decisions are made at the lowest level possible, allowing for quick responses to users' and customers' demands. But empowered individuals and teams will get the most from their autonomy only when they represent diverse points of view, value one another, and respect each other's contributions.

Springfield ReManufacturing Corporation practiced open-book management when its president and CEO, Jack Stack, turned employees, individually and in teams, into **intrapreneurs**—employees who think and act like owners (**entrepreneurs**)—thus changing the ways in which the organization conducted operations. Stack has written a book with Bo Burlingham, *A Stake in the Outcome,* to help managers learn how they can practice his corporation's brand of open-book management in their organizations.

Gifford Pinchot III coined the term *intrapreneur* in his book, *Intrapreneuring, or Why You Don't Have to Leave the Corporation to Become an Entrepreneur.* Intrapreneurs are entrepreneurial individuals in companies, championing new ideas from conception to profitable implementation. The desired result is increased profitability through innovative processes, new products, and new lines of businesses. Innovative companies give intrapreneurs the time and resources to pursue new ideas. Managers need to understand "The Intrapreneurial Bill of Rights" that follows.

organizational climate
An outgrowth of a corporation's culture showing how employees feel about working there

open-book management
Commits organizations and their people to continual learning and requires that well-trained people be allowed to apply, without fear, what they learn

scoreboarding
A technique that routinely keeps employees aware of changes in the critical numbers used to measure a company's processes

empowerment
The sharing of information and decision making

intrapreneurs
Employees who think and act like owners

entrepreneur
Someone who starts and assumes the risk of a business

The Intrapreneurial Bill of Rights

1. **The 10 percent rule:** An employee may use 10 percent of her time to pursue new ideas she believes may be useful to the organization.

2. **The right to form an intraprise:** An employee has the right to form an intraprise if his salary can be covered by revenue from customers or intracapital.

3. **The right to one's intraprise:** An intrapreneurial team that has created a profitable or solvent business has a quasi-ownership right to continue operating it. It cannot be taken and given to others without cause and due process.

4. **The right to join an intraprise:** Every employee has the right to join an intraprise, provided the intraprise is agreeable and is able and willing to pay her salary.

5. **The right to reject team members:** Every intraprise has the right not to accept members it considers unsuitable, and to ask members to leave according to a process designated in the team bylaws. No outside entity can force a team to keep a member it has asked to leave. The larger organization will provide a safety net for employees leaving intrapreneurial teams.

6. **The right to save:** The team, or an individual intrapreneur, has the right to deposit receipts in the intracapital bank, where they cannot be appropriated by any other entity except as the result of due process or corporate taxation at normal rates.

7. **The right of possession:** When an intraprise buys tools or other business assets with its own intracapital, it has a quasi-ownership right to control the use and disposition of those assets for the furtherance of its work.

8. **The right to spend:** Intrapreneurs and intraprises have the right to spend their intracapital as they see fit for any legitimate intraprise or corporate purpose. They may not use it for personal expenditures unrelated to the business unless it is first paid to them as personal compensation in a program approved by human resources.

9. **The right to lead:** The leader of an intrapreneurial team shall not be removed from that position as long as he or she has the support of the team.

10. **Freedom of speech:** Intrapreneurs have the right to speak freely on all matters concerning the governance of the organization.[6]

Leadership

Defined in Chapter 1, *leadership* means influencing others to set and achieve goals. Every leader should encourage and enable followers to give their best. The exercise of leadership, however, is influenced by elements both inside and outside an individual. Each person has a set of beliefs, attitudes, and values— acquired through experience— that composes his or her personality, conscience, and philosophy. An organization's culture and climate also influence those in leadership positions within that organization. Leadership involves setting an example through both words and deeds.

Leaders must "walk like they talk." Nothing can derail efforts for change and improvements more effectively than a leader's hypocrisy, according to Peter Scott-Morgan, a business consultant with Arthur D. Little. "They preach the importance of teamwork—then reward individuals who work at standing out from the crowd. They encourage risk taking—then punish good-faith failures."[7] It takes leadership, not necessarily the traditional type, to cultivate learning. Leadership will create a generative shared vision and will provide the catalyst for perpetual learning.[8] Chapter 12 examines leadership in more detail.

Organizational Structure

The formal structure of a company, a component of the company's internal environment, determines how its activities are conducted. Within each of the three management tiers—top, middle, and first-line—teams may be created to execute such basic tasks as design, production, marketing, finance and human resources management. The formal structure also determines how authority and communications flow from management to employees. Variations in structure are determined by the tasks a company performs, how management wishes to perform them and external factors. External determinants include customer demands, competitors' strategies and government regulations.

The trend today is toward less pyramidal structures, staffed with empowered individuals, empowered teams and autonomous business units. Such structures facilitate more flexibility and a quicker response to customers. Some companies have gone so far as to depend on loose, temporary collections of freelance experts and consultants to create a specific project; the freelancers and consultants then move on to other jobs once they complete their task. The movie industry creates many of its films by using this model. Others, like Bechtel, a worldwide construction company, function with teams of in-house experts brought together to manage projects. Once each project is completed, team members are reassigned to new project teams. Thus, Bechtel's matrix management organizational structure is continually changing.

Boundaryless organizations are not defined or limited by horizontal, vertical, or external boundaries imposed by a predetermined structure. They share many of the characteristics of flat organizations, with a strong emphasis on teams. Cross-functional teams dissolve horizontal barriers and enable the organization to respond quickly to environmental changes and to spearhead innovation. Boundaryless organizations can form relationships (joint ventures, intellectual property, distribution channels or financial resources) with customers, suppliers, and/or competitors. Teleworking, strategic alliances, and customer-organization linkages break down external barriers, streamlining work activities. In order to facilitate interactions with customers and suppliers, Jack Welch, former CEO of General Electric, first used this un-structure.

A boundaryless environment is required by learning organizations to facilitate team collaboration and the sharing of information. When an organization develops the capacity to adapt and survive in an increasingly competitive environment because all members take an active role in identifying and resolving work-related issues, it has developed a learning culture. This design empowers employees because they acquire and share knowledge and apply this learning to decision making. They are pooling collective intelligence and stimulating creative thought to improve performance. Managers facilitate learning by sharing and aligning the organization's vision for the future and sustaining a sense of community and strong culture. Organizational structure is continually changing. Chapters 6 and 7 explore organizational issues.

boundaryless organizations
Organizations not defined or limited by horizontal, vertical, or external boundaries imposed by a predetermined structure

Resources

The primary resource of any organization is its people. Chapter 9 focuses on the management of human resources. An organization needs resources in addition to people to continue its mission and reach specific objectives, however. These resources are the inputs to the system—the elements processed, transformed or used—and they influence the internal environment. Such resources include information, facilities, machinery and equipment, materials and supplies, finances and infrastructure.

Information The word information refers to the facts and knowledge that provide vital nourishment for all the operations of an organization. Without accurate, timely, up-to-date information, neither employees nor managers can make daily decisions effectively and efficiently, nor can they plan ahead. Information from insiders and outsiders is needed to coordinate and execute tasks at every level. Keeping others informed of problems and progress is every employee's duty. Chapter 14 will deal with information management in depth.

Facilities and Infrastructure *Facilities* consist of the physical structures—the work and office spaces and their layouts—required to accomplish the firm's goals. The location, appearance and condition of an organization's facilities can significantly influence employee productivity. The Gensler Workplace Survey series found that the workplace is a significant factor to U.S. workers, with 9 in 10 reporting that the workplace affects their productivity. Many employees report that better design of their workplace would help them be more productive, whether the work involves focus, collaboration, learning or socializing.[9]

The term *infrastructure* refers to the surrounding region or community's permanent framework or foundation of transportation, communication, sewage, water, electric and gas utilities. The framework might include dams, power stations, roads, railways, harbors and airports. Infrastructure projects—such as airports, roads, bridges and pipelines—attract businesses to expand or relocate in an area, driving new jobs for the local community. "One of the biggest drivers of North Texas' economic boom in the 20th century resulted from a huge project...Dallas/Fort Worth International Airport. Today, the massive airport is credited with bringing major companies to North Texas and spurring growth throughout the area."[10] Thus, infrastructure resources support not only individual companies but the community at large. Such resources are generally built at public expense or with government support of one kind or another. Their extent and quality are basic to most businesses, especially manufacturing. From highways and airports to sewage systems and power grids, the operation of modern businesses depends on all these and more.

Machinery and Equipment Computer-directed technologies and all other hardware used to process inputs are part of an organization's machinery and equipment, the tools used in offices, factories and other workplaces. Furniture, fixtures, telephones, computers, printers and robots are but a few examples. The quality of machinery and equipment is a function of its maintainability, efficiency, dependability and speed of operation. Its compatibility with other equipment influences how effectively and efficiently people work together. Current, reliable, and easy-to-use equipment helps to prevent stress to workers. In addition, high-quality equipment encourages people to do their best, freed from interruptions caused by mechanical breakdowns.

Materials and Supplies Taken together, the services, raw materials and parts (components and subassemblies) needed to produce goods and services make up an organization's materials and supplies. The division of General Electric that produces home appliances consumes an astounding amount of goods in this category: miles of wiring, tons of sheet metal, nuts, and bolts; motors; coolants and solvents; plastic; and glass. The division needs all of these items to keep production machinery clean and running. At the facility of a service industry—the home office of Aetna Insurance, for example—the materials and supplies list calls for reams of letterhead and paper, printer ink cartridges, staples, paper clips, file folders and cleaning supplies.

Materials and supplies may be acquired outside the company or within. General Motors (GM) buys windshields and windows from Pittsburgh Plate Glass and tires from Goodyear. But GM's Chevrolet, Buick, Cadillac and Pontiac divisions build most of their engines and transmissions in their own facilities. GM assembly plants are the customers for GM engine and transmission factories. The quality of materials and supplies greatly affects the quality of the goods and services a company can produce. The same can be said for the other resources discussed so far.

Finances The term *finances* means the money available. Finances, which can be generated directly from the sale of the organization's goods and services, can be in the form of cash in bank accounts or a line of credit negotiated with a financial institution (usually a commercial bank). Trade credit is the most significant source of short-term finances. Suppliers grant trade credit whenever they agree to provide materials and supplies in exchange for an organization's promise to pay the invoice, plus interest, within a specified number of weeks.

An important financial resource for U.S. corporations is the sale of stocks and bonds on the open market. Investment brokers and public stock exchanges facilitate such sales. Another source of cash may be the sale of assets. During the last years of Pan Am, the airline was hard pressed to repay massive bank loans. Pan Am managers repeatedly raised needed cash by selling off valuable assets, including its corporate headquarters building in New York and the worldwide routes it had pioneered during better days.

Money is the basis for all of an organization's operations, from acquiring resources to honoring employee paychecks to compensating investors. Money is the lifeblood of an organization. It flows to all operatives and, in turn, allows work to flow. A company's financial health affects its ability to function at every level.

EXTERNAL ENVIRONMENT

External forces exert influences on and are influenced by organizations and their subsystems and present both challenges and opportunities to them. The effects of these influences vary from immediate, constant and of daily concern, to infrequent, modest, and of more long-range concern.

As changes occur in both their internal and external environments, organizations adapt and evolve. Walmart started the "everyday low prices" concept because that market was moving toward its focus—expanding the Walmart brand. Its entry to the internet was a response to changing external economic and market conditions, as was transforming its website to make purchasing products easier for its customers.

Directly Interactive Forces

Of most immediate concern to managers are the **directly interactive forces** shown as the closest colored band surrounding the organization in Figure 3.1. Members of these groups regularly make contact with organization members and subsystems, usually on a daily basis. The major directly interactive forces are an organization's owners, customers, suppliers and partners, competitors and external labor pool.

Owners Owners may actively participate in managing (as they normally do in sole proprietorships and some kinds of partnerships). In other cases they may play no

Describe the directly interactive forces in an organization's external environment

directly interactive forces
An organization's owners, customers, suppliers and partners, competitors, and external labor pool

active role at all. This is the case with stockholders who do not work for the corporations in which they own stock. Both kinds of owners, however, expect a return on their investments and look to all the employees to preserve and advance their interests. From the owners comes the formal authority needed to run the business. In corporations, the board of directors is responsible for protecting the owners' investments and ensuring that management earns an adequate return on them.

Customers The individuals and groups that use or purchase the outputs of an organization are customers. Customers can be either internal or external. Internal customers are employees or work units that receive the work of other employees or units. Internal customers process the work further, use it within their work groups or deliver it outside. The surgeon anxiously awaiting a biopsy report is the customer for a hospital lab. The Southwest passenger-service agent checking the computer screen at the airport is a customer of the reservation department. External customers may be manufacturers, wholesalers, retailers, suppliers or corporate or individual consumers. Ensuring the satisfaction of both internal and external customers is vital in a highly competitive marketplace.

Suppliers and Partners Suppliers provide a company with many of the resources it needs. These resources range from expertise and raw materials to money and part-time employees. Suppliers may be separate, autonomous parts of a company or unaffiliated organizations. Suppliers may also be independent companies brought together through a joint venture or temporary partnership. Wikipedia, the web-based encyclopedia, is maintained by thousands of volunteers. Linux, the free "open source" operating system software, was developed over the internet by thousands of people all over the world. "Loncin, a leading Chinese motorcycle manufacturer, sets broad specifications for products and then lets its suppliers work with one another to design the components, make sure everything fits together, and reduce costs."[11]

Several continuing trends in supplier practices emerged during the 1980s. First, companies increased their use of outsourcing. They selected as suppliers small, efficient businesses that could make resources of higher quality at lower cost than the companies themselves could make. Second, to enhance the effectiveness of working relationships, companies developed close alliances with outside suppliers. An example of this close alliance is exclusive beverage contract some schools have with Coca-Cola or Pepsi, the discussion in this chapter's Ethical Management.

To hasten decision making, suppliers were and continue to be brought into projects early, often at the design stage. One example is the Fridge Pack.

> *The idea grew from Alcoa research into how people cool canned beverages at home, and emerged from brainstorming sessions that included Riverwood package designers and engineers. The team then presented mock-ups to beverage makers. Coca-Cola followed through, renamed the carton the Fridge Pack, and took it to the market, where it has been credited with increasing canned-soda sales by 10 percent. Consumers ask for the Fridge Pack by name, prompting additional applications. Coca-Cola tweaked the carton design for use with Dasani bottled water, and Miller Brewing has now adopted the concept for beer.[12]*

Many companies have merged with suppliers or have bought them outright to guarantee a reliable source of quality goods and services. To strengthen its capabilities in office products, for example, Office Depot acquired Staples. The merger allows the new company to serve individuals, small businesses and large businesses.

Cola Wars on Campus

Coca-Cola and Pepsi have extended their market share war to colleges and universities. They offer schools money if they become the sole beverage provider on campus. The exclusive contracts are the result of bidding wars between the cola giants. Schools have received rewards ranging from commissions as high as 65 percent to the funding of intercollegiate athletic programs. While in some cases this additional funding is necessary, some school officials feel that it ultimately hurts the university when asking for public money.

Such contracts are attractive to many schools. Most have been hit hard by their states' funding cutbacks and are looking for alternate sources of income to help them keep their fees and tuition in check. The cola companies like the school contracts because they create captive markets and help to form the soft-drink habits of thousands of students.

One university vice president in charge of development indicates that his school would not consider such a deal if it were not for state funding cutbacks. He indicated that his school is considering an offer from one of the cola makers to replace lost state funds. One university professor adds that colleges set a bad example when they deprive students of any freedom in selecting soft drinks and that such exclusive contracts actually present state legislators with an additional reason for cutting college funds.

A standard for judging exclusionary contracts is that they also must have foreclosed a rival's ability to get to market with its product in some other way. A key to a company's defense is to claim that its rival wasn't foreclosed from the market by the company's exclusive contracts with partners.

➡ **What do you think about these exclusive contracts?**

➡ **Are exclusive contracts an attack on the basic consumer right of freedom of choice? Why or why not?**

Sources: USDA Food & Nutrition Service Resources, "What does it mean to influence vending contracts?" *http://www.fns.usda.gov/ tn/Resources/g_app2.pdf*; Cornell University Law School Legal Information Institute, "Antitrust: An Overview," *http://www.law.cornell. edu/topics/antitrust.html*.

Third, companies are seeking these "deep" alliances with fewer, more dependable suppliers. And fourth, companies are more willing to procure needed supplies from anywhere in the world, turning more frequently to foreign sources to meet their needs for high quality and low price.

Competitors An organization's competitors are those firms that offer similar products and services in the organization's marketplace. Businesses compete on the basis of price, quality, selection, convenience, product features and performance, and customer services. Customer services include delivery, financing, and warranties. Competition is not merely a contest between Toyota and Ford, NBC and CBS, or JetBlue and Southwest. Instead, competition is an irresistible force at work at every level of commerce in free enterprise systems. Aluminum competes with steel as a manufacturing material; railroads with trucks; network television with cable broadcasters; and long-distance telephone companies with cell-phone service.

For most companies, how managers deal with competition determines whether their companies succeed or fail. In the early 1990s, IBM was struggling to recover leadership in its industry. Many experts said the company's decline derived from the failure of IBM's management to counter the competition. The experts said IBM clung too long to mainframe computers and did not pursue the PC market as aggressively as did other companies. IBM's real resurgence was its shift away from computer hardware to services.[13] Today, IBM sells services and software.

Labor Force The term *labor force* (sometimes used interchangeably with *labor pool* or *workforce*) applies to the people in the "global community" from which an organization can recruit qualified candidates. The key word in the preceding definition is, of course, *qualified.*

The needs of businesses are changing. Jobs in the crafts and trades, which traditionally provided work for the members of labor unions, are giving way to jobs that require proficiency in math, verbal communication and computer sciences. Elaine L. Chao, former U.S. Secretary of Labor reported, "Our economy is making an unprecedented transition into high-skilled, information-based industries. This has created a disconnect between the jobs that are being created and the current skills of many workers."[14]

America's workforce is changing, becoming more culturally segmented and diverse. The notion of cultural diversity applies to communities whose members represent distinctly different ethnic and national backgrounds, language, religious beliefs, lifestyles and age groups. Patterns of social change and widespread immigration are the principal agents of this change. The projections for 2018 from the Bureau of Labor Statistics show an aging and more racially and ethnically diverse labor force.[15]

Indirectly Interactive Forces

An organization's **indirectly interactive forces** are more remote and generally beyond the ability of managers to control or influence to any great extent. They do, however, affect the execution of all management functions to some degree. The major indirectly interactive forces are both domestic and foreign economic, legal/political, sociocultural, technological and natural forces.

Economic Forces The levels of taxes, wages, prices, interest rates, personal spending and saving, business spending and profits, inflation and the state an entire economy is in at any given time—recession, recovery, boom and depression—are called **economic forces.** Economic forces influence management decisions as well as the costs and availability of needed resources. A large chemical producer, Union Carbide (now a subsidiary of The Dow Chemical Corporation), made almost no profits from its core businesses during the 1991–1993 recession. The demand for two of its products—ethyl glycol and polyethylene— was flat until 1994, when it rapidly increased. The company responded by raising prices for the former by 25 percent and raising its prices for the latter by more than 50 percent. This placed the company—the low-cost producer of these chemicals—in an enormously profitable position.[16]

Legal/Political Forces The general framework of statutes enacted by legislatures; precedents established by court decisions; regulations and rulings created by various federal, state and local regulatory agencies; and agreements between and among governments and companies from different nations constitute **legal/political forces.** The U.S. Office of Management and Budget (OMB) released its 2015 Report to Congress on the Costs and Benefits of Federal Regulations and Unfunded Mandates on State, Local, and Tribal Entities.

> *The estimated annual net benefits of major Federal regulations reviewed by OMB from January 21, 2009, to September 30, 2014 (this Administration), for which agencies estimated and monetized both benefits and costs, is approximately $215 billion.[17]*

Determine the indirectly interactive forces in an organization's external environment

indirectly interactive forces
Domestic and foreign economic, legal/political, sociocultural, technological, and natural forces

economic forces
Conditions in an economy that influence management decisions and the costs and availability of resources

legal/political forces
The general framework of statutes enacted by legislatures; precedents established by court decisions; regulations and rulings created by various federal, state, and local regulatory agencies; and agreements between and among governments and companies from different nations

Britain and the Measure of Things

Although most countries have adopted the metric system, it took Britain 800 years. (See a Metrication Timeline—timeline of the adoption of the metric system in the UK—at *http://www.metric.org.uk/metrication-timeline*) The metric system is a decimal-based system of measurement units created by the French in the seventeenth century. Like our money system, units for a given quantity (e.g., length) are related by factors of ten. Calculations involve the simple process of moving the decimal point to the right or to the left. (The United States is the only industrialized country in the world not officially using the metric system.)

Since the thirteenth century, Britain has used pounds, gallons, feet and inches as weights and measures. In 1965, Great Britain, as a condition for becoming a member of the European Common Market, began a transition to the metric system in its trade and commerce. On October 1, 1995, Britain was forced to adopt the metric system's units of weights and measures as a condition of the European Trade Agreement. Yet, Britain's "Metric Martyrs" refused to accept successive governments' attempts to abolish measurements dating back to the Middle Ages (Brogan and Sims). "Sunderland grocer Steve Thoburn inspired the "metric martyr" movement with his defiance of the order to abandon the imperial measurements. In 2001, he was convicted for having weighing scales which had only imperial measurements" (BBC). Metric Martyrs, Neil Herron, explained, "It's about the language and vernacular

with which we relate to each other. Even with kids who have been educated in metric for the past 30 years, watching a football match talk about a penalty kick being 12 yards or the striker being six foot tall" (Kelley).

British retailers sell pints of beer, cider and milk. Land is measured in miles and sold in acres. All of the road signs are in miles. Finally, in 2007, the European Commission gave up the fight and allowed Britain to use its traditional measures "until Kingdom come" (Brogan and Sims).

▶ In the 1980s, Britain converted its money to a decimal system (at the heart of the metric system), abandoning the pounds, shillings and pence it had used for nearly 700 years. So, why won't Britain ever go completely metric?

Benedict Brogan and Paul Sims, "Victory for Britain's Metric Martyrs as Eurocrats give up the fight," *Mail Online* (September 11, 2007), *http://www.dailymail.co.uk/news/article-481129/Victory-Britains-metric-martyrs-Eurocrats-fight.html*

BBC News, "EU gives up on 'metric Britain'," (September 11, 2007) *http://news.bbc.co.uk/2/hi/uk_news/6988521.stm*

Jon Kelley, BBC News Magazine, "Will British people ever think in metric?" (December 21, 2011), *http://www.bbc.com/news/magazine-16245391*

Laws at all levels of government in every country in which a company does business affect all that company's activities. Some regulations, such as antipollution laws, are intended to provide protection for society as a whole; others protect consumers in a variety of ways and preserve or restrict competition in markets. This chapter's Global Applications feature focuses on the impact that Britain's membership in the European Commission has had on its traditional means of weighing and measuring.

Sociocultural Forces The influences and contributions from diverse groups outside an organization constitute **sociocultural forces**. We have already mentioned the value of diverse employees and their subcultures. People don't leave "who they are" at home when they report to work. They bring with them their ethnicity, culture, beliefs and attitudes. In like fashion, groups of diverse people in an organization's external community influence and react to its plans and actions.

When the Walt Disney Company bought 3000 acres near the Manassas National Battlefield in Virginia, it intended to spend about $650 million to develop a Civil War theme park and related businesses. Its plans met strong local and national resistance.

sociocultural forces
The influences and contributions from diverse groups outside an organization

"Critics, including some historians, argued that the … park and adjacent developments would pollute the area and detract from true historic sites only a few miles away."[18] Rather than fight the public's outrage, the project was eventually abandoned.

Technological Forces Processes, materials, knowledge and other discoveries resulting from research and development activities sponsored or conducted by governments, private firms and individuals around the globe give rise to **technological forces**. Research and development have created the technologies that have led to advances in telecommunications, digitization of audio and video satellites, fiber-optic networks, nano technology, robotics and virtual reality, to name but a few. Breakthroughs in technology influence how efficiently businesses operate, as well as the competitiveness and quality of their products and services.

For example, the internet continues to bring many new ways of doing business. Electronic commerce—the worldwide purchases of products and services across the internet—has changed buying and selling. It has forced prices down and resulted in some companies going out of business. Yet, new companies, such as Google, Amazon, and eBay, have become household names. The business rules for selling and buying books, music and travel have been rewritten. Today more than ever, a business's success can be directly linked to how rapidly and effectively it absorbs and adjusts its operations and outputs to the latest technologies.

Natural Forces such as climate, weather, geography and geology that affect how businesses operate and locate their operations are known collectively as **natural forces**. The climate of a region determines a firm's need for energy for such uses as heating and air conditioning. Storms and other natural disasters can disrupt a firm's production and flow of supplies.

When Hurricane Katrina struck Louisiana and Mississippi, it curtailed U.S. energy production by damaging Gulf of Mexico oil rigs and refineries. As a result, energy prices were raised. Higher energy prices mean that businesses have less money to spend on hiring and consumers have less money to spend on discretionary purchases. Furthermore, the hurricane disrupted the Mississippi River, a vital transportation artery. Companies had to seek alternative methods of transportation. Rail and road are more expensive than water. Consumers faced higher prices and shortages of popular products, such as Folgers coffee and Chiquita bananas.

Environments and Management

Environmental forces create challenges, risks, opportunities and changes for every organization. Managers must remain alert to their internal and external environments, sensing changes or shifts, reacting and adapting quickly and imaginatively. They must forecast and plan for the changes they suspect will come and for the changes they wish to initiate. Managers must cultivate a sensible and controlled reactive behavior toward changes that may affect them with little or no warning, and an imaginative program to manage and capitalize on the changes they can foresee and over which they have some control.

SENSING AND ADAPTING TO ENVIRONMENTS

Staying in touch with environments requires that managers monitor events and trends that develop outside their specific areas of influence. The areas could be other departments or divisions within the company, the competition, the economy and all the

---

technological forces
The combined effects of processes, materials, knowledge, and other discoveries resulting from research and development activities

natural forces
Forces such as climate, weather, geography, and geology that affect how businesses operate and locate their operations

Discuss the means available to managers for boundary spanning

other forces that can influence their system or subsystem. This surveillance of out-side areas and factors is called **boundary spanning**.[19] The practice requires current information about what is happening or likely to happen. Boundary spanners look for developments that can influence plans, forecasts, decisions and organizations. Sources of information include feedback from customers and suppliers, competitors' actions, government statistics, professional and trade publications, industry and trade associations and colleagues and professional associates inside and outside the organization. Through boundary spanning, managers keep up to date, establish networks to facilitate the gathering and dissemination of information, and build personal relationships that can lead to increased power and influence over people and events.

boundary spanning
The surveillance of outside areas and factors that can influence plans, forecasts, decisions and organizations. Sometimes called environmental scanning

Sometimes the challenges posed by the environment are clear to everyone. The key to gaining a competitive advantage is how a firm adapts to the challenges. The intensely competitive field of electronics provides an example. In the twentieth century, Samsung was thought of as a cheap producer of copied, electronic products. In the twenty-first century, Samsung is known for its sophisticated product design, especially televisions, cellular phones and other personal electronics. The turnaround at Samsung happened when management began to scan the environment and use this information to produce what consumers wanted. Now, the company can answer the questions, "Who is our customer?" and "What do they want?"

INFLUENCING ENVIRONMENTS

Explain how managers can influence their external environments

Although managers must sense and adapt to environments, they and their organizations can also influence their environments in several ways. In a democratic society, citizens—alone and in groups—have the right to attempt to influence legislation and the rules that determine how the game of business is played. Lobbying allows people to present their points of view to legislators and to push for changes that they see as beneficial. Whether by personal letter to a city official or through a paid professional who lobbies legislators, managers and individual citizens' groups will continue to play vital roles in the shaping of our society.

Managers and organizations use the power of the media to influence public opinion and public policy. Their viewpoints and agendas are constantly reported in advertising, public relations announcements, press releases and in-depth interviews. Industry and trade groups allow businesses to conduct research, build alliances and raise funds to push their agendas for or against change.

MEETING RESPONSIBILITIES TO STAKEHOLDERS

Describe the obligations that organizations have to their stakeholders

Stakeholders are the groups that are directly or indirectly affected by the ways in which business is conducted and managers conduct themselves. Stakeholders include owners, employees, customers, suppliers and society—people in local communities, our economy and the world at large. Members of each of these groups lose or gain depending on how businesses operate. Chapter 9 examines the responsibilities that managers and businesses have to these groups.

stakeholders
Groups directly or indirectly affected by the ways in which business is conducted and by the ways in which managers conduct themselves. Stakeholders include owners, employees, customers, suppliers, and society

Owners To owners, businesses owe a fair return on investment. Managers are obligated to make their best effort to use resources effectively and efficiently. Managers must also give an honest accounting of their stewardship over the owners' assets and interests.

Most states require by law that corporations give a financial accounting in quarterly and annual reports to their shareholders.

In most sole proprietorships and small partnerships, owners are the managers. In corporations, however, owners depend on elected representatives who sit on the board of directors. One of the board's primary duties is to ensure that managers consider owners' interests when they make corporate decisions.

Employees As the most important asset of a business, employees need a safe and psychologically rewarding environment. Such an environment supports honest and open communication and shows evidence of real concern for employees' values, goals and welfare. Employees need nurturing environments that help them grow and become more valuable to themselves and their organizations.

Employees deserve to know the risks, values, rules and rewards to which they are exposed. They have the right to ethical treatment, to fairness and to equity in their relationships with management. Their legal rights must be granted and respected. Businesses that stay focused on the needs of their employees will attract and hold on to them, thus helping to guarantee future success. To most customers, employees are the business in the sense that employees are as important as the product or service in establishing the reputation of the business in the customer's mind.

Customers As stakeholders, customers depend on businesses as places of employment and sources for needed products and services. By law, they have the right to safe work environments, services and products. Ethically, they have the right to fair, honest and equitable treatment.

Suppliers Suppliers provide the services, materials, and parts needed to carry on the vital operations of business. Quality begins with an understanding of its importance and is designed into products and services from their conception. Most suppliers today are involved in product and service design and determine to a great extent the performance capabilities of the end result. Suppliers need honest and open communication from the managers and organizations they serve. They deserve to be paid for the products and services rendered and to have the terms of their contracts honored. Reliable sources of dependable supplies are difficult to find; once found, every effort should be made to keep them.

Society A business's obligations to society begin with its employment base and spread out to the communities in which it does business. A mom-and-pop bakery in Muncie, Indiana, can call the neighborhood in which it operates its piece of society. When the parents in the neighborhood call on the bakery to support a Little League baseball team, the bakery owners are expected to respond with some kind of assistance.

Every business needs to define the portions of society that it must serve. It can serve society in a variety of ways, from following fair employment practices, to donating funds and equipment, to preventing pollution. The United Way charity program is staffed locally by volunteers from businesses whose salaries are donated by their regular employers. Many businesses adopt a school to assist in a variety of ways. Businesses usually concentrate on serving their communities in ways that enrich both the givers and receivers. In this effort, as in all undertakings, businesses need to be both reactive and proactive. They must sense the needs of their communities and plan to implement the kinds of assistance they are best able to provide.

Review What You've Learned

Chapter Summary

1 Discuss why organizations are open systems.

An open system must interact with its external environments (both directly and indirectly interactive ones) and is regularly influenced by the forces in them. Any organization depends on its directly interactive external environment to obtain needed resources. Customers exist in that external environment and they dictate, in part, quality standards.

2 Identify the elements in an organization's internal environment.

An organization's internal environment contains the following elements: core competencies, leadership, culture, climate, structure and available resources. Core competencies are what a company does best; they rest in part in the organization's intellectual capital. Leadership makes things happen by encouraging and supporting people to give their best and set and achieve goals. The culture of an organization contains its shared values, beliefs, philosophies, experiences, habits, expectations, norms and behaviors that give it a distinctive character or personality. Structure refers to the formal arrangements between all the organization's members and details who will perform which tasks. Available resources include people, information, intellectual capital, facilities and infrastructure, machinery and equipment, supplies and finances.

3 Describe the directly interactive forces in an organization's external environment.

These forces are owners, customers, suppliers and partners, competitors, and the labor force. Owners create businesses and share in their profits. They make demands and contributions. Some are active in management; others are merely investors with a stake in the organization's future. Customers exist inside and outside organizations. Their needs are paramount. Meeting and exceeding their expectations is the primary function of any organization. Suppliers and partners help organizations obtain needed resources. An organization's competitors challenge and threaten; they are after the same customers and resources. The labor force is the source for needed human resources.

4 Determine the indirectly interactive forces in an organization's external environment.

These domestic and foreign forces are economic, legal/political, sociocultural, technological and natural. Economic forces include the general state of an economy and levels of spending, saving, taxation, inflation and interest rates. Economics affects nearly every management decision in some way. Legal/political forces include regulatory agencies, legislatures, courts, and law enforcement groups at the federal, state, and local levels, along with international agreements between companies and governments. Laws govern every aspect of business operations and must be complied with to avoid harming the organization, its people, its customers and society at large. External sociocultural forces include an organization's diverse customer groups, the communities in which it does business and society as a whole. Technological forces include the state of the art in manufacturing and methodologies used in any process. To be competitive, one's technology must be competitive. Natural forces include climate, weather, geography and natural resources such as oil and coal. Each country and its markets have their own unique history, language, customs, legal and economic system and culture. All must be understood and considered when operating outside one's native country.

5 Discuss the means available to managers for boundary spanning.

The practice of boundary spanning, or scanning one's external environments, is necessary to gather current information about what is happening or is likely to happen. Boundary spanners look for reliable sources of information on customers, suppliers, competitors, government regulators and regulations, and the state of the economies in which they operate. Sources include customers, competitors' actions, government statistics, professional and trade publications, and industry and trade associations. Professional managers also network through a variety of human contacts to keep themselves in touch.

6 **Explain how managers can influence their external environments.**

Managers, like any other individual or groups of individuals, can influence government at every level by letting their voices be heard. They have the right to try to influence legislation through lobbying efforts, either individually or collectively, through industry or trade groups. They use public relations and advertising to get their messages to the public. Industry and trade groups allow businesses to conduct research, build alliances, raise funds for worthy causes and help their communities in various ways.

7 **Describe the obligations that organizations have to their stakeholders.**

Several groups, already discussed, compose an organization's stakeholders: its owners, employees, customers, suppliers and partners and society as a whole. Owners are owed a fair and honest accounting of how the resources are used and of continual efforts to improve productivity and profitability. Employees are owed ethical, legal treatment and a safe, psychologically rewarding environment. Customers are owed safe products and services that meet or exceed their expectations. Suppliers and partners are owed honest and fair dealings, based on continuing and open communications. Bills must be paid in full and on time. Finally, society as a whole is owed compliance with all the laws that protect the environment and ethical behavior toward all those outside the organization.

KEY TERMS

boundary spanning   80

boundaryless organizations   72

core competencies   66

directly interactive forces   74

economic forces   77

empowerment   70

entrepreneur   70

environmental scanning   64

external environment   65

indirectly interactive forces   77

intellectual capital   66

internal environment   64

intrapreneurs   70

learning organization   64

legal/political forces   77

natural forces   79

open system   64

open-book management   70

organizational climate   70

organizational culture   66

scoreboarding   70

sociocultural forces   78

stakeholders   80

technological forces   79

REVIEW QUESTIONS

1. In what ways does your school or place of employment demonstrate the fact that it is an open system?

2. What are the elements in an organization's internal environment?

3. What is a boundaryless organization?

4. How does a learning organization empower employees?

5. Which forces in an organization's external environments are task or directly interactive? Why are they so?

6. Which forces in an organization's external environments are general or indirectly interactive? Why are they so?

7. How can managers stay in touch with their external environments?

8. What can managers and their organizations do to influence their external environments?

9. What groups compose an organization's stakeholders? What obligations does an organization have to each group?

10. Discuss the importance of customer satisfaction to quality.

DISCUSSION QUESTIONS FOR CRITICAL THINKING

1. How does Walmart differentiate itself from its competitors?

2. Considering the elements in an organization's internal environment, which ones do you think are most important for an organization to grow and prosper? Why?

3. In terms of their importance to any business, what ranking (first, second, etc.) would you give to each of the groups in the task environment?

4. How would your rankings from Question 3 change for a not-for-profit organization? Why the change?

5. Now that the internet has opened up the opportunity for borderless business transactions, what impact does the internet have on how organizations compete?

Social Media Management Exercises

1 Competitive Intelligence and Social Media

Strategic and Competitive Intelligence Professionals (SCIP) define competitive intelligence (CI) as the process of monitoring the competitive environment. Managers use competitive intelligence to understand their competitors' strategies. In his blog, Rion Martin discusses pairing CI with social media to broaden the scope of the CI function.

- Read "Using Social Listening for Competitive Intelligence" at *http://blog.infegy.com/using-social-listening-for-competitive-intelligence.*

- How does pairing CI with social media differ from knowing about how competitors use social media?

- Discuss three ways a company could monitor social media to enhance its competitive intelligence capabilities.

2 Chief Listening Officer

Many businesses don't actively participate in social media. In other words, they will never write a blog post, create a Facebook page or publish a Tweet. Yet, they can listen to the conversations taking place about the business, the products and the services. They could hire a Chief Listening Officer, responsible for gathering, understanding and acting on feedback from customers.

- Do you think companies need a Chief Listening Officer to monitor social media? Explain.

Experiential Learning

Barnes & Noble Refocuses

Leonard Riggio, Founder and former Chairman of Barnes & Noble, Inc., opened his first bookstore in 1965 while still a student at New York University. "He saw bookstores as community centers, places where people could be and become." By 1971, he owned six bookstores and bought the troubled Barnes & Noble, which was located on Fifth Avenue in New York City. (Barnes & Noble, Inc., Our Company.)

Mr. Riggio changed bookselling. Barnes & Noble was the first bookstore to sell books at a discount, to advertise on television and to pioneer the superstore concept. Its stores had restrooms, public seating, magazines, cafés and community events. "The rapid expansion of Barnes & Noble superstores came at a severe price to the independents, and Len Riggio became identified as a kind of publishing Antichrist, a scorn he seems almost to court. By the mid-1990s Riggio was sitting masterfully atop the American publishing industry" (St. John).

Then in 1995, Amazon.com emerged as a formidable competitor, selling books online over the internet, maintaining little or no inventory and ordering directly from manufacturers to fill customer orders received via electronic communications. Barnes & Noble was "Amazoned." That's the industry word for a traditional store chain, such as Barnes & Noble, getting trounced by an internet startup such as Amazon.com.

Mr. Riggio realized that in order to compete with Amazon.com, Barnes & Noble had to have an online presence, so barnesandnoble.com was launched in May 1997. In 2000, barnesandnoble.com refocused and was relaunched, integrating online and in-store elements in an effort to increase sales both online and in the stores. Customers were allowed to return books ordered online to the stores. They could go to the store and check inventory on the web. The website became easier for customers to use.

Today, physical bookstore sales are in decline, while the electronic book market is the fastest-growing segment of the bookselling industry (billyaustindillon). In 2007, Amazon introduced the Kindle, an electronic book reader. In 2009, Barnes & Noble introduced the Nook, a competitor to the Kindle. In 2010, Apple introduced the iPad and iBookstore. By 2010, more electronic books were being sold than paper books. Prices of electronic book readers, which began around $400, began falling. Book apps for phones and tablets can be downloaded for free. Thus, more people are reading books on their smartphones and tablets (Maloney).

Sources: billyaustindillon, "Kindle and Nook Price Cut, iPad eBook Market Share Sales Increase Forecast," *HubPages*, (August 2010), *http://hubpages.com/hub/Kindle-Price-Cut* Warren St. John, "Barnes & Noble's Epiphany," *Wired*, Issue 7.06 (June 1999), *http://www.wired.com/wired/archive/7.06/barnes.html*; Barnes & Noble, *http://www.barnesand noble.com; Amazon, http://www.amazon.com*; Jennifer Maloney, "The Rise of Phone Reading," *The Wall Street Journal*, (August 14, 2015), *http://www.wsj.com/articles/the-rise-of-phone-reading-1439398395*

Questions

1. To which environmental forces is Barnes & Noble responding?

2. What is appealing to customers about ordering on-line?

3. What is appealing to customers about electronic books?

4. Interview 10 other students. Use the following survey. Total your responses and prepare a report. Predict whether or not you think that bookstores will be a thing of the past, like record and CD music stores.

- How many books have you read in the last year?
  - ☐ None
  - ☐ 1
  - ☐ 2-5
  - ☐ 6-10
  - ☐ 10 or more

- How many electronic books have you read in the last year?
  - ☐ None
  - ☐ 1
  - ☐ 2-5
  - ☐ 6-10
  - ☐ 10 or more

- What is the primary devise on which you read electronic books?
  - ☐ computer
  - ☐ phone
  - ☐ iPod
  - ☐ Kindle
  - ☐ Nook
  - ☐ iPad
  - ☐ other (specify)

_____

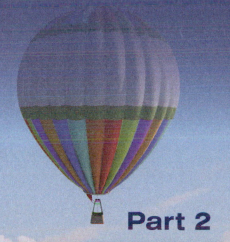

Part 2

Planning

Chapter 4

Planning and Strategy

LEARNING OBJECTIVES

After studying this chapter, you should be able to:

1 Explain the importance of planning

2 Differentiate between strategic, tactical, operational, and contingency plans

3 List and explain the steps in a basic planning process

4 Discuss various ways to make plans effective

5 Distinguish between strategic planning, strategic management, strategy formulation, and strategy implementation

6 Explain the steps involved in the strategic planning process

7 Explain the formulation of corporate-level strategy, business-level strategy, and functional-level strategy

Strategic Thinking

What do you want to accomplish with your life? To be successful, you need to be proactive, look ahead, anticipate change and analyze opportunities. In other words, you need to plan and think strategically. This will help you to determine the potential impact of your actions on other individuals. As a result you will make better decisions.

Strategic thinking involves the gathering and use of data to make significant long-term decisions that will affect future business performance. This process requires examination of the mission, core functions and current performance of a business, the industry in which it operates and the external environment. An important step in becoming a manager is to think strategically. For each of the following statements, circle the number which indicates your level of agreement. Rate your agreement as it is, not what you think it should be. Objectivity will enable you to determine your management skill strengths and weaknesses.

	Almost Always	Often	Sometimes	Rarely	Almost Never
I set clear goals for myself.	5	4	3	2	1
I know what I value.	5	4	3	2	1
I seek advice from others.	5	4	3	2	1
I view problems as opportunities.	5	4	3	2	1
I anticipate how my actions will affect others.	5	4	3	2	1
I evaluate the pluses and minuses of different courses of action.	5	4	3	2	1
I can see the "big picture."	5	4	3	2	1
I stay focused on my long-term goals.	5	4	3	2	1
My goals are achievable.	5	4	3	2	1
I evaluate my results on a regular basis.	5	4	3	2	1

Compute your score by adding the circled numbers. The highest score is 50; the lowest score is 10. A higher score implies you are more likely to be confident about your ability to think strategically. A lower score implies a lesser degree of readiness, but it can be increased. Reading and studying this chapter will help improve your understanding of strategy.

➡ Do you feel confident about your ability to set goals? Do you analyze opportunities and problems from a broad perspective? Do you understand an action's potential impact on others? If not, where do you want to improve?

Assessment adapted from Harvard Manage Mentor, "Strategic Thinking Self-Assessment."
http://www.harvardbusiness.org/harvard-managementor

INTRODUCTION

This chapter begins our examination of the planning function with a self-assessment. After arriving at definitions of planning and planning terminology, we examine the types of plans that managers create, the process used to create plans, commonly used techniques to make planning effective and barriers to successful planning. Our examination extends by analyzing the processes and techniques involved in long-term planning for both an organization and its various subsystems. Through strategic planning, managers, their organizations and the autonomous units or divisions of the organization identify and evaluate how they intend to effectively compete in their markets.

PLANNING DEFINED

1 Explain the importance of planning

planning
Preparing for tomorrow, today

Planning is preparing for tomorrow, today. It provides direction and a unity of purpose for organizations and their subsystems. When planning, managers have five key responsibilities:

1 Construct, review and/or rewrite their organization's mission.

2 Identify and analyze their opportunities.

3 Establish the goals they wish to achieve.

4 Identify, analyze and select the course or courses of action required to reach their goals.

5 Determine resources they will need to achieve their goals.[1]

Vision, Mission, and Core Values

Changing an organization in any significant way is a primary responsibility of top management. Every CEO must sense the need for a change, create a clear statement as to where the organization wants to be in the future—its **vision**—sell that vision to organizational members, create plans to achieve it, commit organizational resources to the effort, lead the effort by removing obstacles and make certain that the organization's progress is monitored. Today's managers require more vision than ever because change is coming faster than ever. Leaders have the ability to make their vision real by engaging the minds, as well as the hearts, of others.

vision
A clear statement as to where an organization wants to be in the future

An organization's **mission** explains its purpose—its primary reason(s) for existence. It affects how every employee and process will operate. When a mission is formalized in writing and communicated to all organizational members, it becomes the organization's **mission statement**. This is the touchstone by which all offerings are judged. America's largest software company, Microsoft, began in 1975 with a one-sentence mission statement: "A computer on every desk and in every home." This mission is interesting because Microsoft makes software, not computers. In addition, in 1975, almost no one had a personal computer at work, much less at home.

mission
A clear, concise, written declaration of an organization's central and common purpose, its reason for existence

mission statement
When a mission is formalized in writing and communicated to all organizational members

The most effective mission statements are easily recalled and provide direction and motivation for the organization. "The mission of Southwest Airlines is dedication to the highest quality of Customer Service delivered with a sense of warmth, friendliness, individual pride, and Company Spirit." Notice the emphasis on quality—meeting customer needs that the organization can meet—in this statement.

Since an organization exists to accomplish something in the larger environment, its specific mission or purpose provides employees with a shared sense of opportunity, direction, significance and achievement. An explicit mission guides employees to work independently and yet collectively toward the realization of the organization's potential. Thus, a good mission statement gets the emotional bonding and commitment needed. It allows the individual employee to say, "I know how I should do my job differently."

For example, many people might think that The Walt Disney Company's mission is to run theme parks. But Disney's mission is always moving toward an expanded view, one of providing entertainment. Also, many people might think that Revlon's mission is to make cosmetics. Yet, Revlon "provides glamour and excitement." Charles Revson, Revlon's founder, understood the importance of mission. He is rumored to have said "In the factory, we make cosmetics; in the store, we sell hope."

While creating a mission statement, management expert Peter Drucker stated that two questions must be answered: What is our business? What should it be?[2] These questions must be raised and answered periodically, not just when forming a business. The answer to the first question is determined in part by the customers an organization currently serves. Meeting their demands and needs has made the organization what it is. The answer to the second question is determined, in part, by the customers that an organization wishes to serve. The specific needs of identified customers, along with the firm's experience and expertise, will dictate what products and services it creates and/or sells, what processes it uses and what their levels of quality will be.

Once Drucker's two questions are answered, the existing mission statement must be confirmed as valid or rewritten. The challenge for management is to transform the organization's concepts and principles into something that anchors everything it does. Keep in mind that the leadership challenge for top management is to create a mission that captures the commitment of organizational members.[3]

core values

Values that should never change; "bedrock principles"

A mission statement usually includes references to an organization's core values and serves as an operational and ethical guide. A company's **core values** are the fundamental principles it will not compromise. One core value any organization should embrace is the continual search for quality and productivity improvement.

Values serve as a baseline for actions and decision making and guide employees in the organization's intentions and interests. The values driving behavior define the organizational culture. Patagonia, a small California-based sportswear maker, has at its core a deep respect for the individual. Patagonia experienced rapid growth, which brought with it a loss of the sense of family that its owner had worked so hard to create. After significant soul-searching, its employees agreed to reduce the size of the company and refuse any new business that would harm this core value. The decision fostered greater loyalty among Patagonia's employees.

A strong value system or clearly defined culture turns beliefs into standards such as best quality, best performance, most reliable, most durable, safest, fastest, best value for the money, least expensive, most prestigious, best designed or styled and easiest to use. If asked, "What do we believe in?" or "List our organization's values," all employees in the organization should write down the same values. For example, McDonald's values are captured in its operating philosophy of "QSC&V," which stands for quality, service, cleanliness and value.

When companies do not ask Drucker's two basic questions regularly or answer them in a less-than-satisfactory manner, they usually experience some rather costly results. For example, before filing one of the biggest-ever corporate bankruptcy cases, Enron had admirable value statements, which included, "We treat others as we would like to be treated ourselves." And, "We work with customers and prospects openly, honestly and sincerely." In reality, Enron kept hundreds of millions of dollars in debt off the company's books in partnerships that were paying millions of dollars in fees to the Enron executives who ran them. Obviously, these values meant little to the company's top managers.

Goals

Goals may be long term or short term. Long-term goals require more than one year to achieve. Southwest Airlines' managers began planning by studying the company's mission statement and determining its expertise. They assessed Southwest's strengths and market opportunities. Only then did they establish the long-term goal of frequent, low-cost flights. This goal capitalized on Southwest's experience, expertise and reputation with existing customers.

Short-term goals can be reached within one year, and many are directly connected to long-term goals. Southwest had several such goals, including expanding service by adding routes in the U.S. and internationally. They've earned a title no other airline in the industry can claim: The *only* short-haul, low-fare, high-frequency, point-to-point carrier in America. Figure 4.1 defines the characteristics that make goals effective.

Plans

A **plan**—the end result of the planning effort—commits individuals, departments, entire organizations and the resources of each to specific courses of action for days, months and years into the future. It provides specific answers to six basic questions in regard to any intended activity—what, when, where, who, how and how much.

plan
The end result of the planning effort—commits individuals, departments, entire organizations and the resources of each to specific courses of action for days, months and years into the future

- *What* identifies the specific goals to be accomplished.
- *When* answers a question of timing: each long-term goal may have a series of short-term objectives that must be achieved before the long-term goal can be reached.

Figure 4.1 Characteristics of Effective Goals and Strategies

Characteristic	Explanation
Specific and measurable	Not all objectives can be expressed in numeric terms, but they should be quantified when possible. Specific outcomes are easier to focus on than general ones, and performance can be more easily measured when then task is defined precisely.
Realistic and challenging	Impossibly difficult objectives demotivate people. Objectives should be challenging but attainable, given the resources and skills available. The best goals require people to stretch their abilities.
Focused on key result areas	It is neither possible nor good practice to set objectives for every detail of an employee's job. Goals should focus on key results—sales, profits, production or quality, for example—that affect overall performance.
Cover a specific period	A measurable objective is stated in terms of the time in which it is to be completed. Sales objectives, for example, may cover a day, month, quarter or year. The period should be both realistic (managers should not require ten months of work in 5 months) and productive (a requirement for excessive reporting can be debilitating, for example). Short-term goals should complement long-term goals.
Reward performance	Objectives are meaningless if they are not directly related to rewards for performance. Individuals, work groups and organization units should receive prompt rewards for achieving objectives.

- *Where* concerns the place or places where the plan will be executed.
- *Who* identifies specific people who will perform specific tasks essential to a plan's implementation.
- *How* involves the specific actions to be taken to reach the goals.
- *How much* is concerned with the expenditure of resources needed to reach the goals—both short- and long-term.

In setting goals, more businesses are "junking" business-as-usual incremental objectives—moving a few grains of sand—and striving instead to hit gigantic, seemingly unreachable milestones called stretch targets."[4] On one hand, top managers are recognizing that achieving incremental improvements invites middle- and lower-level managers, as well as workers, to perform the same comfortable process a little bit better each year. However, even the best-maintained equipment can become obsolete.

stretch goals
Goal that requires great leaps forward on such measures as product development time, return on investment, sales growth, quality improvement, and reduction of manufacturing cycle times

On the other hand, **stretch goals** (dubbed "Big Hairy Audacious Goals" or BHAGS [pronounced bee-hags] by management analyst James Collins) require great leaps forward on such measures as product development time, return on investment, sales growth, quality improvement and reduction of manufacturing cycle times.[5] Walter Todd, the head of operations for PepsiCo UK and Ireland as well as the vice president of sustainability for the company's European operations, explains PepsiCo's use of BHAGS.

One of the ways that we have triggered innovation is by setting big hairy audacious goals. This forces us to look at every area of our operations and encourages ideas to bubble up. We want to engage people about what a future possibility would look like. If you come up with a commitment, say to reduce energy by 3% next year, you will not get people engaged or any real financial engagement. But if you set an engaging vision, you can get a coalition of people excited by the possibilities.[6]

Strategies and Tactics

strategy
A course of action created to achieve a long-term goal

tactic
A course of action designed to achieve a short-term goal—an objective

A course of action created to achieve a long-term goal is called a **strategy**. Strategies may exist for an entire organization or for its autonomous units or functional areas. A course of action designed to achieve a short-term goal—an objective—is called a **tactic**. Mission defines strategy. Objectives must be achieved in order to reach a long-term goal. Therefore, strategies influence and often dictate the choice of tactics.

At Southwest Airlines, creating and successfully managing the company's growth required achieving a sequential set of objectives through a variety of tactics. A strong management team had to be built. People had to be recruited and hired to facilitate the logistics and daily operations of a successful" reliable, low cost" airline. Money had to be raised to finance related activities. New customers had to be adequately served.

One additional example illustrates the connection between a strategy and tactics. An individual seeking a two- or four-year college degree has a strategy (and a goal) that requires two or more years to complete. The strategy requires a sequence of tactics that, semester after semester, will yield the short-term goals—successful completion of courses in their proper sequences—that ultimately lead to the achievement of the strategic goal—a college degree.

Determining Resource Requirements

The best-made plans will not be executed if they lack the resources required. Most plans need various resources, including people, money, facilities, equipment, supplies and information. Among other things, companies need technology to accomplish their plans. An investment in technology can improve business processes and give companies a competitive advantage.

TYPES OF PLANS

For an organization to accomplish its goals at all organizational levels—top, middle and first-line—it must develop three types of mission-based plans: strategic, tactical and operational (as shown in Figure 4.2). Each must work in harmony with the others if the organization's mission and long-term goals are to become reality.

Strategic Plans

A **strategic plan** contains the answers to who, what, when, where, how and how much for achieving strategic goals—long-term, companywide goals established by top management. Strategic goals focus on the changes desired in such areas as productivity, product innovation and responsibilities to stakeholders.[7] Accenture has made valuing the diversity of its employees a strategic goal and—as this chapter's Valuing Diversity and Inclusion feature points out—a duty for all its managers. The strategic plan is concerned with the entire organization's direction and purpose—how it intends to grow, compete, and meet its customers' needs—over the next few years.

strategic plan
Contains the answers to who, what, when, where, how and how much for achieving strategic goals—long-term, companywide goals established by top management

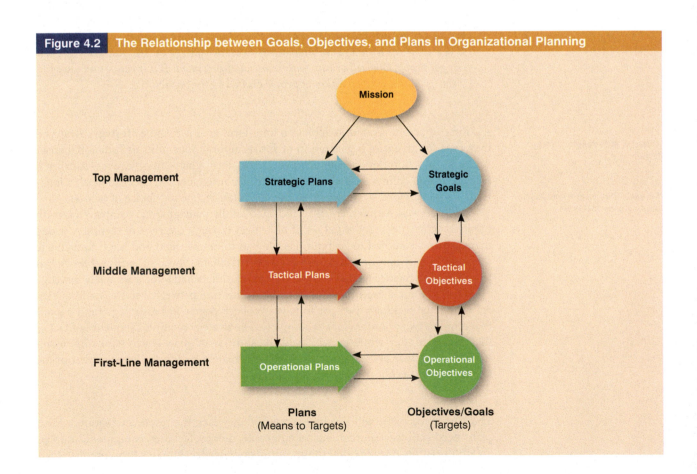

Figure 4.2   **The Relationship between Goals, Objectives, and Plans in Organizational Planning**

Planning for Diversity at Accenture

Accenture—a global management consulting, technology services and outsourcing company—moved women's issues onto the company's global agenda. As part of Accenture's commitment to building a diverse workforce, the company participates in International Women's Day, which honors the economic, political and social achievements of women. The company's Global Women's Initiative offers programs such as mentoring and networking opportunities to ensure that Accenture's women continue to succeed.

Working Mother magazine has named Accenture to its annual list of "100 Best Companies for Working Mothers" for years. In 2015, the magazine had a topic, "What We Love" for each company on the list. For Accenture, the magazine "loved" several things, including the following.

Out-of-town travel to work with clients is a reality for many employees at this management consulting, technology services and outsourcing company. To make sure everything flows smoothly, their employer provides them with numerous flexible work arrangements. Back at the office, everyone can also work remotely, job-share, or compress, reduce and flex their hours. Full-time workers get an average of 25 days of paid time off annually, along with up to two weeks of job-guaranteed unpaid days off to use as they like. Earlier this year, the company doubled parental leave for new moms, who can now take up to 16 fully paid weeks off.

Accenture integrates its diversity initiative with its strategic planning. The company uses International Women's Day to celebrate with employees, while increasing awareness of women's initiatives. Employees have the opportunity to connect and learn from one another.

Like any business goal, there must be quantifiable measures to gauge the progress being made toward achieving it. Accenture uses geographic scorecards, global surveys and performance appraisals to ensure that management remains accountable for the initiative's success. Women at Accenture have advanced since the inception of the initiative. The percentage of female promotions and female "partners," or senior-level executives, has increased.

➡ **Diversity includes the full range of talents, skills, and experiences in a set of individuals. How does Accenture benefit from diversity?**

Sources: Accenture. "Accenture's Global Celebration of International Women's Day," 2015, https://www.accenture.com/us-en/company-accenture-recognizes-international-womens-day.aspx
"Working Mother 100 Best Companies 2015," *Working Mother*, http://www.workingmother.com/accenture

Strategic planning draws heavily on the leadership abilities of managers. A manager's business philosophy should include three key ingredients: (1) define your mission; (2) execute; and (3) "Treat people like you would want to be treated." Regardless of whether a company is large or small, leaders are required to see—have a vision—where the company needs to go and to design the fabric of actions—organize, staff, lead and control—so the future becomes a reality.

Just how far into the future a strategic plan will stretch is determined by the degree of certainty that managers have about the external environmental conditions and the availability of needed resources. Every strategic plan deals with many hard-to-predict but important future events in their external environments: Will there be a recession? Will inflation continue at its current rates? What will be the situation in our industry with regard to local, state and federal regulations? What will the competition do? These things are difficult enough to predict over a one-year period, let alone a five-year span. For this reason strategic plans must be regularly reviewed and adjusted for changes that occur over their time frames. They must be viewed as works in progress.

Just as one person's ceiling can be another person's floor, the completion of one manager's plan marks the beginning of planning efforts by another. Top management's strategic plan becomes the foundation for middle-level managers' planning efforts that produce tactical plans. Figure 4.3 illustrates how tactical and then operational objectives evolve from strategic goals.

Figure 4.3   An Organization's Mission and Level of Goals

Tactical Plans

Developed by middle managers, a **tactical plan** is concerned with what each of the major organizational subsystems must do, how they must do it, when things must be done, where activities will be performed, what resources are to be utilized and who will have the authority needed to perform each task. Tactical plans have more details, shorter time frames and narrower scopes than strategic plans; they usually span one year or less.

Strategic and tactical plans are usually but not always related. Every strategy requires a series of tactical and operational plans linked to each other to achieve strategic goals; middle managers, however, do create plans to reach what are uniquely department, division or team goals, both for the short and long term. The tactical plans are all related to reaching the company's strategic goals. Two such plans might involve the following:

- To reduce fourth quarter unit costs without sacrificing the quality of customer service.
- To consolidate retail stores from nine to six in 5 months.

Following logically from the strategic goals are *tactical objectives:* short-term goals set by middle managers that must be achieved in order to reach top management's strategic goals and the short- and long-term goals of middle managers. Once a company devises the tactical plan, it probably forms teams and assigns team members specific duties.

tactical plan
Developed by middle managers, this plan has more details, shorter time frames, and narrower scopes than a strategic plan; it usually spans one year or less

Operational Plans

operational plan
The first-line manager's tool for executing daily, weekly and monthly activities. Operational plans fall into two major categories: single-use and standing plans

program
A single-use plan for an operation from its beginning to its end

budget
A single-use plan that predicts sources and amounts of income that will be available over a fixed period of time and how those funds will be used

policy
A broad guide for organizational members to follow when dealing with important and recurring areas of decision making. They set limits and provide boundaries for decision makers

procedure
A set of step-by-step directions for carrying out activities or tasks

An **operational plan** is developed by first-line managers—supervisors, team leaders and team facilitators—in support of tactical plans. It is the first-line manager's tool for executing daily, weekly and monthly activities. Operational plans fall into two major categories: single-use and standing plans.

A one-time activity—an activity that does not recur—requires a *single-use plan.* Once the activity is completed, the plan is no longer needed. Two examples of single-use plans are programs and budgets. A **program** is a single-use plan for an operation from its beginning to its end. An example would be to gain influential reviews for a company's new line of computers. Once the reviews were obtained, the plan would cease to be of value. In addition, an example would be a program to handle a company's participation in an industry trade show where it could meet the head buyers for the computer retailers.

Another single-use plan is a **budget**. It is a plan that predicts sources and amounts of income that will be available over a fixed period of time and how those funds will be used. Most companies need several budgets. The company's total operations require a budget each year, and it requires others to back efforts to hire new personnel and to launch new routes. Budgets prepared at various levels help to control spending in an organization and in its autonomous subsystems. When the specified period for a budget ends, it becomes a historical document and often proves useful for future budgeting efforts.

Unlike budgets and programs, a *standing plan* specifies how to handle continuing or recurring activities, such as hiring, granting credit and maintaining equipment. Once constructed, they continue to be useful over many years but are subject to periodic review and revision. Examples of standing plans include policies, procedures and rules.

A **policy** is a broad guide for organizational members to follow when dealing with important and recurring areas of decision making. They set limits and provide boundaries for decision makers. Policies are usually general statements about the ways in which managers and others should attempt to handle their routine responsibilities. Figure 4.4 presents a policy governing the making of hiring and other human resource decisions that was created to conform to federal antidiscrimination guidelines issued by the Equal Employment Opportunity Commission. Policies are not prescriptive. They state a viewpoint the company wants its managers to adopt when conducting ongoing operations. Policies can sometimes be controversial and create ethical issues, as this chapter's Ethical Management feature points out.

A **procedure** is a set of step-by-step directions for carrying out activities or tasks. Companies create procedures for such things as preparing budgets, paying employees, preparing business correspondence and hiring new employees. Like policies, they help to guarantee that recurring, identical activities will be done in a uniform way regardless

| **Figure 4.4** | **Human Resources Policy** |

There shall be no discrimination for or against any applicant or for or against any current employee because of his or her race, creed, color, national origin, sex, marital status, age, handicap or membership or lawful participation in the activities of any organization or union, or refusal to join or participate in the activities of any organization or union. Moreover, in each functional division, the company shall adhere to an affirmative action program regarding hiring, promotions, transfers and other ongoing human resource activities.

Privacy at Work: Company Policy and the Law

Are workers entitled to privacy? Although some companies have clearly told their employees about monitoring and have received their consent as a condition for being hired, others have not done so. Privacy advocates worry that most state laws do not specify how information gathered by employers on employees can be used or with whom it can be shared.

Federal law allows companies to monitor their employees' behaviors and conversations, where the communications relate to the employer's business. Many of these laws rule practically nothing out. Employers are creating policies to keep a tighter rein on employees for a variety of reasons, the least of which determines how they use their time on the job. These policies tell employees that they will be, are being, or can be monitored at work and authorize a variety of monitoring techniques: listening to employees' business-related telephone calls and voice mails, hiring private investigators to pose as workers, reading e-mail and other social media messages, viewing and listening to videos with audio taken by company cameras and smartphones, tracking employees in company vehicles by global positioning system (GPS) and Radio Frequency Identification Devices (RFID).

Many employers monitor their employees (Hoffman, Hartman and Rowe). Electronic evidence is an increasingly important element in litigation. The Privacy Rights Clearing House (2016) summarized the findings of a recent study.

A survey by the American Management Association and the ePolicy Institute found that two-thirds of employers monitor their employees' website visits in order to prevent inappropriate web surfing. And 65% use software to block connections to websites deemed off limits for employees. This is a 27% increase since 2001 when the survey was first conducted. Employers are concerned about employees visiting adult sites with sexual content, as well as games, social networking, entertainment, shopping and auctions, sports, an external blogs. Of the 43% of companies that monitor e-mail, nearly three-fourths use technology to automatically monitor e-mail. And 28% of employers have fired workers for e-mail misuse.

Close to half of employers track content, keystrokes, and time spent at the keyboard. And 12% monitor blogs to see what is being written about the company. Another 10% monitor social networking sites.

Almost half of the companies use video monitoring to counter theft, violence and sabotage. Of those, only 7% state they use video surveillance to track employees' on-the-job performance. Most employers notify employees of anti-theft video surveillance (78%) and performance-related video monitoring (89%).

➡ **What ethical questions are raised when companies create policies authorizing the monitoring of employees?**

➡ **As a manager, under what circumstances would you create a policy authorizing the monitoring of employees?**

Sources: Privacy Rights Clearinghouse, "Workplace Privacy and Employee Monitoring," Revised January 2016, *http://www. privacyrights.org/fs/fs7-work.htm*; AMA, "The Latest on Workplace Monitoring and Surveillance," November 17, 2014, *http://www. amanet.org/training/articles/the-latest-on-workplace-monitoring-and-surveillance.aspx*; Hoffman, W. Michael, Laura P. Hartman and Mark Rowe, "You've Got Mail . . . And the Boss Knows: A Survey by the Center for Business Ethics of Companies' Email and Internet Monitoring," *Business and Society Review*, 2003 *http://www.bentley. edu/cbe/documents/You've_Got_Mail_And_The_Boss_Knows.pdf*.

of who executes them. When followed, procedures give precise methods for completing a task.

Consider the following six-step procedure required to process a customer's return of merchandise at a local discount chain store:

1 Determine customer's need: return and refund or exchange.

2 Verify that purchase (cash or charge) was made at this store.

3 Inspect merchandise for damage.

4 Consult store return policy; apply information obtained in steps 1 to 3.

5 Issue exchange, refund or credit as applicable.

6 Deny return and explain reason(s) in line with store policy.

Only after performing each step in the proper sequence can an employee grant an exchange, refund or credit to a customer.

rule
An ongoing, specific guide for human behavior and conduct at work. Rules are usually "do" and "do not" statements established to promote employee safety, ensure the uniform treatment of employees, and regulate civil behavior

A **rule** is an ongoing, specific guide for human behavior and conduct at work. Rules are usually "do" and "do not" statements established to promote employee safety, ensure the uniform treatment of employees and regulate civil behavior. Unlike policies and like procedures, rules tell employees what is expected in given sets of circumstances.

Managing Social Media

Bring Your Own Device (BYOD)

Most businesses provide employees with a computer, access to e-mail, internet and network access, and software necessary to do their jobs. A common rule is that employees only utilize the software applications supported by the company's information technology (IT) department. The major reason for this rule is security. Downloading software applications and sharing files makes networks vulnerable to viruses and hackers. Furthermore, companies don't want their sensitive corporate data leaked.

Yet, this IT rule keeps employees from doing what they normally do. Today's employees commonly use more technology than those that are supported by the company. Their work lives overlap their private lives, as they use their work devices for personal matters. For example, employees are reading e-mail, sending text messages on their iPhones or other smartphones, Tweeting, connecting with friends on Facebook and checking out video on YouTube. This wide variety of self-provisioned tools can be seen in the graphic below. (Cloud-based services in the graphic are Internet-based services.)

These IT departments are creating barriers and ignoring the 'consumerization of IT' where employees bring their own technology to the workplace. This has been referred to as bring your own device (BYOD) and bring your own technology (BYOT). Also, employees bring their own application (BYOA). For example, employees are using their own e-mail and calendar apps. If IT changes the rules and gives employees access to devices and software applications, employees can create contacts among themselves and with customers. This could lead to improved products and services, as well as increased customer satisfaction.

➥ **Which of the self-provisioned tools depicted in the graphic below do you normally use? What would you think if your employer had a rule that you could not use them at work?**

BYOD
An acronym for a policy permitting employees to bring personally owned devices to work. Bring your own device (BYOD) may be referred to as bring your own technology (BYOT) or bring your own applications (BYOA).

Mobile Cloud Apps and Services

Source for graphic: http://cloudtimes.org/2014/09/05/global-mobile-cloud-apps-and-services-growing-at-37-8-cagr-to-2019/

A rule that prohibits smoking on company premises allows for no exceptions. Many businesses insist that the users only utilize the software applications information technology (IT) supports, as discussed in Managing Social Media.

Procedures and rules offer the advantage of standardizing behavior but restrict individual creativity and encourage blind obedience. The more of both that exist, the less freedom employees have to adjust to changing situations. Figure 4.5 offers some additional insights into policies, programs, procedures and rules.

First-level managers, work groups, and individuals in these groups have specific results expected from them in the form of *operational objectives*. The Boeing first-line manager in charge of a specific assembly operation has regular daily, weekly and

Figure 4.5	The Advantages of and Requirements for Policies, Programs, Procedures, and Rules

ADVANTAGES			
Policies	**Programs**	**Procedures**	**Rules**
Promote uniformity	Provide a plan for an operation from beginning to end	Provide the detail for effective performance	Promote safety
Save time		Promote uniformity	Promote acceptable conduct
Outline an approach	Name participants and detail their duties	Save time	Provide security
Set limitations on management conduct	Coordinate efforts of those seeking the same goal	Provide assistance in training	Provide standards for appraising performance and conduct
Promote effectiveness for managers and the organization		Provide security in operations	Save time
		Promote effectiveness and efficiency	Aid in disciplinary situations

REQUIREMENTS			
Should be in writing	Should be in writing in at least an outline format	Should be in writing	Should be in writing
Need to be communicated and understood	Should answer who, when, where, how and how much	Should be sufficiently detailed	Must be communicated to and understood by all those affected
Should provide some flexibility	Should have clear goals, tactics and timetables	Should be revised periodically	Should be reviewed and revised periodically
Should be consistent throughout the organization and consistently applied	Need to be communicated to all those affected by them	Should be communicated to and understood by those who need to know them	Should serve needed purpose
Should support the organization's strategy			
Need to be based on the mission			

monthly objectives to achieve in areas such as scheduling overtime, completing work on time and on budget, protecting and allocating various resources and reducing waste and scrap.

Unified Hierarchy of Goals

The result of planning should generate a unified framework for the accomplishment of the organization's purposes. The use of the traditional management pyramid as a model for the planning process results in a hierarchy of objectives in which the work of each subsystem complements that of the next; goals at each level mesh with or fit into each other. In Figure 4.6, for illustrative purposes, a single goal occupies each subunit; in reality, multiple goals are the norm. The figure shows that top management has determined the strategic goal for the entire organization. Middle management has established tactical objectives for the functional areas of marketing and manufacturing. Finally, the first-line managers within each functional area have created objectives for their work groups. The outcome is a coordinated hierarchy of objectives.

Figure 4.6   Hierarchy of Unified Goals and Objectives

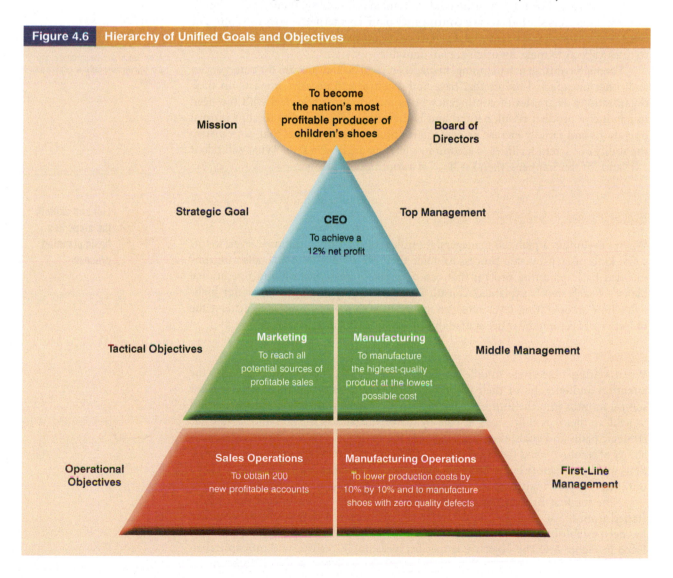

But what happens if an individual manager chooses not to plan within this framework? If a manager develops a set of objectives based on his or her own ambitions, values or goals that oppose or contradict top management's goals, conflicting objectives will result. In the example of the shoe company in Figure 4.6, imagine that the marketing manager has misinterpreted top management's objective. Instead of reaching all potential sources of profitable sales, the marketing manager asks the operating sales manager to seek out all potential buyers. Thus, salespersons will call on and sell to every potential buyer, regardless of the potential size of the order or the cost that the company will incur in servicing that order. The result is bound to be sales to some small or bad-credit accounts that will cause the company losses.

Contingency Plans

Planning should provide the ability to adjust to rapidly changing situations. In most companies, environments change so rapidly that plans must be continually altered as they are being made; at worst, they may actually become useless before they have been totally constructed or fully implemented. To remain as flexible and open to change as possible, managers should create a **contingency plan**: an alternative goal and course or courses of action to reach that goal if and when circumstances and assumptions change so drastically as to make an original plan unusable.

contingency plan
An alternative goal and course or courses of action to reach that goal if and when circumstances and assumptions change so drastically as to make an original plan unusable

Through contingency planning, managers recognize and prepare for emergencies and other unexpected events that have both positive and negative impacts on their organizations. Examples of contingency plans include those that deal with the need to conduct a product recall, natural and human-made disasters that disrupt normal operations and rapidly increasing demand for products and services that can outstrip the ability of current facilities to accommodate. A manager who says, "What will I do if …?" and, "If this happens, then I will …" is a contingency planner.

BASIC PLANNING PROCESS

3

List and explain the steps in a basic planning process

When developing a plan, all managers, regardless of their organizational level, follow some kind of step-by-step process to guide their efforts. Figure 4.7 details a recommended basic planning process that can be used to create tactical and operational plans. As each step is explained, consult Figure 4.8 for applications. The latter highlights how an operating-level manager applied each step in the process to achieve the objective of keeping the office staffed during extended business hours.

Setting Objectives

When setting objectives, middle and operating managers focus and commit the attention and energies of their respective personnel, divisions, and departments for several months into the future. The selection of objectives (and the courses of action to achieve them) is influenced in part by the organization's mission and values; the strategic plans and goals; the standing plans; the environmental conditions; the availability of resources; and the philosophies, ethics, accumulated experience and expertise of its managers. Before being finalized, each objective should possess the characteristics outlined earlier in Figure 4.1.

Note the first-line manager's objective in Figure 4.8—to ensure that the office is staffed from 8 A.M. to 9 P.M., Monday through Thursday. A date for its achievement has been established. The goal has the characteristics for effective objectives previously listed in Figure 4.1. The objective is specific, measurable, realistic and probably chal-

Figure 4.7	Steps in a Basic Planning Process

Step 1: *Setting Objectives*
Establishing targets for the short- or long-range future

Step 2: *Analyzing and Evaluating the Environments*
Analyzing the present position, the internal and external environments and resources available

Step 3: *Identifying the Alternatives*
Constructing a list of possible courses of action that will lead to goal achievement

Step 4: *Evaluating the Alternatives*
Listing and considering the advantages and disadvantages of each possible course of action

Step 5: *Selecting the Best Solution*
Selecting the course of action that possesses the most advantages and the fewest serious disadvantages

Step 6: *Implementing the Plan*
Determining who will be involved, what resources will be assigned, how the plan will be evaluated and how reporting will be handled

Step 7: *Controlling and Evaluating the Results*
Ensuring that the plan is proceeding according to expectations and making necessary adjustments

lenging. It focuses on a key result area, covers a specific time period, and will likely lead to some form of reward for the manager involved.

Analyzing and Evaluating the Environment

Once objectives are established, managers must analyze their current situations and environments to determine what resources they will have available and what other limiting factors such as company policies they must consider as they evaluate possible courses of action or tactics. When assessing the internal environment, managers must consider what human, material, financial, time and informational resources are available and the needs of internal customers. When assessing the external environment, managers must consider such elements as the strengths and weaknesses of suppliers and partners, the availability of additional labor and technology and the needs of external customers. Choices and commitments made by managers as they plan must not jeopardize efforts to continually improve quality, productivity or profitability.

Returning to Figure 4.8, the supervisor has listed the results of an environmental analysis and states limits as well as resources available. The office must be staffed for at least four additional hours, four days per week. Company policies limit overtime and compensatory time and require a limited benefit package for part-time employees working 15 hours per week.

Identifying the Alternatives

Courses of action available to a manager to reach a goal represent alternate paths to a destination. When developing alternatives, a manager should try to create as many roads to each objective as possible. These alternatives may be entirely separate ways to reach a goal, as well as variations of one or more separate alternatives. When listing alternatives, managers usually invite any persons who have the relevant knowledge and experience to contribute suggestions. Allowing those who will have to execute a chosen alternative to be part of the process helps to ensure a commitment on their part to make the alternative work.

Figure 4.8   A First-Level Manager Applies the Basic Planning Process

Objective

To ensure that the office is staffed from 8:00 A.M. to 9:00 P.M., Monday through Thursday. Target date: January 1.

Analysis and Evaluation of the Environment

1 Current staffing situation. Office is staffed by two full-time hourly employees. One works from 8:00 A.M. to 4:30 P.M. and the other works from 8:00 A.M. to 5:00 P.M.

2 Financial resources. Operating budget has sufficient funds to support additional staff at a range of $8 to $10 per hour, but benefits are restricted.

3 Labor supply. The potential number of part-time applicants is uncertain based on the rate of pay available.

4 Company policy. (1) Severe limits are placed on the use of overtime and compensatory time; and (2) a part-time employee becomes eligible for a limited benefit package when he or she works 15 hours per week.

Alternatives

1 Use current office staff by developing a combination package involving overtime and compensatory time.

2 Use the current office staff by altering the work hours of one or both.

3 Hire a part-time staff member to work 5:00 P.M. to 9:00 P.M., Monday through Thursday.

4 Hire two part-time staff members to work two nights each, from 5:00 P.M. to 9:00 P.M.

Evaluation of Alternatives

Alternative 1 Current staff/combination package. Problems with company pay policy and potential reaction of present staff.

Alternative 2 Current staff/altered work hours. Would provide coverage but would affect daytime productivity. Staff reaction— No!

Alternative 3 One part-time staff member. Would provide office coverage but stretch financial resources because the new employee would be eligible for limited benefits.

Alternative 4 Two part-time staff members/two nights each. Would provide coverage and not exceed financial resources or benefits restriction (neither will work 15 hours). Only question: Can labor supply produce two qualified applicants?

Selection of Best Solution

The alternative with the fewest questions and most promise is Alternative 4. The only problem lies in attracting candidates.

Implementation

1 To overcome the potential limitation (supply of qualified candidates), pay the proposed employees the top authorized rate, $10 per hour.

2 Develop advertising by October 1.

3 Advertise the position internally to attract internal referrals.

4 Advertise the position externally, through newspaper advertisements and job placement offices at colleges, private business schools and high schools.

5 Establish November 1 as the cut-off date for applications.

6 Complete screening and interviews by November 21.

7 Make hiring offers by December 1.

Control and Evaluation

1 Check daily to determine the number of applications.

2 Extend the advertising deadline until a sufficient number (20 to 30) of applications are received.

3 If two candidates cannot be found, obtain additional funds and implement Alternative 3.

Notice that in Figure 4.8 the manager has listed four potential alternatives from which to choose. Each alternative represents a possible way to achieve the staffing objective. Which alternative is best, given the situation as outlined, is determined in the next step and should not be determined until then. Attempting to analyze courses of action in this step will only inhibit a free flow of alternatives and thus result in an incomplete listing of possible alternatives.

Evaluating the Alternatives

Each alternative must be evaluated to determine which one or which combination is most likely to achieve the objective effectively and efficiently. Most managers begin their evaluation by constructing a list of advantages (benefits) and disadvantages (costs) for each alternative. Managers then return to the second step to make certain that each alternative fits with the resources available and within the identified limits.

Managers need to know the kind and amount of resources, including time, which each alternative will require. They must create an estimate of the costs for each course of action and relate these to the dollar value of the benefits expected. If, for example, $1000 will be spent to gain an objective valued at a lesser amount, the alternative is inefficient and an unlikely choice.

In addition to financial factors, managers consider the effects each alternative is likely to have on organizational members, the organizational unit and others outside the area of operations in which the planning is taking place. Possibly, certain side effects, both good and bad, will result from the implementation of an alternative. Managers should determine these effects before they finalize the plan.

Notice the evaluation of each alternative in Figure 4.8. All of them have positives and negatives. The manager should choose the one with the greatest number of positives and the fewest or least serious negatives.

Selecting the Best Solution

The analysis of each alternative's benefits and costs should result in determining one course of action that appears better than the others. If no single alternative emerges as a clear winner—the one with the most advantages and the fewest serious disadvantages—managers should consider combining two or more of them, either in part or in their entirety. The alternatives not selected may be considered as possible fallback positions—as choices for a contingency plan.

The supervisor in Figure 4.8 decided on alternative four. The unanswered question is whether available funds will attract the needed two part-timers. If not, the supervisor should choose one of the other alternatives to achieve the staffing objective.

Implementing the Plan

After they have completed the tactical or operational plan, their creators need to develop an action plan to implement it. Among the issues to be resolved: Who will do what? By what date will each task be initiated and completed? What resources will each person have to perform the tasks? In Figure 4.8, the supervisor has listed a time frame by which all necessary activities must be initiated or completed. He or she will do many of the activities with the assistance of the organization's human resources manager, if the latter exists.

Controlling and Evaluating the Results

Once the plan is implemented, managers must monitor the progress being made and be prepared to make any necessary modifications. Since environmental conditions are constantly changing, plans must often be modified. Modifications may also be required because of problems with a plan's implementation. In Figure 4.8, the manager has developed monitoring duties to provide for control and evaluation of the plan. The manager has another alternative ready if the first choice does not work.

4   Discuss various ways to make plans effective

MAKING PLANS EFFECTIVE

All planning is based on assumptions (what planners believe to be true and real) and forecasts (predictions about the probable state of relevant conditions over the span of time covered in their plans). All assumptions and forecasts appear to be reasonable and valid at the time planners make the plans. Managers examine available current data and historical records, consult with others as appropriate, and generate required information they may need to make their assumptions and forecasts. Contingency planning requires the same managers to plan for the "what if?" The assumption behind contingency planning is that circumstances can and are likely to change, and organizations must be ready for the changes.

Managers make assumptions and forecasts. They provide the leadership to grow the business by looking for opportunities that will capitalize on the company's reputation and expertise. Through continual research and the help of knowledgeable outsiders, the manager can successfully predict the future for its products and create most of the company's long-term goals and strategies to become a major player in its market. The top manager must create and execute several additional strategic and tactical plans related to marketing, finance, production and human resources management as he or she gains wisdom and insights through experience.

When done properly, planning should enable managers to avoid making mistakes, wasting resources and experiencing surprises. However, all risks and threats may not be foreseen. For example, the airlines did not expect the terrorist attacks on 9/11 (September 11, 2001).

There are two obvious approaches to making planning more effective: Improve the quality of both assumptions and forecasts. After briefly examining these approaches, two planning tools are discussed. Chapter 5 examines several additional ones as they relate to both planning and decision making.

Improving the Quality of Assumptions and Forecasts

Managers increase the probability of success in planning by beginning the process with quality information. To do so, they must acquire facts and information that are as current and reliable as possible. They must also develop multiple sources for acquiring or generating needed information. By acquiring information internally from various departments and externally from industry research groups, government reports, trade journals, customers and suppliers, managers can include multiple viewpoints in a plan and thus improve the quality of assumptions and forecasts. Information from marketing, sales and customer service can be integrated into a database to estimate (or calculate) the value of each customer.

In **forecasting**, the organization's managers concentrate on developing predictions about the future. Along with internally generated budgets, managers must develop forecasts that will predict with some degree of certainty the conditions likely to exist in all areas of the internal and external environments.

In developing forecasts, managers rely on both internal information and outside resources. This chapter's Global Applications feature, which illustrates both, speaks to

forecasting
A planning technique used by an organization's managers to concentrate on developing predictions about the future

Forecasting Leads Mercedes to Alabama

What led giant Mercedes-Benz to build its first U.S. manufacturing facility in Alabama? The answer lies, in part, with its economic and business forecasts for the U.S. market for all-purpose utility vehicles (APUVs), such as the Jeep Cherokee and Ford Explorer. Mercedes planners saw the United States as the largest and fastest growing market for APUVs. Auto analysts predicted the market was too crowded, but Mercedes planners believed that the company name, its selling price and its quality reputation would be more than adequate to gain the foothold it sought in the United States and to build on it.

Based on their own assumptions and forecasts, several major Mercedes suppliers built factories nearby or geared up to produce greater supply amounts, as did Dunlop Tire in Huntsville, Alabama. All this activity occurred even though the production version of the vehicle had not been finalized!

Original projections were for 65,000 M-Class Sport Utility Vehicles to be built each year. Over the years, based on demand, the factory has increased in size and production has increased to 300,000 vehicles, including GLE-Class SUV, which used to be called the M-Class, as well as the GL-Class SUV, C-Class sedan and GLE Coupe. In addition, the plant is Alabama's largest exporter.

➡ What internal information and outside resources do you think the Mercedes-Benz planners used to develop the forecast for the GLE-class SUV, which used to be called the M-Class?

Sources: Dawn Kent Azok, "Alabama's Mercedes-Benz Plant announces $1.3 billion, 300 job expansion," Alabama Media Group, September 18, 2015, *http://www.al.com/business/index.ssf/2015/09/alabamas_mercedes-benz_plant_a.html*; About Mercedes-Benz U.S. International, *http://www.mbusi.com/about < >*; Sara Lamb and Sherri Chunn, "Mercedes Rolls in with New Age," *Chicago Tribune*, December 3, 1995, sec. 12, p. 7.

the assumptions and forecasts behind the expansion of Mercedes-Benz into the U.S. market.

Planning Tools

Managers can also improve the quality of their planning by applying a variety of planning tools and techniques. Two that apply to tactical and operational planning are management by objectives and linear programming.

Management by Objectives One of the most effective aids to help managers set objectives originated with management expert Peter Drucker.[8] **Management by objectives (MBO)** is a technique that emphasizes collaborative objective setting by managers and their subordinates. The idea behind MBO is that the manager and the subordinate jointly determine objectives for the subordinate. The subordinate proposes objectives to be reached over some agreed-on time period. The manager gives his or her approval or recommends modifications and additional objectives. MBO usually results in employees who are more committed to the achievement of the objectives than they might be if they were not involved in setting them.

Some of the objectives chosen by subordinates are directly linked to those of the manager—that is, the accomplishment of the objectives will assist the manager in reaching his or her goals. Other objectives set by subordinates are for their own growth and development. A set of verifiable, written objectives for the subordinate to achieve should be created, along with priorities and timetables for each.

Although employees are working toward the accomplishment of their objectives, managers should hold periodic review sessions. A supervisor may authorize modifications to the objectives or their timetables as circumstances dictate. At the end of the agreed-on time period, the manager and subordinate hold a final review session to

management by objectives (MBO)
A technique that emphasizes collaborative setting by managers and their subordinates

evaluate the results and repeat the process. The subordinate is evaluated on the basis of whether the objectives were accomplished, how effectively and efficiently they were achieved, and what was learned in the process. Rewards are usually linked to each of these elements. Hoshin Planning is used by quality managers to enhance MBO, as discussed in this chapter's Quality Management highlight.

Quality Management

Hoshin Planning and MBO

Peter Drucker introduced management by objectives (MBO) in his 1954 classic book *The Practice of Management*. Over the years, quality managers have enhanced MBO with Hoshin planning, sometimes referred to as hoshin kanri, strategy deployment or policy deployment. *Hoshin* is Japanese for setting an objective or direction. *Kanri* is Japanese for management.

Hoshin kanri is depicted by a ship's compass, which gives the ship clear direction toward the North Star, especially during a storm. The North Star represents the plan, the compass represents direction and the ship represents the company. Management can measure progress on the plan. When the company gets off plan, clear direction of top management's vision, helps it to get back on plan.

Hoshin planning targets work improvement, especially quality, productivity and customer relationships. Thus, strategy is expressed as key challenges, such as defect-free products and individual problem solving. Managers lead and guide employees as they improve and solve their own problems. Thus, planning is integrated throughout the whole organization.

Hoshin planning is depicted in the graphic below. It provides focus on the vital few strategic priorities, alignment with annual planning, integration with daily management and review by business analysis. It overlaps the Plan-Do-Check-Act (PDCA) cycle, discussed in Chapter 3's Quality Management. Plan the work; establish the objectives and processes to achieve the desired results. Do the work; implement the processes. Check the work; monitor and measure what actually happens against the plan; report the current status and make it visible to all. Act or adjust results to accomplish the plan; continually improve the processes and performance.

➡ **It is the manager's job to make sure employees succeed at their jobs. Hoshin planning requires managers to engage employees and guide them to deeper knowledge and experience. Employees recognize their own problems and solve them jointly. How does this process "develop people before making parts"?**

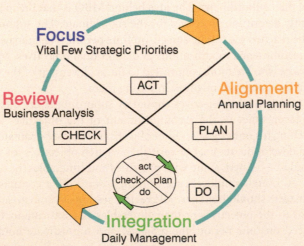

Source for graphic: *http://www.uea.ac.uk/~mg597/hk.htm*

Linear Programming Linear programming is a planning tool that can be used to determine the optimum combination of resources and activities. Consider the situation faced by many small manufacturers such as Armco Products, a producer of patio chairs, loungers and footstools. Although these products share some basic components (metal framing, fabric webbing and plastic feet) and manufacturing processes, they each deliver different costs and profit margins and sell in different quantities. Due to facilities limitations, small companies like Armco usually produce only one product line at any given time (chairs, loungers and so on). Determining just how much to manufacture can be complex, and making the transition from the production of one product line to another is costly and time consuming. Such factories have software programs available to help with linear programming and other types of planning. The programs factor in the effects of dozens of variables and provide a limitless number of optimum solutions for a variety of market conditions.

Barriers to Planning

All managers want their plans to be effective and efficient—to yield the desired results with a minimum of resources. They must be aware of the potential barriers to successful planning and work to avoid or overcome them.

- *Inability to Plan*—People are rarely born with the ability to plan. Until they gain experience, their planning efforts will usually require some improvements. Most people, however, can improve their planning efforts with training and practice.

- *Lack of Commitment to the Planning Process*—Another barrier to effective planning is the lack of commitment to planning. Some managers prefer to react to situations, rather than trying to anticipate events through planning. Another possible reason for a lack of commitment can be fear of failure. This outcome can result if the organizational environment discourages innovation and punishes failures.

- *Inferior Information*—Out-of-date or inaccurate information can have devastating effects on plans. An effective information management system can help prevent such deficiencies (see Chapter 14). Identifying and tracking key variables—indicators that predict "coming business conditions"—is a characteristic of many good management planners.[9]

- *Lack of Focus on the Long Term*—Failure to consider the long term because of emphasis on short-term problems and results will lead to trouble in the future. Too much emphasis on the current year's sales and profits can turn the manager's attention away from long-range goals needed to guarantee survival and future profits. The remedy lies, in part, with evaluating how well managers engage in long-term planning as a portion of their regular performance evaluations. Unless the emphasis on planning long term comes from the top, however, strategic planning will be ignored in favor of tactical planning.

- *Overreliance on the Planning Department*—Many large organizations have planning departments to help managers plan and provide more professional presentations of plans to higher levels. Although these departments may use the latest tools and techniques to conduct studies, build models and generate forecasts, they may ignore the managers they exist to serve. The value of the vast experience acquired by managers outside the planning department gets ignored. Planning departments may assume that the more sophisticated the planning tools and methods, the more reliable the plans. Planning can become, in such cases, an end in itself rather than a means to an end—goal achievement.

- *Overemphasis on Controllable Variables*—Managers may find themselves concentrating on the things and events within their control and failing to adequately consider those factors beyond their control. They may see little value in attempting to devise a plan that includes such variables as future technologies, economic forecasts and possible moves by competitors, because these variables are too difficult to accurately predict. Managers who ignore future developments in these areas, however, risk being surprised and pushed into a reactive planning mode. Managers must make educated guesses about the future, remain flexible by reviewing their plans at regular intervals and make adjustments to the plans as needed.

NATURE OF STRATEGIC PLANNING AND STRATEGIC MANAGEMENT

Distinguish between strategic planning, strategic management, strategy formulation, and strategy implementation

All companies engage in strategic planning as an element of strategic management. **Strategic management** is top management's responsibility; it defines the firm's position, formulates strategies, and guides the execution of long-term organizational functions and processes. The ultimate purpose of strategic planning positions the organization to fit into its environment in order to achieve its goals.

Companies both large and small undertake strategic planning to respond to competitors, cope with rapidly changing environments, and effectively manage their resources—all to ensure that employees and other stakeholders are working toward common goals. With a sharp strategic focus, a company can accomplish all of its goals, a point recognized by Southwest Airlines. Low-fare air service is Southwest's easily articulated strategy.

strategic management
A responsibility of top management, it defines the firm's position, formulates strategies and guides the execution of long-term organizational functions and processes

Elements of Strategic Planning

Strategic planning is designed to help managers answer critical questions in a business:

- What is the organization's position in the marketplace?
- What does the organization want its position to be?
- What trends and changes are occurring in the marketplace?
- What are the best alternatives to help the organization achieve its goals?

The processes involved in strategic planning provide the answers through the development of a strategic plan, which provides the course of action (strategy) required to reach a strategic goal and identifies the resources required to do so. The strategy developed should contain four elements: scope, resource deployment, distinctive competitive advantage and synergy.[10]

Scope The scope of a strategy specifies the position or size (number one in the world or $6 million in profits) the firm wants to achieve—given its environments. It includes the geographical markets it wants to compete in as well as the products and services it will sell.

Resource Deployment Resource deployment defines how the company intends to allocate its resources—material, financial and human—to achieve its strategic goals.

Distinctive Competitive Advantage As discussed in Chapter 3, a firm's core competencies—what it knows and what it does best—gives it a distinctive competitive advantage, a unique position in relationship to its competition.

Customer-driven companies find out what customers value, align it with their core competencies and thrive on it; others don't. For example:

- Why does it take only a few minutes and no paperwork to pick up or drop off a rental car at Hertz but three times as long and several forms to check into some hotels?

- Why can FedEx "absolutely, positively" deliver a package overnight but several major airlines can't take off or land on schedule?

- Why does Amazon remember your last order and your family members' sizes? Instead of trying to be all things to all people, successful companies focus on their competitive edge.[11]

Synergy As discussed in Chapter 2, synergy is the increased effectiveness that results from combined action or cooperation. It is sometimes described as the $2 + 2 = 5$ effect because the result of a synergistic partnership actually exceeds the sum of the production each partner can achieve when acting alone. Synergy occurs when the parts of a single organization or two separate organizations interact, draw on each other's strengths, and produce a joint effort greater than the sum of the parts acting alone can achieve. With synergy, companies can achieve a special advantage in the areas of market share, technology application, cost reduction or management skill.[12]

Responsibility for Strategic Planning

Just who is responsible for strategic planning depends on the organization. As mentioned previously, some companies, like General Motors, hire strategic planning experts and have strategic planning departments. Most often, however, the responsibility for strategic planning belongs to those members of top management who lead the organization's product divisions and regions.

The core group of strategic planners usually includes the senior executives—chief executive officer, division chiefs and chief financial officer. Increasingly, though, large organizations, such as the pharmaceutical maker GlaxoSmithKline, Xerox, the insurer USAA and PepsiCo, want their middle- and lower-level line managers to think and act strategically.[13] They encourage managers at all levels to take the long-term view about where their parts of the organization are going, what major changes will likely occur, and which major decisions will have to be made now to achieve their organization's long-term goals. By encouraging lower-level managers to think and act strategically (it is a significant part of their evaluations), the company not only develops a unified plan but develops its managers.[14]

Strategy Formulation Versus Strategy Implementation

Another important element in understanding the nature of strategic planning is recognizing the difference between strategy formulation and implementation. **Strategy formulation** includes the planning and decision making that goes into developing the company's strategic goals and plans. It includes assessing the environments, analyzing core competencies, and creating goals and plans. On the other hand, **strategy implementation** refers to means associated with executing the strategic plan. These include creating teams, adapting new technologies, focusing on processes rather than functions,

strategy formulation
The planning and decision making that goes into developing the company's strategic goals and plans, including assessing the environments, analyzing core competencies and creating goals and plans

strategy implementation
The means associated with executing the strategic plan. These include creating teams, adapting new technologies, focusing on processes rather than functions, facilitating communications, offering incentives and making structural changes

facilitating communications, offering incentives and making structural changes.[15] Both of these concepts are discussed in more detail later in this chapter.

Levels of Strategy

A final aspect concerned with the nature of strategic planning involves the levels of strategy. As highlighted in Figure 4.9, managers think in terms of three strategy levels: corporate, business and functional.

Corporate-Level Strategy The purpose of **corporate-level strategy** is to answer two questions posed earlier: "What business are we in?" and "What business should we be in?" The answers help to chart a long-term course for the entire organization.

Small companies face the same questions as do large ones. Veda International was an Alexandria, Virginia, maker of flight simulators, focusing its energies on serving commercial customers—American Airlines, Southwest and so on. In exploring the question, "What business should we be in?" Veda International decided to branch into the consumer market by developing a flight simulator that could be sold to amusement parks, resulting in tremendous growth potential. Veda merged with Calspan to become Veridan, which was acquired by General Dynamics.

Business-Level Strategy A **business-level strategy** answers the question, "How do we compete?" It focuses on how each product line or business unit within an organization

corporate-level strategy
Answers the questions: "What business are we in?" and "What business should we be in?"

business-level strategy
Answers the question, "How do we compete?" It focuses on how each product line or business unit within an organization competes for customers

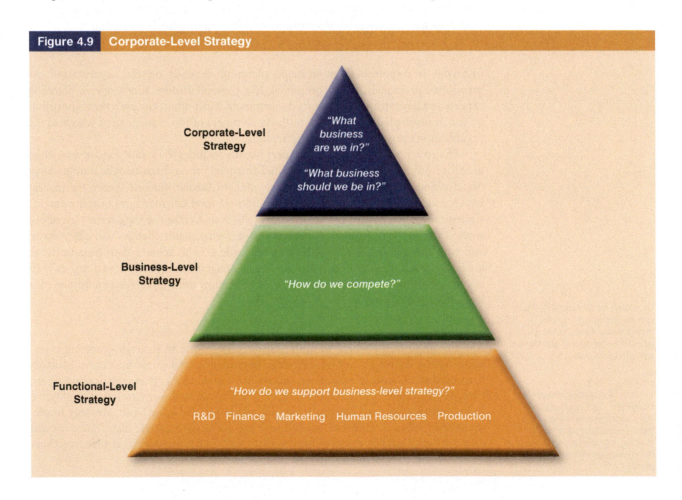

Figure 4.9   Corporate-Level Strategy

competes for customers. The decisions at this level determine how much will be spent on such activities as advertising and product research and development, what equipment and facilities will be needed and how they will be used and whether to expand or contract existing product lines.

Functional-Level Strategy The strategy concern for major functional departments is "How can we best support the business-level strategy?" **Functional-level strategy** focuses on the major activities of the company: human resource management, research and development, marketing, finance and production.

To compete successfully with frequent-flyer programs at other airlines, Southwest Airlines' functional-level marketing strategy called for a pricing incentive for consumers. In addition to a frequent-flyer program, Southwest created Friends Fly Free. For each round-trip ticket purchased at regular full fare at least one day before departure, a ticket holder's friend flies free.[16]

functional-level strategy
Focuses on the major activities of the company: human resources management, research and development, marketing, finance and production

Explain the steps involved in the strategic planning process

STRATEGIC PLANNING PROCESS

At all levels in an organization, the strategic planning process can be divided into several steps, as shown in Figure 4.10. For new ventures, strategic planning begins with the creation of a mission statement and goals. This is the first step (1) shown in Figure 4.10. For ongoing ventures, strategic planning requires managers to continually (2) analyze the internal and external environments by assessing strengths, weaknesses, opportunities, and threats; (3) reassess the organization's mission statement, goals and strategies for continued relevance, making adjustments as necessary; (4) formulate a strategic plan containing goals, strategies, and resources; (5) implement the strategy or strategies; and (6) monitor and evaluate the results.

- The first step for a new enterprise or one considering a total redefinition of itself is to create a mission statement and strategic goals, as discussed previously.

- In executing the second step—analyzing the internal and external environments—strategic planners in established companies scan their internal and external environments (the subjects of Chapter 3). They perform a **situation analysis**—a search for strengths and weaknesses (primarily the result of the internal environment) and opportunities and threats (primarily due to factors in the external environment). This process is often called a SWOT (strengths, weaknesses, opportunities, and threats) analysis. Strengths and weaknesses are internal; opportunities and threats are external. Planners can use the results obtained to reassess the company's mission statement for its continued relevancy and to develop a strategic plan.

situation analysis (SWOT)
A search for strengths, weaknesses, opportunities and threats

Planners can gather external information about threats and opportunities from customers, suppliers, partners, government reports, consultants, trade and professional journals and industry associations. Planners can gather information about internal strengths and weaknesses through financial statements and analyses, employee surveys, progress reports on ongoing operations and statistical analyses of data on such areas as employee turnover and safety. Often by regularly interacting with and observing others, strategic planners can build an adequate assessment of their organization's strengths and weaknesses. Managers often use the expertise of outside consultants to help them obtain as well as analyze the information gathered from both environments.

Figure 4.10 Strategic Planning Process

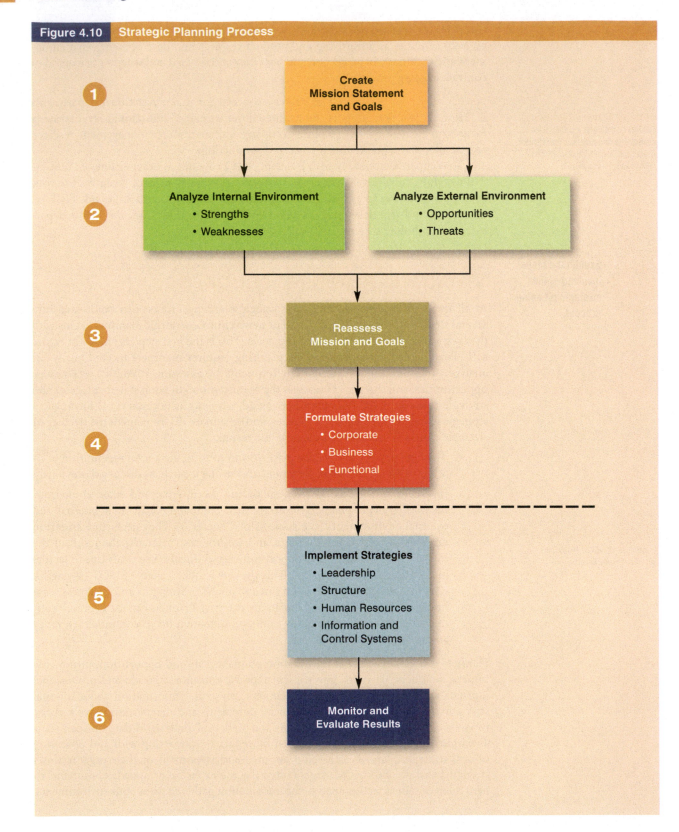

An organization's internal strengths—its core competencies and intellectual capital—are factors the company can build on to reach its goals. Weaknesses inhibit performance capabilities; they are gaps in managers' or organizations' experience and expertise and the unavailability of needed resources. Plans should be designed to compensate for them if they cannot be eliminated. In determining strengths and weaknesses, a company's strategic planners should consider the following:

- *Management factors*—management structure and managers' philosophies and capabilities.
- *Marketing factors*—distribution channels, market share, competitive challenges and levels of customer service and satisfaction.
- *Production factors*—manufacturing efficiency, levels of obsolescence for equipment and technology, production capacity and quality control.
- *Research factors*—research and development capabilities, new product development, consumer and market research and the prospects for technological innovation.
- *Human resource factors*—the quality and depth of employee talent and expertise, degrees of employee job satisfaction and morale, turnover rate and union status.
- *Financial factors*—profit margin, return on investment and various financial ratios.

Management's external assessment focuses on identifying both threats and opportunities. Threats are factors that can prevent the organization from achieving its goals. Opportunities are the opposite; they can help the organization achieve its goals. The following factors should be assessed:

- The threat of new competitors entering the marketplace
- The threat of substitute products
- The opportunity resulting from entering new marketplaces
- The threat or opportunity created by strategy changes of major competitors
- The threat or opportunity resulting from the potential actions and profitability of customers
- The threat or opportunity created by the actions of suppliers
- The threat or opportunity resulting from new (or abandoned) government regulations
- The threat or opportunity created by new technology
- The threat or opportunity from changes in the state of the economy

In reassessing the mission statement and goals step, management leadership is critical. As noted by management consultant Warren Bennis, "The indispensable first quality of leadership is a strongly defined purpose. When people are aligned behind that purpose, you get a powerful organization."[17] The analysis of the external opportunities and threats and the internal strengths and weaknesses can produce one of two outcomes: to reaffirm the current mission statement, goals and strategies or to lead to the formulation of new ones. Once the mission statement is reaffirmed or rewritten, goals and strategies at the corporate, business and functional levels can be formulated. When a new strategy is formulated, it must be implemented. Strategy formulation and strategy implementation are two distinct tasks. If either or both are handled incorrectly, a strategic plan will fail or at least create problems.

Figure 4.10 lists the elements in the "Implement Strategies" step as leadership, structure, human resources and information and control systems.[18]

- **Leadership**—When implementing strategy, the leadership challenge involves the ability to influence others in the organization to embrace the new strategy and adopt the behaviors needed to put it into action. All managers continually face the challenge of convincing people to accept new goals and strategies. To accomplish this, strategic planners create teams and involve lower-level managers and workers in the strategy-formulation process, thus building coalitions that will support change.

- **Organizational Structure**—Implementation can be assisted by change in the structure of the organization as reflected in its organizational chart. Managers can greatly facilitate the implementation of new strategies by changing reporting relationships, creating new departments or business units and providing the opportunity for autonomous decision making.

- **Human Resources**—People are the key to implementing any decision, strategy or plan. Howard Schultz, CEO for Seattle-based Starbucks Coffee Company, has a simple philosophy about the role of human resources in implementing his plans for the gourmet coffee purveyor's expansion both at home and abroad: "I believe in the adage: 'Hire people smarter than you are and get out of their way.'"[19] To manage his company-owned outlets, Schultz recruits experienced fast-food managers from such outlets as Taco Bell and Burger King. These store managers in turn receive and give their staffs—recruited from colleges and community groups, not high schools—"24 hours of training in coffee making and lore—key to creating the hip image and quality service that build customer loyalty."[20]

- **Information and Control Systems**—Management needs to create a proper blend of information and control systems that make use of policies, procedures, rules, incentives, budget and other financial statements to support the implementation phase. Organizational members must be rewarded for adhering to the new system and making it successful.[21]

Once the strategy is implemented, performance must be monitored and evaluated, and modifications must be made as necessary.

Having examined the strategic planning process, let us take an in-depth look at strategy formulation at all three levels of a traditional organization.

FORMULATING CORPORATE-LEVEL STRATEGY

Explain the formulation of corporate-level strategy, business-level strategy, and functional-level strategy

As discussed earlier, corporate-level strategy involves determining in what business or businesses the firm expects to compete. For companies with a single market or a few closely related markets, the corporate-level strategy involves developing an overall strategy. However, most large corporations have complicated organizational structures with stand-alone, often unrelated, business units or divisions each with different products, markets and competitors. The corporate-level strategy then involves making decisions on whether to add divisions and product lines—to manage the corporation's portfolio of businesses. A discussion of both types of corporate-level strategy follows.

Grand Strategies

A **grand strategy** is the overall framework or plan of action developed at the corporate level to achieve an organization's objectives. There are five basic grand strategies—growth, integration, diversification, retrenchment or stability.

- A *growth strategy* is adopted when the organization wants to create high levels of growth in one or more of its areas of operations or business units. Growth can be achieved internally by investing or externally by acquiring additional business units.

- An *integration strategy* is adopted when the business sees a need (1) to stabilize its supply lines or reduce costs or (2) to consolidate competition. In the first situation the company creates a strategy of *vertical integration*—gaining ownership of resources, suppliers or distribution systems that relate to a company's business. The world's largest pork processor and hog producer, Smithfield Foods, has a vertical integration strategy. The company participates in both the hog production and meat processing of the business. *Horizontal integration,* on the other hand, is a strategy to consolidate competition by acquiring similar products or services. Kraft's purchase of Cadbury Schweppes is an example of this strategy. (Previous to this, Cadbury Schweppes had purchased Dr. Pepper/7-Up and A&W Root Beer.)

- A *diversification strategy* is adopted if the company wants to move into new products or markets. This strategy is normally achieved through the acquisition of other businesses and their brands. Altria Group (previously known as Philip Morris) diversified through the purchase of food companies.

- A *retrenchment strategy* is used to reduce the size or scope of a firm's activities by cutting back in some areas or eliminating entire businesses. Xerox and Sears have recently pursued retrenchment strategies. Xerox chose to divest itself of its real estate business ventures and focus on its core competencies. Since the early 1990s, Sears has systematically eliminated virtually all of its nonretail business from its corporate family.

- When the organization wants to remain the same it adopts a *stability strategy*. Sometimes the reason is to have the organization grow slowly; other times such a strategy is adopted to recover immediately after a period of sharp growth or retrenchment. After a growth period that saw expansion to Texas and acquisition of banks in Florida and Ohio, Bank of America, formerly NationsBank and North Carolina National Bank, adopted a strategy of stability.

Portfolio Strategy

Once the managers of a large, diversified organization decide on a grand strategy, they develop a portfolio strategy. A **portfolio strategy** determines the mix of business units and product lines that will provide a maximum competitive advantage. Developing a portfolio begins by identifying **strategic business units (SBUs)**, autonomous businesses with their own identities but operating within the framework of one organization. The SBU concept originated at General Electric in the 1970s to provide managers with a framework for directing GE's many diverse businesses. Typically, an SBU has its own product lines, markets and competitors.

Fortune Brands serves as a case in point. Growing from its roots as the American Tobacco Company, Fortune Brands is now a collection of several companies—autonomous divisions totally unrelated to its original business. Some of these companies include Jim Beam bourbon, Moen faucets, DeKuyper cordials, Titleist golf equipment and Master Lock's family of security devices.

Managing a portfolio of business units is like managing a portfolio of unrelated investments, such as stocks, bonds and real estate. Each SBU must be continually evaluated as to its performance and relevance to the overall grand strategy. Xerox sold its China operations, Xerox Engineering Systems and portions of Fuji Xerox, but kept its famed Palo Alto Research Center (PARC), home of such historic innovations as the personal computer and the mouse.

A technique often employed by organizations to help them evaluate their portfolios is the Boston Consulting Group (BCG) Growth-Share Matrix. The matrix combines growth rates and market share dimensions to identify four types of strategic business units, depicted in Figure below.

1 *Stars.* A star is a high-growth market leader. It has a large market share in a rapidly growing industry. The star is important because it has potential to grow and it will generate profits.

2 *Cash cows.* The cash cow is a principal source of net cash generated. It has a large market share in a stable, slow-growth industry. Because the industry is in slow growth, the business unit can maintain its position with little or no investment. It is in a position to generate cash for the expansion or acquisition of additional SBUs.

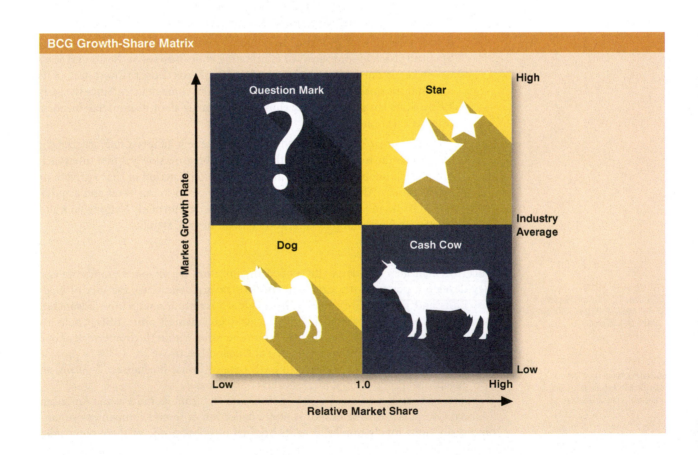

BCG Growth-Share Matrix

3 *Question marks.* The question mark has a small share of the market in rapidly expanding industry. Question marks are risky. A business in this category could become a star, but it could also fail.

4 *Dogs.* The dog is a business with small market share in a low-growth or declining industry.

The BCG Growth-Share Matrix provides a valuable tool for corporate-level strategists. It indicates where expansion should and can take place. It also indicates which business units should be sold off.

FORMULATING BUSINESS-LEVEL STRATEGY

A business-level strategy is the strategy managers formulate for each SBU (or for the firm itself if it is a single-product business), defining how it intends to compete. The many possible strategies available can be grouped as either adaptive strategies or competitive strategies.

Adaptive Strategies

The philosophy behind the adaptive strategies developed by Raymond Miles and Charles Snow is that a business's strategy should be a fit between the internal characteristics of the company—its core competencies—and the external environment.[22] The four adaptive strategies include prospector, defender, analyzer, and reactor.

1 The *prospector strategy* is one based on innovation, taking risks, seeking out opportunities, and expansion. This strategy is appropriate in a dynamic and fast-growing climate, if the organization is flexible, innovative and creative. The prospector strategy has been a good one for 3M Company, maker of Scotch brand products. It has led to cutting-edge products, new applications of technology and market leadership.

2 The *defender strategy* is based on holding current market share or even retrenching. It is almost the exact opposite of the prospector strategy. The defender strategy is appropriate in a stable environment if the organization is concerned with internal efficiency to produce reliable products for regular customers. ExxonMobil and Royal Dutch/Shell use the defender strategy.

3 With the *analyzer strategy* an organization attempts to maintain the current market share while innovating in some markets. It asks managers to perform a kind of balancing act: maintaining the organization in some markets while being aggressive in others. This strategy is appropriate in an environment in which growth is possible and the organization is both efficient and creative. Examples of analyzers include Frito-Lay and Anheuser-Busch. Each has a reliable product base yet innovatively brings new products to the market.

4 An organization adopting the *reactor strategy* could be said to have no strategy. Rather than formulating a strategy to fit a specific environment, reactors respond to environmental threats as they occur. With no clear sense of internal direction, a reactor is doomed until it changes strategies—it simply flails away. Many companies that fail do so because they follow a reactor strategy. Without a strategy, companies fall victim to their competitors and to market changes. They cling to past practices too long, believing that those that worked well in the past will continue to do so. They fail to regularly analyze their environments and reassess their missions, goals and strategies, until changing customer demands overwhelm them. Northwest Airlines got into financial trouble because it was constantly reacting to its competitors' strategies and had none of its own.

Competitive Strategies

The second set of business-level strategies an organization can initiate—the *competitive strategies*—were developed by author and management professor Michael Porter.[23] Whereas adaptive strategies are based on fit between the organization and its environment, competitive strategies are dictated by how the organization can best compete based on its core competencies—internal skills, resources and philosophies. Porter refers to these strategies as generic, as depicted in Figure 4.11, because they can be applied to a firm in any industry. The three potential strategies are differentiation, cost-leadership and focus.[24]

- With a *differentiation strategy* an organization attempts to set its products or services apart from those of other companies. To accomplish this, an organization focuses on basic, core business processes, such as customer service, product design and development, total quality control, and order processing. Lexus and Rolex focus on quality; FedEx and McDonald's focus on service.

- A *cost-leadership strategy* is one focused on keeping costs as low as possible through efficient operations and tight controls. In turn, the company can compete by charging lower prices. Target and Walmart apply this strategy in the growing discount business. Southwest Airlines, Virgin America and JetBlue focus on this strategy in the airline industry.

- When the managers of a firm target a specific market—a particular region or group of potential customers—they are applying a *focus strategy*. It can be either a cost leadership or differentiation strategy aimed toward a narrow, focused market. One example might be a specialty hospital, such as a heart hospital or a children's hospital. Some companies manufacture products for certain buyers. Pro-Line Corporation produces health and beauty aids for African American markets.

FORMULATING FUNCTIONAL-LEVEL STRATEGY

The final level of strategy in the organization is the strategy developed by the major functional departments. These action plans support the accomplishment of the business-level strategies. The major functions include marketing, production, human resources, finance and research and development.

- *Marketing strategy* involves satisfying the customer with decisions on pricing, promotion, distribution and products/services of the organization. When taken together, the decisions in each area become a firm's marketing strategy. Nike continues to commit itself to promote its golf apparel and equipment with Rory McElroy—Underarmour with Jordan Speith. Frito-Lay's Doritos can be purchased in several flavors, such as ranch, nacho cheese, barbecue or regular. Celestial Seasonings has multiple distribution channels—through grocery-store chains, wholesalers and health food stores. Walmart has built its inventories around the fastest-moving merchandise in major consumer goods categories. In the area of marketing services, CVS/pharmacy and Domino's

Figure 4.11	Porter's Generic Strategies

FORCES AFFECTING THE INDUSTRY STRUCTURE	GENERIC STRATEGIES AS DEVELOPED BY MICHAEL PORTER		
	Cost Leadership	Differentiation	Focus
Entry Barriers	Ability to cut price deters potential entrants	Customer loyalty hinders potential entrants	Development of core inimitable competencies
Buyer Power	Ability to offer even lower price to more important buyers	Even large buyers have less power to negotiate due to differentiation	Large buyers have less power to negotiate from core competency
Supplier Power	Better insulation from powerful suppliers	Better position if supplier's price increases	Supplier's price may not have effect at all
Threat of Susbtitutes	Use a low price to ward off substitutes	Customer's attachment to differentiating attributes wards threats	Specialized attributes and core competencies ward off substitutes
Competitive Rivalry	Better competitiveness on price, unmet by competition	Brand loyal can hinder switching to competitors	Rivals cannot meet differentiation developed for customer

Visit us at *http://business-fundas.com*

Source: *http://business-fundas.com/2010/how-the-internet-affects-porters-generic-strategy-models/.*

offer online, text, and telephone ordering, as well as home delivery. Supercuts has a low price to attract volume. Banks have placed ATMs on college campuses to better serve their young customers.

- Functional-level strategy for *production* involves manufacturing goods and providing services. Decisions in this area influence how the organization will compete. Such decisions include choices about plant location, inventory control methods, use of robotics and computer-aided manufacturing techniques, commitments to quality and productivity improvement and the selection and use of outside suppliers.

- For many businesses, such as hotels, restaurants, health care and professional sports, the *human resources strategy* is the fundamental key to survival. These businesses need a specific strategy to execute nearly every employment decision area, such as recruiting, training and developing human resources. Recruiting must result in attracting people who adequately reflect a firm's customer base and the community's workforce. Once acquired, human resources must be trained and developed in order to take advantage of the potentials they have to offer.

- The *financial strategy* of a firm involves decisions about the actions to be taken with profits (distribution to stockholders or retention for future investments), how funds will be spent or invested and how any additional funds will be raised (through borrowing or by attracting new investor capital).

- The functional-level strategy for *research and development* involves the invention and development of new technologies, or new applications for existing technologies, that lead to new products and services. For example, IBM's emphasis is on research.

I.B.M. has laboratories around the world, spends over $5 billion a year on research and development, and generates more patents a year than any other company. Five I.B.M. scientists have won Nobel prizes; the company's researchers attend scientific conferences, publish papers and have made fundamental advances in computing, materials science and mathematics.[25]

Each year companies invest millions of dollars in R&D projects, many of which lead to few if any breakthroughs. Investment for the future, however, is critical so that there will be a future for the enterprise. R&D has led to such breakthroughs in the auto industry as side-mounted airbags, four-wheel antilock brakes and dent- and chip-resistant body panels. All R&D results from strategic management and strategic planning.

Review What You've Learned

Chapter Summary

1 Explain the importance of planning.

Planning helps managers avoid errors, waste, and delays. It provides direction and a common sense of purpose for the organization. Planning sets goals and objectives and selects the means to reach them. It is part of every other management function. Planning allows managers the opportunity of adjusting to, rather than reacting to, expected changes in both their internal and external environments. The planning process for all organizations is built on a framework of an organization's mission, with its accompanying values and principles. An organization's mission statement explains why it exists—what its primary purpose is. Once the mission is defined, all planning efforts must be governed by the mission and should not contradict or oppose it in any way. It becomes an anchor for everything a company does or plans to do.

2 Differentiate between strategic, tactical, operational, and contingency plans.

Plans—the end result of planning—provide answers to the six basic questions: what, when, where, who, how, and how much. Strategic plans establish the steps by which an organization achieves its strategic objectives. They are concerned with the entire organization's direction and the primary responsibility of top management.

Tactical plans are concerned with what the major subsystems within each organization must do, how they must do it, and who will have the responsibility for doing it. As the primary responsibility of middle managers, tactical plans develop the shorter-term activities and goals needed to achieve a strategy.

First-line supervisors develop operational plans as a means to achieve operational objectives in support of tactical as well as strategic plans.

Contingency plans are developed to cope with events that, if they occur, will render primary plans ineffective or obsolete. By planning for changes that have both positive and negative impacts, managers will remain able to deal with worst-case situations and events.

3 List and explain the steps in a basic planning process.

- *Setting objectives.* Establishing targets for the short- or long-range future.
- *Analyzing and evaluating the environments.* Analyzing the current position, analyzing the internal and external environments, and determining the kind of resources that will be available to evaluate courses of action and implement plans.

- *Identifying the alternatives.* Constructing a list of possible courses of action that will lead to goal achievement.

- *Evaluating the alternatives.* Listing and considering the advantages (benefits) and disadvantages (costs) of each possible course of action.

- *Selecting the best solution.* Selecting the course or combination of courses of action that possesses the most advantages and the fewest serious disadvantages.

- *Implementing the plan.* Determining who will be involved, what resources will be assigned, how the plan will be evaluated, and what the reporting structure will be.

- *Controlling and evaluating the results.* Ensuring that the plan is proceeding according to expectations and making necessary adjustments.

4 Discuss various ways to make plans effective.

Aids to effective planning include improving the quality of assumptions and forecasts through the following:

- *Effective communication.* As managers establish their objectives and begin to flesh out their strategic, tactical and operational plans to achieve them, it requires constant communication and exchange of information, ideas and feedback.

- *Quality of information.* A manager increases the probability of success by beginning planning with current, factual and verifiable information.

- *Involvement of others.* Opening the planning process to others can result in better plans, a higher level of commitment to the plan and the long-range development of employees who understand planning is a way of life.

Two planning tools can also improve planning efforts:

- *Management by objectives (MBO).* Mutually-agreed-on objectives are set through planning sessions involving a manager and a subordinate. Whether the objectives are achieved, how they are achieved, and what the subordinate learns through his or her achievement efforts become the foundation for evaluating the subordinate's work and for developing the subordinate's skills.

- *Linear programming.* Mathematics, equations and formulas that factor in the effects of many variables help managers determine an optimum course of action and the best combinations of resources.

There are several major barriers to effective planning:

- *Inability to plan.* Some managers lack experience or do not have the skills. These deficiencies can be overcome by training and practice.

- *Lack of commitment to the planning process.* Some managers claim they do not have time to plan; others fear failure. One way to overcome this is to make the attempt. Experience helps.

- *Inferior information.* Information that is out-of-date, of poor quality or insufficient can be a major barrier to planning. Having an effective organizational management information system as well as prioritizing and promoting the importance of providing reliable information can help to overcome this barrier.

- *Lack of focus on the long term.* Failure to consider the long term because of emphasis on short-term problems can lead to troubles in coordinating plans and preparing for the future. A remedy can be found by including long-term planning as an element of a manager's performance appraisal.

- *Overreliance on the planning department.* Planning specialists often focus on process and lose contact with reality and with line managers. An emphasis needs to be placed on translating the planning department's output into programs for achieving specific goals at defined times.

- *Overemphasis on controllable variables.* Managers can find themselves concentrating on factors within their control and failing to consider outside factors. Variables such as future technology, economic forecasts and expectations about government restrictions must be considered.

5 Distinguish between strategic planning, strategic management, strategy formulation, and strategy implementation.

Strategic planning is the decision making and planning processes that chart an organization's long-term course of action. All companies engage in strategic planning as an element of strategic management. Strategic management is top-level management's responsibility for defining the firm's position, formulating strategies and guiding long-term organizational activities. The ultimate purpose of strategic planning and strategic management is to help position the organization to achieve a superior fit in the environment in order to achieve its objectives.

Strategy formulation includes the planning and decision making that goes into developing the company's strategic goals and strategic plans. It includes assessing the environment—analyzing the internal and external situation—and creating goals and plans. Strategy implementation refers to the processes associated with executing the strategic plan. These processes may include communication, incentives, structural changes or new technology.

6 Explain the steps involved in the strategic planning process.

The strategic planning process involves six steps:

1 *Create mission statement, goals and strategies.* For new enterprises and those desiring to totally redefine themselves, all planning begins with the creation of a mission statement. It is the anchor for every strategy.

2 *Analyze the environments.* Internal and external environments must be assessed and analyzed. In completing this phase, managers perform a situational analysis and search for internal strengths and weaknesses as well as external opportunities and threats.

3 *Reassess mission statement and goals.* The analysis of the external opportunities and threats and the internal strengths and weaknesses can produce two outcomes: to reestablish the current mission, goals and strategies or to define a new mission and supporting goals.

4 *Formulate strategies.* Once the mission and goals are reestablished or redefined, strategies at the corporate, business and functional levels can be formulated.

5 *Implement strategies.* Once strategies are formulated, they must be implemented. Implementation involves the use of four elements: leadership, structure, people and information.

6 *Monitor and evaluate results.* Once the strategy is implemented, performance must be monitored and evaluated and modifications must be made, if necessary.

The assessment of the internal and external environments identifies factors that shape the development of the strategic plan. The analysis (SWOT) of the external opportunities and threats and the internal strengths and weaknesses can produce two outcomes: to reestablish the current mission, goals and strategies or to define a new mission and supporting goals.

In the strategic planning process, managers must have information from external as well as internal sources. External information about opportuni-

ties and threats can be gained from customers, suppliers, government reports, consultants, professional journals and meetings. Internal information about strengths and weaknesses may come from profit and loss statements, ratio analysis, employee morale surveys and budget printouts.

The implementation of a strategy will depend to a great extent on having a good fit between the organizational strategy and culture. The implementation may require changes in the organization's behavior and culture. It achieves implementation through the collaboration of four key elements: leadership, organizational structure, human resources and information and control systems.

7 Explain the formulation of corporate-level strategy, business-level strategy, and functional-level strategy.

- *Corporate-level strategy.* For companies with a single market or a few closely related markets, the corporate-level strategy involves developing a grand strategy. A grand strategy is the overall framework for the organization. Grand strategies include five types: growth, integration, diversification, retrenchment and stability. Large companies that have complicated organizational structures with unique business divisions or that have strategic business units, each with different products, markets and competitors, need a portfolio strategy. After the grand strategy is developed, the portfolio strategy involves determining the power mix of business units and product lines to provide a maximum competitive advantage for the strategic business unit.

- *Business-level strategy.* A business-level strategy is the strategy managers formulate within each SBU (or within the firm itself if it is a single-product business) defining how to compete. Many possible strategies can be chosen; they can be grouped as either adaptive strategies or competitive strategies. Adaptive strategies—prospective, defender, analyzer, and reactor—try to match organizational assets to the external environment. Competitive strategies—differentiation, cost leadership and focus—are dictated by how the organization can best compete based on its core competencies—internal skills, resources and philosophies.

- *Functional-level strategy.* Functional-level strategies are the action plans developed by the major functional departments to support the accomplishment of business-level strategies. The major functions include marketing, production, human resources, finance and research and development.

KEY TERMS

REVIEW QUESTIONS

1. How does planning affect the success of a business?

2. How are mission statements, goals, objectives and plans related?

3. What are the purposes of strategic, tactical, operational and contingency planning? In what situation would an organization use each?

4. How can managers make planning efforts more effective?

5. What are the six barriers to effective planning? How does each interfere with effective planning?

6. What is the purpose of strategic planning?

7. Why is it important to assess the internal and external environments in strategic planning? What four factors are assessed?

8. What is the difference between corporate-level strategies for growth, retrenchment and stability? What is the purpose of the BCG Growth-Share Matrix in the development of business-level plans? What are three of the five functional-level areas of planning? What needs to be considered in each area?

DISCUSSION QUESTIONS FOR CRITICAL THINKING

1. What specific examples can you give that demonstrate the importance of a mission statement to the success of a business and a not-for-profit organization?

2. In what ways can you apply strategic, tactical and operational objectives and plans to your mission of gaining a college education?

3. What evidence can you cite from your experience to prove the value of contingency planning in today's organizations?

4. Would you like to work in an organization that uses management by objectives? Why or why not?

5. Which of the barriers to successful planning have you encountered while making your plans? What was their impact on your plans?

6. What specific examples can you give that demonstrate grand strategies? Competitive strategies? Functional-level strategies?

7. How can you apply a SWOT analysis to your strategic plan for gaining a college education?

8. What specific examples can you cite of organizations capitalizing on their distinctive competitive advantage?

Social Media Management Exercises

1. "Nuts About Southwest" is a leading corporate blog where Southwest Airlines employees share their stories and communicate directly with customers. The blog includes videos, pictures, podcasts and other social media tools. Customers and employees are encouraged to comment.

   • Read the Buzz Binn interview with Southwest's Brian Lusk. How did customer comments on the blog help Southwest change strategic direction on assigned seating and advanced scheduling? *http://www.buzzbinpadillacrt.com/nuts-about-south-west-demonstrates-true-social-interaction*

   • Visit the blog and read "About." Why is the blog moderated? What are the guidelines for posting? *http://www.blogsouthwest.com; http://www.blogsouthwest.com/about*

2. Many corporations resist starting a blog on their own websites because someone might say something negative about the company or brand. Moderation of blog posts by the company is acceptable because it cuts down on inflammatory, offensive, derogatory or obscene comments. But, what if the company has a blog and deliberately withholds comments that do not qualify as inflammatory, offensive, derogatory or obscene?

   • Why would a company withhold comments?

   • Do you think a company withholding comments will be seen as dishonest? Explain.

3. Intel has social media guidelines published online, including moderation guidelines. Read "Intel Social Media Guidelines."

   • What's included as social media?

   • Why should negative content not be moderated?

   • When should negative content be moderated?

   • Prepare a list of Do's and Don'ts for employees using social media.

   http://www.intel.com/content/www/us/en/legal/intel-social-media-guidelines.html

Experiential Learning

Turnaround at IBM

How can one of the most successful companies in the world almost go out of business? It happened to IBM. Competitors and environmental changes threatened IBM. The company was known as a computer maker, especially for its mainframes. Computer prices were falling and IBM's sales were declining. "In 1993, when Louis V. Gerstner Jr. became chairman and chief executive, the question asked about IBM was whether it would survive. And in choosing him, the IBM board had taken a historic gamble on a professional manager with no experience in the computer industry" (Lohr).

Mr. Gerstner was not a technologist, but he was an unabashed champion of the new technology. He traveled all over the world to meet with customers, believing that IBM decisions should be market driven. He found that IBM had two distinct competencies: research and integrated computer solutions (hardware, software, consulting and maintenance) to solve business problems (like manufacturing, purchasing or marketing) for companies.

In 1994, based on feedback from customers, Mr. Gerstner decided that IBM would adopt open systems so that standard software protocols would allow different hardware and software products to talk to each other. IBM had a "networked world" model of computing and embraced the Internet. By 1995, it formed an Internet division, "which was not a product group, but more a corporate SWAT team to make sure the entire company was marching toward the Internet. Then, it carved out its niche, trumpeted in a massive advertising and marketing campaign, beginning in 1997, to push e-business" (Lohr).

Under Gerstner's leadership, from 1993 until 2002, IBM went from "the fallen icon of American technology" to an industry leader. The new strategy relied less on hardware and more on technology services and software. Recurring revenue would come from service contracts and software licenses. The company survived and quickly returned to profitability.

IBM under CEO Samuel Palmisano shed its PC business in 2004 and has focused on technology for corporations. Among other things, the company has moved more aggressively into offering combinations of business software and technology services that help companies and governments solve knotty problems, such as catching welfare fraud (Wire Reports).

Today, IBM helps its customers, who are organizations, to do business.

Questions

1. Work with another student to answer the following questions. What strategy changes did Gerstner use to solve IBM's situation? Develop your answer by selecting specific strategies relating to corporate, business and functional strategy options.

2. IBM was one of the first companies to publish a social policy document, "IBM Social Computing Guidelines," How does the "Add Value" section motivate employees to create thoughtful content?

https://www.ibm.com/blogs/zz/en/guidelines.html

3. The use of social networking by employees can cause problems for businesses. Security issues arise when employees communicate, unregulated, with people outside the organization. Reputation management is a challenge when employees post inappropriate comments on blogs, Twitter and other sites. Work with another student(s) to develop a list of social media "Dos and Don'ts" for employees developing content.

Sources: Wire Reports, "Apple, IBM: Two paths to profit," *The Dallas Morning News*, October 19, 2010, Section D, p. 8; Steve Lohr. "He Loves to Win. At I.B.M., He Did." *The New York Times*, March 10, 2002; IBM: Louis V. Gerstner Jr., http://www.ibm.com/lvg/.

Chapter 5

Making Decisions

LEARNING OBJECTIVES

After studying this chapter, you should be able to:

1 Recognize that decision making is performed at all management levels

2 Distinguish between formal and informal approaches to decision making

3 List the steps in the decision-making process

4 Identify the environmental factors that influence decision making

5 Describe the personal attributes of a manager that influence decision making

6 Discuss the value of group decision making, and identify three techniques of group decision making

7 Explain three quantitative techniques for decision making, and describe the situations in which each is appropriate

8 Determine strategies a manager can use to create a more effective decision-making environment

Decision Making

We all make decisions every day. What time should I get up? What should I wear? What should I eat? What should I say? Where should I go? Some decisions are more important than others. What should be my college major? Where should I live? Which job should I accept?

Decision making involves identifying alternative responses to a business issue, es-timating advantages and disadvantages of alternative responses and choosing the most appropriate alternative in a partially defined situation. Management decisions are im-portant because the out-comes affect people's lives and the success of the organization. But, managers don't always make good decisions. Bad management decisions lead to loss of jobs and business failures.

Managers want to make the right decisions. For each of the following statements, circle the number that indicates your level of agreement. Rate your agreement as it is, not as you would like it to be. Objectivity will enable you to determine your manage-ment skill strengths and weaknesses.

	Almost Always	Often	Sometimes	Rarely	Almost Never
I avoid trying to make a decision until I have defined it.	5	4	3	2	1
I identify several alternative solutions before making a decision.	5	4	3	2	1
I ask others for their opinions before making a decision.	5	4	3	2	1
I research alternative ideas before making a decision.	5	4	3	2	1
I consider points of view different from my own before making a decision.	5	4	3	2	1
I ask lots of questions before considering ways to solve a problem.	5	4	3	2	1
I give my ideas and opinions to help others make decisions.	5	4	3	2	1
I evaluate ideas critically before choosing one.	5	4	3	2	1
I know and use the steps in the decision-making process.	5	4	3	2	1
I evaluate the results of my decisions.	5	4	3	2	1

Compute your score by adding the circled numbers. The highest score is 50; the lowest score is 10. A higher score implies you are more likely to make successful decisions. A lower score implies a lesser degree of readiness, but it can be increased. Reading and studying this chapter will help you to improve your understanding of decision making.

INTRODUCTION

Every organization succeeds or fails based on decisions by its managers. Although many of their critical decisions determine strategic direction, managers make decisions about all aspects of the organization, including organization structures, staffing and control systems. This chapter will thoroughly examine managerial decision making—the steps in the decision-making process, the nature of the decision-making environment, influences on decision making, decision-making techniques and the way managers can create an environment for effective decision making. If you dread decisions, postpone them or simply feel you could use some extra help on the subject, this chapter is for you. By the time you finish reading its ideas, examples and suggestions, you should be more confident in your approach to decision making.

What You Need to Know About Decisions

For many years you have been making decisions. You are reading these words as a direct result of a decision you made to study management. Your entire life is a result of your decisions and those of others. Many decisions are simple: deciding what to eat or what clothes to wear. Others are much more complex: what college to attend or what area in which to major. Regardless of how simple or complex the **decision**, it is a choice made from alternatives.

decision
A choice made from available alternatives

Managers face the same range of decisions; but unlike our individual decisions, the ones managers make in organizations can affect profitability, the lives of thousands of people, or the location of a company's operations. For example, the decision made by Bill Gates and his Microsoft cofounder Paul Allen—licensing its 16-bit operating system, MS-DOS 1.0, to IBM—was the inspiration that set Microsoft apart from its competitors and made it one of the top software sellers in the country.

What Decision Making Is

Decision Making, Problem Solving and Opportunity Management

Decision making is the process of identifying problems and opportunities, developing alternative solutions, choosing an alternative, and implementing it.[1] Decision-making is a process, not a lightning bolt occurrence. In making the decision, a manager is reaching a conclusion—based on considering a number of options or alternatives.

decision making
The process of identifying problems and opportunities, developing alternative solutions, choosing an alternative, and implementing it

Many times, in management the terms *decision making* and *problem solving* are used interchangeably because managers constantly make decisions to solve problems. For example, when an account representative resigns at Verizon, the sales manager has a **problem**—the difference between the current and desired performance or situation.[2] Replacing the person requires a decision: promote from within; hire an experienced person; or recruit an inexperienced college graduate. Each alternative could solve the problem.

problem
The difference between the current and desired performance or situation

But not all decision making is aimed at solving problems; many decisions are made to seize **opportunities**. Managers see a chance, occasion, event or breakthrough that requires a decision to be made. Such was the case with Reed Hastings, Cofounder of Netflix, an innovative online service that started by renting DVDs by mail. Mr. Hastings found that many movie rental customers were dissatisfied with their shopping experience. Seizing the opportunity to address this new set of consumer needs, Netflix was created. Customers don't have to drive to a store, stand in line or pay late charges. Netflix subscribers pay a monthly fee to instantly watch movies or television shows streamed over the Internet on their TV; via any device that streams from Netflix.[3] Subscribers

opportunity
A chance, occasion, event, or breakthrough that requires a decision to be made

electronic commerce
All forms of business transactions involving both organizations and individuals that are based upon the processing and transmission of digitized data, including text, sound and visual images

are offered movie recommendations based on how other subscribers have rated them. Netflix saw an opportunity and took it. Other examples of companies taking advantage of an opportunity are discussed in this chapter's Managing Social Media.

Managing Social Media

Breakthrough Business Models

The Internet has allowed breakthrough business models that were never possible before. A business model is the method by which a company makes money. Early adopters of the Internet were those businesses willing to innovate and to take some risks. The most successful sites online are more than just places to meet, buy and sell. They add value by personalizing access to useful information entertainment and community.

Electronic commerce, is the buying and selling of goods and services, or the transmitting of funds or data, over an electronic network, primarily the Internet. These business transactions occur either business-to-business, business-to-consumer, consumer-to-consumer or consumer-to-business.[4] As business opportunity, is still evolving. The major difference between electronic commerce and traditional commerce is the tools used. Traditional business uses person-to-person contact, as well as mail, faxes and telephone as its primary tools, whereas in electronic business, entire transactions—between businesses and consumers (also known as *business to consumer*—B2C—electronic retailing—e-tailing) or among businesses (also known as *business to business*—B2B)—relies on a computer-to-computer exchange of data. Traditionally, most transactions have been handled manually. Electronic commerce automates this process. Customers can go to a website to get information about a product, order products, make payments and monitor their order status, 24 hours a day, 7 days-a-week.

Electronic commerce continues to grow and evolve because of its potential impact on business practices. These benefits include:

- Reduced costs—Purchasing online reduces the time and overhead cost associated with processing sales.

- Reduced inventory—Storage costs, handling costs and ordering costs are all associated with holding inventory.

- Improved customer service—Customers serve themselves from multiple devices, when and where they choose; with access to many variations of real time customer service support.

- Mobile revenue—It alone is expected to account for 50% of digital commerce in the US by 2017.[5]

- Developing market/product opportunities—An organization can expand its reach, opening markets that would otherwise be inaccessible.

Two unique and successful Internet businesses are Amazon and eBay. Amazon pioneered selling books on the web. Today, Amazon's vision is "to be Earth's most customer-centric company for four primary customer sets: consumers, sellers, enterprises, and content creators."[6] When Jeff Bezos, Amazon's Founder, first heard about the web's high growth potential, he reputedly drew up a list of 20 potential products he could sell over the Internet before he chose books. The books that Amazon sells are exactly the same as the books consumers can buy in their local bookshops. Yet, the site focuses on community, is interactive and tailors itself to each individual shopper. Amazon dominates online retail and allows buyers to review and discuss products. Today Amazon has 25 top-level categories currently represented, the assortment, pricing and competitive dynamics offered through a complex ecosystem.

EBay started as a place for trading Pez dispensers. It is an online auctioneer and now lists millions of items for sale—everything from cars to computer parts to cosmetics. Of course, eBay itself doesn't actually carry the inventory; it just hosts the auctions, charging the sellers a small fee for its services. EBay leveraged Internet technology in a new way by bringing together buyers and sellers of collectibles and creating an online "garage sale." EBay dominates online auctions and allows the community to evaluate sellers.

➡ Amazon and eBay saw opportunities to use the Internet to create new kinds of businesses. For each of these companies, identify one or more companies that failed to innovate adequately, and saw its business suffer as a result.

➡ What decisions about social networking and buyer experiences did the managers at Amazon and eBay make?

UNIVERSALITY OF DECISION MAKING

As noted in Chapter 1, decision making is a key part of all managers' jobs. A manager constantly makes decisions when performing the functions of planning, organizing, staffing, leading and controlling. Decision making is not a separate, isolated function of management but a common core to the other functions, a fact illustrated by Figure 5.1.

Managers at all levels of the organization engage in decision making. The decisions made by top managers, dealing with the mission of the organization and strategies for achieving it, have an impact on the whole organization. Middle-level managers, in turn, focus their decision making on implementing these strategies, as well as on budgeting and allocating resources. Finally, first-level managers deal with tactical decisions associated with repetitive, day-to-day operations. Decision-making is indeed universal.

Managers make big and small decisions every day. Whether they realize it or not, they go through a process to make those decisions. Whether planning a budget, organizing a work schedule, interviewing a prospective employee, coaching a worker on the assembly line or making adjustments to a project, the manager is taking part in a decision-making process.

Recognize that decision making is performed at all management levels

Figure 5.1	**Decision Making in the Five Management Functions**
Planning	What is the mission of the organization? What should it be?
	What are the needs of the customers?
	What are the organization's strengths, weaknesses, threats and opportunities?
	What are the strategic, tactical and operational goals?
	What strategies will achieve the goals?
Organizing	What organizational option will best achieve the objectives?
	What type of departmental structure will result in teamwork?
	How many employees should report to a manager?
	When should a manager delegate authority? How much?
Staffing	How many employees will we need this year?
	What skills are necessary to do this job?
	What type of training will best prepare the employee?
	How can we improve the quality of the performance appraisal system?
Leading	What can we do to have motivated employees?
	What style of leadership is the most effective with an individual?
	What strategies are available to manage conflict?
	How can we build teams?
Controlling	What tasks in the organization need to be controlled?
	Which control technique is the most effective for monitoring finances?
	What is the effect of controls on employee behavior?
	How do we establish acceptable standards of performance?

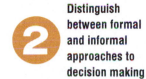

Distinguish between formal and informal approaches to decision making

APPROACHES TO DECISION MAKING

Not all decision-making situations are identical. The nature of the decision often dictates what approach a manager should take. The more complex or uncertain the problem to be solved, the more effective the manager will be if the formal decision-making process is used. This will be described in detail later in this chapter. Less complicated problems or those that a manager has a great deal of experience in solving can be handled less formally by following habit or relying on past solutions. Whether the decision is a programmed or non-programmed each depends on the nature of the situation.

Programmed and Nonprogrammed Decisions

programmed decisions

Decisions that involve problems or situations that have occurred often enough that both the circumstances and solutions are predictable; made in response to recurring organizational problems

Programmed decisions involve problems or situations that have occurred often enough that both the circumstances and solutions are predictable.[7] In other words, programmed decisions are made in response to recurring organizational problems. Examples of programmed decisions include the programmed inventory reorder point at Walmart, the forms necessary to add a person to payroll and the handling of routine correspondence. This chapter's Ethical Management feature identifies a situation in which a programmed decision may have solved a large problem for Facebook. Figure 5.2 presents a model of a programmed decision for processing payroll.

nonprogrammed decisions

Decisions made in response to problems and opportunities that have unique circumstances, unpredictable results, and important consequences for the company

Nonprogrammed decisions are made in response to problems and opportunities that have unique circumstances, unpredictable results, and important consequences for the company. Managers often find themselves in situations that have never occurred before or in which the problem is not thoroughly defined. The decisions made by Bill Gates for Microsoft are examples of non-programmed decisions. There are no programmed decision steps for making software, buying a "shopping experience," or for creating a dazzling marketing strategy. To make these choices, Bill Gates spent hours analyzing the customer, developing and analyzing the alternatives, and making choices. When managers face these difficult, significant choices, they must use a sound decision-making process. Furthermore, in these days of turbulent and disruptive market environments and fierce competition, it becomes even more important to make good decisions.

List the steps in the decision-making process

SEVEN-STEP DECISION-MAKING PROCESS

The decision-making process has seven steps, as shown in Figure 5.3. Each one is essential to the entire process. The sections that follow will examine each step.

Defining the Problem or Opportunity

The initial and most critical step is to define the problem or opportunity. The accuracy of this step affects all the steps that follow. If the problem or opportunity is incorrectly defined, or too broad or narrow in scope, every other step in the decision process will be based on that false start. If a company is losing market share, is the problem poor customer perception, product quality, technical inferiority, a slow warehouse or an inadequate sales force? Managers must pinpoint the problem correctly, because each of these problems requires a different solution.

symptom

Signals that something is wrong and draws the manager's attention to finding the cause—that is, the problem

In problem solving, a manager must differentiate between a problem and a **symptom**. In the previous example, the symptom is dwindling market share; the problem may be poor quality. A symptom signals that something is wrong.[8] It should

Questionable Decision Making at Facebook

Facebook is an online phenomenon with over 1.55 billion monthly active users. "Founded in February 2004, Facebook "gives people the power to share and make the world more open and connected. People use Facebook to stay connected with friends and family, to discover what's going on in the world, and to share and express what matters to them" (About Facebook). It was started in a dorm room by Mark Zuckerberg when he was a student at Harvard to identify and locate other students. Harvard students were automatically connected to all other Harvard students. The user base expanded to include all colleges and universities; next, it expanded to high schools and work networks; and now, anyone can join.

Most people believe that their Facebook information by default is visible only to friends. When a Facebook member joins, he or she gives personal information (name, age, address, hometown and occupation) and sends invitations to friends by e-mail to assemble his or her Facebook online relationships. Each time a member logs on, he or she sees friend's activities and behaviors.

> *Members post all sorts of information about themselves, and a lot of that information is available for the world to see. A report commissioned for Belgium's privacy watchdog found many of the most popular applications (or "apps") on Facebook, including WhatsApp and Instagram, companies that Facebook now owns, were providing user's identification to outside companies, which violated Facebook's privacy rules. An application or app is a dedicated software program that runs on a mobile device or Facebook. "Facebook's acquisition of Instagram and WhatsApp has allowed Facebook to collect more kinds of user data, which enables more detailed profiling. The report also said that it is impossible to add information on Facebook that may not later be used for targeting advertisements." (Fidler)*

Application developers are independents and apps are regarded by Facebook as hosted transactions. The app companies can sell advertising on their applications, even if they lack clear policies for using and storing customer data. When companies have good data-security practices and policies, consumer data still can be misplaced or stolen.

Consumer's personal information and their connections with friends allow online advertisers to use behavioral targeting. Behavioral advertising is the tracking of a consumer's online activities in order to deliver advertising targeted to the individual consumer's interests (FTC). This blurs the boundaries between content and paid advertising (Hagel and Brown).

➤ **What ethical questions are raised by Facebook's privacy breach?**

➤ **User IDs are the unique identifier tied to every person on Facebook, which can be used to find users' names, gender and any information they've made visible to "everyone" on the Internet through privacy settings. How concerned should Facebook members be about the sharing of these IDs?**

➤ **Members may not understand that applications are simply hosted by Facebook. Should Facebook exert control over applications by requiring companies that participate with it to comply with its customer standards?**

➤ **As a consumer, what would be your response to Facebook's ethical practices?**

Sources: Facebook Terms and Policies, *https://www.facebook.com/policies*; Facebook About, *https://www.facebook.com/facebook/info/?tab=page_info*; Stephen Fidler, "Facebook Policies Taken to Task in Report for Data-Privacy Issues," *The Wall Street Journal*, February 23, 2015, *http://www.wsj.com/articles/facebook-policies-taken-to-task-in-report-for-data-privacy-issues-1424725902*; FTC, "FTC Staff Report: Self Regulatory Principles for Online Behavioral Advertising," *http://www.ftc.gov/os/2009/02/P085400behavadreport.pdf*; John Hagel and John Seely Brown, "Life on the Edge: Learning from Facebook," *BusinessWeek*, April 8, 2008, *http://www.businessweek.com/innovate/content/apr2008/id2008042_809134.htm?chan=search*.

draw the manager's attention to finding the cause—that is, the problem. To isolate the problem from the symptoms, a manager needs to develop a sound questioning process and to ask the right questions. "Five Why Analysis "discussed in this chapter's Quality Management Box, is one way for a manager to ask questions.

Figure 5.2   A Programmed Decision Outline for Completing a Routine Payroll

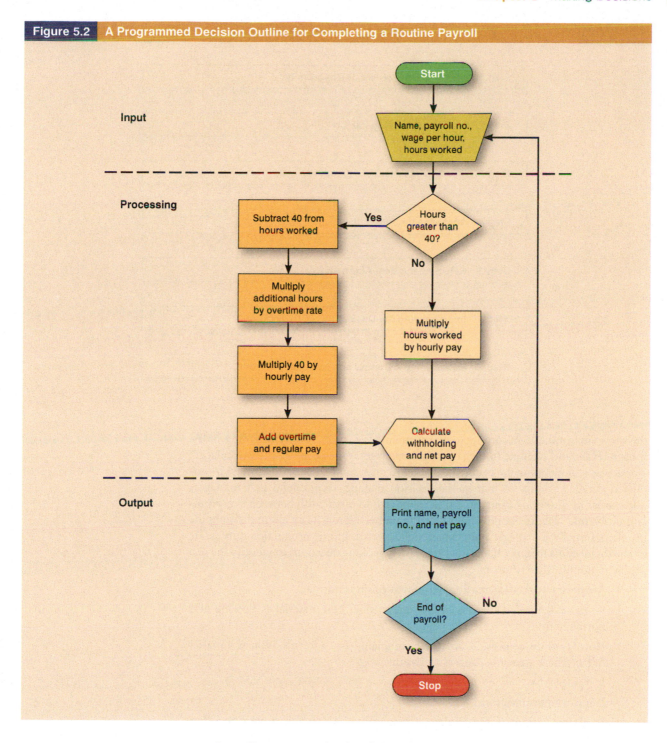

According to Peter Drucker, "The most common source of mistakes in management decisions is the emphasis on finding the right answer rather than asking the right questions."[9] In the process of asking questions, the manager gathers relevant and timely data about the problem. The best way to get good data is for managers to tune in to

Figure 5.3   **The Decision-Making Process**

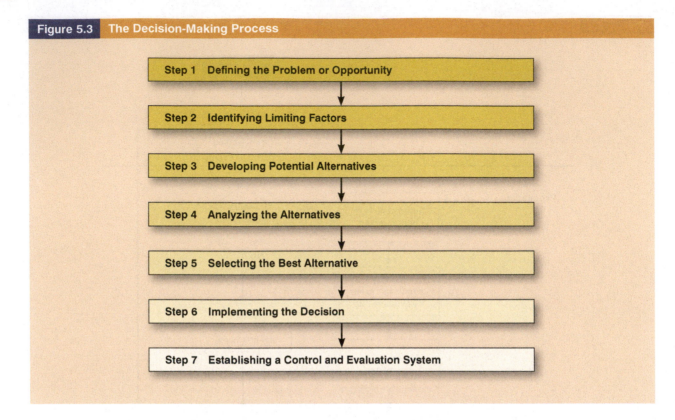

Step 1	Defining the Problem or Opportunity
Step 2	Identifying Limiting Factors
Step 3	Developing Potential Alternatives
Step 4	Analyzing the Alternatives
Step 5	Selecting the Best Alternative
Step 6	Implementing the Decision
Step 7	Establishing a Control and Evaluation System

the work environment. According to management expert Tom Peters, the source of the most relevant and accurate information for a manager is the people in the workplace.[10]

To assist in defining the problem, Charles Kepner and Benjamin Tregoe, who conducted detailed studies of managerial decision making, recommend that managers ask a series of questions using the funnel approach to distinguish between symptoms and problems.[11] Figure 5.4 illustrates how the funnel approach can aid in defining the problem. Initially, a manager notices a problem, such as unmet production quotas. He or she then begins to apply the funnel approach by asking questions to identify the real problem, not just the symptom.

- Are hours worked decreasing? No, absenteeism is normal.
- Is material needed for operations unavailable? No, material is flowing at a normal pace.
- How is employee morale? Are there complaints or concerns? Well, as a matter of fact, there are some rumors of discontent.
- Is it wages? No.
- Is it working conditions? No.
- Is it supervision? Some workers are concerned about the supervision they receive.
- What are their concerns? The supervisor does not answer their questions about technical aspects of the job.

By using the funnel approach, the manager finds out that the supervisor lacks technical skills.

Five Why Analysis

In general, a performance gap exists because the task that was required to transfer a goal to an outcome was either not done or was executed poorly. Analysis includes identifying a business issue, separating it into its component parts and understanding the cause-and-effect relationships among these parts. This is called "Root cause analysis" and can determine why the outcome is not the same as the goal. One way to perform a root-cause analysis is the inductive Five Whys, which originated at the Toyota Motor Corporation.

The idea behind this technique is to ask "Why?" It often takes five "whys" to arrive at the root-cause (underlying reason) of the problem since the answer to the first "why" uncovers another reason and generates another "why." In this way, the symptoms can be separated from the causes of a problem. The process is vastly improved when accomplished by a team.

To diagnose the root causes, the manager conducts a meeting as described below.

1. Assemble a team of knowledgeable people.

2. On a flip chart, white board or smart board, write out a description of what is known about the problem as completely as possible. Come to an agreement on the definition of the problem.

3. Team members ask "Why" the problem as described could occur, and write the answer down underneath the problem description.

4. Repeat steps 3 and 4 until the answer provided solves the problem.

5. The team agrees and attempts a resolution using the answer.

Pascal Dennis, in his book *Lean Production Simplified* (Second Edition, Productivity Press, p. 152) shares "an example which, legend has it, came out of Taichi Ohno's Kamigo Engine plant:"

Problem Statement:

What made 900 units versus a target of 1,200?
Why?
Because the robot stopped
Why?
Because it was overloaded and a fuse blew
Why?
Because the arm wasn't properly lubricated
Why?
Because the lubrication pump wasn't working right
Why?
Because dirt and debris got into the pump shaft
Why?
Because the pump motor was designed without a filter

The root cause of the breakdown would likely be either "inadequate standard"—i.e., we didn't realize the pump motors should have filters to prevent debris from getting into the pump shaft, or "inadequate adherence to standard"—i.e., we had a standard, we just didn't follow it.

➡ **Briefly describe a problem you need to solve. Use Five Why Analysis. Did it help you solve the problem? Why or why not?**

Identifying Limiting Factors

limiting factors
Those constraints that rule out certain alternative solutions; one common limitation is time

Once the problem is defined, the manager needs to identify the limiting factors of the problem. **Limiting factors** are those constraints that rule out certain alternative solutions. One common limitation is time. If a new product has to be on the dealer's shelves in one month, any alternative that takes more than one month will be eliminated. Resources—personnel, money, facilities and equipment, as well as time—are the most common limiting factors that narrow down the range of possible alternatives.

Developing Potential Alternatives

alternatives
Potential solutions to the problem

At this point, the manager should look for, develop and list as many possible **alternatives**—potential solutions to the problem. These alternatives should eliminate, correct or neutralize the problem or maximize the opportunity. Alternative solutions for a manager faced with the problem of trying to maintain scheduled production may be to start an extra work shift, to regularly schedule overtime, to increase the size of the present workforce by hiring employees or to do nothing. Doing nothing about

Figure 5.4	The Funnel Approach to Defining a Problem

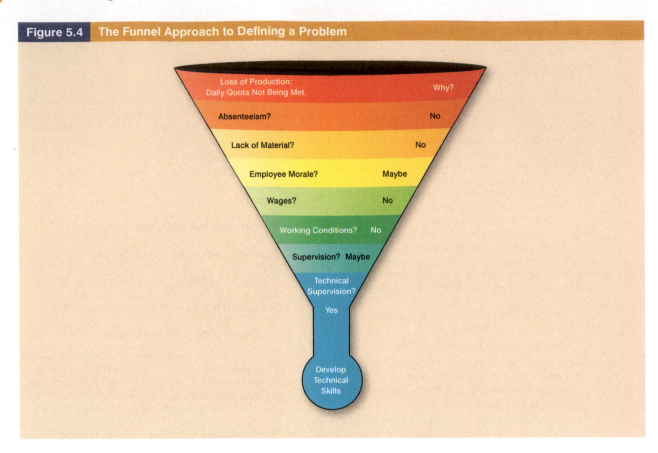

a problem sometimes is the proper alternative, at least until the situation has been thoroughly analyzed. Occasionally, just the passing of time provides a cure. Of course, the more serious or long term the problem, the less likely that is to be the case.

Sources for alternatives include the manager's own experience; other persons whose opinions and judgments the decision maker respects; group opinions, obtained through the use of task forces and committees; and outside sources, including managers in other organizations. (Group decision making will be discussed in detail later in the chapter.)

When building this list of alternatives, a manager should avoid being critical or judgmental about any alternative that arises. Censoring ideas at this stage can needlessly limit the number of alternatives developed.[12] Initially each alternative identified should be a separate solution to the problem or a separate strategy for seizing the opportunity. Alternatives that are simply variations of one another provide less choice in the final analysis. After the initial brainstorming process, variations of the listed ideas will begin to crystallize and combinations will emerge.

When developing alternatives, the goal is to be as creative and wide-ranging as possible. Any decision for which a manager cannot identify more than one alternative is by definition not a decision since more than one choice does not exist. Decision makers must always seek out alternatives to ensure that there are choices to be made, and it is to be hoped that the best choice will result in the best decision.

Analyzing the Alternatives

The purpose of this step is to evaluate the relative merits of each alternative in order to identify the positives and negatives or the advantages and disadvantages of each. To assist in this process the manager should ask two questions:

1 Does the alternative fit within the limiting factors?

2 What are the consequences of using this alternative?

If any alternatives conflict with the limiting factors identified earlier, they must be automatically discarded or a variation must be found—one that does not conflict with those limiting factors. For example, the department has to produce 1,000 motors by the end of the month—an increase of 500 over the normal quota—and this increased quota needs to be accomplished with a maximum of $10,000 of increased expenditures for employee wages. One alternative is to schedule overtime at night and on Saturdays. When the manager evaluates the suggestion, the calculations reveal that this alternative will result in 1,000 additional units produced—but at a cost of $17,000. As a result, this alternative either needs to be rejected or combined with another alternative. Note the fate of Alternatives 1 and 2 in Figure 5.5.

Secondly, the manager needs to identify the consequences of using an alternative. Some alternatives, even though they fall within the guidelines established by the limiting factors, have consequences that make them undesirable. For instance, in order to increase the output of one department, an alternative is to hire more employees; to fund that hiring requires taking money from the operating budgets of other departments. Even though the alternative solves the problem, the political and morale problems caused may require it to be eliminated, as is the case with Alternative 3 in Figure 5.5.

Depending on the type of problem, the manager's analysis of the alternatives can be supported by the application of non-quantitative methods—experience and intuition—or quantitative methods—such as payback analysis, decision trees and simulations. These methods will be discussed in detail later in the chapter.

Figure 5.5	Analyzing Alternatives

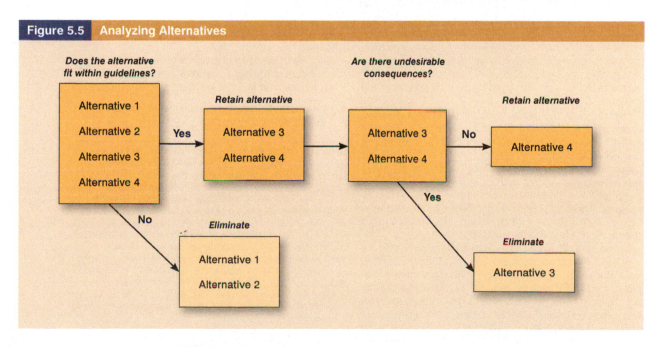

Selecting the Best Alternative

By this step, the most viable alternatives remain, along with their corresponding advantages and disadvantages. Which one(s) should be selected?

The "best" choice or alternative is the one that offers the fewest serious disadvantages and the most advantages. Take care not to solve one problem and create another with your choice. Sometimes the optimal solution is a combination of several of the alternatives. A classic example is the actions taken by Anne Mulcahy when she was named CEO of Xerox in 2001, the company that introduced the copier that transformed office work and later networked printing to "document services." Faced with crippling debt and facing bankruptcy, Mulcahy made some hard decisions. To solve the problem she: (1) raised cash by selling assets; (2) slashed costs by reducing the number of employees; (3) changed inefficient business processes; and (4) re-focused the company on what it did well.

Another excellent example is the topic of this chapter's Global Applications feature. Jochen Zeitz, faced with a company that was almost insolvent, made a series of bold decisions that made PUMA a worldwide creative leader in the sports lifestyle market.

Global Applications

Making the Right Decisions at PUMA

At one point in time, PUMA, a Germany-based company, was one of Europe's also-rans. It was on the brink of insolvency; but when Jochen Zeitz took over in 1993 as chief executive, PUMA's fortunes began to change. Zeitz made a number of critical decisions that had PUMA grabbing sales from the giants.

Initially, Zeitz decided to cut costs and debt. He was convinced that the company had the expertise to become a major player, if it continued to make the right decisions; and PUMA did. It focused on the PUMA brand, combining sports and lifestyle. Most importantly, says Zeitz, the brand was repositioned. "PUMA in the 1980s was a cheap brand. I said let's become premium. Let's bring fashion and style into play" (Davidson). Bjørn Gulden became Chief Executive Officer (CEO) of PUMA in 2013. He repositioned PUMA as the "Fastest Sports Brand in the world" (PUMA Strategy).

In the world of sports, Ricky Fowler has become the face of PUMA; dramatically impacting sales and brand recognition from younger fans across the board; adult golfers and PGA professionals alike. With big wins in 2015, and a Twitter following of almost 1,000,000, he is expected to continue to attract new customers to the PUMA brand. Matt Schalk, PGA director of golf at Colorado National Golf Club, said, "You look at my junior program, which is around 500 kids per summer, and 80% of them are wearing some sort of Rickie Fowler (PUMA) apparel."

CEO Bjørn Gulden's objective is to be fast in reacting to new trends, fast in bringing new innovations to the market, fast in decision-making and fast in solving problems for partners.

▶ **Do you think PUMA will reach this significant milestone?**

Sources: Cameron Morfit, "For Cobra Puma Golf, Rickie Fowler is Driving the Brand," Golf.com, January 29, 2015, *http://www.golf.com/tour-and-news/rickie-fowler-cobra-pumas-golden-child*; Puma's Key Strategic Priorities, March 2016, *http://about.puma.com/en/this-is-puma/strategy*; Karl Lusbec, "Jochen Zeitz to Join PPR, Puma is looking for new CEO," October 18, 2010, *http://karllusbec.wordpress.com/2010/10/18/jochen-zeitz-to-join-ppr-puma-is-looking-for-new-ceo*; Andrew Davidson, "Puma's top cat Jochen Zeitz plays it cool," *The Sunday Times*, February 24, 2008, *http://business.timesonline.co.uk/tol/business/movers_and_shakers/article3422392.ece*; Matt Moore, "Puma Posts 15 Percent Rise in 4Q Profit," ABC News, February 10, 2006; Christopher Rhoads, "Success Stories," *The Wall Street Journal*, September 22, 2003, *http://online.wsj.com/article,SB106382338364356500,00.html*; PUMA Strategy, *http://about.puma.com/en/this-is-puma/strategy*.

Implementing the Decision

Managers are paid to make decisions and to get results from these decisions. A decision that just sits there, hoping someone will put it into effect, may as well never have been made. Everyone involved with carrying out the decision must know what he or she must do, how to do it and why, and when it must be done. Like plans, solutions need effective implementation to yield the desired results. Additionally, a good alternative halfheartedly implemented will often create problems, not solve them. People must know the importance of their roles. Finally, programs, procedures, rules or policies must be thoughtfully put into effect. Figure 5.6 provides some tips on how to translate decisions into actions.

Establishing a Control and Evaluation System

The final step in the decision-making process is to create a control and evaluation system. This system should provide feedback on how well the decision is being implemented, what the positive and negative results are and what adjustments are necessary to get the results that were desired when the solution was chosen. (And point number 6 in Figure 5.6 suggests that the feedback be provided early enough to do something about it.) Often, too, the implementation of a decision produces outcomes that create new problems or opportunities that require new decisions. An evaluation system can help identify those outcomes.

Following these steps gives a manager a greater probability of making successful decisions. Because it provides a step-by-step road map, the manager can move logically

---

Figure 5.6	How to Translate Decisions into Action

1 *Persuade the hostile guns and the foot-draggers.*

From preliminary discussions you know who gave in grudgingly—perhaps after open opposition. Go out of your way to conciliate and persuade.

2 *Determine who needs to be informed and how best to do it.*

Make sure the list absolutely includes people who "need to know." Be sure to let people know the why of the decision. Select the best method—written or verbal—and tune the vocabulary and tone to the reader or listener.

3 *Check for loose ends.*

Double-check to make sure clear assignments have been made and that everyone has the resources to perform the task.

4 *Do a good job of selling the decision.*

Practically none of your decisions will be implemented by you alone. Seek authorization and permission if needed. Provide encouragement to everyone.

5 *Have courage and patience.*

Stand fast when people say, "it can't be done" … "it's too costly" … "it's too soon" … "it's too late."

6 *Arrange for feedback.*

Establish a system that will wave red flags when you are heading into trouble—early enough to do something about it.

Source: Reprinted from Carl Heyel, "From Intent to Implement: How to Translate Decisions into Action," *Management Review* (June 1995), p. 63. © 1995 American Management Association International. Reprinted by permission of American Management Association International, New York. All rights reserved. Permission conveyed through The Copyright Clearance Center.

through decision making and is unlikely to miss an important point. Also, the care taken in identifying and evaluating alternatives helps ensure that the best choice is made. Finally, the creation of a control system helps ensure that the decision is correctly implemented and subsequent outcomes are handled effectively.

To be successful in decision making, the manager must also be aware of the environment in which he or she makes decisions. The following section examines the decision-making environment.

ENVIRONMENTAL INFLUENCES ON DECISION MAKING

Identify the environmental factors that influence decision making

Decision-making, like planning, does not take place in a vacuum. Many factors in the environment affect the process and the decision-maker.

Degree of Certainty

In some situations, the manager has perfect knowledge of what to do and what the consequences of the action will be. In others, the manager has no such knowledge. Decisions are made under the conditions of certainty, risk or uncertainty. As Figure 5.7 illustrates, each condition brings degrees of ambiguity and potential for failure.

In conditions of certainty, the manager has what is known as *perfect knowledge*— he or she knows all the information needed to make the decision.[13] The manager has made this decision before, recognizes the alternatives, and fully understands the consequences of each alternative. In this type of situation, the manager simply chooses the alternative known to get the best results. Ambiguity and fear of failure do not exist. As an example, consider a manager at Verizon who has two new employees and has to provide a desk, chair, and related office equipment for each. Only four companies have been approved to bid on the equipment. The manager needs only to identify the most important factors to him or her and choose the vendor who best supplies these factors. Under conditions of certainty, the manager can rely on a policy or standing plan; so decisions are made routinely. In other words, these can be programmed decisions.

Risk provides a more complex environment. In this situation, the manager knows what the problem is and what the alternatives are but cannot be sure of the consequences of each alternative. Therefore, ambiguity and risk are associated with each alternative. For example, a manager has three candidates for a position. All come from inside the company and have known performance histories, but all three worked in

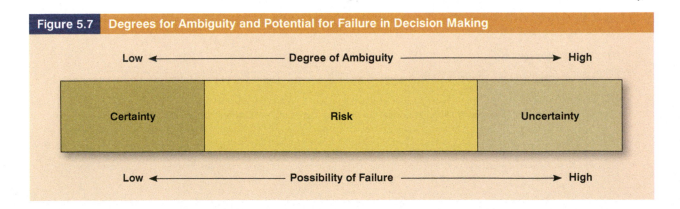

Figure 5.7   Degrees for Ambiguity and Potential for Failure in Decision Making

Low ← —————————— Degree of Ambiguity —————————— → High

| Certainty | Risk | Uncertainty |

Low ← —————————— Possibility of Failure —————————— → High

other jobs, so their performance in the new position is unknown. After extensive interviewing, the manager must make a decision. The dilemma facing the manager is that each candidate has strengths, but none is a perfect fit for the job. The manager has an idea of the probability that they will succeed, but each one has a degree of risk associated with him or her.

Uncertainty is the most difficult condition for a manager. This situation is like being a pioneer. The manager cannot determine the exact outcomes of the alternatives available, either because there are too many variables or too many unknown facts. In addition to the uncertainty associated with the probability of the known alternatives, the manager may not be able to identify all the possible alternatives to be considered.[14] As Figure 5.7 shows, there is high ambiguity and high possibility of failure.

To illustrate this condition, picture a person who has just been promoted into a management position. On the first day an employee reports that a shipment to a highly valued customer has not arrived, and the customer wants the goods—now! The manager can identify some alternatives: send another shipment (but it will take three days) or wait to see if the goods arrive. Unfortunately, the probability of either alternative satisfying the customer is uncertain, and there may be other alternatives the manager has not considered. What can be done? Reliance on experience, judgment and other people's experiences can assist the manager in assessing the value of the alternatives and identifying others.

Imperfect Resources

maximize
Managers want to make the perfect decisions

All managers want to **maximize** their decisions: they want to make the perfect ones. To accomplish this, they need ideal resources—data, information, time, personnel, equipment and supplies. Managers, however, operate in an environment that normally does not provide ideal resources.

satisfice
To make the best decision possible with the time, resources, and information available

Managers in the real world do not always have, for example, the time they need to collect all the information they desire about a problem. They may lack the proper budget to buy printers for every PC or give raises to every employee. Faced with these limits, they choose to do something more realistic: to **satisfice**—that is, to make the best decision possible with the time, resources and information available. If a manager always tries to maximize decisions, the result may be a great deal of time spent gathering information and not making the decision. In addition, managers in organizations typically cannot justify the time and expense of acquiring complete information.

Internal Environment

Decisions cannot solve problems or seize opportunities unless they receive acceptance and support. A manager's decision-making environment is influenced by support (or lack of support) from superiors, subordinates and organizational systems.

Superiors. A major factor in the manager's decision-making environment is his or her boss. Does the manager's superior have confidence in subordinates, want to be informed on progress, and support logical decisions after receiving the information? If so, then the boss can help create a good decision-making environment for the subordinate manager by providing guidance and ongoing feedback.

In contrast, insecure managers may fear the success of their subordinates and may jealously guard the helpful knowledge they possess. Additionally, some superiors are so afraid of being held accountable for failures that they are reluctant to let their subordinates make any decision of consequence. In such an environment, the subordinate manager faces tough choices. He or she can either work over the long run to create a climate of mutual trust, live with the frustration and be ineffective as a decision maker, or leave the environment to find a more acceptable situation.

Subordinates. Subordinates affect a manager's decision-making environment in important ways. Many of the decisions a manager has to make directly affect employees—when they work, who they work with, how they work. Therefore, without subordinates' support, input and understanding of decisions, managers cannot be effective. This situation, in turn, creates a dilemma and thus challenges a manager's leadership ability. When decisions have to be made, what level or degree of involvement should employees have from the range of options shown in Figure 5.8?[15]

Which option should the manager use? Two criteria suggested by Norman Maier influence the choice: the objective quality of the decision needed and the degree to which subordinates must accept the decision for it to succeed.[16] A decision has a high degree of objective quality if it is made in a logical, rational, step-by-step approach. In other words, a decision made by following the formal decision-making process illustrated in Figure 5.3 meets the objective-quality criteria.

A decision has a high degree of acceptance if it has been made with the input of those affected by it. Decisions whose success requires the understanding and support of those affected by them are the kinds of decisions that must meet the acceptance criteria. Examples include decisions about changing procedures, altering the work environment or scheduling vacations.

How can a manager know which factors are important in a given decision, especially when both acceptance and quality criteria can apply to the same decision? Victor Vroom and Phillip Yetton have provided managers with a series of questions that guide the manager to the appropriate option.[17] The model is the **Vroom and Yetton decision tree** shown in Figure 5.9. As each question is asked and answered, the manager learns

Vroom and Yetton decision tree
A series of questions that guide the manager to the appropriate option

---

Figure 5.8	**Five Levels of Subordinate Involvement**

1 The manager makes the decision himself or herself, using information available to him or her at that time. Employees provide no input or assistance.

2 The manager obtains the necessary information from subordinates, and then makes the decision. When obtaining information from them, the manager may or may not tell the subordinates what the problem is. The role played by the subordinates is clearly one of providing the necessary information to the manager, rather than generating or evaluating alternative solutions.

3 The manager shares the situation with relevant subordinates individually, getting their ideas and suggestions without bringing them together as a group. Then the manager makes the decision, which may or may not reflect the subordinates' influence.

4 The manager shares the situation with the subordinates as a group; collectively obtains their ideas and suggestions. Then the manager makes the decision, which may or may not reflect the subordinates' influence.

5 The manager shares the situation with the subordinates as a group. Together they generate and evaluate alternatives and attempt to reach agreement (consensus) on a solution. The manager's role is much like that of chairperson. He or she does not try to influence the group to adopt a particular solution and the manager is willing to accept and implement any solution that has the support of the entire group.

Source: Reprinted from *Organizational Dynamics* (Spring 1973), Victor H. Vroom, "A New Look at Managerial Decision Making," p. 67. Copyright 1973 with permission from Elsevier Science.

more about the nature of the decision. When the manager reaches the circled number at the end of each series of questions, the most effective decision-making method is identified. Those numbers correspond to the options identifying the levels of subordinate involvement in Figure 5.8.

As an example, suppose Kimberly Holland, Barnes & Noble's store manager in Plano, Texas, is developing work schedules. Holland begins the process by asking these questions:

A	Is there a quality requirement that might make one solution more rational than another? Since the answer is no; Holland moves to D.
D	Is acceptance of the decision by subordinates critical to effective implementation? The answer is yes, the subordinates are very concerned; Holland now moves to E.
E	If Holland makes the decision alone, will subordinates be likely to accept it? Since the answer is no, Holland should use option 5 (from Figure 5.8).

Thus, Holland would share the problem with the subordinates as a group. Together they would generate and evaluate alternatives and attempt to reach agreement (consensus) on a solution. Holland should not try to influence the group to adopt her solution, and she must be willing to accept and implement any solution that has the support of the entire group, as long as it fits within Barnes & Noble's policies. In this situation, as in most situations in a work environment, working with and cultivating the support of employees for decisions is critical to a manager. Even the highest-quality decisions will not be effectively implemented if employees do not support them.

Organizational Systems. The organizational system is the final element of the internal environment that affects decision making. Every organization has policies, procedures, programs, and rules that serve as boundaries for a manager's decision making. Sometimes these factors may be obsolete or may cause delays—red tape. If they pose major barriers, it may be wise for a manager to delay a decision and try instead to modify the system.

External Environment

As we noted in Chapter 3 and discussed in Chapter 4, the external environment strongly influences a manager's actions, especially in decision making. Customers, competitors, government agencies and society in general can and do influence decisions. Customers, as has been consistently noted, are a driving force in decisions. The decisions for new products, improved service, an enhanced user experience and longer and more accessible hours of operations are all made as companies respond to meet or exceed customer expectations. Competitors force companies to adjust—Coca-Cola and Pepsi; Domino's, Pizza Hut and Little Caesars; McDonald's, Burger King and Wendy's. The decisions to improve the quality of products and services have been made in response to customer expectations.

In addition, government actions can alter or even reverse the decisions companies make—as Jack Welch, former CEO of GE found out. Welch had postponed his retirement to complete the merger agreement between GE and Honeywell International. When the proposed transaction drew the attention of the European Union, pressure was applied to derail the decision.

Figure 5.9   Applying the Vroom and Yetton Decision Tree for Choosing a Decision-Making Style

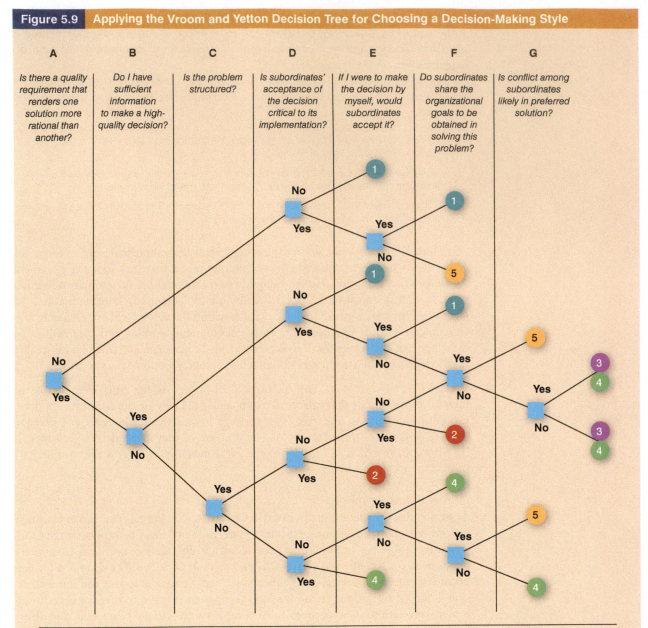

A
Is there a quality requirement that renders one solution more rational than another?

B
Do I have sufficient information to make a high-quality decision?

C
Is the problem structured?

D
Is subordinates' acceptance of the decision critical to its implementation?

E
If I were to make the decision by myself, would subordinates accept it?

F
Do subordinates share the organizational goals to be obtained in solving this problem?

G
Is conflict among subordinates likely in preferred solution?

Source: Adapted and reprinted from *Leadership and Decision-Making* by Victor H. Vroom and Philip W. Yetton, by permission of the University of Pittsburgh Press. © 1973 by University of Pittsburgh Press.

Describe the personal attributes of a manager that influence decision making

INFLUENCE OF MANAGERIAL STYLE ON DECISION MAKING

In addition to the environment in which decisions take place, other factors influence managerial decision making. These are the manager's personal attributes: his or her decision-making approach, ability to set priorities, timing of decisions, tunnel vision, previous commitments and degree of creativity.

Personal Decision-Making Approaches

Not all managers approach decisions the same way. Many have a bias for one of the following three approaches.

Rational/Logical Decision Model This step-by-step approach, illustrated in Figure 5.3, is the one recommended in this chapter. This process focuses on facts and logic and minimizes intuitive judgments. The manager using this method tries to thoroughly examine a situation or problem in an orderly fashion. The manager relies on the decision-making steps and on decision tools such as payback analysis, decision trees and research, which will be discussed later in the chapter.

Intuitive Decision Model Some managers prefer to avoid statistical analysis and logical processes in making a decision. These gut decision-makers rely on their feelings and hunches about the situation. Although it is hard to eliminate all elements of intuition from decision making, the manager who relies on intuition alone for long-range decision making could be courting disaster. The best decisions are often the result of a blend of the decision-maker's intuition (based on experience and hindsight) and the rational step-by-step approach.

Predisposed Decision Model A manager who decides on a solution and then gathers the information to support the decision illustrates this approach. A manager with this tendency is likely to ignore critical information. Such a manager may face the same decision again later.[18]

Another related trait is the tendency of some managers to influence the final solution by favoring specific alternatives. In this way, the manager can distort the value of the preselected alternative.

The critical element is for the manager to know what his or her decision-making tendencies are and to move toward the rational model. A serious problem can result if a manager believes he or she is using one approach but in reality is using a different model.

Ability to Set Priorities

The old saying, "When it rains it pours," seems to be true about decisions. They have a tendency to be called for continuously, possibly in bunches. Thus, a factor that can influence a manager's success at decision making is the ability to establish priorities. Each manager may have a different set of criteria for prioritizing. Some managers may give priority to the decision having the greatest impact on the organization's goals. Others may assign priorities in terms of what their bosses think is important. A third group of managers may make decisions based on likes and dislikes. No matter what criteria are used, managers need to assign priorities and to know why those were the priorities assigned.

For some managers the ability to set priorities may be limited by procrastination—or putting off—difficult decisions. For a procrastinator, decisions don't have a priority; they are made when the procrastinator gets around to them. Avoiding the difficult decisions creates their own priority system— easy decisions are first and difficult decisions are second. Such a practice is dangerous. Tough decisions often cannot be delayed.

Timing of Decisions

After a decision is made, it must be translated into action. Good timing plays an important part in successfully implementing a decision, and improper timing can harm the best decision. A manager should be sensitive to the influence of timing to increase the possibility of success. One example of the importance of timing is provided by American Airlines' decision to purchase Trans World Airlines "five months before the terrorist attacks of September 11, 2001, which ravaged travel demand and helped trigger five straight years of losses."[19]

Starbucks Coffee Company provides another example. Starbucks decided to grow by adding more stores nationally, by entering new markets and by expanding abroad. The reason was timing. In the mid1990s Starbucks' success brought in a host of new competitors each with an eye on Starbucks. In turn, Starbucks wanted to beat the competitors to the punch.[20] Today Starbucks has more than 21,000 locations in over 65 countries.[21]

Tunnel Vision

A manager who approaches a problem with an extremely narrow perspective will likely rely on a limited choice of alternatives. This narrow view, or **tunnel vision**, can result from bias or limited experience. The "glass ceiling" that continues to prevent women from rising in corporate management as often as men might result from the tunnel vision of male managers.[22] In other instances, managers can't "see" another way— another alternative—because they have little or no familiarity with a situation.

tunnel vision
Having a narrow viewpoint

Commitment to Previous Decisions

Managers must frequently make decisions that relate to previous decisions. Consider the CEO who has committed substantial financial resources to the development of a product that could revolutionize the marketplace. He or she might be strongly influenced to commit additional resources, even if the decision seems not to be working. It is difficult to undo a decision, especially with reputations and personal pride at stake. In such instances the implementation of a control mechanism, with benchmarks for follow-up actions, may be helpful.

Creativity

Being innovative and able to see new ways of doing things aid the manager's decision making. Most people possess creativity, but they don't always apply it, often because of situational factors. For example, a shift manager at McDonald's has specific policies, procedures and systems that dictate how and when tasks will be completed. In addition, this same manager works in an environment that can best be described as chaotic during peak times. Neither of the characteristics of the environment provides opportunity for reflection and innovation.

To counter the lack of innovation and creativity, organizations like pioneer 3M, and companies as diverse as Google, Tesla and Panera Bread promote and reward

outside-the-box thinking
To adopt a new perspective and see it work; not get caught up in the old ways

outside-the-box thinking. Instead of approaching a problem at 3M with preconceived ideas and limitations, managers give employees the freedom to take risks and try new ideas. "What we need to do as managers is not get caught up in the old ways, rather we need to tap our corporate brainpower."[23]

Discuss the value of group decision making, and identify three techniques of group decision making

GROUP DECISION MAKING

Earlier in the chapter we noted how subordinates influence a manager's decision-making process. Workers who participate in making decisions are likely to support them. As more organizations and managers accept that real participation in decision making produces ownership of the job and better-quality products, the concept of group decision making will become an increasingly important part of the work environment. Many management experts feel that such involvement is not a maybe, but a must. Front-line employees must become partners with the manager in the decision-making process.[24] Such partnerships are a primary goal of team management, the topic of Chapter 14. But for now, the next section will examine three proven techniques for involving groups in the decision-making process: brainstorming, the nominal group technique and the Delphi technique.

Brainstorming

brainstorming
A group effort at generating ideas and alternatives that can help a manager solve a problem or seize an opportunity

Brainstorming is a group effort at generating ideas and alternatives that can help a manager solve a problem or seize an opportunity.[25] It helps overcome tunnel vision by encouraging any and all ideas while withholding criticism. The following elements are part of a successful brainstorming session:

- A half dozen to a dozen people are gathered in a comfortable setting for a specified time—free from outside interruptions.

- Participants are given the problem (barriers to advancement in the company) or opportunity (new products or new markets) and told that no idea or suggestion is too ridiculous to be voiced.

- The facilitator encourages the free flow of ideas until all opinions have been presented.

- A person acting as the designated scribe records the ideas on a chalkboard or flipchart. After the session, the ideas are sorted and examined in more detail by the manager or another group.

An example of using brainstorming to generate problem-solving ideas can be seen at Deloitte, the accounting firm. Top management discovered a sudden and rapid decrease in the number of women who were seeking employment in other companies. Women were leaving because there were barriers to career advancement. After a series of brainstorming sessions, the company developed a separate career program for women. In addition, it created a companywide task force to recommend policies to support the advancement of women.[26] The Women's Initiative (WIN) helped give Deloitte the intellectual capital to meet aggressive growth targets over the years.

Brainstorming works well when the problem is straightforward and well defined and the atmosphere is supportive of a solution; but it is only a process for generating ideas. The next two techniques offer ways to arrive at a solution.

Nominal Group Technique

Group discussion sessions can be ineffective when only a few people talk and dominate the discussion. The **nominal group technique** eliminates this problem by creating a structure to provide for equal—but independent—participation by all members.[27] As shown in Figure 5.10, the process involves seven steps:

nominal group technique
Creating a structure to provide for equal—but independent—participation by all members

1 *Problem definition.* When the nominal group is assembled, the group leader defines the problem. No discussion is permitted, although questions to clarify the problem may be asked.

2 *Development of ideas.* Each participant writes down his or her ideas about the problem. Once again, there is no discussion.

3 *Round-robin presentation.* Each member of the group presents his or her ideas to the group. The group leader records the ideas on a flipchart or blackboard. The process continues without discussion until all ideas are recorded.

4 *Clarification of ideas.* The group conducts an open discussion of the ideas with members providing explanations when needed.

5 *Initial voting.* In a secret ballot, each member independently ranks what he or she thinks are the best solutions. The solutions with the lowest average ranking are eliminated.

6 *Evaluation of revised list.* The group members question each other on the remaining solutions.

7 *Final voting.* In another secret ballot, all the ideas are ranked. The idea receiving the highest vote total is adopted.

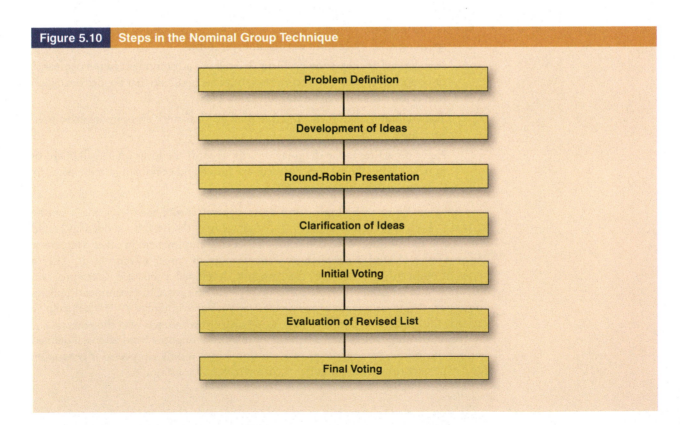

Figure 5.10   Steps in the Nominal Group Technique

In addition to providing a structure for equal participation, the nominal group technique encourages individual creativity. The environment created by the structure provides the opportunity to have an idea developed and presented without interference. The negative associated with this process is that it is time-consuming.

Delphi Technique

Similar to the nominal group technique is the **Delphi technique**. It, too, provides a structure, leads to consensus and emphasizes equal participation—but the Delphi participants never meet. Rather, the decision making is conducted by a group leader through the use of written questionnaires. The process works as follows:

1 The problem is stated to a group of experts through a questionnaire. Each person is asked to provide solutions. The experts do not interact.

2 Each participant completes the questionnaire and returns it.

3 A summary of opinions is developed from the answers received. The summary is distributed to the experts along with a second questionnaire.

4 The experts complete the second questionnaire. In this stage, participants have the benefit of other people's opinions and can change their suggestions to reflect this.

5 The process continues until the experts reach consensus.

Although it is expensive and time-consuming, the Delphi technique works well. It also provides for a thorough, unrushed analysis of information, a factor that aided Sheraton in solving a problem—lower sales caused by a sales force that wasn't viewed as helpful or as knowledgeable as its competitors. To address the problem, Sheraton used its Meetings Advisory Board. By following the Delphi process, the board's experts identified that the major difference between Sheraton and its competitors was that Sheraton was a generalist, whereas the competitors were specialists. The competitors broke business down according to corporate transient, corporate group and association group travel, each of which has different needs. The solution dealt with refining general categories into specific market segments. Sales increased by 31 percent.[28]

Advantages and Disadvantages of Group Decision Making

Regardless of what group techniques a manager chooses to use for decision making, the manager should be aware of the advantages and disadvantages.

Advantages. Groups bring a broader perspective to the decision-making process. The rich Diversity and Inclusion found in today's organizations broadens the views on any topic. The differences in cultures, ethnicity, national origin, gender and age found within provide valuable perspectives in defining a problem and in developing alternatives (a factor emphasized in this chapter's Valuing Diversity and Inclusion feature). When people participate in decision making they are more likely to be satisfied with the decision and to support it, thus facilitating its implementation. Group decision making provides the opportunity for discussion to help answer questions and reduce uncertainty for decision-makers who may not be willing to take risks alone.

Disadvantages Besides the fact that group decision making is time-consuming—is the possibility that the decision reached will be a compromise rather than the optimal outcome. At times individuals can become guilty of **groupthink**. The members become so committed to the group that they become reluctant to disagree with other members. Additionally, groups have difficulty in performing certain tasks. Specifically,

Not Old ... Wise

Joe Borchard will be the first to admit he hasn't always done the right thing when it comes to managing older workers. Three people out of his staff of four are older than him. In many cases they are old enough to be his parents. Admittedly, Borchard made plenty of mistakes—assuming that everyone thought as he did.

After several years as a supervisor, Borchard has a different perspective. As an administrator in the Patterson, New Jersey, school system, Borchard values the Diversity and Inclusion. Individuals look at things differently, regardless of age, culture or race. Older workers are particularly valuable in the operation. They can sometimes point out landmines that are obvious to them from their many years on the job. In full agreement, Borchard knows that older workers have good ideas and may know more. He adds, "You can't put a price tag on experience and being able to draw from that experience. It only helps me out. I'm comfortable in the position that I'm in and confident enough to do the job, and not intimidated to say where I need help."

Roxanne Medina, technology teacher, reports to the much younger Borchard. Medina said she quickly adjusted. "I'm normally a take charge kind of person. But it doesn't drive me crazy not being the boss because I'm not working with an egomaniac." And she's found that, with age, comes wisdom. "If we disagree on something, I don't make an emotional investment in having to be right, or feel the need to say, 'I told you so.' I think that comes with maturity."

➡ **Many mature workers say they'd had problems with their young bosses. How can young managers get along with older workers?**

Source: Barbara Thau. "As more older workers and younger bosses are thrown together, the old workplace order is upended." *NY Daily News.com.* November 8, 2010. *http://www.nydailynews.com/money/2010/11/08/2010-11-08_as_more_older_workers_and_younger_bosses_are_thrown_together_the_old_workplace_o.html#ixzz15CgNdQCg.*

groups struggle when assigned to draft policies and procedures; they do much better at editing or commenting on documents. Also, most groups have difficulty in taking the initiative, instead they tend to react rather than initiate action. A final disadvantage is that in group decision making, no one person has responsibility for the decision.[29]

QUANTITATIVE DECISION-MAKING TECHNIQUES

A manager has several quantitative tools available to help improve the overall quality of decisions. Depending on the type of problem, the application of decision trees, payback analysis and simulations provide several choices.

Decision Trees

Earlier in the chapter, Barnes & Noble store manager Kimberly Holland used a version of a decision tree (Figure 5.9) to help her decide to what degree her employees needed to be involved in developing a new work schedule. Kimberly chose this tool because a **decision tree** shows a complete picture of a potential decision. It allows a manager to graph alternative decision paths, observe the outcomes of the decisions and see how the decisions relate to future events.

To illustrate the value and flexibility of this tool, a decision tree has been developed to help Lisa, a Marketing Manager for Pizza Hut. She must decide whether to spend money either test-marketing in a new market or improving the company's marketing performance in an existing market—the kind of situation that McDonald's, Taco Bell and TGI Friday's face constantly. If the venture into the new market succeeds, Pizza Hut will have a competitive edge. If it fails, competitors (Little Caesars, Domino's) may enter the market and gain so much momentum that Pizza Hut may lose its over-

Explain three quantitative techniques for decision making, and describe the situations in which each is appropriate

decision tree
A graphical representation of the actions a manager can take and how these actions relate to other events

all position. The danger stems from the potential lack of success in the new market and the vulnerability created in the old market by diverting funds and attention away from it.

Lisa's decision tree comprises branches from decision points (squares) and chance or competitive moves (circles). In Figure 5.11, the decision path starts with Lisa's initial decision: to test-market or not to test-market. If the outcome of the decision (shown to the right of the decision point) is to authorize the project, point B is the second point for a decision. At point B the test-market has been successful. Then Lisa must decide between entering the market with a full-scale advertising program or waiting until a later date. With each alternative she will face competitive actions by Little Caesars and Domino's.

Figure 5.11   Decision Tree with Chains of Activities and Events

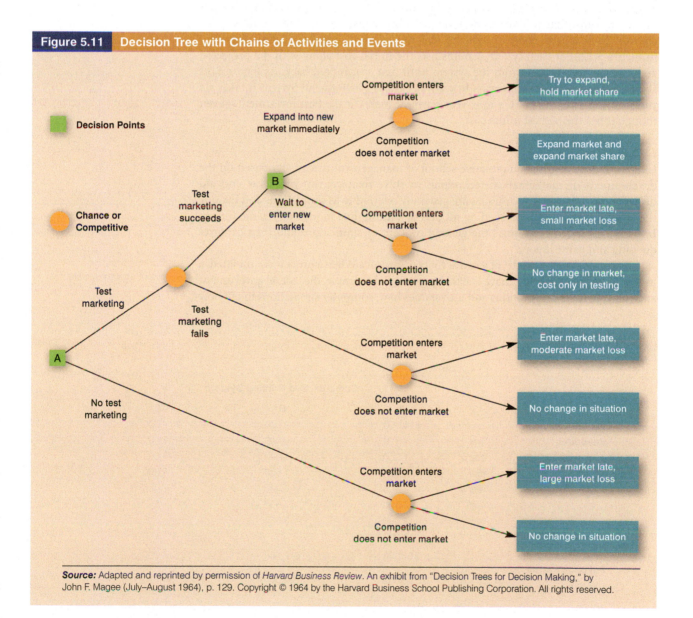

Decision trees require a manager to include only important decisions and events or results—that is, ones having consequences that need to be compared. Note that Figure 5.11 also projects an outcome if Lisa chooses not to begin test-marketing at all.

Payback Analysis

"Out of these three models, which one should I buy? They all have different prices and features. How do you compare apples and oranges?" Sometimes managers face a dilemma in making capital-purchasing decisions. To evaluate alternatives, an excellent strategy is **payback analysis**, a technique that ranks alternatives according to how long each takes to pay back its initial cost. The strategy involves choosing the alternative that has the quickest return.

payback analysis
A technique that ranks alternatives according to how long each takes to pay back its initial cost

Quick Copy owner Tim Collins plans to purchase a computerized printing system. Three suppliers have given him prices for three different systems. Each system has unique features that will affect the revenue to be earned. Which one should Collins choose? To be able to compare systems, Collins prepares a payback analysis as shown in Figure 5.12. For each system, Collins lists the initial cost along with the projected annual revenues derived from the system until that cost is paid back. As Figure 5.12 shows, System A takes seven years to recover Collins's investment; System B takes six years. In this case System C's four-year payback makes it the best investment—even though it has the highest initial cost.

Simulations

Chapter 2 described the quantitative school of management theory. It focused on the development of mathematical techniques to solve management problems and aid decision making. These techniques are generally referred to as simulations and include the specific applications of queuing models or waiting-line models and game theory. Initially this section examines the general concept of simulations and then explores queuing and game theory.

A **simulation** is a model of a real activity or process. When a process is simulated, a model is created that will behave like that process. For example, the federal government and many private corporations and universities have computer simulations to tell how

simulation
A model of a real activity or process

Figure 5.12	An Example of a Payback Analysis

		Computerized Printing System		
		A	**B**	**C**
Initial Cost		$14,000	$12,000	$17,000
Revenues	Year 1	0	500	2,000
	Year 2	1,000	1,000	3,000
	Year 3	1,500	1,500	5,000
	Year 4	2,000	2,500	7,000
	Year 5	2,500	3,000	
	Year 6	3,000	3,500	
	Year 7	4,000		
Payback Period		$\dfrac{\$14,000}{\$2,000} = 7.0$	$\dfrac{\$12,000}{\$2,000} = 6.0$	$\dfrac{\$17,000}{\$4,250} = 4.0$

the economy might respond when various changes are introduced into it. Data on a proposed tax cut or increases in the interest rates can be fed into a computer; what will emerge is a view of the areas of the economy that will be affected and how they will change.

Models may be physical or abstract. The computer model just mentioned is an example of an abstract model, as are a designer's drawings or mathematical or chemical equations. Most of us are more familiar with physical models, because they are tangible and three-dimensional. Manufacturers' prototypes (one-of-a-kind, hand-made models), architectural models of finished structures or beta variations of driver-less cars are just a few examples. As you will soon see when queuing and game theory are discussed, a simulation or model is used in decision making because it allows managers to:

- See the results much more quickly than would be the case if actual changes were made in the real world.

- Anticipate competitive responses to strategy decisions.

- Make decisions under a wide variety of changing conditions.

- Avoid the interruptions of normal business operations that real-life experimentation can cause.

- Avoid the time loss and expense associated with experimenting with actual company assets.

- Avoid annoying the customers and taking facilities out of service while training or experimentation is being conducted.

queuing models or waiting-line models
Models that help managers decide what length of waiting line or queue would be optimal

If you have ever stood in line at a restaurant, movie theater, grocery store or discount store, you will appreciate the value of **queuing models** or **waiting-line models**. These help managers decide what length of waiting line or queue would be optimal. At Walmart, managers have a continuing concern about the length of the checkout line at the cash register and the subsequent time customers must wait in that line. Customers forced to wait too long might take their business to Target. Management must weigh the cost of opening other checkout areas to provide faster service against the risk of losing customers. They must decide what balance between customer dissatisfaction and operating costs is the best.

To help achieve the proper balance, managers can create a model simulating the bottlenecks that form in checkout lines. The neighborhood supermarket opens additional checkout counters when two to three customers are in line. Most movie theaters have created a ticket window where tickets purchased online hours before a show can be picked up.

just-in-time inventory
Delivery of raw materials or other kinds of normal inventories to correspond to production schedules, leading to the elimination of the need to warehouse items

Queues also form in manufacturing, as goods are funneled through a production run. To help solve the problem, companies have devised the **just-in-time inventory** approach. At Texas Instruments, a product is not produced unless the customer has ordered it. Parts used in manufacturing are delivered several times each day, and the goods are sent immediately to where they are needed in the production line. Machinery and people are close together, so that the obstacles that hinder the flow of value are eliminated. Activities are arranged to maximize value and minimize waste. This just-in-time (JIT) delivery of raw materials or other kinds of normal inventories to correspond to production schedules has led to the elimination of the need to warehouse items.

Game theory attempts to predict how people or organizations will behave in competitive situations. It allows managers to devise strategies to counter the behavior of competitors. Managers apply game theory in situations in which organizations compete against one another in regard to price, product development, advertising and distribution systems. If managers at Procter & Gamble were able to predict with a degree of accuracy whether and within what time frame Unilever would initiate a price decrease, the managers at Procter & Gamble could decide whether or not to decrease their own prices.

The use of game theory has been exploding in the last few years in corporate takeovers, negotiations and competitive bidding. Before moving to acquire Medco, a mail-order distributor of low-priced generic drugs, drug maker Merck hired a game theorist to study the impact of health reform on Merck's drug prices—both with and without Medco. In another situation General Reinsurance, worried that it was being used to extract a higher price from a rival, was advised by a game theorist to change the rules—that is, refuse to participate unless there was only a single round of bids. Then General Reinsurance was advised to make unconditional bids that forced the seller to make quick responses. It also gave its rival, General Electric, little time to come up with counteroffers. The rules gave an equal chance to the smaller bidder, and General Reinsurance won the contest in a quick, one-week decision.[30]

CREATING AN ENVIRONMENT FOR EFFECTIVE DECISION MAKING

8 Determine strategies a manager can use to create a more effective decision-making environment

Because managers in today's organizations face complex, challenging and stressful decision-making demands, it is critical that they create an effective decision-making environment for themselves. The following hints can help them do so:[31]

1 *Provide time for decisions to be made.* Don't be pushed—or push others—into making a decision too rapidly. If necessary, negotiate for more time to make a quality decision.

2 *Have self-confidence.* Courage and self-confidence are required for a manager to make the risk-laden decisions called for in today's rapidly changing business environment.

3 *Encourage others to make decisions.* Trust subordinates and allow them the freedom to act.

4 *Learn from past decisions.* The confidence of others is gained by not making the same mistake. Study decisions to see why they worked—and why they didn't.

5 *Recognize the difference in decision-making situations.* All decisions do not have the same degree of risk or priority, nor should all decisions be approached the same way.

6 *Recognize the importance of quality information.* Assume that quality information is available and insist that subordinates support their decisions with data.

7 *Make the tough decisions.* Don't procrastinate or avoid dealing with decisions that could be unpopular. Once the decision is made—whether yes or no—provide an explanation to everyone.

8 *Know when to hold off.* Recognize that sometimes the best decision is no decision; it may be necessary for events to play themselves out or for more information to be gathered.

9 *Be ready to try things.* Today's excellent companies are those that act—that try things. Rather than debating a new product idea, they test-market it. Managers who change the status quo, even on a small scale, can learn more about their market or workforce by watching the effects of those changes than can those who simply observe the status quo.

10 *Be ready to ask for help.* Everyone needs help at some time or another; it isn't a sign of weakness to ask for assistance. In fact, knowing when to ask for help is a sign of wisdom.

Review What You've Learned

Chapter Summary

1 Recognize that decision making is performed at all management levels.

Decision making is a part of all managers' jobs. At all levels of the organization, managers are engaged in decision making. Top managers make decisions dealing with the mission of the organization and strategies for achieving it. Middle-level managers focus their decision making on implementing the strategies, as well as budgeting and allocating resources. First-level managers deal with repetitive day-to-day operations.

2 Distinguish between formal and informal approaches to decision making.

Not all decision making situations are identical. The nature of the decision often dictates what approach to take. Complex problems or situations require the use of a formal decision-making process. Less complicated problems or those that a manager has had a great deal of experience in solving can be handled less formally by following habit or relying on past situations.

3 List the steps in the decision-making process.

There are seven steps in the formal decision-making process: (1) defining the problem or opportunity; (2) identifying limiting factors; (3) developing potential alternatives; (4) analyzing the alternatives; (5) selecting the best alternative; (6) implementing the decision; and (7) establishing a control and evaluation system.

4 Identify environmental factors that influence decision making.

Decision making is influenced by the following environmental factors:

- *Degree of certainty.* Managers make decisions under three conditions of knowledge and ambiguity—certainty, risk and uncertainty.

- *Imperfect resources.* Managers do not make decisions with ideal resources—information, time, personnel, equipment and supplies.

- *Internal environment.* A manager's decision is influenced by superiors, subordinates and organizational systems.

- *External environment.* Customers, competitors, government agencies and society in general are forces that can and do influence decisions.

5 **Describe the personal attributes of a manager that influence decision making.**

The personal attributes of a manager that influence decision making are:

- *Personal decision-making approaches.* Managers may prefer to use the rational/logical decision model, the non-rational/intuitive model, or the predisposed decision model.

- *Ability to set priorities.* Each manager may have a different set of criteria for prioritizing—greatest impact on organizational goals, what the boss wants, likes or dislikes.

- *Timing of decisions.* Timing plays an important part in successfully implementing a decision, and improper timing can harm the best decision.

- *Tunnel vision.* A manager who approaches a problem with an extremely narrow viewpoint will develop a limited choice of alternatives. This tunnel vision may be caused by bias or limited experience.

- *Commitment to previous decisions.* Managers must frequently make decisions that relate to previous decisions. In such situations the manager may be strongly influenced to commit additional resources even if the decision seems not to be working.

- *Creativity.* Although most people possess creativity, they don't always apply it.

6 **Discuss the value of group decision making, and identify three techniques of group decision making.**

Groups bring a broader perspective to the decision-making process. In addition, people who participate in decision making are more likely to be satisfied with it and support it, thus facilitating implementation. Group decision making provides the opportunity for discussion, which helps answer questions and reduces uncertainty for decision makers who may not be willing to take risks alone. Group decision-making techniques include brainstorming, the nominal group technique and the Delphi technique.

7 **Explain three quantitative techniques for decision making, and describe the situations in which each is appropriate.**

- A *decision tree* shows a complete picture of a potential decision. It allows a manager to graph alternative decision paths, observe the outcomes of the decision, and see how the decision relates to future events. Decision trees help the manager think carefully through situations.

- *Payback analysis* can be used in making capital purchasing decisions. It helps the manager rank each alternative according to how long each takes to pay back its initial cost.

- *Simulations* develop models of a real activity. They allow managers to see results much more quickly than would be the case if actual changes were made in the real world. Types of situations include queuing models or waiting-line models, used to help managers decide what length of waiting line is optimal. A second type of simulation, game theory, attempts to predict how people or organizations will behave in competitive situations. It then allows managers to devise strategies to counter the behavior of competitors.

8 **Determine strategies a manager can use to create a more effective decision-making environment.**

To create a more effective learning environment a manager can do the following:

- Provide time for decisions to be made.

- Have confidence.

- Encourage others to make decisions.

- Learn from past decisions.

- Recognize the difference in decision-making situations.

- Recognize the importance of quality information.

- Make the tough decisions.

- Know when to hold off.

- Be ready to try things.

- Be willing to ask for help.

KEY TERMS

REVIEW QUESTIONS

1. For each managerial level, provide examples of the kinds of decisions that managers make at that level.

2. What factors influence whether a manager should use a formal or informal approach to decision making?

3. Identify each step in the decision-making process, and describe briefly what should happen in each step.

4. What four factors in the decision-making environment influence the decision-making process and the decision-maker?

5. What are the three personal decision-making approaches a manager may use? What are the characteristics of each?

6. What are three group decision-making techniques? What is the value of each?

7. Under what circumstances would you use payback analysis? What purpose does payback analysis serve?

8. What are three strategies a manager can use to create a more effective decision-making environment?

DISCUSSION QUESTIONS FOR CRITICAL THINKING

1. What example can you provide to demonstrate the application of the seven-step decision-making process? Take a problem or opportunity you have had and apply the seven-step process.

2. Provide evidence that shows which personal decision-making approach or approaches you use.

3. How do you set priorities for making decisions? What rationale can you give to support your priority setting?

4. What specific applications can you give where organizations have applied queuing models? What examples can you give of companies that need to apply queuing models?

Social Media Management Exercises

1. How safe are you online? Take the security quiz and test your knowledge. How can you make your Internet experience safer, more secure and more private? *https://www.maricopa.gov/technology/pdf/stc_online_safety_quiz.pdf*

2. Facebook began with a closed, friends-only model, and as a result, most college students didn't worry about their privacy on Facebook. Today, Facebook has moved to a more open network, resetting members' default privacy settings. Many users do not realize that Facebook offers privacy controls and security features. But, members must take extra steps to protect personal information. Be proactive and go through all privacy settings. Read Facebook's Privacy Policy and Privacy Guide. Which extra steps will you implement so that not everyone can see everything that you post? *http://www.facebook.com/policy.php* *http://www.facebook.com/privacy/explanation.php*

3. Even if you take precautions online, it's possible your information will be publicly disseminated. For example, friends with access to your site can forward the information to others. Comment on the following statement. "Nothing that you put online is private . . . regardless of any privacy setting."

Experiential Learning

Apple —Failing and Succeeding

Apple and Microsoft were founded within a year of each other. Apple was a pioneer in the personal computer industry. Its Macintosh was the first successful home computer with a graphical interface. In contrast to Microsoft's decision to license its operating system, leadership at Apple decided not to license Macintosh technology. Bill Gates sent a secret memo, dated June 25, 1985, to Apple in which he recommended that Apple license its software to other computer companies.

> Apple's lack of leadership, however, left the decision on whether to license, ultimately, up to the engineers. Not surprisingly, the engineers, led by the enigmatic Jean-Louis Gassée, proved far more interested in hoarding a technology they created than in establishing a standard the rest of the industry could follow (Carlton).

Businesses wanted to save money and preferred Microsoft's Windows software, which could be run on several different manufacturers' machines. According to W3C, which monitors online activity, Microsoft's share of the operating system market, as measured by online activity, is over 90 percent. Apple's share is less than 9 percent. However, "According to NPD, . . . nine out of 10 dollars spent on computers costing $1,000 or more went to Apple" (Wilcox). Apple has total control over its products and chooses not to compete on low price.

The largest commercial success for Apple has been the iPhone, a smartphone. The iPhone has changed the behaviors of its users. People use their smartphones as computers, cameras, global positioning systems (GPS), alarms, to tell time, to make calculations, and to stay in touch. Today, Apple dominates the smartphone market and is one of the world's most valuable companies..

Questions

1. If possible, visit an Apple retail store. Everything in the store represents what it is like to own and use an Apple product. Describe your experience. What products are available? How would you describe the employees? How is the store designed? What is the Genius Bar? What educational classes are offered?

2. How would you classify each of Apple's two decisions—programmed or non- programmed? Explain your answer.

3. What type of decision-making environment—certainty, risk, uncertainty—did Apple have for each decision? Explain your answer.

4. What internal and external factors might have influenced the success of each decision?

5. What quantitative decision techniques might have helped Apple in making its decision to license its software to other computer companies? Explain your answer.

Sources: Forbes, The World's Most Valuable Brands, 2015 Ranking, *http:// www.forbes.com/powerful-brands/list/#tab:rank*; Joe Wilcox. "Apple has 91% of the market for $1,000+ PCs, says NPC." *betanews*. July 22, 2009. *http:// www.betanews.com/joewilcox/article/Apple-has-91-of-market-for-1000-PCs-says-NPD/1248313624*. Jim Carlton, "They Coulda Been a Contender." *Wired*, November 11, 1997; W3C, Browser Statistics, March 30, 2006, *http:// www.w3schools.com/browsers/browsers_stats.asp*; Ina Fried, "Celebrating Three Decades of Apple," *CNET News.com*, March 28, 2006, *http://news. com.com/Apple+celebrates+30+years/2009-1041_3-6053869.html*.

Chapter 6

Management Ethics and Social Responsibility

LEARNING OBJECTIVES

After studying this chapter, you should be able to:

1 Describe the two broad categories of ethical theories

2 Explain what individuals need in order to act ethically

3 Describe the organizational influences on ethical conduct

4 Discuss three primary ways in which businesses can promote ethical conduct

5 Describe the relationship between law and ethics

6 Explain the concept of an ethical dilemma

7 Discuss the guidelines for acting ethically

8 Explain the three approaches by businesses to social responsibility

9 Explain the responsibilities businesses have to stakeholders

10 Describe government's role in promoting socially responsible conduct by businesses

11 Discuss the ways in which businesses can promote socially responsible conduct

Morale-Building

Employees want to work for managers they can trust. Trustworthy managers are ethical; they have moral standards; they know right from wrong; they treat people with respect. Lack of trust among managers and employees often results in low morale in the workplace.

Morale is the attitude of employees toward their work. Low morale causes employees to lose focus. High morale results in a more productive and efficient work climate.

Employees with high morale feel confident and motivated to complete their required tasks.

For each of the following statements, circle the number which indicates your level of agreement. Rate your agreement as it is, not what you think it should be. Objectivity will enable you to determine your management skill strengths and weaknesses.

	Almost Always	Often	Sometimes	Rarely	Almost Never
I show interest in others.	5	4	3	2	1
I express praise and appreciation to others.	5	4	3	2	1
I consult with others before making decisions that affect them.	5	4	3	2	1
I look for opportunities to help others.	5	4	3	2	1
I treat people fairly and equitably.	5	4	3	2	1
I help people to reach agreement.	5	4	3	2	1
I uphold the rights of individuals in the face of group pressure.	5	4	3	2	1
Other people trust me.	5	4	3	2	1
I accept help from others willingly.	5	4	3	2	1
I use positive self-talk to stay focused on my goals.	5	4	3	2	1

Compute your score by adding the circled numbers. The highest score is 50; the lowest score is 10. A higher score implies you are more likely to feel confident about your ability to build morale. A lower score implies a lesser degree of readiness, but it can be increased. Reading and studying this chapter will help you to improve your understanding of business ethics.

INTRODUCTION

This chapter examines the responsibilities that businesses and their employees bear to themselves and to others. It concentrates on what is best for all of an organization's and an individual's constituents, including the recipients of their outputs—their customers. One assumption here is that the best decisions maximize achievement of legitimate goals, conform to high standards of legal and ethical behavior and promote good corporate citizenship. This chapter examines basic principles and methods through which managers and their organizations can strengthen their personal and institutional capacities to act in both an ethical and socially responsible manner.

MANAGING ETHICALLY

Describe the two broad categories of ethical theories

Ethics, you will recall from Chapter 1, is the branch of philosophy concerned with human values and conduct, moral duty and obligation. Specifically, ethics is concerned with what constitutes right and wrong human conduct, values, beliefs and attitudes in light of a specific set of circumstances. The best time for individuals to consider the ethics of their behavior is while they are selecting a course of action and before they actually take the action. Thus, they can identify any possible negative consequences and avoid or, at the very least, consider them before any harm is done.

According to authors Daniel Davidson, et al:

> *There are two broad categories of ethical theories. Ethical theories may be based on consequential principles or nonconsequential principles. Consequential principles judge the ethics of a particular situation by the consequences of that action. Consequential ethics determines the "rightness" or "wrongness" of any action by determining the ratio of good to evil that the action will produce. The "right" action is that action that produces the greatest ratio of good to evil of any of the available alternatives….*
>
> *Nonconsequential principles tend to focus on the concept of duty. Under the nonconsequential approach, a person acts ethically if that person is faithful regardless of the consequences that follow from being faithful to that duty. If a person carries out his or her duties, the greatest good occurs because the duty of the individual is carried out. If each individual carries out his or her duty, society knows what to expect from each individual in any given situation.*[1]

Business ethics addresses the applications of the preceding theories within the context of for-profit organizations and is the primary focus of this chapter. Our main concern is to look at how individuals and their organizations can, in any situation, avoid wrongdoing and do the right thing.

Robert C. Solomon and Kristine R. Hanson, business consultants on ethical issues, have discovered that:

> *Good business begins with ethics. The most successful people and companies are those that take ethics seriously. This is not surprising, since ethical attitudes largely determine how one treats employees, suppliers, stockholders, and consumers, as well as how one treats competitors and other members of the community. Inevitably, this affects how one is treated in return. Ethical managers and ethical businesses tend to be more trusted and better treated and to suffer less resentment, inefficiency, litigation, and government interference. Ethics is just good business.*[2]

business ethics
The rules or standards governing the conduct of persons or members of organizations in the field of commerce

Managers must continually strive to balance diverse and sometimes contradictory demands of multiple constituencies—employees, owners, customers, suppliers and their communities (local and regional)—while allocating and managing limited resources. At the beginning of the twenty-first century, two powerful factors imperil the balance.

First, never have so many conflicting demands been made so insistently on those who manage institutions and hold power: the construction industry, cigarette companies, social networking and technology companies[3], the military, environmentalists, nuclear-power advocates, teachers, school boards, the Baby Boomers and Millennials. The list of powerful special interests is matched only by the list of less powerful general interests: children, the poor and homeless, disadvantaged minorities, the undereducated and the elderly.

Second, the consequences of management decisions affect far more people and environments—and more profoundly—than ever before. Whether directing a medical research laboratory at work on cancer or AIDS, maintaining a fleet of 747s, commanding transoceanic supertankers, supervising a nuclear reactor at Chernobyl or an insecticide plant in Bhopal, leading the police department in Los Angeles, or plotting the future of Ford, today's managers wield unprecedented influence over the world of today and tomorrow. The foundation of the Total Quality Management (TQM) approach to managing the organization is based upon ethics, as depicted in this chapter's Quality Management feature.

With the accelerating rate of change in our society and the explosion of information and technology, the pace of real events approaches that of a video game—with relentless hazards surfacing almost too fast to manage. Pressures to improve quality of products and operations, to increase productivity, to stay close to suppliers and customers, to value diversity and inclusion and to react swiftly to global changes all combine to compress the time managers and their organizations can take to make decisions and choose courses of action. Managers need guidelines to help them to cope with these pressures.

See this chapter's Managing Social Media box for a review of social media ethics terms, as well as ethics to consider in conducting online business.

Explain what individuals need in order to act ethically

INDIVIDUALS AND ETHICAL CONDUCT

Few individuals and organizations would openly endorse cheating, stealing, telling lies, breaking laws and threatening the physical well-being of others. Each of these actions is a violation of commonly held standards in most societies, under most circumstances. Yet, as too many of today's news headlines indicate, people and businesses are accused and convicted of doing these things every day. After a brief look at ethics and individuals, we turn our attention to the organizational influences that affect the ethical conduct of institutions and their members.

A person's ethics are influenced by his or her **morality**—core values and beliefs (i.e., principles and philosophy) that act as a guide (i.e., conscience) when formulating courses of action. Once they are formulated, a person chooses or rejects a course of action based on the action's anticipated effects on both the person doing the selecting and others. "Religious beliefs and training, educational background, political and economic philosophy, socialization through family and peer group influences and work experience all come together to produce a personal moral code of ethical values with associated attitudes."[4] All these factors are usually referred to as an individual's code of

morality

Core values and beliefs that act as a guide (i.e., conscience) when individuals formulate courses of action

Quality Management

TQM Foundation

The philosophy of Total Quality Management (TQM) can be described as the successful implementation of eight elements: ethics, integrity, trust, training, teamwork, leadership, recognition and communication. The elements form four groups: foundation (ethics, integrity and trust), building bricks (training, teamwork and leadership), binding mortar (communication) and roof (recognition). The elements can be depicted as a house, as seen below.

The foundation of TQM includes ethics, integrity and trust.

Trust is a by-product of integrity and ethical conduct. Without trust, the framework of TQM cannot be built. Trust fosters full participation of all members. It allows empowerment that encourages pride of ownership and it encourages commitment. It allows decision making at appropriate levels in the organization, fosters individual risk-taking for continuous improvement and helps to ensure that measurements focus on improvement of process and are not used to contend people. Trust is essential to ensure customer satisfaction. So, trust builds the cooperative environment essential for TQM.

Source: Padhi, Nayantara, iSixSigma, "The Eight Elements of TQM," *http://www.isixsigma.com/index.php?option=com_k2&view=item&id=1333:the-eight-elements-of-tqm&Itemid=179.*

ethics, or moral code and are the primary control device used by individuals to judge and regulate conduct—their own and that of others.

Human behavior derives from discernible causes or motives that can be identified, acknowledged and modified. For this reason, wise individuals cultivate a continuous awareness of their personal priorities, goals, values, needs, beliefs, attitudes and assumptions. Such awareness allows individuals to realistically assess the motivation that underlies their personal choices and actions. All of us must continuously strive to identify the influences on and causes for our motivations and those of our leaders.

Leaders' Ethics

How a leader treats employees influences employee loyalty. "The Walker Loyalty Report for Loyalty in the Workplace" found that 57 percent of employees believed their companies' leaders were people of high integrity. *Loyalty* is defined as an employee being committed to the organization and planning to stay at least two years. Only six percent of employees who believed they were led by less-than-ethical executives were loyal to the company. Conversely, 40 percent of workers with ethical leaders wanted to remain.[5]

In his study of leadership, business writer Danny Cox compiled a list of ten characteristics common to great leaders. The first is "cultivating a high standard of personal ethics." Cox feels that "at the core of any high standard of personal ethics is

Social Media Ethics Terms

Astroturfing is an attempt to falsify a grassroots consumer movement through deceptive means. The term originated in politics and was coined by Senator Lloyd Benson. In social media, astroturf usually manifests itself when people post positive comments about a company on blogs and in online communities without revealing that they are employees and/or representatives of the company. In some cases, companies hire third parties, such as public relations agencies, to engage in astroturfing. Another form of astroturfing is the practice of hiring evangelists who chat favourably about a company on various social networks without revealing their affiliations. The European Union has outlawed the practice.

Blogola typically describes a situation in which a blogger is given free merchandise, often with the request that the blogger review the product. Sometimes this request implies a favorable review in exchange for a "free" product.

The term *blogola* comes from the radio term payola, which originated in the 1950s. In its original usage, payola occurred when record company executives paid DJs to play certain songs and to "talk up" particular artists and records.

Many blogola situations did not begin as deceptions. Mommy blogging, for example, began as an informal way for moms to blog about child raising techniques, nutrition, health, product safety, education, and other topics relevant to other mothers. Manufacturers of relevant products approached these bloggers with requests for product reviews. With the staggering growth of blogging in general, and mommy blogging in particular, what might have started out as a hobby blog, has for some mothers turned into a full-time profession, and in some cases quite a lucrative one, so the ethical standards that might have applied in the "early days" might no longer apply.

Many bloggers have in fact discontinued accepting free merchandise, choosing instead to return all review products to the manufacturer. In some areas this is more difficult than it sounds. For example, a reviewer cannot return food and wine. This can also be an issue in the travel industry, where many professional writers pay their own way but amateurs cannot afford to do so.

Brandjacking is a relatively new term used to describe a situation when a person or company "hijacks" the brand identity of another company. This could include the unauthorized use of the company name, logos, product photography, product names, and even website URLs. Several corporate accounts on Twitter, for example, have turned out to be bogus. This is one of the more blatant forms of brandjacking, in which a person claims to be an official representative of the company.

Another milder form, which occurs often on Facebook, is the unauthorized use in an online discussion group or forum of the company's brand identity by an individual or group. In many cases, this occurs on "fan" pages and groups created by people who are enthusiastic about the company and its products. If the discussions in the group are largely favorable to the company, it may choose not to police this activity, even when it may constitute a violation of copyright or trademark law.

Comment spam attacks blogs and online communities by leaving often innocuous-appearing comments that link to third party sites. Comment spam is predominantly practiced by companies selling pornography, online gaming, and treatments for erectile dysfunction, so it is obviously something companies don't want on their websites. Most blogging software provides filtering for comment spam, and by moderating comments, you can keep comment spam off your blog and other social media sites.

Flog refers to a fake blog designed to deceive consumers and others by simulating a situation or a story favourable to a company. Probably the best known flog is "Walmarting Across America," in which an "average couple" travelled the U.S. in an RV touring Walmart parking lots and writing about their experiences on their blog. The couple turned out to be a professional photographer and a professional journalist hired by Walmart and its agency, Edelman, to write the blog.

A flog, which maliciously deceives to promote the company and its products, should not be confused with a parody blog, such as the Fake Steve Jobs blog, which was open about its artifice and intended strictly for entertainment purposes.

Link Baiting is perhaps one of the grayer areas of social media ethics, and some would argue that it is not unethical at all. Link baiting is the act of engaging in controversial conversation or running some kind of promotion that is intended to generate links to the site. Some of these are blatant offers of a cash reward randomly given to anyone who links to a particular site during a particular time.

Other approaches are more subtle. A blog post titled "Blogs are Worthless" might generate a lot of traffic because it is a fairly outrageous statement coming from a blogger. Some would see this controversial point of view as link baiting, and others would see it simply as good marketing for the blog.

Principally, people are bothered by link baiting because the number of links to a site is a key metric affecting where that site will be placed in search results, and therefore the link baiting strategy is generally intended not to make the site more interesting or relevant but to fool Internet search engines and increase advertising revenue on sites that feature advertising.

Pay Per Post is an arrangement where a blogger is paid a flat rate per post to publish favorable posts about a company's products and services. Drawing its name from payperpost.com, pay per post is another form of blogola, as Michael Arrington wrote on his TechCrunch blog, "How much is your soul worth? Pay Per Post Now Lets Bloggers Set the Price." Pay per post creates confusion among readers as they are generally unaware that the blog they are reading is essentially sponsored by a company that might seem to be receiving objective coverage on the blog.

Screen Scraping is the use of technology to "scrape" content from a blog or website and to republish it on another site without permission. Scraping may violate trademark and copyright protections, and it is also specifically prohibited by user agreements of many websites and social networks. Screen scraping is so named because of using the data output by a program or output from an RSS feed, screen scraping copies, pixel by pixel, the information as displayed on the screen.

Splog or spam blog is a spurious blog set up to capture search engine results and divert them to other blogs or websites. The articles are bogus, sometimes using nonsensical text and other times using text specifically developed to improve search engine rankings.

Source: Joel Postman, *SocialCorp: Social Media Goes Corporate*, New Riders Press (December 18, 2008), pp. 120–123.

continues

Online Business Ethics

Managers can make sure the company considers ethics in conducting business online.

- *Managers should be proactive.* It's not enough to have a great ethics policy that sits on a shelf with the corporate mission statement. Institute regular ethics training and awareness programs. Move ethics away from "rules to be followed" to becoming a way of doing business.

- *Link ethics policies to real-world scenarios that your employees may face.* Establish clear procedures about who employees should contact with ethics-related questions when questionable situations arise.

- *Make clear that your standards of ethical behavior also apply to third-party contractors and on-site consultants working in your company.*

- *If your company doesn't already have one, push for a publicly displayed privacy policy regarding customer data.* Pay attention to how that data is shared within the company, as well as with outsiders.

- *Above all, emphasize that good ethics makes good business sense.* Sacrificing ethics for short-term gain is sure to lose customers and partners in the long run. Ethics is not just a matter of moral correctness—it also means business success.

➡ **What ethical issues are managers grappling with in connection with online business?**

➡ **Many businesses have their own standards—sometimes they're written, sometimes they're just understood. Sometimes they're followed; sometimes they're ignored. And sometimes it comes down to your own personal standards. Where do you go for guidance on ethically ambiguous situations? Explain.**

Source: Clinton Wilder, "Business Ethics for IT Managers— What You Can Do," *InformationWeek.com News*, February 19, 2001, *http://www.informationweek.com/825/ethics_side.htm*.

the declaration of personal responsibility. A person who refuses to accept responsibility lacks the ethical armor to stand against temptation."[6]

Author Verne E. Henderson adds, "Managers and executives who are … unaware of what motivates them are ethical accidents searching for a place to happen."[7] Henderson suggests that when colleagues—including a boss—recommend a course of action, we must consider *their* motives as well as our own. As reasons unfold, watch for rationalizations (self-satisfying but incorrect justifications for one's behaviors) that excuse and bury subtle warnings from our conscience.

Leaders of scandalous corporations such as the Rana Plaza factory in Bangladesh, Enron, Arthur Andersen and certain financial services firms in recent years abdicated responsibility to the community. The nation's media showed many of these leaders being arrested and taken away in handcuffs. Some referred to them as "managers in manacles." Yet, the humiliation suffered by the CEOs has a positive impact on corporate culture, says Arthur Levitt, former Securities and Exchange Commission (SEC) Chairman and author of *Take On the Street: What Wall Street and Corporate America Don't Want You to Know and What You Can Do to Fight Back.* Mr. Levitt served as President of the American Stock Exchange before going into government. He says, "That cultural change is more significant for investor protection than any regulatory rules. The smarter CEOs now know they have to care about the public interest."[8]

A leader with a strong personal code of ethics believes in winning but doing so in the right way. He "walks his talk" as an example and model for his team to follow. He or she has the ethical armor needed to evaluate his choices and balance the competing demands from his constituents.

Describe the organizational influences on ethical conduct

ORGANIZATIONAL INFLUENCES ON ETHICAL CONDUCT

Professors and authors Peter J. Frost, Vance F. Mitchell and Walter R. Nord believe that organizations can have a negative impact on an individual's ability to act ethically: "As organizations become especially central to people, people face strong temptations to do what they perceive to be good for the organization even when it means they act inconsistently with the standards of ethical behavior."[9]

Professor Saul W. Gellerman points out that organizations can encourage (overtly or covertly) unethical behavior in employees in several ways:[10]

- *Offering unusually high rewards.* "Huge bonuses and commissions can distort one's values, in much the same way that too much power can corrupt one's standards of decency. You can motivate people without corrupting them simply by keeping their rewards within the bounds of reason."

- *Threatening unusually severe punishments.* "If people are desperate to avoid what they regard as a calamity, they will go to whatever lengths they must to avoid it. One's conscience will be anesthetized by terror, so the dirty business can be done."

- *Emphasizing results.* If a company places too much value on results, managers will tend to avoid concern for the means employed by subordinates to achieve those results.

In their capacity of setting an example for subordinates, managers teach more about ethics through their actions than they do through their words or what is written in a company's ethics code. An employee who is expected to turn a blind eye to a superior's unethical behavior receives the message loud and clear that ends are more important than means.

Ethics professor Lynn Sharp Paine connects unethical behavior to corporate culture as well. She believes that:

> *Unethical business practice involves the tacit, if not explicit, cooperation of others and reflects the values, attitudes, beliefs, language, and behavioral patterns that define an organization's operating culture. Ethics, then, is as much an organizational as a personal issue. Managers who fail to provide proper leadership and to institute systems that facilitate ethical conduct share responsibility with those who conceive, execute, and knowingly benefit from corporate misdeeds.*[11]

Just as organizations can exert negative influences, they can also exert positive ones.

Discuss three primary ways in which businesses can promote ethical conduct

IMPORTANCE OF ORGANIZATIONAL CONTROLS

Corporate cultures promote values and beliefs that govern the ways in which people interact with others. Several subcultures exist in most organizations, reflecting different work groups or discrete ethnic groups that arise from the workforce. Although these subcultures may display differing sets of values and perceptions, they can achieve a unity of viewpoint: "In a pluralistic society, business is the one place where different cultures and personal values are forced to cooperate and compromise. It is the one place where a single and unifying ethic is essential."[12] To achieve this unified view, organizations rely on the commitment of top management, codes of ethics and compliance programs.

Commitment of Top Management

It is top management's job to ensure that its organization's cultures support ethical conduct and social responsibility. To do this, top management must make organizational integrity a core value. Ethics Professor Paine provides the following explanation of this concept:

> *Organizational integrity is based on the concept of self-governance in accordance with a set of guiding principles. From the perspective of integrity, the task of ethics management is to define and give life to an organization's guiding values, to create an environment that supports ethically sound behavior, and to instill a sense of shared accountability among employees.*[13]

To determine if a corporate culture and its subcultures support or oppose ethical conduct, see Figure 6.1. It is a checklist for examining a company's culture. Every "no" response indicates that some change is necessary to foster ethical as well as socially responsible behavior.

Figure 6.1	**Checklist for Determining If a Corporate Culture Supports Ethical Behavior and Social Responsibility**

Is the company:	Yes	No
1 Concerned about quality in its services, products and operations?	☐	☐
2 Concerned about its employees' quality of life?	☐	☐
3 Proud of its reputation in the industry?	☐	☐
4 Proud of its reputation in the community?	☐	☐
5 Focused on the needs of its customers?	☐	☐
6 6. Honest in its dealings with you?	☐	☐
7 7. Honest in its dealings with customers?	☐	☐
8 8. Honest in its dealings with others?	☐	☐
9 9. Fair and equitable in the ways in which it decides on promotions?	☐	☐
10 Fair and equitable in the ways in which it compensates employees?	☐	☐
11 Open in its communications?	☐	☐
12 Trusting in its relationships with employees?	☐	☐
13 Concerned with developing and keeping its employees?	☐	☐
14 Actively promoting ethical conduct in all its operations and employees?	☐	☐
15 Actively searching for ways to better serve its stakeholders?	☐	☐
16 Carefully monitoring how decisions are made and checking?	☐	☐

Professor Gellerman asserts that the "first line of defense against unethical conduct is each individual's conscience." Managers "have to do everything [they] can to keep it awake. The second line of defense is to eliminate or minimize the circumstances that can overwhelm a conscience or deceive it, or put it to sleep." He recommends three steps that top managers can take to discourage unethical behavior in their areas of responsibility:

- *Draw a clean line between the behavior you'll tolerate and the behavior you'll have to punish.* This step means establishing a code of ethics or conduct that management is willing to commit to and enforce.

- *Invest the time and money in making sure that those distinctions are understood and remembered.* This step requires training, constant oversight and the establishment of rewards for ethical behavior.

- *Put the fear of God into would-be violators by conspicuously raising the risk of exposure.* This step means punishing wrongdoers fairly and swiftly. People will learn from each example of misbehavior and how it is handled by management.[14]

Codes of Ethics

Although there is no generic code of ethics for business, individual organizations often find such codes useful. The Center for the Study of Ethics in the Professions (CSEP) at the Illinois Institute of Technology has posted more than 850 codes of ethics online. (View the codes of ethics at *http://ethics.iit.edu/ecodes/about*)

To be effective and influential in an organization's culture and command structure, codes of ethics must be specific enough to give concrete guidance and must be reinforced by the examples set by key corporate figures. They must be written in such a way as to develop a clear understanding of a company's values and commitment to ethical behavior, both inside the organization and in relation to key outside stakeholders. Codes should deal directly with situations known by a company to have been problematic in the past. Ethical topics might include responsibility, respect, fairness, honesty, compassion, internet use, confidentiality, security and sexual harassment.

Authors Solomon and Hanson outline the following characteristics for codes of ethics:

- They are visible guidelines for behavior at all levels.

- They are an unchallengeable basis for firing an unethical employee, even when his or her action is not, strictly speaking, against either the law or the specific terms of the job.

- They protect all personnel from the pressures of the market, which tend to incite desperation and unethical behavior.

- They remind employees to look beyond the bottom line, and they provide a touchstone for appeals through the hierarchy.[15]

Compliance Programs

Without some means to communicate and enforce codes of ethics and conduct, they will be just words on paper. David Gebler, founder of Working Values Ltd., a Boston corporate governance strategy firm, said, "Andersen and Enron had written codes of business conduct, but there were tremendous cultural gaps. Everything was focused on profits and arrogance."[16] Peter Madsen, Executive Director at Carnegie Mellon

University's Center for the Advancement of Applied Ethics, separates ethics training into two areas:

1 *Compliance training* alerts people to policies, regulations and laws that establish acceptable behavior within a company; and

2 *Cognitive thinking* develops skills to allow people to think through various "moral mazes" with which they may be confronted in the workplace.[17]

Compliance training helps employees understand that laws apply to their jobs. For example, managers who conduct employment interviews need to know if any questions are illegal. Another example would be employees who receive vendor gifts. They need to understand the dollar value limits on any gifts imposed by the government, as well as the organization.

Cognitive thinking includes decision-making models like the Texas Instruments Ethics Quick Test. In order to make ethical decisions, employees are given a card with the following questions:

Is the action legal?

Does it comply with our values?

If you do it, will you feel bad?

How will it look in the newspaper?

If you know it's wrong, don't do it!

If you're not sure, ask.

Keep asking until you get an answer.

(See *http://www.ti.com/corp/docs/company/citizen/ethics/quicktest.shtml*).

According to Andrew C. Sigler of Champion International, "You need a culture and peer pressure that spells out what is acceptable and what isn't and why, and a program involving training, education and follow-up."[18] To make such a program effective, the Business Roundtable, an advisory and research group comprising the chief executives of major corporations, recommends that top management devote a greater commitment to ethics programs, boldly assert management's expectations through clearly written and communicated codes, and conduct surveys to monitor compliance.[19]

Measuring something makes it important even if it wasn't before. In the U.S. Army, the phrase is "don't expect what you don't inspect." The corporate equivalent is, "what the boss watches well gets done well." The same principle applies to the ethical side of enterprise. It only becomes important if and when it's measured.[20]

Several trends are in evidence today. A growing number of corporate boards of directors have ethics committees. The majority of large companies have ethics or compliance officers who are members of top management or report directly to a member. The vision of the Ethics & Compliance Officer Association (ECOA) is "to be the recognized authority on workplace ethics, compliance, and integrity." See Figure 6.2 for ECOA Values.[21]

Since employees are often in the best position to detect fraud, a growing number of companies have adopted policies that encourage, and in some cases obligate, employees who know about wrongdoing to report it. Any employee can report wrong-

Figure 6.2	**The ECOA Values for Business Ethics and Compliance Professionals**

ECOA VALUES

INTEGRITY

As individual ethics and compliance officers, integrity is the essential value inherent in our work; as a professional association, integrity is the foundation supporting our relationships, our commitments, and our business practices. Integrity is the product of an ongoing dedication to honesty, candor, respect, and responsibility and must be demonstrated by our actions.

CONFIDENTIALITY

Essential to the work we do on behalf of our organizations, confidentiality is also a primary expectation and value of the relationships we have within the ECOA. We commit to hold as an absolute trust the information shared with us as fellow ethics and compliance officers, engaging our peers for purposes of support and our continued professional growth.

COLLEGIALITY

Supported by our commitments to integrity and confidentiality, the collegiality of ECOA members is a foundational source of our ability to share in a trusting and frank environment and to draw value from the diversity of cultures and industries represented among our peers.

COOPERATION

In the growing and changing ethics and compliance field, cooperation continues to be a vital strength of ECOA membership. The dynamic relationships that we form and our members' willingness to support one another have allowed ECOA members to better shape their ethics and compliance programs and their careers.

Source: ECOA *http://www.theecoa.org.*

doing anonymously or request ethical assistance in resolving an issue by calling a toll-free telephone number (hotline) with voicemail or visiting a website. Ethics training should include teaching employees how to report ethics violations and where they can go to ask questions or get information.

Ethics training programs don't need to be dull. A growing number of companies are using creative ethics training.

- Lockheed Martin employees play a board game, "DILBERT® Ethics Challenge," in an interactive workshop where players are faced with a selection from different ethical problems.[22]

- Raytheon employees interact with a video featuring the late film critic Roger Ebert using familiar workplace scenes to illustrate the differences between compliance-based actions (one thumb up) and values-based actions (two thumbs up).[23]

- The University of Maryland's Robert Smith School of Business requires students to participate in a field trip to a minimum-security prison, where they come face-to-face with former corporate executives doing time for white-collar crimes. Stephen Loeb, who teaches accounting and business ethics at the school says, "Students find it pretty memorable. They talk to prisoners who were once executives but made errors, and they see how they would live if they made a mistake."[24]

After instructor led in-person training which includes role-playing, ethics training can be reinforced with technology. Web-based training might include employees taking specially designed interactive e-learning courses on their computers or dedicated intranet sites to find answers to ethical questions.

LEGAL CONSTRAINTS

5 Describe the relationship between law and ethics

Competent managers cultivate an informed awareness of the role of the law in organizational and individual conduct. Because ours is a nation of laws, certain presumptions influence decision making at several levels. From the broadest context of constitutional rights to the minutest municipal regulation, companies and their managers are witting and unwitting creatures of the law. One group of business law experts views the relationship of the law to ethics in this way:

> There is a basic problem facing any business in its efforts to be "ethical": there are no fixed guidelines to follow, no formal codes of ethics to set the standards. The legal profession has a Code of Professional Responsibility; the medical profession has its Hippocratic Oath; the accounting profession has a code of ethics; the real-estate industry has a code of conduct; other professions have codes to guide them. But business has no 'road map' of ethical conduct. The closest thing business has is the law. If a business obeys the law, it is acting legally, and it is seemingly meeting its minimum social requirements.[25]

Those minimum requirements offer only a structure, however, void of content and context. Says Peter Madsen,

> Laws and policies form an ethical foundation. But the law is a moral minimum. And no law or policy is going to cover every situation. Sooner or later organizations will have to rely on people to make choices when there is no on-point law or policy to follow. The best ethics training goes beyond legal compliance.[26]

Author Vincent Barry adds,

> Although useful in alerting us to moral issues and informing us of our rights and responsibilities, law cannot be taken as an adequate standard of moral conduct. Conformity with law is neither requisite nor sufficient for determining moral behavior, any more than conformity to rule[s] of etiquette is. By the same token, nonconformity with law is not necessarily immoral, for the law disobeyed may be unjust.[27]

When businesses don't regulate themselves, the government will step in and regulate them. Legal sanctions against individual and corporate criminal behavior can be significant. Since 1909 when the U.S. Supreme Court held that corporations can be "held liable, as individuals can be, for crimes involving intent," corporate liability has translated into fines and jail terms for corporate officials. Criminal penalties can be reduced if companies create ethical compliance programs. In 1991, "federal sentencing guidelines for white-collar crimes stipulated that creating such programs could lead to a 40 percent reduction in penalties for convicted companies or employees."[28]

Federal guidelines cover many offenses that can be committed by employees without a business owner's knowledge. Heavy penalties for a variety of offenses "including serious misrepresentation of a product by a salesperson and bribery of a public official by a subcontractor" are included. "If high-level managers were not involved in the crime and [they] have taken steps to ensure employees' compliance with the law, a firm could pay as little as 5 percent of the base fine." On the other hand, if senior managers "have encouraged or taken part in the law breaking, fines can reach 400 percent of the base rate."[29]

George W. Bush, when President, called for a "new ethic of corporate responsibility" as he signed into law H.R. 3763, the **Sarbanes–Oxley Act (SOX)**. This act adopted tough provisions to deter and punish corporate and accounting fraud and corruption, ensures justice for wrongdoers, and protects the interests of workers and shareholders. Under this law, chief executive officers (CEOs) and chief financial officers (CFOs) must personally vouch for the truth and fairness of their company's disclosures. SOX requires enhanced and timelier disclosures by public companies and mandates significantly increased criminal penalties for violations of the federal securities laws. Corporate officers face prison time if they do so knowing the statements are wrong. Penalties include up to ten years in prison and a $1 million fine for certified statements knowing they are inaccurate; and up to 20 years in prison and a $5 million fine for willfully false certification.

Harsh penalties for white-collar crime were demonstrated by sentences given to convicted U.S. executives in 2005. Former executives at Tyco International (Dennis Kozlowski and Mark Swartz), WorldCom (Bernard Ebbers), and Adelphia (John Rigas and Timothy Rigas) were sentenced to up to 25 years in prison. Unfortunately, these penalties did not deter unethical corporate actions.

The collapse of the economy in 2008 seemed to make many people forget the misdeeds of Enron and Arthur Andersen. Lehman Brothers filed for the largest bankruptcy in U.S. history; Bernard Madoff was arrested for the largest Ponzi scheme in U.S. history; the financial industry (Bear Stearns, AIG, GM, Chrysler, Freddie Mac and Fannie Mae and others) received the largest government bailout in U.S. history.

As a result of the 2007 global financial crisis, the Fraud Enforcement and Recovery Act (FERA) was passed in 2009. It enhances the criminal enforcement of federal fraud laws by expanding the scope of several existing fraud laws; increasing funding for federal agencies that prosecute fraud; re-extending the scope of the False Claims Act; creating the Federal Crisis Inquiry Commission to examine the causes of the financial crisis. In 2010, the Dodd-Frank Wall Street Reform and Consumer Protection Act (the Dodd-Frank Act), the most far reaching Wall Street reform in American history, was passed.

Many managers see self-regulation as a way to avoid legislative or judicial intrusions into their operations. They create a corporate code of conduct, which is also known as a code of ethics or a compliance program. It spells out the company's values and addresses the purpose of the company and its interactions. Ethics codes also help promote tolerance of diverse practices and customs while doing business abroad. One example code of ethics was developed by the United States Department of Commerce International Trade Administration for its corporations doing business internationally. "U.S. Model Business Principles" are the topic of this chapter's Global Applications. (Note: *Business Ethics: A Manual for Managing a Responsible Business Enterprise in Emerging Market Economies* can be viewed at *http://trade.gov/goodgovernance/business_ethics/manual.asp*.)

Figure 6.3 is a simple grid with four quadrants representing the four possible combinations when balancing ethical issues with the law or the absence of a law. Position 1 (upper left) shows a legal and ethical position for the issue in question—smoking in the workplace. Position 4 (lower right) shows an illegal and unethical treatment of the issue. The other two positions represent ethical or legal concerns to a manager.

U.S. Model Business Principles

United States Department of Commerce,
International Trade Administration

Model Business Principles

Recognizing the positive role of U.S. business in upholding and promoting adherence to universal standards of human rights, the Administration encourages all businesses to adopt and implement voluntary codes of conduct for doing business around the world that cover at least the following areas:

1. Provision of a safe and healthy workplace;

2. Fair employment practices, including avoidance of child and forced labor and avoidance of discrimination based on race, gender, national origin, or religious beliefs; and respect for the right of association and the right to organize and bargain collectively;

3. Responsible environmental protection and environmental practices;

4. Compliance with U.S. and local laws promoting good business practices, including laws prohibiting illicit payments and ensuring fair competition;

5. Maintenance, through leadership of all levels, of a corporate culture that respects free expression consistent with legitimate business concerns, and does not condone political coercion in the workplace; that encourages good corporate citizenship and makes a positive contribution to the communities in which the company operates; and where ethical conduct is recognized, valued, and exemplified by all employees.

In adopting voluntary codes of conduct that reflect these principles, U.S. companies should serve as models and encourage similar behavior by their partners, suppliers, and subcontractors.

Adoption of codes of conduct reflecting these principles is voluntary. Companies are encouraged to develop their own codes of conduct appropriate to their particular circumstances. Many companies already apply statements or codes that incorporate these principles. Companies should find appropriate means to inform their shareholders and the public of actions undertaken in connection with these principles. Nothing in the principles is intended to require a company to act in violation of host country or U.S. law. This statement of principles is not intended for legislation.

Source: United States Council for International Business (USCIB) *http://training.itcilo.it/actrav_cdrom1/english/global/guide/usmodel. htm.*

| Figure 6.3 | Legal/Ethical Behavior Model Applied to the Issue of Smoking in the Workplace |

1. Ethical/Legal	**2. Ethical/Illegal**
A decision to allow employees to smoke on the job with no secondhand smoke affecting others	A decision to allow smoking on the job with no secondhand smoke affecting others but in violation of laws
3. Unethical/Legal	**4. Unethical/Illegal**
A decision to allow secondhand smoke to affect others without violation of laws	A decision to allow secondhand smoke to affect others in violation of laws

Explain the concept of an ethical dilemma

ETHICAL DILEMMAS

Ethics is not prescriptive. No simple set of rules tells us how to behave morally or ethically in all situations. Codes of conduct—when they are documented—are written in the manner of company policies as brief, general guidelines. Interpretation varies from one individual to the next. Like policies, codes are meant to give freedom of action within certain boundaries and require interpretation. Professor Gellerman queries and replies:

> How can you tell if a rule "really" applies to what you are doing? How can you avoid crossing a line that is almost never defined precisely? The only safe answer is not even to move in the direction of the line. Here is where the real ethical dilemma begins to emerge, however. Because if you constantly played it safe, and never tested the limits of what you could and couldn't get away with, you'd risk being considered inefficient, or even gutless, by your superiors.[30]

ethical dilemma
A situation that arises when all courses of action open to a decision maker are judged to be unethical

Managers constantly face dilemmas—situations that require a choice between options that are or seem equally unfavorable or mutually exclusive. Dilemmas involve uncertainty and risk over the rightness or wrongness of actions. Besides uncertainty about which course of action is ethical, an **ethical dilemma** also arises when all courses of action open to a manager are judged to be unethical. For example, a company's plant is simply unable to bring work in at a profit. Managers are considering three possible alternatives: (1) shut the plant down and outsource the work to subcontractors who will give the firm the costs it needs; (2) invest in technology that will eliminate half the jobs but make the plant productive enough to continue to operate; or (3) seek wage and benefit concessions from all employees to bring costs into line. Any of these choices will impose immediate hardship on the employees of the plant and those who depend on them—families, local merchants and others.

Because of technology's central role in business, opportunities and innovation, the role of technology managers has become more critical in setting and enforcing ethical standards. In an *InformationWeek Newsletter,* Stephanie Stahl poses several ethical dilemmas:

- It's Monday morning, and you're studying up on a large-scale project that your company intends to bid on. You're well into the details when you realize the company issuing the request for proposals has accidentally included confidential information that could give you a serious leg up on your competitors. What do you do? Pretend you didn't see it? Take advantage of it and act on it? Alert the company to the mistake and remove yourself from the negotiations?

- You find out an employee has been circulating pornographic files via the company e-mail system. Do you ignore it? Give the employee a warning? Fire the employee?

- One of your business partners offers to pay you big bucks for access to your customer data. You've assured customers that such data will remain confidential, but your company is cash-hungry. Do you sell it? Keep your promise to customers?[31]

When managers face such gray areas, Professor Gellerman offers the following suggestions:

- When in doubt, don't.
- Don't try to find out "how far is too far."

- Superiors who push you to do things better, faster, cheaper will turn on you when you cross the line between right and wrong.[32]

Gellerman offers this practical, concrete stratagem:

> *When what you might or might not do is questionable, let the burden of the decision rest on someone who is paid to make the tough decisions. Make your boss earn his [or her] pay. You can't openly condone what policy prohibits. Neither can your boss. That's why bringing the question into the open keeps both of you honest.*[33]

GUIDELINES FOR ACTING ETHICALLY

7 Discuss the guidelines for acting ethically

Someone struggling with a decision, torn between one or another course of action, may well be confronting an issue that involves ethics. The time to consider the ethical dimensions of an act is before acting. Companies and individuals must strive to make ethics a priority in the processes by which they make their decisions.

Different people and groups invoke different criteria for determining if an intended action (or inaction) is the ethical course to follow. The Golden Rule states that we should treat others as we ourselves want to be treated. A variation is to do to others what they want you to do to them. Both work well if the people involved are moral and aware of prevailing social conventions. The utilitarian standard of the greatest good for the greatest number of people provides another ethical test, which works well if the consequences and circumstances surrounding the intended act are fully foreseen and understood.

Authors Solomon and Hanson offer the following rules for contemplating the ethical implications of intended actions:

- Consider other people's well-being, including the well-being of nonparticipants.
- Think as a member of the business community and not as an isolated individual.
- Obey, but do not depend solely on, the law.
- Think of yourself—and your company—as part of society.
- Obey moral rules.
- Think objectively.
- Ask the question, "What sort of person would do such a thing?"
- Respect the customs of others, but not at the expense of your own ethics.[34]

These rules remind us that we are all part of a larger community and that our actions affect others, whose interests must be considered. Keeping these rules in mind can help managers analyze the consequences of their actions before they take any steps. When an individual makes decisions without a moral and ethical base, he or she is adrift and may rely solely on self-interest and economics. People lacking a moral foundation put themselves, their organizations and others at great risk. Risk taking shows up in most managers' job descriptions. "They are paid to know which risks are worth taking. One risk that is definitely not worth taking is the risk of ruining the rest of your career."[35]

Management Professor Kenneth Blanchard and the late, noted cleric Norman Vincent Peale (author of *The Power of Positive Thinking*) wrote a cogent book, *The Power of Ethical Management*. In it they offer a simple sequence of three tests for determining the ethical implications of intended actions:[36]

1 *Is it legal?* Will I be violating either civil law or company policy?

2 *Is it balanced?* Is it fair to all concerned in the short term as well as the long term? Does it promote win–win relationships?

3 *How will it make me feel about myself?* Will it make me proud? Would I feel good if my decision were published in a newspaper? Would I feel good if my family knew about it?

With these inquiries a manager can examine his or her intentions in private and with complete objectivity. When judging the ethical facets of a decision, a person must take ample quiet time, away from pressures and the biases of others, for unhurried reflection on the facts and implications of the decision.

Nature of Social Responsibility

The notion that individuals and organizations have certain obligations, in addition to their business interests, to protect and benefit others and to avoid actions that could harm them is what constitutes **social responsibility**.[37] One reason for the prevalence of this belief in the developed countries of the world is that societies have given businesses tremendous power and rely on them to meet various individual and societal needs.

Businesses are open systems, and most of what they do generates direct benefits and costs for their societies. At one time, businesses did only what they had to do. Today society demands that businesses join in the urgent task of solving societies' problems. Corporations must nourish cultures that promote ethical conduct, and their owners and employees must act with an ethical perspective in order to be socially responsible. Being socially responsible does not mean making everyone happy. Businesses face conflicting demands, and at times a socially responsible action puts the needs of one group of stakeholders ahead of the needs of others—such as donating money to charity rather than paying stockholders higher dividends or giving employees higher raises. Such issues require managers to consider their duty (the course of action required of them by their position or by law) and the priorities of their specific obligations.

Author Rogene A. Buchholz expresses the need for businesses to act in a socially responsible way; "Corporations are more than economic institutions and have a responsibility to devote some of their resources to helping to solve some of the pressing social problems, many of which corporations helped to create."[38] Benjamin Franklin may have been the first American businessperson to advocate such responsible conduct for businesses. Franklin believed that "public service and philanthropy were legitimate concerns … because it is good business to improve the health of the communities from which wealth is derived and because public problems can benefit from private solutions."[39]

Robert D. Haas, former President and CEO of Levi Strauss, persuasively argued the case for businesses to cultivate social responsibility:

> *Corporations can be short-sighted and worry only about our mission, products, and competitive standing. But we do it at our peril. The day will come when corporations will discover the price we pay for our indifference. We must realize that by ignoring the needs of others, we are actually ignoring our own needs in the long run. We may need the goodwill of a neighborhood to enlarge a corner store. We may need well-funded institutions of higher learning to turn out the skilled technical employees we require. We may need adequate community health care to curb absenteeism in our plants. Or we may need fair tax treatment for an industry to be able to compete in the world economy. However small or large our enterprise, we cannot isolate our business from the society around us. Nor can we function without its goodwill.*[40]

---

social responsibility

The notion that, in addition to their business interests, individuals and organizations have certain obligations to protect and benefit other individuals and society and to avoid actions that could harm them

The Harris Interactive Reputation Quotient[SM] (RQ) identifies public perceptions of corporate reputability. It is used as an assessment tool to measure a company's reputation, based on several key areas—social responsibility, emotional appeal, quality of products and services, vision and leadership, workplace environment and financial performance (see Figure 6.4).[41] Companies with the lowest reputations were those that took the government bailouts after the 2008 global financial crisis: General Motors, Freddie Mac, Fannie Mae and AIG. Most admired companies include Berkshire Hathaway, Johnson & Johnson and Google.

APPROACHES TO SOCIAL RESPONSIBILITY

8 Explain the three approaches by businesses to social responsibility

American businesses adopt different approaches to the demands made on them. Some businesses eagerly seek ways to accommodate societal needs, whereas others vehemently resist external obligations. Businesses can adopt any of three primary strategies to manage the issue of social responsibility: to resist, to react and to anticipate.

Resistance Approach Companies adopt the **resistance approach** when they actively fight to eliminate, delay or fend off the demands being made on them. In the earliest days of the Industrial Revolution, businesses were relatively unaffected by government regulation. Labor was cheap and plentiful. Businesses behaved pretty much as they wanted, exerting tremendous influence over their towns, industries and governments. Resistance to government interference and active opposition to demands from both insiders and outsiders marked this early phase of business history. The emphasis was on maximizing profits and the self-interests of owners. The prevailing attitude was that managers owed their allegiance to owners, a view reinforced by the courts. In a

resistance approach
A social responsibility strategy in which businesses actively fight to eliminate, delay or fend off demands being made on them

---

Figure 6.4   Dimensions of Reputation

- **Emotional Appeal**
  - Has a good feeling about the company
  - Admires and respects the company
  - Trusts the company a great deal

- **Products & Services**
  - Stands behind its products and services
  - Develops innovative products and services
  - Offers high-quality products and services
  - Offers products and services that are a good value for the money

- **Financial Performance**
  - Has a strong record of profitability
  - Looks like a low-risk investment
  - Looks like a company with strong prospects for future growth
  - Tends to outperform its competitors

- **Social Responsibility**
  - Supports good causes
  - Is an environmentally-responsible company
  - Maintains high standards in the way it treats people

- **Workplace Environment**
  - Is well-managed
  - Looks like a good company to work for
  - Looks like a company that would have good employees

- **Vision & Leadership**
  - Has excellent leadership
  - Has a clear vision for its future
  - Recognizes and takes advantage of market opportunities

Source: Harris Interactive Inc. "Harris–Fombrun Reputation Quotient (RQ)."

1919 decision, a Michigan court refused to let Henry Ford divert stockholder dividend payments to "certain socially beneficial programs." The court held that directors had an obligation to stockholders and could not renege on that duty.[42] Regulatory agencies were virtually nonexistent. No laws protected consumers or the environment, and both suffered as a consequence.

Even in today's regulatory environment and with so many of society's needs vividly apparent, some businesses persist in doing as little as possible—only what the law demands—and even that they do reluctantly. Government agencies post law enforcement actions against businesses on their websites. For example, see the Federal Trade Commission *www.ftc.gov*, Environmental Protection Agency *www.epa.gov* and the Food and Drug Administration *www.fda.gov*. Many of the companies are not found guilty, but signed consent decrees to avoid lengthy legal action. By signing a consent decree, the business agrees to take specific actions without admitting or denying any wrongdoing for the situation that led to the lawsuit.

reactive approach

A social responsibility strategy in which businesses wait for demands to be made and then react to them, choosing a response by evaluating alternatives

Reactive Approach Businesses taking a **reactive approach** wait for demands to be made on them and then respond to those demands by weighing their options. Anadarko Petroleum, Apache Corp., ChevronTexaco, Tesoro Corp., Marathon Oil, and Unocal bowed to public pressure and acknowledged that global warming is a serious issue. "Most of the oil and gas companies are taking climate change much more seriously than they were just a year ago," said Mindy Lubber, President of Ceres, an investor coalition that has helped coordinate the shareholder resolution filings with the oil and gas companies.[43]

proactive approach

A social responsibility strategy in which businesses continually look to the needs of constituents and try to find ways to meet those needs

Proactive Approach Companies taking the **proactive approach** continually look to the needs of their constituents, constantly staying in touch, sensing their needs and trying to find ways to meet them. Many companies have a variety of programs to help their communities. Some, like the small California sportswear producer Patagonia, encourage their employees to give of their talents in a variety of ways, such as community cleanups, tutoring local schools' students and sponsoring fundraisers to assist local environmental groups. Most companies support the national United Way campaigns and other community-based charitable drives. Some of America's small and most of its largest businesses have established funds or foundations that donate money to worthy causes such as education, the arts, environmental and ecology groups and various communities' human services agencies. According to the American Association of Fundraising Counsel (AAFRC) Trust for Philanthropy's 2009 estimates of charitable giving in the United States, total giving was $358.38 billion. Of this total, individuals contributed $258.51 billion to charitable causes, whereas total corporate giving reached $17.7 billion.[44]

Strategic philanthropy or *financially sound goodwill* refers to corporate donations that provide a return to the giver. Dollars given must support specific efforts, and the results must be monitored. The Conference Board's research indicates that when companies adopt this approach they gain "a better image, increased employee loyalty and improved customer ties."[45]

One example is strategic partnership in education. Realizing that today's students are tomorrow's customers and employees, many companies, such as McDonald's and Sonic, support the school districts in their communities. Others, like Chick-fil-A offer college scholarship opportunities to their high school employees who go on to college. In 2015 Starbucks announced full tuition reimbursement programs for its employees in partnership with Arizona State University One of the initiatives supported by General

Electric's GE Foundation is Developing Futures™ in Education. This encompasses the GE College Bound Program, which is available to high schools in U.S. school districts to help increase the number of students going on to college. The program's success is gauged by how many students go to college.[46]

RESPONSIBILITIES TO STAKEHOLDERS

9 Explain the responsibilities businesses have to stakeholders

Stakeholders are those who have an interest in or who are affected by how a business conducts its operations. In general, the stakeholders in most businesses include their owners and stockholders, employees, customers, suppliers and communities. Society as a whole can be considered a stakeholder, as well, if the business is large enough to affect people and environments beyond its physical location.

Owners and Stockholders A business and its employees owe their best efforts to owners. Assets must be conserved and used effectively and efficiently. Employees must do their best to maximize the return on invested capital and to generate a reasonable profit. Owners and employers should have the right to hire, train, reward, promote, discipline, and remove employees in accordance with ethical, moral, and legal restraints. Owners and employers should have the right to expect ethical, moral and legal conduct from their employees.

Employees Employees should enjoy equal access to the rights, responsibilities and privileges afforded by employers. Employees need to receive fair and equitable compensation, to be dismissed only for just cause and to be treated without discrimination. Employees should experience a quality of work life that provides satisfying jobs. They should receive competent guidance and direction in their work and be accorded due process in disputes. This chapter's Valuing Diversity and Inclusion feature discusses Abbott's proactive approach to valuing diversity and how it links with being ethical.

Employees hold certain rights to freedom of expression, safety, adequate information, privacy and confidentiality in regard to personal concerns. A growing trend in several areas of the country is to fire or charge higher insurance premiums to employees who are obese, consume alcohol or tobacco (both on and off the job) and for working a second job (moonlighting).

> Most states and dozens of municipalities have laws that ban discrimination, and many offer greater protection than federal law. In addition, 29 states and the District of Columbia restrict employers' ability to fire employees for various forms of off-duty conduct. The most common state statutes protect employees' right to use tobacco products. Some states extend the protection to alcohol use, too. Rarest are laws found in four states that protect all legal activities away from the employer's premises.[47]

Customers Businesses and their employees owe fair and honest representation of their products and services to their customers. Such products and services should encompass quality of design, manufacture, distribution and sales. Consumers have a right to be warned of any hazards they may encounter while using a product or receiving a service. The "Consumer Bill of Rights" presented to Congress by President John F. Kennedy in 1962 included the right to safety, the right to be informed, the right to choose and the right to be heard. In short, customers have a right to be treated fairly and with respect.

Many laws have been passed to protect consumers; government inspection of food, drugs and cosmetics is one result of such consumer protection legislation. Nolo

Diversity and Inclusion's Link to Ethics—The Abbott Approach

Abbott is an international leader in advancing health care. Doing business in more than 150 countries places Abbott in an enviable position and offers it a specific challenge: how to take full advantage of the enormous pool of talent that its worldwide workforce represents. It has a program designed to increase the effectiveness of the ways in which all employees work together. Its central purpose is to create a culture of inclusion.

Abbott's Executive Inclusion Council, led by its Chairman and CEO Miles White, meets once per quarter to track major initiatives and to decide which new ones to support. The hiring and advancement of women and ethnic minorities in management are monitored. Programs that support an inclusive work environment are supported. Employee networks include Asian Cultural Leadership Network, Black Business Network, La Voice (Hispanic/Latino), the Part-Time Network, PRIDE (gay/lesbian/bisexual/transgender) and Women Leaders in Action. Inclusion councils support the execution of Abbott's diversity strategies within various divisions across the company.

The company's initial efforts at valuing the diversity of its employees focused solely on race and gender. Management soon realized that this focus would have to be broadened to include the nationalities and customs not only of its employees, but of its customers as well. Mr. White says, "Fostering a diverse and inclusive workplace has helped us cultivate a more innovative and welcoming environment that makes us a better employer, business partner and corporate citizen" (Prince).

➡️ How has Abbott's globalization influenced issues of ethics?

Source: C.J. Prince, "Paying More than Lip Service to Diversity," *Chief Executive*, October 2002; Abbott, An Inclusive Culture. *http://www.abbott.com/careers/diversity-and-inclusion.html*.

---

discusses consumer protection laws by giving several examples.[48] Hundreds of cases have been brought under consumer protection laws. Some examples follow:

- A man sued a department store that ran out of an advertised waffle iron and didn't give him a rain check—a violation of the consumer protection law in his state.

- A homeowner sued a roofing contractor who falsely advertised that it could arrange financing for roof repair jobs.

- A woman sued a health spa that reneged on its promise to return her deposit and cancel her contract if she changed her mind within three days.

Suppliers Suppliers and businesses should build relationships based on mutual trust. Suppliers deserve to receive needed information in time to render quality service and supplies. They, like all parties to business contracts, have the legal right to be treated according to the terms of their agreements.

Fifteen years of combined research into over 1200 organizations published by Logica in association with Warwick Business School found that "well managed outsourcing arrangements based on mutual trust can create a 20 per cent to 40 percent difference on service, quality, cost and other performance indicators over outdated power-based relationships."[49] Thus, contracts with trust-based relationships (flexible working arrangements, willingness to change and frequent and effective communication), rather than power-based relationships (punitive service level agreements and penalties), have a huge impact on return on investment.

Communities Those environments and their governments that are affected by a company's operations constitute its community. The quality of life in a community; its air, land and water quality; and its specific needs all come into play. All its constituents, many of whom may be customers, deserve ethical, legal and moral treatment. A suburban restaurant owner got complaints from neighbors about food-packaging debris on lawns and streets. He now employs a person full-time to patrol the neighborhood and pick up all litter within a square mile of the restaurant.

Pollution is a growing concern around the world, with mounting pressure to produce **green products**—those that minimize energy consumption, reduce carbon footprint and pollutive by-products connected with their manufacture and disposal. Automakers have developed more fuel-efficient, cleaner-burning engines encouraged in no small measure by California's tough environmental laws and the Clean Air Act of 1990. Americans have also embraced the idea of hybrid cars. Hybrid engines boost fuel efficiency by combining a traditional gasoline motor with an electric one. Ford has announced upwards of 40% of its models will be electrified by 2020.

In 2014, Mondelez, producer of brands such as Oreo, Chips Ahoy, Trident gum and Philadelphia cream cheese, bowed to pressures from several sources and agreed to change its food packaging from plastic film to cardboard packaging. McDonald's reduced its packaging for similar reasons in the late 1980s. The fast-food chain has also made attempts to help individuals with vision, hearing and speech impairments by adding Braille menus and picture menus.[50]

green products
Those products with reduced energy and pollution connected with their manufacture and disposal

GOVERNMENT REGULATION: PROS AND CONS

10 Describe government's role in promoting socially responsible conduct by businesses

Corporations have committed acts that harm the environment, consumers, communities and society as a whole. Laws now in existence were brought about largely by these abuses. When society can't depend on the perpetrators to act appropriately, it must compel such action. But the enforcement of many laws depends more on individuals' commitments to social responsibility than it does on government agencies. Governments simply do not have enough money or people to adequately enforce their regulations. Society's best protection rests in an informed citizenry and a formed conscience in each and every owner and employee.

A concerned employee who brings company wrongdoing to the attention of authorities who can do something about it is called a **whistle-blower**. Research shows that people become whistle-blowers for a variety of reasons. Some blow the whistle because of their strong moral and ethical codes. Some do so because they feel a strong obligation to protect others and their communities. Some are participants in the wrongdoing and may blow the whistle out of fear that disclosure may be made by others.[51] Many whistle-blowers believe that their superiors, like themselves, do not want to let their companies or customers be harmed by unethical or illegal conduct and will take action to stop the wrongdoing.

The United States Department of Labor, Occupational Safety and Health Administration (OSHA), Office of the Whistleblower, administers the whistle blowing provisions of seventeen other statutes, protecting employees who report violations of various airline, commercial motor carrier, consumer product, environmental, health care reform, nuclear energy, pipeline, public transportation agency, railroad and securities laws. Unfortunately, all too often the bearer of bad news becomes a victim of retaliation by those individuals and companies that suffer from his or her disclosures. There have been numerous instances made public where they have been isolated, verbally denigrated, harassed, demoted and even fired.

whistle-blower
Individual who takes action to inform bosses, the media or government agencies about unethical or illegal practices within an organization

Ben & Jerry's is an example of a company committed to social welfare. It has taken a stand against the use of a genetically engineered bovine growth hormone. The U.S. Food & Drug Administration (FDA) has approved the hormone, but many consumers are concerned about its possible long-term effects on the safety of dairy products and their users' health. Although it contends that the hormones are perfectly safe, the dairy industry continues to face FDA reprimands in how they label products produced by cows that are given hormones.

The costs of regulation are high and getting higher. Businesses spend billions of dollars and millions of hours reporting to governments and complying with legal mandates. Although regulations, many argue, have made the United States less competitive around the world, they have also brought about needed reforms. It must be remembered that society grants businesses the right to operate. In return, society retains the right to proper treatment and a clean environment. When these fundamental rights are abused, we all suffer.

Unfortunately, after their products are produced and sold, too many businesses do not consider the costs placed on society. Such costs include cleanups of all kinds and the pressing need to recycle. Our nation has created a Superfund to clean up the worst cases of toxic waste; in fact, it spends hundreds of millions of dollars each year to right the wrongs of irresponsible businesses and individuals. Some environmental damage can never be repaired, or will take more than money to make right. Cleaning up such environmental hazards as nuclear waste, toxic dumps and oil spills will take years of commitment by dedicated individuals willing to invest the energy and talent required to remedy what has been done. All of us bear the costs through taxes.

Times, however, are changing. A growing number of individuals and corporations are moving from a reactive to a proactive approach and becoming more socially responsible. These businesses are redesigning processes and products, recycling and repackaging for reduced waste, anticipating needs and facing problems up front to become **sustainable communities**. They are measuring their environmental impact. The goal is to reduce their "carbon footprint" and become "carbon neutral" by offsetting the CO_2 resulting from these processes to wind up with a zero net increase in greenhouse gases.

Businesses are finding that being a good citizen pays off, with dividends that contribute to corporate bottom lines. Many companies have found that pollution prevention is better than pollution control. These organizations have made profits through their efforts to both prevent and reduce pollution. In addition, a growing number of consumers are showing their willingness to pay a premium for products that are environmentally friendly.

sustainable communities
Healthy, livable communities effectively using resources—economic, social and environmental—to meet today's community needs while ensuring that these resources are available to meet the community's future needs.

11 Discuss the ways in which businesses can promote socially responsible conduct

MANAGING FOR SOCIAL RESPONSIBILITY

Managers today must anticipate society's concerns and actively forecast and plan to meet its needs. They must make social responsibility a priority and, as with ethics, build a concern for it as a priority in their cultures and employees as well.

Top-Management Commitment

Executives in top management must commit the time and money necessary to make their organization socially responsible. They need to act as well as talk. They set the tone for their entire operation and establish its priorities. Authors Christopher B. Hunt and Ellen R. Auster recommend the following key elements to top managers who want to make their organizations proactive:

- Top-level commitment and support
- Corporate policies that integrate environmental issues
- Effective interfaces between corporate and business-unit staff
- High degree of employee awareness and training
- Strong auditing programs
- Establishment of responsibility for identifying and dealing with real and potential environmental problems

Figure 6.5 provides components and elements of a generic environmental management system (EMS).

Many organizations have built in a variety of safeguards to promote social responsibility. They usually start with the commitment in words and deeds of top management. Policies are written or revised to include concerns for social responsibility as well as ethics. They create programs for promoting an active role for their organizations in meeting societal needs. Training is given to employees, emphasizing how they can contribute. They encourage people to participate in their communities by granting time off and other incentives. Managers on leave, whose salaries are paid by their business employer, for instance, staff most United Way campaigns. The larger the

Figure 6.5	Components and Elements for Generic Environmental Management System (EMS)
Component	**Element**
Policy	Develop, document and communicate policy
Planning	Identify and track requirements
	Identify vulnerable assets and business and management practices that may impact them
	Identify pollution prevention (P2) opportunities
	Identify, document and rank environmental impacts
	Develop objectives and targets based on environmental impacts
	Establish programs to meet objectives and targets
Implementation	Provide resources (funding, manpower, technical, material)
	Identify training needs and provide training
	Develop and control EMS documentation
	Develop and document standard operating procedures (SOPs) for practices associated with impacts
	Develop and test emergency procedures
Evaluation	Identify, characterize and document problems (compliance and management system)
	Develop corrective/preventive actions (solutions)
	Secure management approval for solutions
	Implement solutions
	Review EMS
Improvement	Aim for continual improvement

Source: U.S. Navy Environmental Quality Assessment Guide, August 31, 1999.

enterprise, the more likely it is to have a separate department to plan for and oversee organizational efforts to be socially responsible and to see to it that environmental, fair employment and safety and health regulations are followed.[52]

Managers are the key to making ethics and social responsibility realities in their organizations. They need fully formed consciences based on sound values. They need to understand the motives that support their decisions and those of others. They need principles, rewards, examples and other forms of guidance and support to keep their commitments to ethical and socially responsible actions. See this chapter's Ethical Management feature for an example of ethical leadership by Jennifer Anastasoff, CEO of BuildingBlocks International. When an organization is truly committed to meeting its social responsibilities, it reflects this commitment in routine management decision making and ongoing planning efforts; and it monitors those efforts to ensure compliance.

Social Audit

To be truly effective, social responsibility needs the backing of all owners, managers and employees. It must be a consideration in daily decisions, not secondary to those decisions. Managers and owners need to know what is being done to meet social obligations, what will be expected in the future, and what past results and contributions have been.

Ethical Management

BuildingBlocks International and U.N. Millennium Goals

Jennifer Anastasoff is Founder and CEO of BuildingBlocks International (BBI), an international nonprofit that works with corporations to develop corporate service fellowships. BBI places professionals within community organizations around the world for between four weeks and a year. The professionals offer their management skills to help a marginalized area of the U.S. or a developing country.

BBI offers a Millennium Promise Marketing Fellowship for leaders who can work across different sectors. Each employee works directly with the world's most vulnerable populations to accomplish the first seven of the United Nations Millennium Development Goals. All 191 United Nations Member States pledged to meet the goals, listed below, by 2015. Progress toward the achievement of the goals has been made, but the target date was not achieved.

United Nations Millennium Development Goals

1 Eradicate extreme poverty and hunger
2 Achieve universal primary education
3 Promote gender equality and empower women

4 Reduce child mortality
5 Improve maternal health
6 Combat HIV/AIDS, malaria and other diseases
7 Ensure environmental sustainability
8 Develop a global partnership for development

➡ **What is the value in taking time off work to volunteer in a developing country?**

➡ **What would the employee volunteer gain?**

➡ **What would the company sponsoring the volunteer gain?**

Sources: BuildingBlocks International, *http://www.bblocks.org*; UN Millennium Development Goals, *http://www.un.org/millenniumgoals*; The Millennium Development Goals Report 2015, *http://www.un.org/millenniumgoals/2015_MDG_Report/pdf/MDG%202015%20rev%20(July%201).pdf*.

The **social audit** is a report on the social performance of a business. No uniform format currently exists, but most proactive firms have devised some method for auditing their efforts and for disclosing the results to both insiders and outsiders. Such an audit usually summarizes corporate activities under the following headings: charitable contributions, support of local community groups and activities, employment of protected groups, political contributions, pollution control and cleanup, health and safety measures and efforts to improve the quality of work life for employees.

Progress may be stated in terms of goals set and met, in monetary terms, or both. Those who benefit are clearly labeled, and the extent to which they benefit is quantified when possible. A company should share the results of the social audit with all constituents and stakeholders so that it can reinforce awareness of and commitment to the programs. Management should continue programs that have been successful, expand them if the need still persists, and eliminate programs that yield few positive results so that it may institute more productive ones. Finally, management should cite and reward people who contribute to successes.

social audit
A report on the social performance of a business

Chapter Summary

1 **Describe the two broad categories of ethical theories.**

Ethical theories can be grouped under two main headings: consequential and nonconsequential. The first deals with the ratio of good to evil flowing from an action. The "right" course is the one that yields the highest good-to-evil ratio.

The nonconsequential theories deal with the obligation to do one's duty to the best of one's ability. If one is faithful to one's duty, the greatest good occurs because the duty of the individual is carried out.

2 **Explain what individuals need in order to act ethically.**

Individuals need a personal moral and ethical code. Morality provides a set of core values and beliefs that act as a guide for evaluating intended actions. This code is acquired through life experiences. In addition, individuals must be able to cultivate a continuous awareness of their personal priorities, goals, values, needs, beliefs, attitudes and assumptions and how these influence their personal choices.

3 **Describe the organizational influences on ethical conduct.**

In addition to individuals' moral and ethical codes, environmental influences affect their choices within the context of their organizational affiliations. An organization's culture, the person's superiors and the core values and working climate send value messages as to what is essential to survive. Individuals are tempted to place the good of the organization above their personal ethics and the interests of other stakeholders. Ethics, thus, becomes as much an organizational issue as a personal one.

4 **Discuss three primary ways in which businesses can promote ethical conduct.**

Organizational controls on employee behaviors and practices can be summarized as a commitment of top management to promote an ethical culture based on organizational integrity through the establishment of codes of ethics and compliance programs. Training, "walking the talk," providing rewards as well as punishments, and establishing clear guidelines and limits are all part of an ethical culture. A variety of mechanisms are used by companies, including hotlines, committees, ethics and compliance officers and the encouragement of whistle-blowing.

5 **Describe the relationship between law and ethics.**

The law is an ethical and moral minimum. Individuals must take care to think beyond the law to what is best for all concerned and the effects of their actions. Conforming to the law cannot guarantee ethical conduct. Some laws may be immoral or unjust. No law may exist to forbid an action that can result in unethical behavior.

6 **Explain the concept of an ethical dilemma.**

An ethical dilemma exists when people are required to make a choice between options that are or seem equally unfavorable or mutually exclusive. An ethical dilemma also arises when all courses of action open to a manager are judged to be unethical.

7 **Discuss the guidelines for acting ethically.**

Many ethical tests exist. Most rely on an individual's personal morals and on a focus beyond the individual or organization. People must think as members of a broad community. They need to recognize that actions can affect many in subtle and not so subtle ways. Consideration for others' welfare is a must. Start with the law and move beyond it. Respect your moral code and those of others. Ask yourself, "What sort of person would take the action I intend to take?" Consider balance: Is there a win–win situation? Finally, ask yourself if you would be willing to tell those you love and the public in general about your intended actions.

8 **Explain the three approaches by businesses to social responsibility.**

The three approaches are resistance, being reactive and being proactive. In the resistance approach, an organization fights to eliminate, delay or fend off the demands being made on it. In the reactive approach, organizations wait for demands to be made and then respond to them by evaluating their alternatives. The proactive approach leads organizations to actively seek ways to be socially responsible. They continually look at their operations for ways in which to make them more environmentally friendly. They encourage their employees to be active in community causes. They look at the needs of constituents, constantly staying in touch, sensing their needs and trying to find ways to meet them. An emerging trend, called *strategic philanthropy* or *financially sound goodwill,* encourages businesses to get something in return for what they give.

9 **Explain the responsibilities businesses have to stakeholders.**

Stakeholders are owners, employees, external customers, suppliers and the communities affected by business operations. To owners, a business owes its most effective and efficient use of resources and an adequate return on owners' investments. To employees, it owes respect for their legal rights, fair and equitable treatment, competent guidance and due process. To external customers, a business owes quality and safe products and services, honest dealings, warnings about any hazards and fair and equitable treatment. To suppliers, a business owes relationships built on integrity and mutual trust, conformance to the law governing business dealings and honest conformance to all contractual obligations. Finally, to the communities on which it has an impact, a business owes socially responsible behavior and ethical con-

duct. It must, at a minimum, obey all laws affecting its interactions.

10 **Describe government's role in promoting socially responsible conduct by businesses.**

Businesses exist because government allows them to. Government is the referee in a capitalist society, setting rules and boundaries for economic activity. It must seek a balance between the rights of the individual and those of the various groups in the society it represents. For its laws to be effective, governments depend on individuals throughout society to know and obey them and assist in their enforcement. Additionally, it must put in place various sanctions that will encourage compliance.

11 **Discuss the ways in which businesses can promote socially responsible conduct.**

As with ethical conduct, businesses must have leadership at the top that makes socially responsible behavior a core value. If top management is committed, then awareness training, auditing and rewards for those who act on the core value will follow. Quality of working life will improve, and the company will reap the benefits that result from being a good corporate citizen.

KEY TERMS

business ethics   164

ethical dilemma   177

green products   184

morality   165

proactive approach   181

reactive approach   181

resistance approach   180

Sarbanes–Oxley Act (SOX)   175

social audit   188

social responsibility   179

sustainable communities   185

whistle-blower   184

REVIEW QUESTIONS

1. How can simply doing your duty be considered to be acting ethically?

2. In what ways are a person's morals and ethics linked? Can an individual's moral code be an ethical code as well?

3. How can an organization's culture influence the ethics of its members?

4. What can organizations do to promote ethical conduct from their members?

5. What, if anything, is wrong with this statement: "If it's legal, it's ethical."

6. You have been ordered to reduce your ten-person staff, all of whom are quite competent, by two people. What are the possible ethical dilemmas you may face?

7. What guidelines do you use to determine if an intended action is ethical?

8. When a company hires lawyers to find ways around a new environmental law, what approach to social responsibility is it exhibiting?

9. Who are a company's stakeholders? What obligations does the company have to each?

10. How does government promote socially responsible conduct on the part of businesses?

11. How can a business ensure its socially responsible conduct?

DISCUSSION QUESTIONS FOR CRITICAL THINKING

1. A car wash in your neighborhood has decided to increase its business by showcasing bikini-clad ladies drying cars as the cars exit the washing operations. The company proposes to begin offering the new process next week. As a neighborhood resident, what are the ethical and social responsibility issues here? As an alderman in the city government that must approve the proposed change, would you give it your approval? Why or why not?

2. A city ordinance has been proposed for your community. It would require that all sales of alcoholic beverages take place no closer to churches or schools than two city blocks. If it is enacted into law, six businesses (restaurants and taverns) would be forced to relocate or cease doing business. The ordinance is a response to calls for action by church-sponsored community groups and parent–teacher associations. What are the ethical and social responsibility issues here?

3. For both ethical and socially responsible behavior to take place within organizations, their top management must commit to making this happen. Why is top management's commitment essential?

4. Your boss has asked you to alter your time sheets so that more of your time can be allocated to a government project and less of it allocated to business customers. What will you do in response to this request?

Social Media Management Exercises

Some people don't trust business. They think companies lie, exaggerate or omit facts about their products. Given the vast amount of information people can access, they look to other people before they look to companies for information. Social media tools allow people to talk to others about products and companies. Thus, some companies are afraid of social media. They don't allow their employees to use social media on the job. They believe it is a waste of time. They fear the company name might be damaged. Yet, companies can benefit from thoughtful application of Social Media tools. More and more, people are already using social media in their daily lives. They expect interactive communications and engagement from companies.

- Choose a big-ticket item, like a car or a flat-screen TV that you would like to purchase. Read online reviews, ask friends for their experience and opinions, and then visit the company's website. Identify the product and websites. What does the company say about itself on its website? Does it match the online reviews? What about your friends' experiences? Compare and contrast the company website to online reviews and your friends' experiences and opinions. What social media tools would you recommend to the management of the company? (Consider an interactive "ask management" page; a blog to provide additional information and discussion of the company's product(s); Twitter to call attention to new blog postings, news releases or website updates, etc.)

Experiential Learning

Tenet: Does Getting Lean Mean Getting Mean?

Tenet Healthcare Corporation grew to become one of largest hospital chains by acquiring other health care providers and turning them into profit centers. When Tenet decided to enter a geographic area, it typically purchased two or more health care providers, consolidated their services, pooled their talent and reduced their costs. One tactic for improving efficiency was to replace high-skilled jobholders, such as registered nurses, with lesser-skilled and lower-paid nurse's aides. Because of its size—49 acute care hospitals in 11 states and 64 outpatient centers (About Tenet Healthcare)—Tenet negotiated price concessions from many of its suppliers, saving it millions each year. Although Tenet's stockholders and managers seemed happy, many of its competitors believed the company's tactics ignored what was best for patients and their communities.

Tenet hospital CEOs are given an incentive plan, thus enlisting their help in and commitment to generating revenues. Such incentives put pressure on executives to inflate prices. Off and on since the 1990s the company has been investigated and prosecuted by the U.S. Department of Health and Human Services. The company has settled fraud charges for admitting psychiatric patients who did not need hospitalization, carrying out unnecessary heart surgeries and overbilling Medicare. (Search Tenet Healthcare at the Justice Department, *www. justice.gov*.)

A special Medicare "outlier" fund compensates hospitals for caring for sicker-than-average patients by granting extra payments when the cost of a patient's care exceeds a threshold. The Stark Statute prohibits hospitals from billing Medicare for services rendered to patients by doctors with whom the hospital has a financial relationship, unless the financial relationship falls within specified exceptions. Tenet Healthcare's settlement is one of the largest from the False Claims Act recovery that the United States has obtained from a single hospital arising out of alleged violations of the Stark Statute. Settlements included corporate integrity agreements and fines.

Questions

1. In what ways might Tenet's drive for profits place patient care in jeopardy?

2. What ethical issues do you see in this case?

3. What issues relating to social responsibility exist for Tenet and its rivals?

4. Should servant leadership training be required for all Tenet Healthcare managers? (In a confidential employee survey at TDIndustries (a mechanical contracting and service company), 94 percent of employees agreed with the statement, "Management is honest and ethical in its business practices." TDIndustries garners that sort of loyalty with a management philosophy of *servant leadership,* which emphasizes the leader's role in helping employees develop their careers. Read more at http://www.tdindustries.com/AboutUs/ServantLeadership.aspx.)

Sources: U.S. Department of Justice, http://www.justice.gov; Tenet Healthcare, *http://www.tenethealth.com*.

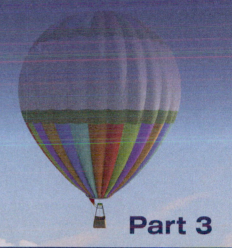

Part 3

Organizing

Chapter 7

Organizing Principles

LEARNING OBJECTIVES

After studying this chapter, you should be able to:

1 Explain the relationship between planning and organizing

2 Determine the importance of the organizing process

3 List and discuss the five steps in the organizing process

4 Describe and give an example of the four approaches to departmentalization

5 Define authority, and explain how line, staff, and functional authority differ

6 Explain the concept of power and its sources

7 Discuss the following major organizing concepts and how they influence organizing decisions:
   a. Unity of direction
   b. Chain of command
   c. Line and staff departments
   d. Unity of command
   e. Delegation
   f. Responsibility
   g. Accountability
   h. Span of control
   i. Centralization and decentralization

8 Explain the term "informal organization"

9 Compare the informal organization to the formal organization

Management in Action

Power

In order to accomplish anything, managers need power to influence people to do what they are asked to do with the resources that they are given. Position in the organization is one source of power. Additional sources of power come from expertise, information and personality. Managers can increase their power and influence by using all sources of power.

For each of the following statements, circle the number which indicates your level of agreement. Rate your agreement as it is, not what you think it should be. Objectivity will enable you to determine your management skill strengths and weaknesses.

	Almost Always	Often	Sometimes	Rarely	Almost Never
I put forth more effort and take more initiative than expected.	5	4	3	2	1
I upgrade my skills and knowledge.	5	4	3	2	1
I support organizational ceremonial events and activities.	5	4	3	2	1
I form a broad network of relationships with people at all levels.	5	4	3	2	1
I strive to generate new ideas, initiate new activities and minimize routine tasks.	5	4	3	2	1
I send personal notes to others when they accomplish something significant or when I pass along important information to them.	5	4	3	2	1
I express friendliness, honesty and sincerity toward others.	5	4	3	2	1
I find something in which I can specialize that helps meet others' needs.	5	4	3	2	1
I reward others for agreeing with me, thereby establishing a condition of reciprocity.	5	4	3	2	1
I avoid using threats or demands to impose my will on others.	5	4	3	2	1

Source: 2012 Critical Skills Survey, AMA, December 2012.
Retrieved from *http://playbook.amanet.org/wp-content/uploads/2013/03/2012-Critical-Skills-Survey-pdf.pdf.*

Compute your score by adding the circled numbers. The highest score is 50; the lowest score is 10. A higher score implies you are more likely to obtain power and influence others. A lower score implies a lesser degree of readiness, but it can be increased. Reading and studying this chapter will help you to improve your understanding of gaining power.

Adapted from David A. Whetton and Kim S. Cameron, *Developing Management Skills*, Eighth Edition (Prentice Hall, 2011), p. 26.

INTRODUCTION

"You can't tell me what to do; only Larry can—he's my boss!"

"When did the research and development department start reporting to marketing? I thought I was part of the production group."

"All I want is a decision on this engineering drawing. Can't anyone make a decision? Who's in charge here, anyway?"

The second managerial function is organizing. Every enterprise continually wrestles with the problem of how to organize or reorganize to pursue a new strategy, to respond to changing market conditions or to successfully respond to customer expectations. The enterprise wants to achieve systematic, continuing improvement—what the Japanese call *kaizen* (Chapter 2).

In earlier chapters you learned that an organization's success begins with a mission, goals, objectives, strategies and tactics. They develop these through integrated planning and decision making. But, planning is just the beginning. Organizing converts plans into reality; it makes things happen.

A company that has taken the time, energy and money to develop quality plans needs to organize its employees to attain these objectives and needs managers who understand the importance of organizing. Organizing, like planning, is a process that must be carefully worked out and applied. This process involves deciding what work is needed, assigning those tasks and arranging them into a decision-making framework (an organizational structure). This framework provides a structure for all jobs, making clear who has responsibility for what tasks and who reports to whom. An organization without structure can result in confusion, frustration, loss of efficiency and limited effectiveness.

This chapter will examine the fundamental organizing concepts; which determine the organizing steps, the types of departmentalization, authority, delegation, the span of control and the decentralization that managers use to organize. Chapter 8 will apply the concepts to the problems of organizational design and change.

The Formal Organization

Remember that a business is an organization. Owners and managers create businesses to achieve specific goals and objectives: to provide a quality product or service to a customer at a profit. When managers create an organization, then, they are actually developing a framework in which to create the desired product or service and provide a profit. This framework establishes the operating relationships among people: who supervises whom, who reports to whom, what departments are formed and what kind of work each department performs. This framework is known as a **formal organization**—the official organizational structure that top management conceives and builds. A formal organization does not just happen; managers develop it through the organizing function of management.

formal organization
The official organizational structure that top management conceives and builds

Organizing Process

Organizing is the management function that establishes relationships between activity and authority. It has five distinct steps that will be examined later in the chapter. The result of the organizing process is an organization—a whole consisting of unified parts (a system) acting in harmony to execute tasks that achieve goals effectively and efficiently and accomplish the company's mission.[1]

organizing
The management function that establishes relationships between activity and authority

Explain the relationship between planning and organizing

RELATIONSHIP BETWEEN PLANNING AND ORGANIZING

The managerial functions of planning and organizing are intimately related. Organizing begins with and is governed by plans that state where the organization is going and how it will get there. An organization must be built or an existing one modified to ensure that those plans are executed and objectives achieved. The organization must be able to concentrate its resources in a unified way to translate plans from intentions to realities.

An organizational structure is a tool of management to achieve plans. As the plans change, the structure should be responsive. The ability to change and keep up with the global society is the way to profits and existence. Examples of the relationship between planning and organizing—more specifically, how changes in plans affect the organization—can be seen in the changes taking place throughout business and industry.

Although these plans and organizational changes are primarily aimed at growth strategies, sometimes plans call for **downsizing**. Also known as *rightsizing,* downsizing calls for shrinking both the size of the company and the number of employees. Companies like General Electric (GE) have used this strategy to fuel strategic turnarounds. GE restructured—sold or collapsed divisions, pulled layers of middle management out of the organization, eliminated jobs and changed reporting relationships—many times, most recently with the 2016 announcement of its transformation into a digital-industrial company.[2]

Other times, plans call for **outsourcing**, the use of outside resources to perform a business process. UPS Supply Chain Solutions lets companies outsource everything from computer repairs to customer call centers. In this way, a company can focus on its core competencies and outsource support work that doesn't produce revenue.

Many American-based companies maintain that outsourcing business processes—such as call centers, processing loan applications or accounting processes—to low-cost, low-wage countries helps to keep down their own cost of doing business. When many people think of outsourcing, they think of India-based offshore outsourcing companies, the subject of this chapter's Global Application. Offshore employees receive information over the Internet, input the information into databases, and send the processed information back over the Internet. The flow of an outsourced health insurance claim is depicted in Figure 7.1.

Research paints a fairly consistent picture; layoffs alone don't work. And for good reason. In *Responsible Restructuring,* University of Colorado professor Wayne Cascio lists the direct and indirect costs of layoffs: severance pay; paying out accrued vacation and sick pay; outplacement costs; higher unemployment-insurance taxes; the cost of rehiring employees when business improves; low morale and risk-averse survivors; potential lawsuits, sabotage, or even workplace violence from aggrieved employees or former employees; loss of institutional memory and knowledge; diminished trust in management; and reduced productivity.[3]

Before we move on to examine the benefits of the organizing process, remember that organizational changes influence the staffing, leading and controlling functions. Hiring and training plans are quite different when a structure is expanding and when it is downsizing. The same is true for leading, if the company reorganizes into teams. Control systems, too, will need to be created to monitor effectiveness.

downsizing

Also known as rightsizing, it calls for shrinking both the size of the company and the number of employees

outsourcing

The use of outside resources to perform a business process, such as payroll, insurance records, health claims, or credit card applications

Figure 7.1   **Outsourcing**

Workers at an offshore company data entry center in New Delhi, India, look at digital images of medical claim forms and enter the information into a database. The client's system can decide whether to approve or deny the claim. The hospital and the insurance company are informed of the decision.

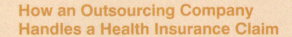

How an Outsourcing Company Handles a Health Insurance Claim

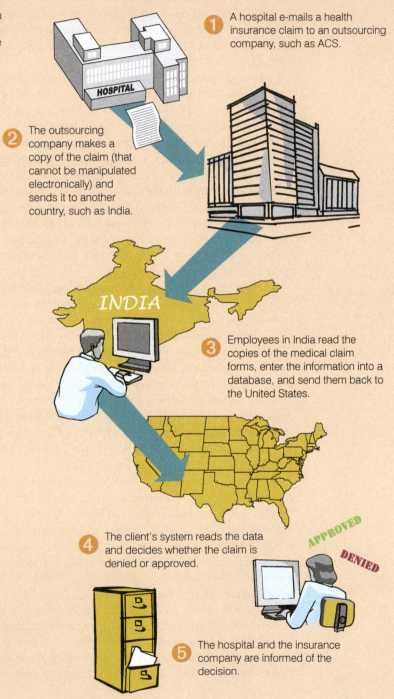

1 A hospital e-mails a health insurance claim to an outsourcing company, such as ACS.

2 The outsourcing company makes a copy of the claim (that cannot be manipulated electronically) and sends it to another country, such as India.

3 Employees in India read the copies of the medical claim forms, enter the information into a database, and send them back to the United States.

4 The client's system reads the data and decides whether the claim is denied or approved.

5 The hospital and the insurance company are informed of the decision.

Rightsizing by Outsourcing Hollywood to India

American-based companies, including IBM, GE and Accenture, maintain that business process outsourcing (BPO) to India is attractive because it has a vast pool of college-educated, English-speaking, low-wage workers. The low-costs and low-wages help to keep down their costs of doing business. One industry that has found India especially attractive is the American movie industry.

Hollywood has seen increasing costs in producing and marketing movies. At the same time, revenues have declined because more people are downloading movies online, and fewer people are buying DVDs. Furthermore, movies compete with online games, video games and independently-produced video content on sites such as YouTube.

Companies in India are providing Hollywood with post production, animation and local production support. Post production services include processing, printing, and digital and audio editing. Pre-production services include script writing, storyboarding, character designing, color model creation, conceptual artwork, key layouts, key animation and key background.

"At present, animation is the biggest player when it comes to outsourcing Hollywood to India," says [Dileep Singh] Rathore [producer and founder of the Mumbai-based On the Road Productions and the Los Angeles-based Directors Guild of America]. "India's cutting-edge IT skills, the large pool of highly-educated English speakers and lower manpower costs are the main reasons for outsourcing, on projects as diverse as Game of Thrones and Inter-

stellar. A typical half-hour 3D animation TV episode costs between $70,000 and $100,000 to produce in India, compared to $170,000 to $250,000 in America. U.S. animators can cost $125 an hour; in India, they cost $25 an hour. India offers animation at 25% to 40% lower rates than other Asian studios and much lower than those of American studios. The total cost of making a full-length animated film in the U.S. is estimated to be $100 million to $175 million. In India, it can be made for $15 million to $25 million."

➤ Downsizing in America has wiped out hundreds of thousands of jobs, disrupted the lives of employees, and changed the face of employment. How might rightsizing affect employment in Hollywood?

➤ In the past, India outsourcing companies have been known for improving business processes through reengineering, but now, they are moving into more knowledge-intensive services. Do you think that Hollywood is in danger of losing a sizable piece of its knowledge-based movie industry to India in much the same way Detroit lost its lead to Japan in the in the automotive industry?

Source: Nivedita Bhattacharjee, "Witches and thrones: Indian animators cash in on special effects boom," Reuters, (October 12, 2015), *http://www.reuters.com/article/us-india-outsourcing-animation-idUSKCN0S625Y20151012.* Knowledge@Wharton, "BPO Goes to Hollywood," (October 31, 2006), *http://knowledge.wharton.upenn.edu/india/article.cfm?articleid=4110.*

Determine the importance of the organizing process

Discuss the following major organizing concepts and how they influence organizing decisions:
• Unity of direction
• Chain of command

unity of direction
The establishment of one authority figure for each designated task of the organization

BENEFITS OF ORGANIZING

As noted, the organizing process is important as a way to help the organization attain its mission. It has four primary functions:[4]

1 *It clarifies the work environment.* Everyone understands what to do. The tasks and responsibilities of all individuals, departments and major organizational divisions are clear. The type and limits of authority are determined.

2 *It creates a coordinated environment.* Confusion is minimized and obstacles to performance are removed because it defines the interrelationships of the various work units and establishes guidelines for interaction among personnel.

3 *It achieves the principle of unity of direction.* The principle of **unity of direction** calls for the establishment of one authority figure for each designated task of the organization; this person has the authority to coordinate all plans concerning that task. The importance of this principle can be illustrated by the following example of its absence: various government agencies develop separate plans on the same topic because no one agency or person is in control of the task or can coordinate plans.

4 *It establishes the chain of command.* The **chain of command** is the unbroken line of reporting relationships from the bottom to the top of the organization. It defines the formal decision-making structure and provides for the orderly progression up and down the hierarchy for both decision making and decision-making communication. As a result, the confusion highlighted by the question, "Who's in charge here, anyway?" should not occur.

By applying the organizing process, management will improve the possibilities of achieving a functioning work environment.

chain of command
The unbroken line of reporting relationships from the bottom to the top of the organization

FIVE-STEP ORGANIZING PROCESS

Figure 7.2 illustrates the organizing process at the Excelsior Table Saw Corporation. At Excelsior—as in all organizations—organizing includes five steps:

1 Reviewing plans and goals

2 Determining work activities

3 Classifying and grouping activities

4 Assigning work and delegating authority

5 Designing a hierarchy of relationships

List and discuss the five steps in the organizing process

As you read and study the following description of the five-step process, refer to Figure 7.2 to see an example of how you build an organizational structure.

Reviewing Plans and Goals

A company's goals and its plans to achieve them dictate its activities. Excelsior Table Saw plans to make and sell a top-quality table saw, which will dictate its activities. Some purposes, and thus some activities, are likely to remain fairly constant once a business is established. For example, the business will continue to seek a profit and it will continue to employ people and other resources. In time and with new plans, however, the ways in which it carries out basic activities will change. The company may create new departments; it may give old ones additional responsibilities; some departments may cease to exist. New relationships between groups of decision makers may come into being as well. Organizing will create the new structure and relationships and modify the existing ones.

Businesses adjust their organizational structures in response to new plans. When a company seeks new opportunities, it does so as well. Business magazines and daily newspapers frequently carry announcements about companies making structural changes. Each company adjusts structures to mesh with plans aimed at helping it compete in the world economy.

Determining Work Activities

In the second step, managers ask what work activities are necessary to accomplish these goals. Creating a list of tasks to be accomplished begins with identifying ongoing tasks and ends with considering the tasks unique to this business. Hiring, training and record-keeping are part of the regular routine for running any business. What, in addition, are the unique needs of this organization? Do they include assembling, machining, shipping, storing, inspecting, selling and advertising? Identifying all necessary activities (as Figure 7.2 illustrates for Excelsior Table Saw) is important.

Figure 7.2 The Organizing Process in Action

Step 1
Reviewing Plans and Goals

Excelsior Table Saw Corporation
Our aim: To manufacture and market the Mark IV Table Saw at a 10% return on investment

---

Step 2
Determining Work Activities

Hiring	Training	Assembly	Sales
Grinding	Shipping	Payroll	Collections
Bookkeeping	Inspection	Recruiting	Compensation
Machining	Pricing	Advertising	Packaging

Step 3
Classifying and Grouping Activities

Marketing	**Finance**	**Human Resources**	**Production**
Sales	Pricing	Recruiting	Machining
Advertising	Payroll	Hiring	Grinding
Packaging	Bookkeeping	Training	Assembly
Shipping	Collections	Compensation	Inspection

Step 4
Assigning Work and Delegating Authority

Benny Salazar **Sales**	Marcia Padilla **Bookkeeping**	Pat McCormick **Payroll**	Jacob Finsterbush **Hiring**
Sanjay Patel **Collections**	Lee Mai **Advertising**	Melody Kwan **Assembly**	Renée Montaigne **Recruiting**
Bill Vlasic **Machining**	Joyce Sabha **Training**	Frank Peña **Shipping**	Celeste Golushko **Grinding**

Step 5
Designing a Hierarchy of Relationships

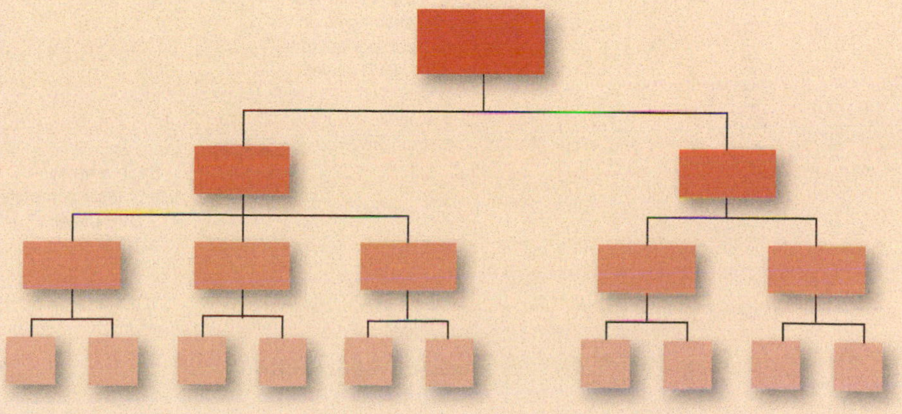

Specialization or Division of Labor An important concept in specifying tasks is **specialization of labor** or **division of labor**. Both terms refer to the degree to which organizational tasks are subdivided into separate jobs.[5] When using specialization of labor, a manager breaks a potentially complex job down into simpler tasks or activities. The result is that one person or group may complete only that activity or a related group of activities. Figure 7.3 shows three different degrees of work specialization in the job of producing a DVR player—low, moderate, or high specialization. The shaded bars at the side, top, and bottom of Figure 7.3 illustrate the relationship of specialization, efficiency and job satisfaction.

An advantage of work specialization is that work can be performed more efficiently if employees are allowed to specialize.[6] In addition, because employees are allowed to specialize in one area, they can gain skill and expertise. Specialization facilitates the process of selecting employees as well as decreasing training requirements. Finally, it allows managers to supervise more employees. Because each job is simplified, managers know what performance standard to expect and can detect job-related performance problems quickly.

Disadvantages of Work Specialization Despite its advantages, specialization can create problems. When specialization is overdone, jobs can become too simplified. When employees do one simple task—for example, tightening a nut—for eight hours a day, five days a week, they become bored and tired. In turn, when employees become bored and tired, safety problems and accident rates increase, absenteeism rises and the

specialization of labor or division of labor
Breaks a potentially complex job down into simpler tasks or activities

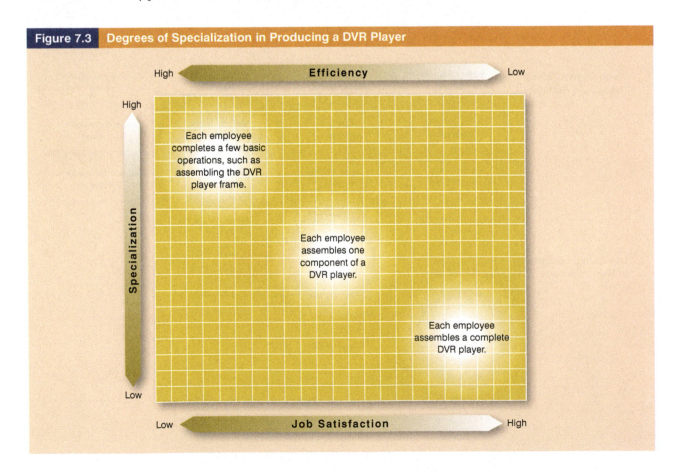

Figure 7.3   Degrees of Specialization in Producing a DVR Player

High ◄ **Efficiency** ► Low

High — Specialization — Low

Each employee completes a few basic operations, such as assembling the DVR player frame.

Each employee assembles one component of a DVR player.

Each employee assembles a complete DVR player.

Low ◄ **Job Satisfaction** ► High

quality of work may suffer.[7] Some companies have tried to overcome this disadvantage by job redesign (Chapter 10 describes this approach). Other companies have moved to the development of teams responsible for an entire product (Chapter 13 describes teams).

The process of specialization leads to designing a job. This job and the abilities required of a person to do the job are clearly stated in a job description and a job specification. These documents serve as the basis for staffing the organization (see Chapter 9).

4 Describe and give an example of the four approaches to departmentalization

CLASSIFYING AND GROUPING ACTIVITIES

Once managers know what tasks must be done, they classify and group these activities into manageable work units. This third step takes the jumble of Excelsior's tasks and creates four related and identifiable groups of like activities (Figure 7.2). When managers group tasks that are similar in terms of tasks, processes or skills, they are grouping them by the principle of *functional similarity*, or similarity of activity. This guideline is simple to apply and logical.

Managers apply the principle in three steps:

1   They examine each activity identified to determine its general nature. Normally, identifiable areas include marketing, production, finance and human resources.

2   They group the activities into these related areas.

3   They establish the basic department design for the organizational structure.

In practice, the first two steps occur simultaneously. Sales, advertising, packaging and shipping can be considered marketing-related activities. Thus, they are grouped under the marketing heading. Machining, grinding, assembly and inspection are manufacturing processes; they can be grouped under production. Personnel-related activities include recruiting, hiring, training and compensation; they are grouped under human resources.

As the tasks are classified and grouped into related work units (production, marketing, finance and human resources), the third step, **departmentalization**, is being finalized; that is, a decision is being made on the basic organizational format or departmental structure. Groups, departments and divisions are being formed on the basis of the organization's objectives. Management can choose one of four departmental types. Although Chapter 8 will describe these in detail, we will briefly discuss the options here.

Functional departmentalization involves creating departments on the basis of the specialized activities of the business—finance, production, marketing and human resources. Note in Figure 7.2, Step 3, that the managers at Excelsior Table Saw used this type of departmentalization. For most businesses the functional approach is the logical way to organize departments. It is simple, groups the same or similar activities, simplifies training, allows specialization, and minimizes costs.[8]

Geographical departmentalization groups activities and responsibilities according to territory. To be near customers, expanding companies often locate production plants, sales offices and repair facilities in their market areas. This grouping allows the company to serve customers quickly and efficiently and helps the company stay abreast of the changing needs and tastes of the customer. Disney—with theme parks in Anaheim, Orlando, France and Japan—uses geographical departmentalization for

departmentalization
The basic organizational format or departmental structure for the company

functional departmentalization
Creating departments on the basis of the specialized activities of the business—finance, production, marketing and human resources

geographical departmentalization
Grouping activities and responsibilities according to territory

that aspect of its business. FedEx pursues its mission by using a geographic design, as shown in Figure 7.4.

Product departmentalization assembles the activities of creating, producing, and marketing each product into a separate department. This option is adopted when each product of a company requires a unique marketing strategy, production process, distribution system or financial resources. As shown in Figure 7.5, United Technologies has six product categories and capitalizes on this approach.

Customer departmentalization groups activities and responsibilities in departments based on the needs of specific customer groups. As shown in Figure 7.6, companies like Johnson & Johnson that markets products to three different customer groups—pharmaceutical, professional and direct to consumer—face an extremely difficult task. Because each customer group has its own demands, needs and preferences, Johnson & Johnson must use tailored strategies that are not necessarily compatible. Another example can be found at the Hoffman Agency, a small public relations firm that is the subject of this chapter's Valuing Diversity and Inclusion feature. By using customer departmentalization, Hoffman was better able to focus on customer needs and eliminate problems caused by functional departmentalization.

Although these department types have been presented individually, in reality most companies use a combination of types to meet their needs.

product departmentalization
Assembling the activities of creating, producing, and marketing each product into a separate department

customer departmentalization
Grouping activities and responsibilities in departments based on the needs of specific customer groups

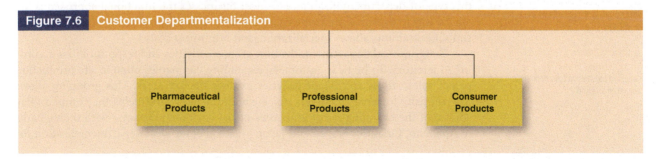

Figure 7.4   Geographical Departmentalization

Southern Region   Western Region   Eastern Region   Northern Region

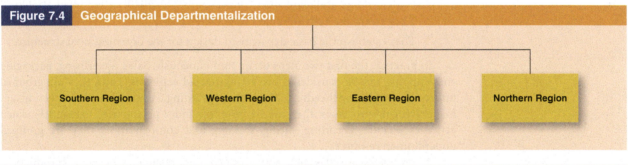

Figure 7.5   Product Departmentalization

Helicopter Division   Power Systems Division   Elevator Products Division   Aircraft Engine Division   Heating and Air Conditioning Systems Division   Aerospace and Industrial Systems Division

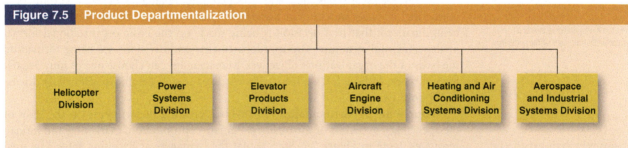

Figure 7.6   Customer Departmentalization

Pharmaceutical Products   Professional Products   Consumer Products

Reorganizing to Maximize Talent

"Delegation and empowerment are great words," states Lou Hoffman, "but they don't have much meaning if people don't know one another well enough to resolve things on their own." That was the problem at Hoffman's San Jose, California, public relations firm. The number of employees at the Hoffman Agency had doubled in two years, and Hoffman found himself dealing with issues that were a direct by-product of two factors—the departmental structure and the increasing ethnic diversity of the staff. If someone from the accounting department was dissatisfied with something coming out of the editing group, it wound up on Hoffman's desk. All the talent brought by the diverse staff was being short-circuited by the departmental structure.

Hoffman's solution: He restructured his departments to mesh the different functions and the staff's diversity. The new departmental design, focused on the customer base, not only combined accounting, editing and creative elements but also captured the diversity and inclusion in each former functional department. The teams were purposely designed to incorporate young and old, as well as different genders, ethnicities and cultures. To nudge the new structure along and help develop camaraderie and cooperation, Hoffman offered to pick up the tab for any two employees on the team who dined at the restaurant down the road. Moreover, he offered a special prize to anyone who lunched with every other person on the team. Over a two-month period, Hoffman spent $2100. The results: Delegated authority was used more effectively, all employees developed a better understanding of the workings of the agency, and the diverse backgrounds were combined to meet customer needs.

In an e-mail, Mr. Hoffman evaluated the "Out to Lunch" campaign. "It was more about helping our staff members get to know each other (since people tend to gravitate towards those on their respective account teams). The 'Out to Lunch' campaign was particularly effective since we had one large client which constituted roughly 40 percent of our revenue. As a result, it was only as if there were two agencies within our company. The 'Out to Lunch' campaign helped to break down this barrier."

Today, Hoffman's client revenue is nicely spread across several clients, so this dynamic no longer exists. Hoffman says, "As a professional services firm, it's all about the people. We've continued to implement things out of the norm to cultivate what we'd like to think is a unique culture. For example, we implemented what we call 'Building Bridges' in which a person takes a two-week assignment in one of our overseas offices in Europe or Asia. While less grand, our summer hours in which we shut down the office early on Friday afternoon so folks can get an early start on their weekend was a hit last year and will be repeated this year."

Lou Hoffman was named one of the 2015 most influential tech agency PR executives in the world.

➡ **What are some of the major concerns or problems a manager might face in a culturally diverse organization?**

➡ **How did Lou Hoffman advance the idea of diverse employees getting to know each other better?**

➡ **Which of these ideas did you like the best? Why?**

Sources: Tom Lytton-Dickie, "The 100 most influential tech agency PR executives globally," *Hot Topics*, *https://www.hottopics.ht/stories/infographic/the-100-top-tech-pr-executives-in-the-world/*; 2014; Jennifer Fishsbein, "Balancing Work and Life," *BusinessWeek*, June 9, 2008, *http://www.hoffman.com/v3/pop/lou_bizwk.html*; e-mail interview with Lou Hoffman, April 5, 2006; Donna Fenn, "Out to Lunch," *Inc.*, June 1995, 89; Hoffman Agency, *http://www.hoffman.com*.

There is no such thing as the one right organization. There are only organizations, each of which has distinct strengths, distinct limitations and specific applications. It has become clear that organization is not an absolute. It is a tool for making people productive in working together. As such, a given organizational structure fits certain tasks in certain conditions and at certain times.... In any enterprise ... there is need for a number of different organizational structures coexisting side by side.[9]

Companies like Verizon and AT&T incorporate departments arranged by function, geography, product and customer to meet their objectives.

Assigning Work and Delegating Authority

After identifying the activities necessary to achieve objectives and classifying and grouping them departmentally, managers must assign these activities to individuals and give these employees the appropriate authority to accomplish the task. This step, critical to the success of organizing, is based on the principle of **functional definition**—in establishing a department, its nature, purpose, tasks and performance must first be determined as a basis for authority. This principle means that the activities to be performed determine the type and quantity of authority necessary. How much is needed to accomplish the tasks?

functional definition
The activities to be performed determine the type and quantity of authority necessary

Designing a Hierarchy of Relationships

The last step requires managers to determine the vertical and horizontal operating relationships of the organization as a whole. In effect, this step puts together all the parts of the organizing puzzle.

The vertical structuring of the organization results in a decision-making hierarchy that shows who is in charge of each task, each specialty area and the organization as a whole. Levels of management are established from bottom to top in the organization. These levels create the chain of command, or hierarchy of decision-making levels, in the company.

The horizontal structuring has two important effects: (1) it defines the working relationships between operating departments, and (2) it makes the final decision on the **span of control** of each manager. Span of control is the number of subordinates under the direction of a manager.

span of control
The number of subordinates under the direction of a manager

The result of this step is a complete organizational structure. An **organization chart** shows this structure visually. Look closely at Excelsior Table Saw's organization chart in Figure 7.7 below. As do all organization charts, it tells us the following:

organization chart
The complete organizational structure shown visually

1   *Who reports to whom.* This specifies the chain of command.

2   *How many subordinates work for each manager.* This is the span of control.

3   *The channels of official communication.* Communication channels are shown by the solid lines that connect each job.

4   *How the company is departmentalized.* This could be by function, customer or product, for example.

5   *The work being done in each position.* The labels in the boxes describe each person's activities.

6   *The hierarchy of decision making.* This details where the ultimate decision maker for a request, problem, appeal or grievance is located.

7   *The types of authority relationships.* Solid connections between boxes illustrate line authority, dotted lines show staff authority, and broken lines trace functional authority. These types of authority will be explained in the next section.

In addition, the chart serves as a troubleshooting tool. In the design (or redesign) stage, managers can create alternative structures to study their effectiveness and spot difficulties. In the operational stage, it can help managers locate duplications and conflicts that result from awkward arrangements. The chart does not, however, show the degrees of authority, informal communication channels and informal relationships—all keys in managing successfully. We will discuss these later in the chapter.

The organizing process draws heavily on the leadership skills of the management group. Very much like building a ship to carry the company across the ocean, the initial

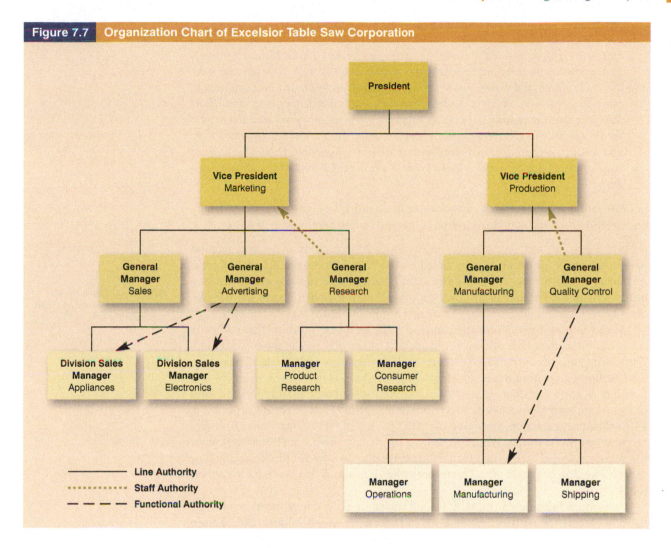

Figure 7.7 Organization Chart of Excelsior Table Saw Corporation

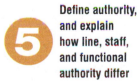

application of the process results in the company's first organizational structure and organization chart. Then, like a launched ship, the organization begins its journey in pursuit of its goals. Management is called on to monitor and control its actions, successes, or failures. Leadership will also be necessary—as was the case at the Hoffman Agency—to realign or redesign the structure in a new application of the organizing process.

5 Define authority, and explain how line, staff, and functional authority differ

MAJOR ORGANIZATIONAL CONCEPTS

The organizing process requires managers to draw on and integrate a number of major organizational concepts. To organize effectively, leaders/managers need to master concepts, including authority, power, delegation, span of control and centralization/decentralization.

Authority

One hears a great deal today about "the end of hierarchy." This is blatant nonsense. In any institution there has to be a final authority, that is, a "boss"—someone who can make the final decision and who can then expect to be obeyed in a situation of common peril—and every institution is likely to encounter it sooner or later. If the ship founders, the captain does not call a meeting; the captain gives an order. And if the ship is to be saved, everyone must obey the order, must know exactly where to go and what to do and do it without "participation" or argument. Hierarchy, and the unquestioning acceptance of it by everyone in the organization, is the only hope in a crisis.[10]

Because authority plays such a central a role in organizations, managers should fully understand its nature, sources, importance, variations and relationship to power.

Nature, Sources, and Importance of Authority   All managers in an organization have authority in different degrees, based on the level of management they occupy. **Authority** is the formal and legitimate right of a manager to make decisions, give orders and allocate resources. It holds the organization together, because it provides the means of command. How does a manager acquire authority?

It has been said that "authority comes with the territory," meaning that authority is vested in a manager because of the position he or she occupies in the organization. Thus, authority is defined in each manager's job description or job charter. The person who occupies a position has its formal authority as long as he or she remains in that position. As the job changes in scope and complexity, so should the amount and kind of formal authority possessed. As Albert Bersticker, former CEO of Ferro Corporation, a diversified organization composed of 100 SBUs, noted, "The Ivory Tower isn't dictating all corporate moves. What I stress from my management team is that they make the decisions. I won't tell a divisional manager what to do—I want him to decide how to fix it, tweak it, or get rid of it. The authority for decisions is theirs—that's what their job is."[11]

Johnson & Johnson's former CEO Ralph Larsen sings the same tune. When Robert Croce took over the reins at Ethicon Endo-Surgery, a Johnson & Johnson SBU, Larsen did not tell Croce what the latter's growth and earnings targets should be but let Croce decide instead. Croce was far more ambitious than Larsen expected, claiming he would control half of the world's staple and endosurgery business and be profitable in three years.[12]

Types of Authority   In an organization, three different types of authority are created by the relationships between individuals and departments.

Line authority defines the relationship between superior and subordinate. Any manager who supervises operating employees—or other managers—has line authority, allowing the manager to give direct orders to those subordinates, evaluate their actions and reward or punish them. At Johnson & Johnson, Corporate Chairman William C. Weldon, has line authority over the CEOs of the 250 SBUs, who, in turn, have line authority over their vice presidents. In an organization, line authority, shown by solid lines with arrows in Figure 7.8, flows downward directly from superior to subordinate.

Staff authority is the authority to serve in an advisory capacity. Managers who provide advice or technical assistance are granted advisory authority. This staff or advisory authority provides no basis for direct control over the subordinates or activities

authority
The formal and legitimate right of a manager to make decisions, give orders and allocate resources

line authority
The relationship between superior and subordinate; any manager who supervises operating employees—or other managers—has line authority

staff authority
The authority to serve in an advisory capacity; it flows upward to the decision maker

of other departments with which the person holding staff authority consults; however, within the staff manager's own department, he or she can exercise line authority over subordinates. Staff authority—in the form of advice or assistance—flows upward to the decision maker. In Figure 7.9, both the legal department and the research and development department provide advice to the president, as shown by the dotted lines.

functional authority
The authority that permits staff managers to make decisions about specific activities performed by employees within other departments

Functional authority permits staff managers to make decisions about specific activities performed by employees within other departments. Staff departments often use functional authority to control their procedures in other departments. For example, as Figure 7.10 illustrates, the human resources manager monitors and reviews compliance of recruiting, selecting, and evaluation systems in operating departments.

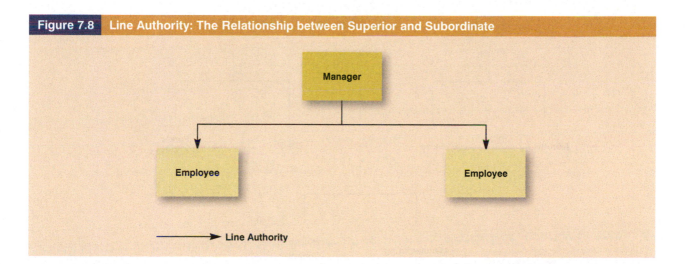

Figure 7.8   Line Authority: The Relationship between Superior and Subordinate

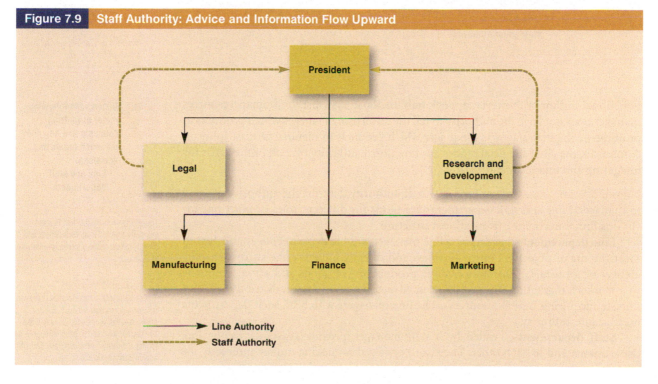

Figure 7.9   Staff Authority: Advice and Information Flow Upward

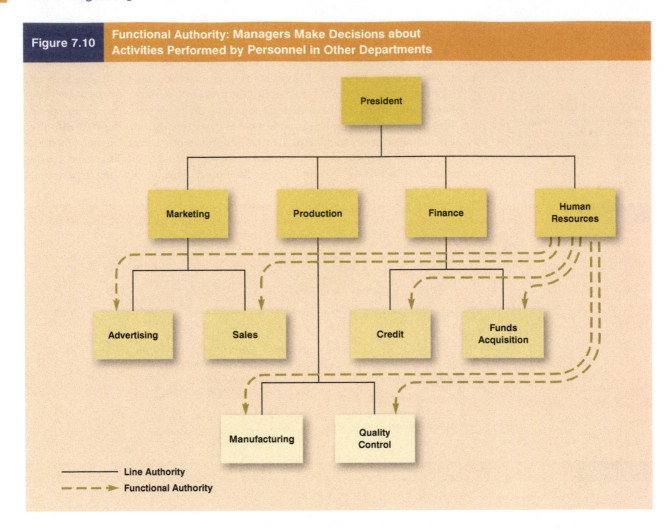

Figure 7.10   **Functional Authority: Managers Make Decisions about Activities Performed by Personnel in Other Departments**

Functional authority, however, applies only to those systems; the human resources manager does not have the authority to tell the advertising manager which products to promote or the manufacturing manager which products to manufacture. At Johnson & Johnson, the chief financial officer has functional authority over all of the SBUs for budgeting and financial reporting.

Line and Staff Departments Line and staff authority describe the authority granted to managers; *line* and *staff* departments are terms for different roles or positions for various functions in the organizational structure.

   Line departments, headed by a line manager, are the departments established to meet the major objectives of the business and directly influence the success (profitability) of a business. Examples include production (of goods and services for sale to a market), marketing (to include sales, advertising and physical distribution), and finance (acquiring capital resources). The line managers who head such departments exercise line authority.

   Staff departments, headed by a staff manager, provide assistance to the line departments and to each other. They can be viewed as making money indirectly for

Discuss the following major organizing concepts and how they influence organizing decisions:
 • Line and staff departments

line departments
The departments established to meet the major objectives of the business and directly influence the success (profitability) of a business

staff departments
The departments—including legal, human resources, computer services, and public relations—that provide assistance to the line departments and to each other, making money indirectly for the company through advice, service and assistance

the company—through advice, service and assistance—rather than directly contributing to achieving the company's major objectives. Traditional staff departments include legal, human resources, computer services and public relations. Staff departments meet the special needs of the organization. As an organization develops, its need for expert, timely and ongoing advice becomes critical. If the organization's resources can support the existence of a staff department, one can be created to fill the special needs gap. Staff departments can play a vital role in the success of a company. Staff department heads have line authority over their subordinates but staff authority in relation to other departments.

Line–staff interactions offer some real dangers of which all managers should be aware. Because staff people must sell their ideas, line personnel may view them as pushy or, in extreme cases, as undermining the line managers. Staff managers need to develop tact and persuasive skills along with ideas. They also need to foster credibility for their ideas to be accepted. Bad advice can result in no audience the next time. Another problem is that line managers are inclined to feel that "the buck stops" with them. In other words, because staff personnel are not responsible for the performance results of the line managers' unit and the line managers ultimately make the decisions, they don't have to take staff advice seriously.

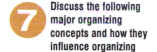

Discuss the following major organizing concepts and how they influence organizing decisions:
• **Unity of command**

unity of command
The organizing principle that states that each person within an organization should take orders from and report to only one person

Unity of Command

A concern of all managers in applying staff and functional authority is violation of the principle of **unity of command**, one of Henri Fayol's management principles (Chapter 2). The principle requires that each person within the organization take orders from and report to only one person.[13]

Unity of command should guide any attempt to develop operating relationships. Although each person should have only one boss, the operating relationships developed through staff departments mean that workers may have more than one supervisor in a given situation—or at least perceive that they do from the style with which advice is given. A departmental manager or subordinate may receive guidance or directives on a given day from human resources on employment practices, from finance on budget time frames and from data processing concerning computer procedures. If possible, these situations should be minimized, or at least clarified, for the sake of all affected.

> *It is a sound general principle for all kinds of organizations that any member of the organization should have only one "master." There is wisdom in the old proverb of the Roman law that a slave who has three masters is a free man. It is a very old principle of human relations that no one should be put into a conflict of loyalties—and having more than one master creates such a conflict.*[14]

Explain the concept of power and its sources

power
The ability to exert influence in the organization; power is personal

POWER

Two managers could occupy positions of equal formal authority, with the same degree of acceptance of this authority by their employees, and still not be equally effective in the organization. Why? Because one manager possesses more power than the other.

Power is the ability to exert influence in the organization. As Figure 7.11 shows, having power can multiply managers' effectiveness to influence people beyond what they can attain through formal authority alone. Authority is positional—it will be there when the incumbent leaves; and, as Figure 7.11 shows, it is part of the larger concept of power. Power is personal; it exists because of the person. A person does not

| Figure 7.11 | Power Increases a Manager's Ability to Influence |

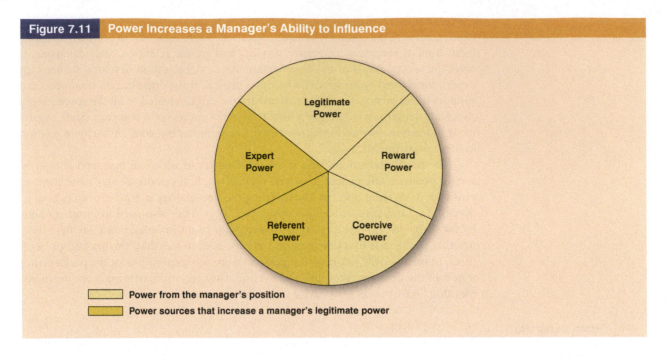

Power from the manager's position
Power sources that increase a manager's legitimate power

need to be a manager to have power. Some administrative assistants of top managers have considerable power, but no authority. Managers can acquire power from several different sources.

Legitimate or Position Power comes from holding a managerial position with its accompanying authority, providing a manager with a power base. The manager has the right to use this **legitimate power** because of the position. The higher a manager sits in the organization hierarchy, the greater is the *perceived power* (or, power thought by the subordinates to exist—whether or not it really does). Vice presidents wield or can wield a lot of power.

Reward Power is the opposite of coercive power. **Reward power** comes from the ability to promise or grant rewards. Managers have the ability to decide on raises, promotions, favorable performance appraisals and preferred work shifts.

Coercive Power is dependent on fear. A person reacts to this power out of the fear of the negative results that may happen if one fails to comply. Managers, because of their position, have the ability to punish by assigning unpleasant or boring work, withholding raises or promotions and suspending or dismissing an employee.

Referent Power is based on the kind of personality or charisma an individual has and how others perceive it. A manager who is admired by others—the latter perhaps demonstrating this admiration by their desire to identify with or emulate the manager—has referent power. The manager can use this power effectively to motivate and lead others.

Expert Power is possessed by persons who have demonstrated their superior skills and knowledge. They know what to do and how to do it. Others hope to stay on this expert's

legitimate power
The power possessed by managers and derived from the positions they occupy in the formal organization

reward power
The power that comes from the ability to promise or grant rewards

coercive power
The power dependent on fear of the negative results that may happen if one fails to comply

referent power
The power that is based on the kind of personality or charisma an individual has and how others perceive it

expert power
Influence due to abilities, skills, knowledge or experience

good side to be able to benefit from his or her expertise. A seasoned manager exercises power with newcomers. Knowledge of budgets, systems or company culture that others need provides a basis for the manager's power. Later in the chapter, in our discussion of the informal organization, the concept of power will be discussed. Chapter 13 also provides a discussion on power as a basis of leadership.

Discuss the following major organizing concepts and how they influence organizing decisions:
  • Delegation

delegation
The downward transfer of formal authority from one person to another

DELEGATION

Delegating authority takes place as a company grows and more demands are placed on a manager or because a manager wishes to develop subordinates' skills. **Delegation** is the downward transfer of formal authority from one person to another. Superiors delegate or pass authority to subordinates to facilitate the accomplishment of work.

Importance of Delegation is that no person can do it all in an organization. Therefore, managers should delegate authority to free themselves from some management areas to be able to focus better on more critical concerns. Having capable subordinates can increase the ability of a manager. Delegation is also a valuable tool in training subordinates.

When authority is truly shifted to the hands of non-managers and is accompanied by shared information, needed training and relationships based on mutual trust and respect, delegation becomes empowerment. Employees are given ownership of their tasks, along with the freedom to experiment and even fail, without fear of reprisal. As noted in Appendix A, empowerment is a key to quality and customer service.

Armstrong World Industries empowered employees in steps. "The first steps were taken in the 1960s and 1970s when they began recognizing and rewarding employees through pay-for-knowledge or pay-for-skills systems. The 1980s shifted the focus from individual workers to high-performance work teams. The 1990s pushed empowerment even further by emphasizing the work, or output, itself rather than the job."[15] The 21st century global environment requires individual workers or work teams to make choices and to transform those choices into desired actions and outcomes. Bob Price, a 7-Eleven store manager in The Colony, Texas, now tracks daily orders and leftovers of fresh sandwiches and pastries; then he figures in weather reports, special events in the area, and other factors that could affect demand. Using the information he has gathered, he maps out future orders. "Before this, we had no say about what we needed in our store. Either you had a field consultant come in and say we need to have more of something, or else they'd automatically ship the stuff. Now we have to make the decisions."[16]

Fear of Delegation "When you fail to delegate, the monkey on your back gets fatter and fatter until it squashes you," says Paul Maguire, a senior partner of a management consulting firm.[17] Even when they know the potential of empowerment, some managers still do not delegate. Some managers fear giving up authority or lack confidence in subordinates. Others worry that the employee may perform the job better than they can, are impatient, or are too detail oriented to let go. Some managers simply don't know how to delegate. Learning how to delegate is like learning to ride a bicycle—you have to learn to let go.[18] Delegation is not only a tool for survival, it is one of the key factors in a manager's success or failure. The process involves two of the most critical concepts in management: responsibility and accountability.

Delegation Process When managers choose to delegate authority, they create a sequence of events.

- *Assignment of tasks.* The manager identifies specific tasks or duties to assign to the subordinate, then approaches him or her with those tasks. As an example, at Grimpen Advertising, Sharon's manager assigns her the task of designing an advertising campaign for the company's new client, a styling salon called The Hair Connection.

- *Delegation of authority.* For the subordinate to complete the duties or tasks, the manager should delegate to the subordinate the authority necessary to do them. A guideline for the amount of authority to be delegated is that it be adequate to complete the task—no more and no less. In Sharon's case, she receives the authority to spend $10,000 on the campaign and to hire a graphic designer.

- *Acceptance of responsibility.* **Responsibility** is the obligation to carry out one's assigned duties to the best of one's ability. A manager does not delegate responsibility to an employee; rather, the employee's acceptance of an assignment creates an obligation to do his or her best. When Sharon takes on The Hair Connection account and agrees to complete it by the deadline and within the budget, she becomes responsible to her boss for the project.

- *Creation of accountability.* **Accountability** is having to answer to someone for your actions. It means accepting the consequences—either credit or blame—of these actions. When a subordinate accepts an assignment and the authority to carry out that assignment, he or she is accountable, or answerable, for his or her actions.

Delegation does not relieve managers of responsibility and accountability. Managers are responsible and accountable for the use of their authority and for their personal performance as well as for the performance of subordinates. If Sharon goes beyond the deadline, spends more than the budgeted amount, or does not develop an acceptable advertising campaign, she must answer to her boss. Her boss, in turn, is accountable to his or her boss for assigning the project to Sharon. On the positive side, if Sharon completes the project as designed, she will receive the credit and the praise, and so will Sharon's boss—for having delegated authority well. This chapter's Ethical Management feature focuses on the nature of responsibility and accountability for companies involved in payoffs and kickbacks.

The sequence of events outlined here should ensure that the process of delegation produces clear understanding on the part of the manager and the subordinate. The manager should take the time to think through what is being assigned and to confer the authority necessary to achieve results. The subordinate, in accepting the assignment, becomes obligated (responsible) to perform, knowing that he or she is accountable (answerable) for the results. Figure 7.12 provides some quick tips for successful delegation of authority.

SPAN OF CONTROL

As managers design the organizational structure, they are concerned with the span of control—the number of subordinates a manager directly supervises.

Wide and Narrow Spans of Control As a general rule, the more complex a subordinate's job, the fewer subordinates with those jobs should report to a manager. The

Discuss the following major organizing concepts and how they influence organizing decisions:
- **Responsibility**
- **Accountability**

responsibility
The obligation to carry out one's assigned duties to the best of one's ability

accountability
The need to answer to someone for your actions; it means accepting the consequences—either credit or blame—of these actions

Discuss the following major organizing concepts and how they influence organizing decisions:
- **Span of control**

Payoffs and Kickbacks — Who Pays?

In order to obtain or retain business, or to secure an improper advantage, unethical businesses might offer payoffs and kickbacks. A payoff is given before the sale is made; a kickback is paid after the sale is made. Some of the employees and managers accepting these "gifts" have something in common. They got caught.

- One of the most famous incidents of payoffs coincided with the rise in popularity of rock 'n' roll. This was before the Internet, I heart radio and iTunes.. It was even before DVDs, CDs, cassette tapes and 8-track tapes. Radio disk jockey Alan Freed coined the term *rock 'n' roll*. In 1962, he admitted that he had accepted payoffs from record companies for playing specific records on the radio. "The term *payola* was coined to describe this practice, combining *pay* and *Victrola* (the name of an early popular record player)." Congress amended the Federal Communications Act in 1960 to prohibit the payment of cash or gifts in exchange for airplay.

- A famous incident of kickbacks coincided with rise in popularity of the online trading marketplaces. It is detailed in one of the largest corporate scandals in American history, the "Enron Scandal" of accounting fraud. Before its bankruptcy in 2001, Enron was one of the world's leading energy companies. Part of Enron's accounting fraud included kickbacks. Michael J. Kopper, former Enron executive, paid kickbacks to Enron ex-Chief Financial Officer Andrew Fastow to make Enron look more profitable. David M. Howard, Kopper's lawyer, stated, "Michael has admitted that he misused his position at Enron to enrich himself and others, and in so doing violated his duties as an Enron employee." Enron's auditor, Arthur Andersen, one of the five largest ("Big Five') accounting firms, was dissolved in 2002 as a result of the scandal. The Sarbanes-Oxley Act was passed in 2002. In the Senate, it is referred to as the 'Public Company Accounting Reform and Investor Protection Act' and in the House as the 'Corporate and Auditing Accountability and Responsibility Act.'

➤ How do these two situations relate to the concept of responsibility?

➤ Who (middle-level or top-level management) will be held accountable?

➤ How could these actions be known but go uncorrected by management?

Sources: Shirley Biagi, *Media/Impact: An Introduction to Mass Media*, (2014 Wadsworth Publishing); Mary Flood and Tom Fowler, "Kopper Admits Kickback," *Houston Chronicle*, August 22, 2002, Section A, p. 1, 3 Star Edition, http://www.chron.com/CDA/archives/archive. mpl?id=2002_3574885.

| **Figure 7.12** | **Quick Tips for Successful Delegation of Authority** |

- **Develop a good attitude**
  - Give up some control
  - Trust your employees
  - Stay calm and patient

- **Decide what to delegate**
  - Delegate whenever possible
  - Consider skill, motivation, and work load

- **Select the right person**
  - Match skills and interests with tasks
  - Motivate your employees

- **Communicate responsibility**
  - Set and prioritize clear goals
  - Share possible pitfalls
  - Develop performance standards
  - Develop reasonable deadlines for progress reports and project completion

- **Provide support**
  - Let everyone know how and when you can help
  - Share your resources
  - Don't overrule decisions

- **Monitor the delegation**
  - Record progress
  - Ask for feedback on how well you are delegating

- **Evaluate the delegation**
  - Compare results with goals
  - Evaluate the employee's role
  - Discuss and give feedback

more routine the work of subordinates, the greater the number of subordinates that can be effectively directed and controlled by one manager. Because of these general rules, organizations always seem to have narrow spans at their tops and wider spans at lower levels.[19] The higher one goes in the organization's hierarchy, the fewer subordinates, as Figure 7.13 illustrates.

Finding a factory production supervisor with fifteen or more subordinates is not uncommon. Workers, who can be well trained to follow procedures will, once they master their tasks, require less of their supervisor's time and energies. They will know what they must do and exactly how to do it to meet their performance standards. The topic of this chapter's Quality Management is the changing roles of supervisors and production personnel.

Conversely, looking again at Figure 7.13, finding a corporate vice president with more than three or four subordinates is uncommon.[20] Middle and upper managers perform little that is routine. Their tasks usually require ingenuity and creativity; and, because the problems are more complex, they are more difficult to resolve. Managers

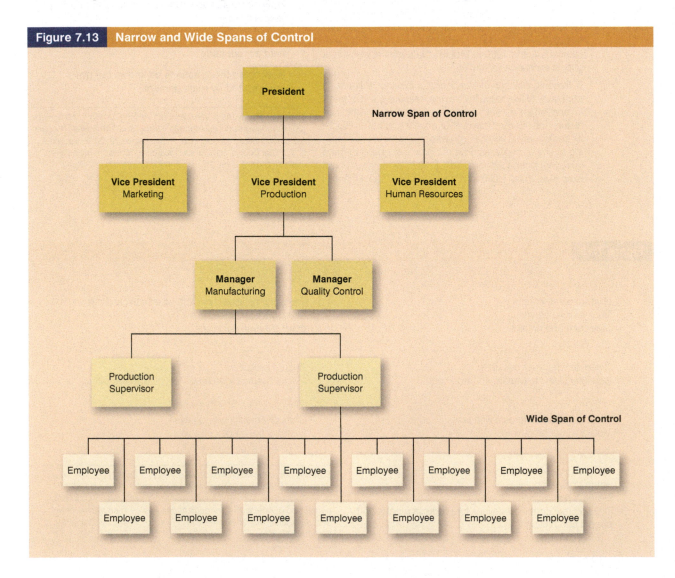

Figure 7.13   Narrow and Wide Spans of Control

Lean Defined

The MEP Lean Network defines **Lean** as "a systematic approach to identifying and eliminating waste (non-value added activities) through continuous improvement by flowing the product at the pull of the customer in pursuit of perfection."

We've all heard, "Time is money." This is especially true in manufacturing. Companies need customers and customers need products. In the above definition of lean, "pull of the customer" means that the customer places an order. Thus, pull means that the production process reacts to customer demand. Once a customer orders a product, the company doesn't get paid until the product is delivered. So, if the production time of the product can be shortened, the company will get its money sooner.

The lean manufacturing system is designed to "flow the product" through the production process in as short a time as possible. The production process begins with the raw materials and ends with the finished product. Flow, producing or moving one item at a time, is accomplished by the physical layout in product cells. All of the machines and employees needed to create a product are in one prescribed space. To flow (make one, move one), the product must stay busy and move through the system until it is finished and ready to be delivered.

Production time can be reduced by eliminating or minimizing waste or non-value added activities. Wastes can be remembered by the acronym "DOWN TIME."

Lean = Eliminating Wastes

- **D**efects
- **O**verproduction
- **W**aiting
- **N**on-Value Added Processing
- **T**ransportation
- **I**nventory
- **M**otion
- **E**mployees Underutilized (Knowledge, Skills, Abilities)

Quality is at the source of reducing the time the product spends in production. The proximity of machines in a product cell cuts down on waste that comes from having to transport materials from one department to another and offers employees an opportunity to be cross-trained on a variety of machines. Production costs decline as quality improves. Eliminating waste creates more value for customers. Lean shrinks the time from order to cash.

➡ **"Less is more." This statement applies to Lean manufacturing. But what if you aren't in manufacturing? How does the definition of Lean apply to other types of businesses?**

Lean
A systematic approach to identifying and eliminating waste (non-value added activities) through continuous improvement by flowing the product at the pull of the customer in pursuit of perfection. (The MEP Lean Network)

at these levels require more time to plan and organize their efforts. When they turn to their bosses for help, those bosses need to have the time available to render the assistance required. The only way to ensure having that time is to limit the number of people who will approach that boss for help—thus creating a narrow span of control.[21]

Proper Span of Control Given these general rules, how many subordinates should any one manager have? The answer depends on many factors and must be determined in terms of a specific manager:

- The complexity and variety of the subordinates' work
- The ability of the manager
- The ability and training of the subordinates themselves
- The supervisor's willingness to delegate authority
- The company's philosophy for centralization or decentralization of decision making

Setting an effective span of control for each manager is crucial to effectiveness. If a manager has too many people to supervise, his or her subordinates will be frustrated by their inability to get immediate assistance from or access to their boss. Time and other resources could be wasted. Plans, decisions and actions might be delayed or made without proper controls or safeguards. On the other hand, if a manager has too few people to supervise, the subordinates might be either overworked or feel over supervised and could become frustrated and dissatisfied.

Two managers who hold jobs at the same level in the organization should not automatically be assigned identical spans of control because their abilities and those of their subordinates will differ. Managers' and subordinates' qualifications and experience must be considered when spans of control are created. The more capable and experienced the subordinates, the greater the number who can be effectively supervised by one competent manager. The less time needed to train and acclimate employees, the more time is available to devote to producing output. In general, spans can be widened as the experience and competence of personnel grow—thus the continuing need for training and development. Of course, this generalization applies only up to the middle-management level of the organization; once there, the need for limited spans of control due to complexity becomes paramount.

The company's philosophy toward centralization or decentralization for decision making can also influence the span of control of a manager. We will next examine the concept of centralization and then explain how it relates to span of control.

CENTRALIZATION VERSUS DECENTRALIZATION

Discuss the following major organizing concepts and how they influence organizing decisions:
• **Centralization and decentralization**

The terms **centralization** and **decentralization** refer to a philosophy of organization and management that focuses on either systematically retaining authority in the hands of higher-level managers (centralization) or systematically delegating authority throughout the organization to middle- and lower-level managers (decentralization).[22] Management's operating philosophy determines where authority resides. Management can decide either to concentrate authority for decision making in the hands of one or a few or to force it down the organization structure into the hands of many. Johnson & Johnson's extraordinary success is attributed to the art of decentralized management. Behind the art is the philosophy held by CEO Alex Gorsky and four of his predecessors, William C. Weldon, Jim Burke, Robert Wood Johnson, and Ralph Larsen. Decentralized decision making is a core value and a core competency at Johnson & Johnson.

Centralization and decentralization are relative concepts when applied to organizations. Top management may decide to centralize all decision making: purchasing, staffing and operations. Or it may decide to decentralize—setting limits on what can be purchased at each level by dollar amounts, giving first-level managers hiring authority, or letting operational decisions be made where appropriate.

centralization
A philosophy of organization and management that focuses on systematically retaining authority in the hands of higher-level managers

decentralization
A philosophy of organization and management that focuses on systematically delegating authority throughout the organization to middle- and lower-level managers

Why Decentralize? To be effective, authority should be decentralized to the management level best suited to make the decision in question. A company president should not decide when to overhaul the engine in a forklift. Authority for that decision should be decentralized to the lowest possible level, in this case the plant maintenance manager or, if the company believes in empowerment, to the worker. Empowerment, discussed in Chapter 5, is the maximum expression of a decentralized philosophy. More companies are decentralizing authority to the people who know the jobs the best—the workers. This is especially true with team management, the topic of Chapter 13.

More and more organizations see decentralization as a means to achieving greater productivity and rebuilding the organization. Decentralization allows managers to be closer to the action and get closer to the consumer. As more organizations move toward "flatter" organizational structures, with fewer levels of management, decentralization and accountability are becoming watchwords for management success.[23] For example, Staples, an office-supply retailer, has committed to the principle of decentralization to develop "customer intimacy." Staples already provides great prices on papers, pens, fax machines and other office supplies; however, it plans to grow by providing customers with the best solutions to their problems. With a level of management removed, Staples encourages and empowers store managers and employees to solve customers' problems.[24] For example, when a customer wanted to buy an unusual variety of map pins, a salesclerk was empowered to:

- Telephone the manufacturer of a similar pin
- Fax the information on the pins to the customer after the customer returned to his own place of business
- Deliver the $20 order of pins to the customer

Guidelines for Judging Decentralization Research and experience have developed guidelines to follow in determining the degree to which a company is decentralized:

1 The greater the number of decisions made at the lower levels of management, the more the company is decentralized.

2 The more important the decisions made at lower levels, the greater the decentralization. Purchasing decisions are a good measure. A company with a purchasing limit of $100,000 at the first level is more decentralized than another company in the same industry with a first-level limit of $1000.

3 The more flexible the interpretation of company policy at the lower levels, the greater the degree of decentralization.

4 The more widely dispersed the operations of the company geographically, the greater the degree of decentralization.

5 The less a subordinate has to refer to his or her manager prior to making a decision, the greater the decentralization.

Relationship of Centralization to Span of Control A company's philosophy of centralization or decentralization in decision making can influence the span of control of lower and middle managers. It also can influence the number of levels in an organization. Centralized decision making produces narrow spans of control and more levels of management. With centralized management, top-level managers delegate little authority and must closely supervise those who report to them. Recall from our discussion on span of control, if a manager closely supervises subordinates, the manager has committed his or her time to a limited few. Given the philosophy of centralization, successive levels of managers will follow the same practice. Thus, there will always be narrow spans of control and the company will need many levels of management to reach first-line supervisors, seen in Figure 7.14.

Conversely, a philosophy of decentralized decision making generally means that the company will have wider spans of control and fewer levels of management. Such firms delegate authority and decision making down the organization to lower levels of management. Decentralization relieves managers of time commitments and allows them to spend time with more subordinates. As managers at each successive level follow this philosophy, two outcomes should be predictable: (1) a manager can supervise more subordinates and thus can have a wider span of control, and (2) a company needs fewer management levels to do the same job because people operate more independently. Review Figure 7.14 to examine an organization chart of a decentralized organization.

Despite the logic of this interrelationship of decision making and span of control, it does not often happen in practice. Managers with wide spans of control may choose not to delegate authority, and they are frequently not as effective as they could be if they did delegate. Another problem with this generalization is that other factors, as noted in the discussion on span of control, can influence how many subordinates report to a manager.

THE INFORMAL ORGANIZATION

8 Explain the term "informal organization"

Functioning within the formal organization designed by management—the organization of departmental structure, designated leaders (managers), decision-making guidelines, policies, procedures and rules—is a system of social relationships. These relationships, collectively, constitute the informal organization. Managers need to understand this informal organization because it influences the productivity and job satisfaction of all members of the organization—managers as well as non-managers. Managers find out through experience that not everything in an organization takes place within the squares on the organization chart. People by nature refuse to "stay in the boxes" as drawn. They choose to operate within the confines of and with the support of the informal organization.

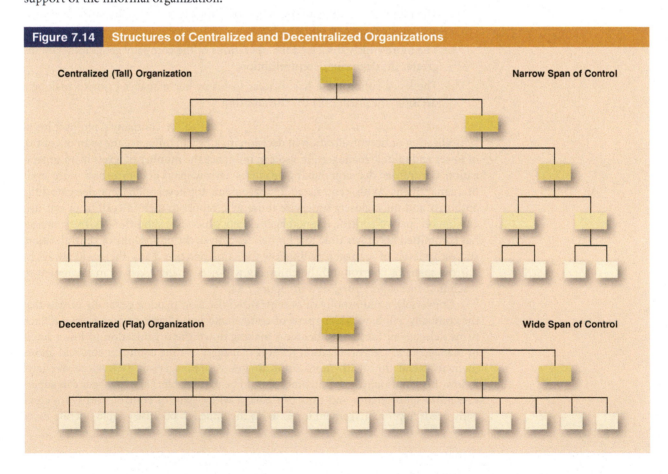

Figure 7.14   Structures of Centralized and Decentralized Organizations

Informal Organization Defined

informal organization
A network of personal and social relationships that arise spontaneously as people associate with one another in a work environment

The **informal organization** is a network of personal and social relationships that arise spontaneously as people associate with one another in a work environment.[25] It consists of all the informal groupings of people within a formal organization. Memberships in most informal organizations change with time. Members join together through the need for or enjoyment of one another's company; they find membership beneficial to them in one or more ways.

The informal organization challenges a manager because it consists of actual relationships that have real consequences on workers' behavior but that are not prescribed by the formal organization and, therefore, not shown on the company's organization chart.

The informal organization knows no boundaries. It cuts across the organization because it results from personal and social relationships, not prescribed roles. When two workers, at break or after work, gossip and share their perceptions of company affairs and fellow workers, their action is an example of the informal organization. Another example is an employee assisting someone in another department in solving a work problem. The informal organization should not be thought of as the domain of only workers. Managers form informal groups that cut across departmental lines. In addition, they actively participate in other groups with non-managers. The informal organization exists everywhere. The lunch bunch, the coffee break group and the employees who run, jog or walk together at lunch are other examples of informal groups. Social networking friends on Facebook, connections on LinkedIn and followers on Twitter are some more recent examples of informal groups. Monitoring corporate image on social networks is the topic of Managing Social Media.

Compare the informal organization to the formal organization

INFORMAL AND FORMAL ORGANIZATIONS COMPARED

The informal organization puts emphasis on people and their relationships; the formal organization puts emphasis on official organizational positions. The leverage or clout in the informal organization is informal power that attaches to the individual. In the formal organization, the formal authority comes directly from the position; and the person has it only when occupying that position. Informal power is personal and authority is organizational, as noted in Figure 7.15

Informal power does not come from within a person but is, instead, given by group members; informal power does not follow the official chain of command. Authority, in contrast, is delegated by management and creates a chain of command. Workers may grant power to a coworker at the same level or to someone in another department. Power is much less stable than authority; it comes from how people feel about each other and may change rapidly.

A manager probably has some informal power along with his or her formal authority, but the manager does not necessarily have more informal power than does anyone else in the group. The manager and the informal leader can be—and often are—two different individuals.

Formal organizations may grow to be extremely large, but informal organizations tend to remain smaller in order to maintain the personal relationships. As a result, large corporations like UPS tend to have hundreds of informal organizations operating within them.[26]

Monitoring Corporate Image

Personal relationships in informal groups are more visible than ever before through social networking sites. Three of the most popular social networking sites are Facebook, LinkedIn and Twitter. As many of you saw in the movie, "The Social Network" Facebook, the largest social network, was started by Harvard student Mark Zuckerberg in 2004 and only students at universities were allowed to join. Now, everyone can join can join several networks at once, linking them to their schools, workplaces and cities. LinkedIn is a social network originally designed for connecting career-minded professionals. It was created in 2003 by Reid Hoffman. Members can search for jobs, trade resumes and find other professionals. Now with over 400 million professionals, it is a hub for finding talent, partners and enabling marketing and sales. Twitter started in 2006. It is a networking service that lets members send out short, 140-character messages called *tweets*. Members broadcast what they're doing and thinking on the Twitter website, as well as using instant messenger (IM) or e-mail to read and post updates.

Businesses embracing social networking technologies are sharing information, innovating and collaborating. Yet, some managers question the benefits of social networking.

Within companies there is plenty of doubt about the benefits of online social networking in the office. Results from the third annual global survey about social media use in the workplace by Proskauer, an International Labor & Employment Law Group, found an increase in the number of businesses taking measures to stop employees from using social media at work. They found 36 percent of employers actively block access to such sites, compared to 29 percent the previous year and 43 percent of businesses permit all of their employees to access social media sites, a fall of 10 percent since their last survey (Proskauer).

A survey of 1,400 chief information officers conducted by Robert Half Technology, a recruitment firm, found that many companies were blocking Facebook and Twitter altogether. The executives' biggest concern was that social networking would lead to social "notworking," with employees using the sites to chat with friends instead of doing their jobs. Some bosses also fretted that the sites would be used to leak sensitive corporate information.

Businesses want to protect themselves from litigation and public relations problems. Employees should realize that the company has access to all e-mails and browsing history (sites visited on the Internet) from company computers. These are typically backed up or saved and are subject to review. Furthermore, there are sophisticated software solutions that allow businesses real time monitoring of posts or references on social media, and managers to view "alerts" to those which could prove troublesome." Monitoring can help managers ensure that employees aren't breaking laws using company computers or leaking confidential information.

➤ **The use of company communications technology is blurring the lines between personal and professional time. Employees use work computers for more than business. They work at the office, on the road and at home. How can we keep our work and personal lives from being intertwined?**

Source: Proskauer, "Social Media in the Workplace Around the World 3.0," (2013/2014), *http://www.proskauer.com/files/uploads/social-media-in-the-workplace-2014.pdf*; Martin Jiles, "A World of Connections," *The Economist*, January 28, 2010m *http://www.economist.com/node/15351002*; Sarah E. Needelman, "For Companies, a Tweet in Time Can Avert a PR Mess," *The Wall Street Journal*, August 4, 2009, *http://online.wsj.com/article/SB124925830240300343.html*.

Figure 7.15	Comparison of Informal and Formal Organizations

INFORMAL ORGANIZATION	FORMAL ORGANIZATION
Unofficial organization created by relationships	Official organization created by management
Primary area of emphasis is on people and their relationships	Primary area of emphasis is official organization positions
Leverage is provided by power	Leverage is provided by authority
Source of power: given by the group	Source of authority: delegated by management
Functions with power and politics	Functions with authority and responsibility
Behavior guidelines provided by group norms	Behavior guidelines provided by rules, policies and procedures
Sources of control over the individual are positive or negative sanctions	Sources of control over the individual are rewards and penalties

Emergence of the Informal Organization

The informal organization emerges within the formal organization. Because of the relationships and alliances in the informal group, workers' behavior differs from what managers may have expected based on the reporting relationships, procedures and rules established in the formal organization. Several factors contribute to these differences. First, employees sometimes act differently than anticipated. They may work faster or slower than expected, or they may modify a work procedure based on their experience and knowledge. Second, employees often interact with people other than those the formal organization specifies or with specified people more or less often than their job requires. Gene may seek advice from Joy instead of Larry, for example. Cindy may spend more time helping Buddy than she does helping Maceo. Third, workers may adopt a whole set of beliefs and attitudes that differ from those the organization expects of them. The company may expect loyalty, commitment and enthusiasm, but some employees may become totally unenthusiastic; whereas others may act rebellious and alienated. Values or attitudes that employees as a group accept as standards of behavior are known as **norms**. A norm serves as a guideline of behavior and an internal control device on members. Fourth, the groups of workers that form begin to display cohesion. **Cohesion** is a strong attachment to the group and a closeness measured by a singleness of purpose and a high degree of cooperation. As a result, a manager has dual sets of behavior to monitor—the activities, interactions and beliefs required by the formal organization and the ones that develop as people interact.[27]

norms
Values or attitudes that employees as a group accept as standards of behavior and that serve as a guideline of behavior and an internal control device on members

cohesion
A strong attachment to the group and a closeness measured by a singleness of purpose and a high degree of cooperation

interaction chart
A diagram that aids in identifying the informal organization structure by spotlighting the informal interactions people have with one another

Structure of the Informal Organization

Because individuals constantly enter and exit an informal organization, it continually changes. Its structure can be identified through the communication and contact people have with each other. Figure 7.16, an **interaction chart**, aids in identifying the informal organization structure by spotlighting the informal interactions people have with one another. Notice that the contacts don't always follow the formal organizational chart. The arrows indicate which person initiates contact with others.

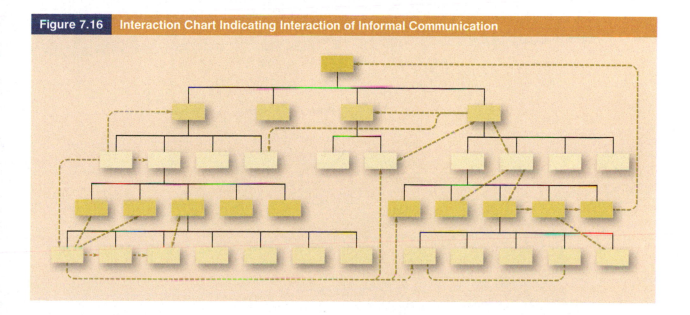

Figure 7.16 Interaction Chart Indicating Interaction of Informal Communication

Leadership of the Group As in a formal organization, the informal group develops leader–follower relationships. Because of the number of informal groups in an organization, a person may be a leader in one group and a follower in another. To determine why a person assumes the leadership role, you have to look at the groups and the individual members.

When you look at a group, each member has identifiable characteristics that distinguish him or her from the others—for example, age, seniority, level of earnings and technical ability. Each of these elements can provide status to its holder, based on what the group members value. The employee with the most status in the informal organization emerges as its informal leader. This person possesses great informal power. In some groups, charismatic leadership (leadership based on the person's personality) is common. In others, the leader may be the most senior person or the person holding the highest position in the formal organization.

A group might have several leaders of varying importance to perform different functions. The group might look to one person as the expert on organizational matters and to another as its social leader. A third might be consulted on technical questions. Even in a situation of multiple leaders, however, one leader usually exerts more influence on the group than do the others.

Nonleader Roles for Members Members of an informal group play other roles besides leader. As Figure 7.17 illustrates, an informal group normally has an inner core, or primary group; a fringe group, which functions within and outside of the larger group; and an out-status group, which, although identified with the larger group, does not actively participate in the larger group's activities.[28]

Figure 7.17	Composition of an Informal Group

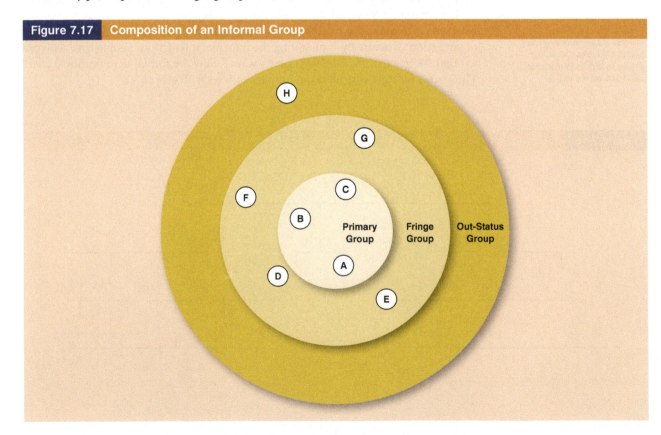

Working with the Informal Organization The three steps a manager must take in order to work with the informal organization are as follows:

1 Recognize that informal groups exist.

2 Identify the roles members play within those groups.

3 Use that information to work with the informal groups.

Managers need to understand the personality, values and culture of each group. They need to know how the groups' values and norms differ from those of the formal organization—if, indeed, they do. Managers also need to be able to identify the leaders of these groups and work with them to influence the total group. Trying to influence a group by appealing to a fringe member will fail. Managers need to approach the leaders at the core of decision making. Managers can also use the communication network of the informal organization to spread the word about a new company policy or to learn about how workers perceive a new company head.

Impact of the Informal Organization

The informal organization can affect the formal organization positively and negatively, as shown in Figure 7.18.

Positive Impact The informal organization has the potential to be helpful to managers in the following ways:[29]

- *Makes the total system effective.* If the informal organization blends well with the formal system, the organization can function more effectively. The ability of the informal group to provide flexibility and instantaneous reactions can enhance the plans and procedures developed through the formal organization.

- *Provides support to management.* The informal organization can provide support to the individual manager. If the manager will accept assistance, the informal organization can fill in gaps in the manager's knowledge through advice or through actually doing the needed work. When the group performs effectively and positively, it builds a cooperative environment. This, in turn, can lead the manager to delegate more tasks to the employees.

- *Provides stability in the workplace.* The informal organization provides acceptance and a sense of belonging. These feelings of being wanted and part of the group can encourage employees to remain in the workplace environment, reducing turnover. Additionally, the informal organization provides a place for the person to vent frustrations. Being able to discuss them in a supportive environment may relieve emotional pressures.

Figure 7.18   Positive and Negative Potential of Informal Organizations

POSITIVES	NEGATIVES
+ Makes the total system effective	– Develops pressure for conformity
+ Provides support to management	– Creates conflicts
+ Provides stability in the workplace	– Resists change
+ Provides a useful communication channel	– Initiates rumors and processes false information
+ Encourages better management	– Exposes weak management

- *Provides a useful communication channel.* The informal organization provides employees with the opportunities for interacting socially, for discussing their work and for understanding what is happening in the work environment.

- *Encourages better management.* Managers should be aware of the power of the informal organization in what is actually a checks-and-balance system. Planned changes should be made with an awareness of the ability of the informal group to make the plan successful or unsuccessful.

Negative Impact There are potential problem areas associated with the informal organization:[30]

- *Develops pressure for conformity.* The norms of informal groups strongly pressure group members to conform. The more cohesive the group, the more accepted are the behavioral standards. An informal group often uses rewards or penalties, called **sanctions**, to persuade its members to conform to its norms. Nonconforming can result in gentle verbal reminders from the group, but such a situation can escalate to outright harassment—ostracism, hiding supplies or sabotaging computer files.

- *Creates conflict.* The informal group can create two masters for an employee. In an attempt to satisfy the informal group, the employee may come in conflict with the formal organization. The lunch bunch enjoys going together as a group, eating a leisurely meal and analyzing the company. The lunch bunch enjoys its 60-minute lunch each day even though management has authorized only a 30-minute lunchtime. The employees' social satisfaction conflicts with the employer's need for productivity.

- *Resists change.* The informal organization can resist change. In an effort to protect its values and beliefs, the informal group can place roadblocks in the path of any work modifications. Establishing a four-day workweek or hiring younger workers could infringe on the values of the informal group, resulting in resistance to the change.

- *Initiates rumors and processes false information.* The informal communication system—the grapevine—can create and process false information or rumors. Rumors can upset the balance of the work environment. The grapevine will be discussed further in Chapter 10.

- *Exposes weak management.* Although skilled managers can see the relationships of the informal organization, less practiced managers can be stymied by them. The result may be a work group that does not perform and a manager who does not last.

sanctions
Rewards or penalties used by an informal group to persuade its members to conform to its norms

Chapter Summary

1 Explain the relationship between planning and organizing.

Planning and organizing are intimately related. Organizing begins with and is governed by plans that state where the organization is going and how it will get there. An organization must be built, or an existing one modified, to ensure that those plans are executed and objectives achieved.

2 Determine the importance of the organizing process.

The organizing process results in the creation of an organization—a whole consisting of unified parts (a system) acting in harmony to execute tasks that achieve goals effectively and efficiently and accomplish the company's mission. Additionally, the organizing process clarifies the work environment, creates a coordinated environment, achieves the principle of unity of direction, and establishes the chain of command.

3 List and discuss the five steps in the organizing process.

1 *Reviewing plans and goals.* A company's goals and its plans to achieve them dictate its work activities.

2 *Determining work activities.* Managers need to ask what work activities are necessary to accomplish the objectives. Both ongoing and unique tasks need to be determined.

3 *Classifying and grouping activities.* Once managers know what tasks must be done, they classify and group these activities into manageable work units—departments. Grouping tasks is accomplished by applying the principle of functional similarity. Departmentalization may be functional, geographical, product or customer.

4 *Assigning work and delegating authority.* After grouping the activities into departments, managers must assign the units to individuals and give them the appropriate authority to accomplish the task.

5 *Designing a hierarchy of relationships.* The last step requires managers to determine the vertical and horizontal operating relationships of the organization as a whole. Vertical structuring results in a decision-making hierarchy. Horizontal structuring defines working relationships between operating departments and makes the final decision on the span of control of each manager.

4 Describe and give an example of the four approaches to departmentalization.

Approaches to departmentalization:

- Functional departmentalization is logical and simple; it involves creating departments on the basis of specialized activities of the business—finance, production, marketing and human resources.

- Geographical departmentalization groups activities and responsibilities according to territory—for example, northern region, southern region. It allows companies to be close to, and adapt to, the needs of customers.

- Product departmentalization assembles the activities of creating, producing and marketing each product into a separate department—for example, elevator products division, aircraft products division. It is adopted when each product requires unique marketing strategies, production processes, distribution systems or financial resources.

- Customer departmentalization groups activities and responsibilities in departments organized on the needs of specific customer groups—for example, pharmaceutical, professional or final consumer.

5 Define authority, and explain how line, staff, and functional authority differ.

Authority is the formal and legitimate right of a manager to make decisions, give orders and allocate resources.

- Line authority is supervisory authority. It allows managers to give direct orders to subordinates, evaluate their actions and reward or punish them.

- Staff authority is the authority to serve in an advisory capacity. Managers who provide advice or technical assistance are granted advisory authority.

- Functional authority permits staff managers to make decisions on specific activities performed by personnel within other departments.

6 **Explain the concept of power and its sources.**

Power is the ability to exert influence in the organization. Whereas authority is positional, power is personal—it exists because of the person. There are five sources of power: legitimate or position power, coercive power, reward power, referent power and expert power.

7 **Discuss the major organizing concepts and how they influence organizing decisions.**

The major organizational concepts include:

• *Unity of direction.* A principle of organizing that calls for the establishment of one authority figure for each designated task of the organization. This person has the authority to coordinate all plans concerning that task.

• *Chain of command.* The unbroken line of reporting relationships from the bottom to the top of the organization. It defines the formal decision-making structure and provides for the orderly progression up and down the hierarchy for both decision making and communications.

• *Line and staff departments.* Organizations operate with line and staff departments. Line departments meet the major objectives of an organization and directly influence its success. Staff departments contribute indirectly—through advice, service and assistance.

• *Unity of command.* Each person within the organization takes orders and reports to only one person. It should guide any attempt to develop operating relationships.

• *Delegation.* The downward transfer of formal authority from one person to another. It involves assignment of tasks, delegation of authority, acceptance of responsibility and creation of accountability. Delegation frees managers from some management areas to be able to focus on more critical concerns. It can increase the ability of a manager.

• *Responsibility.* The obligation to carry out one's assigned duties to the best of one's abilities. Responsibility cannot be delegated to an employee; rather, the employee's acceptance of an assignment creates an obligation to do his or her best. Responsibility is a step in the delegation process.

• *Accountability.* Having to answer to someone for your actions. Accountability means accepting the consequences—either credit or blame—for these actions. Accountability is a step in the delegation process.

• *Span of control.* Refers to the number of employees a manager directly supervises. There is no correct number for the span of control, but it is normally narrower at the top of the organization than at the bottom. Generally, the more complex a subordinate's job, the fewer such subordinates should report to a manager. The more routine the work, the greater the number to be supervised.

• *Centralization and decentralization.* A philosophy of organization and management that focuses on either the concentration (centralization) or disposal (decentralization) of authority within the organization. Management determines where authority resides in an organization—either to concentrate authority for decision making in the hands of the few or to force it down the organization structure into the hands of many.

8 **Explain the term "informal organization."**

The informal organization is a network of personal and social relationships that arise spontaneously as people associate in a work environment. It consists of all the informal groupings of people within a formal organization.

9 **Compare the informal organization to the form organization.**

The informal organization puts emphasis on people and their relationships; the formal organization puts emphasis on official organizational positions. The leverage or clout in the informal organization is informal power—it attaches to the person. In the formal organization, the formal authority comes directly from the position, and the person has it only when occupying that position. Informal power is given by group members; management delegates authority. Informal power does not follow the chain of command; authority does. Power is much less stable than authority. Formal organizations may grow to be extremely large, but informal organizations tend to remain smaller. As a result, large corporations tend to have hundreds of informal organizations operating throughout them.

KEY TERMS

accountability 214

authority 208

centralization 218

chain of command 200

coercive power 212

cohesion 223

customer departmentalization 204

decentralization 218

delegation 213

departmentalization 203

division of labor 202

downsizing 197

expert power 212

formal organization 196

functional authority 209

functional definition 206

functional departmentalization 203

geographical departmentalization 203

informal organization 221

interaction chart 223

Lean 217

legitimate power 212

line authority 208

line departments 210

norms 223

organization chart 206

organizing 196

outsourcing 197

power 211

product departmentalization 204

referent power 212

responsibility 214

reward power 212

sanctions 226

span of control 206

specialization of labor 202

staff authority 208

staff departments 210

unity of command 211

unity of direction 199

REVIEW QUESTIONS

1. How do the functions of planning and organizing relate to each other: (a) in the initial development of a company; and (b) during the modification of the company's structure?

2. Identify and explain three important benefits of the organizing process.

3. List the five steps in the organizing process. Draft a one-sentence description of each.

4. Identify the four popular approaches to departmentalizing. Specify which approach you would recommend for each of the following organizations and defend your choices:

   a. A retail hardware store
   b. A company that manufactures and markets one product
   c. A company with sales offices in forty states
   d. A retail department store

5. Identify and explain the three types of authority.

6. What is power? What are its sources? How does it differ from authority?

7. Explain the importance to managers of each of these organizing concepts or principles:

   a. Unity of direction
   b. Chain of command
   c. Line and staff departments
   d. Unity of command
   e. Delegation of authority
   f. Responsibility
   g. Accountability
   h. Span of control
   i. Centralization/decentralization

8. What does the term *informal organization* mean? Of what does the informal organization consist?

9. How does the formal organization differ from the informal organization?

DISCUSSION QUESTIONS FOR CRITICAL THINKING

1. What type of departmentalization does your company or college use in its organizational structure? Diagram the structure and explain your answer.

2. Develop a different way to departmentalize your company or college. What are the specific advantages of your form of departmentalization over the current departmentalization design?

3. Which type of department (line or staff) is most important to an organization? Why? Could an organization function without either of them? Why or why not?

4. At your company or college, what is the span of control for the president? A vice president? A first-line supervisor or chair of a department? Why do different spans of control exist among these managers?

Social Media Management Exercises

Listening

E-mail flattens hierarchies within the bounds of an office. It is far easier to make a suggestion to your manager and colleagues via e-mail than it is to do so in a pressure-filled meeting room. Anytime when you have something that is difficult to say, e-mail can make it easier.

Social media flattens hierarchies *outside* the bounds of an office *across* the organization and *into* the online community. Customers, journalists, investors, competitors and employees are talking about companies and their products and services. These conversations are displayed for all to see, even if it is not flattering. Employees need to understand company policy. Anything they say—rightly or wrongly—could be tied back to the company. If they put the company name in their profile or online conversations, they need to follow corporate guidelines. If an employee violates that policy, it's management's job to assess the situation and take appropriate action.

Online content can be searched, sorted, indexed and summarized. Managers can gather feedback, respond to it, and take action based on that feedback. Listening is an important part of managing, because it lets people know that they have been heard, allowing managers to create a real connection with employees.

- Google Alerts tracks keywords and sends an e-mail to you when those keywords are found. Visit Google Alerts via e-mail at *http://www.google.com/alerts*.
- Google News aggregates headlines from news sources worldwide at *http://news.google.com*.
- Twitter Search allows you to see conversations in real-time at *http://search.twitter.com*.
- Choose a company and identify it.
- Find out what is being said by automating listening technology. Search for the company at Google Alerts, Google News and Twitter. Was the company in the news? What was being said about the company and its products and services?
- Was the company on the main social media sites like Facebook, LinkedIn, YouTube and Twitter? Which ones?

Experiential Learning

Merlin Needs a Magician

After getting a master's degree in business, spending time as a stockbroker on Wall Street, and working as a manager in a traditionally organized manufacturing company, Ashley Korenblat was hired as President of Merlin Metalworks. Korenblat, fresh from her experience at a large company, was anxious to try out her own theories at the small, Albany, New York-based producer of bicycles. In short order, Korenblat had to contend with the following organizational problems:

- Two welders, unable to get a decision from their supervisor, requested time off. One welder had a dentist appointment and the other needed to leave early to pick up an anniversary present.
- A review of the previous day's shipping log revealed that nothing had been shipped. The reason: a customer had called about a problem bottom bracket—the place where the bicycle pedals attach—which made the customer's $4000 bike useless. The customer service department had the authority to stop everything to solve a customer's problem. In this case, it meant turning off the final threading machine for a day, which brought the shipments to a halt.
- After little discussion, Korenblat made a decision to redesign the brakes on road bikes, believing it would be less expensive. Shortly after the first production run began, the person in charge of purchasing insisted on rehashing the decision. It turned out that the new design would lead to a series of new expenses—adding up to more than the expected savings.
- In an effort to have the employees make decisions and be more independent, the machine department was developing the production schedule, determining the size of the production runs, and coordinating the 35 operations in any given production run—some of which were linear, others which proceeded simultaneously. All went well until the company approached

a six-month backlog in a seasonal business. To respond, Korenblat kept increasing the size of the runs—"I know you made 200 57-centimeter road bikes last week, but this week we need 250 58-centimeter bikes." The result: the machine shop came to a standstill, waiting for the next command.

Questions

1. For each of the four situations noted, what organizational concepts apply? Identify the concept and explain the related problem.

2. As an adviser to President Ashley Korenblat, how would you resolve each problem?

Chapter 8

Organizational Design, Culture, and Change

LEARNING OBJECTIVES

After studying this chapter, you should be able to:

1 Define organizational design and describe the four objectives of organizational design

2 Distinguish between mechanistic and organic organizational structures

3 Discuss the influence that contingency factors—organizational strategy, environment, size, age, and technology—have on organizational design

4 Describe the characteristics, advantages, and disadvantages of functional, divisional, matrix, team, and network structural designs

5 Define organizational culture and describe the ways that culture is manifested

6 Explain the role of managers and employees in creating culture and making a culture effective

7 Define change and identify the kinds of change that can occur in an organization

8 Explain the steps managers can follow to implement planned change

9 Identify the organizational qualities that promote change

10 Explain why people resist change and what managers can do to overcome that resistance

11 Explain why change efforts fail

12 Explain the purpose of an organizational development program

232

Organizational Culture

An organization's culture is similar to an individual's personality. Each has unique behaviors. Organizational culture was defined in Chapter 3 as a dynamic system of shared values, beliefs, philosophies, experiences, customs and norms of behavior that give an organization its distinctive character.

Most people prefer one type of organizational culture over others. Where would you prefer to work? A personal place where the people seem like extended family? An entrepreneurial organization with people who like to take risks? A results-oriented organization with competitive people? A controlled and structured organization with formal rules?

For each of the following statements, circle the letter next to the description with which you most agree.

1. A leader should be:
   A. mentoring, facilitating, nurturing
   B. entrepreneurial, innovative, risk-taking
   C. no-nonsense, aggressive, results oriented
   D. coordinating, organizing, smooth running efficiency

2. Management of employees should include:
   A. teamwork, consensus, participation
   B. individual risk taking, innovation, consensus and participation
   C. hard-driving competitiveness, high demands and achievement
   D. security of employment, conformity, predictability, stability in relationships

3. People in organizations need:
   A. loyalty and mutual trust
   B. commitment to innovation, being on the cutting edge
   C. emphasis on achievement and goal accomplishment
   D. formal rules and policies, maintaining smooth running operations

4. Strategic emphasis should be:
   A. high trust, openness, participation
   B. acquiring new resources and creating new challenges
   C. trying new things and prospecting for opportunities
   D. permanence and stability, efficiency, control and smooth operations

5. Criteria of success should be:
   A. human resources, teamwork, employee commitment, concern for people
   B. most unique or newest products, product leader and innovator
   C. winning in the marketplace and outpacing the competition, competitive market leadership
   D. efficiency, dependable delivery, smooth scheduling and low-cost production are critical

Note the statements that you circled. If you circled mostly "A"s, you prefer to work in a personal place where the people seem like extended family. The most important requirement for employees in this culture is to fit into the group. Cohesion, a humane working environment, group commitment and loyalty are valued. If you circled mostly "B"s, you prefer to work in an entrepreneurial organization with people who like to take risks. The culture is fast-paced and high risk. New opportunities to develop new products, new services and new relationships are valued. If you circled mostly Cs, you prefer to work in a results-oriented organization with competitive people. Results are more important than process. The organization values competitiveness and productivity through emphasis on partnerships and positioning. If you circled mostly Ds, you prefer to work in a controlled and structured organization with formal rules. This culture offers a stable environment. Standardization, control and a well-defined structure for authority and decision making are valued.

INTRODUCTION

Managers frequently must rethink and reorganize to pursue their mission and strategic goals. As companies focus or refocus their attention on the customer—whether in manufacturing or marketing a product or providing a service—it becomes necessary to modify structures or drastically overhaul the organization.

Chapter 7 identified and examined the concepts and process of organizing. This chapter will focus on organizational structure as a tool. It will examine how managers integrate departmentalization, decentralization and span of control into an organizational design to achieve specific objectives. Initially the chapter will examine the nature of organizational design and its objectives and then introduce potential design outcomes. A discussion of the organizational structure options available to a designer are discussed. Then, the nature of organizational culture, manifestations of culture and how culture is created are explored. The chapter will conclude with a discussion of the nature of change—sources of change, types of change, rates of change and how to successfully manage and implement change.

1 Define organizational design and describe the four objectives of organizational design

DESIGNING ORGANIZATIONAL STRUCTURES

Organizational Design Defined

What is organizational design? Quite simply, when managers create or change an organization's structure, they engage in **organizational design**.[1] They develop the overall layout of the positions and departments as well as the interrelationships of the departments. Most importantly, these managers create the means to implement plans, achieve goals and objectives and ultimately accomplish the organization's mission—to satisfy the customer. Designers make decisions critical to success. As management consultant Frank Ostroff rightly noted, "The right organizational structure can take you from 100 horsepower to 500 horsepower."[2]

For organizational designers, organizational design is like putting together a giant jigsaw puzzle, with two differences. Unlike a jigsaw puzzle, an organization offers no picture to tell the designer what the final outcome should look like; and organizational design often involves billions of dollars to put the correct pieces together!

organizational design
The creation of or change to an organization's structure

Objectives of Organizational Design

Organizations have certain common elements: they operate with authority, they have departments, and they use line and staff positions. As alike as they might seem, however, no two organizations are exactly the same. Some, like Starbucks, rely on functional departmentalization; others, like Verizon, choose product groups. Some, like Sears, centralize decision making; others, like Honda, decentralize. Some, like Matsushita, have narrow spans of control; others, like American Airlines, have developed wide spans. The decisions made by managers on the various elements determine the organizational design; and organizations continually evolve to suit their operational requirements.

Regardless of whether managers are responsible for organizational design work for ExxonMobil or Campbell's Soup, they have the same objectives: respond to change, integrate new elements, coordinate the components and encourage flexibility.

Responding to Change "Nothing lasts forever" could be the slogan of organizational designers. For a firm to stay competitive, it must respond to changes in the environment—competition, technology, the global economy and consumer needs—as well as to changes that emerge from the company's evolutionary development. To remain static in the face of warning signals could eventually result in making change an arduous process. One company that needed to trim down to be competitive in a changing environment was Alcoa. Sometimes meeting the objective, however critical, creates consequences for employers, as this chapter's Ethical Management feature illustrates.

Integrating New Elements As organizations grow, evolve and respond to changes, they add new positions and new departments to deal with factors in the external environment or with new strategic needs. The objective of organizational design is make these changes *seamless*—that is, integrating these new elements into the overall fabric of the organization with positive impact and minimal friction. Accomplishing this objective may require adding a department to a level in the organization or virtually restructuring the company. The strategic need to provide quality customer service may require the dismantling of functional departments, creating teams and re-delegating authority.

Coordinating the Components Simply placing a department in an organization structure is not enough. Managers need to find a way to tie all the departments together to ensure coordination and collaboration across the departments. If this objective is not accomplished, the departments might not work together. Whether through reporting relationships, teams or task forces, departments must collaborate to avoid conflict and problems and to meet customer needs.

Ethical Management

Profits and Layoffs

Pittsburgh, Pennsylvania-based Alcoa, the aluminum manufacturer, reorganized after demand for aluminum fell to its lowest point in 20 years. Alcoa concluded that it could save money by moving assembly jobs used in manufacturing to India. By 2009, the mammoth restructuring shaved thirteen percent of the company's global workforce and shuttered plants to maintain profitability. The reorganization resulted in numerous job cuts by Alcoa's subcontractors. "Those layoffs netted Alcoa $325 million in cash savings", noted Alcoa Chief Financial Officer Charles D. McLane Jr." (Steverman).

Even in an industry plagued by massive cutbacks, Alcoa's downsizing appeared drastic. The Alcoa layoffs created a reverse multiplier effect. When a company takes away jobs, the reverse multiplier effect removes additional support and service jobs throughout the community, and economic developers become concerned. Manufacturing companies such as Alcoa pay higher wages than a retailer, and thus pump more money into communities where they operate.

➡ **Can layoffs used as a management tool become a matter of ethical concern?**

➡ **Did Alcoa's management owe a greater duty to its stockholders than to its employees?**

➡ **What ethical guidelines would you recommend to Alcoa's management to use when determining which operations, offices and jobs to eliminate?**

Sources: Ben Steverman, "Layoffs: Short-Term Profits, Long-Term Problems," *Bloomberg Businessweek*, January 13, 2010, *http://www.businessweek.com/investor/content/jan2010/pi20100113_133780.htm*.

Encouraging Flexibility The final objective of organizational designers is flexibility. Designers want to build into the organization—with all its authority, chains of command and bases of departmentalization—flexibility for decision making, for responding to and redirecting energies and for spotlighting people's talents. Flexibility for decision making differs from the aim of responding to change.

Range of Organizational Design Outcomes

Remember that the organizational designer specializes in creating a structure to accomplish the company's objectives and mission. The elements that a designer has to work with—chain of command, centralization/decentralization, formal authority, types of departments and span of control—fit together to form an overall structural approach. Depending on the balance of the elements, the design outcome can be very different. Some organizations see the need to use the formal, vertical hierarchy as a means of control and coordination. Other organizations decentralize decision making, create teams and provide managers with loosely structured jobs. The range of options can be described as tight (mechanistic) structures or loose (organic) structures.

MECHANISTIC ORGANIZATIONAL STRUCTURES

2 Distinguish between mechanistic and organic organizational structures

A tight, or **mechanistic**, **structure** is characterized by rigidly defined tasks, formalization, many rules and regulations and centralized decision making (Figure 8.1) shows the characteristics of a mechanistic structure). In an organization with a mechanistic structure, the vertical structure is very tight, with emphasis on control from top levels down. Tasks are broken down into rigidly defined, routine jobs. Many rules exist and the hierarchy of authority is the major form of control. Decision-making is centralized, and communication is vertical—it follows the chain of command.[3] The most vivid example of a mechanistic structure is the military.

mechanistic structure
A tight organizational structure characterized by rigidly defined tasks, formalization, many rules and regulations and centralized decision making

Organic Organizational Structures

A flexible, or **organic structure** is free flowing, has few rules and regulations and decentralizes decision making right down to the employees performing the job. Often referred to as the horizontal structure, the organic structure is a highly adaptive form that is as loose and workable as the mechanistic organization structure is rigid and stable. Rather than having standardized jobs and regulations, the organic structure allows changes to be made rapidly as the needs require. Organic structures have a division of labor, but the jobs people do are not standardized. Organizations with organic structures frequently redefine tasks to fit employee and environmental needs.[4] They have few rules, and base authority on expertise rather than on the hierarchical position of the person. Decision-making is decentralized and communication is horizontal, rather than being vertical up and down the chain of command. They empower employees to make decisions. Figure 8.1 contrasts the characteristics of organic organizations with those of mechanistic structures.

organic structure
A flexible, free-flowing organizational structure that has few rules and regulations and decentralizes decision making right down to the employees performing the job

Although the companies we have identified represent mechanistic and organic organizations, it is difficult to categorize an organization as purely mechanistic or organic. In actuality, most organizations favor one or the other, depending on how designers have integrated contingency factors— which is the topic of our next section.

| **Figure 8.1** | **Mechanistic Structures versus Organic Structures** |

Vertical Structure Dominant

- Fixed and Specialized Tasks
- Centralized Decision Making
- Formal Vertical Communication
- Rigid Hierarchical Relationships
- Many Rules
- Strict Hierarchy of Authority

Horizontal Structure Dominant

- Adaptable and Shared Tasks
- Decentralized Decision Making
- Informal Horizontal Communication
- Vertical and Horizontal Collaboration
- Few Rules
- Relaxed Hierarchy; Authority by Expertise

Mechanistic Structure   **Organic Structure**

Discuss the influence that contingency factors—organizational strategy, environment, size, age, and technology—have on organizational design

CONTINGENCY FACTORS AFFECTING ORGANIZATIONAL DESIGN

The dilemma facing managers charged with the responsibility for organizational design is to determine how mechanistic or organic the structure should be, for the organization to be successful? Studying the contingency factors that affect organizational design, strategy, environment, size of the organization, age of the organization and technology, provides the solution. The manager designs a structure to fit these contingency factors. If the organization structure is incorrect, problems occur.

Strategy

Managers build organizational structures to achieve objectives. Logically then, structure follows strategy; and when strategy changes, structure must change. Ford serves as an example. At the corporate level, the foundation for strategy is the vision. For Ford this is "People working together as a lean, global enterprise to make people's lives better through automotive and mobility leadership."

To achieve leadership, that meant selling off the sexy, high profile brands Land Rover, Jaguar, Aston Martin and Volvo. It meant bringing back the Taurus—a once hugely successful car that the company had abandoned—and completely redesigning it. It meant shifting emphasis away from bigger trucks to more fuel-efficient cars.

Then to carry out strategic goals, a company develops a business-level strategy. Chapter 4 introduced different business-level strategies that companies can adopt to achieve their goals. For example, if Dell Inc. chooses to pursue a prospector strategy, it must innovate, seek new markets, grow and take risks. An organic structure providing for flexibility and decentralization matches best with this strategy.[5] In contrast, if a top manager at ExxonMobil adopts a defender strategy—holding on to its current market and protecting its turf—a mechanistic structure providing for tight control, stability, efficiency and centralization would be the best fit.[6]

Firms can also select differentiation or cost-leadership strategies.[7] With a differentiation strategy, the company attempts to develop new products for the market.

Internally, it requires coordination, flexibility and communication. The proper fit is an organic structure. A strategy of cost leadership, in contrast, focuses on internal efficiency. A mechanistic structure is appropriate to achieve these objectives because it provides structured organization and responsibilities. Figure 8.2 provides a comparison of strategy–structure alternatives.

Environment

Chapter 5 demonstrated the impact of environment on decision making—specifically, the difficulty of making decisions in an uncertain or unpredictable environment. As in decision making, the organizational environment provides a major influence on the design of organizational structure. The stability and predictability of the environment has a direct bearing on the ability of the organization to function effectively. An unstable environment that changes rapidly and is less predictable raises two issues:

1 The organization must be able to adapt to change. It needs to be flexible and responsive.

2 The flexible organization needs greater coordination between departments. The individual departments cannot become isolated, creating their own goals and ignoring each other. In fact, departments tend to work more autonomously during periods of instability, which creates barriers.

As seen in Figure 8.3, the organizational structure must fit the environment for the organization to succeed. In a stable and predictable environment, the organization should have a mechanistic structure. Centralized decision making, wide spans of control and specialization "fit" in such an atmosphere. An uncertain environment calls for an organic structure that emphasizes flexibility, coordination and less formal procedures.[8]

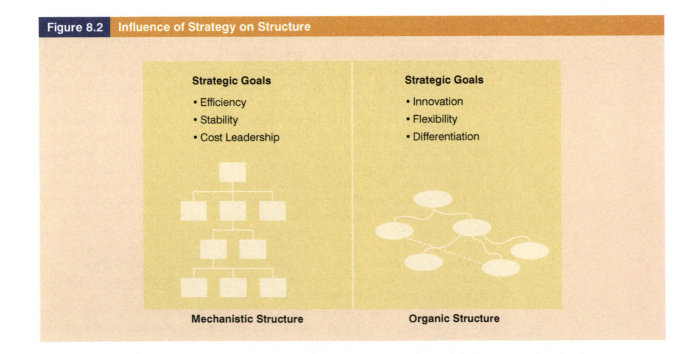

| **Figure 8.2** | **Influence of Strategy on Structure** |

Strategic Goals

- Efficiency
- Stability
- Cost Leadership

Strategic Goals

- Innovation
- Flexibility
- Differentiation

Mechanistic Structure

Organic Structure

Figure 8.3   Relationship between Environment and Structure

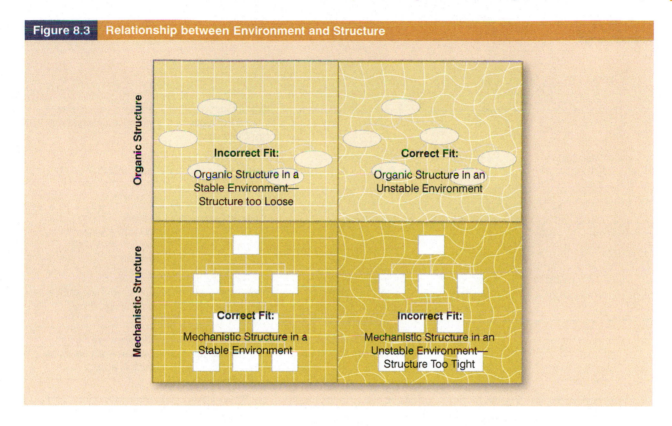

Size of the Organization

The size of an organization is normally measured by the number of employees. Research has found that large organizations differ structurally from small ones. Small organizations—for example, De Mar Plumbing and Tony's Café—have little division of labor, few rules and regulations, informal performance appraisals and budget development procedures. These characteristics describe an organic system. Large organizations, with tens of thousands of employees—for example, ExxonMobil and American Airlines—are mechanistic. They have a greater division of labor, more rules and regulations and more elaborate internal systems to control performance appraisals, rewards and creativity.[9] These large organizations—including Ford Customer Service Division and DuPont—have, however, begun to recognize the limitations of mechanistic structures and are moving toward more organic structures. In some cases they accomplish change by shifting structures; but more often, by downsizing, defined in Chapter 7. Although downsizing normally results in helping the organization in the long run, it often costs employees' jobs.

Age of the Organization

The longer an organization operates, the more formalized it is likely to become. With age comes standardized systems, procedures and regulations. Therefore, older companies take on characteristics of mechanistic structures.

Organizations, like people, evolve through stages of a life cycle. Within this **organizational life cycle**, businesses follow observable and predictable patterns. Figure 8.4 presents the four stages: birth, youth, midlife and maturity. Each stage involves changes in the overall structure.[10]

organizational life cycle

The stages an organization goes through: birth, youth, midlife and maturity, where each stage involves changes in overall structure

Figure 8.4	Relationship between Organizational Life Cycle and Structural Characteristics			
Structural Characteristics	**Birth Stage**	**Youth Stage**	**Midlife Stage**	**Maturity Stage**
Division of labor	Overlapping tasks	Some departments	Many departments, well-defined tasks, organization chart	Extensive—small jobs, written job descriptions
Centralization	One-person rule	Top leaders rule	Decentralization to department heads	Enforced decentralization (top management overloaded)
Degree of formal control	No written rules	Few rules	Policy and procedures	Extensive—most activities covered manuals by written manuals
Administrative staff	Secretary, no professional staff	Increasing clerical and maintenance, few professional staff members	Increasing size of professional support staff	Large—multiple professional and clerical staff departments
Internal systems (information, budget, planning, performance)	Nonexistent	Crude budget and information system	Control systems in place—budget, performance, operational reports	Extensive— planning, financial, and personnel systems added

Source: Based on Robert E. Quinn and Kim Cameron, "Organizational Life Cycles and Shifting Criteria of Effectiveness: Some Preliminary Evidence," *Management Science* 29 (1983), 33–51. Copyright 1983, The Institute of Management Sciences, now the Institute for Operations Research and the Management Sciences (INFORMS), 901 Elkridge Landing Road, Suite 400, Linthicum, MD 21090.

Birth Stage In the birth stage, an entrepreneur creates the organization. The informal organization has no professional staff, no rules, and no regulations. Decision making is centralized with the owner, and tasks are not specialized. Frito-Lay was in the birth stage when Elmer Doolin, making corn chips with his family in his mother's kitchen from a Mexican proprietor's recipe, began to sell to the neighborhood grocery store.

Youth Stage In the youth stage, the organization is growing. Its product or service succeeds and it hires more employees. A division of labor begins to emerge, as do a few formal rules and policies. Decision-making is still centralized with the owner, although it is shared with an inner circle. Frito-Lay was in the youth stage when Elmer Doolin began a partnership with Herman W. Lay. They combined their resources, opened two plants and began limited regional distribution.

Midlife Stage In the midlife stage, the company has done well and grown quite large. It now has an extensive set of rules, regulations, policies and systems to guide specialized employees. Control systems are put in place. Professional and clerical staff are hired to undertake specialized support activities. Top management decentralizes many tasks and assigns authority to functional departments; but in the process, it loses flexibility and innovation. Frito-Lay moved into this stage when it was purchased by PepsiCo and became one of its SBUs. PepsiCo, in turn, provided professional management to expand the product line, perk up promotions and expand national distribution.

Maturity Stage In the maturity stage, the organization is large and mechanistic. The vertical control structure becomes overwhelming. Rules, regulations, specialized staffs, budgets, a refined division of labor, and control systems are in place. The company—as happened with General Motors (GM) and DuPont—faces stagnation. Innovation and aggressiveness can only come with moves to decentralize and increase flexibility through reorganization. When Frito-Lay entered the maturity stage, it had layers of management and specialists and was not responding to competitors. The company underwent a major downsizing and restructuring, which reshaped its fortunes and competitiveness.

The critical point of these discussions is for managers to shape and adjust the structure to minimize or eliminate the mechanistic outcome of the maturity stage. As we have seen, Frito-Lay reached this stage but was able to restructure to gain flexibility and responsiveness.

Technology

technology

The knowledge, machinery, work procedures and materials that transform the inputs into outputs

Every organization uses some form of technology to convert its resources into outcomes. **Technology**, as a generic term here, is the application of knowledge to solve problems or invent something. The technology required by ExxonMobil to produce oil differs from the technology employed by Revlon to produce cosmetics, but both use some kind of technology. Production technology directly influences organizational structure. The structure must fit the technology, as well as work with an organization's strategy, external environment, age and size.

An example of this would include the changing roles of supervisors, the subject of this chapter's Quality Management feature.

Quality Management

Changing Roles of Supervisors and Production Personnel

In some organizations, employees are not expected to think, but they are in the Lean enterprise. Everyone's knowledge, creative and physical skills and abilities (KSA's) are needed to help the organization succeed. The roles of supervisors and production personnel are changing.

Supervisors direct the work of others and have more need to delegate, more need to develop teams and more responsibility for improvement. To do this, they need two types of knowledge and three types of skills. Knowledge needed by the supervisor to do the job is unique to the company and/or the industry. This includes knowledge of the work and knowledge of responsibilities. Knowledge training is the responsibility of each company, and supervisors will learn these when they go through management training. Three types of skills that are required for supervisors to perform within their role, regardless of the industry, are skill in leading, skill in instruction and skill in methods. The original supervisor training manuals developed for production during World War II by

the Training Within Industry Service Bureau of Training, War Manpower Commission—*TWI Job Relations Manual*, *TWI Job Instruction Methods Manual*, *TWI Job Methods Manual*—are available free on the Internet.

In the lean enterprise, employees are expected to participate more, interact more and communicate more. Total employee involvement is expected. Employees are given a clear understanding of the benefits of lean. They are asked for positive, constructive ideas for solving any relevant issues. In addition, employees are allowed to express their feelings and ideas. In fact, their participation is measured. Accountability is determined by daily, weekly and monthly checks.

➡ Do an Internet search to find and download one of the wartime manuals mentioned above. Present day Lean Enterprise training deviates little from these original manuals. How can training from World War II be still relevant today?

STRUCTURAL OPTIONS IN ORGANIZATIONAL DESIGN

Because no single organizational design suits all circumstances, managers must carefully consider their company's situation—strategy, environment, age, size and technology—before designing a structure for it. When the contingency factors favor a more mechanistic design, there are options from which to choose. If the need is for an organic design, there are other viable choices.

Before discussing the options, we must make one other point. Some options are more clearly mechanistic or organic in practice, but the majority of them are not purely one way or the other. Figure 8.5 arranges the five options—functional, divisional, matrix, team and network—on a continuum from mechanistic to organic. As you can see, most fall in the middle rather than reflecting either extreme.

Describe the characteristics, advantages, and disadvantages of functional, divisional, matrix, and network structural designs

Functional Structure

The **functional structure** groups positions into departments based on similar skills, expertise and resources. Functional structure is an expanded version of functional departmentalization, introduced in Chapter 7. In an organization with functional structure, activities are grouped under headings common to nearly every business—headings such as finance, production, marketing and human resources. The entire organization is then divided into areas such as the one shown in Figure 8.6.

functional structure
An organizational design that groups positions into departments based on similar skills, expertise and resources

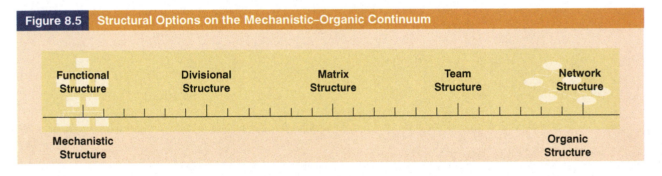

Figure 8.5   Structural Options on the Mechanistic–Organic Continuum

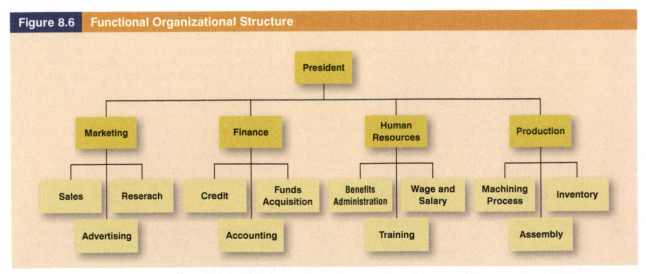

Figure 8.6   Functional Organizational Structure

Advantages of the Functional Structure Putting specialties together results in economies of scale and minimizes duplication of personnel and equipment. Employees tend to feel comfortable in a functional structure because it gives them the opportunity to talk the same language with their peers. Because the structure acknowledges occupational specialization, it also simplifies training.

Organizationally, the functional structure offers a way to centralize decision making and provide unified direction from the top. Within each department, communication and coordination are excellent. Finally, the functional structure increases the quality of technical problem solving because it gives workers quick access to those with technical expertise.

Disadvantages of the Functional Structure The functional structure also has inherent disadvantages. Because functions are separate from one another, employees may have little understanding of and concern for the specialty areas outside their own functional area. This narrowness can lead to barriers in communication, cooperation and coordination. Departments may develop their own focus rather than a company focus. Also, because a functional structure has rigid and separate chains of command, response time to changes in the environment may be slow. Managers in a functional structure also become focused on their functional area, both long and short range. Problems are seen from one perspective, and individuals become isolated. In addition, this narrowness carries over to long-range development. The specialization does not give managers a broad perspective on the company or other functional areas. This lack of a broad general perspective minimizes the training for future chief executives.

Divisional Structure

divisional structure

An organizational design that groups departments based on organizational outputs; these divisions are self-contained strategic business units that produce a single product

An alternative to the functional structure is the **divisional structure**, which groups departments based on organizational outputs. As shown in Figure 8.7, divisions are self-contained strategic business units that produce a single product. As we noted in Chapter 4, each SBU or division is responsible for the management of a given product

---

Figure 8.7   **Divisional Organizational Structure**

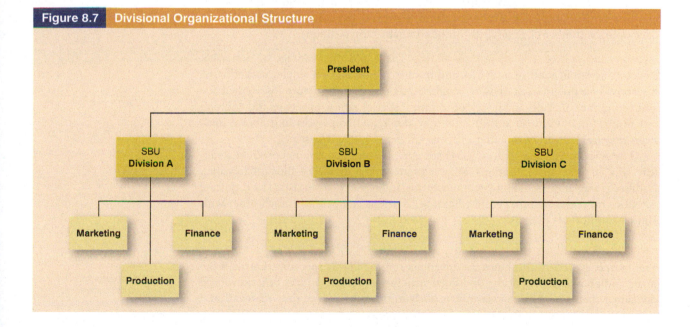

or product family. Within each division, diverse departments—for example, production and marketing—are brought together to accomplish the division's objective.

The divisional structure creates a set of autonomous mini-companies. In a large company such as PepsiCo, each division has its own market, competitors and technologies. At PepsiCo, the divisions include Frito-Lay, Pepsi-Cola, Quaker, Gatorade and Tropicana. In addition to organizing by product, a company can organize divisions by customer or geography.

A customer divisional structure is called for when customers are distinct enough in their demands, preferences and needs to justify it. For large customers—say, state and federal governments—as well as for commercial accounts with a certain line of products, the company can group all the skills necessary and establish divisions to serve those customers full time. The structure provides a company focus for the employees. We reference again the three divisions established at Johnson & Johnson: direct to consumer, medical devices and diagnostics and pharmaceutical. One focuses on consumers, a second on professionals and the third on pharmaceutical buyers.

Managers create geographic divisions when a company needs to group functional skills for a specific region—international, national or regional. This structure tries to capitalize on situations in which the geography dictates differences in such factors as laws, currencies, languages and taxation. Some department stores, such as JCPenney and Sears, have created regional divisions. On an international scale, McDonald's has structured geographically based on continent—European, North American and Asian divisions.

Advantages of the Divisional Structure The divisional structure focuses the attention of employees and managers on results for the product, the customer or the geographical area. Divisional structure is flexible and responsive to change, because each unit focuses on its own environment. Coordination among different functions within the division benefits from singleness of purpose. Because each division is a self-contained unit, responsibility and accountability for performance are easier to target. The divisional structure is also an excellent vehicle for developing senior executives. Division managers gain a broad range of experience in running their autonomous units, which are, in essence, companies. An organization that has a large number of divisions is developing a number of generalists for the company's top positions.

Disadvantages of the Divisional Structure The major disadvantage of divisional structure is duplication of activities and resources. Instead of a single marketing or research department, each division maintains its own. The structure loses efficiency and economies of scale; and a lack of technical specialization, expertise and training can result. Interdivisional coordination may suffer, and employees in different divisions may feel they are competing with one another—a mixed blessing.

Historically, General Motors (GM) has operated with a divisional product structure, and its inherent limitations. For each automobile division—Buick, Chevrolet, Cadillac—a separate marketing, manufacturing and research area exists. The duplicate activities reduce overall corporate efficiency. Divisions compete with each other with almost identical car designs.

Matrix Structure

The **matrix structure** combines the advantages of functional specialization with the focus and accountability of the divisional structure. A matrix utilizes functional and divisional chains of command simultaneously in the same part of the organization.[11]

matrix structure
An organizational design that utilizes functional and divisional chains of command simultaneously in the same part of the organization

To achieve this combination, the matrix structure employs dual lines of authority. As Figure 8.8 shows, the functional hierarchy of authority runs vertically from the functional departments—production, materials purchasing, human resources and so on—and project authority runs laterally from group to group. This combination of function and project authority creates a grid or matrix. As a result each employee has two bosses, with a dual chain of command based on both the department and individual projects.[12]

A matrix structure can be created when any division established for a specific product, program or project is combined with a functional structure. In general, a matrix design will most likely be used when a firm offers a diverse set of products, or has a complex environment requiring functional expertise.

Second, the matrix organization is used when managers want to maximize economies of scale and shared resources. Resource duplication is minimized by having

Figure 8.8	Matrix Organizational Structure

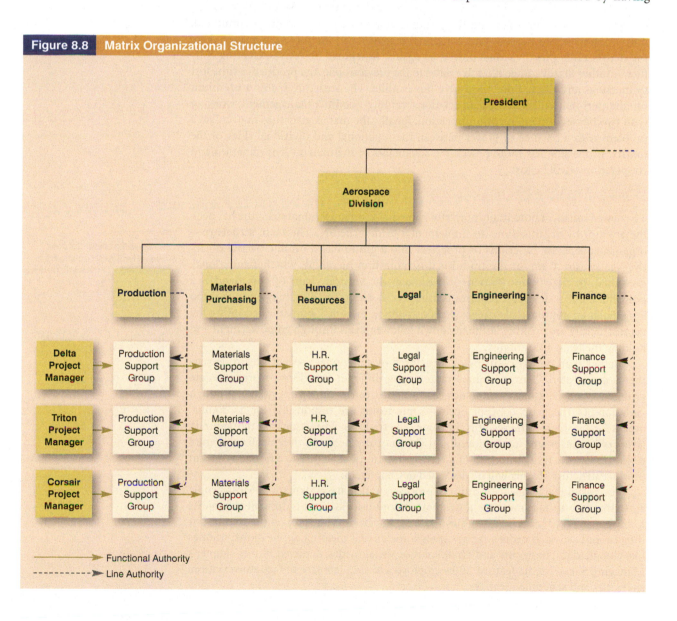

—————▶ Functional Authority

- - - - - -▶ Line Authority

employees work for more than one division or by transferring employees among divisions as requirements change. The manager in charge of the engineering department shown in Figure 8.8 can assign engineers as the needs of each project demand.

Advantages of the Matrix Structure Monsanto, Dow Chemical and Asea-Brown Boveri (ABB) have used the matrix structure successfully. It has proven to be flexible; teams can be created, changed and dissolved without a major problem. Communication and coordination are increased. Lars Ramquist was so impressed with the advantages of the matrix structure that his first move as CEO of Sweden's L. M. Ericsson Corporation was to solve organizational problems by installing a matrix structure.

The matrix structure increases the motivation of individual employees, often bringing a sense of commitment and satisfaction. The structure also provides training in functional and general management skills.

Disadvantages of the Matrix Structure The most obvious disadvantage is the potential conflict, confusion and frustration created by the dual chain of command. Employees have two bosses—the functional manager and the project manager. Also, the matrix often pits divisional objectives against functional objectives, creating conflict. Another disadvantage directly relates to the previous one: the productive time lost to meetings and discussions to resolve this conflict. The structure places a premium on interpersonal skills and human relations training—conflict management, working with two bosses and open communication. Finally, the matrix structure may create a problem with a balance of power between the functional and divisional sides of the matrix. If one side has more power, the advantages of the matrix—coordination and cooperation—will be lost.

Team Structure

The newer and most potentially powerful approach to organizational structure has been the attempt by organizations to implement a team structure. The **team structure**—organizing separate functions or processes into a group based on one overall objective—takes direct aim at the traditional organization hierarchy, whether functional, divisional, or matrix and flattens it. Although the vertical chain of command is a powerful control device, it requires passing decisions up the hierarchy and takes too long. Such an approach also keeps responsibility at the top. Companies adopting the team structure are pushing authority down to lower levels through empowerment and holding the team accountable.

team structure
An organizational design that places separate functions or processes into a group according to one overall objective

Rather than departments being structured by functional specialty, team departments are created. Team members representing different functions or processes are grouped together; a number of such teams report to the same supervisor. Although variations of the team concept occur—some teams are responsible for a product, others for a process—the result is the same. The traditional functions are reorganized, layers of management are removed and the company becomes decentralized. Figure 8.9 illustrates the reorganization of a vertical functional structure to a horizontal team product structure. Teams will be discussed in Chapter 13.

Successful teams discuss products, processes and share information. Most people agree that face-to-face meetings are important for business. Yet it is difficult to achieve. Many coworkers are too busy to meet on a regular basis. They talk on the phone, but they cannot see each other's facial expressions. Virtual meeting applications, utilities like Google docs, hangouts and SharePoint or social media, depicted in this chapter's Managing Social Media feature, allow employees to simulate face to face conversation, share files and schedule meetings.

Figure 8.9   Development of a Team Structure

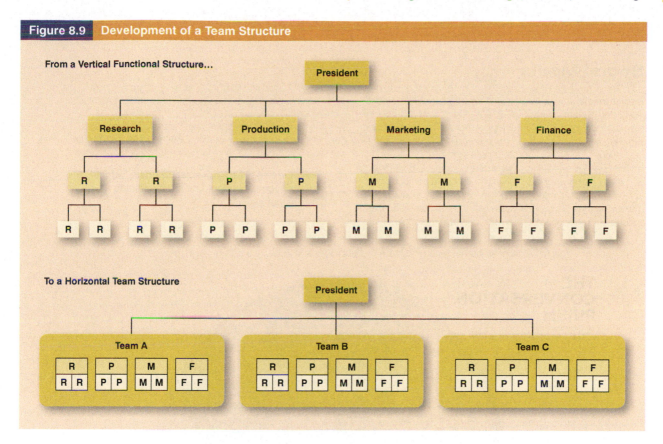

From a Vertical Functional Structure...

To a Horizontal Team Structure

Advantages of the Team Structure The team concept breaks down barriers across departments because people who know one another are more likely to compromise than would strangers. The team structure also speeds up decision making and response time. Decisions no longer need to go to the top of a hierarchy for approval. Employees are strongly motivated. They take responsibility for a project rather than for a narrowly defined task, and the result is enthusiasm and commitment. Decentralization of authority is accompanied by the elimination of levels of managers, which results in lower administrative costs. Finally, team structure is an improvement over the matrix structure in that it does not involve the problem of double reporting.

Disadvantages of the Team Structure The team structure depends on employees who learn and train for success. If the company won't provide training, performance suffers. Also, a large amount of time might be required for team meetings, thus increasing coordination time.

Network Structure

The final approach to structure is known as the *dynamic network* organization. In the **network structure** a small central organization relies on other organizations to perform manufacturing, marketing, engineering or other critical functions on a contract basis.[13] In other words, rather than these functions being performed under one roof, they are really free-standing services. Nike and Esprit Apparel, both of whom have booming businesses even though they own no manufacturing facilities, use the

network structure

An organizational design option in which a small central organization relies on other organizations to perform manufacturing, marketing, engineering or other critical functions on a contract basis

Social Media

Social media refer to online platforms that facilitate discussions and sharing of content. It is a very convenient way for teams to collaborate. Technologies include blogs (Blogger, Tumblr), wikis (Wikipedia), microblogging (Twitter), social networking (Facebook), professional networking (LinkedIn), videos (YouTube), slides (Slideshare), pictures (Instagram) and many more. Each employee working on a particular project can access content, read the documents posted, and make changes to these documents. Other features might include a bulletin board, a group calendar, personal calendars, virtual meeting rooms for real-time chat and private messaging.

"The Conversation Prism" by Brian Solis and JESS3, depicted below, is a view of the social media universe, categorized and organized by how people use each network.

➡ **After studying "The Conversation Prism," identify the networks you think would be most useful to teams. Explain your answer.**

Social Media Universe: The Conversation Prism v.4 by Brian Solis and JESS3

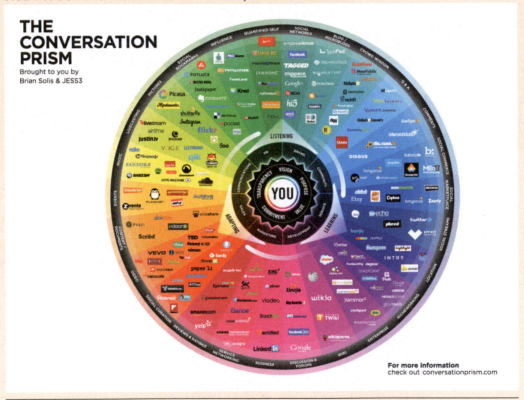

Source: *http://www.theconversationprism.com/.*

network structure concept seen in Figure 8.10. Rather than create the functions internally, they connect independent designers, manufacturers and sales representatives to perform needed functions on a contract basis.[14]

Advantages of the Network Structure The network structure provides flexibility because a company purchases only the specific services needed. Administrative overhead remains low because large teams of staff specialists and other administrative personnel are not needed.

social media
A set of online technologies enabling a community of participants to collaborate

Figure 8.10	Network Organizational Structure

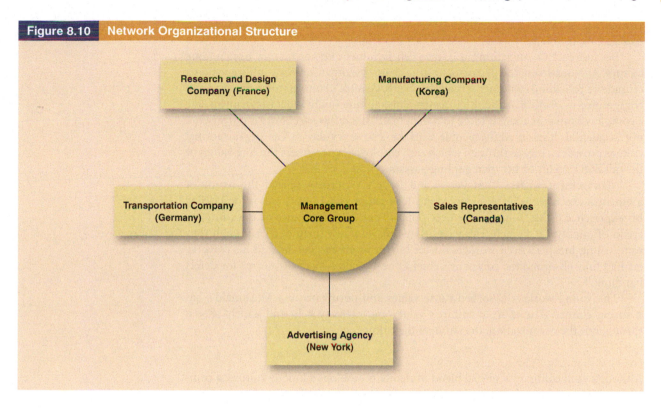

Disadvantages of the Network Structure The major shortcoming of this type of structure is lack of control. The management core must rely on contractors. This limitation can be minimized if management is willing and able to work closely with the suppliers. The reliability of supply, however, is less predictable than it would be if the company owned the means of supply. If a supplier fails to deliver, goes out of business or suffers a plant breakdown, the central hub of the network is endangered. Also, if an organization relies on contract work, central managers may lack technical expertise to resolve problems effectively.

Define organizational culture and describe the ways that culture is manifested

ORGANIZATIONAL CULTURE

Organizational Culture Defined

In Chapter 3 we introduced a critical concept in the successful management of a company—organizational culture. As you remember, organizational culture is a dynamic system of shared values, beliefs, philosophies, experiences, habits, expectations, norms and behaviors that give an organization its distinctive character. More importantly, that system—the organizational culture—defines what is important to the organization, the way decisions are made, the methods of communication, the degree of structure, the freedom to function independently, how people should behave, how they should interact with each other, and for what they should be striving. Sharing these beliefs, values, and norms helps employees develop a sense of group identity and pride—both valuable contributors to organizational effectiveness. The norms for behavior develop around a set of values and create an *invisible hand*—a consensus and driving force for goal accomplishment.

Because each organization has its own beliefs, values, and norms, each has a unique culture. At Nordstrom, the department store chain, the organizational culture makes a crusade of providing customer service. Procter & Gamble's culture stresses quality and competitive marketing. Although organizational culture might seem suspiciously like a company's mission, there is more to it than that. "At Southwest, culture is purposeful, not accidental. It's something people work hard at every day."[15] The organizational culture provides a means through which each employee can translate the core values of the mission into his or her own guiding passion.

Management writers Tom Peters and Robert Waterman related the words of a business executive who had worked at McDonald's as a 17-year-old. In describing his experience at McDonald's, the exec pointed out the importance of the company credo of quality: "If French fries were overdone, we threw them out." Although they were young inexperienced workers on the burger assembly line, he and his coworkers had fully absorbed the company's chief value—quality—and the norms for defect handling.[16]

The young workers absorbed those values and norms because McDonald's has a strong culture. The more a culture's values are intensely held and widely shared throughout the organization, the stronger the culture.

Factors Shaping Culture

Although each company's special blend of elements develops a unique culture, a comparison of many organizations identifies seven culture-shaping factors:

- Key organizational processes
- Dominant coalition
- Employees and other tangible assets
- Formal organizational arrangements
- Social system
- Technology
- External environment

As shown in Figure 8.11, these factors interact with each other. In fact, no single ingredient is independent of the others. Let us examine each of these factors.[17]

Key Organizational Processes At the core of every organization, and fundamental to it, are the processes people follow to gather information, communicate, make decisions, manage work flow and produce a good or service. How managers communicate to employees, how they share decision making, and how they structure the flow of work define the organization. These processes affect and are affected by the other six factors that influence organizational culture.

Dominant Coalition An organization's culture is greatly affected by the objectives, strategies, personal characteristics and interrelationships of its managers, who form the dominant coalition. Managers' leadership styles (discussed in Chapter 12) determine how employees are treated and how they feel about themselves and their work. The dynamic energy and vision of Bill Gates at Microsoft made his company the world leader in computer software and networks. Herb Kelleher of Southwest Airlines created a culture that values having fun at work and that stresses the importance of contri-

| **Figure 8.11** | **Factors that Shape Organizational Culture** |

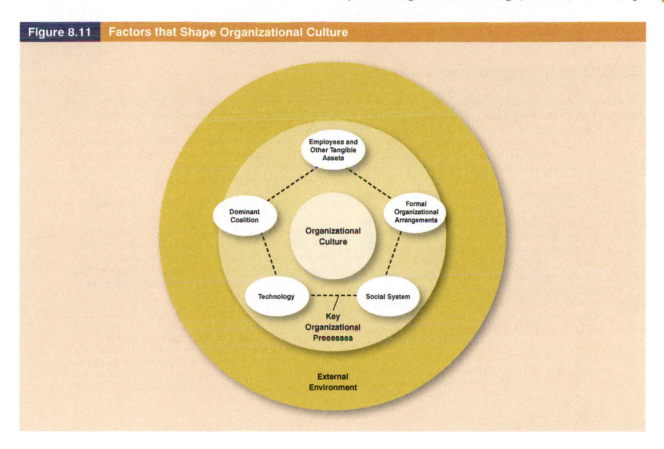

bution from each employee. Deloitte, the subject of this chapter's Valuing Diversity and Inclusion feature, launched its Initiative for the Retention and Advancement of Women and changed a culture that spurned women to one that valued and retained them.

Employees and Other Tangible Assets An organization uses its resources—employee population, plant and offices, equipment, tools, land, inventory and money—to carry out its activities. These assets are the most visible and complex of the factors that influence organizational culture. Their quantity and quality have a major effect on organizational culture and performance. For example, Procter & Gamble attributes much of its success to the quality of its people—who, in turn, are proud to be part of an organization that describes itself as "special," "great," "excellent" and "unique among the world's business institutions."

Formal Organizational Arrangements The formal arrangements that organize tasks and individuals constitute another factor that affects organizational culture. These arrangements include the structure of the organization and its procedures and rules. Specific mandated behaviors are also a part of organizational arrangements.

Social System The social system, which contributes norms and values to organizational culture, includes the set of employee relationships that relate to power, affiliation and trust. It also includes the grapevine and the informal organization, thus helping

Deloitte Changes the Culture

For ten years, Cynthia Turk inched her way up the ladder at the accounting firm of Deloitte & Touche. Eventually she became a partner—when fewer than ten percent of the partners were women—but she wasn't welcomed openly. "I walked into a culture that wasn't used to having women in very senior positions. It wasn't warm, welcoming, or nurturing" (Lawlor). Three years later, Turk left, still feeling unaccepted.

Since Turk, together with many other women, left, few firms have made a more public commitment to top-to bottom cultural change than has Deloitte. Following a fact-finding study to determine why, after years of hiring women for 50 percent of the entry-level jobs, fewer than ten percent of those promoted to partner were female, a task force was formed. A strategic plan with top-down accountability was developed.

To change a culture where women, once they had a family, were perceived as less committed, Deloitte embarked on an ambitious program in 1993, known as the Women's Initiative (WIN). Focused at all parts of the culture, the program included gender awareness training for partners and managers, formal career planning for all female partners and senior managers and succession planning for senior women. The program also involved more flexible work arrangements, including the possibility of becoming a partner on a part-time basis. Also, partners are monitored to ensure they give their female managers challenging, growth-oriented assignments, rather than clerical work.

WIN helped Deloitte change its culture and close the gender gap. Cathy Engelbert, a 30-year Deloitte veteran, made history in March 2014 when she became the first woman to be named CEO of a Big Four firm in the U.S.

➡ Sharon Allen (Chairman of the Board, Deloitte) addressing the Wharton Women in Business Conference, said, "Forget the negative things you might read and hear and forget the statistics that detail a tough business world where success is hard to come by. There's never been a better time to be a woman in business." Do you agree with Ms. Allen? Explain your answer.

Sources: http://www.us.deloitte.com, Inclusion, http://www2.deloitte.com/us/en/pages/about-deloitte/articles/deloitte-inclusion.html; Douglas M. McCracken, "Best Practice—Winning the Talent War for Women: Sometimes It Takes a Revolution," *Harvard Business Review*, November–December, 2000; Angela Briggins, "Win-Win Initiatives for Women," *Management Review*, June 1995, 6; Julia Lawlor, "Executive Exodus," *Working Woman*, November 1994, 39–41, 80–87.

render it one of the most important factors of organizational culture. Because people are the organization, their relationships are crucial to defining what the organization is like.

Technology The major technological processes and equipment that employees use and how they use them also affect organizational culture. Is a machine or process intended to replace human labor or enhance workers' skills and productivity? The answer sends a message about the values of employees in the organization. Assembly-line technology promotes an impersonal, uninvolved culture. Many years ago, Volvo of Sweden embraced quality and worker satisfaction as corporate values. As a result, Volvo managers adopted team organizations and unconventional layouts in Volvo facilities. These changes helped shift the organizational culture away from the mechanistic values of the assembly line.

Manifestations of Culture

An organization's culture is nurtured and becomes apparent to its members in various ways. Some aspects of culture are explicit; some must be inferred. The chief evidences of culture include statements of principle, stories, slogans, heroes, ceremonies, symbols, climate and the physical environment.

Statements of Principle

Some corporations have developed written expressions of basic principles central to organizational culture. Many years ago Forrest Mars developed the "Five Principles of Mars," which established fundamental beliefs for the company.[18] Mars's principles still guide the company today:

1 *Quality.* No one at Mars has the word *quality* in his or her job title; quality control is everywhere, and everyone is responsible for it.

2 *Responsibility.* All employees are expected to take on direct and total responsibility for results, exercising initiative and making decisions.

3 *Mutuality.* In all dealings—with the consumer, other employees, a supplier or distributor, or the community at large—employees are to act so that everyone can win.

4 *Efficiency.* All of the company's factories operate 24 hours a day, 7 days a week. As a whole, the company uses 30 percent fewer employees than its competitors do.

5 *Freedom.* The company provides freedom to allow employees to shape their futures, and profits that allow employees to remain free.

Stories

Shared stories illustrate the culture. Telling stories acquaints new employees with the culture's values and reaffirms those values for existing employees. For example, all new employees at Nordstrom learn the importance of being a "customer service hero" by seeing, hearing, and reading "true tales of incredible customer service."[19] This gives Nordstrom employees a standard to aspire to—and even surpass.

Slogans

A slogan is a phrase or saying that clearly expresses a key organizational value. The late Sam Walton's slogan, "The customer is the boss," keeps the culture of Walmart focused on providing high-quality customer service. A slogan, however, should not be confused with a company's advertising campaign, unless the slogan is genuinely backed by the actions of the company and becomes a company value.

Heroes

A hero is a person in the organization who exemplifies the values of the culture, as Southwest Airlines former CEO Herb Kelleher does. To his employees, Kelleher embodied what Southwest stands for—customers first, quality service and have fun while doing it. A true hero? When Herb Kelleher was CEO, all of Southwest's employees secretly contributed to buying a full-page ad in *USA Today* for National Boss Day.

Ceremonies

Managers hold ceremonies to exemplify and reinforce company values. Awards ceremonies for outstanding service, top producers or high-performance teams promote the values of the culture and allow recipients and colleagues to share the experience of achievement. Awards ceremonies at Mary Kay Cosmetics are legendary in the cosmetics industry. At these lavish affairs, high-achieving sales representatives receive furs, pins and cars. Whereas ceremonies at Mary Kay are simmering with sophistication, the same could hardly be said at Henkel Consumer Adhesives, a manufacturer and marketer of Duck brand duct tape. Henkel's celebrations are raucous and fast moving. To celebrate successes, people in yellow duck outfits ("duct" sounds like "duck") waddle through the halls; do the Henkel Consumer Adhesives cheer at the beginning of every meeting; and celebrate at the Duck Challenge Day each year.[20]

Many companies use a ceremony to mark the advancement of a new hire from trainee to full-fledged employee. Ceremonies also include rituals that honor promotions. These events increase the employee's identification with the organization's values.

Symbols

An object or image that conveys meaning to others is a symbol. Some organizations use symbols to embody their core values. Walt Disney created an entire symbolic language to reinforce his company's core values. At the Disney theme parks:

- Employees are "cast members."
- Customers are "guests."
- A crowd is an "audience."
- A work shift is a "performance."
- A job is a "part."
- A uniform is a "costume."
- The personnel department is "casting."
- Being on duty is "on stage."
- Being off duty is "off stage."[21]

The Gold Standards of the Ritz Carlton are famous for ensuring each employee is a committed ambassador for their world class service values. Symbols may include job titles and perks, such as the location of a reserved parking space, the size and location of the office or the size of the desk.

Climate

As defined in Chapter 3, organizational climate is the quality of the work environment experienced by employees—that is, how it feels to work there. Climate is largely a function of how workers feel about the organization. Do they work hard and apply themselves to the task, cooperating with management goals and directives; or do they drag their feet, resenting management instructions and resisting demands for output?

A company with a healthy climate encourages everyone to tap into the other person's expertise, empowers people and rewards them for taking risks and provides lots of celebrations where peers cheer peers. An unhealthy climate is found in enterprises where management has different values, is in conflict, and has widely divergent goals.

Physical Environment

Last but not least in the discussion of culture-shaping factors is a simple but powerful force: the physical environment of an organization. It is no coincidence that Sears & Roebuck, a hierarchical organization, built one of the world's tallest buildings. The Sears Tower (renamed Willis Tower in 2009) dominates the Chicago skyline and reflects the multilayered structure and centralized culture of the organization that it built. A software developer or computer maker, on the other hand, may create a campus like environment to promote the free exchange of ideas. Such enclaves are common in California's Silicon Valley.

Explain the role of managers and employees in creating culture and making a culture effective

CREATION OF CULTURE

The efforts of managers and employees combine to create an organizational culture. Managers like Walt Disney deliberately set out to instill certain values. In other cases the culture simply emerges from a pattern of behaviors that may not be consciously planned.

Role of Managers

Managers at all levels in an organization help develop the culture. Quite simply, managers set the tone, control the resources and have the means to influence the results. Management helps create culture in the following ways:

- Clearly defining the company's mission and goals
- Identifying the core values
- Determining the amount of individual autonomy and the degree to which people work separately or in groups
- Structuring the work in accordance with the corporation's values to achieve its goals
- Developing reward systems that reinforce the values and goals
- Creating methods of socialization that will bring new workers inside the culture and reinforce the culture for existing workers

The task of defining the culture often begins with the organization's founder. Both Walt Disney and Sam Walton created and put their stamp on strong organizational cultures. Sometimes, though, managers in charge of existing organizations wish to change that organization's culture. For example, a new manager might find a culture that is hierarchically oriented and frowns on confrontation. Decisions are made too slowly. People don't take risks.

Such an organization needs a new spirit with a willingness to compete. To begin the transformation, a new mission focusing on fulfilling the needs of the customer is required. Core values—such as respect for the individual, integrity, trust, credibility and continuous improvement—will help build the culture.

Regardless of whether the manager is the organization's founder, a second generation CEO or a newly positioned chief executive, James C. Collins and Jerry I. Porras point out that truly visionary managers and companies "translate their ideologies into *tangible* mechanisms aligned to send a consistent set of reinforcing signals. They indoctrinate people, impose tightness of fit, and create a sense of belonging to something special."[22] Figure 8.12 presents a summary of practical ways Collins recommends for building culture.

Role of Employees

Employees contribute to organizational culture to the extent that they accept and adopt the culture. Workers at Disney theme parks are renowned for their sunny disposition and friendliness to patrons. The training they receive after hiring clearly succeeds in making them see themselves as performers who give enjoyment.

Also, workers contribute to organizational culture by helping to shape the values it embodies. Employees who shirk the tasks at hand—and influence newcomers to do the same—have a significant effect on quality, regardless of what top managers may say about quality as a value. Employees who give each other a hand to meet a deadline

| **Figure 8.12** | **Practical Ways to Build a Culture** |

- Orientation and ongoing training programs that have ideological as well as practical content, teaching such things as values, norms, history and traditions.
- Internal "universities" and training centers.
- On-the-job socialization by peers and immediate supervisors.
- Rigorous up-through-the-ranks policies—hiring young, promoting from within, and shaping the employee's mind-set from a young age.
- Exposure to a pervasive mythology of "heroic deeds" and corporate exemplars (for example, customer heroics letters, marble statues).
- Unique language and terminology (such as "cast members," "Motorolans") that reinforce a frame of reference and the sense of belonging to a special, elite group.
- Corporate songs, cheers, affirmations or pledges that reinforce psychological commitment.
- Tight screening processes, either during hiring or within the first few years.
- Incentive and advancement criteria explicitly linked to fit with the corporate ideology.
- Awards, contests and public recognition that reward those who display great effort consistent with the ideology. Tangible and physical penalties for those who break ideological boundaries.
- Tolerance for honest mistakes that do not breach the company's ideology ("non-sins"); severe penalties or termination for breaching the ideology ("sins").
- Buy-in mechanisms (financial, time, investment).
- Celebrations that reinforce successes, belonging and specialness.
- Plant and office layouts that reinforce norms and ideals.
- Constant verbal and written emphasis on corporate values, heritage and the sense of being part of something special.

Source: James C. Collins and Jerry I. Porras, *Built to Last* (New York: HarperBusiness, 1993), p. 136. Copyright © 1994 by James C. Collins and Jerry I. Porras. Reprinted by permission of Jim Collins.

create a feeling of teamwork that exists regardless of management's decisions about structuring work.

Finally, workers play a role in influencing organizational culture by forming subcultures. A **subculture** is a unit within an organization that is based on the shared values, norms and beliefs of its members. The values of the subculture may or may not complement those of the dominant organizational culture. Unionized employees constitute a subculture. Groups of workers who share a common background or interest or who work in the same department may also form subcultures. When workers form a subculture, their shared experiences take on a deeper meaning because they also share values, norms and beliefs. Subcultures influence their members' behavior; managers should, therefore, consider them important. If a subculture's values and norms conflict with those of the dominant culture, managers must take action.

subculture
A unit within an organization that is based on the shared values, norms and beliefs of its members

Factors Contributing to the Effectiveness of Culture

Culture affects performance. In a study of hundreds of firms, John P. Kotter and James Heskett found a dramatic difference between effective and ineffective cultures:

We found that firms with cultures that emphasized all the key managerial constituencies (customers, stockholders, and employees) and leadership from managers at all levels outperformed firms that did not have those cultural traits by a huge margin.[23]

Kotter and Heskett went on to warn that managers must do more than promote an effective culture; they must be constantly on the lookout for the signs of an ineffective culture.

Corporate cultures that inhibit strong long-term financial performance are not rare; they develop easily, even in firms that are full of reasonable and intelligent people. Cultures that encourage inappropriate behavior and inhibit change to more appropriate strategies tend to emerge slowly and quietly over a period of years, usually when firms are performing well.[24]

Three factors help determine the effectiveness of an organizational culture: (1) coherence; (2) pervasiveness and depth; and (3) adaptability to environment.

Coherence In discussions of organizational culture, coherence refers to how well the culture fits the mission and other organizational elements. A culture like the one at Walmart, which values customer service and a low-cost strategy, must train employees to recognize customer needs. It must also empower them to make decisions to meet those needs, create processes and structures that will achieve the goals of low inventory cost and low overhead, and employ technology to meet those goals.

Pervasiveness and Depth The phrase *pervasiveness and depth* refers to the extent to which employees adopt the culture of an organization. The greater the acceptance of and commitment to organizational values, the stronger the culture.[25] By training theme-park employees extensively, Disney helps guarantee that employees deeply hold its values. In applicant interviews, Southwest Airlines' employees ask the interviewee, "What did you do on your last job to have fun?" This perpetuates the fun-loving environment at Southwest.

Adaptability to the External Environment If organizational culture fits the external environment, managers and employees have the mind-set they need to compete. For decades, American Telephone & Telegraph (AT&T) enjoyed a monopoly on long-distance telephone service. In the 1980s, when long-distance service was deregulated, AT&T employees found they did not have the mind-set to compete in their new environment; their organizational culture was a poor fit in terms of the real world. The new external environment had created new demands, and it required a new way of thinking—a new culture.

Of the three factors that determine the effectiveness of an organizational culture, the degree of fit with the external environment is perhaps the most critical. Its importance lies in the fact that the environment changes. Just ask managers at Sears, IBM, or GM about the importance of change in the external environment. These three organizations fell on hard times because they were not adaptable enough. Managers must not only achieve the difficult task of building a culture strong enough to compel commitment and unwavering support; but be flexible enough to allow change in the face of emerging external demands.

We now turn to understanding change and learning how to manage change.

Define change and identify the kinds of change that can occur in an organization

NATURE OF CHANGE

Not since the Industrial Revolution has U.S. business environment experienced so much change. In the past decade, almost every industry has been rocked by change. Telecommunications has been changed by divestitures and continuous innovation.

Pharmaceuticals, banking and transportation have all undergone consolidation, pressure to adopt new technologies and increasing regulatory oversight. Manufacturers battle an increase in foreign competition, and the high tech industry must constantly accommodate innovation from hordes of new and established competitors. One constant is as soon as they adjust to one change, they must readjust to accommodate another.

Change is any alteration in the current work environment. The shift may be in the way things are perceived or in how they are organized, processed, created or maintained. Every individual and organization experiences change. Sometimes change results from external events beyond the control of a person or an organization. Other times the change results from planning. When a company lowers its prices to increase market penetration, for example, the change in price is purposeful.

change
Any alteration in the current work environment

This section explores change by discussing its sources and types. The sections that follow will examine the kinds of changes that confront an organization during its typical life span and how change affects managers at each level.

Sources of Change

Change originates in either the external or internal environments of the organization.

External Sources Change may come from the political, social, technological or economic environment. Externally motivated change may involve government action, technology, competition, social values and economic variables. Developments in the external environment require managers to make adjustments. New government regulations, for example, can require that a manufacturer install pollution-control devices, a bank keep higher levels of capital and deposit insurance or that a restaurant raise the wages of its workers to meet a new minimum. The actions of competitors certainly put demands on a business. When one U.S. airline launches new low fares, other domestic airlines in the same markets feel compelled to follow suit.

Internal Sources Internal sources of change include managerial policies or styles; systems and procedures; technology; and employee attitudes. When managers change the standards by which they measure job performance, new job requirements or when a new manager takes over a department or company, employees must adapt their behavior to fit the new situation.

New conditions in the external environment clearly can bring about changes within the organization; but internal change can also cause external change. Whether internal change affects the external environment depends on the extent of the internal change and on whether the change affects a part of the organization that has impact on the environment. New internal policies requiring employees to check their e-mail at least once each day will unlikely have any impact on the external environment.

Types of Change

Change can also be understood on the basis of its focus; which can be strategic, structural, process oriented, or people centered. Such changes can have dramatic impact on the organizational culture.

Strategic Change As discussed in Chapter 4, sometimes managers find it necessary to change the strategy or the mission of the organization. Organizations that decide to focus on a single mission often need to divest themselves of unrelated businesses, as Motorola did when it sold off its semiconductor group. Managers who want to expand operations to new areas may move to acquire another company, as eBay did in its purchase of PayPal, Skype and the 2015 acquisition of Twice (a second hand "e"clothing marketplace).

Achieving strategic changes can require, in turn, a change in other organizational elements. When a company adopts quality as a key to its competitive strategy, it has to adopt quality work as a corporate value too.

Structural Change Managers often find it necessary to change the structure of their organizations, such as team building or downsizing. These changes have usually been made to make operations run more smoothly, improve overall coordination and control or empower individuals to make their own decisions. Because structural change has a major impact on an organization's social system and climate, it greatly affects organizational culture.

Process-Oriented Change Many changes aim at process improvement, such as using new technology, shifting from human to mechanical labor employ robotics for manufacturing or adopting new procedures. If process-oriented change takes the form of reengineering, it may have dramatic effects on the organization and its culture. As defined earlier, reengineering is the fundamental rethinking and radical redesign of business processes to achieve dramatic improvements in critical, traditional measures of performance, such as cost, quality, service, and speed. Reengineering first determines what process is needs improvement, then how to do it.[26]

As illustrated in Figure 8.13, most business processes involve activities in more than one department. When the steps have been completed in one department, the

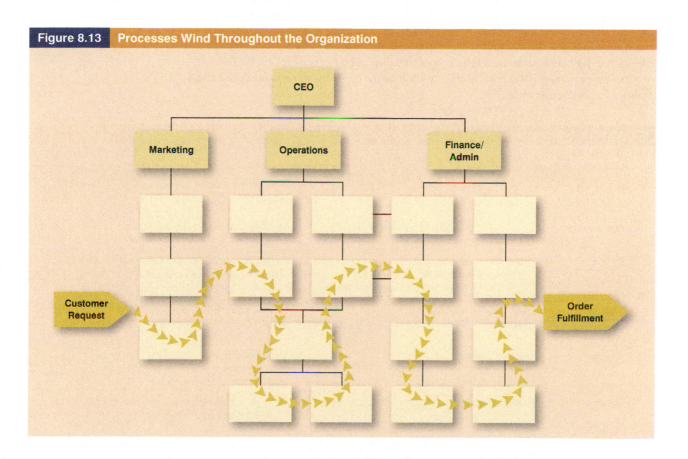

Figure 8.13   Processes Wind Throughout the Organization

process continues in the next department. In most instances the result is an inefficient and ineffective process.[27] Reengineering takes aim at these processes to optimize the workflow and productivity. Changing or reengineering the processes may change the entire organization.

People-Centered Change Many changes are directed at the attitudes, behaviors, skills or performance of the company's employees. These changes can be achieved through retraining, replacing current employees, or increasing the performance expectations of new employees. The task of changing attitudes and behaviors falls into the domain of behavioral training. As an aspect of organizational development, behavioral training will be discussed later in this chapter.

Rates of Change

Change can also be viewed based on its pace—that is, either evolutionary or revolutionary. **Evolutionary change** focuses on the incremental steps taken to bring about progress and change. Organizations like Johnson & Johnson show a strategy for incremental change. Visionary companies have a philosophical commitment to constant change, but at a measured pace.[28] Figure 8.14 illustrates a comparison between evolutionary and revolutionary changes.

Revolutionary change focuses on bold, discontinuous advances. To the observer, these "leaps" bring about dramatic transformations in organizational strategies and structure. Organizations and managers involved in revolutionary change push the envelope and practice outside-of-the-box thinking. By his actions, Jack Welch, former CEO of GE, was a supporter of revolutionary change. In transforming GE, Welch opted for immediate rather than incremental change. Welch, using a tool of revolutionary change, challenged the company by setting a BHAG (as described in Chapter 4, a BHAG is a Big Hairy Audacious Goal). Welch challenged GE executives "to become #1 or #2 in every market [it] serves" and revolutionize the company to have the speed and ability of a small enterprise.

evolutionary change
The incremental steps taken to bring about progress and change

revolutionary change
Bold, discontinuous advances that bring about dramatic transformations in organizational strategies and structure

Figure 8.14	Examples of Evolutionary and Revolutionary Change

Factors	Evolutionary Change	Revolutionary Changes
Time Period	Longer	Shorter
Strategy	Strategy refocused on core business Noncore businesses sold	Strategy focused on downsizing Older plants closed Jobs eliminated
Structure	New unit created Reorganize several units into one unit Experienced manager hired to lead new unit	Large percentage of headquarters staff eliminated Large percentage of management eliminated Many non-managerial employees eliminated
Culture	Core values identified Culture reshaped to stress accountability, quality, and cycle time	Organization focused on cost cutting Cultural change bypassed
People	Morale positive Future bright Communication open	Morale negative Future uncertain Communication sporadic
Finance	Debt reduced by sale of noncore businesses	Debt eliminated by the stream-lining of operations and the selling of assets

As previously discussed, business process reengineering (BPR), is another tool of revolutionary change. It calls everything into question—what no longer needs to be done, what must be done, and how better to execute the latter. Reengineering changes the fundamental ways in which people and their organization handle their processes. Typical results of BPR have been to dramatically change organization's missions, visions, values, activities and structures.

Managing Change

Each level of management faces change in a different way. Top-level managers are more likely to be involved in changes in strategy, structure and process. Because such changes have a major impact on culture and on the way an organization does business, the effects of change decisions made by top managers ripple throughout an organization. By scanning the external environment, they may be able to see when internal changes are needed to fit new circumstances and meet new opportunities.

Middle managers will likely face structural, process-oriented or people-centered changes, although they may well have some input into strategic change. They might reorganize staff or work flow. They might develop training programs to introduce new technology or processes. In any case, the changes implemented by middle managers are likely to have a wide impact.

First-line managers are unlikely to make decisions about strategic issues. First-line managers institute process-oriented and people-centered change, and must understand how to manage change for their employees.

A company can deal with change by anticipating the need for it and planning for it. This is called **planned change**. When managers plan for change—whether employing an evolutionary approach or a revolutionary style—they are more likely to predict the results and control events. The alternative—**management by reaction**—can invite disaster.

The **change agent** implements planned change. The change agent could be the manager who conceived of the need to change; it could be another manager within the organization who is delegated the task; or it could be an outsider, a consultant brought in specifically to help an organization adopt a new way of doing things. Jack Welch at GE and Lou Gerstner at IBM fall into this last category of deploying outside change agents, as considered to be more objective, less influenced by existing politics and people.

The next section will examine planned change by looking at the kinds of changes that managers can expect, the steps involved in planned change and the attitudes that underlie an effective approach to change.

Need for Change: Diagnosing and Predicting It

Managers can diagnose and predict the need for organizational change by studying the typical phases of change. Recall the organizational life cycle of birth, youth, midlife and maturity and some of the crises commonly experienced by organizations at each stage. Management consultant Larry Greiner has graphed these predictable phases of organizational evolution (see Figure 8.15).[29]

Phase 1: Creativity This birth stage of the organization is marked by concerns for product and market, by an informal social system and by an entrepreneurial style of management. Soon the need for capital, new products, new markets and new employees forces the organization to change. A crisis of leadership occurs when management becomes incapable of reacting to the growing organization's needs.

planned change
Trying to anticipate what changes will occur in both the external and internal environment and then developing a response that will maximize the organization's success

management by reaction
A management method that does not anticipate change but merely reacts to it

change agent
A person who implements planned change

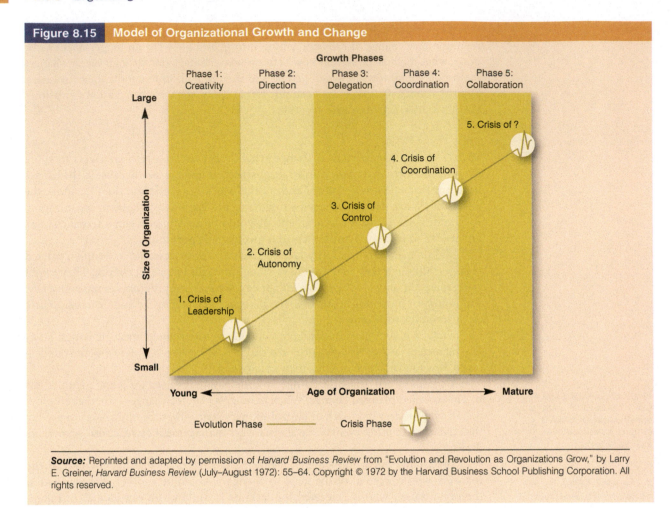

Figure 8.15   Model of Organizational Growth and Change

Phase 2: Direction The second phase is characterized by the implementation of rules, regulations and procedures. A functional organizational structure is introduced; an accounting system is created; incentives, budgets and work standards are established; and formal, impersonal communications begin. Eventually, lower-level managers demand greater decision-making authority, which brings on another crisis and launches the organization into the next phase.

Phase 3: Delegation Decentralization is the key to the third phase, in which top management creates profit centers under territorial managers who are given leeway to act and held accountable for the results. Communication from the top becomes less frequent. Eventually, top managers sense that they have lost control of the organization. This realization brings on another crisis and another major change.

Phase 4: Coordination Responding to their sense of loss of control, managers attempt to seize control by emphasizing coordination. Decentralized work units are merged, formal organization wide planning is introduced, capital expenditures are restricted and staff personnel begin to wield greater power. The price of this phase: Red tape and interpersonal distance between line and staff and between headquarters and the field develop. A new crisis takes place.

Phase 5: Collaboration The final phase introduces a new people-oriented and flexible system, with managers exhibiting more spontaneity. Characteristics of this phase include problem solving by teams, reductions in headquarters staff, simplification of formal systems and encouragement of an attitude of risk taking and innovation.

The heart of Greiner's model shows a key point about change. The solution to one set of problems eventually creates another set of problems that require solving. In other words, the need for change is constant.

STEPS IN PLANNED CHANGE

8 *Explain the steps managers can follow to implement planned change*

Once committed to planned change, a manager or an organization must create a step-by-step approach to achieve it. Figure 8.16 presents the steps that a manager can use to implement change. As an example, the following paragraphs will show how Wendy, a manager, can use this process to change her company's policy about smoking.

Recognizing the Need for Change The first step in the change-implementation process is to identify the need for a change. Recognition can come as a result of factors inside or outside an organization. In Wendy's case, suppose the company's health insurance carrier notifies her that it will conduct a rate-structure review in light of research about the effects of smoking. Meanwhile, an internal force, a group of employees, requests a policy statement about smoking in the workplace. In this case, external and internal forces contribute to the recognition of the need for change.

Developing Goals As in any planning process, a key step is the identification of goals. Managers must ask what they wish to achieve. In Wendy's case, the manager's goals become (1) to develop a smoking policy for the organization that will be widely accepted, and (2) to prevent insurance costs from rising.

Selecting a Change Agent With goals in mind, the next issue is to determine who will manage the change. Wendy asks the leader of the group concerned about smoking to assist her as a change agent.

Figure 8.16 **Nine Steps for Implementing Planned Change**

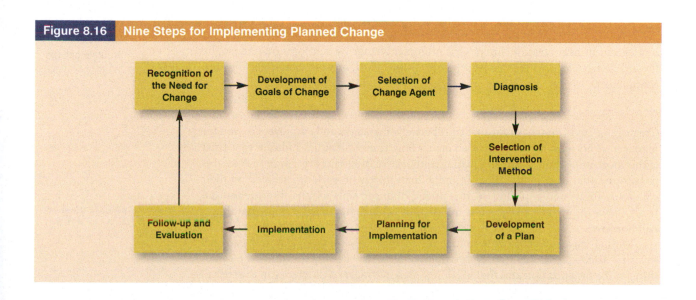

Diagnosing the Problem In the next step, the manager gathers data about the problem and analyzes the data to identify the key issues. The two change agents in the current example find that other companies control health insurance costs by instituting smoking restrictions. They also learn that whether employees support or oppose smoking in the workplace, smoking is an emotional issue.

Selecting the Intervention Method In the fifth step, the manager must decide how to achieve the change. Because smoking is such an emotionally charged issue, the change agents in the current example decide not to create the needed policy themselves. Instead, they form a task force that includes representatives from all departments. They believe that large-scale participation will help ensure the facilitation of the change.

Developing a Plan This step involves actually putting together the "what" of the change. The task force must decide if the company will have a no smoking policy or will designate areas that permit smoking.

Planning for Implementation In this phase, the decision maker must decide the "when," "where" and "how" of the plan. The task force in Wendy's case must decide when the policy will go into effect, how it will be communicated and how its impact will be monitored and evaluated.

Implementing the Plan After a plan is created, it must be put into effect. Implementing the plan requires notifying the employees who will be affected by the change. Notification may consist of written messages, briefings or training sessions. The choice depends on the depth of the change and the impact it will have on people. With a major change, such as the adoption of work teams, training might be necessary for some time. In Wendy's case, the task force decides to settle the smoking issue by announcing the plan and holding briefings.

Following Up and Evaluating Once a change has been implemented, the manager must follow up by evaluating it. Evaluation consists of comparing actual results to goals. If the new smoking policy receives widespread employee acceptance and holds the line on insurance costs, then the change was worthwhile.

QUALITIES PROMOTING CHANGE

Identify the organizational qualities that promote change

Managers can help create a climate that promotes change by developing a philosophy toward change that includes three elements: mutual trust, organizational learning and adaptability.

Mutual Trust

Creating an environment of mutual trust between managers and employees is vital for managers who wish to implement change. Many research studies indicate that trust is the most important factor in creating an effective, well-run organization.[30] In this context, mutual trust is the ability of individuals to rely on each other based on their character, ability and truthfulness. In a period of uncertainty and hard times, **mutual trust** allows individuals to continue to function while maintaining a hope that things will improve.

Mutual trust includes two essential ingredients: sense of adequacy and personal security. Adequacy means that each employee feels that he or she counts for something in the organization and that his or her presence makes a difference in the overall

mutual trust
The ability of individuals to rely on each other based their character, ability and truthfulness

performance of the firm. Personal security is the degree to which each person feels safe when speaking honestly and candidly.

Mutual trust can lessen fear of change, which can help managers implement change. When trust is present, employees will feel comfortable as the organization moves through change even though change is threatening.

Organizational Learning

organizational learning
the ability to integrate new ideas into an organization's established systems to produce better ways of doing things

The term **organizational learning** refers to the ability to integrate new ideas into an organization's established systems to produce better ways of doing things. A manager can view organizational learning as either single looped or double looped.[31]

A single-looped learning situation is one in which only one way of making adjustments exists. An organization with single-looped learning has a prescribed way of doing things. When actions do not follow the prescription, the actions are adjusted to meet the standards. An organization with this belief is inflexible; it does not change its attitude, only its responses.

Double-looped learning, on the other hand, is based on the realization that more than one alternative exists. Double-looped learning facilitates change because they allow for more than one way to do something. If a manager believes there are numerous ways of reaching a goal, each employee can freely share ideas and the assumptions underlying the ideas. Double-looped learning provides for a change in both attitude and behavior.

Adaptability

Managers can either plan for change or react to it. Being adaptive takes energy, commitment and caring, but the wear and tear of the reactive approach is far worse. Adaptiveness means being open to new and different ways of doing things; it means being flexible rather than rigid.

According to James C. Collins, adaptiveness means changing without losing the company's core values. Companies have done so by grasping the differences between timeless principles and daily practices.

Explain why people resist change and what managers can do to overcome that resistance

IMPLEMENTATION OF CHANGE

To implement a program of change, a manager must be aware of why people resist change, why change efforts fail and what techniques can be used to modify behavior.

Resistance to Change

One of the greatest difficulties faced by managers trying to institute change involves overcoming the resistance of those who must change. In his book, *The Reengineering Revolution,* the late MIT professor-consultant Michael Hammer called people's innate resistance to change "the most perplexing, annoying, distressing, and confusing part" of the change process.[32] Nevertheless, resistance must be overcome or the change cannot take place.

Sources of Resistance People resist changes for many reasons. The following list includes some of them:

- *Loss of security.* Change scares people. Individuals tend to find security in traditional methods; the familiar is comfortable. New technology, new systems, new procedures and new managers can threaten that security and thus cause resistance.

- *Fear of economic loss.* Sometimes people resist change because they foresee, or fear, an economic loss. Workers might disapprove of new processes because they feel that the result will be layoffs or reduced wages.

- *Loss of power and control.* Change often poses problems of power and control. "Will my influence still exist?" "Where will I end up in the pecking order?" These questions reflect the anxiety caused by change. Some reorganizations clearly indicate that specific people will lose power. These people are likely to wish to preserve the status quo.

- *Reluctance to change old habits.* Habits provide a programmed method for decision making and performing. Someone who needs no initiative to solve problems might think, "I can do this job blindfolded." Learning new processes requires rethinking or learning to think again; it's hard work.

- *Selective perception.* A person who has a biased interpretation of reality is guilty of selective perception. To someone with selective perception, reality is what the person thinks it is. Employees prone to selective perception tend to think in terms of stereotypes, and these stereotypes can permeate their logic. Faced with a change at work, a person with selective perception might think, "It's a management plot to do away with us." An employee with such an attitude is difficult for a manager to deal with. If the employee's views are extreme, he or she regards all actions of management as suspect.

- *Awareness of weaknesses in the proposed change.* Sometimes employees resist change because they see that the change may cause problems. This type of resistance can be constructive. By listening to the objections of these employees, managers can help the organization avoid problems and save time, money and energy. For employees to have a constructive effect, they must be encouraged to express their concerns through constant communication.

Techniques for Overcoming Resistance Managers can use five techniques to overcome resistance to change:

1 *Participation.* Participation can be as simple as saying "we changed" instead of "they changed." A person involved in the process of change understands the goals and feels more strongly committed to the change than someone who did not participate. Organizations have recognized and have responded by implementing cross-functional teams (one of the topics in Chapter 14).

2 *Open communication.* Uncertainty breeds fear, which creates rumors, which causes more uncertainty. Managers can reduce the likelihood of this unsettling cycle by providing timely, complete and accurate information. Holding back information destroys trust.

3 *Advance warning.* Sudden change can have the same effect as an earthquake. People adapt better to change if they are prepared for it. As managers sense a need for change or know that change is imminent, they should inform the employees who will be affected. Continuous education and training help people prepare for change. Continuous learning seems to enhance adaptability.

4 *Sensitivity.* When implementing change, managers must work with those affected to learn each employee's concerns and respond to them. In other words, managers must be sensitive to the effects the change has on each person. Sensitivity minimizes resistance to the change.

5 *Security.* People are much more willing to accept change if the fear of dire consequences can be removed. In many cases, managers can reassure workers simply by explaining that the change will not affect income and job security. Of course, such a commitment is meaningful only if it's true. When managers break promises, they are taking the first step to employee discontent.

11 Explain why change efforts fail

WHY CHANGE EFFORTS FAIL

Not all change efforts are successful. Even when they undertake change for the best of reasons, managers cannot always bring about desired changes. Normally, failure can be traced to one of the following causes.

Faulty Thinking Managers can fail to achieve change by not analyzing the situation properly. A classic example of faulty thinking is California's tomato industry, which was threatened because of a lack of laborers to harvest the tomatoes. Managers thought the problem could be solved by a mechanical tomato harvester, but the machine crushed the tomatoes. Instead of changing the machine, the problem was solved "by breeding a firmer-skinned tomato—also known as the square tomato—that the machine could not crush, thus keeping California's tomato industry alive."[33]

Inadequate Process Sometimes change efforts fail because of the process used to bring them about. A change might fail because the manager did not follow the steps for change shown in Figure 8.16 or because he or she did not follow them properly. Perhaps the manager chose an inappropriate change agent or neglected a step in the process. In any case, an incomplete approach usually leads to failure.

Lack of Resources Some changes require a significant expenditure of time and money. If those resources aren't available, the change effort may be doomed from the beginning.

Lack of Acceptance and Commitment If individuals, both managers and employees, do not accept the need for change and commit to it, change will not occur. Lack of commitment typically occurs in organizations whose managers frequently announce change but do not follow through to implement it. In such a situation, employees begin to see each new announcement as merely a program of the month—entertaining per-haps, but nothing to be taken seriously.

Lack of Time and Poor Timing Some situations do not allow enough time for people to think about the change, accept it and implement it. In other instances, the timing is poor—for example, an economic downturn might lower revenue, employees might be occupied with other commitments or a competitor might release a new product. A company might invest years and millions of dollars into a change, only to find that the environment has evolved so much that the plan devised for success no longer applies.

A Resistant Culture In some cases the cultural climate of an organization needs to be changed before anything else can be.

Methods of Effecting Change

This section will explore how to change behavior on the individual level. Most first-line managers need to understand this kind of change, because their change efforts will be directed at modifying or altering their subordinates' behavior. Change in individuals usually relates to a change in skills, knowledge or attitude. The paragraphs that follow explore two approaches: the three-step approach and force-field analysis.

Three-Step Approach Many psychologists and educators have observed that different people react differently to pressures to change. Most will accept the need to learn new skills and update their knowledge, but most resent efforts to change their attitudes. Kurt Lewin provided a useful approach to changing attitudes in a lasting way.[34] His method, called the **three-step approach**, which consists of three phases: unfreezing, change and refreezing.

three-step approach
A technique of behavior modification to change attitudes in lasting ways; it consists of three phases: unfreezing, change and refreezing

- The first step, **unfreezing**, challenges managers who spot deficiencies in a subordinate's behavior to identify the causes of that behavior. They confront the individual with the behavior and the problem it causes; they then begin trying to convince him or her to change by suggesting methods and offering incentives. This step may include pressure on the individual that makes him or her uncomfortable and dissatisfied. When the person is upset enough, step two may begin.

  For example, say that Jessica wants to improve the productivity of Jane, a staff member in the Information Center. By spending too much time on her work, Jane increases the workload of others in the department. To resolve the problem, Jessica must first explain to Jane that her work is inadequate and that her coworkers must unfairly carry her burden. She may mention that the others are starting to complain about Jane. Having reviewed Jane's work, Jessica thinks that the basic problem is lack of training. As a result, she suggests that Jane undertake a special weeklong training course offered by the company. She could offer an incentive, too—pointing out that the higher productivity could mean a better chance at a salary increase.

- In the second step, **change**, the individual's discomfort level rises. When it rises high enough, he or she will look for ways to reduce the tension. This leads the employee to question his or her motives for the current behavior and provides the manager with the opening to present new role models that promote the desired behavior. As the individual adopts that behavior, performance will improve; but the manager must support and reinforce that behavior if it is to last.

- In step three, **refreezing**, the manager recognizes and rewards new and approved attitudes and behaviors. If any new problems arise, the manager must identify and discourage them; in other words, the process begins again. The three-step process is continuous. Managers must watch that the new behaviors do not become counterproductive. If they do, the behaviors must be unfrozen and replaced by a new, more desirable behavior.

Force-Field Analysis Kurt Lewin also developed **force-field analysis**, another useful tool for managing change. As Figure 8.17 shows, to achieve change a manager must overcome the status quo—the balance between forces that favor change and forces that resist change. The change forces are known as *driving forces*, and the resisting forces are known as *restraining forces*. Managers trying to implement a change must analyze the balance of driving and restraining forces, then attempt to tip that balance by selectively removing or weakening the restraining forces. The driving forces will then become strong enough to enable the change to be made.

force-field analysis
A technique to implement change by determining which forces drive change and which forces resist it

To see how force-field analysis works, we look at the example of Jane, a worker in the Information Center. To convince Jane to change, Jessica must first identify the

| Figure 8.17 | Forces that Contribute to a Force Field |

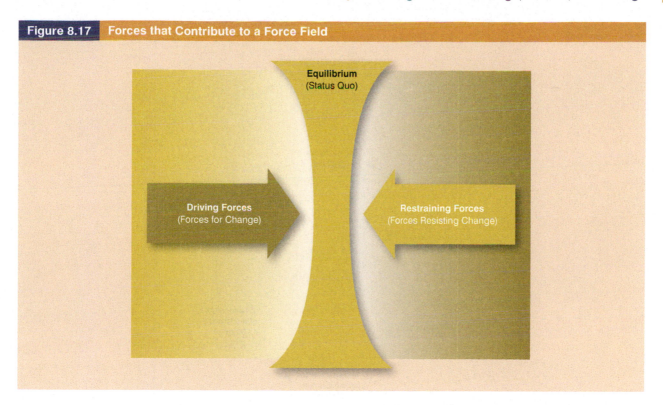

driving forces: self-esteem, the regard of peers and increased monetary compensation. The key restraining forces might be Jane's lack of desire to expend the effort to improve and her unfamiliarity with the computer. Jessica can weaken the restraining forces by having one of Jane's coworkers tell Jane how the training program helped the coworker. This information may strengthen the driving forces and alter the balance of the forces, leading Jane to accept the change.

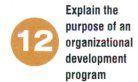

Explain the purpose of an organizational development program

organizational development (OD)

A process of conducting a thorough analysis of an organization's problems and then implementing long-term solutions to solve them

ORGANIZATIONAL DEVELOPMENT

Managing change is an ongoing process. If a manager does it well, he or she can maintain a positive organizational climate. Some organizations make thorough analyses of their problems and then implement long-term solutions to solve them. Such an approach is called **organizational development (OD)**.

Purposes of Organizational Development

The main purpose of OD, according to one management writer, is "to bring about a system of organizational renewal that can effectively cope with environmental changes. In doing so, OD strives to maximize organizational effectiveness as well as individual work satisfaction."[35] Organizational development is the most comprehensive strategy for intervention. It involves all the activities and levels of management in ongoing problems that respond to external and internal sources. The OD process is cyclical, as Figure 8.18 shows.

Figure 8.18   **Model of the Organizational Developmental Process**

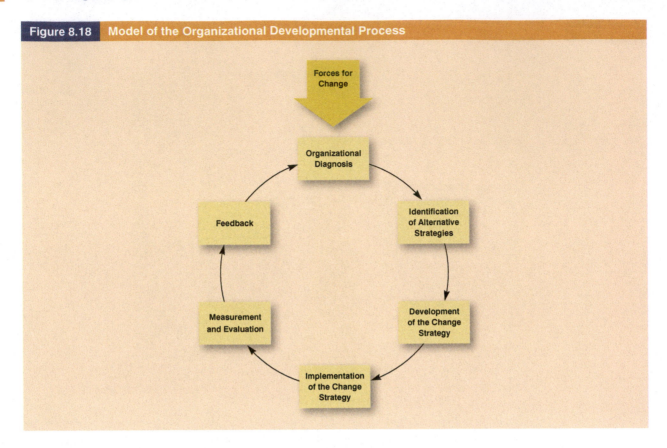

Strategies of Organizational Development

Managers may choose one or more of the tools and strategies of OD described in Figure 8.19. The choice depends on the circumstances. Restrictions the managers might have to take into account include limits on time and money and lack of skill at implementing a strategy.

The choice of a strategy usually results from conferences and discussions involving those who will be most directly affected. The experiences, feelings, and perceptions of conference participants help determine if their parts of the organization are ready for change and for OD techniques. The success of OD depends on a high level of receptiveness to change.

Evaluating the Effectiveness of Organizational Development

Since OD requires an ongoing, long-term effort to bring about lasting change in an organization's technology, structure and people, a successful OD program takes a significant investment of money and time. Both are needed for managers to adequately diagnose the problem, select the strategy and evaluate the effectiveness of the program.

Managers can measure the effectiveness by comparing the results of the program to the goals before it was implemented. Were the goals met? If not, why not? Perhaps they were too rigid and too hard to achieve. Perhaps the problems were inadequately defined, and the inadequate definition resulted in the choice of an inappropriate solution. Perhaps managers tried to institute changes before people were prepared for

Figure 8.19	Tools and Methods for Applying Organizational Development Strategies

Diagnostic Strategies	
Consultants	This strategy consists of bringing in objective outsiders (consultants) to analyze and conduct audits of existing policies, procedures, and problems. Consultants can be individuals or groups and may act as change agents as well.
Surveys	Surveys consist of interviews or questionnaires used to assess the attitudes, complaints, problems, and unmet needs of employees. Surveys are usually conducted by outsiders and guarantee anonymity to participants.
Group discussions	Group discussions are periodic meetings conducted by managers to uncover problems and sources of their subordinates' discomfort and dissatisfaction.
Change Strategies	
Training programs	Training programs are ongoing or special efforts to improve or increase skill levels, change or instill attitudes, or increase the knowledge needed to per-form jobs more effectively and efficiently.
Meetings and seminars	As change strategies, meetings or seminars are gatherings held to explore mutual problems and seek mutually agreeable solutions. Such group sessions may be chaired by insiders or outsiders and may be used to prepare people for changes in advance of implementation.
Grid OD	Grid OD is a six-phase program based on the Leadership Grid. Its purpose is management and organizational development. The first two phases focus on management development. The last four phases are devoted to organizational development. The six phases are laboratory training, team development, intergroup development, organizational goal setting, goal attainment and stabilization.

them. Regardless of the cause, the results of the OD analysis will provide feedback needed for later changes.

In the final analysis, as is the case with any other management effort, the effectiveness of OD depends on the quality of its inputs and the skills of those making the analysis. Successful OD depends on solid research, clear goals and implementation by effective change agents who use appropriate methods.

OD is an expression of managers' efforts to stay flexible. Managers recognize that events inside and outside the organization can happen quite suddenly and can create pressure for change. OD provides the personnel and mechanisms to deal with change; control its evolution; and direct its impact on organizational structure, technology and people.

Chapter Summary

1 Define organizational design and describe the four objectives of organizational design.

Organizational design is the creation of or change to an organization's structure. It involves developing the overall layout of the positions and departments as well as establishing the interrelationships among the positions and departments.

The managers responsible for organizational design have four objectives in creating organizational structures. They design structure to:

1 *Respond to change.* To stay competitive the company must respond to changes in the environment as well as to changes that emerge from its evolutionary development.

2 *Integrate new elements.* As organizations grow, evolve and respond, new positions and new departments must be integrated into the fabric of the organization.

3 *Coordinate the components.* Managers need to find a way to tie all departments together to ensure coordination and collaboration across the departments.

4 *Encourage flexibility.* Designers need to institutionalize the ability to respond to change.

2 Distinguish between mechanistic and organic organizational structures.

Depending on how organizational concepts are balanced, the design produced can be a tight, or mechanistic structure or a flexible or organic structure. A mechanistic structure is characterized by rigidly defined tasks, formalization, many rules and regulations and centralizes decision making right down to the employees performing the job.

3 Discuss the influence that contingency factors— organizational strategy, environment, size, age, and technology—have on organizational design.

Whether an organization will be mechanistic or organic is influenced by the meshing of five factors:

1 *Organization strategy.* The mission, corporate-level strategy and business-level strategy influence design. Structure is a tool to accomplish strategy.

2 *Organization environment.* Whether a company operates in a stable or in a dynamically changing environment influences structure. A mechanistic structure functions well in a stable environment; an organic structure functions better in a changing environment.

3 *Organization size.* Large companies tend to have mechanistic structures. Small companies have organic structures.

4 *Organization age.* Older, mature companies tend to have mechanistic structures. New or young organizations tend to have organic structures.

5 *Organization technology.* Every organization uses some form of technology to convert resources to outputs. The type of technology—small batch, mass production or continuous process—influences the type of structure. Small batch and continuous process favor organic structures. Mass production technology favors a mechanistic structure.

4 Describe the characteristics, advantages, and disadvantages or functional, divisional, matrix, team and network structural designs.

The organizational design alternatives include a functional structure, divisional structure, matrix structure, team structure and network structure.

• The functional structure groups positions into departments based on similar skills, expertise and resources used. The functional structure has the advantages of economies of scale, minimizes duplication of personnel and equipment, makes employees comfortable and simplifies training. Disadvantages include the lack of understanding and concern for other specialty areas, communication barriers, lack of cooperation and coordination and slow response time to changes in the environment.

• The divisional structure groups departments based on organizational outputs. Divisions become self-contained strategic business units (SBUs). The divisional structure focuses the attention of the employees and managers on the results for the product, customer or geographical area. It is flexible and responsive to change, performance is easier to target and it aids in developing senior executives. Disadvantages include duplication of activities and resources; lack of technical specialization, expertise and training; lack of coordination across positions; and competition among divisions.

- The matrix structure combines the advantages of functional specialization with the focus and accountability of the divisional structure. It utilizes the functional and divisional chains of command simultaneously in the same part of the organization. To achieve this, the matrix structure uses dual lines of authority. The matrix organization is flexible, communication and coordination are increased, motivation is increased for the individual employee, and technical training is provided for both functional and general management skills. Disadvantages include potential conflict, confusion and frustration created by the dual chain of command, the danger of creating conflict by pitting divisional objectives against functional objectives, time lost in meetings to resolve conflicts and the problem of balance of power between the functional and divisional sides of the matrix.

- The team structure organizes separate functions or processes into a group based on one overall objective. The team concept breaks down barriers across departments; speeds up decision making and response time; motivates employees by developing employee responsibility; eliminates levels of managers, resulting in lower administrative costs; and eliminates the double reporting problem associated with the matrix structure. Disadvantages include the dependence on employee learning and training for the system to succeed and the large amount of time required for meetings.

- The network structure features a small central organization that relies on other organizations to perform critical functions on a contract basis. The network structure provides flexibility and reduces administrative overhead. Disadvantages include the lack of control, the unpredictability of supply and the lack of internal managerial technical expertise to effectively resolve technical problems.

5 Define organizational culture and describe the ways that culture is manifested.

Organizational culture is the distinctive character of an organization comprising its shared values, beliefs, philosophies, experiences, habits, expectations, norms and behaviors. Seven factors influence organizational culture: key organizational processes, the dominant coalition, employees and other tangible assets, formal organizational arrangements, the social system, technology and the external environment.

The culture becomes apparent through the following manifestations:

- *Statements of principle*—written expressions of basic principles central to the organizational culture
- *Stories*—illustrations of the culture used to acquaint new employees with the cultural values and to reaffirm those values to existing employees
- *Slogans*—a phrase or saying clearly expressing a key organizational value
- *Heroes*—people in the organization who exemplify the values of the culture
- *Ceremonies*—presentation of awards to provide examples of and reinforce company values
- *Symbols*—objects or images that convey meaning to others
- *Climate*—the quality of the work environment experienced by employees
- *Physical environment*—the structure of the work setting, which often reflects the cultural values

6 Explain the role of managers and employees in creating culture and making a culture effective.

Managers help develop culture by identifying core values, defining the company's mission, determining the amount of individual autonomy and the degree to which people work separately or in groups, structuring the work in accordance with the corporation's values, developing reward systems that reinforce values and creating methods of socialization that will bring new workers inside the culture and reinforce the culture for existing workers. Employees contribute to defining the culture by the extent to which they accept and adopt it, by shaping the organization's norms and values and by forming subcultures.

Three factors that make a culture effective:

1 *Coherence*—how well the culture fits the organization's mission and other organizational elements

2 *Pervasiveness and depth*—the extent to which employees adopt the culture of an organization

3 *Adaptability to the external environment*—the degree to which a culture is flexible enough to allow change in the face of emerging external demands

7 **Define change and identify the kinds of change that can occur in an organization.**

Change is any alternative in the current work environment. Change can occur in strategy, structure, process and people.

Evolutionary change focuses on incremental steps to bring about progress. Its techniques include *kaizen,* total quality management, quality circles and benchmarking. Revolutionary change focuses on bold, discontinuous advances. Its techniques include BHAGS and reengineering.

Planned change involves trying to anticipate what changes will occur in both external and internal environments and then developing a response that will maximize the organization's success. Unplanned change involves reacting to events rather than anticipating them.

8 **Explain the steps managers can follow to implement planned change.**

To implement planned change, managers should follow these steps: recognize the need for change, develop goals, select a change agent, diagnose the problem, select the intervention method, develop a plan, plan for implementation, implement the plan and follow up and evaluate.

9 **Identify the organizational qualities that promote change.**

The organizational qualities that promote change include mutual trust, organizational learning and adaptiveness.

10 **Explain why people resist change and what managers can do to overcome that resistance.**

People resist change because of loss of security, fear of economic loss, loss of power and control, reluctance to change old habits, selective perception and awareness of weaknesses in the proposed change. To overcome resistance, managers might develop techniques including participation, open communication, advance warning, sensitivity and security.

11 **Explain why change efforts fail.**

Change efforts fail for a number of reasons, including faulty thinking or an inadequate process, lack of resources or commitment, poor timing or a resistant cultural climate.

12 **Explain the purpose of an organizational development program.**

The purpose of an organizational development program is to bring about a system of organizational renewal that can effectively cope with environmental changes. In doing so, OD strives to maximize organizational effectiveness as well as individual work satisfaction.

KEY TERMS

REVIEW QUESTIONS

1. When managers are engaged in organizational design, what are they developing?

2. Identify and discuss the four objectives of organizational design.

3. What are the characteristics of a mechanistic organization? What are the characteristics of an organic organization?

4. Name factors that influence organizational design. How does an organization's strategy influence organizational design? What types of structure are appropriate for the three types of technology? What two needs in organizational design result from a volatile environment?

5. What are the characteristics of a functional organization structure? What are the advantages of a divisional structure? What are the characteristics of a matrix organizational structure? What are the characteristics of teams? What are the advantages and disadvantages of networks?

6. What are the seven factors that influence culture? Use specific examples to explain how they interact.

7. How is culture evidenced?

8. What is the role of managers in creating culture? What is the role of employees in creating culture?

9. How does culture influence organizational effectiveness? What factors contribute to an effective culture?

10. What are the four kinds of change that can occur in an organization?

11. What are the steps of planned change?

12. What organizational qualities promote change?

13. Describe three reasons that people resist change, and explain what managers can do to overcome that resistance.

14. What are three reasons that change efforts fail?

15. Why do organizations adopt an organizational development program?

DISCUSSION QUESTIONS FOR CRITICAL THINKING

1. In which structural design options—functional, divisional or matrix—would you prefer to work? Least prefer? Explain your answers.

2. What examples can you provide to demonstrate the application of the team structure? Was the team organized by process or by function?

3. The discussion on contingency factors affecting organizational design states that organizational structure follows strategy. Other observers suggest that strategy should fit the organization's structure. With which position do you agree? Why?

4. What specific examples can you give to demonstrate the manifestations of culture (statements of principle, stories, slogans, symbols, heroes, etc.) in an organization with which you have been involved?

5. Can a change made in one area of a company—in strategy, for instance—lead to a change in other areas? Why or why not?

6. If appointed CEO of a troubled company, would you adopt a revolutionary or evolutionary change agent style? Why? Which would be more effective?

7. Demonstrate your understanding of force-field analysis by applying it to a change with which you have been involved.

8. In order to be proactive, instead of reacting to change, managers must anticipate and make change happen. List some rules for leading change.

Social Media Management Exercises

- Organizational culture includes shared values, which help give an organization its distinctive character. (Organizational culture was defined in Chapter 3; core values were defined in Chapter 4). Social Media values openness, ease of use and sociability. Popular culture values influence, success, status, recognition and wealth. Ethical virtues include peace, love, integrity and justice. Choose one word from each area—Social Media, popular culture, ethical virtues—that is most important to you. What do the words mean to you? If others in a company share these similar values and beliefs, how might it influence worker behavior?

- Use the "The Conversation Prism" to identify the networks you use and the ones you are missing.

Experiential Learning

A Cultural Mismatch

North American Chrysler merged with Germany's Daimler-Benz AG to form DaimlerChrysler in May 1998. Chrysler's profit performance and leadership in minivans during the 1990s made it an attractive partner for Daimler. The core management, engineering, manufacturing, purchasing and design operations of Chrysler were located at one place in Auburn Hills, Michigan, facilitating decentralized and quick decision making.

"Chrysler's primary reason for teaming with Daimler-Benz is to extend its international reach" (Smith). Daimler-Benz AG's Mercedes Benz brand stood as a symbol of Germany's economic might, but Daimler-Benz AG was known as an autocratic decision maker. "From the beginning, the high command in Stuttgart issued orders to Detroit about everything from where the headquarters would be located (Germany) to what kind of business cards would be used" (Jamieson).

Chrysler was successful before the merger but began to flounder soon after the merger. In fact, many began to believe that the deal was not a merger of equals but was really an acquisition. Soon after the merger, top American managers at Chrysler were replaced by German managers and plants were closed. Furthermore, Germans headed all divisions, while Americans were laid off.

Nine years after the $36 billion dollar merger, Chrysler was sold for just $7.4 billion. Dave Healy, an analyst with Burnham Securities, said, "You had two companies from different countries with different languages and different styles come together yet there were no synergies. It was simply an exercise in empire-building by Juergen Schrempp (Daimler-Benz chairman at time of merger). Basically Daimler paid Cerberus Capital Management to take Chrysler off its hands" (ArticlesBase).

Chrysler immediately had major problems with the change.

- It was hard to imagine two more different cultures than those of Chrysler and Daimler-Benz AG.

- Chrysler is based in the heart of an American industrial neighborhood. Daimler-Benz AG sits an ocean away in Europe.

- Chrysler's workers make decisions from the bottom up. Daimler-Benz's managers make decisions from top down.

- Chrysler's management is low key and creates autonomy. The management at Daimler is intense, precise and controlling.

Questions

1. Based on the experiences of Chrysler and Daimler-Benz AG, what is the importance of culture in the change process?

2. What specific cultural factors caused problems in the change process? Cite examples to support your answer.

3. What specific mistakes did Chrysler and Daimler-Benz AG make in the change process? Cite examples to support your answer.

4. Using as your guide the nine steps for planned change discussed in this chapter, construct a change process to successfully merge Chrysler with Daimler-Benz AG.

Sources: David C. Smith, "Is Bigger Really Better—DaimlerChrysler merger faces hurdles," *Ward's Auto World*, June 1, 1998; Bob Jamieson, "Far From a Merger of Equals," *ABC News*, January 25, 2001; ArticlesBase "How Daimler, Chrysler Merger Failed," May 18, 2007, *http://www.articlesbase. com/automotive-articles/how-daimler-chrysler-merger-failed-149797. html#ixzz19cyiPFdU*.

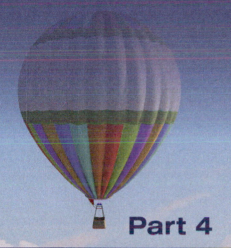

Part 4

Staffing

Chapter 9

Staffing the Workforce

LEARNING OBJECTIVES

After studying this chapter, you should be able to:

1 Determine the importance of the staffing function

2 List and explain the eight elements of the staffing process

3 Describe the three primary staffing environments

4 Identify the four activities related to human resource planning

5 List and describe the primary screening devices used in the selection process

6 Explain the differences and similarities between training and development

7 Discuss the purpose of a performance appraisal

8 Describe the four primary employment decisions

9 Determine the purposes and components of compensation

Intrapreneur/Entrepreneur

Entrepreneurs start businesses. They are self-employed; they are their own bosses. Intrapreneurs are employed by businesses but embody the entrepreneurial spirit to come up with new and innovative ideas that may become profitable products and services for the business. They look for opportunities, and they work like they own the company. Thus, entrepreneurs and intrapreneurs have similar motivations.

Do you want to pursue your own ideas like an entrepreneur but work for a large corporation? For each of the following statements, circle the number that indicates your level of agreement. Rate your agreement as it is, not what you think it should be. Objectivity will enable you to determine your management skill strengths and weaknesses.

	Almost Always	Often	Sometimes	Rarely	Almost Never
I am passionate about a product or service.	5	4	3	2	1
I am willing to work long hours.	5	4	3	2	1
I am a salesperson for the product or service I'm passionate about.	5	4	3	2	1
I am willing to take risks.	5	4	3	2	1
I am good at making decisions.	5	4	3	2	1
I feel confident about my ability to make the right decision.	5	4	3	2	1
I am responsible.	5	4	3	2	1
I am willing to take on more responsibility.	5	4	3	2	1
I handle stress well.	5	4	3	2	1
I can maintain work/life balance.	5	4	3	2	1

Compute your score by adding the circled numbers. The highest score is 50; the lowest score is 10. A higher score implies you are more likely to enjoy working innovatively for yourself or for a company that will encourage you to be creative. A lower score implies a lesser degree of readiness, but it can be increased. Reading and studying this chapter will help you to improve your understanding of staffing.

INTRODUCTION

The primary purposes of **staffing** are to attract, hire, train, develop, reward, and retain the required number of good people, helping them meet their needs while they help the organizations meet their needs. Texas entrepreneur Courtland L. Logue has created or managed 28 companies—running them for a time, then selling some and acquiring others. Here is what he thinks about the importance of finding and hiring the right number of good people:

> *"First, get good people. If you don't have good people, that's your fault. Remember, .200 hitters don't win championships. Overpay and get .300 hitters. Just don't hire more of them than you need."*[1]

staffing
Efforts designed to attract, hire, train, develop, reward, and retain the people needed to accomplish an organization's goals and promote job satisfaction

"Good" people are those with proven performance records or potential that demonstrates they will or do fit into the organization's culture and climate. Frank Sonnenberg, business author and consultant, adds this insight: "The point is, you don't just hire bodies, but seek employees that you value enough to invest in."[2] Since most job applicants have some deficiencies, the key issue is the employer's willingness and ability to help applicants remedy their deficiencies. Providing needed investments (training, for example) makes good people even better, making them more confident and capable and more valuable to their organizations.

Once good people are on board, organizations must retain them. This goal leads to the second part of staffing: helping employees meet their needs while they help the organization to meet its needs. Lorry Lokey, Founder and CEO of Business Wire, a wireless news provider, believes the following: "My people spend a fourth of their lives—or more—working for this company, so they deserve to have their needs taken care of." His financial chief, Constance Cummings, adds, "There's no fear here because we believe in doing everything we can to hold on to good employees and to improve the quality of their lives." These few words sum up the essence of the company's staffing philosophy.[3]

Staffing, which follows organizing, links people and processes. People create an organization's *intellectual capital*—that which makes the organization unique and separates it from its competition. Without dedicated, knowledgeable, and motivated employees, the best-laid plans cannot bear fruit. The Society for Human Resource Managers (SHRM) reports that 25 percent of the workforce turns over yearly. "Turnover is expensive, so it's important to support new employees with comprehensive onboarding to ensure their success." **Onboarding** is the process by which new hires get adjusted to the social and performance aspects of their jobs quickly and smoothly, and learn the attitudes, knowledge, skills, and behaviors required to function effectively within an organization."[4] Empowered people working in a diverse and open climate—one based on mutual trust and respect—can make bad plans work and good plans better.

onboarding
The process by which new hires get adjusted to the social and performance aspects of their jobs quickly and smoothly, and learn the attitudes, knowledge, skills and behaviors required to function effectively within an organization

This chapter examines many major investments that organizations make in their human resources, along with the laws, principles and processes that affect staffing in the United States. Appendix B includes staffing concerns for organizations operating in an international environment.

Responsibility for Staffing

In small organizations, every manager is responsible for the staffing function; even worker teams can participate. A large firm usually establishes a separate department dedicated to staffing. A subunit that focuses on staffing is usually called a personnel or human resource department. Managers of such a department—**human resource**

human resource manager or personnel manager
A manager who fulfills one or more personnel, or human resource, function

managers or **personnel managers**—assist others by planning, organizing, staffing, coordinating, controlling and sometimes executing specific personnel and human resource (P/HR) management functions.

Some human resource managers and practitioners are specialists who focus on a specific aspect of P/HR management—compensation, training or recruiting for example. Others are generalists responsible for several functions. This book will use the terms *human resource manager* and *human resource specialist* to refer to both groups.

List and explain the eight elements of the staffing process

STAFFING PROCESS

Figure 9.1 summarizes the eight elements of the staffing process. The list that follows briefly describes each element:

1 *Human resource planning.* This aspect of staffing involves assessing current employees, forecasting future needs and making plans to add or remove workers. To adapt to changing strategies and changing needs, managers must continually update their plans.

2 *Recruiting.* In this step, managers with positions to fill look for qualified people inside or outside the company.

3 *Selection.* This step involves testing and interviewing candidates and hiring the best available.

4 *Orientation.* In this phase of staffing, new employees learn about their surroundings, meet their coworkers, and learn about the rules, regulations and benefits of the company.

5 *Training and development.* To train and develop employees, employers establish programs to help workers learn their jobs and improve their skills.

6 *Performance appraisal.* As part of the controlling function of management, managers must establish the criteria for evaluating work, schedule formal sessions to discuss evaluations with employees, and determine how to reward high achievers and motivate others to become high achievers. All these tasks are part of the performance-appraisal element of staffing.

7 *Compensation.* This aspect of staffing relates to establishing pay and, in some cases, benefits.

8 *Employment decisions.* Workers' careers involve transfers, promotions, demotions, layoffs and firings. Making decisions about these career developments is part of the staffing process.

Figure 9.1	Eight Elements of the Staffing Process

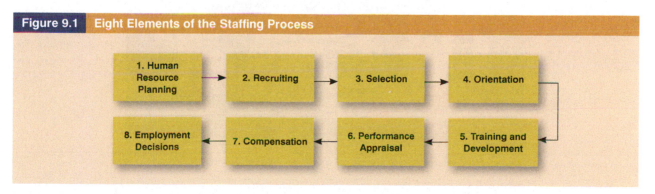

Not all the elements of the staffing process are components of every staffing problem. Recruiting, for example, is not necessary unless new employees are needed. Some elements are constants, however. Planning, training and appraisal accompany the primary management functions. Therefore, every manager must be concerned about staffing.

STAFFING ENVIRONMENTS

3 Describe the three primary staffing environments

Staffing, like other managerial functions, is subject to outside influences. Events and pressures from many sources in an organization's external environment—customers, suppliers and competitors, for example—influence staffing and dictate the human resource plans and strategies necessary to carry them out.

Economic Environment
An indicator of the strength of the economy is employment rates.

In recent decades, a growing number of stable employment relationships have given way to something more armslength, from contract situations to temporary employment to oneoff job opportunities, or "gigs", arising from subcontracting, outsourcing and other forms of "fissuring." Technological change is driving some of these developments, but these broad workplace trends are unfolding across both high and lowtech sectors. Because these trends are taking place in many traditional sectors of the economy, hospitality, manufacturing, healthcare, etc.—as well as emerging sectors, they are already affecting a broad swath of the working population.[5]

The **sharing economy** has led to the **gig economy**. The **sharing economy** refers to the peer-to-peer rental market. In both cases, temporary positions are common and organizations contract workers to rent rooms, rides or other assets as depicted in Figure 9.2 below, using mobile Apps or the Internet. Sharing companies like Uber Technologies and Airbnb do not use employees. The contingent workers monetize their cars for Uber and extra rooms in their homes for Airbnb.

sharing economy
The peer-to-peer rental market

gig economy
Independent contractors or self-employed people work for short-term engagements

Figure 9.2	The Rise of the Sharing Economy

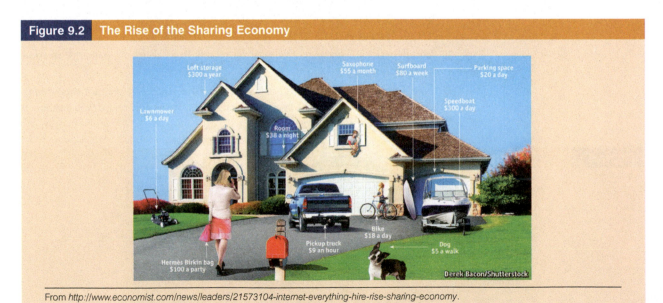

From *http://www.economist.com/news/leaders/21573104-internet-everything-hire-rise-sharing-economy.*

independent contractors
Self-employed workers hired by companies with a verbal agreement for a short term or under terms specified in a contract

These companies use **independent contractors** who are available on demand. Since independent contractors have a particular expertise and are self-employed, they are often hired by companies with a verbal agreement for short-term assignments or under terms specified in a contract. This allows workers to be flexible and companies to lower overhead with respect to planning. The company does not pay contractors overtime or benefits, such as health insurance, Social Security or FICA taxes.

Legal Environment

The laws and principles that govern a community inevitably affect the way companies do business. Consider just a few of the legal issues that pertain to even the smallest company: contracts, criminal law, negligence and equity. A legal concept that has a great impact on organizations today is the idea that the law is a tool to correct and prevent wrongs to individuals and groups. Laws and legal principles act as controls on managers who discharge staffing responsibilities.

Executive orders and laws generated by federal, state, county and city agencies regulate how companies, usually those with 15 or more employees, must conduct staffing. So complex are these regulations, and so great is the potential for harm due to noncompliance, that many large companies and institutions hire attorneys and specialists to deal with reporting and disclosure requirements.

Figure 9.3 highlights federal laws regarding three topics: equal employment opportunity, affirmative action and sexual harassment. The following paragraphs discuss these topics in more detail.

Figure 9.3	U.S. Federal Legislation Related to Staffing

Federal Legislation	Description of Provisions
Equal Pay Act of 1963	Prohibits paying employees of one sex less than employees of the opposite sex for doing roughly equivalent work. Applies to private employers.
Title VI 1964 Civil Rights Act	In staffing decisions, prohibits discrimination based on race, color, religion, sex or national origin. Applies to employers receiving federal financial assistance.
Title VII 1964 Civil Rights Act (amended 1972)	Prohibits discrimination based on race, color, religion, sex or national origin. Applies to private employers of 15 or more employees; federal, state and local governments; unions; and employment agencies.
Executive Orders 11246 and 11375 (1965)	In staffing decisions, prohibits discrimination based on race, color, religion, sex or national origin. Establishes requirements for affirmative action plans. Applies to federal contractors and subcontractors.
Age Discrimination in Employment Act of 1967 (amended 1978)	Prohibits age discrimination in staffing decisions against people over 40 years of age. Applies to all employers of 20 or more employees.
Title I 1968 Civil Rights Act	Prohibits interference with a person's exercise of rights with respect to race, color, religion, sex or national origin.
Rehabilitation Act of 1973	In staffing decisions, prohibits discrimination based on certain physical and mental handicaps. Applies to employers doing business with or for the federal government.
Vietnam Era Veterans Readjustment Act of 1974	In staffing decisions, prohibits discrimination against disabled veterans and Vietnam-era veterans.

continues

| Figure 9.3 | U.S. Federal Legislation Related to Staffing (continued) |

Federal Legislation	Description of Provisions
Privacy Act of 1974	Establishes the right of employees to examine letters of reference concerning them unless the right is waived.
Revised Guidelines on Employee Selection (1976, 1978, and 1979)	Establishes a single set of guidelines that define discrimination on the basis of race, color, religion, sex and national origin. The guidelines provide a framework for making legal employment decisions about hiring, promoting and demoting and for the proper use of tests and other selection procedures.
Pregnancy Discrimination Act of 1978	Prohibits discrimination in employment based on pregnancy, childbirth or related medical conditions.
Equal Employment Opportunity Guidelines of 1981—Sexual Harassment	Prohibits sexual harassment when such conduct is an explicit or implicit condition of employment, if the employee's response becomes a basis for employment or promotion decisions, or if it interferes with an employee's performance. The guidelines protect men and women.
Equal Employment Opportunity Guidelines of 1981—	Identifies potential national-origin discrimination to include fluency-in-English job requirements and disqualification due to foreign training or education.
National Origin	Identifies national-origin harassment in the work environment to include ethnic slurs and physical conduct with the purpose of creating an intimidating or hostile environment or unreasonable interference with work.
Equal Employment Opportunity Guidelines of 1981—Religion	Determines that employers have an obligation to accommodate religious practices of employees unless they can demonstrate that doing so would result in undue hardship. Accommodation may be achieved through voluntary substitutes, flexible scheduling, lateral transfer and change of job assignment.
Mandatory Retirement Act (amended 1987)	Determines that employees may not be forced to retire before age 70.
Workers Adjustment and Retraining Act of 1988	Employer of 100 or more workers must provide to employees a 60-day notice of mass layoffs or plant closures so that they have ample time to search for other jobs.
Americans with Disabilities Act of 1990	Prohibits discrimination on the basis of physical or mental handicap.
Civil Rights Act of 1991	Permits women, persons with disabilities, and persons who are religious minorities to have a jury trial and sue for punitive damages if they can prove intentional hiring and workplace discrimination. Also requires companies to provide evidence that the business practice that led to the discrimination was not discriminatory but was job related for the position in question and consistent with business necessity.
Genetic Information Nondiscrimination Act of 2008	Prohibits discrimination based on a person's genetic information.

Equal Employment Opportunity Federal laws prohibit discrimination in employment decisions. **Discrimination** means using illegal criteria in staffing. Laws that prohibit discrimination are designed to guarantee **equal employment opportunity**. The Equal Employment Opportunity Commission (EEOC) enforces antidiscrimination laws. Claims of discrimination filed with the U.S. Equal Employment Opportunity Commission are based on race/color, national origin, gender, religion, age or disability.

discrimination
Using illegal criteria when making employment decisions. Discrimination results in an adverse impact on members of protected groups

equal employment opportunity
Legislation designed to protect individuals and groups from discrimination

According to the U.S. Senate, it is unlawful for an employer to do either of the following:[6]

1 To fail or refuse to hire or to discharge an individual solely on the basis of race, color, religion, sex, age, national origin or handicap

2 To limit, segregate or classify employees or applicants for employment in any way that would tend to deprive the individual of employment opportunities solely on the basis of race, color, religion, sex, age, national origin or handicap

A company's best defense against accusations of discrimination or bias in hiring is to be certain that any employment practice or device adheres to the following:

- Analyze the duties, functions, and competencies relevant to jobs. Then create objective, job-related qualification standards related to those duties, functions, and competencies. Make sure they are consistently applied when choosing among candidates.

- Ensure selection criteria do not disproportionately exclude certain racial groups unless the criteria are valid predictors of successful job performance and meet the employer's business needs. For example, if educational requirements disproportionately exclude certain minority or racial groups, they may be illegal if not important for job performance or business needs.

- Make sure promotion criteria are made known, and that job openings are communicated to all eligible employees. (Source: U.S. Equal Employment Opportunity Commission, Best Practices for Employers and Human Resources/ EEO Professionals, *http://www.eeoc.gov/eeoc/initiatives/e-race/bestpractices-employers.cfm.*)

Protected Groups The federal government has created several protected groups— people against whom it is illegal to discriminate. These groups are women, the disabled or differently abled and minorities. Federal law lists socially disadvantaged individuals as follows:

- Black Americans
- Hispanic Americans
- Asians Pacific Americans
- Native Americans
- Subcontinent Asian American

As defined under federal law, the differently abled in America are those who have a physical or mental impairment that substantially limits one or more major life activities, have a record of such impairment, and are regarded as having such impairment.

Two major laws govern the protection of people with such disabilities: the Rehabilitation Act of 1973 (covering firms doing business with the federal government) and the Americans with Disabilities Act of 1990 (covering nearly every firm with 15 or more employees). On September 25, 2008, the President signed the Americans with Disabilities Act (ADA) Amendments Act of 2008. The ADA contains a broad definition of disability.

Protection is extended to people with current or past physical and mental conditions. Examples of those protected are people with dependency on legal drugs whose dependency does not impair work performance; people with a history of cancer, heart trouble or a contagious disease, providing that their conditions do not pose a significant risk to coworkers or render them unable to perform their work; and people who have undergone or who now are undergoing rehabilitation for their drug dependencies.

Under both laws employers must make reasonable accommodations (that cause no *undue hardship*) for the disabled. Jobs may have to be redefined, removing those tasks that the person with a disability cannot perform. Prerequisites such as passing a physical exam may have to be waived when parts of that exam are not job related. Physical facilities may have to be altered to accommodate access by persons with disabilities. Signs in Braille and wheelchair ramps are but two examples.

The Job Accommodation Network (JAN), a service of the U.S. Department of Labor's Office of Disability Employment Policy (ODEP), conducts a survey on the cost of accommodation. Each year the survey continues to indicate that the cost of accommodation in dollars is low, while the impact to the workplace is positive in many ways. JAN surveys employers who call for accommodation information to obtain feedback on the cost and benefit of accommodation. Study results show that more than half of accommodations needed by employees and applicants with disabilities cost absolutely nothing. Of those accommodations that do cost, the typical expenditure by employers is $500. The most frequently mentioned direct benefits were: (1) the accommodation allowed the company to retain a qualified employee; (2) the accommodation increased the worker's productivity; and (3) the accommodation eliminated the costs of training a new employee.[7]

In 1998, the U.S. Supreme Court ruled that Title VII of the 1964 Civil Rights Act covers claims of same-sex sexual harassment but does not include claims of "sexual orientation discrimination" (*Bibby v. The Philadelphia Coca-Cola Bottling Co.*). Several states, counties and municipalities have added the category of sexual orientation to fair housing, employment, public accommodations and credit laws that already protect people in the preceding categories from discrimination. Almost half of the states have laws protecting lesbians and gay men against workplace discrimination. In addition, many companies, including Microsoft, Levi Strauss, Hewlett-Packard, Fox Inc., Ben & Jerry's and Disney, have adopted nondiscrimination policies with regard to sexual orientation. A few states and cities, however, specifically exclude protecting people from discrimination on the basis of their sexual orientation.

By law, managers must refrain from employment decisions that produce a disparate impact on these protected groups. A **disparate impact** is any result that harms one group more than another. Not hiring an applicant because she is a woman causes a disparate impact. Using an employment test that eliminates a significantly greater percentage of protected groups than unprotected groups also causes a disparate impact. The actions in both these cases are considered discriminatory under law. The organization and the managers involved in the discriminatory decisions would be subject to criminal penalties.

disparate impact
The result of using employment criteria that have a significantly greater negative effect on some groups than on others

Title VII of the 1964 Civil Rights Act requires parties who file discrimination complaints to do so within 180 days of the alleged violation. It provides two basic remedies when discrimination is proved: reinstatement and recovery of lost pay. The Civil Rights Act of 1991 amended the 1964 Civil Rights Act to allow for the recovery of punitive damages if it can be proved that a company engaged in a discriminatory practice with malice or with reckless indifference to the law. Limits placed on these damages are as follows:

- Between 15 and 100 employees: $50,000
- Between 101 and 200 employees: $100,000

- Between 201 and 500 employees: $200,000
- More than 500 employees: $300,000

affirmative action
A plan to give members of specific groups priority in hiring or promotion

Affirmative Action Some laws go beyond prohibiting discrimination. Laws that mandate **affirmative action** require employers to make an extra effort to employ protected groups. Affirmative action laws apply to employers that have, in the past, practiced discrimination or failed to develop a workforce that is representative of the whole population of their community. (Under current laws, affirmative action is not required with regard to disabled Americans.)

The fact that an organization has an affirmative action plan does not necessarily mean that the organization practiced unfair employment practices in the past, however. Managers of many organizations choose to develop affirmative action plans even when the law does not require them to do so. Affirmative action plans must include goals and timetables for achieving greater representation of and equity for protected groups.

sexual harassment
Unwelcome verbal or physical conduct of a sexual nature that implies, directly or indirectly, that sexual compliance is a condition of employment or advancement or that interferes with an employee's work performance

Sexual Harassment Title VII of the 1964 Civil Rights Act and guidelines established by the EEOC prohibit sexual harassment. **Sexual harassment** includes unwelcome sexual advances, requests for sexual favors and other verbal or physical conduct of a sexual nature when any of these three conditions are present:

1 Submission to such conduct is an explicit or implicit term or condition of employment.
2 Submission to or rejection of such conduct is used as a basis for any employment decision.
3 Such conduct has the purpose of unreasonably interfering with the individual's work performance or creating an intimidating, hostile or offensive working environment.

Sexual harassment creates anger, suspicion, fear, stress, mistrust, victims and costs in a workplace. Costs are both psychological and financial. Companies experience losses in employee morale, loyalty, company reputation and, correspondingly, reductions in quality and productivity. According to research by Ellen Bravo and Ellen Cassedy:

- In general, men and women have different views of what constitutes harassment.
- Most harassers are men, but most men are not harassers.
- Intentional harassment is an exercise of power, not romantic attraction.
- Ninety percent of harassment cases involve men harassing women; 9 percent involve same-sex harassment; one percent involve women harassing men.[8]

Preventing sexual harassment is no easy task; efforts to do so begin with top management. They must create a clear policy and communicate to everyone that sexual harassment will not be tolerated. Every employee must be made aware of what sexual harassment is and is not. In most organizations, creating awareness means bringing in outside experts who will conduct training. The National Association of Working Women, 9 to 5, offers these guidelines for creating a meaningful policy:

- Involve all employees.
- Clearly define procedures to protect the complainant and the accused.
- Investigate promptly, using a team of impartial investigators.
- Give several options for reporting, including informal channels.
- Indicate appropriate discipline, including counseling.[9]

Sociocultural Environment

The U.S. labor force is becoming more diverse (see Figure 9.4). On the last Labor Day of the 20th century, Secretary of Labor, Alexis M. Herman, delivered a report titled "Futurework—Trends and Challenges for Work in the 21st Century." This report examined where the United States has been, where the United States is, and where the country is going.

> In 1995, the United States was estimated to be 83 percent white, 13 percent black, one percent American Indian, Eskimo, and Aleut, and four percent Asian and Pacific Islander. Ten percent of Americans, mostly blacks and whites, were also of Hispanic origin. Nearly one in eleven Americans was foreign born.... Trends show that whites will be a declining share of the future total population while the Hispanic share will grow faster than that of non-Hispanic blacks. By 2050, minorities are projected to rise from one in every four Americans to almost one in every two. The Asian and Pacific Islander population is also expected to increase.[10]
>
> Nearly 83 percent of all adults ages 25 and over have completed high school, and 24 percent have obtained a bachelor's degree or more.[11]
>
> Since 1950, the proportion of men in the labor force has declined from 86 percent to 75 percent. In contrast, the trend for women is on the rise. In 1950, one-third of women worked outside the home. Almost 50 years later, 60 percent of women are in the labor force.[12]

Cultural Diversity Differing sociocultural groups both inside and outside organizations make demands on and contribute to those organizations. They constitute any

Figure 9.4   How Workplace Demographics are Evolving

The U.S. workforce of the future will be:

SMALLER

LESS MALE

MORE ETHNICALLY DIVERSE

Elderly population will increase 80% by 2025, working age adults and children by only 15%.

Women composed almost half of the work force in 2015.

By 2025, nearly 40% of workers will be Hispanic, African American, or Asian.

Source: U.S. Department of Commerce

Source: From "Meeting the Challenge of Tomorrow's Workplace," in *CEO Perspectives*, an online supplement to *Chief Executive*, August/September 2002. Reprinted with permission.

organization's stakeholders, help shape its culture and climate and must have adequate representation in all staffing activities.

In the past, most managers tried to create a homogeneous workforce—to treat everyone in the same way and make people fit the dominant corporate culture. These efforts did not always build a stable, committed group of employees. What was needed—and what is rapidly appearing in enlightened corporations—is respect for what workers from different backgrounds bring to the workplace. Across America, managers are participating in workshops designed to facilitate understanding among diverse groups, not just tolerance of one another's existence. See this chapter's Valuing Diversity feature for a workshop example.

Glass Ceilings and Glass Walls The terms *glass ceiling* and *glass wall* refer to invisible barriers of discrimination that block the careers of women and other protected groups.[13] A glass ceiling is discrimination that keeps individuals from protected groups out of upper-level management jobs; a glass wall prevents them from pursuing fast-track career paths. Nearly a quarter of a century after the Glass Ceiling Commission report, Blacks, Hispanics, Asian Americans and women are underrepresented (when compared to their representation in the whole workforce) in senior management positions in the nation's largest companies.

Catalyst, a nonprofit research organization that focuses on women's issues in the workplace, updated the Glass Ceiling Commission recommendations and published *Cracking the Glass Ceiling: Strategies for Success.* Stereotyped as support providers, women end up in staff positions. One reason for the perpetuation of the stereotype is that many men, especially those in the upper ranks of management, feel uncomfortable dealing with women. Additionally, Catalyst research discovered that talent management systems can be vulnerable to pro-male biases, which results in even less

Valuing Diversity and Inclusion

"Avoid This Workplace" Top-10 List

G. Neil, a provider of human resources solutions based in Florida, has developed a "Harassment Prevention Program" to be used for training. Part of the training includes a list of things that wrongheaded people have said.

What harassment allegations might be brought against a manager for saying the following? To check your responses, check the answer key that follows.

1 "This report is retarded."
2 "What are you, senile or something?"
3 "What's wrong with you? Are you on your period or something?"
4 "Men. They're all pigs!"

5 "What are you, crippled or something?"
6 "These numbers don't sound kosher to me."
7 "That's a man's job."
8 "You're in no condition to travel."
9 "Speak English. This is America."
10 "With a name like Jeff Chang, I'm sure he's good with computers."

Answer Key: (1) disability; (2) age; (3) gender; (4) gender; (5) disability; (6) religion; (7) gender; (8) disability (pregnancy); (9) national origin; (10) national origin

Source: G. Neil, *http://www.gneil.com.* Used with permission.

diverse employee pools. Below is the list, "Catalyst's Top Ten Tactics to Cracking the Glass Ceiling."[14]

- Measure women's advancement.
- Move women into line positions.
- Find mentors for women.
- Create women's networks.
- Make culture change happen.
- Promote women.
- Get women into nontraditional work.
- Promote women in professional firms.
- Support customized career planning.
- Make flexibility work.

According to "Holding Women Back," a special report from talent management consultancy DDI's Global Leadership Forecast 2014/2015,[15] barriers still exist in the career opportunities offered to women. The study measured the impact of leadership development initiatives around the world. The research revealed that female leaders are under-represented in higher levels of leadership. Many companies recognize that glass ceilings and glass walls exist and have worked hard to eliminate them. The number of women and minorities in top management jobs is gradually increasing. Each year there are more leading large companies than there were the previous year.

AIDS and Drug Testing Acquired immune deficiency syndrome (AIDS) is a frightening condition that—until medical progress can prevent it—eventually leads to death. HIV, the virus that causes AIDS, cannot be casually transmitted, but fear of AIDS is a reality in the workplace.

Federal law prohibits discrimination against employees suffering from AIDS and any other contagious diseases.[16] Will a company accommodate the employee who does not want to work with an employee who has HIV? What will management do when an employee's routine physical reveals that he or she is HIV positive? Companies need policies telling employees and managers how to deal with the issue.

Most of America's largest companies have had experience with employees who are suffering from some sort of drug addiction. Employees with drug or alcohol dependencies can and do cause losses to their companies, themselves and others. A Substance Abuse and Mental Health Services Administration (SAMHSA) study revealed that workers reporting current drug use were more likely to have worked for three or more employers, to have voluntarily left an employer in the past year, and skipped one or more days of work in the past month.[17] Workers with drug problems compromise safety, quality and productivity.

Many companies require drug testing for all applicants, and some require random testing of current employees involved in work that is potentially hazardous to themselves or others. Figure 9.5 shows why the lingering effects of drugs are of such concern to many companies. (Where a workforce is unionized, it is wise to involve the union in any drug-testing efforts before they are instituted.) Workplace safety is the most common reason given by employers for drug testing. In those occupations identified with the highest rates of drug information and policies in the workplace, employees reported significantly lower rates of current drug use and heavy drinking.[18]

Figure 9.5	Duration of Detectability of Drugs in Urine

Drug	Retention Time During Which Detectable
Amphetamines and methamphetamines	48 hrs.
Barbiturates	short-acting (e.g., secobarbital), 24 hrs. long-acting (e.g., phenobarbital), 7 or more days
Benzodiazepines	3 days if therapeutic dose ingested
Cocaine metabolites	2–3 days
Opiates	2 days
Propoxyphene (Darvon)	6–48 hrs.
Cannabinolds	single use, 3 days moderate smoker (4 times/week), 5 days heavy smoker (daily), 10 days chronic smoker, 21–27 days
Methaqualone	7 or more days
Phencyclidine (LPCP)	approximately 8 days

Note: Retention times may vary depending on variables including drug metabolism and half-life, patient's physical condition, fluid intake, and method and frequency of ingestion.

Source: From "Scientific Issues in Drug Testing," *Journal of the American Medical Association*, 1987, v. 257 (22), p. 3112. Reprinted with permission from the American Medical Association.

According to the Americans with Disabilities Act, drug-addicted employees are protected from discrimination if they are currently enrolled in legitimate drug-intervention programs or have completed such programs and are drug free. Testing for drugs raises issues about employee privacy, because most drug tests involve blood and urine analysis. These tests can reveal conditions that an employer has no business knowing about. In addition, drug tests can produce false positive results.

Genetic Screening Medical tests of a person's genetic makeup can identify his or her predisposition to diseases like heart disease and certain types of cancer. Such tests were used in the past to deny employment, insurance and advancement.[19] The Genetic Information Nondiscrimination Act of 2008 (GINA) is a Federal law that prohibits discrimination in health coverage and employment based on genetic information. Employers with 15 or more employees cannot request genetic testing or consider someone's genetic background in hiring, firing or promotions. They cannot ask employees for their family medical histories.

Union Environment

According to the U.S. Bureau of Labor Statistics in 2015 more than 14 million or almost 11.3 percent of wage and salary workers were union members. This is down from a high of 20.1 percent in 1983, the first year for which comparable union data are available.[20] Most union members belong to unions affiliated with the American Federation of Labor and Congress of Industrial Organizations (AFL–CIO).

Companies that employ unionized workers must bargain collectively to create a contract, to enforce that contract and to process complaints (called grievances) about how the contract is enforced. Unions typically bargain for their members' wages, hours and working conditions. Whether the issue is employment, work methods, equipment, safety or productivity improvement, a union can impede or support changes that managers want to make.

Collective Bargaining In **collective bargaining**, negotiators from management and a union sit down together and try to agree on the terms of a contract that will apply to the union's members for a fixed period of time. Both parties prepare for these negotiations by analyzing past problems and agreements, polling their constituents, building a list of demands and creating strategies. Both want what they perceive to be the best deal for themselves, given their respective needs and priorities. Negotiations usually begin before an existing contract expires, and negotiators try to reach a new agreement while the contract is still in effect.

collective bargaining
Negotiation between a union and an employer in regard to wages, benefits, hours, rules and working conditions

Grievance Processing A labor agreement (contract) provides a process by which managers and workers can file *grievances,* complaints alleging that a contract violation has taken place. The process of filing a grievance usually begins at the lowest level. If no settlement can be reached at that level, the complaint is brought before those at successively higher levels. A grievance can progress to the point that it becomes a focus for top managers and union officials. When these parties cannot agree, a third party may be called in. Third parties are usually neutral professionals hired to recommend or enforce a settlement. A third party might be a mediator or an arbitrator. Mediators make recommendations. Arbitrators suggest settlements that are enforced. Arbitrators have the power to hold hearings, gather evidence and render a decision to which both parties agree in advance to adhere.

HUMAN RESOURCE PLANNING

Identify the four activities related to human resource planning

In planning to meet staffing needs, managers must know their organization's plans and what human resources are available. They study existing jobs by performing job analyses. They review their firm's past staffing needs, inventory current human resources, forecast personnel needs in light of strategic plans and compare their human resource inventory to the forecast. Then, with line managers, they construct plans to expand the company's employee roster, maintain the status quo, or reduce the number of jobs. Figure 9.6 illustrates this process.

Job Analysis

Before managers can determine personnel needs, they must perform a **job analysis** for each job. The first step in a job analysis is to prepare up-to-date descriptions that list the duties and skills required of each jobholder. Then managers must compare all the analyses to ensure that some jobholders are not duplicating the efforts of others. This comparison enhances effectiveness and efficiency in the organization.

job analysis
A study that determines the duties associated with a job and the human qualities needed to perform it

To prepare an in-depth study of jobs, some companies employ job analysts. To do their work, job analysts: (1) observe the jobholder executing his or her duties; (2) review questionnaires completed by the jobholder and supervisor; (3) conduct interviews with both; or (4) form a committee to analyze, review and summarize the results. Job analysts may study more than one jobholder in a job category over several months.

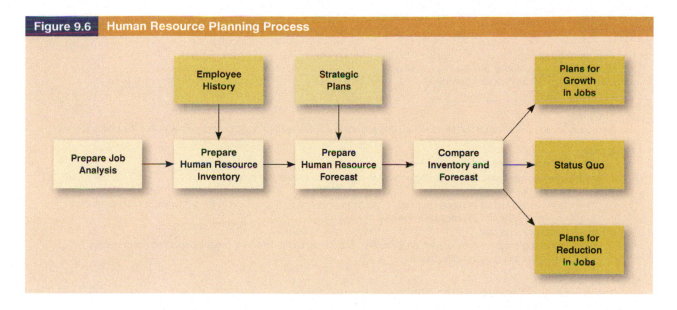

Figure 9.6 Human Resource Planning Process

The job analysis produces two coordinated documents: a job description and a job specification. Figure 9.7 presents an example of a job description. A job description cites the job title and the purpose of the job. It lists major work activities, the levels of authority above and below the jobholder, the equipment and materials the jobholder must use, and any physical demands or hazardous conditions the job may involve.

Figure 9.8 presents an example of a job specification. A job specification lists the human dimensions that a position requires. These include education, experience, skills, training and knowledge. To avoid even the appearance of discrimination, those who create job specifications must take care to list only those factors directly linked to successful work performance.

Managers should review job descriptions and specifications regularly (usually each year) to ensure that they continue to reflect the positions to which they refer. Jobs evolve with time as changes in duties, knowledge bases and equipment take place; the documents should reflect that evolution. When new positions are added to the organization, job descriptions and specifications must be created.

Human Resource Inventory

The human resource inventory provides information about an organization's current personnel. The inventory is a catalog of the skills, abilities, interests, training, experience and qualifications of each member of its current workforce. A human resource inventory tells managers the qualifications, length of service, responsibilities, experiences and promotion potential of each person in the firm. This information is updated periodically and supplemented by the most recent appraisals given to jobholders. What emerges is something similar to Figure 9.9, a plan for staffing changes in management ranks. Developing such a chart makes managers aware of strengths and weaknesses in the current personnel base and allows them to develop a managerial succession plan.

Human Resource Forecasting

When forecasting an organization's personnel requirements, managers need to consider the strategic plans of the company and its normal level of attrition. Strategic

Figure 9.7	**Example of a Job Description**

I. Job Identification
Position Title: Customer Service Representative
Department: Policyholders' Service
Effective Date:

II. Function
To resolve policyholders' questions and make corresponding adjustments to poli-cies if necessary after the policy is issued

III. Scope
(a) Internal (within department)
   Interacts with other members of the department in researching answers to problems
(b) External (within company)
   Interacts with Policy Issue in regard to policy cancellations, Premium Accounting in regard to accounting procedures, and Accounting in regard to processing checks
(c) External (outside company)
   Interacts with policyholders, to answer policy-related questions; client-company payroll departments, to resolve billing questions; and carriers, to modify policies

IV. Responsibilities
The jobholder will be responsible for
(a) Resolving policyholder inquiries about policies and coverage
(b) Initiating changes in policies with carriers (at the request of the insured)
(c) Adjusting in-house records as a result of approved changes
(d) Corresponding with policyholders regarding changes requested
(e) Reporting to the department manager any problems he or she is unable to re-solve

V. Authority Relationships
(a) Reporting relationships: Reports to the manager of Policyholders' Service
(b) Supervisory relationship: None

VI. Equipment, Materials, and Machines
Personal computer, calculator and video display terminal

VII. Physical Conditions or Hazards
95 percent of the duties are performed sitting at either a desk or video display ter-minal

VII. Other
Other duties as assigned

plans determine the company's direction and its need for people. A long-term plan to stabilize the company at its current employment level will mean the need to replace those who leave.

Consider how a fictional furniture-making company translates strategic plans into actual personnel requirements. Suppose managers decide to increase production by 30 percent to meet a forecast increase in long-term demand. They analyze current capabilities, reject the use of overtime, and decide to add a third shift within three months. Using up-to-date job descriptions and specifications for the jobs to be added, managers determine how many and what kinds of employees to hire: nine production workers. Then the managers look at anticipated turnover in the existing shifts and support personnel. They decide to hire two new employees over the next three months to replace retiring employees. Therefore, the managers must acquire eleven new hires over the next three months.

Figure 9.8	**Example of a Job Specification**

I.   Job Identification
Position: File/Mail Clerk
Department: Policyholders' Service
Effective Date:

II.   Education
Minimum: High school or equivalent

III.   Experience
Minimum: Six months of experience developing, monitoring, and maintaining a file system

IV.   Skills
Keyboarding skills: Must be able to set up own work and operate a computer. No minimum WPM.

V.   Special Requirements
(a) Must be flexible to the demands of the organization for overtime and change in work load
(b) Must be able to comply with previously established procedures
(c) Must be tolerant of work requiring detailed accuracy (the work of monitoring file signouts and filing files, for example)
(d) Must be able to apply systems knowledge (to anticipate the new procedures that a system change will require, for example)

VI.   Behavioral Characteristics
(a) Must have high level of initiative as demonstrated by the ability to recognize a problem, resolve it and report it to the supervisor
(b) Must have interpersonal skills as demonstrated by the ability to work as a team member and cooperate with other departments

Inventory and Forecast Comparison

By comparing the inventory and the forecast, managers determine who in the organization is qualified to fill the projected openings and which personnel needs must be met externally. At the furniture company, managers decide that most of the needed personnel must come from outside, because many of the positions are entry-level jobs and members of the existing workforce will be needed to replace retiring workers.

If the managers decide to try to fill some of the vacancies from within, the first question is whether current employees qualify. If so, the managers must advertise the jobs within the company and encourage employees to apply for them. If current employees do not qualify, the next question is whether, through training and development, they can achieve the qualifications. If so, and if the company can afford the money and time, managers should prepare a plan to provide the needed training and development.

RECRUITMENT, SELECTION, AND ORIENTATION

Recruitment

recruiting
Efforts to find qualified people and encourage them to apply for positions that need to be filled

With the forecast and inventory complete and job descriptions and specifications in hand, managers begin **recruiting**—the process of locating and soliciting a sufficient number of qualified candidates. Sources of applicants should include employed and unemployed prospects and temporary-help services. Managers may also want to investigate the option of leasing employees. This option involves working with a company that hires workers to lease to a client firm. The lease company hires, fires, complies with

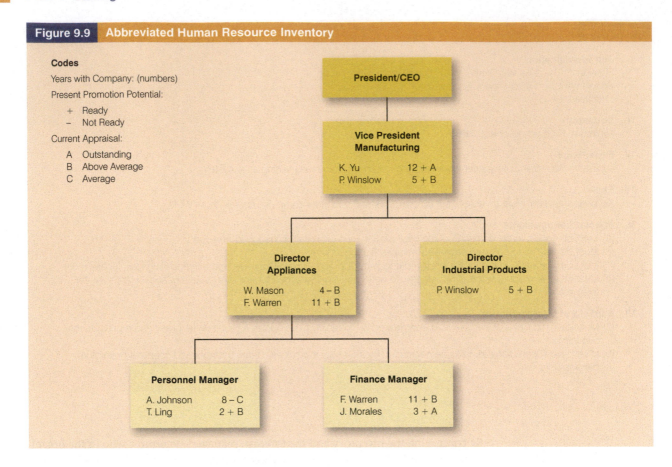

Figure 9.9   Abbreviated Human Resource Inventory

Codes

Years with Company: (numbers)

Present Promotion Potential:

+   Ready
−   Not Ready

Current Appraisal:

A   Outstanding
B   Above Average
C   Average

President/CEO

Vice President Manufacturing

K. Yu   12 + A
P. Winslow   5 + B

Director Appliances

W. Mason   4 − B
F. Warren   11 + B

Director Industrial Products

P. Winslow   5 + B

Personnel Manager

A. Johnson   8 − C
T. Ling   2 + B

Finance Manager

F. Warren   11 + B
J. Morales   3 + A

all government regulations, pays the leased employees and is responsible for all human relations functions.

Company policies define strategies for and limits on filling vacancies. Among the concerns many companies have are the issues of nepotism—employing spouses or other relatives of existing employees—and of employing friends of employees. See this chapter's Ethical Management feature for some recent research in this area.

Strategies for Recruiting

At our fictitious furniture-making company, managers decide to look outside for the needed applicants. This decision presents several options. They can call private or state-operated employment services. They can run ads on the Internet, in newspapers and in other publications, including trade journals and papers that appeal to racial and ethnic minorities. They can ask current employees to recommend qualified friends and relatives. (Many companies offer bonuses to employees who refer people who are eventually hired.) They can contact schools and offer a training program, and they can participate in job fairs. The managers can ask neighborhood and community groups to help them reach minorities and other protected groups and encourage them to apply for the jobs. If the company employs union labor, managers can contact trade unions in their search for skilled workers.

Many companies like to recruit for entry-level positions through internship programs. These offer a person, usually a student, a chance to gain some full-or part-

Coping with Workplace Romances

Many organizations have policies that prevent the hiring of an existing employee's spouse. Others forbid two employees, once they marry, from continuing to work at the organization; one of them must quit or be fired. But Microsoft, like a growing number of companies, sees advantages to employing married couples. The company's Seattle headquarters has several married couples who met and courted during their long workdays. People who work together have, almost by definition, similar backgrounds, talents and aspirations. Microsoft ought to know. Its billionaire CEO, Bill Gates, married one of his executives.

The most likely outcome of workplace romances is marriage of the people involved in the office romance. But, workplace romances can lead to organizational conflict. Outcomes with less favorable results include complaints of favoritism by workers outside of the relationship, claims of sexual harassment and decreased productivity of those involved in the office romance.

The annual office romance survey by CareerBuilder.com, a jobs and career website, found that nearly 40 percent of respondents said they had been in an office romance. Nearly one third married someone that they started dating at work. Most managers think that it is unacceptable to date a superior or subordinate. Yet, one quarter said they had dated someone with a higher position in their organization.

CareerBuilder offers the following tips for workers who may want to spark a workplace romance:

- **Check the Company Handbook**—Some companies have strict policies around office romances. Acquaint yourself with the rules before turning a professional relationship into a personal one.

- **Proceed with Caution**—Some romances lead into marriage, but others can lead into disaster. Seven percent of workers who have dated a co-worker reported having to leave their jobs because their office romance soured. Take the time to get to know someone first and carefully weigh risks and benefits.

- **Compartmentalize**—Keep your work life separate from your home life. Avoid showing public displays of affection in the office and don't involve co-workers in personal disagreements.

- **Think Before You Post**—Be careful what you post on social media. You can end up outing your relationship before you're ready to discuss it.

➡ What experiences that relate to this ethical issue can you share with your classmates?

➡ If you were a manager, what would you do if you found out about an office romance?

Source: CareerBuilder, "Thirty eight Percent of Workers Have Dated a Co-Worker, Finds Annual CareerBuilder Valentine's Day Survey," February 12, 2014 <http://www.careerbuilder.com/share/aboutus/pressreleasesdetail.aspx?sd=2%2F13%2F2014&id=pr803&ed=12%2F31%2F2014>.

---

time experience in his or her specialty area while assisting an employer. Networking with associates in various professional groups and trade associations often leads to referrals of likely prospects. See this chapter's Managing Social Media feature for recruiting with LinkedIn. Another option involves the use of public and private employment agencies. Industry-specific search firms may help companies locate the best employees in the field, despite the price.[21] Fees for hiring through private search firms can run as high as a new hire's first year's salary.

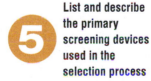

5 List and describe the primary screening devices used in the selection process

selection
Evaluating applicants and finding those best qualified to perform a job and most likely to fit into the culture of the organization

Selection Process

Selection is the process of deciding which candidate out of the pool of applicants possesses the qualifications for the job to be filled. Selection begins where recruiting ends. Its goal is to eliminate unqualified candidates through use of the screening devices shown in Figure 9.10.

Application Form Usually, a prospective employee must fill out an application form as part of the selection process. An application form summarizes the candidate's education, skills and experiences relating to the job for which he or she is applying. To avoid discrimination in the selection process, employers must not ask for information that is

Recruiting with LinkedIn

The Internet is one of the methods employers use to find employees. One of the methods used by employers on the Internet is LinkedIn, a social network for business professionals. Members have a profile page detailing their work history, career aspirations and references. LinkedIn allows members to look at the profiles of anyone they know, and in turn anyone those people know, growing their network exponentially. A few direct contacts can translate to hundreds of business users.

LinkedIn members can adjust their settings to indicate that they are interested in career opportunities and that they will accept messages from other members. Recruiters use keywords to search for people in their desired field and send them job queries. "Keywords" are nouns that meet a set of job criteria. In addition to nouns, skill and experience verbs may be used. Specific keywords are found in job descriptions and classified ads for those positions.

Job seekers maximize keyword exposure by using variations of the same word within their profiles. For example, both "managing" and "manager" can be used at different places on the profile. Also, if an acronym such as "AMA" is mentioned in a profile, "American Management Association" might be used at another place in the profile.

Once a potential candidate is found, the recruiter can delve deeper by reading the candidate's profile. How complete is the profile? How well does it communicate the candidate's qualifications? The recruiter may review the candidate's references, contact list, group membership and involvement in groups. Who are the references? Who is in the network? What does the candidate contribute? Does the candidate ask questions? Does the candidate answer questions? This review gives the recruiter additional information for qualifying the job candidate.

Find LinkedIn at *http://www.linkedin.com*.

unrelated to the candidate's ability to perform the job successfully. Questions regarding home ownership, marital status, age, ethnic or racial background and place of birth are usually irrelevant. When used properly, the completed application yields needed information. In addition, it indicates a person's ability to follow simple instructions and use basic language skills.

Preliminary Interview In small firms, a job candidate's first interview at a firm may be conducted by the very manager for whom the person hired will work. In large companies, someone from the human resource staff may be the designated screening interviewer. In very large or sophisticated firms, a human relations specialist may conduct the preliminary interview. If a team has authority to hire, several team members may question each applicant. This procedure is usually the case if the team is self-managing.

A preliminary interview may be structured—scripted with specific questions—or unstructured. An unstructured format allows an applicant relative freedom to express thoughts and feelings. An interviewer uses the preliminary meeting to verify details from the application form and to obtain information needed to continue the selection process. Interviewers must avoid topics that are not related to the applicant's abilities to perform successfully on the job. Ability necessary to perform a job is called a bona fide occupational qualification. For example, if a job involves work in a men's locker room, a question about the gender of the applicant is probably not discriminatory because it asks about a bona fide occupational qualification.

Employers and job candidates must be particularly sensitive to the potential for discrimination in interviews. Both parties must avoid sensitive issues; Figure 9.11 presents some interviewing guidelines prepared by one state employment agency.

Testing According to Equal Employment Opportunity Commission guidelines, a **test** is any criterion or performance measure used as a basis for any employment decision. Such measures include interviews, application forms, psychological and performance

test
Any criterion or performance measure used as a basis for an employment decision

Figure 9.10 Screening Devices of the Selection Process

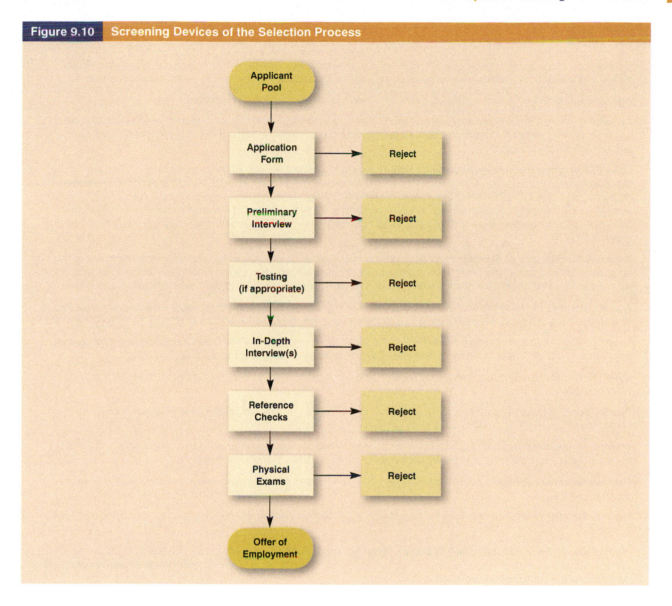

exams, physical requirements for a job, and any other device that is scored and used as a basis for selecting an applicant.[22] All tests used for screening should attempt to measure only performance capabilities that have been or can be proven to be essential to successful performance of the job.[23]

Regardless of the tests used, employers must avoid producing a disparate impact—that is, creating a test that one demographic group is more likely to perform better on than another. Employers must also ensure that each test has validity. A test with validity is a predictor of future performance on a specific job. A person receiving a high score on a valid test will be able to perform the related job successfully. Those who perform poorly on the test would perform poorly on the job. If test performance does not correlate to job performance, the test is probably invalid.

| **Figure 9.11**   **Employment Application Forms and Interviews: Potentially Discriminatory Inquiries** |

The best general guideline to follow on employment application forms and in interviews is to ensure that information elicited relates to qualifications for effective performance on the job. The topics listed in bold in this figure are especially sensitive.

Age? Date of birth? In general, asking whether a candidate is under 18 or over 70 is permissible.

Arrests? Since an arrest is no indication of guilt and because, proportionally, minorities are arrested more than those in other segments of the population, questions about arrests are probably discriminatory. Such an inquiry is prohibited by the Illinois Department of Human Rights.

Convictions (other than traffic violations)? Military record? Questions about convictions are generally inadvisable, though they may be appropriate for screening candidates who have been convicted of certain offenses and are under consideration for certain kinds of jobs. Questions about less-than-honorable military discharges are likewise inappropriate unless the job involves security issues. In general, a candidate can be asked what branch of service he or she served in and what kind of work the candidate did. If information about convictions or military discharge is necessary, exercise care in how it is used; avoid possible discrimination.

Available for Saturday or Sunday work? Although knowing when employees are available to work is important, a question about availability on certain days may discourage applicants from certain religious groups. If business requirements necessitate such a question, indicate that the employer will make an effort to accommodate the religious needs of employees.

Age and number of children? Arrangements for child care? Although the intent of these questions may be to explore a source of absenteeism or tardiness, the effect can be to discriminate against women. Do not ask questions about children or their care.

Credit record? Own a car? Own a home? Unless the person hired must use personal credit, a personal car, or do business from a home he or she owns, avoid these questions. They could discriminate against minorities and women.

Eyes? Hair color? Eye and hair color are not related to job performance and may serve to indicate an applicant's race or national origin.

Fidelity bond? Since a bond may have been denied for an arbitrary or discriminatory reason, use other screening considerations.

Friends or relatives? This question implies a preference for friends or relatives of employees and is potentially discriminatory because such people are likely to reflect the demography of the company's present workforce.

Garnishment record? Federal courts have held that wage garnishments do not normally affect a worker's ability to perform effectively on the job.

Height? Weight? Unless height or weight relates directly to job performance, do not ask about it on an application form or in an interview.

Maiden name? Prior married name? Widowed, divorced, separated? These questions are not related to job performance and may be an indication of religion or national origin. These inquiries may be appropriate, however, if the information gained is needed for a pre-employment investigation or security check.

Marital status? A federal court has held that refusal to employ a married woman when married men occupy similar jobs is unlawful sex discrimination. Do not ask about an applicant's marital status.

Sex? State and federal laws prohibit discrimination on the basis of sex except where sex is a bona fide occupational qualification necessary to the normal operation of business.

NOTE: If certain information is needed for postemployment purposes, such as in the administration of affirmative action plans, the employer can obtain it after the appli-cant has been hired. Keep this data separate from data used in career advancement decisions.

Source: Illinois Department of Employment Security.

Assessment centers specialize in screening candidates for managerial positions. Tests administered at assessment centers attempt to analyze a person's ability to communicate, decide, plan, organize, lead, and solve problems. The testing techniques used include interviews, in-basket exercises (tests that present a person with limited time

assessment center
A place where candidates are screened for managerial positions, which usually involves extensive testing and hands-on exercises

to decide how to handle a variety of problems), group exercises intended to uncover leadership potential and the ability to work with others, and a variety of hands-on tasks. The assessments usually last several days and take place away from the usual job site. Many large companies use assessment centers to determine who will make it into a company or up its corporate ladder. The results from assessment centers are usually more accurately predictive than paper-and-pencil exercises that assess managerial ability. Figure 9.12 presents the advantages and disadvantages of different types of assessment instruments.

In-Depth Interview An in-depth interview is almost always conducted by the person or persons for or with whom the applicant will work if hired. The goal of an in-depth interview is to determine how well the applicant will fit into the organization's culture and the subsystem in which he or she would work. Eaton Corporation, for example, screens its applicants to be certain they will be willing to share authority. In-depth interviews may or may not be structured. They can be used to relay information

Figure 9.12	Main Advantages and Disadvantages of Different Types of Assessment Instruments

Type of Assessment Instrument	Advantages	Disadvantages
Ability tests	• Mental ability tests are among the most useful predictors of performance across a wide variety of jobs • Are usually easy and inexpensive to administer	• Use of ability tests can result in high levels of adverse impact • Physical ability tests can be costly to develop and administer
Achievement/proficiency tests	• In general, job knowledge and work-sample tests have relatively high validity • Job knowledge tests are generally easy and inexpensive to administer • Work-sample tests usually result in less adverse impact than ability tests and written knowledge tests	• Written job knowledge tests can result in adverse impact • Work-sample tests can be expensive to develop and administer
Biodata inventories	• Easy and inexpensive to administer • Some validity evidence exists • May help to reduce adverse impact when used in conjunction with other tests and procedures	• Privacy concerns may be an issue with some questions • Faking is a concern (information should be verified when possible)
Employment interviews	• Structured interviews, based on job analyses, tend to be valid • May reduce adverse impact if used in conjunction with other tests	• Unstructured interviews typically have poor validity • Skill of the interviewer is critical to the quality of interview (interviewer training can help)
Personality inventories	• Usually do not result in adverse impact • Predictive validity evidence exists for some personality inventories in specific situations • May help to reduce adverse impact when used in conjunction with other tests and procedures • Easy and inexpensive to administer	• Need to distinguish between clinical and employment-oriented personality inventories in terms of their purpose and use • Possibility of faking or providing socially desirable answers • Concern about invasion of privacy (use only as part of a broader assessment battery)

continues

| Figure 9.12 | Main Advantages and Disadvantages of Different Types of Assessment Instruments (*cont.*) | |

Type of Assessment Instrument	Advantages	Disadvantages
Honesty/integrity measures	• Usually do not result in adverse impact • Have been shown to be valid in some cases • Easy and inexpensive to administer	• Strong concerns about invasion of privacy (use only as part of a broader assessment battery) • Possibility of faking or providing socially desirable answers • Test users may require special qualifications for administration and interpretation of test score • Should not be used with current employees • Some states restrict use of honesty and integrity tests
Education and experience requirements	• Can be useful for certain technical, professional, and higher level jobs to guard against gross mismatch or incompetence	• In some cases, it is difficult to demonstrate job relatedness and business necessity of education and experience requirements
Recommendations and reference checks	• Can be used to verify information previously provided by applicants • Can serve as protection against potential negligent hiring lawsuits • May encourage applicants to provide more accurate information	• Reports are almost always positive; they do not typically help differentiate between good workers and poor workers
Assessment centers	• Good predictors of job and training performance, managerial potential and leadership ability • Apply the *whole-person approach* to personnel assessment	• Can be expensive to develop and administer • Specialized training required for assessors; their skill is essential to the quality of assessment centers
Medical examinations	• Can help ensure a safe work environment when use is *consistent* with relevant federal, state and local laws	• Cannot be administered prior to making a job offer. Restrictions apply to administering to applicants post offer or to current employees • There is a risk of violating applicable regulations (a *written policy*, consistent with all relevant laws, should be established to govern the entire medical testing program)
Drug and alcohol tests	• Can help ensure a safe and favorable work environment when program is consistent with relevant federal, state, and local laws	• An alcohol test is considered a medical exam and applicable law restricting medical examination in employment must be followed • There is a risk of violating applicable regulations (a *written policy*, consistent with all relevant laws, should be established to govern the entire drug or alcohol testing program)

Source: U.S. Department of Labor Employment and Training Administration, "Testing and Assessment: An Employer's Guide to Good Practices," (2000) pp. 4–11, 12 <*https://www.onetcenter.org/dl_files/empTestAsse.pdf*>.

specifically related to the job and its environment, as well as to talk about benefits, hours, and working conditions. Applicants who have passed through the initial screenings and progress to in-depth interviews need the endorsement of the person for whom they will work. Without this person's commitment to the success of the new hire, the applicant's future at that firm is in doubt. As is the case with application forms and preliminary interviews, interviewers must take care to avoid topics that could lead to accusations of employment discrimination.

Reference Checks Since September 11 (9/11/01), employers are conducting more rigorous reference checks. "In some cases, employers may look at credit reports, civil court records, driving records, workers' compensation claims and criminal records going back 10 or more years. Some are conducting background checks on current employees as well as new hires."[24]

Checking an applicant's past can present problems. First, employers must avoid background checks that could be discriminatory. Checks of credit history and arrest records, for example, are discriminatory. Second, checking references can be difficult because most former employers refuse to cooperate. They may avoid saying anything negative for fear of a defamation-of-character lawsuit by the ex-employee. Background checks must comply with the Fair Credit Reporting Act. "The employer must obtain consent for a check, and if a company wants to check a current employee, they must get permission from the employee at the time they intend to do the investigation. The employer must provide the employee with the results of the check."[25]

David Blumenthal, who owns Flash Creative Management, a small company focused on information technology, provides an interesting twist to reference checking. He requires applicants to "call his references (most of whom are customers) in order to really understand what kind of company they are trying to enter." Why? Blumenthal believes that by doing so, job candidates will truly "understand his commitment to customer service and what he expects of employees.... Blumenthal asks his customers for their opinions of prospective hires.... Would the customer feel comfortable working with that applicant?"[26]

Physical Exam Employers use physical exams and medical histories to prevent insurance claims for illnesses and injuries that occurred prior to employment. Physical exams also detect communicable diseases and certify that an applicant is physically capable of performing his or her job. If the job description cites physical demands, they must be valid. According to the Americans with Disabilities Act, employers must make reasonable accommodations for the physically impaired and not use physical barriers as an excuse for not hiring.

Offer of Employment At this point in the selection process, the manager or team offers the job to the top-rated applicant. This step may involve a series of negotiations about salary or wages, work schedule, vacation time, types of benefits desired and other special considerations. With the diversity of today's workforce, an employer might have to accommodate an employee's disability, make time for him or her to get children off to school or be at home when they return, or to arrange for day care. Federal law requires that within 24 hours from the time of hiring, the new employee must furnish proof of U.S. citizenship or the proper authorization needed to work in the United States as a legal alien.

Orientation

The previous steps in the selection process have done much to familiarize the newcomer with the company and the job. What the new hire needs now is a warm welcome so he or she can begin contributing as soon as possible. The newcomer needs to be introduced to his or her workstation, team and coworkers. Managers and coworkers should answer the new employee's questions promptly and openly. Someone should explain work rules, company policies, benefits and procedures, and fill out the paperwork necessary to get the new person on the payroll. All employee assistance programs should be explained, and the new hire should be told how to take advantage of them.

All of this can be done in stages and by several different people. Human resource specialists may handle the paperwork; team members or a supervisor may take charge of introductions to the work area and coworkers. All equipment, tools and supplies that the newcomer needs should be in place when he or she reports for work.

A new employee's first impressions and early experiences should be realistic and as positive as possible. **Orientation** is the beginning of a continuing socialization process that builds and cements employees' relationships, attitudes and commitment to the company. Orientation should be thoroughly planned and skillfully executed.

orientation
Introducing new employees to the organization by explaining their duties, helping them meet their coworkers, and acclimating them to their work environment

TRAINING AND DEVELOPMENT

Training teaches skills for use in the present and near future. Development focuses on the future. Both involve teaching the particular attitudes, knowledge and skills a person needs. Both are designed to give people something new, and both have three prerequisites for success: (1) Those who design training or development programs must create needs assessments to determine what the content and objectives of the programs should be; (2) the people who execute the programs must know how to teach, how people learn and what individuals need to be taught; and (3) all participants—trainers, developers and those receiving the training or development—must be willing participants.

In most U.S. businesses, training and development are continual processes. According to the American Society for Training and Development (ASTD) research report, *2014 ASTD State of the Industry Report,* total training expenditures on a per-employee basis average $1200.[27]

6 Explain the differences and similarities between training and development

training
Giving employees the knowledge, skills, and attitudes needed to perform their jobs

Purposes of Training

Training has five major aims: to increase knowledge and skills, to increase motivation to succeed, to improve chances for advancement, to improve morale and the sense of competence and pride in performance, and to increase quality and productivity. To understand just how important training is and will be, consider the following quote from former U.S. Secretary of Labor, Elaine L. Chao, in her report on the American workforce.

> *Our economy is making an unprecedented transition into high-skilled, information-based industries. This has created a disconnect between the jobs that are being created and the current skills of many workers.*[28]

Today's corporate emphasis on downsizing and flattening hierarchies only leads to greater efficiency and customer satisfaction when it is accompanied by redesigning organizational processes. If it is otherwise, all that will happen is that the same amount of work must be done by fewer people, who will quickly become stressed out and overburdened.

Reengineering the right way inevitably means "better technology, better processes, and fewer, better workers. The ideal: technology that actually helps workers make decisions, in organizations that encourage them to do so.[29] Moving to open-book management and empowering workers, however, means preparing people for these changes through training. Also, since technology keeps changing, both workers and managers need to continually train to become and remain technically competent.

Technically competent, multi-skilled workers are the nucleus of both temporary and permanent, empowered cross-functional teams that are so pervasive today. Before people can function effectively in team environments, however, team members, team leaders, and team facilitators need various types of training to gain the skills, knowledge, and attitudes necessary for teaming.

Challenges of Training

Findings from the U.S. Department of Labor indicate that more than 20 percent of America's workforce has serious problems with basic literacy skills (see Figure 9.13). For this reason, many firms need to conduct remedial training so that workers can cope with job demands and prepare themselves for positions of greater responsibility.

One answer to language and illiteracy problems is job redesign. The redesigned jobs avoid, as much as possible, the need to rely on English and math. "Some warehouses use computers with speech capability to tell forklift operators who cannot read where they should go in the warehouse. Some construction firms rely on portable computers with touch-activated display screens that allow workers to record their reports by touching appropriate pictures on the screens."[30]

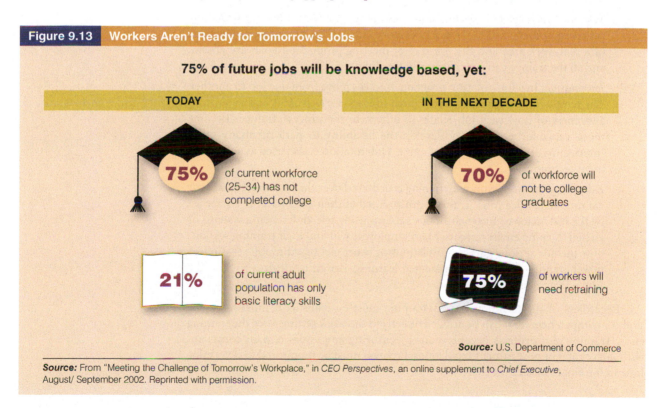

Figure 9.13   **Workers Aren't Ready for Tomorrow's Jobs**

75% of future jobs will be knowledge based, yet:

TODAY	IN THE NEXT DECADE
75% of current workforce (25–34) has not completed college	**70%** of workforce will not be college graduates
21% of current adult population has only basic literacy skills	**75%** of workers will need retraining

Source: U.S. Department of Commerce

Source: From "Meeting the Challenge of Tomorrow's Workplace," in *CEO Perspectives*, an online supplement to *Chief Executive*, August/September 2002. Reprinted with permission.

Another challenge is America's increasingly diverse workforce. In the culturally diverse workforce of today, employees often need to improve their ability to handle English, to gain an appreciation of the organization's diverse cultures, and to learn how to cope with the many changes that occur on the job, such as new technologies, methods and duties.

Immigrants, many highly educated in their home countries, bring motivation and skills to the workplace. They also bring cultural values and norms that may make it difficult for them to find well-paying jobs. Aside from their language difficulties, their views about the value of time, the relative importance of work and family and how people should interact at work, may not mesh with those of the dominant culture or the current mix of cultures.

Techniques of Training

A company may train employees in various places. For example, a trainee may be sent to a job site, a corporate training center, a college classroom or various workshops, seminars and professional gatherings. When the employer does training in-house, it commonly takes the following forms:

- *On-the-job training (OJT).* In this approach, an employee learns while performing the job. Training proceeds through coaching or by the trainee observing proficient performers and then doing the work. Apprenticeships and internships are on-the-job training programs.

- *Machine-based training.* In this technique, trainees interact with a computer, simulator, or other type of machine. The environment is usually controlled and the interaction is one-on-one. The trainees proceed at their own pace or at a pace set by the training equipment.

- *Vestibule training.* This system simulates the work environment by providing actual equipment and tools in a laboratory setting. The noise and distractions of a real work area and the pressure of meeting production goals are absent, and so the trainee can concentrate on learning.

- *Job rotation.* In a job-rotation program, trainees move from one job to another. The temporary assignments allow them to learn various skills and acquire an awareness of how each job relates to others. In the process, trainees become more valuable because they develop the flexibility to perform many tasks. Internships utilize this form of training. (Job rotation is also used as a development technique.)

- *E-learning.* In this technique, training is delivered over the Internet, Intranet or via mobile applications. Trainees can proceed at their own pace, at a pace set by the instructor or in synchronous sessions using teleconferencing systems or virtual learning environments. Many employees will find their training sessions now include serious games, simulations or short fact based mobile sessions A newer trend is the rise in augmented learning, driven by devices such as the Apple Watch and Google Glass.

Regardless of the techniques used, training must be realistic. It must teach the skills or competencies that can be applied directly to the work setting once the training ends. Training also protects organizations by ensuring employees remain compliant with safety rules or government regulations. Progress must be monitored to determine how well trainees master the material.

development
Efforts to acquire the knowledge, skills, and attitudes needed to move to a job with greater authority and responsibility

Purposes of Development

Development is a way of preparing someone for new and greater challenges he or she will encounter in another, more demanding job. Workers seek development opportunities to prepare for management positions; supervisors need development to prepare for a move into middle management. All development is really self-development. Without a personal commitment, development cannot occur. People can be pressured into training just to keep their jobs, but development, when offered, can be rejected.

Employees cannot depend on their employers for development opportunities. Small companies cannot afford it, and many large employers will not pay for development when it is not directly related to an employee's current job or career track.

Techniques of Development

Development techniques include job rotation, sending people to professional workshops or seminars, sponsoring memberships in professional associations, paying for an employee's formal education courses, and granting a person a sabbatical (leave of absence) to pursue further education or engage in community service. An employee should regard a company-sponsored program as a reward and a clear statement about his or her value to the company. Such programs are conduits through which workers can gain prestige, confidence and competence.

Development efforts should never end; indeed, they can be part of a daily routine. By reading professional journals and business publications regularly and by interacting with experts at professional meetings, employees can help keep themselves up to date. Another approach to development involves volunteering for difficult assignments. Meeting tough challenges encourages a person to expand his or her abilities.

Mentoring is another form of development that can be extremely significant. Mentors are professionals who are one or two steps above a person in his or her profession. Mentors can come from a person's current environment or from another organization. Whatever their affiliation, mentors are willing to share experiences and give competent advice about handling advancement opportunities, company politics, and self-development. See Appendix D for some ideas on developing mentor relationships.

7

Discuss the purpose of a performance appraisal

performance appraisal
A formal, structured comparison between employee performance and established quantity and quality standards

PERFORMANCE APPRAISAL

In most organizations, some assessment of job performance takes place every day, at least informally. When results for a given period are summarized and shared with those being reviewed, **performance appraisal** becomes a formal, structured system designed (in line with legal limits) to measure the actual job performance of an employee by comparing it to designated standards. These standards are introduced and reinforced in the selection and training processes.

Purposes of Performance Appraisal

Most organizations use appraisals to:

- Provide feedback about the success of previous training and disclose the need for additional training.
- Develop individuals' plans for improving their performance and assist them in making such plans.
- Determine whether rewards such as pay increases, promotions, transfers or commendations are due or whether warning or termination is required.

- Identify areas for additional growth and the methods that can be utilized to achieve it.

- Develop and enhance the relationship between the person being evaluated and the supervisor doing the evaluation.

- Give the employee a clear understanding of where he or she stands in relation to the supervisor's expectations and in relation to the achievement of specific goals.

Company policy establishes the frequency and form of the appraisal. Whatever form evaluations take, managers should provide daily feedback to an employee about performance. The employee's team members should do the same. If feedback is continual, the formal annual or semiannual performance appraisal will contain no surprises.

Components of Appraisal Systems

Performance appraisal systems include three major components:

- The criteria (factors and standards) against which the employee's performance is measured. Criteria could include quality of work, efforts at improvement, specific attitudes and quantity of output.

- The rating that summarizes how well the employee is doing.

- The methods used to determine the ratings. Methods could involve specific forms, people and procedures.

Different personalities, jobs, organizations and subsystems call for different criteria, ratings and methods. According to Susan Resnick-West, coauthor of *Designing Performance Appraisal Systems,* the major predictor of the effectiveness of a performance system is whether it is tailored for individuals. Factors that system designers should consider include task competency, previous experience, educational levels and individual preferences.[31]

Appraisal systems can be classified as subjective or objective. Subjective systems allow raters to operate from their own personal points of view. Raters may be allowed the freedom to create factors, define what each factor means, and determine the employee's proficiency in each category. Figure 9.14 shows how one rater uses a simple matrix of four categories—Time Management, Attitude, Knowledge of Job and Communication—and the proficiency categories Excellent, Good, Fair and Poor. What do these words mean? How is the rater defining each? In comparison to another person or to an ideal? Definitions used by one rater using this form may vary from those of another. Worse, the evaluator's stereotypes of and prejudices against an employee may become factors in the evaluation. Subjective methods and forms are difficult to justify

Figure 9.14	Subjective Performance Appraisal System			
	Excellent	**Good**	**Fair**	**Poor**
Time Management		✔		
Attitude		✔		
Knowledge of Job	✔			
Communication			✔	

when faced with accusations of discrimination. An employer should make every effort to keep subjectivity out of ratings.

Objective performance appraisals attempt to remove rater biases. Criteria are clearly defined and shared with the employee well in advance of the actual rating. Figure 9.15 shows just how concrete standards can be. An objective approach causes little confusion about the factors used for evaluation.

Appraisal Methods

Four appraisal methods dominate current practice: management by objectives, behaviorally anchored rating scales, computer monitoring and 360-degree feedback. After a brief look at each type, this chapter will examine the legal constraints on all rating methods.

Management by Objectives Recall from Chapter 4 that a management by objectives (MBO) system requires a manager and subordinate to meet periodically to agree on specific performance goals for the subordinate over a fixed period. At the end of that period, an employee working under MBO is evaluated in regard to the number of goals met, how effectively and efficiently each one was achieved, and the growth that took place during the effort. Evaluators take into account the difficulties that the employee had to overcome to reach those goals.

Figure 9.15	Portion of an Objective Performance Appraisal System

PERFORMANCE ASPECT	1	2	3	4	5
1. Self Improvement Consider the desire to expand current capabilities in both depth and breadth. ❑ No opportunity to observe.	Has no interest in learning additional duties.	Has limited interest in expanding job assignments. Has little interest in preparing for advancement.	Has demonstrated interest in additional assignments. Has shown some interest in and preparation for advancement.	Has shown extra effort to learn additional duties. Has undertaken advancement preparation.	Is very inquisitive concerning all phases of job-related assignments. Has undertaken advancement preparation.
2. Attendance Consider the regularity with which the employee reports to work.	Excessively absent	Frequently absent	Occasionally absent	Rarely absent	Almost never absent
3. Punctuality Consider number of occasions late. ❑ Punctuality is not essential.	Excessively tardy	Frequently tardy	Occasionally tardy	Rarely tardy	Almost never tardy
4. Work Planning Consider how the work load is planned and organized for maximum efficiency. ❑ No opportunity to observe.	Unsystematic, unable to organize work load.	Fair on routine, but unable to organize variations effectively.	Efficient under normal conditions. Gives priority to important jobs.	Skillful in organizing and planning work. Meets emergencies promptly.	Exceptional efficiency. Keeps priority items in proper perspective.

Behaviorally Anchored Rating Scales BARS, or behaviorally anchored rating scales, identify important dimensions of job performance anchored by specific behaviors that correspond to different levels of performance. Each behavior corresponds to a numeric rating. Figure 9.16 illustrates a rating scale for the job of quality control inspector on the dimension of "Quality Strategy: Knowledge of Inspection Methods." The employee's overall rating is the sum of the points earned in each category.

Computer Monitoring A computer monitoring system tracks an employee's performance as it is taking place. The performance of those who work with computers or computerized equipment can be evaluated in terms of the amount of time their machines are operating productively, the number of keystrokes per minute or total output. Managers can compare the ratings of various employees in similar jobs and rank workers according to productivity. Performance averages can be used by managers to set or confirm existing standards. Retailers, banks, insurance companies, telephone companies and transport firms use computer monitoring as one objective measure of employee performance.

360-Degree Feedback Feedback is sought from all or most of the constituencies with which an employee has contact, particularly coworkers and customers. The goal of 360-degree feedback is to increase employees' self-awareness so that they can improve their work performance. This is also known as multirater feedback, multisource feedback, full-circle appraisal and group performance review.

Legality of Appraisals

An analysis of U.S. Supreme Court rulings over the past 25 years reveals that performance appraisals are likely to be illegal if any of these situations hold:

- The instruments used are invalid.
- Standards are not job related and objective (quantifiable and observable).
- The results of the process have a disparate impact on women, the disabled or minorities.
- The scoring method is not standardized.
- People who are performing similar jobs are evaluated differently, using different forms, factors or processes.

Figure 9.16	Example of a BARS for Quality Control Inspectors

Quality Strategy; Knowledge of Inspection Methods. This area of performance concerns the ability of a quality control inspector to test and measure assembled parts and contribute to the strategic prevention of defects.

High	5—Based on mechanical and electronic inspections, makes recommendations on process and materials that will result in fewer defective assemblies 4—Using specialized tools and electronic devices for measurement and calibration, ensures that all components meet established standards and assemblies operate correctly
Average	3—Visually and mechanically inspects assembled objects and makes minor repairs/modifications as needed 2—Visually inspects assembled objects to ensure all component parts are present and operating correctly
Low	1—Visually inspects assembled objects to ensure all component parts are present

Source: Adapted from Landy, Jacobs and Associates. Reprinted with permission.

**Note: This example is from Bohlander and Snell, *Managing Human Resources 15E*, p. 385.

- Evaluative criteria are not developed according to EEOC guidelines.
- Employees are not warned of declining or substandard performance.
- The evaluation is not based on the employee's current duties.

Raters must be trained to carry out performance appraisals consistently and in accordance with legal requirements. Also, women, disabled people and minorities in a proportion that is representative of the community at large should fill the ranks of performance appraisers. Lawrence H. Peters, Professor of Management at Texas Christian University, gave practical advice to raters and ratees: "It's hard to remember what the employee did 12, 11 or 10 months ago. It's important for managers to keep information as it occurs, and if you don't, stop and take time to collect your thoughts before the performance review. Employees should do the same." In addition, raters need to reserve adequate facilities and time to review appraisals with subordinates.

Describe the four primary employment decisions

IMPLEMENTATION OF EMPLOYMENT DECISIONS

As you recall, employment decisions include decisions about promotions, transfers, demotions and separations (voluntary or involuntary). These changes are influenced by appraisals and by how an organization recruits, hires, orients and trains. All employment decisions mean change—change that has a ripple effect throughout an organization's subsystems and its ability to interact with the external environment.

Promotions

promotion

A job change that results in increased status, compensation and responsibility

Promotions are job changes that lead to higher pay and greater authority and that reward devoted, outstanding effort. They serve as incentives as well, offering the promise of greater personal growth and challenges to those who seek them. Employees usually earn a promotion by exhibiting superior performance and going beyond that which is expected.

Sometimes past performance is not the sole criterion for a promotion. Affirmative action requires that underrepresented groups such as women and minorities be better represented at all levels within an organization. Therefore, affirmative action goals may dictate that members of these groups be given special status in hiring and promoting decisions. In many union agreements, seniority is the most significant factor influencing promotion decisions.

Transfers

transfer

Moving an employee to a job with similar levels of status, compensation and responsibility

Opportunities for promotion are not as available now as they were only a few years ago. The leaner, flatter management structures of today and the trend toward teams mean there simply are not a large number of openings. **Transfers** are lateral moves that require new skills. They comprise one way for companies to retain talent.

For years companies have used lateral moves in attempts to train and develop employees. Job rotation is one way of exposing people to different aspects of an operation and helping them see the big corporate picture. Transfers can help people advance by moving them from an area where few opportunities exist to an area that offers a less-congested career track.

Demotions

demotion

A reduction in an employee's status, pay and responsibility

A **demotion** is a reassignment to a lower rank in an organization's hierarchy. In today's business climate, demotions are rarely used as punishment. (Ineffective performers are fired, not retained.) Demotions are used to retain employees who lose their positions through no fault of their own. Some people prefer taking a lower-status, lower-paying job to the alternative of being laid off. Others choose a demotion to decrease stress, allow them more freedom to pursue outside interests, or meet challenges such as having to care for children or an elderly parent.

Some companies have established what have become known as *mommy tracks*—temporary career interruptions for parents. Mommy tracks allow a parent to take care of children from pregnancy through the preschool years. By offering adjustments such as part-time work, a mix of telecommuting and in-house office hours, and flexible work schedules, companies help valued employees cope with new interests and demands on their time. As Joan Beck notes, however, some of these arrangements have drawbacks:

> *Unfortunately, many employers still exact a steep price for non-standard work arrangements. Part-time work typically pays low wages and usually includes few if any benefits. Even women at middle-management levels or on fast professional tracks find that cutting back on work hours and trying other strategies to eke out more time for family cuts chances for promotion.*[32]

Separations

A **separation**, the departure of an employee from an organization, may be voluntary or involuntary. Voluntary separations include resignations and retirements. Involuntary separations include layoffs and firings. Employers sometimes encourage voluntary separation by offering incentives to encourage employees to retire early. Involuntary separations seem to be on the rise in U.S. business. Layoffs due to declining business, personal performance or company bankruptcies (as in the cases of Enron and Lehman Brothers) have cost millions of Americans their jobs. See this chapter's Global Applications feature for a discussion of Japan's custom of lifetime employment.

separation
The voluntary or involuntary departure of employees from a company

Layoffs Although downsizing can make companies more competitive, it can also undermine the loyalty of employees threatened with layoffs. A disgruntled employee might destroy data or leave behind a computer virus that will sabotage the system after the employee has left. An information security consultant, William H. Murray, says that the best way to protect a company against sabotage is to take steps to prevent employee disaffection—to treat those who must leave as well as possible before the layoff and compensate remaining employees fairly. According to Murray, most revenge comes from those who conclude that their contributions are unrecognized. People need to know they are appreciated day by day.[33]

As alternatives to layoffs, many companies are implementing other strategies. Some have enacted hiring freezes, which allow normal attrition to reduce the workforce. Other strategies include job sharing, restricting the use of overtime, retraining and redeploying workers, reducing hours and converting managers to paid consultants. Southwest Airlines hasn't had a layoff in its history. Southwest managers find useful employment for displaced workers by relying on moves and reassignments.

Managers everywhere have good reasons to avoid layoffs. See this chapter's Quality Management feature for a discussion of lean factories avoiding layoffs, which can be extremely expensive. Processing paperwork, closing facilities and paying severance costs and higher unemployment-insurance premiums may cost thousands of dollars. The psychological costs are high as well. Those left behind after layoffs are fearful and insecure; those laid off are more likely than employed people to experience family problems, suffer divorce or commit suicide.

The End of Japan's Lifetime Employment

In the past, three principles dominated Japan's employment system: company unions, pay for seniority and lifetime employment. The latter was a result of informal industry agreements formed after World War II, which restricted competition for labor by companies in the same industry. One could not hire another's employees. It was not so much company loyalty that kept Japanese workers from job-hopping; it was the lack of opportunity for another job in their industries.

In the 1980s, Japan became the world's second-largest economy. "Then the bubble burst in 1991, and stock and real estate markets tumbled. To recover, leaders jolted Japan's entrenched corporate culture, giving companies new freedom to replace "lifetime employment" with part-time and contract laborers" (Osnos). In 2010, China passed Japan to become the world's second-largest economy.

Technology and the global economy continue to change Japan's system. The Internet allows manufacturers worldwide to find supply routes that are faster and cheaper. Furthermore, foreigners are now allowed to invest in long-shielded sectors of the Japanese economy.

Yet, lifetime employment persists for core employees, those comprising the foundational group in the company. In a management briefing seminar, Norm Bafunno, President Toyota Motor Manufacturing Indiana, Inc., was asked, "Why didn't Toyota layoff any workers during the difficult times?" He said, "It was an easy decision. We used the time to RE-TAIN and RE-TRAIN our team members." He related a quote from Akio Toyoda, president of Toyota Motor. "There is a Japanese proverb: After the rain… the ground hardens," he said. "I am very confident; we will look back and say, the company has become more focused, on our customers and safety, because we went through this period" (Bafunno).

➡ In Japan, an employee can no longer expect a job for life. Do you think that the changes in the Japanese employment systems will encourage more people to start their own business? Why or why not?

Sources: Norm Buffano, "2010 Management Briefing Seminar," Toyota USA Newsroom, *http://pressroom.toyota.com/pr/tms/2010-management-briefing-seminar-165695.aspx*; Evan Osnos, "Behind Japan's growth lies economic divide," *The Dallas Morning News*, May 7, 2006, p. 36A.

Exit Interviews Exit interviews are voluntary discussions between managers and employees who are being laid off or who are leaving voluntarily. Because the costs of laying off and replacing workers are high, a manager should use exit interviews to find out about factors that could cause employees to leave. Once the manager identifies a problem, he or she should fix it. In its *Study of Retention Practices,* the Society for Human Resource Management (SHRM) found that nine out of ten respondents conduct exit interviews.[34]

> The study revealed that more than half of those that conduct exit interviews have initiated changes, including reviewing salary structures, forming employee satisfaction/retention committees, establishing alternative work schedules, providing more training, reimbursing employees for expenses such as cell-phone usage, instituting casual-dress policies and introducing bonus plans.

Managers should realize, however, that exit interviews have a limitation. Because department employees may not wish to leave a negative impression, they may not be totally open and honest. The fact that exit interviews do not reveal a cause for employee dissatisfaction does not necessarily mean that a cause does not exist.

Lean Factories Avoid Layoffs

Production goes up and down in factories that have adopted Lean, but labor remains steady. Lean production means doing more with less by cutting wastes during the production process. Today's customers are more powerful than ever before. They have many product choices, access to a wealth of information and expect high quality products at reasonable prices.

"A decade ago, most factories tended to do "batch" work, with large groups of employees churning out endless runs of the same pieces. Since many workers did identical tasks, it was easier for companies to cut people during downturns" (Aeppel and Lahart). Today, lean operations require fewer, but more highly trained employees running more sophisticated equipment.

The ultimate objective of lean production is to achieve continuous flow of the product. This is done by arranging operators, equipment and materials right next to each other so that they can complete processing steps in sequential order. "Streamlined production and technological improvements also mean fewer jobs need to be cut in a downturn" (Aeppel and Lahart). Lynn Mahuta, CEO of Germantown, Wisconsin-based Mahuta Tool Corp., which makes items such as 600-pound screws used in cranes, sums it up this way. "The highly skilled person, you're not going to lay them off. You will find other work for them to do" (Aeppel and Lahart).

Toyota Alabama did not lay off any team members during the last recession. James Bolte, president of Toyota Motor Manufacturing Alabama Inc. in Huntsville, said, "During the economic crisis, Toyota Alabama focused on improvement efforts that allowed us to accomplish more with fewer resources. For example, we became more efficient with various production processes and cross-trained team members to expand their skill sets" (Armstrong).

➡ Employers with Lean factories maintain stable workforces at all costs. Others lay off workers seemingly at the drop of a hat. What differences could explain these two extremes in human resources management policy?

Source: Jessica Armstrong, "Lessons from the Recession," Business Alabama, May 2014, *http://www.businessalabama.com/Business-Alabama/May-2014/Lessons-from-the-Recession/*; Timothy Aeppel and Justin Lahart, "Lean Factories Find It Hard to Cut Jobs Even in a Slump," *The Wall Street Journal*, March 9, 2009, A1, *<http://online.wsj.com/article/SB123655039683165011.html>*.

COMPENSATION

9 Determine the purposes and components of compensation

compensation
All forms of financial payments to employees. Compensation includes salaries, wages and benefits

Compensation includes all forms of financial payments to employees: salaries and wages, benefits, bonuses, gain sharing, profit sharing and awards of goods or services. The trend today is to offer increases in compensation in response to increases in performance that add value to the organization, its services or its products. Increasing compensation is a way of retaining employees who have proved themselves valuable. This response makes sense. As employees become more valuable, losing them becomes more costly.

Purposes of Compensation

Compensation has three primary purposes: to attract, help develop and retain talented performers. The level of compensation offered by a firm can either increase or decrease a company's attractiveness to job seekers. Compensation should encourage workers to continually improve their performance and to make themselves more valuable, both to themselves and to their employers. Also, compensation must anchor valued employees to the company, discouraging them from leaving to find other employment. People who consider their compensation fair and adequate feel that they are being treated with recognition and respect. They feel that the organization is giving them a fair return on their investment of time, energy and commitment. Finally, compensation should give employees a sense of security, freeing them to unleash their full energies without the distraction that comes with the inability to meet financial needs.

Factors Influencing Compensation

When designing a compensation package for employees, managers should be concerned about being equitable, meeting legal and strategic requirements, and linking compensation philosophy to various market factors. When certain types of workers are in short supply, managers may have to offer premium compensation to attract or hold them. Similarly, managers who decide to make their organization a leader in terms of the compensation it offers will probably be able to attract and keep the best employees.

The U.S. Fair Labor Standards Act, passed in 1938 and amended many times, relates to the payment of wages and overtime to workers under 18 years of age. Other federal laws address the level of wages that must be paid to workers in companies doing business with the federal government. Some local and state laws affect compensation systems, and union contracts set wages and restrict compensation decisions in the organizations that are party to them.

Wages and Salaries

job evaluation
A study that determines the worth of a job in terms of its value to an organization

To determine the worth of each job and establish a compensation package for each that is fair in relation to all jobs, organizations use a process called **job evaluation**. Human resource compensation specialists usually do job evaluations. To complete the evaluation process, the specialist works with a manager with firsthand knowledge of the job and the employee or employees who hold the job.

One common job evaluation method involves grouping jobs by type and then choosing factors common to each type. For example, two groups of jobs that job evaluation specialists often define are manufacturing jobs (wage jobs) and sales jobs (salary jobs). An evaluation might involve examining each type of job in light of the responsibility, education, skills, training, experience and working conditions that are common to it. Then the evaluator assigns various levels within each factor and assigns point values to each level as measures of achievement.

To illustrate this process, suppose the job being analyzed is that of an industrial products sales professional. The evaluator chooses experience as an evaluation factor and defines experience as number of years in the selling profession. The levels for this factor might be one year or less of experience, one to three years of experience, three to five years of experience, and more than five years of experience. By assigning points to each level, the specialist shows the relative value the organization places on each. If the top level is worth ten points and the previous one is worth five points, the organization is saying that more than five years of experience is twice as valuable as three to five years of experience.

Once all jobs have been evaluated, they can be grouped by total points into what are usually called job grades or classifications. Evaluators then rank, by point total, jobs within each grade. For example, all jobs with point totals between 0 and 200 might be in the same grade. What emerges is a "job ladder" that shows jobs with the fewest total points at the bottom. At the top are the jobs with the most points. Evaluators assign a salary range to jobs in the same grade. Figure 9.17 shows the result of a typical job evaluation.

Figure 9.17   **Result of a Typical Job Evaluation**

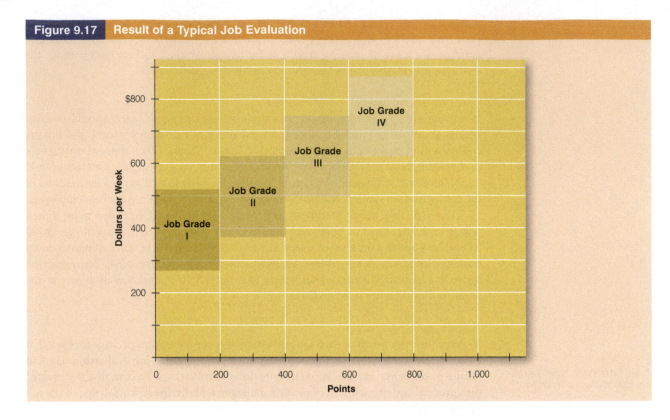

Job evaluation requires skill, up-to-date job descriptions and specifications, knowledge and ample time. Many companies conduct pay surveys within their industries as a base for beginning the job evaluation process or as a substitute for it. Pay surveys show what competitors pay for comparable jobs. These rates of pay may be available through industry and trade associations as well as from the federal government. Not all jobs are compared with the survey results; the evaluator compares only those that are representative of their grades or classes. Compensation for other jobs are established in relation to the jobs being compared.

In the final analysis, the minimum and maximum compensation assigned to a job are determined by an organization's ability to pay, market conditions for specific types of jobs, and the organization's strategies and philosophy about employee compensation.

Benefits

Each year employers spend about an additional 40 percent of their payroll costs on employee **benefits**—the additional or indirect compensation employees receive beyond their direct compensation (wages and salaries). Benefits can be divided into two general types: *legally required*, and *voluntary*. The first type includes Social Security, unemployment compensation, and worker's compensation insurance. The second type includes variable work schedules, life and health insurance, pension and savings plans, payment for hours not worked (sick days), leaves of absence, profit-sharing and bonus plans (usually one-time payments), and employee assistance programs (EAPs).

EAPs have gained in popularity over the years. Most can be classified as health and wellness programs that deal with either prevention of health-related problems

benefit

Legally required or voluntary compensation provided to employees in addition to their salaries or wages

or coping with chronic work-related problems. Stop-smoking clinics, weight-loss programs and exercise facilities are examples of prevention efforts. Stress-reduction workshops, day-care facilities and financial and psychological counseling concentrate on coping with work-related problems.

An organization offers benefits, like other forms of compensation, so that it can attract, develop, motivate and retain talented and committed workers. As with wages and salaries, managers plan benefits according to their organizations' financial resources and strategies and the market conditions the organization faces. An organization should provide tailored benefits to appeal to a variety of needs for its diverse workforce. Tailored benefits can help an organization achieve its goals; among them, developing a core of committed managers and workers. As with wages and salaries, however, benefits must be constantly reviewed for their relevance and economic feasibility.

Executive Compensation

In addition to salaries and the benefits all other employees in their firm receive, executives—members of top management—may also receive benefits unique to their status. These benefits are called perquisites, commonly known as **perks**.[35] Most perks are financial—actual cash or goods and services that have a measurable cash value. Such items include shares of the company's stock, stock options (rights to purchase a company's stock at a discount), bonuses based on overall company performance, use of a company's airplane and regional residential suites, generous travel and lodging allowances, paid-for housing, no-interest loans and memberships in various clubs and associations. In recent years, discussion of "excessive" executive compensation has appeared in popular periodicals and the business press.

perk
A payment or benefit received in addition to a regular wage or salary

Chapter Summary

1 Determine the importance of the staffing function.

Staffing breathes life into an organization. It acquires and nurtures the human resources needed to execute tasks and functions. People are the key to everything in organizations. They are the organization's most valuable resources. As such, they must be selected, trained, developed, rewarded and retained for effective and efficient use of the organization's other resources. Staffing is every manager's concern.

2 List and explain the eight elements of the staffing process.

1 Human resource planning begins with job analysis. Performing a job analysis involves creating descriptions and specifications of all jobs and their human qualifications. Next, an inventory of people on hand and their abilities to meet current and future needs is determined. Planning also includes forecasting—attempting to predict the future human resource needs. Finally, forecasts are compared to the inventory and needs to recruit or reduce personnel are determined.

2 Recruiting brings enough qualified people into a hiring pool. Care must be taken to find sufficient numbers of people from all ethnic and racial groups. Existing employees must be trained and developed to become eligible for future openings.

3 Selection involves a series of pre-employment screening devices used to determine each candidate's ability to provide the organization what it needs. Care must be taken to determine a fit with the company's cultures and to avoid discrimination.

4 Orientation includes a set of activities designed to introduce and welcome newcomers to their new company and working environments. Rights and duties are explained, along with the introduction of existing personnel to the new ones.

5 Training and development increase and change employee knowledge, skills and attitudes. Training is focused on the near term; development focuses on the future. Both help companies to meet their needs and make employees more valuable to both themselves and their organizations.

6 Performance appraisal measures outcomes and behaviors of employees against established and taught standards. Appraisals become the basis for rewards, punishments, promotions and terminations, and affect nearly every employment decision made by managers. They provide necessary feedback, helping to keep people motivated and focused on their most essential duties.

7 Compensation includes all financial and psychological rewards and incentives provided to employees. Direct compensation is largely composed of wages and salaries. Indirect compensation includes financial and nonfinancial rewards and incentives such as benefits, bonuses, gain and profit sharing, leaves of absence and employee assistance programs.

8 Employment decisions include transfers, promotions, demotions, layoffs and firings. All have their specific appropriate applications and must be performed without discrimination.

3 Describe the three primary staffing environments.

The environments are legal, sociocultural and union. The legal environment sets limits and provides guidelines for conducting all staffing activities. Specifically, it attempts to provide protection for employees and groups from discrimination and in the areas of health and safety. The sociocultural environment is a collection of diverse individuals and groups, both inside and outside an organization, that make demands on and contribute to it. The union environment affects some companies more than others. Union contracts govern work rules, wages and conditions of employment. Wages and benefits established in some industries are often duplicated or exceeded by nonunion organizations.

4 Identify the four activities related to human resource planning.

In job analysis, groups of jobs are studied to determine their basic duties and the human qualities needed to perform them. A human resource inventory determines who are on board, along with their current qualifications and future prospects. The human resource forecast is based on both short- and long-term plans and strategies for the company and its various parts. Finally, a comparison is made between the inventory and the forecasted needs to determine if contraction, expansion or keeping the status quo is the correct plan to follow.

5 List and describe the primary screening devices used in the selection process.

All selection devices must be job related and validated in order to avoid discrimination. The application provides essential personal data—job history, education, aspirations—about a person's suitability for a particular job. Preliminary interviews verify the data on applications and provide an initial face-to-face encounter for both applicant and employer. Testing may include any paper-and-pencil exercise or performance that will be used to make a hiring decision. In-depth interviews are usually conducted by the person or persons for whom and with whom the new person, if hired, will work. Reference checks provide verification of key facts about a job applicant such as work history, compensation earned, and successes in various positions. Physical exams help to avoid bringing newcomers into an environment that could be injurious to their health.

6 Explain the differences and similarities between training and development.

Training increases knowledge and skills, motivation to succeed, chances for advancement, morale, pride in performance and quality and productivity. It is usually provided to keep people current in the jobs and to prepare them for changes to those jobs. Development focuses on preparing people for new and different positions, challenges and opportunities. It also imparts skills, knowledge and attitudes. Training is usually provided by organizations. Development is each person's individual responsibility and may or may not be aided by one's organization.

7 Discuss the purpose of a performance appraisal.

The primary purpose is to provide feedback on one's performances and outputs, enabling rewards and

needed improvement efforts to take place. It helps to evaluate the results of previous training and to determine any additional training needs. It helps individuals and teams plan for their improvement and choose the methods they will utilize. Appraisals also help to improve the relationships between the evaluator and the evaluated. People know how they are doing—what's right and wrong—and the expectations for their future performances.

8 Describe the four primary employment decisions.

Promotions lead individuals to higher levels of responsibility, greater demands on their talents and improvements in earnings. They are often earned rewards for current performance and development efforts undertaken to qualify them for a new, more demanding position. Transfers are often temporary lateral movements to cross train and provide additional experiences. Demotions are the opposite of promotions and are primarily used to save good people until more appropriate positions become available. Separations are voluntary and involuntary. Resignations and retirements are examples of the first; layoffs and firings are examples of the latter.

9 Determine the purposes and components of compensation.

Compensation in all its forms is intended to help organizations attract, train, develop, reward and retain good people. Compensation is direct and indirect. Wages, commissions, piece rates and salaries are direct because they link directly to hours or days worked or outputs achieved. Indirect compensation includes financial and psychological rewards beyond the preceding. Benefits include the largest segment. These include such items as insurance, pay for time not worked, gain sharing, profit sharing, pensions and employee assistance programs such as wellness programs. Psychological rewards include satisfaction achieved through work and various alterations to one's working schedule.

KEY TERMS

affirmative action **287**

assessment center **300**

benefit **316**

collective bargaining **292**

compensation **314**

demotion **311**

development **307**

discrimination **284**

disparate impact **286**

equal employment
   opportunity **284**

gig economy **282**

human resource manager **280**

independent contractors **283**

job analysis **292**

job evaluation **315**

onboarding **280**

orientation **304**

performance appraisal **307**

perk **317**

personnel manager **281**

promotion **311**

recruiting **295**

selection **297**

separation **312**

sexual harassment **287**

sharing economy **282**

staffing **280**

test **298**

training **304**

transfer **311**

REVIEW QUESTIONS

1. Why is staffing so important to organizations?

2. What are the components of staffing, and in what order do they occur?

3. Which external environments affect the staffing process most directly? How do they affect it?

4. What takes place under the heading of human resource planning?

5. What are the primary screening devices used in staffing?

6. How are training and development similar? How are they different?

7. What are the primary purposes of appraising employees?

8. Under what circumstances would an organization perform each of the following: promotion, transfer, demotion and separation?

9. What purposes do organizations try to achieve through compensation? What forms can compensation take?

DISCUSSION QUESTIONS FOR CRITICAL THINKING

1. Why are the concepts of equal employment opportunity and affirmative action so important to organizations today?

2. How would an organization recruit if it is looking for electrical engineers with knowledge of the latest technologies? If it is looking for medical technicians with at least three years of experience?

3. What kind of compensation do you think is most important to each of the following: People five years away from retirement? Single people in their twenties? Young marrieds with their first child on the way?

4. How are you appraised in your classes? At work? What value do you find in such appraisals?

Apply What You Know

Social Media Management Exercises

Network with Twitter

Dan Schawbel, managing partner of Millennial Branding, LLC, is an authority on personal branding. He is author of *Promote Yourself and Me 2.0,* which includes a section on how to use social networks for job search and career development (*http://danschawbel.com*). He likes Twitter (*www.twitter.com*) because it is a *public* network.

1. Build your network. Identify the type of job you desire, i.e. accounting, finance, human resources, marketing, public relations, etc.

2. Identify 3 to 5 companies where you would like to work.

3. Choose 3 to 5 locations where you would like to live and work.

4. Prepare a Twitter list with the names of those you would like to follow.

5. The people you follow on Twitter can see that you are following them. You can retweet (RT) what they tweet, which means to share that tweet with your followers. Reflect on your Twitter list. How relevant do you think preparing a Twitter list would be to your job search? Explain.

6. A direct message (DM) allows you to send a private message to someone via Twitter. Compose a direct message to someone on your Twitter list. How do you think this direct message could help you with your job search?

Experiential Learning

Try a New Platform

Some people open a social media account in each new platform. They want answers to the following questions. How does it work? Who's using it? Is it useful? Social media platforms for networking include Facebook, Friendster, LinkedIn, Ning, Twitter and many others.

- Identify a new social media platform that could help you network.

- How does it work?
- Who is using it?
- How is it useful?
- List the pros and cons.
- Would you use it for job networking? Why or why not?
- Will you continue to use it?

Chapter 10

Communication: Interpersonal and Organizational

LEARNING OBJECTIVES

After studying this chapter, you should be able to:

1 Discuss the importance of communication in organizations

2 Diagram the communication process and label all its parts

3 List and explain the barriers to interpersonal communication and suggest remedies to overcome them

4 Describe the uses of downward, horizontal, and upward communication channels

5 Explain the informal communication channel known as the grapevine

6 List and explain the barriers to organizational communication and suggest remedies to overcome them

7 Describe the responsibilities of senders and receivers during the communication process

Communicating Skills

Communicating skills include speaking, listening, reading and writing. These are some of the most important skills needed to succeed in the workplace. Managers speak to employees and listen when employees speak to them. They read and write reports; they create documents and make presentations. When managers communicate effectively, understanding takes place. Mistakes are minimized. Productivity is increased.

For each of the following statements, circle the number which indicates your level of agreement. Rate your agreement as it is, not what you think it should be. Objectivity will enable you to determine your management skill strengths and weaknesses.

	Almost Always	Often	Sometimes	Rarely	Almost Never
Before I speak, I think about what I will say.	5	4	3	2	1
When I write, I make clear statements.	5	4	3	2	1
I keep my communications brief and concise.	5	4	3	2	1
People understand what I've said.	5	4	3	2	1
When people talk to me, I listen actively and alertly.	5	4	3	2	1
When I talk to someone, I pay attention to their body language.	5	4	3	2	1
When I finish writing, I review it carefully before sending.	5	4	3	2	1
I use pictures, diagrams and charts to clarify my ideas.	5	4	3	2	1
If I don't understand something someone has written or said, I ask for clarification.	5	4	3	2	1
Before communicating, I think about the best way to get my message across—face-to-face, telephone or e-mail.	5	4	3	2	1

Compute your score by adding the circled numbers. The highest score is 50; the lowest score is 10. A higher score implies you are more likely to be an effective communicator.

A lower score implies a lesser degree of readiness, but it can be increased. Reading and studying this chapter will help you to improve your understanding of communication.

INTRODUCTION

Communication is the process through which people and organizations accomplish objectives. By communicating with others we share attitudes, values, emotions, ambitions, wants and needs. Behind most successes is effective communication— well planned and thoughtfully executed. The process of communication, however, is difficult. Failed plans are often the result of failed attempts at communicating.

Successful managers effectively communicate their vision to a work unit and the company as a whole. At Walmart, Founder Sam Walton's vision to make the customer number one led his company to become the most successful retailer in American history. The late Sam Walton offered his thoughts about the importance of communication:

> *Communicate everything you possibly can to your partners. The more they know, the more they'll understand. The more they understand, the more they'll care. Once they care, there is no stopping them. If you don't trust your associates to know what's going on, they'll know you don't really consider them partners. Information is power, and the gain you get from empowering your associates more than offsets the risk of informing your competitors.*
>
> *Listen to everyone in your company. And figure out ways to get them talking. The folks on the front lines—the ones who actually talk to the customer—are the only ones who really know what's going on out there. You'd better find out what they know. This really is what total quality is all about. To push responsibility down in your organization, and to force good ideas to bubble up within it, you must listen to what your associates are trying to tell you.*[1]

Organizations must continually ask, "How can our customers find us to communicate with us?" Customers can communicate with employees face-to-face in the store, on telephones and corporate websites with real time chat or social media. This allows employees to respond instantly in real time to customer needs.

People in organizations need one another. They must coordinate and pool their efforts to achieve their goals and avoid waste and confusion. They must focus on the needs of the customers, those inside as well as outside the company. They must be able to articulate their needs so that they can work cooperatively. They must be free to express what they know and believe in order to capitalize on opportunities for meaningful change. Managers who really believe that their people are the organization's most valuable resource will make communicating with those people their most vital process.

Communication Process

Communication is the transmission of **information**—data in a coherent, usable form—from one person or group to another. Rational communicators strive to achieve a common **understanding**—agreement about the meaning and intent of the message—among all parties in each communication. Although much of the information that managers rely on is in numeric form, the greatest portion of managerial activity depends on verbal communication and competent use of language. Able communicators respect the conventions of language—spelling, grammar and punctuation. They know precisely what they wish to say and thoughtfully select the best way to say it. In addition, communicators need to be certain that the people who receive the information actually understand the message.

Communication is a process—a set of steps usually taken in a definite sequence. The initiator of communication is called the **sender**; the person or group that gets the

communication
The transmission of information and understanding from one person or group to another

information
Processed data that is useful to the receiver

understanding
The situation that exists when all senders and receivers agree about the meaning and intent of a message

sender
The person or group who initiates the communication process

receiver
The person or group for whom a communication effort is intended

message
The information the sender wants to transmit

medium
The means by which a sender transmits a message

feedback
Information about the receiver's perception of the sender's message

communication is the **receiver**. The information that the sender wants to transmit is the **message**. The means chosen by the sender to transmit the message is the **medium**, or channel. Finally, the process must provide mechanisms through which both sender and receiver can determine if the intended communication has taken place and mutual understanding has been achieved. That mechanism offers **feedback**—information the receiver provides to show how he or she perceived the sender's message. In supplying feedback, the receiver becomes a sender and the original sender becomes a receiver; the process of sending and receiving messages proceeds until both communicators believe that understanding has taken place. The more carefully crafted and unambiguous the message is, the less feedback will be required to achieve understanding. Figure 10.1 provides a model of the communication process.

To illustrate the communication process, consider an example involving Harry Trent, a manufacturing director. Harry calls Anita Raton, the human resource manager for his company, and says, "I need a replacement employee." In response to the message, Anita says, "What kind of skills do you need? For which department?" The receiver is seeking clarification of the original message and becomes a sender in doing so. Harry now shifts to being a receiver and must clarify his original message before responding and becoming a sender again. Many conversations flow in this manner because the sender transmits an incomplete message—one that requires the receiver to ask for additional information so that understanding can take place. Harry failed to refine his message before he initiated the communication process.

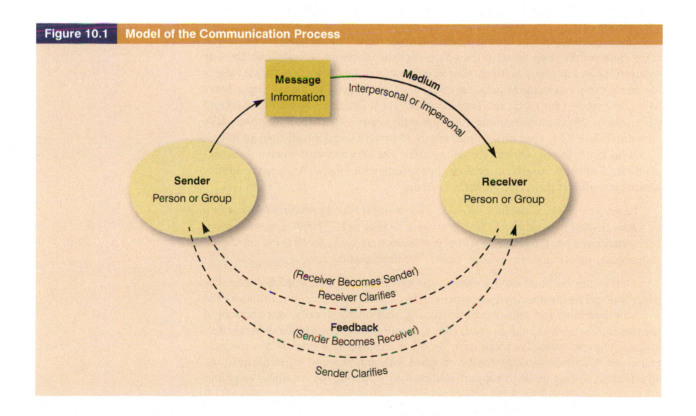

Figure 10.1   Model of the Communication Process

MEDIUMS OF COMMUNICATION

Communication mediums are verbal (spoken or written words) and nonverbal (images, facial expressions, gestures and body language).

2 Diagram the communication process and label all its parts

Verbal Communication

Spoken verbal messages can be delivered face-to-face or by electronic means, such as telephone, voice mail and voice messaging. Written verbal mediums fall into two categories: traditional printed matter and digital delivery systems. Printed matter includes memos, letters, manuals, newsletters and reports. Individuals connect and communicate with the outside world digitally by computers, tablets, cell phones, and smartphones. In 2013, according to the U.S. Census Bureau, 83.8 percent of U.S. households reported computer ownership, with 78.5 percent of all households having a desktop or laptop computer, and 63.6 percent having a handheld computer; 74.4 percent of all households reported Internet use, with 73.4 percent reporting a high-speed connection. In 2015, Pew Research Center reported that 68 percent of adults had a smartphone, up from 35 percent since mid-2011.[2]

The sender's choice of medium is influenced by several factors: the content of the message, the importance of feedback, the number of intended receivers, the receiver's and sender's preferences and characteristics, the sender's and receiver's locations and environments and the technologies available. Communication requiring immediate two-way feedback and a personal touch should be oral and in person. If the message is complicated and requires a considered response, communication should be written. Most companies choose electronic mediums for their obvious advantages of speed and accuracy. No human can keep records of suppliers and parts in so many locations, keep them current, search through them and then schedule shipments as swiftly as computers can.

Conversation, perhaps the most common communication medium for managers, takes place on the shop floor, in the office, over the telephone, at lunch, on the way to meetings and in group settings. Conversation should be used when the message is for one person and requires personal contact, or when give and take is vital. Henry Mintzberg studied five CEOs and found that they spent 78 percent of their time talking with others. These conversations were generally short—49 percent of their daily encounters lasted less than nine minutes; only 10 percent lasted longer than an hour.[3]

John Kotter found virtually the same results. The fifteen executive general managers he studied spent 76 percent of their time talking with others.[4] As Suzanne Rinfret Moore, who directs three companies, reported:

> *Someone can say to me in 30 seconds what it might take 15 minutes to write in a memo—and it generates the ability to think on your feet.... [Oral communication] fosters creativity for yourself and the people you work with. Access is critical. I want people who can come to my door. They're not time bandits.*[5]

Oral communication cannot always substitute for the written word, however. The process of preparing a written document allows careful consideration. Initiators can precisely determine and control the content, organization, complexity, tone and style of the message. Receivers can digest such communication according to their own schedule and at their own pace. They can draw on other resources and prepare a considered responses. A written message can be enriched with graphics and other illustrations. In addition, writing tends to support confidentiality. Among the countless variations of written communications are e-mails, letters, memos, outlines, reports, procedures manuals, press releases, newsletters, contracts, advertisements and forms. Figure 10.2 suggests conventional applications for common written communication tools.

Written forms of communication have disadvantages. They are impersonal, do not provide the immediacy of face-to-face contact and do not elicit immediate feedback.

Some forms of written communication—such as notices on bulletin boards, handbooks and newsletters—are, by their nature, impersonal. Do not rely on these tools when timely feedback or elaboration is needed, or when the message is critical. Receivers read these communications casually. If communication is vital, use tools of this nature as supplements to immediate tools.

Nonverbal Communication

nonverbal communication
Images, actions and behaviors that transmit messages

Nonverbal communication consists of messages transmitted without the use of words. Nonverbal transmitters include facial expressions, gestures and body language (posture, placement of limbs and proximity to others). Photographs, graphs, charts, animations and videos also convey information nonverbally. Visual transmitters are powerful and persuasive tools that enable senders to impart messages that are nearly impossible to communicate verbally. For example, a product's distinctive name, appearance and packaging communicate messages to consumers. See this chapter's Ethical Management feature about simulating packaging of name brand products. To further understand how valuable images can be, try to convey the drawing in Figure 10.3 using words alone.

A picture can communicate more effectively than words can. Boeing provides a good example of how computer graphics can be used to aid workers:

Researchers are developing head-mounted displays that put computer graphics to uses that are … helping workers do complex wiring or place the perfect rivet…. Cables connect the headset to a computer, which generates the image and changes it when the worker turns or proceeds to a new task; a magnetic or ultrasonic receiver on the helmet helps the system track its position … so the wearer sees a diagram superimposed on whatever he's working.[6]

Like pictures, gestures and body language convey messages. Research and your own experiences indicate that a sender's body language and other nonverbal expressions help

Figure 10.2	Five Written Forms of Communication
Letters	For correspondence with persons or groups outside an organization. Usually produced in a format—a form letter or block-style letter, for example.
Memos	For routine correspondence with superiors, subordinates and peers. Memos should contain the date, the names of intended receivers and their titles, the subject of the correspondence (ideally only one subject per memo), the message and the name and title of the sender. The ideal memo is no more than one page long.
Outlines	For indicating the structure of a lecture, report or agenda and to order major and minor points. Outlines are useful in developing tables of contents and summaries.
Reports	For reporting the results of an investigation or routine and ongoing activities. Report formats range from fill-in-the-blank styles to manuscripts with or without statistical data. The format is often prescribed.
E-mail	For routine correspondence. E-mails should contain a descriptive subject line, be clear and brief, be polite, and include a signature.

| **Figure 10.3** | **Exercise in Nonverbal Communication** |

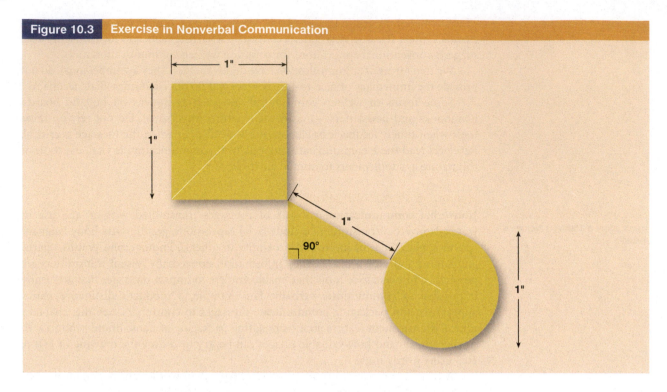

a receiver to understand the sender's feelings and intent. The upset boss communicates emotions through tortured facial expressions, clenched fists, aggressive gestures, a louder-than-normal voice, closer-than-normal physical presence and burning eye-to-eye contact—expressions that are all direct and intense.

Suppose a manager remains seated behind the desk when a visitor arrives, refuses to look at the person and grunts an acknowledgment of the visitor's presence. These behaviors transmit one or more of the following messages to the visitor: "This person is not pleased to see me," "I have done something to annoy this person," "This person does not respect me," or "Maybe this is not a good time to visit with this person." The manager sends quite a different set of messages if he or she rises and extends a hand, seeks eye contact, smiles broadly, and says, "It's great to see you. Have a seat!"

Senders and receivers must be aware of the messages inherent in nonverbal communication. When nonverbal cues seem to contradict the sender's verbal messages, the receiver tends to believe the nonverbal message.

Interpersonal Communication

Interpersonal communication involves real-time, face-to-face, or voice-to-voice (telephone) conversation that allows instant feedback. Interpersonal communication is appropriate for discussing matters that require give-and-take between participants. Applications include discussions about a performance appraisal; management by objectives (MBO) sessions; conversations in which praise or criticism is given; and coaching, counseling or training sessions. Meetings and conferences are useful forms of interpersonal communication when the issues affect others or require input from

interpersonal communication
Face-to-face or voice-to-voice (telephone) conversations that take place in real time and allow instant feedback

Profits through Imitation

How would you like to work for a company that makes most of its profits by imitating the best that name-brand cereal makers can create? That's what Ralcorp Holdings Inc., now a subsidiary of Treehouse Foods and a leader in private-label (or store-brand) foods, does to earn most its profits.

Compared with the high-priced national brands, Ralcorp's knockoffs sell for about $1 less per box at retail, while delivering more profit per box to retailers, who get their names on the box as well. Another positive result of private-label growth has been virtual wholesale price freezes on name-brand cereals.

Ralcorp works hard to simulate the look, taste and packaging of the name brands it mimics. In its plants, the company uses technology that helps it reproduce, as precisely as possible, the original recipes. Also, Ralcorp's names mimic those of the originals: Tasteeos for Cheerios, Fruit Rings for Froot Loops and Apple Dapples for Apple Jacks. Because cereals are made with routine manufacturing methods, the legality of copying most types of cereal is not an issue.

➡ Is what Ralcorp does a form of "legalized" theft?

➡ Why does Ralcorp try to imitate the packaging of name-brand cereals?

➡ What additional ethical issues do you see in this case?

Source: Ralcorp Holdings Inc., *http://www.ralcorp.com*.

---

more than one or two parties. Brainstorming sessions, quality circles, committee meetings and contract negotiations are but a few uses for interpersonal communication.[7]

Communication and Teams

Teams are taking an increasingly large role in organizations. Managers find that by putting workers together, they can get better work. Chapter 13 will explore team dynamics in detail; this chapter will focus on the management of team communication.

Team members generally engage in four kinds of communication. They exchange views, discuss work, deliberate on a problem or issue and transmit information.

Whether a team is a permanent work group or temporarily gathered to address an issue, team members share a leader, a goal or goals, related activities (though each member may have a distinct role) and mutual dependency. Each individual possesses unique traits, of course, but the shared characteristics build group identity. In fact, group members often develop common perspectives about management and the organization. These shared viewpoints arise first from the fact that group members affect each other but also from the fact that communications within the group transmit and reinforce similar attitudes. One key to managing intergroup communication, then, is to ensure that the viewpoints being shared are positive and match the organization's culture and goals.

Often disputes arise between group members and must be competently handled. Ellen Lord leads a team at Textron's Davidson Interiors plant in New Hampshire. She has "found that to keep teams happy, managers must have the patience and presence of mind to act like a parent, teacher and referee all at once."[8] As her team was forming, its members found a variety of issues to argue over. "A neatnik sitting next to a slob lost his cool. People were becoming emotional about what kind of coffee was brewing in the pot.... No matter how bad it gets you must keep people together and talking until they feel comfortable, a process that can take months."[9] See Figure 10.4 for a checklist that covers productive group and team communication.

Figure 10.4	Checklist for Ensuring Effective Communications between Groups and Group Members

1 Are members clear about the group's purposes and goals?   _____

2 Is each group member clear about his or her role?   _____

3 Do members know the procedures?   _____

4 Does mutual trust and respect exist between group members?   _____

5 Do all members have access to the information they need?   _____

6 Are formal discussions properly led and their results recorded?   _____

7 Do groups and their members receive prompt feedback on the results of their efforts?   _____

8 Do members periodically evaluate the effectiveness of their group and individual members' contributions?   _____

9 Are groups and their members given recognition and rewards for their valuable contribution?   _____

Much team communication revolves around getting the job done—copywriters talk to product managers about a product's features and target market, and designers discuss page layouts with copywriters. In this kind of communication, a manager is mainly concerned with ensuring that people send and receive accurate information, that all team members get the information they need when they need it, and that team members show sensitivity to one another's ideas and issues.

Team communication is vital when a group meets to explore an issue, determine how to implement a procedure, solve a technical problem or make a pricing decision. Group decision making offers many benefits. Hearing multiple perspectives can help a person generate more ideas than he or she could generate alone; the interaction of people can create a powerful synergy. In addition, participation increases commitment to the decision (see Chapter 5). Group deliberations, however, must be carefully managed to ensure that they are effective. Managers must set a clear agenda for the meeting and keep the discussion to the point. They need to ensure that all group members participate by channeling discussion to avoid domination by a few. They must keep an eye on the clock so the meeting does not waste time. See this chapter's Quality Management feature for an example of a Six Sigma team's communication plan.

Intra-team communication often involves the transmission of information. Whether a manager is informing team members about a new organizational policy or a team member is passing on the details of a telephone conversation, a team meeting is ideal for this kind of communication. Telling five people at once is far more efficient than seeking out and telling each one individually. Also, when information is transmitted to several people at a time, the chance of each team member receiving the same information increases. Finally, having the team assembled to hear this kind of message provides the opportunity for members to discuss its implications.[10]

BARRIERS TO INTERPERSONAL COMMUNICATION

List and explain the barriers to interpersonal communication and suggest remedies to overcome them

Leonard R. Sayles and George Strauss identify common barriers to interpersonal, or face-to-face, communication.[11] The paragraphs that follow summarize the barriers they define. These barriers can be overcome in large measure by following the guidelines for improving communication that appear toward the end of this chapter.

Quality Management

Communication Plan

Six Sigma is a quality management program that strives for near perfection. The first step in a Six Sigma project is to develop a project charter, which is an agreement between management and the Six Sigma team. It includes an overview of the project and its expected outcomes. A communication plan, as seen below, provides information to the team. It displays what will be communicated, who will do the communicating, when the communication will take place, to whom the communication will be delivered, how the communications will be delivered and where the information will be stored. [Note: A champion is the leader. A black belt is a Six Sigma expert. A war room is an area where project measures and progress are displayed for all to see. TBD is to be determined. COB is close of business.]

➤ Identify a group of which you are a member. List 2 or 3 projects the group would like to accomplish. Choose one of the projects and complete a communication plan for it.

Source: iSixSigma, "A Project Charter Communication Strategy is Essential," http://www.isixsigma.com/index.php?option=com_k2&view=item&id=1469:a-project-charter-communication-strategy-is-essential&Itemid=212.

SIX SIGMA PROJECT CHARTER COMMUNICATION PLAN

What	To Whom	When	Who	How	Where	Comments
Project team meetings	Project team, invitees	Weekly (every Thurs @ 9 a.m.)	Black Belt	Notices, agendas sent out one week ahead	War Room	
Meeting minutes	Distribution list	By next day COB	Black Belt or team scribe	Via e-mail	MS Word file on shared drive	
Team work/action items	Project team, Champion	TBD	Black Belt	Via e-mail	Nature of file TBD, placed on shared drive	
Status reports, including timeline	Project team, Champion, customer/client	Weekly (every Friday at COB)	Black Belt	Via e-mail	MS Word file on shared drive, e-mail to customer rep	
Project budget	Champion, project financial analyst, quality dept head	TBD	Black Belt or project financial analyst	Via e-mail	MS Excel file on Six Sigma database	
Project reviews	Project team, Champion, quality dept head	TBD (monthly)	Black Belt	Notices sent out one week ahead	Six Sigma conference room	
Project storyline	Deployment Champion, quality dept head, senior management	TBD	Black Belt or team members	Gallery walk notices sent out two weeks prior	Six Sigma gallery room	

diction
The choice and use of words in speech and writing

semantics
The study of the meanings of words

Diction and Semantics Diction—the choice and use of words in speech and writing—significantly affects communication. **Semantics**, the study of the meanings of words, confirms that words may possess different meanings for different people. In everyday usage, abstract words such as *liberal, conservative* and *motivate* can create different images for senders and receivers. Business terms can cause the same problems. Terms such as *discipline* and *grievance* can convey both negative and positive connotations and may elicit a strong emotional response. The effective communicator is sensitive to such effects.

In today's culturally diverse workplaces, English is a second language to many. To overcome problems related to this situation, companies are providing basic English courses. They are also capitalizing on America's racially diverse population by sharing experiences within teams. This chapter's Valuing Diversity feature discusses some of the benefits of racial diversity.

Jargon—the specialized or technical language that develops in trades, professions, subcultures and other groups—poses its own set of hazards. Each corporate culture, subculture, unit and division has its own unique terminology and slang expressions. Computer experts talk about *bits, bytes* and *boilerplate.* Financial managers use terms like *leverage, equity* and *depreciation.* When members of these subcultures use these expressions in an attempt to communicate outside their group, confusion can result.

jargon
The specialized or technical language of a trade, profession, subculture or other group

The lesson for communicators is clear. Strive for language that means the same thing to both receiver and sender. The sender who has any doubt about the possible interpretation of unusual, specialized, or vague words should take extra care to ask receivers if they understand the terms. Newcomers to U.S. culture and language deserve special attention. Slang can be treacherous to those new to the United States. A simple phrase like, "Hang on, I'm going to IM Jerrod on my cell and bounce this idea off him," will confuse most newcomers. In fact, they might look at you as if you had just switched to an alien dialect—and in terms of classroom English, you have.

Expectations of Familiarity How many times have you been in a conversation and tuned out the speaker because you absolutely knew what he or she was going to say? People do this because they are familiar with a speaker's thoughts on particular topics. The speaker begins with a statement and tone that sounds similar to openings used in

Valuing Diversity and Inclusion

Benefits of Racial Diversity

According to Harvard Business School Professors Robin Ely and David Thomas, racial diversity results in a more productive company. Professor Ely defines cultural diversity as "group differences in identity, particularly concerning groups that are socioculturally distinct and have different power positions in society." He further asserts, "Sociocultural distinctions may be race, ethnicity, gender, religion, nationality and sexual orientation" (Lagace). Ely and Thomas studied racial diversity in work groups in a large commercial bank in the northeastern United States.

Their study yielded three distinct perspectives on racial diversity in work groups (Lagace):

1. **Discrimination and fairness perspective.** The work groups aspire to being color blind, so conversations around race are limited. They believe there is no connection between race and the work, but racial bias can end up being destructive in the work group.

2. **Access and legitimacy perspective.** There is diversity only in certain parts of the organization. People are effectively shunted onto segregated career tracks and told, "This is what you're good at."

3. **Integration and learning perspective.** Group members are encouraged to bring all relevant insights and perspectives to bear on their work.

Only the third perspective, integration and learning, resulted in performance gains.

➡ **How can work groups learn from members' different experiences rather than ignore or suppress them?**

Source: Martha Lagace, "Racial Diversity Pays Off," *HBS Working Knowledge,* June 21, 2004.

the past. At that moment, listening stops. When a parent begins by saying, "When I was your age …," the child tunes out. When the boss begins with "When I did your job, I …," the subordinate tunes out. Failure to listen because of the listener's expectation of familiarity is a factor that inhibits communication.

When addressing people on familiar topics, senders should engage their receivers by asking questions about their understanding and current knowledge of the topic. If receivers already know what a sender wants to communicate, no further effort is needed. If what is about to be sent is new, senders should state that fact and proceed to convey the new data.

Source's Lack of Credibility If a sender has credibility in the receiver's mind, the message will be received more readily than if the sender lacks credibility. When a person proven to have knowledge and a successful track record speaks about his or her specialty, people tend to listen. The finance manager is presumed to have more expertise in budgetary matters than the marketing manager. The experienced plant manager's ideas about how to handle a maintenance problem should prevail over those of his or her apprentice. New and inexperienced employees, however, often bring a fresh, unbiased approach to problems. They may spot more effective or efficient ways to get things done. Their ideas deserve a hearing. Empowering employees means giving them the freedom and authority to offer suggestions and devise new solutions.

Preconceived Notions If the new and different viewpoint the receivers hear contradicts what they "know" to be true, the receivers do not accept it. In reacting this way, the receivers close their minds and inhibit growth and change. They shut others out even though the others could be the means of the receivers' own growth and development.

Differing Perceptions Most organizations include people from different social, economic and cultural backgrounds. These people may hold a variety of values, beliefs, expectations and goals. They may even speak different languages. These differences contribute to differing **perceptions**—ways of observing and the bases for making judgments. Predetermined sets of conventional and oversimplified beliefs about groups of people—**stereotypes**—can elicit an array of typical reactions, both positive and negative, to those groups. "He's Hispanic, so he must be …," "Women just don't …," and "Germans always …" are expressions of stereotypes. Stereotypes can inhibit interaction and communication. Everyone needs to keep an open mind.

perceptions
Ways in which people observe and the bases for their judgments about the stimuli they experience

stereotypes
Predetermined beliefs about a group of people

Conflicting Nonverbal Communication A person who frowns while saying, "I feel great," is sending conflicting messages. The manager who squirms in her seat and keeps checking her watch while telling us to continue a conversation is really telling us to stop.

A person's physical appearance and behavior send messages. Suppose a manager urges employees to strive for thoroughness. The urgings are likely to go unheeded if the manager always looks sloppy. Whatever a manager says about the need for continual improvement may be mitigated if he or she is never on time for meetings. Tardiness says that other things are more important, that the meeting is unnecessary, or that other people's time has no value.

Emotions Tempers interfere with reason and understanding; therefore, they inhibit communication. Sender and receiver become opponent and adversary. When the head coach of the Chicago Bears lost his temper on the sidelines during a football game, sports commentators and some team members claimed that it turned the momentum in favor of the opposing team. The Bears had a fourteen-point lead at the time but scored no more points and lost the game. Attempts at achieving a meeting of the minds dissolved into name calling and offensive remarks and behaviors. Messages communicated in anger can be damaging to people and their relationships for some time thereafter. Once offensive words are spoken, they cannot be unsaid. Apologies will not erase the hurt that receivers feel.

The best way to overcome the barriers to communication emotions can pose is to develop a sense of *timing*. This important sense helps a sender know when best to initiate a communication. Sam shows sensitivity to timing when he says, "I wouldn't see the boss today. He's just heard that his new budget was rejected." Similarly, the end of a tiring workday, when people are less open to communication, is not the best time to attempt to convey complex messages.

Noise Anything in the environment that interferes with the sending and receiving of messages is **noise**. If you have ever tried to speak over the roar of machinery or over a telephone with a bad connection, you know how noise interferes with communication. When people have to shout to be heard or are overburdened with irrelevant messages, they are experiencing noise.

noise
Anything in the environment of a communication that interferes with the sending and receiving of messages

ORGANIZATIONAL COMMUNICATION

Now that we understand how people communicate on an interpersonal level, we are ready to explore organizational communication. This section will begin by discussing the **formal communication channels**, the channels that result from a company's organizational structure. These designated pipelines for messages run in three directions: upward, downward and horizontally. Managers are charged with the responsibility of creating, using and keeping these channels open and available to organization members. The channels act as connections between members and outsiders and as paths through which official communications flow.

One look at a company's formal organization chart will reveal who is connected to whom and, therefore, in which directions communications will flow. Figure 10.5

formal communication channels
Management-designated pipelines—running up, down and across the organizational structure—used for official communication efforts

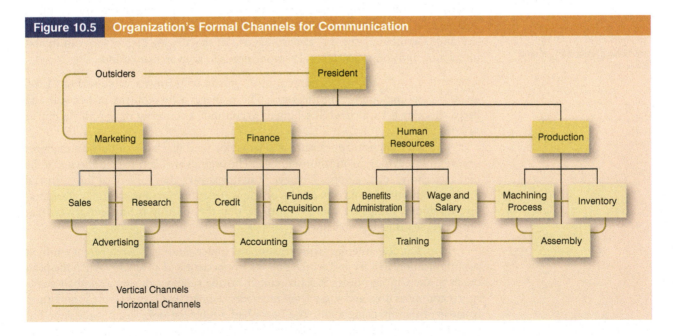

Figure 10.5 **Organization's Formal Channels for Communication**

shows a formal organization chart and the communication links between line and staff managers. Remember that communication is a two-way effort, so these channels carry messages from, as well as to, the persons they link.

In the not-too-distant past, formal communication flowed down from the top and rarely in any other direction. A strict chain of command existed at each level in every work unit or subsystem. Feedback efforts were difficult and time-consuming. A great dependence on paper and written communication was the norm. Orders were given, procedures were written, and those who received them obeyed them.

Today organizations emphasize electronic means of communicating, empowerment of employees, flexibility and integrated teams. Therefore, compared with the past, more communication flows from the bottom up and from side to side.

Communications currently are faster, more direct and subject to less filtering than in the past. Computer networks, satellite communications and teleconferencing link those who must work together—even if they are in another part of town or in another country. With a computer or smart phone and a connection to the Internet an employee is never out of touch. These days, managers and workers occupy offices that are, in effect, without walls.

4 Describe the uses of downward, horizontal, and upward communication channels

Formal Downward Channels

Downward communication conveys the kinds of information shown in Figure 10.6. Along with the messages themselves, managers should communicate the reasoning behind the messages—why things are being done and the advantages and disadvantages that may result. Sharing reasons has the effect of bringing others into the decision-making process. As Chapter 5 reported, the results can be extremely beneficial.

Figure 10.6	Subjects for Downward, Horizontal, and Upward Communication

DOWNWARD COMMUNICATION	
CEO's vision	Job designs
Changes in rules or procedures	Performance appraisals
Company mission	Policies
Delegation of authority	Solutions
Development	Staff managers' advice
Feedback	Strategic goals
Incentives	Training

HORIZONTAL COMMUNICATION	
Coordination efforts	Information to and about customers
Efforts to seek assistance	Information to and about suppliers
Feedback	Group-member interactions

UPWARD COMMUNICATION	
Complaints	Requests for assistance
Feedback	Status reports
Recommended solutions	Research results

Downward communication takes place daily, in on-the-job conversations and interactions between managers or team leaders and their subordinates. It can be one on one or take place in large meetings. Typical devices used to carry downward communication are company procedure manuals, newsletters, public relations announcements, annual statements, and various types of memos, reports, letters and directives.

The cofounders of Zingerman's Deli in Ann Arbor, Michigan, began their company newsletter when the deli got too large for them to talk to all 130 employees. The cofounders justified the cost of the newsletter because it gave them a way to communicate with their workers. As Ellen Spragins reports, the cofounders give three reasons for the newsletter's positive reception:

1   *Nothing gets published that is offensive or a put-down.*

2   *The editor receives extra pay for producing the newsletter. Therefore, the editor has an incentive for producing a quality communication that will appeal to the workers.*

3   *Some 30 percent of the newsletter's content is created by the frontline employees (the remainder comes from the managers and cofounders).*[12]

The newsletter has become so popular that outsiders are willing to pay for a subscription to it. Zingerman's website, *zingermans.com*, shares four different electronic newsletters (enews), a blog and a Facebook page. *Zingerman's Guide to Good Leading, Part 1: A Lapsed Anarchist's Approach to Building a Great Business* is the first in a series of books by Zingerman's co-founding partner Ari Weinzweig. He writes about the management principles and methods that have made Zingerman's Community of Businesses successful. Zingerman's uses its network to get more and better information about great food out there where people can use it.

Formal Horizontal Channels

As Figure 10.6 implies, horizontal channels connect people of similar rank and status within an organization (such as engineers and team members) and outside stakeholders (such as dealers and customers) with those insiders who can best meet their needs. Through horizontal channels, workers and managers provide feedback, keep teammates informed, coordinate activities, seek assistance and stay in contact with customers.

Toll-free, long-distance telephone lines for customers are horizontal channels that connect consumers with people in the company, no matter what level, who can best answer their questions or meet their needs. Transmitting voice over the Internet has become a catalyst in the continuing drop in international telecommunications rates. Net2Phone was the first company to bridge the Internet with telephone networks. Internet telephony, known as VoIP or voice over Internet protocol, is the technology that enables the real-time transmission of voice signals over the IP network. Voice is transmitted over the Internet by using public telephone switching networks for the minimum portion of the call and the Internet to carry the call over the widest distance.

Real-time communication over the Internet adds a customer service dimension and enhances a website. For example, customers leaving e-mail messages or sending a text may be "guaranteed" a return call from a "live" company representative within a specified time parameter. Or customers entering questions or queries may be answered through Internet telephony, shared browsing or real-time text chats, as depicted in Figure 10.7.

Figure 10.7   Real-Time Customer Support

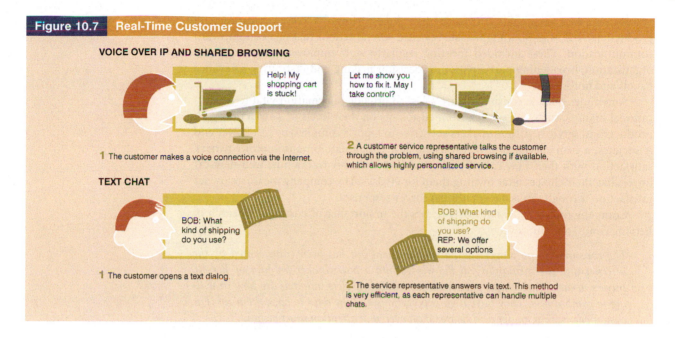

VOICE OVER IP AND SHARED BROWSING

Help! My shopping cart is stuck!

Let me show you how to fix it. May I take control?

1 The customer makes a voice connection via the Internet.

2 A customer service representative talks the customer through the problem, using shared browsing if available, which allows highly personalized service.

TEXT CHAT

BOB: What kind of shipping do you use?

BOB: What kind of shipping do you use?
REP: We offer several options

1 The customer opens a text dialog.

2 The service representative answers via text. This method is very efficient, as each representative can handle multiple chats.

A number of companies now use satellite-transmitted videoconferences for interpersonal communication. A retailer, for example, can regularly run videoconferences between its managers at headquarters and those in its stores nationwide. The managers at headquarters make a presentation, and the store managers are invited to ask questions.

Horizontal communication channels are used to: set goals; define roles; create, examine and improve methods; enhance working relationships; define, investigate and solve problems; and gather, process and distribute information.

Horizontal communication is becoming increasingly important as managers institute more and more work teams. One observer pointed out the advantages of horizontal communication and the team approach: "Information moves straight to where it's needed, unfiltered by a hierarchy. If you have a problem with people upstream from you, you deal with them directly, rather than asking your boss to talk to theirs." Professor Shoshana Zuboff of Harvard University calls for all companies to "informate" employees by placing the corporation at their fingertips—giving them real-time access to all the information and experts in the system.[13]

Formal Upward Channels

Upward communication provides the feedback required by downward communication. It allows workers to request assistance in solving some problems, and it provides a means for workers to recommend solutions to other problems. Upward communication also permits workers to provide status reports and inform higher authorities about employee complaints. The tools of upward communication are employee surveys; newsletters; regular meetings between managers and their subordinates; suggestion systems; team meetings; and an open-door policy, which offers employee access to managers.

When asked what their companies had done to improve communication and productivity, CEOs responding to a survey cited several actions that related to upward communication. These included meeting regularly with employees, delayering the organization, broadening participation in decision making and instituting grievance panels and hotlines.[14]

Sometimes outside consultants are asked to provide information vital to organizational matters, such as feedback from customers on their levels of satisfaction with products and services. All automakers subscribe to reports compiled by J.D. Power and Associates, a firm specializing in gathering and selling data on automobile owners' satisfaction with their new cars. Its most celebrated survey tracks how well new-car buyers like their choices after owning them for 90 days. The company measures owner satisfaction through thousands of annual survey responses.

Company founder J.D. Power III relates the importance of customer research in helping companies improve.

> *The consumer is no longer the passive recipient but has been transformed by the Internet and the availability of knowledge into a powerbroker for him or herself. Buyers in auto dealerships, patients in hospitals, travelers in hotels are now unwilling to compromise. They have high expectations and the data to back them up. The customer's voice is louder and clearer than ever, and attention must be paid.*[15]

The challenge for many organizations is how to use customer feedback to improve their customer experience. Measurement is just the first step. When Chrysler vehicles did not rate well in J.D. Power and Associates' surveys, Chrysler hired Detroit-based Process Development Corporation (PDC) to help the company improve its ratings. According to Tom Kowaleski, a Chrysler spokesperson, PDC's job was to study the survey's questions—what they rate and how—and "what we should look at when we build a car."[16] Chrysler has learned that such things as the "feel" of a knob, switch or dial and the "location" of cup holders and ashtrays are as important as smooth-running engines and transmissions. As a result, the company considered removing equipment that prompted complaints from those interviewed by J.D. Power.[17]

Formal Communication Networks

Formal communication networks are electronic links between people and their equipment as well as between people and databases that store information. Organizations have linked their desktop computers for years. Computers began as an engineering tool and later as a means of storing data. Today they are essential to business. The timeline of computer use in business is discussed in Chapter 14.

Informal Communication Channels

The formal communication channels designed by management are not the only means of communication in an organization. **Informal communication channels** carry casual, social and personal messages on a regular basis in or around the workplace. These channels are often called, collectively, the **grapevine**. Informal communication channels disseminate rumors, gossip, accurate as well as inaccurate information, and on occasion, official messages. Anyone inside or outside an organization can originate a grapevine message. Grapevine messages are transmitted in many ways—face-to-face and by telephone, e-mail, fax or social networks.

Messages transmitted through informal channels usually result from incomplete information from official sources, environmental influences in the organization or

formal communication networks
Electronic links between people and their equipment and between people and databases

Explain the informal communication channel known as the grapevine

informal communication channels
The informal networks, existing outside the formal channels, which are used to transmit casual, personal and social messages at work

grapevine
An informal communication channel

outside it, and the basic human need to socialize and stay informed. When changes occur, people like to speculate about what they will mean. When people feel insecure or fearful because of cutbacks and layoffs, rumors fly about what will happen next. When Jill is absent from her job, friends and coworkers want to know why. People who are the first to know something special usually want to share their new knowledge with others. Figure 10.8 shows how messages might travel through the grapevine. The grapevine has a number of characteristics:

- It can penetrate the tightest security.
- It is fast (with or without electronic links).
- It tends to carry messages from anonymous sources.
- Its messages are difficult to stop or counter once they get started.
- It is accessible to every person in an organization.
- It can be supportive of or an obstacle to management's efforts.

In most organizations, a relatively small number of individuals disseminate most of the grapevine messages. These people create networks through which the messages are carried. Managers need to be attuned to the grapevine—that is, they should be aware of the messages it carries and the people who control it. They should not, however, use it as a formal communication channel. But inaccurate messages must be countered with the truth as soon as possible.

Figure 10.9 illustrates four common grapevine configurations. The most common is the cluster chain. Through it, an initiator—A, in this case—sends a message to a cluster, or group, which consists of B, E and L. Through their own connections, these three send the message to others. Each party involved often distorts the message. Not all recipients carry the message to others. If a recipient has no interest in a grapevine communication or disagrees with it, he or she probably does not pass it along.

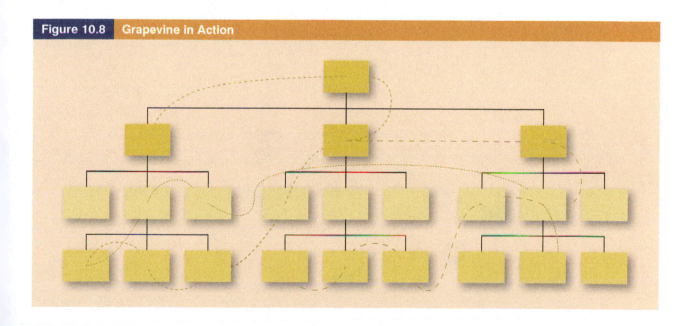

Figure 10.8   Grapevine in Action

Figure 10.9   **Four Common Grapevine Configurations**

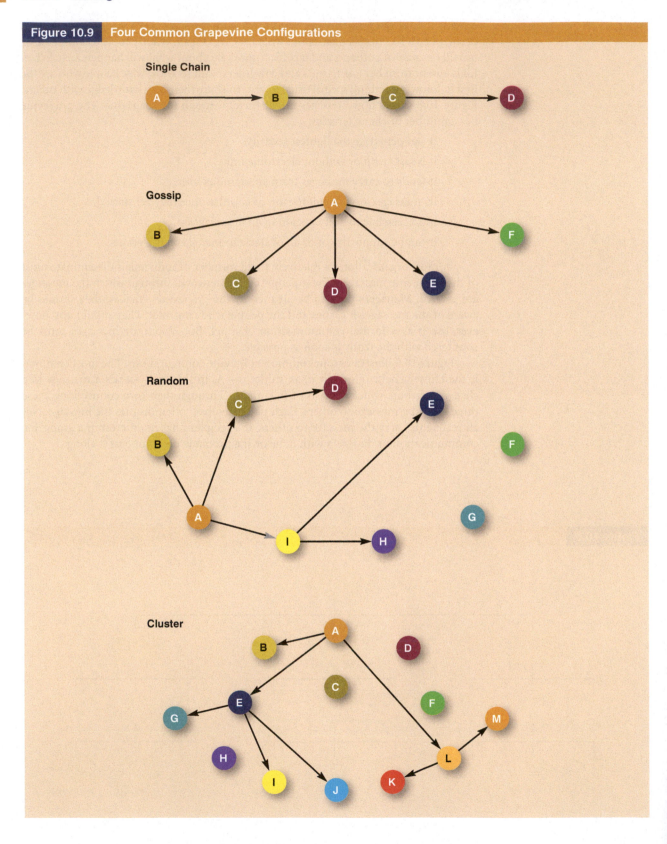

List and explain the barriers to organizational communication and suggest remedies to overcome them

BARRIERS TO ORGANIZATIONAL COMMUNICATION

Communication in organizations can be blocked by interpersonal barriers and by barriers that are part of the organizational environment. The way workstations are positioned in an office or factory can enhance or hinder communication, for example. People who cannot see each other or who are not in close physical proximity may find it difficult to stay in touch, although telephones, e-mail and social networks can diminish the difficulty.

The paragraphs that follow will review several barriers to organizational communication.

Overload In the context of communication, the term *overload* means too much information. Everyone receives dozens of pieces of junk mail at home each week. The same thing occurs in plants and offices every day. People receive information they do not want or need. This overload is a type of noise, and employees are forced to waste time trying to sort through it. One job for a company's management information system specialist is to make certain that people receive only what they need and that they receive it in the form that is most useful to them.

Filtering by Levels The management levels in a company can become barriers to communication. According to Keith Davis, the more levels information has to pass through, the more it can be embellished or filtered.[18] The message the last receiver acquires may bear little resemblance to the original communication. The current trend toward flattened organizational structures should help to prevent such distortion.

Alcoa, the subject of this chapter's Application Case, reengineered its organizational structure and working relationships from the mechanistic to the organic. One reason for this action was to remove physical and structural barriers that delayed decision making and responses to rapidly changing customer needs. By reducing levels of management and grouping people together in open workspace, Alcoa greatly improved communications and coordination.

Timing Communications that must pass through several hands can delay the process. Anything in an organization that prevents the free and quick flow of needed information impedes communication. The spread of high-speed communication technologies (such as e-mail) and the growing use of teams (whose members are trained to recognize the need to share information) are expected to reduce barriers to prompt communication. For example, employees can connect and communicate more efficiently with the company, customers, suppliers and others with the aid of communication tools. "These include real-time channels (mobile phones, audio conferences), near-real-time channels (instant messaging, paging) and messaging (e-mail, fax, voice mail)."[19] Some guidelines for e-mail courtesy, known as *netiquette,* can be seen in Figure 10.10.

Lack of Trust and Openness Companies that are secretive about sharing vital information with employees lack openness; such behavior says that they do not trust their workers. Today, organizations are expected to be transparent, participating and collaborating not only with employees, but with customers and stakeholders as well.

The importance of both trust and transparency is noted in the 2016 Edelman Trust Barometer®, an annual survey, which gauges attitudes about the state of trust in business, government, NGOs (non-governmental organizations) and media across 23 countries. "Trust in institutions is no longer automatically granted on the basis

Figure 10.10	**E-mail Courtesy (Netiquette)**

When sending e-mail messages, practice e-mail etiquette by following these guidelines:
- Use a descriptive subject line in your mail header.
- DON'T PUT YOUR MESSAGES IN ALL UPPERCASE LETTERS. Readers will think you are shouting.
- Use the * (asterisk) before and after a word for emphasis. Avoid bold and underline.
- Remember, anything you send could become common knowledge. Reread your message before sending.
- Include your name, position and affiliation at the bottom of e-mail messages.

of hierarchy or title. In today's world, that trust must be earned," observed Edelman president and CEO Richard Edelman.[20]

Consumers will bestow trust on companies who deliver quality products, communicate frequently and honestly, and consider the role of business in society. An opportunity exists for companies to commit to open communication and a collaborative approach that benefits society. One way to keep the communication channels open is through social media, the topic of this chapter's Managing Social Media.

Insufficient openness in organizational communications derives from a lack of trust or from the fear that wrongdoing will be exposed. That's what happened when Don Carty, former top manager of American Airlines, kept information about executive retention packages from the unions.

> *American issued a statement saying labor leaders had been informed of the [executive] retention package but did not tell their members. Labor leaders went ballistic, since it turned out this statement was not true. When American later retracted its statement, the gap of credibility widened even further. Carty then issued an apology saying, "it was not my intent to mislead anyone." He acknowledged, "My mistake was failing to explicitly describe these retention benefits, and because of that, many employees felt*

Managing Social Media

Social Media for Communications

Social media is transforming the way businesses communicate with their customers, partners, and employees. Richard Hughes, Director of Social Strategy at Broad Vision and the author of *The Business Communication Revolution*, relates that there are three types of social networks used by business:

- **The Public Social Network** includes Facebook, Twitter, Google+, YouTube, Pinterest, LinkedIn, Instagram, Tumblr, etc. These are used for making contact with customers.

- **The Social Extranet** is made up of private communities and are used for deeper customer conversations. Customer communities encourage peer-to-peer, as well as company knowledge, to solve customer problems. The business can collaborate with vendors and agencies.

- **The Social Intranet** is private employee social networks connecting employees to each other allowing them to share knowledge throughout the organization.

Source: *http://communication-revolution.biz/.*

they were kept in the dark." The apology rang hollow. Carty's credibility was gone. And within six days of these developments, so was he.[21]

Workers and managers at some companies use team-building exercises to develop good working relationships and mutual trust. Everyone from the chairman of the board to the customer-service representatives undergo the same training program. The programs may consist of games such as blindfolded dart throwing. Blindfolded throwers have little chance of hitting the target unless others coach them, which helps foster a sense of trust and cooperation.

Inappropriate Span of Control If a manager supervises more people than time and energy permit, communication suffers. The manager who has too few people to oversee may become overbearing and overwhelm subordinates with too much contact. The more that leaders empower their people by delegating authority and providing quick access to needed information, the less they need to worry about keeping communication effective. Well-trained, self-managing work teams know that when they require help, all they have to do is seek it. Until then, the manager should observe, track and facilitate as needed.

Change Changes anywhere in a company can hurt or hinder communication. When a new manager takes over, he or she invariably introduces changes in goals, methods and communication style. What matters is how well people are prepared to cope with the changes. Larry Senn, head of Senn-Delaney Leadership Consulting Group, in California, has this advice: "Take the time to describe your expectations to people. In a small organization, one person who's not open to change and not a team player can really gum up the works."[22]

Rank or Status in the Company Unfortunately, in too many organizations the higher a manager is in the hierarchy, the less available he or she seems to be to others. Faced with rank or status, some subordinates can become timid and hesitant to communicate, or willing to communicate good news only. Some people in high positions begin to imagine that they are something special, an attitude that leads them to avoid listening to what subordinates have to offer.

In *Riding the Runaway Horse*, Charles C. Kenney examines the fall of Wang Laboratories. He attributes the company's decline to, among other things, an unwillingness to respect diverse opinions and stay close to customers. An Wang, the founder, created two classes of stock to avoid stockholder influences on his decisions. He delayed moving into the personal computer field until that field fell to others. He announced the development of new products when the products were nothing but ideas on paper. And, on his deathbed, he fired his son and president, Fred Wang, so that Fred would be blamed for the company's failures. In the words of a former president at Wang, John Cunningham, An Wang had become "a humble egomaniac."[23]

Managers' Interpretations Managers, like everyone else, are people with biases, stereotypes, values, needs, morals and ethics. How they perceive their world determines how they will react to it. Managers will communicate where, when, what and to whom they believe they must. As an example, consider the manager who is facing a crisis and asks for emergency funding for additional overtime. He needs the approval quickly, but the finance manager who receives the request is in no hurry. She wants to defer the request until next year's budget kicks in, a wait of about two months. When pressured for a decision, she responds: "You'll get the money you requested when I decide to give it." Both managers have different needs and agendas. Both have differing perspectives, priorities—and notions of courtesy.

Electronic Noise Modern electronics have added yet more noise to the work environment. Breakdowns, overloads, static on the line, slow loading websites and ill-trained operators are barriers to organizational communication. Voicemail systems can be barriers to communication. If a manager leaves a voicemail and asks the receiver to share the information at a meeting, the receiver may misinterpret the message, creating message noise. Customer frustration grows when individuals cannot get through the voicemail system to find the answers to their questions. Furthermore, if users don't receive proper training on the appropriate uses of hardware and software, potential electronic noise will be experienced. Employees waste time and make mistakes trying to work through unnecessary noise.

IMPROVEMENT OF COMMUNICATION

Describe the responsibilities of senders and receivers during the communication process

Being adept at communicating involves individual skills as well as organizational frameworks and aids. Both the sender and the receiver have distinct responsibilities in the communication process. Meeting those responsibilities can help both parties avoid or overcome barriers to communication.

Responsibilities of Senders

Those who send messages must shape them and be aware of how they are received. The paragraphs that follow discuss the sender's responsibilities.

Being Certain of Intent The sender's first task is to be clear about the intent of the message. Figure 10.11 lists some typical goals of communication. As the exhibit shows, the goals often vary according to the receiver. One goal common to all messages is that the receiver understands them.

Knowing the Receiver and Constructing the Message Accordingly The sender should acquire as much information as possible about the individual or group that is to receive the message. The sender needs to know the receiver's job, experience, personality, perceptions and needs. If the sender and receiver use different native languages, are from different cultures, or have had significantly different experiences, the sender must be aware of the barriers these differences could pose. For instance, pictures and

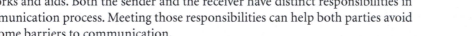

Figure 10.11	Typical Communication Goals

When communicating with superiors
- To provide responses to requests
- To keep them informed of progress
- To solicit help in solving problems
- To sell ideas and suggestions for improvement
- To seek clarification of instructions

When communicating with peers
- To share ideas for improvement
- To coordinate activities
- To provide assistance
- To get to know them as individuals

When communicating with subordinates
- To issue instructions
- To persuade and sell
- To appraise performance
- To compliment, reward and discipline
- To clarify intentions and instructions
- To get to know them as individuals

charts may be the best way to communicate when senders and receivers do not speak the same native languages.

The sender must choose, rather than his or her own words, those with the receiver's vocabulary in mind. While composing a message, the sender should try to get into the head of the receiver; would the receiver understand the message as conveyed? One basic goal of all communication is to help the receiver view the content of the message as the sender does. The sender should emphasize aspects of the message that relate to the receiver. If the message announces a change, the sender should point out the advantages that will result for the receiver. If the purpose is to ask for assistance, the sender should cite what the receiver will gain by providing it.

Selecting the Proper Medium The choice of the medium to carry the message depends in part on the content of the message. Confidential information and praise always call for a personal touch. If the receiver is in a remote location or if the matter is complex and lengthy, putting it in writing might be the best choice. If the receiver prefers a given medium, the sender should try to use that method. A sightless person may prefer a voice message or one encoded in Braille. A person who has a hearing difficulty may prefer a visual presentation. Finally, the sender must consider the physical and emotional environment to be faced when attempting to communicate. What kind of noise will there be?

Timing the Transmission The timing of the communication affects its success. The sender's needs, along with the receiver's, must be considered in determining the best time. A supervisor may want to talk with a subordinate at 4:00 P.M., but if the worker's day ends at 3:30, another meeting time must be agreed upon. Business communications should be delivered under the proper circumstances, and to people who are in a receptive mood. Important discussions about a new budget would be inappropriate at a company picnic or when people are on their breaks. People who are clearly overwhelmed with work when a sender contacts them cannot give their full attention to the message.

Seeking and Giving Feedback A sender has the primary responsibility to make certain that his or her message has been received and understood. The only way to make certain is to get feedback. The sender cannot settle for the response, "I understand." If the receiver has no questions, then the sender should pose some. One technique to assess understanding is to ask the receiver to restate the message using his or her own words. Another approach is to ask questions to check on the receiver's grasp of specifics.

As the receiver engages in feedback, he or she may ask questions that require responses from the sender. At this time the sender must assess how the receiver has interpreted the message and then take the actions needed to clear up any misunderstandings.

Responsibilities of Receivers

Just as senders have specific obligations, so do receivers. The paragraphs that follow discuss these responsibilities.

Listening Actively Receivers must listen attentively to the message being sent. Listening attentively requires that receivers block out distractions that can interfere with communication. Because people tend to speak more slowly than listeners can process words, listeners' minds can often wander. Receivers must not attempt to pass judgment on the sender or the message until the message has been completely transmitted. Being critical distracts from listening. According to John J. Gabarro, a professor of human resource management at the Harvard Business School, "The greatest barrier to effective communication is the tendency to evaluate what another person is saying and therefore to misunderstand or to not really 'hear.'"[24]

Active listeners take notes and list any areas where a sender's meanings are unclear. Good listeners ask questions to clarify messages. They observe gestures, tone of voice, facial expressions and body language, and look for any contradictions that might occur among them. If necessary, they seek explanations for the contradictions.

Being Sensitive to the Sender Senders communicate because they believe they must. They pick a certain medium, time and receiver because they see these elements of communication as appropriate. Receivers should approach every communication with the assumption that the message is important to the sender. They should try to discover why that is so and what value the message has for them as receivers. Being sensitive means not interrupting or distracting the speaker. If a sender is having trouble making the message clear, the receiver must try to help or act to postpone communication until the sender is better prepared.

Indicating an Appropriate Medium Receivers can often facilitate communication by stating a preference for a certain medium. Many managers want to receive important messages in writing so that they can study and store them. E-mail, faxes, letters, memos and reports can meet these requirements. Sometimes the request is for a face-to-face meeting so that two or more people can interact. Expressing a preference speeds up a communication effort and removes possible guesswork by the sender. Both parties, therefore, should be more comfortable. Of course, company rules and procedures or a union contract often specify preferred mediums for the handling of routine communications.

One advantage of e-mail is being able to prioritize messages, whereas with voice mail or answering machine messages the receiver must listen to them in sequence no matter how unimportant. When e-mail messages are checked, a list of senders and topics are displayed on the computer screen. Receivers can use the subject lines to prioritize messages and select which message to read first, and then reply immediately by clicking a reply button, typing a response and clicking "send." Junk mail and other mail that is not pertinent can be deleted without opening it. E-mail software allows users to filter and categorize their e-mail. Receivers can let senders know if they don't want to be on someone's group mailing list. All the people on a group mailing list should want to be there.

Initiating Feedback The receiver bears the primary responsibility for providing feedback. Until the receiver states his or her interpretation of the message, the sender will never know if it was understood. Similarly, the receiver cannot be certain that he or she has understood the sender's intentions until the receiver summarizes the message and obtains confirmation that the summary was correct. When a receiver cannot restate a message, it is a sure sign that he or she did not understand it. Samsung, the topic of this chapter's Global Applications feature, uses customer feedback to improve its product quality and design.

Ten Commandments of Good Communication

The American Management Association International has prepared guidelines for effective communication that serve as a useful summary of, and offer additional insights into, much of what we have examined in this chapter. Figure 10.12 presents these guidelines.

Samsung Buys Quality and Design Message

South Korea's Samsung is one of the world's leading brands in electronics and appliances. Yet it wasn't always a leader. In 1969, Samsung began making televisions with technology borrowed from Sanyo. Its models carried low sticker prices, but the televisions compared poorly in quality to sets made by other manufacturers.

Then in 1988 the company entered the mobile phone market with a commitment to quality. In 2001 the company's Spanish subsidiary, Samsung Electronica Espanola SA (SESA), was certified in the Hardware category for the quality control system known as Technology Leadership 9000 (TL9000). Samsung Electronica is distinguished as being the first company to receive such certification. Based on ISO 9001, TL9000 is the most advanced quality control system in the telecommunications industry.

Next, in 1993, the company decided that in addition to quality, its products would emphasize design. "Samsung's design focus goes well beyond just the look and feel of its products. The company is working to improve the way people use and control gadgets" (Rocks and Ihlwan). By 2004, Samsung was the best-selling brand in high-end TVs in the United States. "Good design is the most important way to differentiate ourselves from our competitors," said CEO Kang Yun Je (Rocks and Ihlwan).

"With its Galaxy Note series, Samsung introduced a new category of smartphone—the phablet—which has been widely copied by competitors. Design is now so much a part of its corporate DNA that top leaders rely on designers to help visualize the future of the entire company" (Yoo & Kim).

➤ Chung Kook Hyun, the Senior Vice President who runs design operations for Samsung says, "Just as a lizard cuts off its own tail to move on, we will have to break with the past to move forward." How do you think feedback has helped Samsung move forward?

Source: Youngjin Yoo and Kyungmook Kim, "How Samsung Became a Design Powerhouse," *Harvard Business Review*, September 2015, https://hbr.org/2015/09/how-samsung-became-a-design-powerhouse; David Rocks and Moon Ihlwan, "Samsung Design," *Business Week*, November 29, 2004, http://www.businessweek.com/magazine/content/04_48/b3910003.htm.

Figure 10.12	The American Management Association International's Ten Commandments of Good Communication

1. Clarify your ideas before communicating. The more systematically you analyze the problem or idea to be communicated, the clearer it becomes. This is the first step toward effective communication.

2. Examine the true purpose of each communication. Before you communicate, ask yourself what you really want to accomplish with your message—obtain information, initiate action, change another person's attitude? Identify your most important goal and then adapt your language, tone and total approach to serve that specific objective.

3. Consider the total physical and human setting whenever you communicate. Meaning and intent are conveyed by more than words alone.

4. Consult with others, when appropriate. Frequently, it is desirable or necessary to seek the participation of others in planning a communication or developing the facts on which to base it.

5. Be mindful, while you communicate, of the overtones as well as the basic content of your message. Your tone of voice, expression and apparent receptiveness to the responses of others has tremendous impact on those you wish to reach.

6. Take the opportunity, when it arises, to convey something of help or value to the receiver. Consideration of the other person's interests and needs will frequently highlight opportunities to convey something of immediate benefit or long-range value to the receiver.

7. Follow up your communication. Unless you follow up, your best efforts at communication may be wasted and you may never know whether you have succeeded in expressing your meaning and intent.

8. Communicate for yesterday and tomorrow as well as today. Although a message may be aimed primarily at meeting the demands of an immediate situation, you must plan it with the past in mind if it is to maintain consistency in the receiver's view. More important, it must be consistent with long-range interests and goals.

9. Be sure your actions support your communications. In the final analysis, the most persuasive kind of communication is not what you say but what you do. When a person's actions or attitudes contradict his or her words, we tend to discount what that person has said.

10. Seek not only to be understood but to understand—be a good listener. When we start talking, we often cease to listen in that larger sense of being attuned to the other person's unspoken reactions and attitudes.

Source: Adapted from "Ten Commandments of Good Communication," *Management Review* (October 1955). © 1955 American Management Association International. Reprinted by permission of American Management Association International, New York. All rights reserved. Permission conveyed through the Copyright Clearance Center.

Chapter Summary

1 Discuss the importance of communication in organizations.

Communication is the process through which people and organizations accomplish objectives. By communicating with others, we share a common understanding of one another's attitudes, values, emotions, ambitions, wants and needs. People must coordinate and pool their efforts, electronically and otherwise, to please their customers. Prompt communication about problems is essential for creating and adapting to change. Quality, productivity, and profitability depend on accurate and timely communications on a variety of issues. All employees must have feedback during their communication efforts and work performance.

2 Diagram the communication process and label all its parts.

Figure 10.1 illustrates the process. It begins with the sender (a person or group) planning the effort. The sender's ideas are formulated into a message. An appropriate medium is chosen and used to deliver the message to the intended receiver. Finally, efforts to ensure mutual understanding and seek clarification (feedback) are engaged in by both sender and receiver.

3 List and explain the barriers to interpersonal communication and suggest remedies to overcome them.

1 *Diction and semantics:* The use of words, terms and symbols that are abstract or have multiple meanings and elicit emotional responses.
Remedy: Choose clear and precise language, keeping your receiver's understanding in mind.

2 *Expectations of familiarity:* The assumption that you know what the sender is sending before you receive the entire message.
Remedy: Don't draw any conclusions until the entire message has been delivered and received. Read and listen with an open mind.

3 *Source's lack of credibility:* The receiver's perception that the sender lacks sufficient credibility in the subject area.
Remedy: Hear the sender out; fresh perspectives often bring new and better suggestions and solutions.

4 *Preconceived notions:* The negative reaction to ideas that differ from your own.
Remedy: Try to keep an open mind on every subject, especially those most familiar to you.

5 *Differing perceptions:* The different way each person observes and makes judgments. Most people stereotype other individuals, for better or worse, prejudging their motives as well as who they are.
Remedy: Judge people on their individual merits. What matters is who they are as individuals.

6 *Conflicting nonverbal communication:* The noncorrelation of body language, expressions, and gestures with other messages being sent.
Remedy: Actions speak louder than words. At the very least, try to determine what might explain the contradiction; stress and emotions can confuse the process.

7 *Emotions:* The clouding of logic and judgment by emotion. Sender and receiver may become adversaries rather than partners in a process.
Remedy: Avoid the communication process when either the sender or receiver is in an emotional, and definitely when either is in an irrational state.

8 *Noise:* Anything in the communication environment that can interfere with the sending and receiving of messages.
Remedy: Avoid the process until you can eliminate or avoid the sources of noise. Don't try to compete with those sources for a receiver's attention.

4 Describe the uses of downward, horizontal, and upward communication channels.

Downward channels send messages from managers to non-managers and from top management to all others in the company. Mission, vision, feedback to requests from below, policies, solutions, goals and appraisals are typical subject areas.

Horizontal channels connect people of similar rank and status, insiders connect with outsiders, and team members interact with one another.

Upward channels provide feedback required by downward communication. They provide input for decisions at higher levels and status reports on the conditions throughout the organization.

5 **Explain the informal communication channel known as the grapevine.**

The grapevine arises spontaneously through social interactions and carries all nonofficial messages between and among organization members. It is usually word of mouth and can penetrate the tightest security. It is fast, difficult to stop, and may be a support for or an obstruction to management efforts.

6 **List and explain the barriers to organizational communication and suggest remedies to overcome them.**

1 *Overload:* The sending and receiving of too much information, given the circumstances surrounding the communication.
Remedy: As a sender, deliver only what your best judgment and observations during the effort suggest your receiver can handle. As a receiver, inform the sender when incoming data becomes excessive.

2 *Filtering by levels:* The increased embellishment and filtering of information as it passes through successive levels.
Remedy: Try to deliver messages in the most direct way possible; avoid nonessential handling. Use written formats that can pass unaltered through several layers or hands.

3 *Timing:* The sending of information too late to be of use or without consideration for the receiver's receptivity.
Remedy: Use technology to speed the flow and store the message until the receiver is receptive.

4 *Lack of trust and openness:* The guarding and control of information and access to it by key people, resulting in a closed culture and climate. Such cultures and climates ignore individuals and operate on fear and suspicion.
Remedy: Training to create trust, promoted ethical behavior, and "walking your talk" are cures for this barrier.

5 *Inappropriate span of control:* Too many, or too few, subordinates or team members under any one leader.
Remedy: Reorganize and reassign personnel to more appropriate groupings.

6 *Change:* Change in processes, systems or leadership that creates new demands for communication; fear causes resistance.
Remedy: Remove fear through forewarning and by making standards and requirements clear. Point out the positives and similarities to what exists, before communicating the differences.

7 *Rank or status in the company:* Differences in rank and status that inhibit communication when a person is intimidated by someone of higher position. Self-image can become distorted if a person is surrounded by yes-men and no opposition.
Remedy: Instituting appraisals by one's subordinates and peers using objective, measurable standards is helpful. Hold people accountable for how well they serve their particular customers' needs. Downplay and eliminate artificial barriers.

8 *Managers' interpretations:* The perhaps-flawed judgment of managers. Managers are most often the initiators of the communication process. Like those they manage, they have their virtues and vices. Their judgment about the when, where, how, and why of the process is not flawless.
Remedy: Provide training in how to communicate in all the various media.

9 *Electronic noise:* Breakdowns, overloads, static on the lines and poorly trained operators, resulting in miscommunication. Electronic media both help and hinder communication efforts.
Remedy: Provide training for all in the proper use and maintenance of various pieces of equipment and software programs before people are authorized to use them.

7 **Describe the responsibilities of senders and receivers during the communication process.**

Senders have the following responsibilities:

- Being certain of intent before attempting communication
- Knowing the receiver and constructing the message accordingly
- Selecting the proper medium, given the particular circumstances
- Timing the transmission for maximum effect
- Seeking and giving feedback

Receivers have the following responsibilities:

- Listening actively
- Being sensitive to the sender
- Indicating an appropriate medium
- Initiating feedback

KEY TERMS

communication **324**

diction **331**

feedback **325**

formal communication channels **334**

formal communication networks **338**

grapevine **338**

informal communication channels **338**

information **324**

interpersonal communication **328**

jargon **332**

medium **325**

message **325**

noise **334**

nonverbal communication **327**

perceptions **333**

receiver **325**

semantics **331**

sender **324**

stereotypes **333**

understanding **324**

REVIEW QUESTIONS

1. Why is communication so important in organizations?

2. What are the essential elements in any effort to communicate?

3. What are the barriers that can interfere with interpersonal communication efforts?

4. What are the major uses for downward, horizontal and upward communication channels?

5. How does the grapevine work in organizations?

6. What are the barriers that can interfere with organizational communication efforts?

7. What must a sender do before attempting to communicate?

8. What must a receiver do when entering into the communication process?

DISCUSSION QUESTIONS FOR CRITICAL THINKING

1. What barriers exist in your working or school environment that inhibit your ability to get information you need on a timely basis? Are these organizational, interpersonal, or both?

2. What kind of barriers to communication is a company like American Airlines likely to experience with its heavy reliance on electronic linkages to customers?

3. Find individuals in class or at work who own a Samsung product. Ask them why they purchased their Samsung and whether their motivations match up with those stated in this chapter's Global Applications feature.

4. Phones are used for voice calling and for *texting*, sending short messages or *texts*. Most adults use their phones for voice calling, but texting has reached the mainstream. Sherri Elliott-Yeary, author of *Ties to Tattoos: Turning Generational Differences into a Competitive Advantage*, hands out bookmarks titled

"RU in the know?" to help older people at work understand business texting. Below are some of her abbreviations.

RU in the know?

*$	Starbucks
4COL	For crying out loud
AAMOI	As a matter of interest
AB2	About to
B4N	Bye for now
CMU	Crack me up
CYE	Check your e-mail
DIY	Do it yourself
DQYDJ	Don't quit your day job
E123	Easy as 1, 2, 3
F2F	Face to face
G2G	Got to go
H&K	Hugs and kisses
h/o	Hold on

I 1-D-R	I wonder
IDK	I don't know
J2LYK	Just to let you know
KYFC	Keep your fingers crossed
LMSO	Laughing my socks off
M4C	Meet for coffee
MLAS	My lips are sealed
Nm,u	Not much, you?
NRG	Energy
NUFF	Enough said
OIC	Oh, I see
PMC	Please call me
PPL	People
QT	Cutie
TC	Take care
W8	Wait
WIP	Work in progress

WTG	Way to go
XME	Excuse me
^5	High five

Source: Cheryl Hall, "Making Peace Among Generations," *The Dallas Morning News*, January 30, 2011, D1.

Would you classify text messages as formal or informal communications? Explain.

5. Businesses use text messages to send reminders and/ or bills to their customers. What are some other ways businesses might use text messages?

6. Make a list of smart phone activities. (What can people do with a smart phone or a phone connected to the Internet?) How could your college use a phone application to improve communication with students?

Apply What You Know

Social Media Management Exercises

Foursquare, Geolocation-Based Social Network

Service businesses in local neighborhoods (casual restaurants, health clubs, grocery stores, dry cleaners, shoe repair, spas, dentists, doctors, insurance agents, etc.) are filling the shopping needs of consumers. Shoppers need these businesses to run their weekly errands. Consumers can't exercise, eat or get their cars fixed on the Internet. Thus, local service businesses don't compete with businesses on the Internet. Yet, the Internet can help these errand friendly neighborhood businesses satisfy their customers.

Foursquare is a geolocation-based social network, making a neighborhood easier to use. It is a smartphone application that reveals user's locations. Once downloaded, it links a person's smartphone contacts, Facebook friends and Twitter followers. Smartphone technology includes GPS (global-positioning-system) data and proximity to cell towers. This allows Foursquare to know the location on a map.

Users win prizes and meet people by using their smartphones to "check in" at local establishments, which depend on customer traffic, such as bars, restaurants, stores and events. Friends tell friends where they are physically located. They can give tips, suggestions and recommendations about the establishment. An advantage to using Foursquare is that it only takes a few seconds for someone to check in and/or write a text message.

Businesses who participate in the program would potentially see more sales. Nearby establishments can send special offers, such as discounts or points. Frequent patronage or loyalty can be rewarded. "Badges" or digital emblems and points are earned and awarded by visiting certain locations and for completing activities. If someone checks in to a location more than anyone else, he or she can become the "mayor" of that location. This allows businesses to connect with people and retain customers. Furthermore, many businesses have replaced their coupons and loyalty cards by using Foursquare.

Visit *www.foursquare.com*. Read the information at the site and watch the video.

1. How would using Foursquare make your neighborhood easier to use?

2. Besides retailers and restaurants, what other types of establishments in your neighborhood could benefit from geolocation-based social networks? Give a brief justification for each type of establishment listed.

3. Identify a local establishment that depends on customer traffic, which you frequently visit. Is it listed on Foursquare at foursquare.com/search? If so, is it linked to their Twitter feeds and Facebook pages? If not, will you tell the manager about Foursquare?

4. Besides the business concepts mentioned above, what are 2–3 other ideas you would suggest for this establishment to harness Foursquare for their communication efforts? (Examples might include rewards programs, games and coupons.) For each suggestion listed, briefly discuss how it would enhance your customer experience.

Experiential Learning

Alcoa's Open Work Spaces

Companies increase communication when workers and managers alike inhabit open work spaces rather than private offices. Marilyn Farrow, member of IIDA: International Interior Design Association College of Fellows, explains,

> The 'Old Thinking' of entitlement; one person, one workspace, one site; job title, years of service, status; square feet per person; windows, corners, and level of finish are giving way to 'New Thinking' which values people as a source of knowledge; empowered people contribute more; two heads are better than one; faster, better, cheaper; open communication is good—'need to know' not the rule; serendipitous talk is not idle talk; informal communications have value. Workers want to win within this new scenario, and enabled by an appropriate workplace, they can (Smith).

Alcoa's Corporate Center is an example of a building with open work spaces. Alcoa is the world's leading producer of primary aluminum, fabricated aluminum and alumina combined. The corporate center in Pittsburgh is located on the Allegheny River and houses employees in a unique open environment. No one has an office, not even the top executives. The organic environment allows employees to meet and form problem-solving groups anywhere within the facility at any time.

Some managers have found that people seek each other out more often in a building equipped with escalators than in one with stairways or elevators. Escalators, they believe, offer relative privacy and allow senders and receivers to pay more attention to each other.

"The offices at Alcoa are designed around a central escalator where people can see one another on many floors. Elevators do not allow for visibility between floors and do not allow for as much visibility of people coming and going. Companies use their open stairway space for social interactions and for impromptu knowledge exchange" (Smith).

Office floors at Alcoa have desk-storage areas and small conference tables with ports (for easy connections between employees' laptop computers and the devices of customers and suppliers). Also, it is possible for employees to plug in laptop computers randomly at meeting tables and elsewhere, even on the deck near the cafeteria. There are at least two paneled work spaces on each floor for employees to view videos or to improve their computer skills away from their desks.

Questions

1. What barriers to organizational communication are overcome by this type of working situation?

2. What problems can arise in such an open environment?

3. What kind of workers or work might suffer in such an environment?

4. Of all of the elements described in this open environment, which one appeals to you the most? Which ones do not appeal to you? Explain.

Sources: Laurie A. Smith, "Space SIG 10: Workspace and Learning Organizations," *KnowledgeBoard*, January 14, 2004, *http://www.knowledgeboard.com/item/1181/23/5/3*; Donald Miller, "Alcoa Corporate Center: A Triumph over Pretension," *Post-Gazette*, September 18, 1998; Alcoa Inc., *http://www.alcoa.com*.

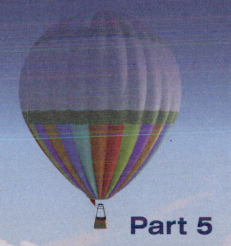

Part 5

Influencing

Chapter 11

Motivation

LEARNING OBJECTIVES

After studying this chapter, you should be able to:

1 Discuss the factors that stimulate and influence motivation

2 Differentiate between content and process theories of motivation

3 List the five levels of needs according to Maslow and give an example of each

4 Discuss the impact of hygiene and motivation factors in the work environment

5 Explain the characteristics of a person with high-achievement needs

6 Identify the needs associated with ERG theory

7 Discuss the relationship between expectations and motivation

8 Explain the relationship between reinforcement and motivation

9 Explain how equity influences motivation

10 Explain how goals influence motivation

11 Discuss the importance of a manager's philosophy of management in creating a positive work environment

12 Describe how managers can structure the environment to provide motivation

Management in Action

Empowerment

Motivation at work is influenced by the work environment, and the organization influences within the work environment. An empowered organization provides the direction, resources and respect employees desire. It supports facilitation and rewards responsible ownership. An empowered manager allows employees to make decisions about how to do their own jobs. Thus, the manager gives the employees more power. The empowered manager provides information and facilitates work processes. He or she helps employees learn and trusts their abilities. The empowered employee seeks responsibility and takes prudent risks. He or she has a personal stake in work, generates ideas and makes decisions. Empowered employees perform their job in a way that delivers optimal value to the organization.

For each of the following statements, circle the number which indicates your level of agreement. Rate your agreement as it is, not what you think it should be. Objectivity will enable you to determine your management skill strengths and weaknesses.

	Almost Always	Often	Sometimes	Rarely	Almost Never
I have control over my own destiny.	5	4	3	2	1
I take responsibility for what I do.	5	4	3	2	1
I take advantage of leadership opportunities.	5	4	3	2	1
I make good decisions.	5	4	3	2	1
I take advantage of learning opportunities.	5	4	3	2	1
I make the right choices.	5	4	3	2	1
I learn from my mistakes.	5	4	3	2	1
I am competent in what I do.	5	4	3	2	1
I am a valued team member.	5	4	3	2	1
What I do makes a difference.	5	4	3	2	1

Compute your score by adding the circled numbers. The highest score is 50; the lowest score is 10. A higher score implies you are more likely to be empowered. A lower score implies a lesser degree of readiness, but it can be increased. Reading and studying this chapter will help you to improve your understanding of empowerment.

INTRODUCTION

When you ask people what motivates them at work, most will tell you, in a tone usually reserved for children and in-laws, that they do it for the money. But this doesn't explain people like Warren Buffett or Bill Gates. Their combined net worth is greater than the GDP of Luxembourg, and yet these billionaires throw themselves into their jobs as if their next meal depended on it. So if it's not about the money, what is it?

This chapter will help provide the answers. First, the chapter presents the basics of motivation. Then it continues with an analysis of motivation theories that focus on employee needs and ones that focus on behaviors. The chapter concludes with a description of how managers can structure the environment to provide motivation.

Challenge of Motivation

What do Southwest Airlines, SAS Institute and the Container Store have in common? One answer is success. If you entered each workplace, you would notice another similarity. In each organization the morale is excellent. **Morale** is the attitude or feelings the workers have about the organization and their total work life.[1] The CEOs of each company and their management teams have created a positive work environment. Each, in his or her own unique way, has taken steps to enhance the **quality of work life (QWL)**.[2] Efforts at increasing QWL focus on improving workers' dignity, physical and emotional well-being, and workplace satisfaction. By developing a positive work environment, managers can capture the commitment of their employees. "SAS CEO Jim Goodnight's philosophy is simple, but effective: Treat employees like they make a difference and they will."[3] The result is employees who are truly motivated— want to do their jobs well. Such commitment, combined with the skill to do the job, creates an energetic, highly competent labor force working in partnership with management. Figure 11.1 shows the factors that contribute to the quality of work life.

The managers at Southwest Airlines, SAS, and Semco (the latter the subject of this chapter's Global Applications feature) have met one of the great management challenges. They have discovered how to motivate employees. These managers recognize that motivation is not magic but a set of processes that influences behavioral choices.[4]

BASICS OF MOTIVATION

Modern researchers and enlightened managers have discovered that motivation is not something that is done to a person. It results from a combination of factors, including an individual's needs and his or her ability to make choices, as well as an environment that provides the opportunity to satisfy those needs and to make those choices. **Motivation** is the result of the interaction of a person's internal needs and external influences, which determine how a person will behave.

People make conscious decisions for their own welfare. Why do you do what you do? Why do you choose to go to college and someone else does not? Why do you choose to study hard and someone else does not? Why do some employees at Southwest Airlines take outside education classes and others do not? Why do some Nordstrom employees adopt the culture and become "Nordies" and others do not?[5] The study of motivation is concerned with what prompts people to act, what influences their choice of action, and why they persist in acting in a certain way. The starting point is to look at a person's needs by using a motivation model.

morale
The attitude or feelings workers have about the organization and their total work life

quality of work life (QWL)
Factors in the work environment contributing positively or negatively to workers' physical and emotional well-being and job satisfaction

1 Discuss the factors that stimulate and influence motivation

motivation
The result of the interaction of a person's internal needs and external influences—involving perceptions of equity, expectancy, previous conditioning, and goal setting—which determine how a person will behave

Figure 11.1   Factors that Enhance the Quality of Work Life

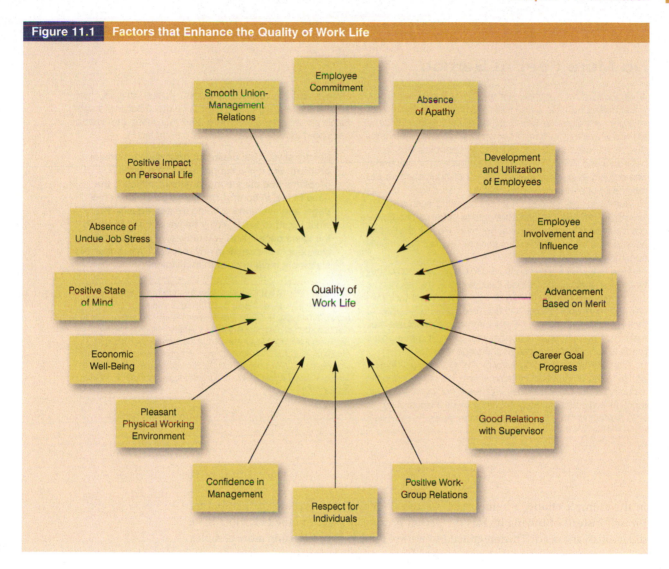

needs

Physiological or psychological conditions in humans that act as stimuli for behavior

Motivation Model

A person's needs provide the basis for a motivation model. **Needs** are deficiencies that a person experiences at a particular time. They can be physiological or psychological. Physiological needs relate to the body and include requirements for air, water, and food. Psychological needs include the need for affiliation and self-esteem. Needs create a tension (stimulus) that results in wants. The person then develops a behavior or set of behaviors to satisfy his or her wants. The behavior results in action toward goal achievement.[6]

Figure 11.2 offers a rudimentary example of the motivation model. A person feels hunger (a need). Recognition of the need triggers a want (food). The person chooses to cook a hamburger (behavior) and then eats it (takes action to achieve the goal). Satisfied, he feels no hunger (feedback). When the model is modified to reflect the fact that behavior is subject to many influences, it grows more complex. Why did the person

No More Fear at Semco

When Ricardo Semler took over the family business, Semco, which makes propellers and rocket-fuel propellant mixers for satellites, among other products, looked much like any other old-line Brazilian company. Fear was the governing principle. Guards patrolled the factory floor, timing people's trips to the bathroom and frisking workers who left the plant. Anyone who was unlucky enough to break a piece of equipment had to replace it out of his or her own pocket.

Semler initially carried on in this style but soon revolted, vowing to remake his company into a "true democracy, a place run on trust and freedom, not fear." He has created an environment where people want to work—Semco has virtually no turnover.

Now employees are empowered to run the company. They wear what they want, choose their own bosses, and come and go as they please. A third of them actually set their own salaries, with one crucial "hitch." They have to reapply for their jobs every six months. Production workers evaluate their managers once a year and post the score. If a manager's grade is consistently low, he or she steps down.

Also, Semler shares company profits, regularly distributing profits to the employees. He also shares his title. Six people, including a woman, rotate as CEO, each putting in six-month tours. In addition, even though Semler owns the company, his vote carries no more weight than anyone else's.

In a country that barely blinks at high inflation, mere survival is a feat; but Semco has done much better than that. Sales per employee are more than four times the average compared with the sales of Semco's competitors.

➡ Semler says, "The desire for uniformity is a major problem. But it is a subproduct of the same problems that plague management, which is the need to feel in control, that we're all on the same page, and everyone is being treated equally. But what I want to ask is, 'Why do we all need to be on the same page?' And you realize, of course, that no two people are equal in any respect." What does his statement have to do with motivation?

Sources: NPR, "What Happens When You Run a Company with (Almost) No Rules?" May 5, 2015, *http://www.npr. org/2015/04/24/401742828/what-happens-when-you-run-a-company-with-almost-no-rules*; Brad Wieners, "Ricardo Semler: Set Them Free," *CIO Insight*, April 1, 2004, *http://www.cioinsight. com/ article2/0,1397,1569009,00.asp*; Ricardo Semler, *The Seven Day Weekend*, Viking/Penguin, 2003; Ricardo Semler, *Maverick: The Success Story Behind the World's Most Unusual Workplace*, Warner Books, 1995.

in the example choose a hamburger, not cereal? Why did he prepare the hamburger himself instead of buying it? Has the person previously practiced the behavior? If so, did it satisfy the need? The integrated motivation model—by addressing more complex influences on motivational choices—provides these explanations.

Integrated Motivation Model

Unsatisfied needs stimulate wants and behaviors. In choosing a behavior to satisfy a need, a person must evaluate three factors:

1 *Past experiences.* All the person's past experiences with the situation at hand enter into the motivation model. These include the satisfaction derived from acting in a certain way, any frustration felt, the amount of effort required, and the relationship of performance to rewards.

2 *Environmental influences.* The choices of behaviors are affected by the environment, which in a business setting make up the organization's values as well as the expectations and actions of management.

3 *Perceptions.* The individual is influenced by perceptions of the expected effort required to achieve performance and by the value of the reward both absolutely and in relation to what peers have received for the same effort.

Figure 11.2   Basic Motivation Model

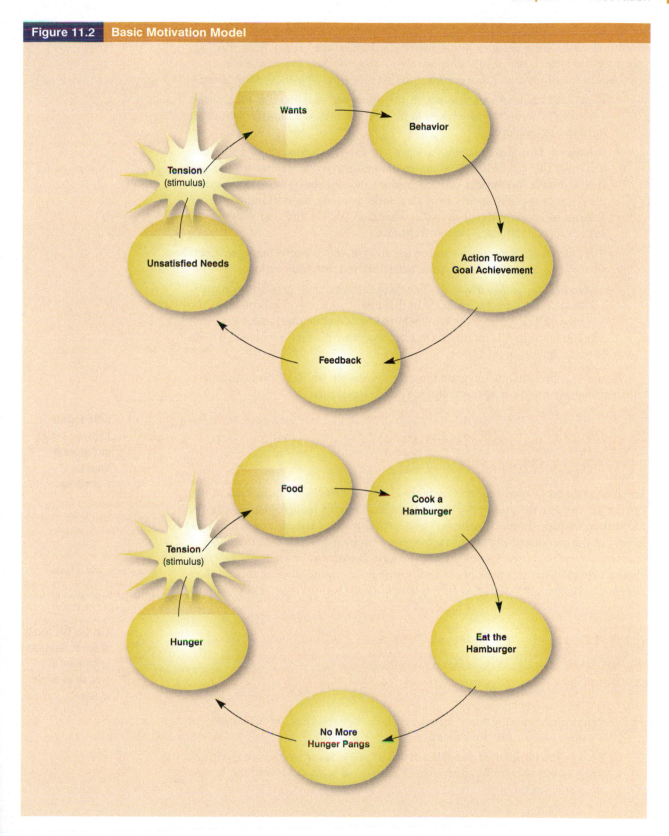

In addition to these three variables, two other factors are at work: skills and incentives. Skills are a person's performance capabilities; they result from training. Incentives are factors created by managers to encourage workers to perform a task.

Look at the motivation process again, but this time from a business perspective:

- *Unsatisfied needs stimulate wants.* In this situation a first-level manager feels a need to be respected. She wants to be recognized by top management as an outstanding employee.

- *Behavior is identified to satisfy the want.* The first-level manager identifies two behaviors that can satisfy the want: volunteering to write a report or seeking a special project. To consider which behavior to choose, she consciously evaluates the rewards or punishments associated with the performance (incentives); her abilities to accomplish the activities identified (skills); and past experiences, environmental influences, and perceptions.

- *The individual takes action.* Based on her analysis, the first-level manager selects what she considers the best option (behavior) and then takes action.

- *The individual receives feedback.* The response the manager gets from top management constitutes the feedback in this case. If the response is positive, the top manager has done more than help the first-level manager meet her need. The top manager has increased the likelihood that the first-level manager will behave similarly in the future.

Figure 11.3 presents the integrated motivation model, which shows how experience, environment, and perception influence decision making.

CONTENT AND PROCESS THEORIES OF MOTIVATION

Differentiate between content and process theories of motivation

The integrated motivation model is useful in exploring theories of motivation in two categories: content theories and process theories. **Content theories** emphasize the needs that motivate people. If managers understand workers' needs, they can include factors in the work environment to meet them, thereby helping to direct employees' energies toward the organization's goals. **Process theories** explain how employees choose behaviors to meet their needs and how they determine whether their choices were successful.[7]

content theories
A group of motivation theories emphasizing the needs that motivate people

process theories
A group of theories that explain how employees choose behaviors to meet their needs and how they determine whether their choices were successful

CONTENT THEORIES: MOTIVATION THEORIES FOCUSING ON NEEDS

List the five levels of needs according to Maslow and give an example of each

Maslow's Hierarchy of Needs

Psychologist Abraham H. Maslow[8] based his study of motivation on a hierarchy of needs. His theory is based on four premises:

1. *Only an unsatisfied need can influence behavior; a satisfied need is not a motivator.* Thus, someone who has just eaten is unlikely to want food until the hunger need arises again.

Figure 11.3   Integrated Motivation Model

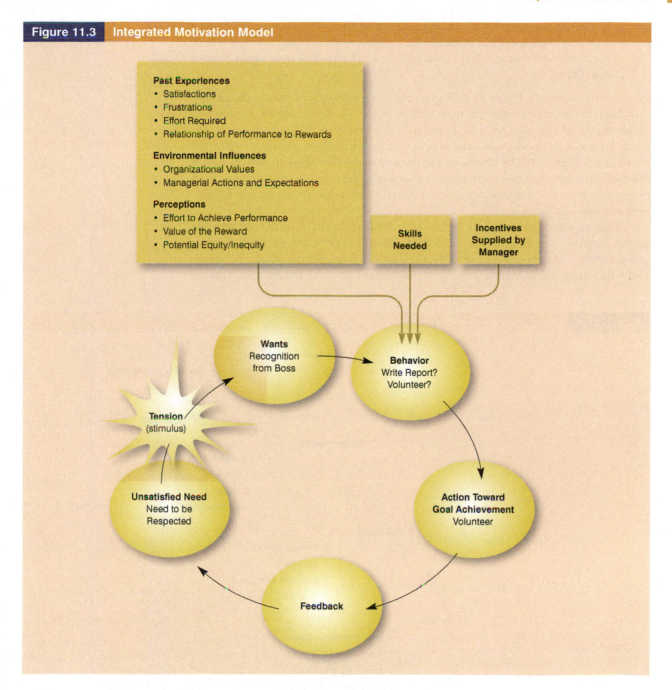

2   *A person's needs are arranged in a priority order of importance.* The hierarchy goes from the most basic needs (such as water or shelter) to the most complex (esteem and self-actualization).

3   *A person will at least minimally satisfy each level of need before feeling the need at the next level.* Someone must obtain companionship before desiring recognition.

4   *If need satisfaction is not maintained at any level, the unsatisfied need will become a priority once again.* For example, for a person who is already feeling a lack of social connectedness, safety could become a priority need once again if he or she is fired.

Five Levels of Needs Figure 11.4 displays Maslow's hierarchy of needs. The exhibit lists the needs in order of priority, from bottom to top. The first category is composed of physiological (physical) needs. These are the primary, or basic-level, needs: the needs for water, air, food, shelter and comfort. In the working environment, managers try to satisfy these needs by providing salaries and wages that allow employees to buy the basic necessities. While the employee is at work, the manager meets these needs by providing water fountains, clean air, no objectionable odors or noises, comfortable temperatures and lunch breaks.

When physiological needs are met to the individual's satisfaction, the next priority becomes safety—the need to avoid bodily harm and uncertainty about one's well-being. Safety is closely allied to security, the freedom from risk or danger. Behaviors that reflect safety needs include joining unions, seeking jobs with tenure, and choosing

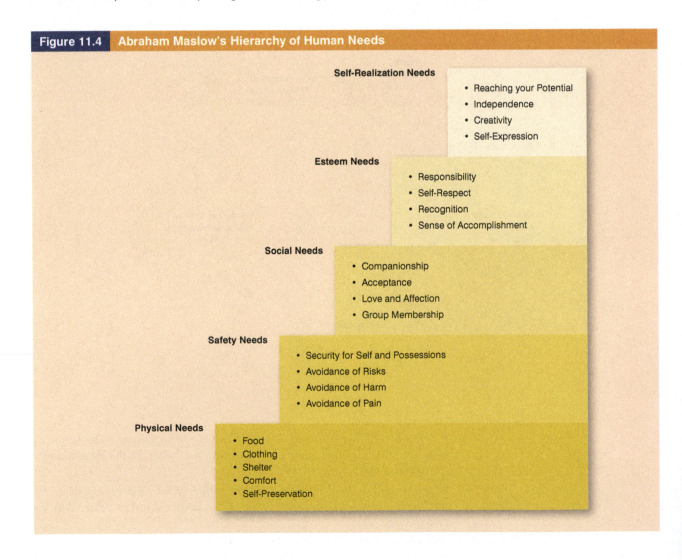

Figure 11.4   Abraham Maslow's Hierarchy of Human Needs

Self-Realization Needs
- Reaching your Potential
- Independence
- Creativity
- Self-Expression

Esteem Needs
- Responsibility
- Self-Respect
- Recognition
- Sense of Accomplishment

Social Needs
- Companionship
- Acceptance
- Love and Affection
- Group Membership

Safety Needs
- Security for Self and Possessions
- Avoidance of Risks
- Avoidance of Harm
- Avoidance of Pain

Physical Needs
- Food
- Clothing
- Shelter
- Comfort
- Self-Preservation

jobs on the basis of health insurance and retirement programs. All of us desire a work environment in which we can be free from threats to our physical and emotional senses of security.[9] Managers attempt to satisfy safety needs by providing salaries, benefits, safe work conditions and job security.

One such manager is Robert M. Thompson, Founder of Michigan's largest asphalt paving contractor, Thompson-McCully Company. When Thompson sold his company to Oldcastle Materials, a subsidiary of Ireland's CRH plc, he recognized his employees' contributions to his success by giving the 550 company employees and retirees a special bonus of $128 million total. Also, he paid the taxes on the bonus. He chose Oldcastle Materials because of its record of not dismantling companies or firing workers. One of Thompson's employees happily reports that his safety needs had been met:

> *"It was unbelievable. It is hard to tell you how I felt," says Frank Azzopardi, quarry manager [of Thompson-McCully] in Newport, MI, who received an annuity that kicks in at 55. He says he now has a "secure feeling" because retirement funding "was always a big worry." Azzopardi says he "started on the end of a shovel as a laborer" and worked his way up. "I never thought 14 years ago that I would be a manager in this company or that I would share in the proceeds.[10]*

Unfortunately, not all companies treat employees as well, as this chapter's Ethical Management feature illustrates.

Ethical Management

Unannounced Layoffs

Companies pay management consultants hundreds of thousands of dollars to help them create work environments in which employees can be productive. One of the basic themes promoted by consultants is valuing and respecting the individual. For most it is a lesson quietly internalized, but evidently not at IBM.

Former CEO, Samuel J. Palmisano, sent employees an e-mail inferring that IBM would not cut costs like other companies, by writing, "Most importantly, we will invest in our people" (Lohr). The next day, more than 1,400 employees were notified that their jobs would be eliminated. More layoffs followed and about 4,600 North America IBM jobs vanished. IBM's overall employment in the United States declined, while its foreign employment increased.

IBM reports revenue by three geographic regions: Americas; Europe, Middle East and Africa; and Asia Pacific, but it no longer reports where its employees are located. It stopped disclosing headcounts in 2010. Ron Hira, an associate professor of public policy at the Rochester Institute of Technology, said, "By hiding its offshoring, IBM is doing a disservice to America—through omission the company is providing misleading labor market signals and information to policymakers" (Thibodeau).

➤ What does this situation say about the company's value system?

➤ If you were an employee, what effect would this action have on your morale?

➤ What is your reaction to the Professor Hira's statement?

Source: Patrick Thibodeau, "IBM Stops Disclosing U.S. Headcount Data," March 12, 2010, *Computerworld*, http://www.computerworld. com/article/2520399/it-outsourcing/ibm-stops-disclosing-u-s-headcount-data.html; Steve Lohr, "Piecemeal Layoffs Avoid Warning Laws," *The New York Times*, March 5, 2009, http://www.nytimes. com/2009/03/06/business/06layoffs.html.

Social needs become dominant when safety needs have been minimally gratified. People desire friendship, companionship and a place in a group. Love needs include the needs for giving and receiving love.[11] At work employees meet social needs by interacting frequently with fellow workers and through acceptance by others. The familiar gathering at the water cooler reflects employees' needs to interact socially as well as in their official business roles. The groups that employees form at lunchtime are also a result of their need to be social. Managers can meet these needs by supporting employee get-togethers—birthday parties, lunches and sports teams.

The next level in the hierarchy, esteem needs, includes the desire for self-respect and for the recognition of one's abilities by others. Satisfaction of these needs gives one pride, self-confidence and a genuine sense of importance. Lack of satisfaction of these needs can result in feelings of inferiority, weakness and helplessness. Work-related activities and outcomes that help meet individual esteem needs include successfully completing projects, being recognized by peers and superiors as someone who makes valuable contributions and acquiring organizational titles. Walmart Founder Sam Walton recognized the importance of this need in creating Sam's Rules for Building a Business. He discusses the esteem need in Rule 5: "Appreciate everything your associates do for the business … nothing else can substitute for a few well-chosen, well-timed, sincere words of praise."[12]

Maslow's highest need level, self-realization, relates to the desire for fulfillment. Self-realization (also called self-actualization) represents the need to maximize the use of one's skills, abilities and potential.

Implications for Managers Maslow's needs theory applies to all environments, not specifically to the workplace. Nevertheless, it presents a workable motivation framework for managers. By analyzing employees' comments, attitudes, quality and quantity of work and personal circumstances, the manager can hope to identify the particular need level that individual workers seek to satisfy. Then the manager can attempt to build into the work environment the opportunities that will allow individuals to satisfy their needs. To see how a manager satisfies workers' needs by applying Maslow's theory, review Figure 11.5. Also refer to the figure for ways the manager can facilitate need satisfaction.

Because people are unique in their perceptions and personalities, applying the needs theory poses some difficulties. Just as one motive may lead to different behaviors, similar behaviors in individuals can spring from different motives. The act of working hard on a new project, for instance, can arise from many needs. Some people apply themselves in order to grow and develop; others do so to be liked; still others wish to earn more money to enhance their sense of security; and yet others want the recognition that success will bring. For this reason, managers must use care when assessing motives simply by observing behavior.

An unmet need can frustrate an employee. It will continue to influence his or her behavior until it is satisfied, either on the job or off. The means of satisfaction might mesh with the organization's goals and processes. However, it could compete or even conflict with them. The esteem need, for example, can be satisfied by involvement with work-related groups or groups outside the work environment.

The level of need satisfaction constantly fluctuates. Once a need is satisfied, it ceases to influence behavior, but only for a time. Needs do not remain satisfied over the long term.

Figure 11.5 **Five Common Worker Needs and Appropriate Managerial Responses**

Worker's Circumstances	LEVELS OF NEEDS	
	Demanding Satisfaction	Need-Satisfying Actions
Employee has two children entering college next year	Physiological/safety	Increase pay or train and promote employee to higher-paying job, if justified; confirm job security.
Worker feels concern about a competitor's purchase of the firm	Safety	If possible, reassure worker that jobs will not be eliminated; otherwise, frankly admit that certain jobs will be abolished. Encourage and assist those affected to seek employment elsewhere.
Worker feels uncomfortable as a new addition in a closely knit work group	Social	Invite subordinates to a social evening at your home creating an opportunity for the newcomer to meet peers in an informal setting. Encourage the new worker to participate in company recreational activities. Sponsor the new worker for membership in professional organizations.
Employee feels unappreciated	Ego/self-esteem	Examine the employee's job performance and find reasons for praise. Accept the employee's suggestions where applicable. Build closer rapport.
Worker wants to get ahead in the organization and has a general idea of an ultimate employment goal in the company	Self-realization/ self-actualization	Provide specific guidance in pinpointing ultimate goal; help chart career path. Facilitate educational improvement. Provide opportunities for job experience and recognition.

4 Discuss the impact of hygiene and motivation factors in the work environment

hygiene factors
Maintenance factors (such as salary, status, working conditions) that do not relate directly to a person's actual work activity, but when of low quality are the cause of unhappiness on the job

Herzberg's Two-Factor Theory

Psychologist Frederick Herzberg[13] and his associates developed a needs theory called the two-factor, or hygiene-motivator, theory. Herzberg's theory defines one set of factors that lead to job dissatisfaction; these factors are called **hygiene factors**. The theory also defines a set of factors that produce job satisfaction and motivation; these factors are called motivators.

Hygiene Factors According to Herzberg, a manager's poor handling of hygiene factors (often referred to as *maintenance factors*) is the primary cause of unhappiness on the job. Hygiene factors are extrinsic to the job—that is, they do not relate directly to a person's actual work activity. Hygiene factors are part of the job environment; they are part of the context of the job, not its content. When the hygiene factors that an employer provides are of low quality, employees feel job dissatisfaction. Even when the factors are of sufficient quality, they do not necessarily act as motivators. High-quality hygiene factors are not necessarily stimuli for growth or greater effort. They seek only to prevent employees' job dissatisfaction.[14] Hygiene factors are as follows:

- *Salary.* To prevent job dissatisfaction, a manager should provide adequate wages, salaries and fringe benefits.

- *Job security.* Company grievance procedures and seniority privileges contribute to high-quality hygiene.

- *Working conditions.* Managers ensure adequate heat, light, ventilation and hours of work to prevent dissatisfaction.

- *Status.* Managers who are mindful of the importance of hygiene factors provide privileges, job titles and other symbols of rank and position.

- *Company policies.* To prevent job dissatisfaction, managers should provide policies as guidelines for behavior and administer the policies fairly.

- *Quality of technical supervision.* When employees are not able to receive answers to job-related questions, they become frustrated. Providing high-quality technical supervision for employees prevents frustration.

- *Quality of interpersonal relations among peers, supervisors and subordinates.* In an organization with high-quality hygiene factors, the workplace provides social opportunities as well as the chance to enjoy comfortable work-related relationships.

Motivation Factors According to Herzberg, **motivation factors** are the primary cause of job satisfaction. They are intrinsic to a job and relate directly to the real nature of the work people perform. In other words, motivation factors relate to job content. When an employer fails to provide motivation, employees experience no job satisfaction. With motivation, employees enjoy job satisfaction and provide high performance. Different people require different kinds and degrees of motivation factors—what stimulates one worker might not affect another. Motivation factors also act as stimuli for psychological and personal growth. These factors are as follows:

motivation factors
The conditions, intrinsic to the job, that can lead to an individual's job satisfaction

- *Achievement.* The opportunity to accomplish something or contribute something of value can serve as a source of job satisfaction.

- *Recognition.* Wise managers let employees know that their efforts have been worthwhile and that management notes and appreciates them.

- *Responsibility.* The potential for acquiring new duties and responsibilities, either through job expansion or delegation, can be a powerful motivator for some workers.

- *Advancement.* The opportunity to improve one's position as a result of job performance gives employees a clear reason for high performance.

- *The work itself.* When a task offers an opportunity for self-expression, personal satisfaction, and meaningful challenge, employees are likely to undertake the task with enthusiasm.

- *Possibility of growth.* The opportunity to increase knowledge and personal development is likely to lead to job satisfaction.

Figure 11.6 illustrates the hygiene and motivation factors. The hygiene factors relate to responses that range from no dissatisfaction to high dissatisfaction. The motivators, if present in the work environment, can provide low to high satisfaction. If not present, a complete lack of satisfaction can result.

Implications for Managers Herzberg's theory relates specifically to the work environment. Managers can use their knowledge to ensure that hygiene factors are in place in the environment as a foundation on which to build motivation. The absence of quality hygiene factors can lead to dissatisfaction in the workforce—a lesson quickly learned by Chuck Mitchell at GTO Inc. The company, located in Tallahassee, Florida, was a deteriorating five-year-old maker of automatic gate openers. When Mitchell replaced the founder, who had suffered a fatal heart attack, he inherited greatly disillusioned

Figure 11.6   Results of Hygiene Factors and Motivation Factors

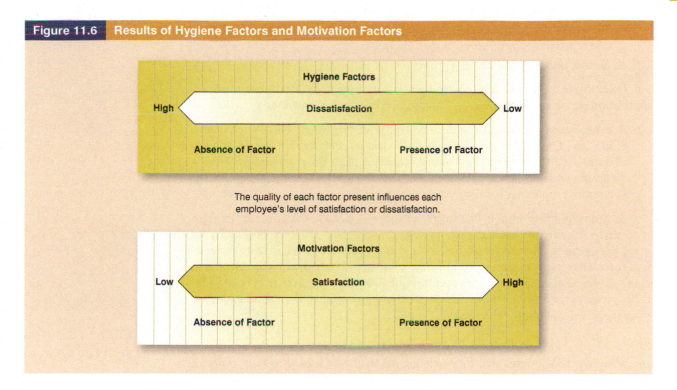

The quality of each factor present influences each employee's level of satisfaction or dissatisfaction.

workers in a work environment where hygiene factors had been neglected. It had been common practice for the founder to do the following:

- Harangue employees for filing claims on the company's health insurance policy.
- Begrudge employees ten-minute breaks every two hours.
- Have no budget funds available for machine repairs.
- Insist that hourly workers work overtime without premium pay.
- Direct employees to repair antique cars, install basketball backboards, and build fences for the owner on company time.
- Require employees to bring their own coffee and supplies for the break room.

After Mitchell gained a sense of some of the higher-priority items among the employees, there were certain hygiene factors he knew he could improve immediately. As Mitchell notes, "The little things often mean more to people, and they show that management cares about everybody." So for starters, Mitchell took some high-profile steps:

- He bought coffee and supplies for the break room.
- He hired a roofer to patch the leaking building.
- He encouraged employees to bring in their personal cars so they could use some of GTO's tools to repair them over the weekend.
- He changed the health insurance policy from one with a $300 employee deductible to one featuring a $5 co-payment.
- He introduced company-paid employee disability insurance.
- He gave employees keys to the building.

- He provided a "blank check" when employees needed money for machine parts and repairs.
- He instituted a profit-sharing program.[15]

Once top management has provided satisfactory hygiene factors, it can focus, on motivation factors, as the founder of Thompson-McCully demonstrates:

> Bob Thompson *"challenges people to achieve more by giving them more responsibility,"* says Office Manager Marlene Van Patten, *an annuity recipient who joined Thompson-McCully when it purchased Spartan Asphalt ten years earlier. "He is a demanding person, but extremely fair. He always has wanted to be the best and he has wanted his people to be the best."*[16]

A critical point to note is that nearly all supervisors have the power to increase motivation in the workplaces they manage by granting more responsibility to employees, praising their accomplishments, and making them feel that they are succeeding. Top managers at Southwest Airlines have come to the same conclusion. Motivated employees believe they have control over their jobs and can make a contribution.[17] This belief provides the basis for team management, empowerment and *intrapreneurship*— to be discussed later in this chapter.

McClelland and the Need for Achievement

In the needs theory developed by psychologist David McClelland, certain types of needs are learned during a lifetime of interaction with the environment.[18] He described three specific needs:

1. *Achievement,* or the desire to excel or achieve in relation to a set of standards
2. *Power,* or the desire to control others or have influence over them
3. *Affiliation,* or the desire for friendship, cooperation and close interpersonal relationships

Achievement relates to individual performance. Power and affiliation, by contrast, involve interpersonal relationships.

Studies of achievement motivation have produced two important ideas: (1) a strong achievement need relates to how well individuals are motivated to perform their work; and (2) the achievement need can be strengthened by training.

McClelland's needs theory recognizes that people may have different mixtures or combinations of the needs; an individual could be described as a high achiever, a power-motivated person or an affiliator.

High Achiever McClelland and associate David Burnham defined the characteristics of the high achiever.[19] They believed the high achiever does the following:

Explain the characteristics of a person with high-achievement needs

- *Performs a task because of a compelling need for personal achievement, not necessarily for the rewards associated with accomplishing the task.* The desire to excel applies to both means and end; the high achiever, in addition to wanting to do a good job, wants to do the job more efficiently than it has been done before.
- *Prefers to take personal responsibility for solving problems rather than leaving the outcome to others.* Achievers may be viewed as loners. At times they may appear to have difficulty delegating authority.
- *Prefers to set moderate goals that, with stretching, are achievable.* For the achiever, easy goals with a high probability of success provide no challenge and thus no

satisfaction. Difficult goals with a low probability of success would require an achiever to gamble on success. Because the achiever likes to be in control, an outcome that depends on chance is unacceptable.

- *Prefers immediate and concrete feedback about performance, which assists in measuring progress toward the goal.* The feedback needs to be in terms of goal performance (rather than personality variables) so the achiever can determine what needs to be done to improve performance.

Power-Motivated Person The person with a strong desire for power needs to acquire, exercise and maintain influence over others. Such persons compete with others if success will allow them to be dominant. The power-motivated person does not avoid confrontations.

Affiliator The person with a high need for affiliation wants to be liked by other people, attempts to establish friendships, and seeks to avoid conflict. The affiliator prefers conciliation.

Implications for Managers Based on McClelland's theory, managers should work to identify and encourage the development of high achievers. Managers should capitalize on high achievers' goal-setting ability and on their desire for responsibility. This can be accomplished by providing them with opportunities for participation, by delegating authority to them, and by using management by objectives as discussed in Chapter 4. To work effectively with high achievers, managers should provide immediate, concrete feedback. For example, Tom Warner, president of Warner Corporation, a Washington, D.C.-based plumbing, heating, ventilation and air-conditioning contractor, structured a unique program to capitalize on his high achievers.[20] Considered revolutionary in the mundane world of stopped-up sinks and balky furnaces, Warner appointed 80 area technical directors (ATD) in his 260-person business. The directors have their own businesses to manage within their assigned zip codes. Warner prepares the ATD with training in sales and marketing, budgeting, negotiating, cost estimating and customer service. Then he empowers them to build up the business in their assigned locations. Says Warner, "The guys who gravitate to the ATD program want more, with more effort. If you want a 9-to-5 job, it's not for you." Because the program is geared toward high achievers, it is not for everyone. Eight out of the first twelve ATDs decided the program wasn't for them; they wanted to remain ordinary mechanics.

When dealing with the power-motivated person of McClelland's theory, managers should recognize that the use of power is a necessary part of corporate life and that those who are motivated by power can serve as necessary and useful members of the organization. Managers should be aware, however, of the negative aspect of power as a motivator. Many individuals seek power solely for personal benefit. The power-motivated person may not, therefore, have the organization's best interests at heart.

In working with employees whom McClelland labeled affiliators, managers must be aware that these employees desire to avoid conflict, which may prevent them from handling organizational conflict effectively.

Figure 11.7 shows how the three needs theories relate. Each theory provides the manager with a different viewpoint from which to understand the cause of behavior. Herzberg's hygiene factors relate to Maslow's lower-level needs; Herzberg's motivation factors relate to the higher-level needs, as do McClelland's needs for power and achievement.

Figure 11.7	Comparison of the Theories of Maslow, Herzberg, and McClelland

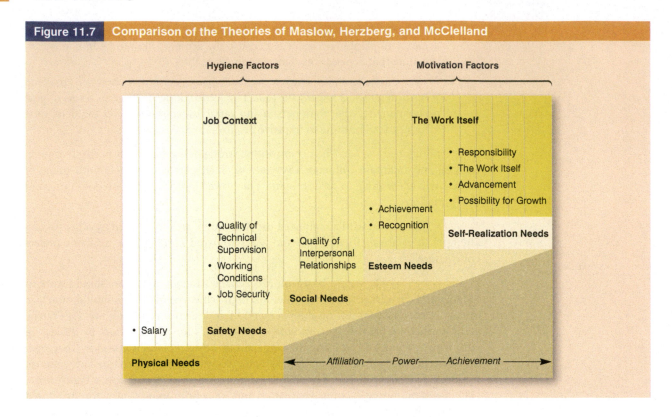

Alderfer's ERG Theory

Psychologist Clayton Alderfer proposed a needs theory that compressed Maslow's five levels of needs into three:[21]

1. *Existence.* Existence needs relate to a person's physical well-being. (In Maslow's model, existence needs include physiological and safety needs.)

2. *Relatedness.* This level includes needs for satisfactory relationships with others. (Relatedness needs correspond, in Maslow's model, to social needs.)

3. *Growth.* Growth needs call for the realization of potential and the achievement of competence. (In Maslow's model, growth needs become esteem and self-realization needs.)

Alderfer's theory is called the **ERG theory**. The name derives from the first three letters of each of the needs Alderfer defined.

Maslow and Alderfer agreed that an unsatisfied need is a motivator, and that as lower-level needs are satisfied they become less important. Alderfer believed, however, that higher-level needs become more important as they are satisfied. If a person fails in an attempt to attain a higher need, the individual might return to a lower-level need. For example, the employee frustrated in an attempt to achieve more growth could redirect energies to, say, becoming part of a group. When high-tech computer-related businesses in Silicon Valley began to retrench after a period of expansion, managers who had been focusing on furthering their growth needs began to seek new organizations to meet their existence needs. Figure 11.8 illustrates the relationship between the theories of Maslow and Alderfer.

6 Identify the needs associated with ERG theory

ERG theory
A motivation theory establishing three categories of human needs: existence needs, relatedness needs and growth needs

Figure 11.8 Comparison of the Theories of Maslow and Alderfer

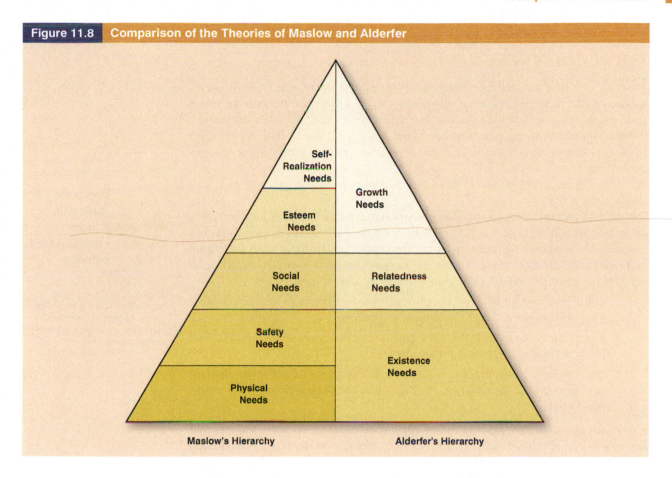

Maslow's Hierarchy — Self-Realization Needs, Esteem Needs, Social Needs, Safety Needs, Physical Needs

Alderfer's Hierarchy — Growth Needs, Relatedness Needs, Existence Needs

Implications for Managers According to Alderfer, managers should realize that a person may willingly slip down the needs hierarchy if attempts to achieve needs are frustrated. To maintain high levels of performance, managers should provide opportunities for employees to capitalize on higher-order needs. Managers can do this by recognizing employees and encouraging participation in decision making. For example, at Silicon Graphics Inc., 40 people are chosen each year by their peers as the employees who best represent the culture and spirit of the company. The winners are announced with great fanfare, and each receives a trip for two to Hawaii. At least equally important to the trip is the recognition by peers, which meets esteem needs.

The importance of fulfilling growth and self-realization needs is illustrated by the comments of Ocelia Williams, an hourly worker at Cincinnati's Cin-Made, a small manufacturer of mailing tubes and other cardboard-and-metal containers, and a practitioner of open-book management. "I couldn't see how the company could make it unless we all took our share of responsibility. I now know what is going on, and where I fit. What I do does make a difference." What Ocelia and other employees do is share responsibility. Hourly workers now do all of Cin-Made's purchasing and have a voice in every hiring decision. They schedule their own hours, hire and supervise all temporary employees, oversee the company's safety program, and administer its skill-based pay system.[22]

PROCESS THEORIES: MOTIVATION THEORIES FOCUSING ON BEHAVIORS

Now that we have examined four motivation theories relating to the individual's needs, we can explore four theories about why people choose a particular behavior to satisfy their needs. This section will discuss four behavior-oriented theories: expectancy theory, reinforcement theory, equity theory, and goal-setting theory. Each derives from the factors summarized in Figure 11.3: past experiences, environmental influences and perceptions.

Expectancy Theory

Developed by Victor Vroom, **expectancy theory** states that before choosing a behavior, an individual will evaluate various possibilities on the basis of anticipated work and reward.[23] Motivation—the spur to act—is a function of how badly we want something and how likely we think we are to get it. Its intensity functions in direct proportion to perceived or expected rewards. Expectancy theory includes three variables:

1   *Effort–performance link.* Will the effort achieve performance? How much effort will performance require? How probable is success?

2   *Performance–reward link.* What is the possibility that a certain performance will produce the desired reward or outcome?

3   *Attractiveness.* How attractive is the reward? This factor relates to the strength or importance of the reward to the individual and deals with his or her unsatisfied needs.

To see how expectancy theory can be applied, consider an example. Suppose that late one Friday afternoon, John Friedman's boss asks him to develop a presentation of the six-month budget results. The presentation is due the following Monday. John realizes he can complete the four-hour project in one of two ways. He can stay at the office and do the work, or he can take the work home over the weekend.

John evaluates the first option, which involves staying at work for the necessary four hours. He realizes that staying will result in a completed presentation by Monday (effort–performance link). He knows from past experience that a completed project will result in recognition by his boss (performance–reward link). John has a high regard for this recognition, because it will eventually lead to a promotion. Working late on Friday will, however, interfere with existing plans and might cause domestic problems. (The domestic problems affect the attractiveness of the reward.)

As John evaluates the second option of having to take work home, he realizes that the effort–performance link and the performance–reward link will be the same as in the stay-at-work option. By taking the work home, however, John can avoid the negative consequences of interfering with social plans. (This makes the reward seem more attractive.) John chooses the second option.

In his decision making, John asked himself a series of questions: "Can I accomplish the task?" Yes, it will take four hours, but I can do it. "What's in it for me?" When I do the task it can bring both positive and negative results (option 1), or just positive results (option 2). "Is it worth it?" The positive is, but the negative isn't. Study Figure 11.9 and determine the stage of the expectancy theory to which each question pertains.

Implications for Managers According to expectancy theory, behavior is heavily influenced by perceptions of the outcomes of behavior. The individual who expects

7 Discuss the relationship between expectations and motivation

expectancy theory
A motivation theory stating that three factors influence behavior: the value of rewards, the relationship of rewards to the necessary performance, and the effort required for performance

Figure 11.9   Model of Expectancy Theory

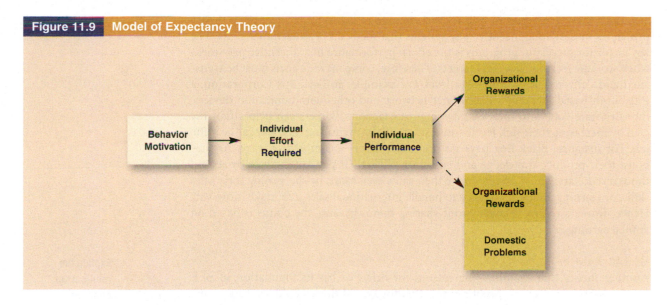

an outcome, possesses the competence to achieve it, and wants it badly enough will exhibit the behavior required by the organization. The person who expects that a specific behavior will produce an outcome perceived as undesirable will be less inclined to exhibit that behavior. A manager who knows each subordinate's expectations and desires can tailor outcomes associated with specific behaviors to produce motivation.[24,25] To motivate behavior, managers must do the following:

- *Understand that employees measure the value associated with the assignment.* As a manager, you get from your people what you reward, not what you ask for.

- *Find out what outcomes are perceived as desirable by employees and provide them.* Outcomes may be intrinsic (experienced directly by the individual) or extrinsic (provided by the company). A feeling of self-worth after doing a good job is intrinsic; the promotion that the job produces is extrinsic. For an outcome to be satisfying to an employee, the employee must recognize it as an outcome that relates to his or her needs and one that is consistent with his or her expectations of what is due.[26]

- *Make the job intrinsically rewarding.* If the employee feeling good about successfully completing a job is a valued outcome, it is critical for managers to provide experiences that enhance an employee's feeling of self-worth.

- *Effectively and clearly communicate desired behaviors and their outcomes.* Employees need to know what is acceptable and what is unacceptable to the organization.

- *Link rewards to performance.* Once the acceptable performance level is attained, rewards should quickly follow.

- *Be aware that people differ in their goals, needs, desires, and levels of performance.* The manager must set a level of performance for each employee that is attainable by that person.

- *Strengthen each individual's perceptions of his or her ability to execute desired behaviors and achieve outcomes by providing guidance and direction.* The manager trains and coaches, and then must trust employees to do their jobs.

With these guidelines in mind, some companies incorporate expectancy theory principles in designing incentive pay systems that focus on organizational goals. The key factor for successful programs is the effort–performance link. Incentive pay works when workers feel they can meet targets. Therefore, companywide goals must be translated and delivered at the employee level. For example, at Black Box Corporation, a Pittsburgh-based marketer of computer network and other communication devices, the corporate goal is to increase customer satisfaction. Workers can help attain the goal by increasing their skill levels—and substantially increasing their pay in the same job. For instance, Black Box pays starting order takers a competitive wage. As they boost their product knowledge and customer skills, their pay can increase by several thousand dollars. Those who improve their skills even more, by sharpening their sales skills, or learning another language to handle international sales, can make more still. Hence, workers receive a larger profit-sharing bonus because the bonus is based on annual earnings.[27]

Reinforcement Theory

Another theory that examines the reasons for behavior has its foundation in B. F. Skinner's work in operant conditioning.[28] **Reinforcement theory** holds that a person's behavior in a situation is influenced by the rewards or penalties experienced in similar situations in the past. John, the employee who was faced with the task of preparing a last-minute budget presentation, received praise from his boss for expending extra effort in the past. This positive reinforcement influenced John's behavior when the boss had another similar request.

Reinforcement theory introduces a major point that managers should understand. Much of motivated behavior is learned behavior.[29] The employee learns over time what type of performance is acceptable and what is unacceptable. This learning influences future behavior. Figure 11.10 shows how reinforcement affects behavior.

Types of Reinforcement Managers can choose from four main types of reinforcement: positive reinforcement, avoidance, extinction and punishment. Of these four

8 Explain the relationship between reinforcement and motivation

reinforcement theory
A motivation theory that states a supervisor's reactions and past rewards and penalties affect employees' behavior

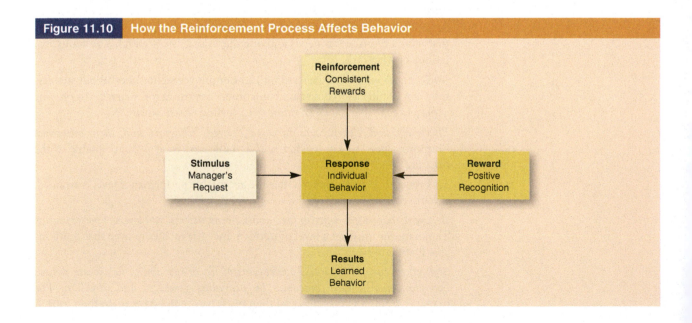

| Figure 11.10 | How the Reinforcement Process Affects Behavior |

approaches, positive reinforcement most often leads to long-range growth in individuals by producing lasting and positive behavioral changes.

1 *Positive reinforcement.* To increase the probability that an individual will repeat a desired behavior, a manager provides positive reinforcement as soon as possible after the desired behavior occurs. Positive reinforcers can offer praise, pay or promotions—elements normally regarded as favorable by employees.

2 *Avoidance.* This method of reinforcement attempts to increase the probability that a positive behavior will be repeated by showing the consequences of behavior the manager does not desire. The employee avoids those consequences by displaying the desired behavior. For example, a manager has a policy of penalizing all employees who do not turn in reports on time. As long as the threat of punishment is there, employees will be motivated to meet the required deadline.

3 *Extinction.* Managers are using extinction when they choose to ignore the behavior of subordinates in order to weaken the behavior. This approach is most effective when behavior is temporary, atypical and not serious in its negative consequences. The supervisor's hope is that the behavior will soon go away or disappear if it is ignored. Extinction might also be appropriate in a situation of changed circumstances. Say a manager and an employee have developed the habit of talking during working hours about off-the-job topics. After the manager is promoted to another job in another area, the employee continues to drop by, a practice that makes the manager uncomfortable. If the manager continues to work while the employee is there, the employee will eventually get the message and the behavior will be extinguished.

4 *Punishment.* Managers might attempt to decrease the recurrence of a behavior by applying negative consequences, or punishment. Loss of privileges, docked pay and suspension are forms of punishment. The trouble with punishment as a response to behavior is that the person will learn what not to do but will not necessarily learn the desired behavior.

Reinforcement is affected by time. The closer the reinforcement is to the behavior, the greater the impact it will have on future behavior.

Implications for Managers Reinforcement theory has several implications for managers. First, managers should bear in mind that motivated behavior is influenced by the employee's learning what is acceptable and unacceptable to the organization.[30] In addition, in working with employees to develop motivated behavior, managers should do the following:

- *Tell individuals what they can do to get positive reinforcement.* The establishment of a work standard lets all individuals know what behavior is acceptable.

- *Tell individuals what they are doing wrong.* The person who does not know why rewards are not forthcoming may be confused. Information allows a person to improve motivated behavior.

- *Base rewards on performance.* Managers should not reward all individuals in the same way. If the manager gives the same rewards to all employees for all degrees of performance, poor or average performance is reinforced and high performance may be ignored.

- *Administer the reinforcement as close in time to the related behavior as possible.* To achieve maximum impact, the appropriate reinforcement should immediately follow performance.

- *Recognize that failure to reward can also modify behavior.* If a manager does not praise a subordinate for meritorious behavior, the subordinate can become confused about the behavior the manager wants.

By applying these guidelines, managers can, as they help employees focus on organizational objectives, modify employee behavior at the same time. For example, CEO Steve Wilson of Mid-States Technical Staffing Services, in Davenport, IA, used positive reinforcement to develop teamwork, follow-through and initiative. After teaching everyone to understand company financial statements and to take responsibility for budget items, Wilson told employees, "Every time you hit $75,000 in net earnings, I'll pay a bonus." As Wilson notes, "The light dawned slowly. At first employees thought, 'Great, I don't have to wait 'til Christmas for my bonus,' but when we paid out the second one two months after the first, that's when they changed." Now, employees watch weekly budget and income numbers like hawks, and move heaven and earth if they think they are falling behind set goals or are within reach of a target. Salespeople help one another out instead of hoarding customers. Office workers, each of whom has responsibility for certain expenses, find other departments eager to cooperate in cutting spending.[31]

Equity Theory

Another view of motivation is found in **equity theory**. According to this theory, people's behavior relates to their perception of how fairly they are treated. Most professional athletes use equity arguments to support their salary demands. They point to publicized salaries received by peers as justification for their negotiating stands. Equity theory also involves the fairness that an individual perceives in the relationship between effort expended and reward.

People determine equity by calculating a simple ratio: the effort they are expected to invest on the job (their input) in relation to what they expect to receive after investing that effort (their outcome or reward). As Figure 11.11 shows, this input-outcome ratio should provide a means of comparison with the ratios of other individuals or groups. Equity exists when the ratios are equivalent. Inequity exists when, in the employee's mind, inputs exceed the relative or perceived values of outcomes.[32]

9 Explain how equity influences motivation

equity theory
A motivation theory in which comparisons of relative input-outcome ratios influence behavior choices

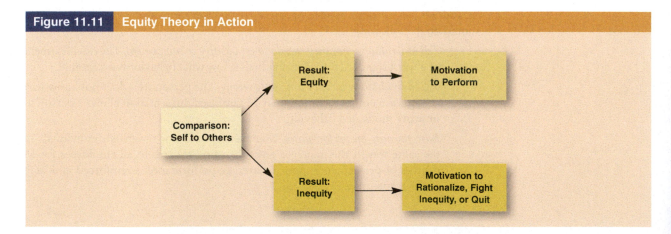

Figure 11.11	Equity Theory in Action

Comparison: Self to Others

Result: Equity → Motivation to Perform

Result: Inequity → Motivation to Rationalize, Fight Inequity, or Quit

Example of Equity Theory Ellen McCann has been working as a salesperson for ten months. In this time, she has gone to sales school three times (achieving superior ratings in all categories), consistently achieved 125 percent of sales quota, and has won two local sales contests. In recognition of this achievement, Ellen's boss has given her a $150 per month raise. Ellen's motivation has dropped noticeably in the past month, however. Why? She learned that a salesperson with no prior experience had been hired at $2,750 per month—$50 more than Ellen is making! As Ellen said, "It's not fair! If they can do that, I'm going to start to look around for an employer who will appreciate me."

This example leads to two points about equity theory. First, when an individual perceives himself or herself as the victim of inequity, one of three responses occurs. The person can decide to escape the situation ("I quit"), put the input-outcome ratios in balance ("I'll do less" or "I want a raise"), or attempt to change perceptions ("It's actually fair because …").

The second important point about equity theory concerns the referent the person selects for comparison. There are two categories: other and system. In the example of professional athletes, the "other" category includes those persons in the same job, same team, or same league, or those with similar backgrounds or in the same circle of friends. The system is the referent when the individual recognizes the presence of organization-wide policies and procedures: "If those people are allowed overtime, I should have overtime when I need it to complete my work."[33]

Implications for Managers Equity theory emphasizes that employees are motivated by both the absolute and relative rewards available in the system. More important, employees make conscious comparisons of equity, and these comparisons have the potential to influence employee motivation levels. Therefore, managers must make conscious efforts to establish and maintain equity in the work environment. In addition, managers need to recognize that perceptions of equity are constantly in flux. Current perceptions are affected by past perceptions. By bearing this in mind, a manager may be able to identify the incident that served as the straw that broke the camel's back.

Whenever everyone in a company has a small open cubicle, including the chairman, and no one gets a reserved parking spot, the organization has applied equity theory.

Goal-Setting Theory

Explain how goals influence motivation

goal-setting theory
A motivation theory stating that behavior is influenced by goals, which tell employees what they need to do and how much effort they need to expend

According to the final behavior-oriented theory, **goal-setting theory**, people's behavior is influenced by the goals that are established. In essence, goals tell an employee what needs to be done and how much effort will need to be expended.[34] "Other practices that leaders like Robert Thompson, of Thompson-McCully, tend to endorse include promoting from within and setting achievable stretch goals for managers and workers alike. When you think that you are doing the best you can do, 'he can get a little more out of you,' says CFO Gregg Campbell."[35]

Goal-setting theory is similar to the concepts associated with expectancy theory in that it focuses on the conscious choices a person makes. According to the theory, there are two approaches to goal setting: (1) managers may set goals for the employees; or (2) employees and managers develop employee goals together.

Implications for Managers According to goal-setting theory, managers should

- *Work with employees in setting goals.* Help them provide targets for motivation.
- *Make goals specific rather than general.* The goal "Do your best" is not as effective as "Complete the project by June 15 with no budget overruns."

• *Provide feedback on performance.* Feedback acts as a guide to behavior. It helps identify shortcomings in performance and provides the means for corrective action.

Jere Stead, former CEO of AT&T's Global Information Solutions (now NCR Corporation), led business transformations five times by relying on goal-setting theory. Notes Stead, "At GIS all objectives must clearly link to key results: customer or shareholder satisfaction and profitable growth. The goal-setting links the organization, provides a basis for gauging progress, and gives specific measures for rewards."[36]

BUILDING A PHILOSOPHY OF MANAGEMENT

11

Discuss the importance of a manager's philosophy of management in creating a positive work environment

The theories of Maslow, Herzberg, McClelland and Alderfer offer valuable insight into the needs that drive motivation. The theories of expectancy, reinforcement, equity and goal setting reveal the *why* of motivation—why employees display different types of motivated behavior. Each theory makes an important contribution to understanding the motivation of an employee, and each provides input for the motivation model. Familiarity with theories of motivation allows a manager an educated viewpoint from which to consider how to foster motivation in workers, capture commitment and develop a positive work environment.

One significant factor that sets the foundation for creating a positive work environment is a manager's **philosophy of management**, or attitude about work and the people who do the work. A manager's philosophy of management incorporates and reflects personal beliefs about human nature in the work setting—about worker attitudes and characteristics, employee maturity and the influence of management expectations on behavior. Ed Armatis, an operator and mechanic at the oil blending facility at Thompson-McCully, describes Bob Thompson this way: "He is a fair guy, but very demanding. You don't see him around much if you do your job."[37] A manager's philosophy influences the motivation approaches he or she will select. Managers who think subordinates are ambitious and eager, wish to do work well, want to be independent, and enjoy work will take far different actions than managers who think subordinates are lazy and work only to attain security.

To develop a philosophy of management, there are three concepts describing human nature that should be incorporated: Theory X and Theory Y, Argyris's maturity theory and the development of management expectations.

philosophy of management
A manager's attitude about work and the people who perform it, which influences the motivation approaches he or she selects

Theory X and Theory Y

Douglas McGregor, a professor of industrial management, said that an individual's management philosophy reflects one of two sets of assumptions about workers.[38] He called the two sets Theory X and Theory Y. **Theory X** is a philosophy of management that negatively perceives subordinates' potential for work and attitudes toward work. It assumes that subordinates dislike work, are poorly motivated, and require close supervision. A manager with these beliefs tends to control the group, use negative motivation, and refuse to delegate decision making. Figure 11.12 lists the components of Theory X.

Theory Y is a philosophy of management that positively perceives subordinates' potential for and attitudes toward work. It assumes, as Figure 11.12 shows that subordinates can be self-directing, will seek responsibility, and find work as natural as play or rest. The outcome of this belief is a manager who encourages people to seek responsibility, involves people in decision making, and works with people to achieve their goals.

Theory X
A philosophy of management with a negative perception of subordinates' potential for and attitudes toward work

Theory Y
A philosophy of management with a positive perception of subordinates' potential for and attitudes toward work

Figure 11.12　Assumptions about Workers According to Theory X and Theory Y

THEORY X	THEORY Y
People basically dislike work and avoid it whenever possible.	Most people find work as natural as play or rest and develop an attitude toward work based on their experience with it.
Because most people dislike work, they have to be closely supervised and threatened with punishment to reach objectives.	People do not need to be threatened with punishment; they will work voluntarily toward organizational objectives to which they are committed.
Most people prefer to be told what to do, have little ambition, want to avoid responsibility, and want security above all else.	The average person working in an environment with good human relations will accept and seek responsibility.
Most people have little creativity. They are not capable of solving problems. Rather, they must be redirected.	Most people possess a high degree of imagination, ingenuity and creativity with which to solve organizational problems.
Most people have limited intellectual potential. Contributions above basic job performance should not be expected.	Although people have intellectual potential, modern industrial life utilizes only part of it.

The important point about Theory X and Theory Y is that a manager's philosophy influences the kind of work climate he or she endeavors to create and, ultimately, shapes how the manager treats people.

Argyris's Maturity Theory

A manager's philosophy incorporates his or her attitude toward employee maturity. The work of Chris Argyris, who is most noted for his models of organizational learning, summarized these attitudes.[39] Argyris related the development of individual maturity to the structure of organizations. He believed that people develop along a continuum from immaturity to maturity. People who have reached maturity:

- Tend to be active rather than passive.
- Are independent rather than dependent.
- Are self-aware rather than unaware.
- Are self-controlled rather than controlled by others.

Argyris's concern was that a mature personality conflicts with typical organizations in four ways:

1 The formal chain of command limits self-determination, making individuals passive and manager dependent.
2 The span of control decreases a person's self-determination.
3 Unity of direction places objectives under the control of one manager. It limits the employee's ability to define objectives.
4 Specialization of labor limits initiative and self-determination.

Managers who create work environments that are obstacles to mature employees set up themselves and their organizations for failure. Mature people confronted with rigid, limiting circumstances become passive and dependent. They cannot grow, and they can rarely see long-term implications. Recognition of these realities in recent years has fueled the growth of the movement to employee empowerment, which this chapter will discuss in the next section.

Development of Expectations

In developing a philosophy of management, a manager must consider the importance of expectations. "If the employees are happy, they make the customers happy," says SAS CEO Jim Goodnight. "If they make the customers happy, they make me happy."[40] A manager must communicate his or her expectations directly to employees. John L. Single reports that:

- Subordinates do what they believe they are expected to do.

- Ineffective managers fail to develop high expectations for performance.

- Managers perceived as excellent create high performance expectations that their employees can fulfill.[41]

The last point, that employees fulfill their manager's expectations, is often referred to as the self-fulfilling prophecy. It is a key management concept. Sam Walton believed in it so much that it became Rule 3 of Sam's Rules for Building a Business: "Motivate your partners. Money and ownership aren't enough…. Set high goals, encourage competition, and then keep score."[42]

Incorporating expectations into management requires two phases. The first consists of developing and communicating expectations of performance, group citizenship, individual initiative and job creativity. The second involves consistency. The manager must be consistent in his or her expectations and in communicating them. Consistency will produce reinforcement and, in the end, promote stability and reduce anxiety. Employees will know what the boss expects.

MANAGING FOR MOTIVATION

12 Describe how managers can structure the environment to provide motivation

With a well-rounded, people-centered philosophy in place, a manager is ready to motivate by creating a positive, supportive work environment. In the next few pages we will discuss how to manage for motivation: how to treat people as individuals, offer support, recognize and value Diversity and Inclusion, foster empowerment, provide an effective reward system, redesign jobs, promote intrapreneurship, and create flexibility in work.

Treating People as Individuals

All of us are different. We think differently; we have different needs and wants; and we cherish different values, expectations, and goals. Each of us wants to be treated as a special person because each of us is special. What is more, we change. Today, a person's link to others may be paramount; a year from now, recognition for accomplishment may be the driving passion.

Looking at today's workforce brings the concept of individuality into sharp focus. Companies manage four generations of employees: [43]

- *Silents* are also known as Veterans or Traditionalists and were born between 1925 and 1946. They grew up during the Great Depression, and then fought World War II. Tom Brokaw called them "the greatest generation." They are hardworking and loyal, with a strong commitment to teamwork and collaboration.

- *Baby Boomers* were born between 1946 and 1964. After World War II, birth rates rose sharply and this population explosion is referred to as a "boom." Boomers lived through civil rights and the Vietnam War. They are willing to work long hours, putting work before their personal lives. They equate success with salaries and work commitment.

- *Generation Xers* were born between 1965 and 1980 and are more independent than previous generations. They grew up with both parents working and many were "latch-key" kids, since they had no parental supervision after school. Many are entrepreneurial, self-reliant and self-starters. They trust others less. They don't like rigid work schedules or working in teams. Sometimes they are referred to as slackers because they want to balance their work and personal life.

- *Millennials* are also known as Generation Y or Echo Boomers, children of the Baby Boomers. They were born after 1980 and are the most educated and technologically advanced generation. They have grown up with computers, the Internet and cell phones. They are connected 24/7 (24 hours a day, 7 days a week), and are willing to share their network. See this chapter's Managing Social Media for a discussion about Millennials' use of computers and technology. Millenials work well in teams, but are more demanding than other generations. They were overindulged by their parents, and are challenged by responsibility and accountability. Yet, they work well with a mentor to help them navigate the professional world.

Characteristics of the four generations at work can be seen in Figure 11.13.

Successful managers recognize people as individuals and work with their particular differences. Such recognition goes a long way. The successful manager knows that, because each of us is an individual, each of us is motivated differently. The more managers know about motivation, the more successful they will be in working with people.

Managing Social Media

Tech Savvy Millennials

Millennials are the first generation to be raised with computers. They quickly adopted the Internet and online social media. Electronic gadgets enable them to talk, type, listen and text. Silents and Baby Boomers aren't as adept at computers and technology, so tech savvy Millennials are at an advantage in the workplace.

Instead of reading newspapers or watching television like preceding generations, Millennials get their information from social media sites, which include blogs, microblogs, social networks and photo- and video-sharing sites. Online, Millenials post and share their personal profiles, which include photos as well as descriptions of interests and hobbies.

⮕ Neil Howe and William Strauss, co-authors of the book *Generations*, came up with the name *Millennials*. The authors say, "They don't waste time trying to change things. Our message for employers is you want to organize them in groups and structure the work and give them constant feedback." What else could managers do to structure the environment to provide motivation for Millennials?

Figure 11.13	Workplace Characteristics

	Veterans (1922–1945)	Baby Boomers (1946–1964)	Generation X (1965–1980)	Generation Y (1981–2000)
Work Ethic and Values	Hard work Respect authority Sacrifice Duty before fun Adhere to rules	Workaholics Work efficiently Crusading causes Personal fulfillment Desire quality Question authority	Eliminate the task Self-reliance Want structure and direction Skeptical	What's next Multitasking Tenacity Entrepreneurial Tolerant Goal oriented
Work is...	An obligation	An exciting adventure	A difficult challenge A contract	A means to an end Fulfillment
Leadership Style	Directive Command-and-control	Consensual Collegial	Everyone is the same Challenge others Ask why	*TBD
Interactive Style	Individual	Team player Loves to have meetings	Entrepreneur	Participative
Communications	Formal Memo	In person	Direct Immediate	E-mail Voicemail
Feedback and Rewards	No news is good news Satisfaction in a job well done	Don't appreciate it Money Title recognition	Sorry to interrupt, but how am I doing? Freedom is the best reward	Whenever I want it, at the push of a button Meaningful work
Messages that Motivate	Your experience is respected	You are valued You are needed	Do it your way Forget the rules	You will work with other bright, creative people
Work and Family Life	Ne'er the twain shall meet	No balance Work to live	Balance	Balance

*As this group has not spent much time in the workforce, this characteristics has yet to be determined.

Source: Greg Hammill, "Mixing and Matching Four Generations of Employees," *FDU Magazine* (Winter/Spring 2005) http://www.fdu.edu/newspubs/magazine/05ws/generations.htm.

Providing Support

To develop motivated employees, a manager must provide a climate in which each employee's needs can be met. A starting point is to facilitate attainment of the employee's goals. The manager does this by removing barriers, developing mutual goal-setting opportunities, initiating training and education programs, encouraging risk taking and providing stability.

Two other actions can provide support and enhance the environment. The first is the open appreciation of employees' contributions. Jill Barad, former President of Mattel USA, has this to say about appreciation:

> *Taking time to tell people how good they are is one of the best ways management can reward people for their efforts. We in management tend to focus on what's not being done, how people are not performing instead of recognizing that our people are performing. We must constantly remind people of their strengths so they can make the most of those behaviors.*[44]

Barad's point is echoed by Jere Stead, formerly of AT&T Global: "Even middle managers, who often have little money and few promotions to dispense, have plenty they can give: 'Attaboys', letters, notes, trips, cash—really pound out rewards."[45]

The second action managers can take is to show sensitivity to employees' needs for equity. Each employee must feel that he or she is receiving a fair exchange for his or her input into the company and in comparison to other employees. This point is supported by Norman Brinker, Chairman of Brinker International: "Compensation has to be equitable. From the top to the bottom of the organization, the program must recognize the value of inputs into the company. Everyone is aware of everyone else."[46]

Recognizing and Valuing Diversity and Inclusion

As we have discussed throughout the text, part of working with people as individuals is the ability to recognize and incorporate the value of Diversity and Inclusion within the workplace. The composition of the workforce is changing—and with it, workers' needs, goals and values. As noted in Chapter 1, managers are no longer managing a homogeneous workforce. Rather, the workforce of present-day organizations manifests a kaleidoscope of Diversity and Inclusion: young and old; all races, colors, ethnicities, cultures, national origins; male and female—all with differing mental and physical capabilities—as well as full time, part time and temporary.[47]

Managers need to respond to this Diversity and Inclusion by understanding, appreciating and utilizing the differences. If they do not, according to former Xerox Regional Vice President Tracy Whitaker, "30 percent of your intellectual capital is not participating in your organization."[48]

As the Diversity and Inclusion in the workforce continues to change, traditional programs for training, monitoring and compensation may have to be modified.[49] One example of an organization that has recognized the need to modify its policies and practices is Umanoff & Parsons, a New York City bakery. Umanoff & Parsons' senior management team is composed of three women and three men from five diverse cultures: they are Jamaican, American, Haitian, Hispanic and Russian. Half the bakery's workforce is foreign born; the workers come from Haiti, Trinidad, Grenada, the Dominican Republic and Russia. The Diversity and Inclusion brings contrasting viewpoints, experiences and needs to the work environment. With these in mind, the company has devised innovative training and mentoring programs, it has gathered these varied individuals into cross-cultural teams.

A Diversity audit allows a company to determine whether Diversity exists among the managers and employees. In order to conduct a Diversity audit, managers must first determine Diversity and Inclusion goals. Next, essential questions to ask in a Diversity audit must be determined. This chapter's Valuing Diversity and Inclusion feature is an example of questions that might be used. The audit seeks to identify strong and weak areas with regard to where the organization currently stands on its Diversity goals.

Empowering Employees

"You want motivated workers?" asks Peter C. Fleming, vice president of Prudential Insurance Company.[50] "Just empower them and you will see what motivation and ownership means." As discussed in Chapter 5, leaders empower employees by sharing authority and information, providing needed training, listening to employees, developing relationships based on mutual trust and respect and acting on employee recommendations. As noted management consultant Tom Peters says, empowerment occurs when individuals in an organization are "given autonomy, authority, trusted, and encouraged to break the rules in order to get on with the job."[51]

Workplace Diversity and Inclusion Audit

Recruiting and retaining a diverse workforce involves much more than simply placing a job ad. It demands an environment that welcomes and values people of all backgrounds. The following Diversity audit can help employers evaluate how their recruitment, retention and advancement practices meet the needs of culturally diverse employees and job candidates. The audit was provided by Graciela Kenig & Associates, a consulting firm specializing in multicultural work issues.

Indicate whether each statement below is:

- True (2 points),
- Somewhat True (1 point), or
- Not at All True (0 points).

Add up your points on each question to determine your organization's total score. Then, interpret your score by referring to the guidelines at the end of the assessment.

Regarding Human Resources (HR)

1 Our HR recruiting staff understands cultural differences that may affect the interview experience (e.g., meaning of eye contact, use of I ,boasting, type of information shared).
2 Our HR recruiting staff is comfortable interacting with people from different cultural backgrounds.
3 Our reception areas and interview rooms are culturally appealing to various populations (pictures, publications, decorations, etc.).
4 There is cultural Diversity among the people a job candidate will meet/see on his or her first visit to the company.

Regarding Supervisors/Managers Who Interview Candidates

1 Our leadership is comfortable interacting with people of different backgrounds.
2 More than 30 percent of our leadership is culturally diverse.
3 Appreciation of differences can be seen in the rewards managers give, the work schedules they allow, and the vacation needs they meet.

Regarding Recruitment

1 My company is successful in recruiting diverse employees.
2 Our recruitment strategy includes advertising in publications and websites geared to specific ethnic markets.
3 Our recruitment strategy includes relationships with community organizations.
4 Our ads use culturally appropriate language.
5 Our ads highlight benefits that appeal to specific diverse populations.
6 Our employee affinity groups are involved in recruitment and interviewing of job candidates.
7 We use feedback from our current ethnically diverse employees to describe our benefits to job candidates.

General

1 Diversity and Inclusion means more than numerical representation and is evident at all levels.
2 Affinity groups are visible and active.
3 Employees of different backgrounds interact well.
4 Employees of different backgrounds are encouraged to apply for higher-level positions.
5 All employees participate actively in meetings.
6 When food and drink are offered, they reflect cultural awareness.

Interpreting your score. The overall score has a range of 0–40. The higher number of points, the more effectively your organization is managing and capitalizing on Diversity and Inclusion.

Over 35 points indicates that appealing to diverse candidates is a top priority.

25–34 points indicates that your company is making an effort to adapt its recruitment, retention and advancement practices to meet the needs of culturally diverse candidates.

Less than 25 points suggests the company's recruitment, retention and advancement practices should be revised if a diverse workforce is a high priority.

Source: HRTools, *http://www.hrtools.com/hiring/forms/workplace_Diversity_audit.aspx.*

Empowerment is designed to unshackle the worker and make the job—not just part of the job—the worker's. In the words of James Champy,[52] managers must be willing "to let go of control, in terms of letting people make decisions, particularly when they affect customers." An example of this approach is Chesapeake Packaging Co.'s Baltimore box plant, which created eight employee-managed, so-called internal companies. Customer service is the providence of a "company" called Boxbusters. A "company" called Bob's Big Boys runs the flexigraphic-printing department. Like any business, the internal companies manage their own affairs. Employees track and measure output and figure how to improve it. They watch costs. If they need new equipment, they order it. They get involved in the annual plantwide planning and budgeting process. The members of each "company" review one another's performance and take part in hiring and disciplinary decisions.[53]

Employees, by being empowered, make decisions that formerly were made by the manager. Empowerment results in greater responsibility and innovation and a willingness to take risks. Ownership and trust, along with autonomy and authority, become a motivational package.

Another company that is reaping the benefits of empowered workers is Reflexite Corporation of Avon, Connecticut. CEO Cecil Ursprung says of the employees, "They wanted more than money—they wanted to be committed to something, and they wanted power over the decisions affecting their work lives. Give them that and they would repay the company a thousand times over."[54] Empowerment, in the form of work teams responsible for production and quality, has given employees control over the decisions affecting their work lives. The teams plan the production operation, work with suppliers, respond to customer questions and are accountable for bottom-line decisions. The quality team, composed of members from all production operations, has established individual responsibility for quality assurance as an organizational value. At Reflexite the results can be seen in increased productivity, attainment of quality goals and a committed workforce.

Providing an Effective Reward System

To motivate behavior, an organization must provide an effective reward system. Given the belief that all people are individuals with different needs, values, expectations and goals, the reward system must accommodate many variables.

According to David Van Fleet, an effective reward system has the following characteristics:

- *Rewards must satisfy the basic needs of all employees.* Pay, for example, must be adequate, benefits reasonable, and vacations and holidays appropriate.

- *Rewards must be comparable to those offered by competitive organizations in the same area.* For example, the pay offered for the same job should be equal to that offered by a competitive company. In addition, benefit packages and other programs should be equal to those provided by a competing company.

- *Rewards must be equally available to people in the same positions and be distributed fairly and equitably.* People performing the same job need to have the same options for rewards and also be involved in the decisions governing which rewards they receive. When employees are asked to complete a special task or project, they should have the opportunity to determine the reward they value—a day off or extra pay.

- *The reward system must be multifaceted.* Because all people are different, managers must provide a range of rewards that focus on different aspects— pay, time off, recognition or promotion. In addition, managers should provide several different ways to earn these rewards.[55]

This last point is worth noting. With the widely developing trend toward empowerment in American industry, many people are beginning to view traditional pay systems as inadequate. In a traditional system, workers are paid according to the positions they hold, not the contributions they make. As organizations adopt approaches built on teams, customer satisfaction and empowerment, workers need to be paid differently.

Companies like Procter & Gamble and Monsanto have already responded to this change in perspective. P & G has a pay system that provides rewards based on skill levels. Monsanto has more than 60 pay plans at various operations around the world. "Each is different," says Barry Bingham, the company's Director of Compensation. "All have been built from the bottom up by employee design teams."[56]

Redesigning Jobs

Jobs are important motivational tools because what they contain may provide a means to meet an employee's needs. Managers need to know what elements of a job provide motivation and then apply the concepts of **job redesign**—the application of motivational theories to the structure of work—to increase output and satisfaction.

job redesign
The application of motivational theories to the structure of work, to increase output and satisfaction

Principles of Job Redesign

Recent trends in management have attempted to increase output and satisfaction in several ways. Jobs and organizations have been reexamined with the aim of providing greater challenges and offering other psychological rewards at work. To this end, managers have assigned less interesting repetitive tasks to robots and other kinds of computer-assisted machinery. Training and development programs have been devised that enable people to perform more demanding tasks and jobs.

Job redesign requires a knowledge of and concern for the human qualities that people bring with them to the organization—such things as their needs and expectations, perceptions and values, and levels of skill and abilities. Job redesign also requires knowledge of the qualities of jobs—their physical and mental demands and the environment in which they are performed. Job redesign usually tailors a job to fit the person who must perform it. The beginner who holds a redesigned job gets pieces of the work in measured increments until he or she masters the tasks required to complete the whole job. Workers who have more experience and who are becoming bored with their jobs may be given more challenging tasks and more flexibility or autonomy in dealing with them.

The two approaches to job redesign relate to job scope and job depth. **Job scope** refers to the variety of tasks incorporated into a job. **Job depth** refers to the degree of discretion the employee possesses to alter the job. Job redesign alternatives include job enlargement, job rotation and job enrichment.

job scope
An element of job redesign that refers to the variety of tasks incorporated into a job

job depth
An element of job redesign referring to the degree of discretion an employee has to alter the job

Job Enlargement To increase the number of tasks in a job, rather than its quality or challenge, is to implement **job enlargement**. Often called *horizontal loading*, job enlargement may attempt to demand more of the same from an employee or to add other tasks containing an equal or lesser amount of meaning or challenge. Under-worked employees can benefit from job enlargement. These people want and need to be kept constantly busy and occupied with routine tasks that they understand and have mastered. Their sense of competence improves as their volume of output does. Some people, however, seek more variety, not more tasks; job enlargement is not an appropriate strategy for the latter.

job enlargement
Increasing the variety or the number of tasks in a job, not the quality or the challenge of those tasks

Job Rotation Temporarily assigning people to different jobs or tasks is **job rotation**. The idea is to add variety and to emphasize the interdependence of a group of jobs. Managers involved in job rotation gain knowledge about the operations of departments outside their own. Assembly-line workers may be assigned one set of tasks one month and another set the following month. Office workers may swap jobs for a time to learn other aspects of the operation, to gain added insights, and to enable them to substitute for one another in times of need.

job rotation
Temporarily assigning people to different jobs or tasks on a rotating basis

At the Tony Lama Company—a boot manufacturer in El Paso, Texas—customer-service department employees work in the store for one week. Similarly, salespeople work a week in the shipping department. The experiences broaden employees' perspectives. Job rotation can be used for cross training, or to facilitate permanent job transfers or promotions. Workers who can benefit from job rotation are those who are interested in or ready for promotion and those who need variety.

Job Enrichment Frederick Herzberg pointed out that jobs can allow workers to satisfy some of their psychological needs.[57] **Job enrichment** results when jobs are designed that can enhance psychological satisfaction. (Herzberg referred to job enrichment as *vertical job loading*.) Job enrichment should include the following elements:

job enrichment

Designing a job to provide more responsibility, control, feedback, and authority for decision making

- *Variety of tasks.* An enriched job introduces an employee to new and more difficult tasks he or she has not previously handled.

- *Task importance.* An employee with an enriched job handles a complete natural unit of work and also handles specific or specialized tasks that enable him or her to become an expert.

- *Task responsibility.* An employee with an enriched job is accountable for his or her own work and can exercise authority in the course of job activities.

- *Feedback.* Workers in enriched jobs receive periodic and specialized reports that are delivered directly to them.

Experiments with job enrichment vary widely in their approach, scope and content. Most efforts at job enrichment increase the workers' control over work. For example, Volvo pioneered the concept of having a team take over the entire automobile-assembly operation to produce a single car. The result was increased employee commitment and productivity, and fewer quality defects. Many manufacturers have allowed skilled machine operators to set up their machines and maintain them, to plan their own work flow and pace, and to inspect their own output. See this chapter's Quality Management feature for a discussion of the changing roles of supervisors and production personnel.

In some companies like Cin-Made, which practice open-book management, employees are given the knowledge to help them shape and control their jobs. As discussed in Chapter 5, in an open-book company employees understand why they are being called on to solve problems, cut costs, reduce defects and give the customer better service. Furthermore, employees:

- See—and learn to understand—the company's financial reports, along with all the other numbers that are critical to tracking performance.

- Learn that, whatever else they do, part of their job is to move the numbers in the right direction.

- Have a direct stake in the company's success. If the business is profitable, they get a cut of the action; if it's not, they don't.[58]

Regardless of the approach selected, for job enrichment to be successful, participation must be voluntary and management must be competent in its day-to-day operations as well as in its efforts at job enrichment. However, managers and workers can be expected to resist some efforts at job enrichment. (See Chapter 8 for an analysis of resistance to change.) Also, once introduced, changes do not yield improvements overnight; mistakes can be made in the implementation of job enrichment programs and setbacks can occur. Nevertheless, companies that undertake job enrichment find higher morale and improved productivity.

Changing Roles

The United States remains the number one manufacturing country in the world. Higher productivity means a leaner manufacturing labor force that's capitalized on efficiency. Fewer workers making more goods means that supervisors need to delegate more to production personnel. Furthermore, production personnel must participate more and communicate more. Employees are expected to think. Thus, the roles of supervisors and production personnel have changed. Employees are making decisions that formerly were made by managers.

Total employee involvement is the key to lean production. Management must involve all employees and allow them some "say" in their work. Employees need to have a clear understanding of the benefits of lean production and provide positive, constructive ideas for solving relevant issues. They need to feel free to express their opinions and ideas.

Supervisors lay the foundation for good relations with employees. Good relations get good results; poor relations get poor results.

➤ Make the best use of each person's ability. Get to know people. What have they done before? What do they know?

➤ Treat people as individuals. Let each worker know how he or she is getting along. If not, employees are working in a vacuum.

➤ Give credit when it is due. Recognition cements a relationship of trust between the supervisor and the employee.

➤ At the end of the day, ask each employee, "What kind of job did you do today? Good? Bad? OK?

➤ When you left work last Friday, did you know what kind of job you did? Explain the job and how you know how you did. (If you don't work, interview someone you know.)

Promoting Intrapreneurship

As an organization grows, it has a tendency to establish rules, policies and procedures—to become mechanistic in nature. The formal control systems that become established along with bureaucratic procedures cause it to lose innovative energy. The corporate environment can stifle the creative spirit of entrepreneurial employees. To meet their need for creativity, these employees often leave and build their own organizations.

Recognizing this problem—and the losses their organizations suffer as a result—the top managers of many large corporations are trying to foster environments that promote corporate entrepreneurship, or intrapreneurship.[59] **Intrapreneurship** occurs when entrepreneurship exists within the boundaries of a formal organization. It is, in essence, a process whereby an individual pursues an idea and has the authority to develop and promote it within the boundaries of the formal organization. As discussed in Chapter 5, these individuals become *intrapreneurs*—employees who think and act like owners. They take responsibility for an idea or project and are empowered to make it successful. According to Donald Kuratko and Richard Hodgetts, a manager can foster intrapreneurship by following these guidelines:

intrapreneurship
Entrepreneurship within an organization, allowing employees flexibility and authority in pursuing and developing new ideas

- Encourage action.
- Use informal meetings whenever possible.
- Tolerate—do not punish—failure, and use it as a learning experience.
- Be persistent.
- Reward innovation for innovation's sake.
- Plan the physical layout to encourage informal communication.
- Reward and/or promote innovative personnel.
- Encourage people to go around red tape.

- Eliminate rigid procedures.
- Organize people into small teams to pursue future-oriented projects.[60]

Managers who really want a climate of intrapreneurship cannot be timid. True intrapreneurs are not comfortable with structure—they will figure a way around orders that block their dreams. They will do any job that will make the project successful, always being true to their goals.[61]

A company that thrives on intrapreneurship is 3M. Its first president, William McKnight, "wanted to create an organization that would continually self-mutate from within, impelled forward by employees exercising their individual initiative." McKnight's approach is captured in these phrases that are a part of 3M's culture: [62]

- "Listen to anyone with an original idea, no matter how absurd it might sound at first."
- "Encourage; don't nitpick. Let people run with an idea."
- "Encourage experimental doodling."
- "If you put fences around people, you get sheep. Give people the room they need."

This philosophy created a climate for intrapreneurs to dabble, take chances, and make mistakes. Spurred along by such traditions as the 15 percent rule (technical people are encouraged to spend up to 15 percent of their time on projects of their own choosing) and Genesis Grants (an internal venture capital fund that distributes parcels of up to $50,000 for researchers to develop prototypes and market tests), 3M-ers have brought wide-ranging products to the market—reflective highway signs, electrical connectors, air filters, stethoscopes, surgical drapes and tape and Post-it® Notes.

Creating Flexibility

Another way managers can motivate workers is to provide them with flexibility in work through flextime, a compressed workweek, or job sharing. Flexibility in work is also facilitated through the use of e-mail communication.

flextime
An employment alternative allowing employees to decide, within a certain range, when to begin and end each workday

Flextime allows employees to decide, within a certain range, when to begin and end each workday. It thus allows them to take care of personal business before or after work and to vary their daily schedules, thereby giving them more control over their lives. Companies that have adopted this approach—Northeast Utilities, a Hartford, Connecticut, power company, for example—have reported decreases in absenteeism, lower turnover, less tardiness and higher morale. Employees caught in the work–family pressure cooker of juggling conflicting demands are virtually unanimous in choosing flexibility as a solution.[63]

compressed workweek
A schedule that allows employees to fulfill weekly time obligations in fewer days than the traditional five-day workweek

A **compressed workweek** allows employees to fulfill their work obligation in fewer days than the traditional five-day workweek. The most often used model is four 10-hour days. The approach—like flextime—provides more time for personal business and recreation. Employees who adopt it report improved job satisfaction. Nevertheless, not all managers are supportive of the idea. Some managers think compressed workweeks make scheduling too difficult. They fear that providing employee coverage at all times may be impossible if people are in and out. Other managers fear loss of control.[64]

job sharing
A technique to provide flexibility by permitting two part-time workers to divide one full-time job

Job sharing, or *twinning*, permits two part-time workers to divide one full-time job. Such an occupational buddy system is ideal for parents who are raising school-aged children or people who prefer part-time employment. The benefit from an employer's standpoint is that creative input comes from two sources, and the cost is only one salary and one set of benefits.

Review What You've Learned

Chapter Summary

1 Discuss the factors that stimulate and influence motivation.

Motivation results from a combination of factors, including the individual's needs, the ability to make choices, and an environment that provides the opportunity to satisfy those needs and make those choices. In choosing behavior to satisfy a need, a person evaluates past experiences, environmental influences, perceptions, skills and incentives.

2 Differentiate between content and process theories of motivation.

Content theories emphasize the needs that motivate people. Process theories explain how employees choose behaviors to meet their work needs and how they determine whether their choices were successful.

3 List the five levels of needs according to Maslow and give an example of each.

The five levels of needs are physiological (water, food); safety (avoiding bodily harm); social (friendship); esteem (recognition); and self-realization (maximizing abilities).

4 Discuss the impact of hygiene and motivation factors in the work environment.

Hygiene factors (salary; job security; working conditions; status; company policies; quality of technical supervision; and quality of interpersonal relationships among peers, supervisors and subordinates) are the primary elements involved in job satisfaction. When present in sufficient quality, they have no effect; when absent, they can lead to job dissatisfaction. Motivation factors (achievement, recognition, responsibility, advancement, the work itself and possibility of growth) are the primary elements involved in job satisfaction. When present, they can stimulate personal and psychological growth.

5 Explain the characteristics of a person with high-achievement needs.

A person with high-achievement needs:

- Performs a task because of a compelling need for personal achievement, not necessarily for the rewards associated with accomplishing the task.
- Prefers to take personal responsibility for solving problems rather than leaving the outcome to others.

- Prefers to set moderate goals that, with stretching, are achievable.
- Prefers immediate and concrete feedback on performance, which assists in measuring progress toward the goal.

6 Identify the needs associated with ERG theory.

The ERG theory identifies three categories of needs: existence, relatedness and growth. Existence needs relate to a person's well-being. Relatedness needs include needs for satisfactory relationships with others. Growth needs call for realization of potential and the achievement of competence.

7 Discuss the relationship between expectations and motivation.

Motivation is a function of how badly a person wants something and how likely the person thinks he or she will get it. The intensity of motivation functions in direct proportion to perceived or expected rewards.

8 Explain the relationship between reinforcement and motivation.

Much of motivated behavior is learned behavior. Learning, in turn, is influenced by the rewards or penalties that individuals have experienced in similar situations in the past. Employees learn over time what type of performance is acceptable and what is unacceptable. This learning then influences employees' subsequent behavior.

9 Explain how equity influences motivation.

Employees' behavior relates to their perception of how fairly they are treated. Employees consciously compare the rewards they receive and their expended effort with the rewards and efforts of other employees. These comparisons influence their levels of motivation.

10 Explain how goals influence motivation.

A person's behavior is influenced by the goals that are set. The goals tell an employee what needs to be done and how much effort will need to be expended.

11 **Discuss the importance of a manager's philosophy of management in creating a positive work environment.**
A manager's philosophy of management can set the foundation for a positive work environment. Because this philosophy incorporates and reflects personal beliefs about human nature in the work setting—about worker attitudes and characteristics, employee maturity and the influence of management expectations on behavior—it affects the motivation choices the manager will make.

12 **Describe how managers can structure the environment to provide motivation.**
Managers can structure the environment to provide motivation by treating people as individuals, offering support, recognizing and valuing Diversity and Inclusion, empowering employees, providing an effective reward system, redesigning jobs, promoting intrapreneurship and creating flexibility at work.

KEY TERMS

compressed workweek   389

content theories   360

equity theory   376

ERG theory   370

expectancy theory   372

flextime   389

goal-setting theory   377

hygiene factors   365

intrapreneurship   388

job depth   386

job enlargement   386

job enrichment   387

job redesign   386

job rotation   386

job scope   386

job sharing   389

morale   356

motivation   356

motivation factors   366

needs   357

philosophy of management   378

process theories   360

quality of work life (QWL)   356

reinforcement theory   374

Theory X   378

Theory Y   378

REVIEW QUESTIONS

1. What stimulates motivation? What three factors influence the behavior an individual will choose to satisfy a stimulus?

2. On what do content theories of motivation focus? What theories are included in this category? On what do process theories of motivation focus? What theories belong in this category?

3. List and explain the five categories of human needs identified by Abraham Maslow. Why are the needs arranged in a hierarchy?

4. Define Frederick Herzberg's hygiene and motivation factors and give three examples of each. What is the importance of each set of factors to a manager?

5. Why is a high achiever likely to focus on goal setting, feedback, individual responsibility and rewards?

6. What three needs does Clayton Alderfer's ERG theory identify?

7. What is the relationship between expectancy and motivation? What is the relationship among effort–performance link, performance–reward link and attractiveness?

8. List and explain the four main types of reinforcement.

9. Describe the two factors a person uses to determine equity in a work situation.

10. What influence on behavior and motivation is the result of employee goal setting?

11. What is the importance of a manager's philosophy of management in creating a positive work environment?

12. How can a manager influence motivation through empowerment, intrapreneurship and recognition of Diversity and Inclusion?

DISCUSSION QUESTIONS FOR CRITICAL THINKING

1. Would a person with high-achievement needs be a good manager? Why or why not?

2. How does expectancy theory apply to your classroom experience? Discuss your motivation for grades in relationship to the value of the reward (grade), the relationship of the reward to performance (tests, papers) and the amount of effort required to receive the grade (time spent in class and studying).

3. What two experiences can you cite to demonstrate the influence of reinforcement theory on your behavior (motivation)?

4. Which of the eight motivational concepts discussed in this chapter's Managing for Motivation section would be your first priority as manager? Which would be your last priority? Why?

5. The winning formula of late founder Sam Walton was to provide "everyday low prices" to the American working class. Current Walmart managers veered away from that formula, trying to reach higher-income shoppers. As a result, Walmart lost sales to dollar stores, discount grocery chains and online merchants. How do you think this change in management philosophy affected the work environment?

6. There are challenges that come along with managing across generations and overseeing staffs made up of people of different ages. Baby boomers still are in the majority among U.S. employees, but increasingly they're supervising, being supervised by or working closely with Generation X'ers and the even-younger "Millennials," Gen Y employees. Motivating these employees, with their different mindsets, requires managers to relinquish a one-style-fits-all approach. **Identify your generation.** Do you think managers understand what inspires members of your generation? What are those things that are most important to you when it comes to getting a job done? What tactics worked best for you?

Apply What You Know

Social Media Management Exercises

Workplace Wikis

Empowered employees need to feel free to express their opinions and ideas. One way to do this is to use wikis, websites that allow users to add and edit content at will. The best known wiki is Wikipedia, the online encyclopedia. Many organizations use workplace wikis to aggregate employee knowledge and enhance productivity. The collaborative tool allows users to add and maintain content for their specific business area.

Gartner classifies wikis as one of several social collaboration technologies. Others include blogs, instant messaging, collaborative office, and crowdsourcing. By 2016, Gartner predicts that social technologies will be integrated with most business applications.

- Visit Wikipedia and read the coverage on motivation. Choose an area in motivation that interests you. Prepare at least a three paragraph wiki entry which could be submitted to Wikipedia as your contribution to the topic of motivation. The entry should focus on *one* important person, place, thing, event, fact, concept or principle. *Note*: Each paragraph should consist of at least five sentences organized around a single topic sentence and have a header that explains what the paragraph is about (e.g., Introduction, History, Early Career, etc.). Cite your references.

http://en.wikipedia.org/wiki/Motivation.

Source: Gartner Press Release
http://www.gartner.com/newsroom/id/1454221.

Experiential Learning

Container Store: Intense Employee Commitment

The Container Store, originator of the storage and organizational retail concept, has been at the top of *Fortune* magazine's list of the 100 Best Companies to Work For in America sixteen years in a row (1999–2015). To develop the list, *Fortune* asked randomly selected employees at several hundred candidate companies to complete The Great Place to Work Trust Index (an employee survey that evaluates trust in management, pride in work and the company, and camaraderie). The companies provide *Fortune* with the entry-level salary for both professional and production or service workers and the number of workers in each category.

The Container Store operates retail, mail order and online business devoted to storage products such as closet organization systems, decorative shelving and wire and plastic bins. Garrett Boone, Chairman, and Kip Tindell, CEO, opened their first store in Dallas, TX, in 1978. The Container Store's philosophy is centered on strict merchandising, superior customer service and intense employee commitment. The passion for the company that employees at The Container Store feel comes from the top. Garrett and Kip can be found selling, dusting shelves, and helping with customer carry-outs.

One of The Container Store's core business philosophies is that three good people equal one great person in terms of business productivity. Elizabeth Barrett, Vice President of Operations, describes the characteristics of an indispensable employee: "One who has tremendous vision and relentless dedication to The Container Store's philosophy, culture and customer service level. That employee has a great enthusiasm for his or her job and a work ethic that is equally enthusiastic and comes from loving the job that they do" (*Dallas Morning News*).

Most employees at The Container Store were customers first. Barrett is an example. "I moved to Dallas from New York immediately after graduation from college. In September of 1981, I went into one of our original stores … looking for some part-time work that would keep me busy until my 'real' career began. I figured that I would put my liberal arts degree and my French major to use at a later time. I fell in love with the way The Container Store treats its customers and its employees, and here I am, 19 years later!" (*Dallas Morning News*)

Questions

1. Using Figure 11.1 as a guide, evaluate the quality of work life at The Container Store. Provide examples from the case that relate to specific factors contributing to the quality of work life.

2. Which motivation theories do Garrett and Kip apply in developing their overall motivation strategy? Provide examples of specific elements of each theory to support your answer.

3. Do Garrett and Kip focus on content theories, process theories or both? Explain your answer.

Sources: "100 Best Companies to Work For," *Fortune*, 2015; The Container Store press release, March 5, 2015, *http://www.containerstore.com* ; "Employment: Success Story," *Dallas Morning News*, September 3, 2000.

Chapter 12

Leadership

LEARNING OBJECTIVES

After studying this chapter, you should be able to:

1   Discuss leadership traits, skills, and behaviors

2   Differentiate between management and leadership

3   Describe the five sources of power leaders may possess

4   Differentiate between positive and negative motivation

5   Describe the three decision-making styles used by leaders

6   Explain the two primary approaches leaders can take: task centered and people centered

7   Describe the three theories of situational leadership

8   Discuss the three challenges facing leaders

Leadership

Effective leaders don't have to be the smartest people in the company. They usually don't have the highest IQs, but they combine mental intelligence with emotional intelligence. In other words, they are smart and they have common sense. Leaders understand their own strengths and weaknesses, while grasping what others want and need. As a result, they work on their own and others' emotional development. The best leaders have strengths in several key emotional-skill competencies.

For each of the following statements, circle the number which indicates your level of agreement. Rate your agreement as it is, not what you think it should be. Objectivity will enable you to determine your management skill strengths and weaknesses.

	Almost Always	Often	Sometimes	Rarely	Almost Never
I deal calmly with stress.	5	4	3	2	1
I believe the future will be better than the past.	5	4	3	2	1
I deal with changes easily.	5	4	3	2	1
I set measurable goals when I have a project.	5	4	3	2	1
Others say I understand and am sensitive to them.	5	4	3	2	1
Others say I resolve conflicts.	5	4	3	2	1
Others say I maintain relationships.	5	4	3	2	1
Others say I inspire them.	5	4	3	2	1
Others say I am a team player.	5	4	3	2	1
Others say I helped to develop their abilities.	5	4	3	2	1

Compute your score by adding the circled numbers. The highest score is 50; the lowest score is 10. A higher score implies you are more likely to understand your strengths. A lower score implies a lesser degree of readiness, but it can be increased. Reading and studying this chapter will help you improve your understanding of leadership.

INTRODUCTION

Leading is one of five functions of management. It is vital to the execution of the other four. Leading people and their organizations requires the ability to do many of the activities we have discussed so far in this text. The principles governing communication, decision making and motivation form the foundation of leading. At the top of any organization, leading is most concerned with

- Establishing values, culture and climate.
- Defining a mission.
- Identifying core competencies.
- Scanning environments.
- Sensing the need for change.
- Creating a vision for the future.
- Enlisting cooperation and support for that vision.
- Keeping people and processes focused on satisfying various customers.
- Unleashing the full potential in and soliciting contributions from all the organization's human resources through training, development and empowerment.

People with the ability to lead, however, must exist at all organizational levels and within each of its units and teams.

Howard Schultz, founder and CEO of Starbucks, encourages participation from his employees. He says that people are the secret to the company's success. Ashley Woodruff, analyst at Bear Stearns who follows Starbucks, explains, "Howard Schultz's leadership style makes employees feel like partners, not hourly workers. That's one of the reasons why the people behind the counter in the stores are so friendly and passionate. They're not just selling coffee. They have a relationship with customers."[1]

Leadership Defined

Leadership, in its management application, is the process of influencing individuals and groups to set and achieve goals. **Influence** is the power to sway other people to one's will or views. Leaders—those who practice leadership—guide, direct, persuade, coach, counsel and inspire others. How well they do this depends on several variables.

Leadership involves three sets of variables: the leader, those being led, and the circumstances and situations they find themselves facing. All three are constantly changing. The leader, like those being led, is a human being with various skills, traits, knowledge and attitudes developed through experience that shape his or her personality, personal philosophies and ethical beliefs—that is, his or her *moral compass*. These factors can contribute to or detract from the leader's ability to influence others. They are the sources of the individual's strengths or weaknesses.

What qualities must a leader have? As Carol Kleiman reported, Jeffrey Christian, President and Chief Executive Officer of a Cleveland-based executive search firm, looks for managers

> *who are high impact players, change agents, drivers and winners—people who are extremely flexible, bright, tactical and strategic, who can handle a lot of information, make decisions quickly, motivate others, chase a moving target and shake things up. Previously, corporate recruiting emphasized credentials [schooling] and experience, which are still important, but ... you can't teach good leadership or how to be excited about life.*[2]

leadership
The process of influencing individuals and groups to set and achieve goals

influence
The power to sway people to one's will or views

Robert Greenleaf, former Director of Management Research at AT&T and Founding Director of the Center for Applied Ethics, said, "The leader exists to serve those whom he nominally leads, those who supposedly follow him. He (or she) takes their fulfillment as his (or her) principal aim."[3] The servant–leader takes people and their work seriously, listens to and takes the lead from the troops, heals, is self-effacing, and sees himself or herself as a steward.[4]

Discuss leadership traits, skills, and behaviors

LEADERSHIP TRAITS

Early theories about leadership suggested that excellent leaders possessed certain traits, or personal characteristics, that lay at the root of their ability to lead. Following World War II, the U.S. Army surveyed soldiers in an attempt to compile a list of traits shared by commanders whom soldiers perceived as leaders. The resulting list, which included 14 traits, was clearly inadequate to describe leadership. No two commanders displayed all the traits, and many famous commanders lacked several.

More recently, Gary Yukl constructed a list of traits and skills commonly associated with effective leaders.[5] Figure 12.1 presents these traits. Yukl's list suggests that a leader is strongly motivated to excel and succeed.

No list of leadership traits and skills can be definitive, however, because no two leaders are exactly alike. Different leaders working with different people in different situations need different traits. If people in charge possess what is needed when it is needed, they should be able to exercise effective leadership.

William Peace is a former executive with Westinghouse and United Technologies and consultant with Doctus Management Consultancy of Chester, England. In the course of his career, Peace learned certain traits served him well in management jobs. In an article for *Harvard Business Review*, Peace noted the importance of intelligence, energy, confidence and responsibility. He differed from some observers in his emphasis

---

| Figure 12.1 | Traits and Skills Commonly Associated with Effective Leadership |

TRAITS	SKILLS
Adaptable	Cleverness (intelligence)
Alert to social environment	Conceptual ability
Ambitious and achievement oriented	Creativity
Assertive	Diplomacy and tact
Cooperative	Fluency in speaking
Decisive	Knowledge about the group task
Dependable	Organizational (administrative) ability
Dominant (desires to influence others)	Persuasiveness
Energetic (high activity level)	Social ability
Persistent	
Self-confident	
Tolerant of stress	
Willing to assume responsibility	

Source: Leadership in Organizations, p. 70 by Gary Yukl. © 1981 by Prentice-Hall, Inc. Adapted with permission of Pearson Education, Inc., Upper Saddle River, NJ 97458.

"Male" and "Female" Approaches to Leadership

Do men and women approach leadership differently? Meta-analyses revealed no significant difference between male and female executive leadership. However, gender has an important leadership role in management.

As author Alice Eagly puts it:

There is considerable evidence that female leaders have a somewhat more participative, androgynous, and trans-formational leadership style than their male counterparts. There are also multiple indications that women, compared with men, enact their leader roles with a view to producing outcomes that can be described as more compassionate, benevolent, universalistic, and ethical, thus promoting the public good.

Men and women manage similarly, but talk about it differently.

The author believes that, "women leaders act more on behalf of the public good." She cautions, "To find out whether our societies would thrive and prosper if women shared power equally with men, more women would have to hold the reins of power."

➡ Select an image that represents leadership, and then write a 100-word essay explaining why you selected that image. Compare your image to that of your classmates. Do men and women (in your class) represent leadership differently?

Source: Alice H. Eagly, "Women as Leaders: Leadership Style Versus Leaders' Values and Attitudes," 2013 Presidents and Fellows of Harvard College, *http://www.hbs.edu/faculty/conferences/2013-w50-research-symposium/Documents/eagly.pdf.*

---

on candor, sensitivity and a, "certain willingness to suffer the painful consequences of unpopular decisions." Peace called using these traits in management "soft management."[6] As this chapter's Valuing Diversity and Inclusion feature points out, personal traits are often perceived as masculine or feminine.

Leadership Skills

A person's skills are the competencies and capabilities he or she possesses. Look again at Figure 12.1 and notice that many of the skills Yukl identified are primarily useful in dealing with others. These skills include diplomacy, fluency in speech (communication skills), persuasiveness and social ability. Some of the traits listed imply the existence of skills. For example, being decisive means that one has skill in making decisions by both rational and intuitive means.

Chris Carey, former president of Datatec a global ICT solutions and services group, believes subordinates should evaluate their bosses in what he calls *reverse performance reviews.* He had his 318 employees score their managers' skills in areas such as coaching, listening, praising and responsiveness. Employees rated upper managers in terms of support of employees, articulation of goals, attention to employee ideas and fairness. The surveys were anonymous, and the results were shared. Formal, top-down appraisals followed within a month. "Scheduling the reviews back-to-back underscores the fact that everyone can perform better and everyone has a chance to say how that will happen."[7]

Leadership Behaviors

Gary Yukl and his colleagues determined 19 categories of "meaningful and measurable" leadership behavior.[8] Figure 12.2 presents the Yukl group's categories along with definitions and examples. As you examine these behaviors—the things leaders do in the everyday exercise of leadership—relate them to the traits and skills discussed earlier. Then link the concepts to what you know about human behavior and motivation as described in Chapter 11.

Figure 12.2 | **The Yukl Group's 19 Categories of Leadership Behavior**

1. **Performance emphasis:** The extent to which a leader emphasizes the importance of subordinate performance, tries to improve productivity and efficiency, tries to keep subordinates working up to their capacity, and checks on their performance.

   Example: My supervisor urged us to be careful not to let orders go out with defective components.

2. **Consideration:** The extent to which a leader is friendly, supportive and considerate toward subordinates and strives to be fair and objective.

   Example: When a subordinate was upset about something, the supervisor was sympathetic and tried to console him.

3. **Inspiration:** The extent to which a leader stimulates subordinates' enthusiasm for the work of the group and says things to build subordinates' confidence in their ability to perform assignments successfully and attain group objectives.

   Example: My boss told us we were the best design group he had ever worked with, and he was sure that our new product was going to break every sales record in the company.

4. **Praise-recognition:** The extent to which a leader provides praise and recognition to subordinates with effective performance, shows appreciation for their special efforts and contributions, and makes sure they get credit for their helpful ideas and suggestions.

   Example: In a meeting, the supervisor told us she was satisfied with our work and she appreciated the extra effort we had made this month.

5. **Structuring reward contingencies:** The extent to which a leader rewards effective subordinate performance with tangible benefits. Such benefits include pay increases, promotions, preferred assignments, a better work schedule and time off.

   Example: My supervisor established a new policy that any subordinate who brought in a new client would earn 10 percent of the contracted fee.

6. **Decision participation:** The extent to which a leader consults with subordinates and otherwise allows them to influence decisions.

   Example: My supervisor asked me to attend a meeting with him and his boss to develop a new production schedule. He was very receptive to my ideas on the subject.

7. **Autonomy-delegation:** The extent to which a leader delegates authority and responsibility to subordinates and allows them to determine how to do their work.

   Example: My boss gave me a new project and encouraged me to handle it as I think best.

8. **Role clarification:** The extent to which a leader informs subordinates about their duties and responsibilities, specifies the rules and policies that must be observed, and lets subordinates know what is expected of them.

   Example: My boss called me in to inform me about a rush project that must be given top priority, and she gave me some specific assignments related to this project.

9. **Goal setting:** The extent to which a leader emphasizes the importance of setting specific performance goals for each important aspect of a subordinate's job, measures progress toward the goals, and provides concrete feedback.

   Example: The supervisor held a meeting to discuss the sales quota for next month.

10. **Training-coaching:** The extent to which a leader determines training needs for subordinates and provides any necessary training and coaching.

    Example: My boss asked me to attend an outside course at the company's expense and said I could leave the office early on the days classes were to be held.

11. **Information dissemination:** The extent to which a leader keeps subordinates informed about developments that affect their work, including events in other work units or outside the organization; decisions made by higher management; and progress in meetings with superiors or outsiders.

    Example: The supervisor briefed us about some high-level changes in policy.

12. **Problem solving:** The extent to which a leader takes the initiative in proposing solutions to serious work-related problems and acts decisively to deal with such problems when a prompt solution is needed.

    Example: The unit was short-handed due to illness, and we had an important deadline to meet. My supervisor arranged to borrow two people from other units, so we could finish the job today.

13. **Planning:** The extent to which a leader decides how to organize and schedule work efficiently, plans how to attain work-unit objectives, and makes contingency plans for potential problems.

    Example: My supervisor suggested a shortcut that allows us to prepare our financial statements in three days instead of the four days it used to take.

continues

Figure 12.2	The Yukl Group's 19 Categories of Leadership Behavior (*cont.*)

14. Coordinating: The extent to which a leader coordinates the work of subordinates, emphasizes the importance of coordination, and encourages subordinates to coordinate their activities.

Example: My supervisor encouraged subordinates who were ahead in their work to help those who were behind. By helping each other, all the different parts of the project will be ready at the same time.

15. Work facilitation: The extent to which a leader obtains for subordinates any necessary supplies, equipment, support services or other resources; eliminates problems in the work environment; and removes other obstacles that interfere with the work.

Example: I asked my boss to order some supplies, and he arranged to get them right away.

16. Representation: The extent to which a leader establishes contacts with other groups and important people in the organization, persuades them to appreciate and support the leader's work unit, and influences superiors and outsiders to promote and defend the interests of the work unit.

Example: My supervisor met with the data processing manager to ask for revisions to the computer programs. The revised programs will meet our needs more effectively.

17. Interaction facilitation: The extent to which a leader tries to get subordinates to be friendly with each other, cooperate, share information and ideas, and help each other.

Example: The sales manager took the group out to lunch to give everybody a chance to get to know the new sales representative.

18. Conflict management: The extent to which a leader restrains subordinates from fighting and arguing, encourages them to resolve conflicts in a constructive manner, and helps settle disagreements between subordinates.

Example: Two members of the department who were working together on a project had a dispute about it. The manager met with them to help resolve the matter.

19. Criticism-discipline: The extent to which a leader criticizes or disciplines a subordinate who shows consistently poor performance, violates a rule or disobeys an order. Disciplinary actions include official warnings, reprimands, suspensions and dismissals.

Example: The supervisor, concerned that a subordinate repeatedly made the same kinds of errors, made sure the subordinate was aware of expectations concerning quality.

Source: *Leadership in Organizations*, p. 70 by Gary Yukl. © 1981 by Prentice Hall, Inc. Adapted with permission of Pearson Education, Inc., Upper Saddle River, NJ 97458.

The first behavior Yukl listed, performance emphasis, remains a popular focus for managers and business writers. The movement in business today is to pay people for what they learn and to reward them for their individual and group performance. At Lyondell Petrochemical, "Managers and workers tackle new undertakings in teams, which get bonuses if their ideas fly."[9] By putting their emphasis and money where their words are, company managers emphasize performance and productivity.

MANAGEMENT VERSUS LEADERSHIP

2 Differentiate between management and leadership

Management and *leadership* are not synonyms. Managers plan, organize, staff, lead and control. They might or might not be effective in influencing their subordinates or team members to set and achieve goals. Ideally, leadership and management skills combine to allow a manager to function as a leader, as Figure 12.3 suggests. The manager who gives orders and explicit instructions to experienced people, for instance, is not leading but actually impeding productivity. Planning effectively helps one to become a manager; enabling others to plan effectively is leading. Leaders empower—they give people the things they need to grow, to change and to cope with change. Leaders create and share visions, generating strategies to bring the visions to reality.

| Figure 12.3 | Relationship between Management and Leadership |

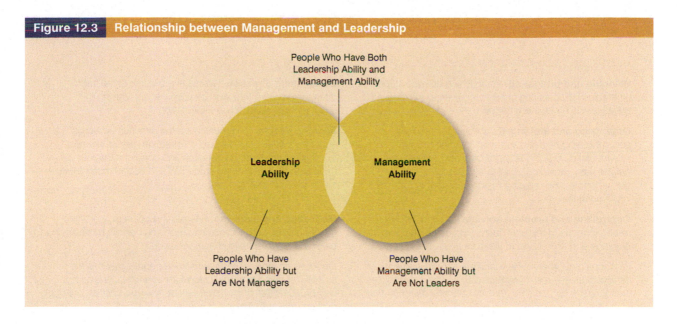

As the leaders' visions and strategies were conveyed, they won allies and became role models for other managers. "Their ability to change and play a useful leadership role signaled that others could also."[12] Such leaders are often called *transformational leaders* because they are able to create fundamental changes in their organizations' values, missions and cultures. Figure 12.4, which is based on John Kotter's work, further differentiates between management and leadership. Notice how Kotter's list of leadership behaviors emphasizes people skills and motivational connections.

For Wegmans Food Markets, a Rochester-based grocery chain and a Fortune 100 Best Companies to Work For, empowering people requires a corporate culture that makes empowerment a core value. The company worked hard to create a culture that has as its core values: caring, high standards, making a difference, respect, and empowerment."[10]

John Kotter and James Heskett, in *Corporate Culture and Performance*, listed organizations that had made major cultural changes. The leaders of these organizations first had to realize that change was needed. Then they had to communicate to employees the facts that pointed to a crisis or potential crisis so the employees would perceive the need to change. Finally, as Kotter and Heskett described, these leaders

> developed or clarified their visions of what changes were needed…. After perceiving some minimum readiness on the part of their managers, the leaders then began communicating their visions of what changes were necessary. These visions always carried some general message about key constituencies, especially customers…. [Also] included was information about more specific strategies and practices that were seen as needed to deal with the current business climate or competitive situation.[11]

As the leaders' visions and strategies were conveyed, they won allies and became role models for other managers. "Their ability to change and play a useful leadership role signaled that others could also."[12] Such leaders are often called *transformational leaders* because they are able to create fundamental changes in their organizations' values, missions and cultures. Figure 12.4, which is based on John Kotter's work, further differentiates between management and leadership. Notice how Kotter's list of leadership behaviors emphasizes people skills and motivational connections.

Kotter notes that, "A few … corporate change efforts have been very successful. A few have been utter failures. Most fall somewhere in between, with a distinct tilt toward the lower end of the scale."[13] Why so few big successes? Management can get stuck in the planning phase or be trapped with a culture, a decision structure, practices and people who resist change. "A paralyzed senior management often comes from having too many managers and not enough leaders."[14]

Figure 12.4	Differences between Management and Leadership

MANAGEMENT	LEADERSHIP
Planning and budgeting. Establishing detailed steps and timetables for achieving needed results and the resources necessary to make them happen.	**Establishing direction.** Developing a vision of the future, often the distant future, and strategies for producing the changes needed to achieve that vision.
Organizing and staffing. Establishing a structure for accomplishing plan requirements, staffing that structure with individuals, delegating responsibility and authority for carrying out the plan, providing policies and procedures to help guide people, and creating methods or systems to monitor implementation.	**Aligning people.** Communicating the direction by words and deeds to all those whose cooperation may be needed to influence the creation of teams and coalitions that people, understand the vision and strategies and accept their validity.
Controlling and problem solving. Close monitoring of results in terms of the plan, identifying deviations, and then planning and organizing to solve these problems.	**Motivating and inspiring.** Energizing people to overcome major political, bureaucratic and resource barriers by satisfying basic, but often unfulfilled human needs.
Produces a degree of predictability and order and consistently achieves the key results expected by various stakeholders (for customers, being on time; for stockholders, being on budget).	*Produces change, often to a dramatic degree, that has the potential of being extremely useful (for example, developing new products that customers want or new approaches to labor relations that help make a firm more competitive).*

Source: Reprinted with the permission of The Free Press, a division of Simon & Schuster Adult Publishing Group from, *A Force for Change: How Leadership Differs from Management*, p. 6, by John P. Kotter. Copyright © 1990 by John P. Kotter, Inc. All rights reserved.

To enlist support for change and gain progress toward it, consultant Peter Scott-Morgan believes that although. "humans are amazingly adaptable, you have to make it logical for them to want to change."[15] Former Integra Financial wanted to shift from a superstar culture to one based on teamwork. It, "developed a carefully crafted system of evaluations and rewards to discourage hot-dogging, grandstanding, filibustering and other ego games. The best team players get the goodies; the worst get a gentle dressing down…. One thing that you can count on: Whatever gets rewarded will get done."[16] See this chapter's Ethical Management feature for a discussion on how peer reviews can be used to identify true leaders in an organization.

As is the case at Starbucks, corporate culture begins with a leader that leads by example ("walks like they talk") and creates a vision, a strategy to achieve it, and a coalition consisting of empowered people at every level committed to change. Leadership is the ability to articulate a vision and to inspire the best efforts of followers in the service of that vision. Howard Schultz focuses on social interactions with the people of Starbucks, fostering an atmosphere of mutual trust and mutual commitment to the interests of the organization as a whole.

POWER AND LEADERSHIP

Describe the five sources of power leaders may possess

Power gives people the ability to exert influence over others, to get them to follow; it makes leadership possible. Leaders possess power, as do all managers whether or not they are leaders. Possessing power can increase the effectiveness of managers by enabling them to inspire people—to get them to perform willingly, without relying solely on formal managerial authority. Formal authority grants a manager legitimate

Peer Reviews at Risk International

Peers rating peers (workers rating workers and managers rating other managers of equal rank) is one approach to appraising employees in industry. Many employees fear receiving such ratings and having the responsibility for rating workmates. Among their ethical concerns are confidentiality and privacy.

Ohio-based Risk International was one of the first companies to discover a way to make such reviews pay off and is pleased with the results. The risk-management company employees rate, "only those [peers] they work with directly" once each year through a standardized form (Gruner). Eleven specific, equally weighted areas are evaluated on a scale of 1 (the highest rating) through 4 (unacceptable) along with an "unknown." A 3 means improvements are needed; a 2 is a satisfactory rating; a 1 denotes a strength. The first item on the form asks how well a peer, "demonstrates high ethical standards and personal integrity" (Gruner). The other areas deal with how well an employee deals with quality and customer service, solves problems and makes judgments, gets his or her work out, conducts him- or herself on the job, manages resources, communicates, works in teams, markets company services, exhibits personal excellence and understands the company and its operations.

The results are tabulated, but who said what is not disclosed. The results are shared with rated persons through meetings with their supervisors, at which time plans are made for improvements. Risk International has discovered its "quietly competent workers" who are no longer ignored; it has identified superstars and those who exhibit true leadership traits and behaviors.

Eric Mosley, CEO and co-founder of Globoforce, a social recognition firm, thinks annual evaluations should be replaced by real-time peer reviews. He writes, "By providing instant and continuous recognition of positive behavior, typically via a public social platform, they yield more and richer data on employees, offering managers a clearer picture of a team or company's strengths and weaknesses and everyone a better sense of how they're performing" (Mosely).

➡ **What do you think about evaluating and being evaluated by your peers?**

➡ **What additional ethical issues can you identify with such a process?**

Sources: Eric Mosely, "Creating an Effective Peer-Review System," *Harvard Business Review*, August 19, 2015, *https://hbr.org/2015/08/creating-an-effective-peer-review-system*; Risk International, *http://www.riskinternational.com*; Stephanie Gruner, "The Team-Building Peer Review," *Inc.*, July 1995, 63–65.

power; but coercive, reward, expert, and referent power exist as well. A brief review of these five foundation stones of leadership is in order here.

Legitimate Power

Managers' formal authority derives from their positions in their organizations, which each position's job description usually specifies. A manager's formal authority grants power or influence because it enables the holder to use organizational resources, including other employees. An employee's instructor, manager or team leader has the right to assign work, establish standards for its execution, and apply those standards to both outcomes and behaviors of subordinates. All employees recognize they have a fundamental duty to comply with lawful and ethical orders, rules and standards established by those in formal positions of authority.

According to United States Immigration and Customs Enforcement (ICE), the agency responsible for enforcing the nation's immigration laws, millions of people live in the United States illegally. Undocumented workers use fraudulent means to obtain employment. In most cases, those who are employed respect and fear managers because of the legitimate power they possess. Managers use the power of their formal positions. See this chapter's Global Applications feature for a discussion of employing illegal immigrants.

Employing Illegal Immigrants

In today's tough economy, some employers try to save money by employing illegal immigrants. The use of illegal workers appears to benefit a company, its shareholders, and managers by minimizing the company's costs, and it benefits consumers by helping hold down prices. Companies profit, and thousands of foreign workers are able to earn more than they could back home.

But the system also has its costs. Workers may be forced to work seven days a week, not be paid overtime, and often endure harsh conditions. Furthermore, foreigners get jobs that Americans might want. And taxpayers sometimes end up paying for the illegal workers' emergency health care or their children's education in American schools.

Some companies use subcontractors and claim they are not responsible for anything a subcontractor does wrong. The Immigration and Customs Enforcement agency says that managers should know whether contractors have a history of hiring illegal immigrants. ICE's IMAGE (ICE Mutual Agreement between Government and Employers) Program strives to reduce unauthorized employment and the use of fraudulent identity documents by educating employers on proper hiring procedures. Employers learn how to implement IMAGE best practices, establish an immigration compliance program, develop proper hiring procedures, detect fraudulent documents and use E-verify to ensure employees are eligible for employment in the U.S.

➠ **When a company is raided by ICE, the illegal immigrant employees are arrested and sent back home. Do you think the immigrants are paid for their work during the week they were arrested?**

➠ **What do you think about hiring illegal immigrants?**

➠ **What can companies do to ensure subcontractors don't hire illegal workers?**

Source: U.S. Immigration and Customs Enforcement (ICE), *http://www.ice.gov*.

Coercive Power

One result of the exercise of legitimate power—a person's formal authority—is punishment for a subordinate's unacceptable outcomes and performances. People with authority and, therefore, influence over others usually have the right to punish or withhold rewards from them. A few of the possible results from the exercise of coercive powers include oral and written warnings, suspension and firing. If these punishments are to act as deterrents for inappropriate behaviors, however, people subjected to them must believe they will be administered in a timely and appropriate manner.

Reward Power

The opposite of coercive power is reward power—the right to promise or grant rewards, such as raises, praise, promotions and so on. It, too, is often the result of exercising legitimate power. As Chapter 11 has pointed out, people usually work hard to please those who can reward or punish them. The attractiveness of the reward is important; it must have a strong appeal to the person being influenced or it may have little impact on that person's motivation. When rewards are promised and not granted in a timely manner, however, they can actually have a negative impact on an individual's motivation. Finally, rewards must be earned before being granted; to do otherwise is to lessen their value and importance to the individual.

Expert Power

A person's abilities, skills, knowledge and experience can exert influence when others value them. A seasoned practitioner exercises expert power with newcomers and apprentices. A trainer or coach uses it to impart his or her knowledge, skills and attitudes to trainees. Physicians, lawyers and other licensed professionals earn their living by selling their expertise. A person in need of legal advice, however, may find a production manager's expertise to be of little value. Unlike legitimate, coercive and reward power, expert power may reside in and be exercised by nearly everyone, whether inside or outside an organization.

Referent Power

Power that comes to people because of the kind of personality or personal attractiveness they have to others is known as referent or charismatic, power; it creates in people a desire to associate with or emulate the person who has it. Your personality, sense of humor, openness, honesty and other endearing traits can draw others to you. Many of this chapter's leadership traits generate referent power in those who possess them. Like expert power, referent power is possessed by nearly everyone to some degree; but not all people are attracted to the same personalities or traits. Another may consider what one admires unappealing.

Howard Schultz of Starbucks understands the people he is leading. He gets to know his followers, and the followers see him as their leader. In other words, they trust him and he trusts them. He is accepted because he possesses legitimate, referent and expert power.

A few years ago Starbucks changed its focus from the customer to growth. Sales began to decline. CEO Schultz announced the new strategy would focus on the customer. As a result sales increased. In a *Wall Street Journal* (WSJ) interview, he explained the success.

> **WSJ**: *What led to the turnaround?*
>
> **Schultz**: *Putting our feet in the shoes of our customers, understanding what they were dealing with and the anxiety of the [financial] crisis. In addition to that, getting our own people to understand what was at stake and specifically asking them to be more accountable. We were growing the company with such speed and aggression that we lost sight of the customer experience.*[17]

Starbucks was fortunate to overcome the mistake of losing focus on the customer. Other companies might not be as lucky. They have to stay focused on the customer in order to survive. Employees and CEO Schultz had mutual trust and worked together to help Starbucks recover. Implementing a quality management system requires mutual trust, as this chapter's Quality Management feature discusses.

Managers can become leaders when they couple their formal authority (legitimate power) with the other types of power. As the foregoing indicates, it is possible to be a leader without being a manager and a manager without being a leader. A major goal for many organizations is to develop and tap into the leadership potential that exists in nearly every employee.

Possessing power and using it wisely are two different things. Power gives individuals and groups the means to influence for both good and evil, as Chapter 6, titled, "Management Ethics and Social Responsibility," points out. Leaders without moral and ethical values or who disregard the law can do others, themselves and their organizations great harm. The use of power in any organization must not contradict its core values. Mickey Mantle, a baseball great, held a press conference following his liver transplant in 1995. He admitted to years of alcohol abuse, a primary cause for his liver's failure. He cautioned all his fans and admirers to not emulate him, fearful that his behavior had or would become a model for others.

Mutual Trust

Consumers expect quality products. Thus, in order to remain competitive in the global marketplace, many manufacturers have implemented a quality management system to produce quality products. Developing a world class operation involves changing from a company focused on volume to one focused on the customer. When people are asked to change, they become cautious and suspicious. They won't embrace the opportunity for the company unless mutual trust exists.

In order for employees to accept change, they need to trust management. Companies can implement quality management because they have developed mutual trust that everyone will do their best to serve the customer. Employees want to feel that management takes their problems seriously and that management will look for solutions. Anytime someone brings a problem to a manager, the manager should say, "Thank you;" "Let's work the problem;" and "Let's figure this out together."

Trust is a learned skill. When it exists throughout the organization, the business will be more efficient and more profitable.

Mutual trust enables collaboration and innovation. Without it, empowerment and teamwork eventually will fail. With mutual trust, companies can attract and retain employees because the employees are engaged in executing the strategy.

Mutual trust needs to be reinforced continuously. Managers and employees need leadership training to solve problems, communicate with all levels of staff and execute plans. When mutual trust exists, managers help employees, and employees help managers.

➡ The late Stephen M.R. Covey, co-founder of CoveyLink Worldwide LLC, said the following about trust. "Trust is an economic driver, not just a social virtue. It's an ability to collaborate, to innovate, to attract and retain people, to satisfy, to engage, to execute your strategy. High trust pays dividends; low trust is a tax." What does he mean when he says 'low trust is a tax'? (See Cheryl Hall, "Son of '7 Habits' author says trust pays off," *The Dallas Morning News,* March 6, 2011, p. D1)

Leadership Styles

From the discussion of leadership and its power bases, we turn now to the dynamic interaction between a leader and other people. The perceived approaches and behaviors a manager uses to influence others constitute the manager's **leadership style**.[18] Managers' leadership styles result from their philosophies about motivation, their choices of decision-making styles, and their areas of emphasis in the work environment—whether they focus on tasks or people.

leadership style
The perceived approaches and behaviors a manager uses to influence others

POSITIVE VERSUS NEGATIVE MOTIVATION

4 Differentiate between positive and negative motivation

Leaders influence others to achieve goals through their approach to motivation. Depending on the style of the manager, the motivation can take the form of rewards or penalties.[19] Figure 12.5 presents a continuum containing positive and negative motivations. Leaders with positive styles use positive motivators. They motivate by using praise, recognition, or monetary rewards or by increasing security or granting additional responsibilities.

A negative leadership style incorporates coercion known as sanctions—fines, suspensions, termination, and the like. The manager who says, "Do it my way or else" employs negative motivation. Implied in the statement is the manager's willingness to exercise disciplinary powers; the subordinate's failure to comply would be an act of insubordination.

Positive leadership styles encourage development of employees and result in higher levels of job satisfaction.[20] Negative leadership styles are based on the manager's ability to withhold items of value from employees. The result of negative leadership

| **Figure 12.5** | **Motivation Continuum** |

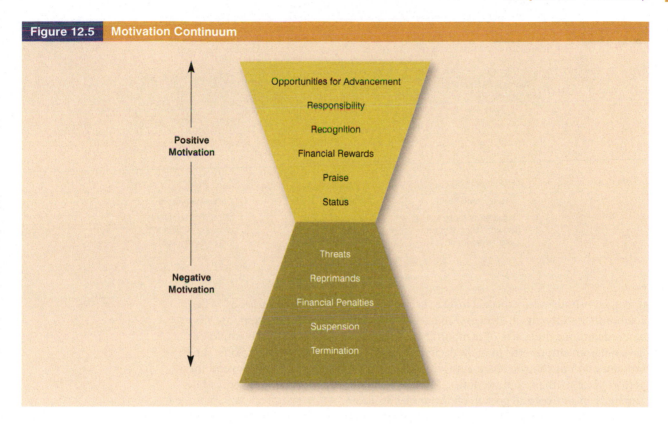

may be an environment of fear, where managers are viewed with distrust and seen as dictators rather than leaders or team players.

Describe the three decision-making styles used by leaders

DECISION-MAKING STYLES

Another element in a manager's leadership style is the degree to which he or she shares decision-making authority with subordinates. Managers' styles range from not sharing at all to completely delegating decision-making authority. Figure 12.6 shows the degrees of sharing as a continuum, with the range of styles categorized in three groups: autocratic style, participative style and free-rein style. Which style a manager chooses should relate to the situation encountered.

autocratic style

A leadership approach in which a manager does not share decision-making authority with subordinates

Autocratic Style A manager who uses the **autocratic style** does not share decision-making authority with subordinates. The manager makes the decision and then announces it. Autocratic managers may ask for subordinates' ideas and feedback about the decision, but the input does not usually change the decision unless it indicates something vital has been overlooked. The hallmark of this style is that the manager, who retains all the authority, executes the entire process. Consequently, the autocratic style is sometimes called the "I" approach.

Under certain conditions, the autocratic style is appropriate. When a manager is training a subordinate, for instance, the content, objectives, pacing and execution of decisions properly remain in the hands of the trainer. (The manager should elicit feedback from the trainee, however.) During a crisis—a hazardous-materials spill or bomb

| **Figure 12.6** | **Leadership Styles and the Distribution of Decision-Making Authority** |

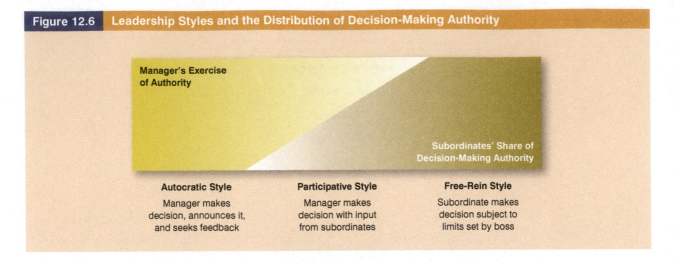

threat, say—leaders are expected to take charge, issue orders and make decisions. When a subordinate directly challenges a manager's authority, an autocratic response may be needed to preclude acts of insubordination. In circumstances in which employees have not been empowered to make decisions, supervisors must make them. Some subordinates do not want to share authority or become involved in any way beyond the performance of their routine duties. Managers should respect these preferences but also make incentives and growth opportunities available.

To use the autocratic style effectively, managers must know what needs to be done, and they must possess expert power. The autocratic style is effective when managers face issues they are best equipped to solve, create solutions whose implementation does not depend on others, and desire to communicate through orders and instructions. If these conditions do not exist, one of the other two leadership styles is probably more appropriate.

Participative Style Managers who use the **participative style** share decision-making authority with subordinates. The degree of sharing can range from the manager's presenting a tentative decision that is subject to change, to letting the group or subordinate participate in making the decision. Sometimes called the "we" approach, participative management involves others and lets them bring their unique viewpoints, talents and experiences to bear on an issue. This style is strongly emphasized today because of the trends toward downsizing, employee empowerment and worker teams.

A consultative and democratic approach works best for resolving issues that affect more than just the manager or decision maker. People affected by decisions support them more enthusiastically when they participate in the decision making than when decisions are imposed on them. Also, if others in a manager's unit know more than the manager does about an issue, common sense urges their inclusion in decisions concerning it.

Before subordinates can be brought into the process, mutual trust and respect must exist between them and their managers. The subordinates must be willing to participate and be trained to do so. People need training in rational decision making. They must also possess the related skills and knowledge needed to cope with the problems they are expected to solve. It takes time to give people the confidence and competence needed to make decisions. Managers must have the time, means and

participative style
A leadership approach in which a manager shares decision-making authority with subordinates

patience to prepare subordinates to participate. When employees participate, they devise solutions they feel they own. This sense of ownership increases their commitment to making the solutions work.

Inc. magazine reported that the participation of Datatec employees is encouraged even in the matter of their bosses' appraisals. Datatec managers believe that

> *giving employees the chance to appraise their bosses forces a company to live up to its commitment to participative management. [Managers are asked] to conduct one-on-one reverse appraisals with subordinates. Employees who find appraising their bosses simply too discomforting may choose to talk to another manager. [President] Carey wants to make sure that problems don't get buried just because they're prickly ones.*[21]

Limits on subordinates' participation must be clearly spelled out beforehand; there should be no misunderstandings about who holds authority to do what. Mistakes will be made and some waste will occur, but the power of the participative style to motivate and energize people is great. In many organizations, managers must use this style; corporate culture and policies demand it.

free-rein style

A leadership approach in which a manager shares decision-making authority with subordinates, empowering them to function without direct involvement from managers to whom they report

Free-Rein Style Often called the "they" approach, or spectator style, the **free-rein style** empowers individuals or groups to function on their own, without direct involvement from the managers to whom they report. The style relies heavily on delegation of authority and works best when the parties have expert power, when participants have and know how to use the tools and techniques needed for their tasks. Under this style, managers set limits and remain available for consultation. The managers also hold participants accountable for their actions by reviewing and evaluating performance.

Free-rein leadership works particularly well with managers and experienced professionals in engineering, design, research, and sales. Such people generally resist other kinds of supervision.

In most organizations managers must be able to use the decision-making style that circumstances dictate. Lee is new, so his manager needs to use an autocratic approach until he develops the confidence and knowledge to perform independently or until he joins a team. Kim, experienced in her job and better at it than anyone else, will probably do well under a participative or free-rein approach. Because people and circumstances constantly change and because subordinates must be prepared for change, the effective manager switches from one leadership style to another as appropriate.

6 Explain the two primary approaches leaders can take: task centered and people centered

TASK ORIENTATION VERSUS PEOPLE ORIENTATION

Yet another element of leadership style is the manager's philosophy about the most effective way to get work done. Leaders can adopt a focus on task (a work, or task, orientation) or a focus on employees (a relationship, or people-centered, approach). Depending on the manager's perspective and situation, these two approaches can be used separately or in combination.

A task focus emphasizes technology, methods, plans, programs, deadlines, goals and getting the work out. Typically, the manager who focuses on a task uses the autocratic style of leadership and issues guidelines and instructions to subordinates. A task focus works well in the short run, especially with tight schedules or under crisis conditions. Used over the long term, however, a task focus can create personnel problems.

It might cause the best performers, who desire flexibility and freedom to be creative, to leave the group; and it might increase absenteeism and decrease job satisfaction.[22]

The manager who focuses on employees emphasizes workers' needs. He or she treats employees as valuable assets and respects their views. Building teamwork, positive relationships, and mutual trust are important activities of the people-centered leader. By focusing on employees, a manager can increase job satisfaction and decrease absenteeism.[23]

University of Michigan Studies Researchers at the University of Michigan compared the behaviors of effective and ineffective supervisors. The researchers' findings indicated that supervisors who focused on their subordinates' needs (employee-centered leaders) were the most effective, building high-performance teams that reached their goals. The less-effective supervisors (job-centered leaders) tended to focus on tasks and were more concerned with efficiency and meeting schedules.[24]

The Ohio State University Studies Researchers at The Ohio State University surveyed hundreds of leaders. The researchers studied their behavior in terms of two factors: consideration and initiating structure. Consideration was defined as concern for subordinates' ideas and feelings (what the University of Michigan studies referred to as an employee focus). Leaders who rated high in consideration communicated openly, developed teams and focused on subordinates' needs. Initiating structure was defined as concern for goal achievement and task orientation (what the Michigan studies called job focus). Leaders who rated high in initiating structure were concerned with deadlines, planning work and meeting schedules.[25]

The researchers found that leaders had one of four combinations of the two behaviors: high consideration and low initiating structure, low consideration and high initiating structure, low consideration and low initiating structure and high consideration and high initiating structure. The researchers concluded that the last combination resulted in the greatest job satisfaction and performance by subordinates.[26]

Since the Ohio State studies, additional research suggests the approach a manager takes should vary, depending on the people involved and the situation. In a crisis, managers should focus on task. When training people to become a self-managing work team, managers should focus on people—learn their needs to cooperate, get to know one another and develop relationships. Managers, these studies suggest, must be flexible and provide the kind of leadership their people and situations require.

The Leadership Grid® In its original version, Figure 12.7 was published as the Managerial Grid by Robert R. Blake and Jane S. Mouton. Along with the Grid theory itself, the figure has evolved through the years to its present configuration and is now referred to as The **Leadership Grid®**. It presents two axes: the vertical axis measures concern for people; the horizontal axis measures concern for production. (The axes correspond to employee- and job-centeredness in the University of Michigan studies and to consideration and initiating structure in the Ohio State studies.) The positions on the grid are stated in terms of a 9-point scale, with 1 representing a low concern and 9 representing a high concern. The grid effectively summarizes positions that managers and leaders can take under a variety of circumstances and with different employees.

The Leadership Grid® provides a framework for understanding leadership. Karen McCormick of Grid International, Inc., gives the following explanation:

> *The premise behind Grid theory is that there is one basic set of principles by which to manage that is appropriate to all situations. The different "styles" in the theory are*

Leadership Grid®
Blake and Mouton's two-dimensional model for visualizing the extent to which a manager focuses on tasks, employees, or both

Figure 12.7   The Leadership Grid®

9,1 Grid Style: CONTROLLING
(Direct & Dominate)

I expect results and take control by clearly stating a course of action. I enforce rules that sustain high results and do not permit deviation.

1,9 Grid Style: ACCOMMODATING
(Yield & Comply)

I support results that establish and reinforce harmony. I generate enthusiasm by focusing on positive and pleasing aspects of work.

5,5 Grid Style: STATUS QUO
(Balance & Compromise)

I endorse results that are popular but caution against taking unnecessary risk. I test my opinions with others involved to assure ongoing acceptability.

1,1 Grid Style: INDIFFERENT
(Evade & Elude)

I distance myself from taking active responsibility for results to avoid getting entangled in problems. If forced, I take a passive or supportive position.

PATERNALISTIC Grid Style
(Prescribe & Guide)

I provide leadership by defining initiatives for myself and others. I offer praise and appreciation for support, and discourage challenges to my thinking.

OPPORTUNISTIC Grid Style
(Exploit & Manipulate)

I persuade others to support results that offer me private benefit. If they also benefit, that's even better in gaining support. I rely on whatever approach is needed to secure an advantage.

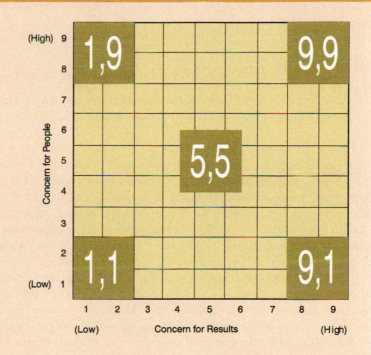

9,9 Grid Style: SOUND
(Contribute & Commit)

I initiate team action in a way that invites involvement and commitment. I explore all facts and alternative views to reach a shared understanding of the best solution.

Source: This image is an adaptation of the Leadership Grid® figure as it appears in *The Power to Change*, Rachel McKee and Bruce Carlson (Austin, TX: Grid International, Inc.), p. 16. Copyright © 1999 by Grid International, Inc. Reproduced by permission of the owners.

behavioral generalizations that manifest themselves as a result of the axes of "concern" and depict how a person characterized by that style of behavior would react (positively or negatively) given that same set of basic management principles. Grid theory does not recommend the use of any particular style but holds up fundamental principles as a yardstick against which the behavior styles are measured. When a person is characterized as a certain "style" on the Grid, this is a characterization of his or her behavior in relation to this ideal set of principles that remain unchanged.

For example, when faced with conflict in the workplace, a 1,9-oriented person would tend to smooth over conflict and ease feelings and hope it just "goes away." (But as anyone who has ever experienced workplace conflict knows, it never does—it just festers.) The 9,9-oriented leader, on the other hand, would confront the conflict, determine the root causes, and create ways to eliminate the source of the conflict. This represents management by a basic, unchanging set of principles across the board, rather than situational management where the very foundation on which one manages is subject to change at the whim of external circumstances.

The next section will examine three theories of leadership that incorporate situational elements: the contingency model, the path–goal theory, and the life-cycle theory.

THEORIES OF SITUATIONAL LEADERSHIP

Three general theories of leadership address adaptation of leadership to situations. All have strong roots in the motivational theories discussed in Chapter 11.

Fiedler's Contingency Model

Fred Fiedler holds that the most appropriate style of leadership for a manager depends on the manager's situation.[27] Fiedler's model of management, the **contingency model**, suggests a manager should choose task or employee focus according to the interaction of three situational variables: leader–member relations, task structure and leader position power. Because Fiedler's model emphasizes the importance of the situation, Fiedler's work is sometimes called the theory of situational leadership. Figure 12.8 shows Fiedler's contingency model.

The solid line plotted at the top of Figure 12.8 reveals the recommended focus for specific situations. To understand the recommendations and how they were reached, we must understand the variables the model uses.

The scale of leader–member relations refers to the degree to which the leader is or feels accepted by the group. Measured by the observed degree of mutual respect,

contingency model

A leadership theory stating that a manager should focus on either tasks or employees, depending on the interaction of three variables—leader–member relations, task structure, and leader position power

7 Describe the three theories of situational leadership

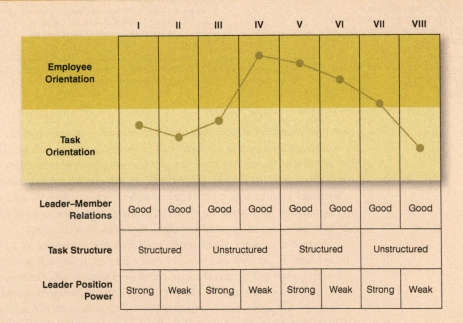

| **Figure 12.8** | **Fiedler's Contingency Model, Depicting the Interaction of Leadership Orientations with Situational Variables** |

trust and confidence, this acceptance is rated as good or poor. In a good relationship, the leader should be able to inspire and influence subordinates. If the relationship is poor, the manager might have to resort to negotiating or to promising favors to get performance.

The task structure ratings relate to the nature of subordinates' jobs or tasks. A structured task is or can be broken into procedures. It is narrowly defined and may be machine-paced, and it tends to be full of routines that are repeated regularly. Data entry clerks, file clerks and supermarket checkers hold structured jobs. An unstructured job includes complexities, variety and latitude for creative expression. Researchers, managers, design engineers and most professionals hold unstructured jobs.

The ratings for leader position power describe the organizational power base from which the leader operates. To what degree can the leader reward and punish? With whom is the leader allied? The leader's connections, legitimate power, expert power and referent power determine weakness or strength—the ability to exercise a little influence or a great deal of influence inside the organization. Note position I in Figure 12.8. In a situation displaying good leader–member relations, structured tasks and strong leader position power, the contingency model tells the leader to adopt a task orientation. At position VII, a nearly equal blend of employee and task orientation is best. Employee-oriented leaders perform best under conditions associated with positions IV, V and VI. When a manager is promoted or given a temporary assignment—as project leader or product design team leader, for example—he or she will find a new combination of people and circumstances. Each combination calls for a fresh assessment of Fiedler's three variables.

House and Mitchell's Path–Goal Theory

path–goal theory
A view of management asserting that subordinates' behaviors and motivations are influenced by the behaviors managers exhibit toward them

Robert House and Terrence Mitchell developed the **path–goal theory** of leadership.[28] Their theory relates to the behaviors a leader can use to stimulate subordinates' motivation to achieve both personal and organizational goals and rewards.[29] The path–goal theory suggests that a leadership style is effective or ineffective on the basis of how successfully leaders influence and support their subordinates' perceptions of the following:

- Goals that need to be achieved
- Rewards for successful performance
- Behaviors that lead to successful performance

According to the path–goal theory, leaders can influence subordinates' motivation by (1) teaching employees the competencies they will need to perform successfully and gain rewards, (2) tailoring rewards to meet employees' needs, and (3) acting to support subordinates' efforts. Teaching (coaching, development and training) builds confidence and competencies. Adapting rewards to the specific needs of individual employees makes them more appealing. Supportive behaviors assist subordinates as necessary, enabling them to achieve both personal and organizational goals.

The path–goal theory has its basis in the expectancy theory of motivation. In that theory, employees' motivations are influenced by their perceptions of what a task requires, their confidence in their abilities to perform, the attractiveness of the reward being offered and the relationship of the reward to the accomplishment of the task. The more self-confidence and the greater the desire for the reward, the more willing employees will be to perform as required. According to the path–goal theory, leadership behaviors and situational factors influence the motivational process.

Leadership Behaviors House and Mitchell based their theory on the following two assumptions: [30]

1 A leader's behavior is acceptable and satisfying to subordinates to the extent that they view it as either an immediate source of satisfaction or as an instrument to some future satisfaction.

2 A leader's behavior will increase subordinates' efforts if it links satisfaction of their needs to effective performance and supports their efforts to achieve goals.

These two assumptions tell managers to increase the number of ways in which performance can be deemed successful, to clear away barriers to successful outcomes, and to help subordinates see these outcomes as desirable. [31] To enable leaders to do these things, the theory provides four kinds of leadership behavior:

1 *Instrumental behavior (task-oriented)*. This behavior, sometimes called directive behavior, involves the planning, directing, monitoring and task-assignment aspects of leadership. It can be prescriptive. A manager who uses instrumental behavior establishes precise procedures, goals and timetables and utilizes the autocratic style of leadership. This behavior can be used to increase an employee's work effort or to clarify outcomes.

2 *Supportive behavior (employee-oriented)*. This behavior creates a climate of mutual trust and respect between leaders and followers. It involves the coaching, counseling and mentoring aspects of leadership. Supportive behavior requires open communication and a leader's honest concern for subordinates' needs. This type of behavior builds teams.

3 *Participative behavior (employee-oriented)*. In this behavior a leader solicits and uses subordinates' ideas and contributions and involves subordinates in decision making. During the planning and execution phases of an operation, the manager tries to obtain input from everyone concerned. Supportive behavior promotes participative behavior. The reverse is true as well. Participative behavior builds team spirit, values individuals and their contributions, and encourages development through exposure to others' points of view and experience.

4 *Achievement-oriented behavior (employee-oriented)*. A leader who shows this type of behavior helps subordinates grow and increases their competencies through training and development. The leader's primary aim is to improve subordinates' abilities and performance, thus making the employees more valuable to themselves and their organization. Instrumental behavior, supportive behavior and participative behavior increase a leader's ability to engage in achievement-oriented behavior, which paves the way for subordinates' advancement.

Companies like NTT Data and Deloitte use gamification for leadership development. Gartner defines **gamification** as, "the use of game mechanics and experience design to digitally engage and motivate people to achieve their goals."

The key elements of the definition are:

• *Game mechanics* describes the use of elements, such as points, badges and leaderboards that are common to many games.

• *Experience design* describes the journey players take with elements, such as game play, play space and story line.

gamification
Gartner defines gamification as, "the use of game mechanics and experience design to digitally engage and motivate people to achieve their goals"

- Gamification is a method to *digitally engage*, rather than personally engage, meaning that players interact with computers, smartphones, wearable monitors or other digital devices, rather than engaging with a person.

- The goal of gamification is to *motivate people* to change behaviors or develop skills, or to drive innovation.

- Gamification focuses on enabling players to *achieve their goals*. When organizational goals are aligned with player goals, the organization achieves its goals as a consequence of players achieving their goals. [32]

Situational Factors Two situational factors are important components in the path–goal theory: the personal characteristics of subordinates and the work environment. These two factors influence the behavior a leader should choose.

The personal characteristics of subordinates include their abilities, self-confidence, personal needs and motivations and perceptions of their leaders. When subordinates exhibit low levels of performance, leaders must be ready to provide coaching, training and direction. The leader must ensure that the rewards offered for outstanding performance are rewards that appeal to employees.

Factors in the work environment include the organization's culture and subcultures, the philosophy of management, how power is exercised, policies and rules, and the extent to which tasks are structured. These factors are environmental pressures beyond the abilities of employees to control, but they affect employees' abilities to accomplish tasks and achieve goals.

Leaders must know what their people want from work, what their motivations are, and what stands between them and successful performance. Leaders must provide to each person the appropriate leadership, depending on the employees and the environmental conditions. Where skills are weak, instrumental behavior is called for; when subordinates lack motivation, achievement-oriented behavior may be appropriate.

Managers at Collins & Aikman, a floor coverings manufacturer, decided to give their employees what they needed: new technology. Instead of opting for cheap labor overseas as a means to stay competitive, the company chose to invest in its U.S. workforce and operations and install state-of-the-art equipment. In their Georgia plant, the primary tufting and shearing machines were to be linked to computers. But the prospect of working with computers terrified many of the firm's 560 employees. Almost one-third of the workers had not finished high school; some could not read or write. [33]

A needs assessment revealed that only eight percent of the workers possessed the skills needed to adjust to the new high-tech environment. Collins & Aikman provided basic literacy training at a cost of about $1200 per worker, and the employer implemented other in-house training programs as well. Productivity and employee self-confidence rose, and so did a flood of workers' suggestions about how to improve just about every phase of the operation. Production rejects fell by 50 percent, and workers needed less assistance from supervisors. [34]

Hersey and Blanchard's Life-Cycle Theory

life-cycle theory
A view of management that asserts that a leader's behavior toward a subordinate should relate to the subordinate's maturity level. The focus on tasks and relationships should vary as the subordinate matures

Paul Hersey and Kenneth Blanchard developed the **life-cycle theory** of leadership. The life-cycle theory relates leadership behavior to subordinates' maturity levels. [35] Immature employees (new and inexperienced) require leadership with a high task–low relationship focus. As people learn and mature in their jobs, they become increasingly able to direct themselves and participate in decision making. Employees develop relationships with their coworkers, team members and superiors that lead to mutual respect and trust. New skills and knowledge make employees more valuable to themselves and their organizations. As they progress in their organizational lives, employees require from their leaders first a high task–high relationship focus, followed by a high relationship–low task approach, and finally a low task–low relationship focus.

For new employees needing high direction, an autocratic leadership style would be appropriate. As employees progress, the manager should move to a participative style. For experienced employees needing little direction, the free-rein style is appropriate. Stated in terms of path–goal theory behaviors, new employees call for instrumental behavior. As employees progress, they call for supportive, participative and achievement-oriented behaviors. By the time employees attain experience, they should be operating in a relatively autonomous way, turning to the manager or higher authority on an as-needed basis.

Hersey and Blanchard built on and combined ideas from The Leadership Grid® and path–goal theory. Their theory does not allow for changes in situations, however, and it assumes leaders are capable and mature.

CHALLENGES FACING LEADERS

8 Discuss the three challenges facing leaders

Leaders provide vision. They also supply incentives that enlist the support of others in making the vision a reality. Leaders keep people focused on what is important and what must be done. They set examples and foster values that become part of their organizations' cultures. Leaders are change agents, sensing the need for change and creating strategies that will help to initiate it.

An example of a leader who takes his role as a change agent seriously is Harold McInnes, the former CEO of AMP, a business that supplies electronic and electrical connectors. From its headquarters in Pennsylvania, AMP does business through its companies located in 150 countries around the globe. While he was CEO, McInnes's vision was to build on his company's position by devoting 11 to 12 percent of sales dollars to research & development each year. He believed this investment would allow the company to move from being a supplier of connectors to being a provider of larger, more complete subsystems. McInnes called the process "moving up the food chain." One strategy for achieving McInnes's vision was to couple AMP's sales engineers with product-design teams at customers' locations. "That way, when computer whizzes sit down to formulate next-generation products, AMP people are right there determining which AMP subsystems can be designed into them." Harold McInnes developed plans to ensure that his company would thrive in the future.[36]

Leadership Throughout an Organization

It is not enough to have a leader at the top of an organization. Leadership must be exerted at all levels, or change will be resisted and blocked. Leaders must occupy top, middle and supervisory ranks. Workers in self-directed teams need leaders too. Staff development and training efforts (see Chapter 9) should encourage and empower people to become leaders at every level. As this chapter's Managing Social Media feature discusses, social media allows open leadership.

If one story illustrates the value of leadership at all levels of a company, it is the dramatic turnaround of Harley-Davidson, the motorcycle maker. Harley-Davidson tried various approaches to improving the quality and dependability of its motor-

Open Leadership

Social media give managers the ability to form new relationships with their customers and employees. In her book, *Open Leadership*, Charlene Li defines open leadership as:

> *Having the confidence and humility to give up the need to be in control while inspiring commitment from people to accomplish goals.*

She offers the following five rules.

New Rules of Open Leadership

1 *Respect that your customers and employees have power.* Once you accept this as true, you can begin to a have a real, more equal relationship with them. Without this mind-set, you will continue to think of them as replaceable resources and treat them as such. And if you ever need a reminder of what that customer and employee power looks like, just go read a social media monitoring report on your company from a vendor like Radian6, BuzzMetrics, or Cymfony—you'll quickly be humbled by the power of these people.

2 *Share constantly to build trust.* At the core of any successful relationship is trust. Trust is typically formed when people do what they say they will do. But in today's increasingly virtual, engaged environments, trust also comes from the daily patter of conversations. The repeated successful interchange of people sharing their thoughts, activities, and concerns results in relationships. New technologies like blogs, social networks, and Twitter remove the cost of sharing, making it easy to form these new relationships.

3 *Nurture curiosity and humility.* Often, sharing can quickly turn into messaging if all of the outbound information isn't accompanied by give and take. Expressing curiosity about what someone is doing and why something is important to that person keeps sharing grounded and focused on what other people want to hear, balanced with what you want to say. The natural outgrowth of curiosity is humility, which gives you the intellectual integrity to acknowledge that you still have a lot to learn, and also to admit when you are wrong.

4 *Hold openness accountable.* In relationships, accountability is a two-way street—it makes clear the expectations in the relationship, as well as the consequences if they are not met. So if your product causes someone problems, what's the first thing you should do? Apologize and figure out how to resolve the problem. Likewise, if you give someone the ability to comment on your site and they misuse it, they should understand that you will deny them future access.

5 *Forgive failure.* The corollary to accountability is forgiveness. Things go wrong all the time in relationships, and the healthiest ones move on from them, leaving behind grudges and blame. This is not to say that failure is accepted; rather, that it is acknowledged and understood.

➡ **How can adopting the new rules for open leadership speed the pace of innovation and collaboration among managers, employees and customers?**

Source: Charlene Li, "The New Rules of Open Leadership," http://www.charleneli.com/resources/new-rules.

cycles. Results were insignificant until managers discovered the power within its own workforce.

In the 1980s, Harley-Davidson managers decided to replace the obsolete manufacturing system in its Pennsylvania plant and introduce a just-in-time inventory system. To implement the new system, the company took a step that was unusual for that time. Managers involved employees in deciding how to handle the changeover. Instead of having managers and engineers make all the decisions and announce them to workers, managers spent several months discussing the desired changes with everyone. After all parties helped decide on the changes, everyone cooperated to make them work.[37]

Employee involvement worked so well that management decided to enlist employees in solving quality problems. Employees learned how to use statistical tools for monitoring and controlling the quality of their own work; managers and supervisors were trained as team leaders. Both quality and morale improved. Employee involvement, just-in-time inventory and statistical operator control became part of what Harley-Davidson came to call its productivity triad.[38] Employees were empowered to monitor their own work, resolve problems and implement their own solutions. Managers worked with teams, sharing authority and supporting team efforts in every way possible.

Leadership and Rapid Response

Constantly changing demands challenge a leader's effectiveness. As culturally diverse organizations evolve, the leader's constituencies grow increasingly complex. Different circumstances and demands call for different kinds of direction, change and strategies. In a business world based on high technology, speed is essential. In Sam Walton's words, a company must be able to "turn on a dime."[39]

In complex times, people are anxious and emotional. Thus, to lead in a culture of change, leaders must develop strong emotional intelligence competencies to achieve outstanding leadership performance. Leaders influence others emotionally. **Emotional intelligence (EI)** concerns how leaders manage personal emotions and social relationships.

The term emotional intelligence was made popular by Daniel Goleman in his book of the same name.[40] Goleman contends that emotional intelligence is twice as important as purely cognitive abilities (IQ) to an individual's job success.[41] For example, one study compared highly successful executives with those who failed in their job. "He found that the managers who failed were all high in expertise and IQ. In every case their fatal weakness was in emotional intelligence—arrogance, overreliance on brainpower, inability to adapt to the occasionally disorienting shifts in that region and disdain for collaboration or teamwork."[42] Kevin Murray, former director of communications with British Airways told Goleman, "Organizations going through the greatest change are those who need emotional intelligence the most."[43]

Emotion is important to leadership. Understanding that others are influenced by emotions is an essential skill in leading people. Leaders in similar situations who get their employees emotionally engaged accomplish far more. Goleman identified four sets of emotional competence, divided into two domains of personal competence and social competence.[44]

Personal competence is made up of self-awareness and self-management. *Self-awareness* is the ability to know one's inner self and recognize how it impacts other people. A self-aware leader would be able to understand personal strengths and handle emotions. *Self-management* is the ability to manage one's emotions and impulses. In order to regulate one's emotions, a leader would need greater awareness of one's inner self. Thus, managing others begins with managing oneself.

Social competence is made up of social awareness and relationship management. *Social Awareness* is the ability to understand the feelings, needs and concerns of other people and the impact on the organization. *Relationship Management* is the ability to develop rapport with others. It is the knowledge of how to regulate the emotions of others.

Effective leadership depends on improving emotional intelligence, which can be learned. Leaders who are able to find the best in themselves can influence people even under the most demanding circumstances. Marriott Hotels have gained customer loyalty by empowering their frontline employees—those who have direct contact with guests. Their primary concern is to delight their guests and turn them into repeat customers. Through careful screening of new hires, investments in training, sharing of management authority and reengineering its processes, the hotel giant lowered its turnover and costs; increased employee commitment, enthusiasm and efficiency; and provided superior service to its guests.[45]

emotional intelligence (EI)
A set of competencies that distinguishes how people manage feelings, interact and communicate. Effective leaders combine mental intelligence with emotional intelligence to handle themselves and others. The four main sets of emotional competence are self-awareness, self-management, social awareness and relationship management

The company's First Ten program concentrated on making each guest's first 10 minutes pleasurable and memorable. Marriott guests can preregister by using a credit card. When they arrive, a "guest service associate," or GSA, greets them at the door. His or her responsibility is to, "pick up your key and paperwork from a rack in the lobby and then [escort] you directly to your room."[46] No hassles, no waiting in line, no confusion about your reservations. Each GSA can do what it takes to make a guest happy without clearance from on high.

Leadership and Tough Decisions

Anyone can lead when decisions are easy and please constituencies. Leaders must often, however, make unpopular, difficult decisions that adversely affect people inside and outside an organization. Leaders need the courage to see their decisions through and to face the consequences. Leaders must have the ability to do—within legal, moral, and ethical boundaries—what is best for their organizations.

Rudolph Giuliani became a global symbol of a leader responding to crisis after the terrorist attacks of September 11th. The former mayor of New York City relied on his beliefs to get him through something he never thought he'd experience—the attacks on the World Trade Center. Giuliani defines a leader in his book, *Leadership:* "Someone who has his own ideas. Someone who can see beyond today, into tomorrow and the next day. Someone who can see where we have to be."[47] *TIME* magazine selected Giuliani as "2001 Person of the Year" and cited him, "for having more faith in us than we had in ourselves, for being brave when required and rude when appropriate and tender without being trite, for not sleeping and not quitting and not shrinking from the pain all around him."

Top managers must be prepared for a disaster. They make plans for a crisis. In a crisis, a company may turn to an outsider for guidance. Niagara Mohawk Power of Syracuse, New York, turned to an insider, Bill Donlon. Maintenance problems had caused the shutdown of a nuclear power station, forcing the company to buy electricity from rival producers. Cost overruns from the construction of a second nuclear plant were also hurting the bottom line. Donlon turned the company around by bringing in 20 new senior officers, reassigning key staff, terminating poor performers, reassessing the functions of all 11,000 employees, and enlisting everyone's help in establishing changes and productivity savings. "The whole system just wasn't working any longer," said Donlon. "It was apparent to me that we had to change."[48]

Making tough decisions is how Indra Nooyi, PepsiCo's President and CEO, earned her reputation and promotions. The India-born American had to make a number of hard decisions at PepsiCo. Her overriding concern has always been to do what's best for the company, given the people and circumstances. PepsiCo spin-offs formed two new companies, Yum Brands and Pepsi Bottling Group. Says Nooyi,

You have to think of a business like any investment. You have to know when to get in, but more important, when to get out. Getting out can be a lot tougher, especially if you develop an emotional tie to the business. But the world changes, and so should the models we apply to our businesses.[49]

How Managers Can Become Better Leaders

Becoming a better leader begins with efforts to know oneself. Each manager has diverse values, needs, goals, ethics, strengths and weaknesses; these determine how he or she will use the arts of management and leadership. An individual's philosophy about work and about the people who perform it will influence approaches to leadership. Managers who respect individuals will value diversity and inclusion and treat each person with dignity. Managers who value security above all else may be too cautious, unwilling to make tough decisions and take the consequences of those decisions. Conversely, managers who value growth and challenge will seek new approaches, take on tough assignments, and willingly endure personal sacrifice to improve themselves, their subordinates and their organizations. Such managers will encourage others to do the same.

Because leadership is situational, leaders must be adaptable. They must build teams and work with them. Leaders must willingly and ably exercise different leadership styles and utilize the behaviors discussed in this chapter. Only by doing so will their businesses be able to turn on a dime—a capability that the business environment of today requires. Managers must provide a vision and "sell" it to their constituents. They need to sense the need for change, prepare themselves and their team members for change, and articulate what is needed for change. Then they must act as change agents. They can do all these things only by staying current in their fields, remaining open to what is new and different, and committing themselves to constant efforts at self-improvement through the adoption of the *kaizen* philosophy.

Leaders must be willing to suppress what may seem best for themselves and implement what is best for others—subordinates, customers and their organizations. As a servant who tailors leadership style and behavior to fit others' needs, the true leader excels by doing what is best for others. Being a manager is tough; being a leader–manager is tougher still.

Chapter Summary

1 Discuss leadership traits, skills, and behaviors.

Leadership traits are specific personal characteristics possessed by individuals that can both help or hinder their ability to lead and manage. Being dependable, for example, is a must for building mutual trust and respect between oneself and others. Without it, people discount or ignore a person and his or her contributions. With a proper mix of traits, given the circumstances and the available resources, a leader can be a source of influence over others.

Skills are a person's ability to demonstrate knowledge and competencies. They are capabilities to perform some process or task. Communicating effectively requires many skills, such as critical thinking, listening actively and fluency with one or more languages. Skills represent employment security, provided they are not obsolete and are in demand. Skills move people from knowing to doing. As such, certain types of skills are essential to leading people and are a source of power over others.

Behaviors for leaders are detailed in Figure 12.2. Each requires specific knowledge, traits, and skills. Praise recognition, for example, requires such traits as decisiveness, willingness to assume responsibility and dominance. Skills required are diplomacy and tact, fluency in speaking and writing and knowledge about individual and group task performances. The key concept is: If what is needed in any situation is available in an individual or team, leadership can take place.

2 Differentiate between management and leadership.

Some managers may be leaders, some leaders may be managers, and leadership can be exhibited by other than management personnel. Leading may be done in or out of a leadership or management position. Leading is a management function that can be exercised by any employee. Leadership is based on five sources of power (discussed in Learning Objective 3), and may be exercised by people regardless of their job descriptions. The key difference between these two concepts is the willingness of a person's subordinates to follow that person's direction. Leaders persuade, guide, direct, counsel, coach and inspire others. They do so because they possess more than one source of power.

3 Describe the five sources of power leaders may possess.

The five kinds of power are legitimate, coercive, reward, expert and referent. Legitimate power flows from a person's formal authority, as denoted in his or her job description. Coercive power is defined as the ability to punish or deny rewards. It rests in both managers' job descriptions and in various group members who can exert peer pressure. Reward power, the opposite of coercive power, is the ability to bestow rewards. Like coercive power, it is held by managers and non-managers. Expert power is based on a person's knowledge and expertise—what one knows or is able to do. Anyone with skills, knowledge, or capabilities needed by others can exercise this kind of power. Finally, a person's traits, characteristics, and personality are a source of influence over others. A person with referent power is attractive to others—those attracted want to associate with or emulate the person possessing it. Referent power is the basis for friendships.

4 Discuss between positive and negative motivation.

Positive motivation is practiced by true leaders. Using Herzberg's (Chapter 11) motivational factors, leaders engineer jobs and offer the kinds of rewards desired by individuals to bring out their best and keep them motivated. Challenges and opportunities are offered and supports are provided to meet or exceed those challenges. People are encouraged to take risks, to welcome responsibilities, and to develop their talents.

Negative motivation relies primarily on fear. It uses coercive power to threaten and punish. It tends to work in a crisis or for the short run but cannot stimulate lasting motivated behaviors. It becomes too stressful and eventually leads to employee dissatisfaction and loss of commitment. What behavior is not acceptable is made clear; but what behavior is necessary is often vague and uncertain.

5 Describe the three decision-making styles used by leaders.

The three styles are the autocratic, the participative and the free rein. The autocratic style is an "I" approach to leadership. The leader keeps the decision-making authority but may consult with followers when making decisions. This style is appropriate when handling crises, instructing others, and exerting maximum focus on the task.

The free-rein style asks subordinates and followers to take over the decision-making process—to solve and resolve the problem. It is the ultimate expression of empowerment. Experienced experts desire and usually must have such a style. It treats people as though they were self-employed—giving them the ultimate authority and responsibility for solving problems. Leaders know they must be able to use all three styles as circumstances and individuals dictate. Using the wrong style with an individual can inhibit his or her motivation.

6 **Explain the two primary approaches leaders can take: task centered and people centered.**

When leading, leaders and managers can take a task-centered approach, a people-centered approach, or an approach that blends the two. Which one they choose is usually dictated to them by what their followers or subordinates need and what the situation requires. Task orientation is usually practiced when people must focus on getting their work or the job done, as is the case in a crisis. People orientation helps build teams and cooperation between and among individuals and within groups. In most situations leaders must give some emphasis to both people and tasks.

7 **Describe the three theories of situational leadership.**

The three theories are Fiedler's contingency model, House and Mitchell's path–goal theory, and Hersey and Blanchard's life-cycle theory. Fiedler links focus on task or people to conditions in three variables: leader–member relations (good or poor), task structure (structured or unstructured), and leader position power (weak or strong). All three relate to a leader's situation at any given time and underscore the need to be flexible in adopting any orientation.

House and Mitchell's path–goal theory holds that leaders can influence subordinates' motivation by (1) teaching employees the competencies they need to perform to standards and gain rewards, (2) tailoring

rewards to meet employees' needs, and (3) acting to support subordinates' efforts. This theory is the basis for the expectancy theory of motivation (Chapter 11). It links subordinates' success to examples and supports provided by their leaders.

Hersey and Blanchard's life-cycle theory states that throughout one's career, the style of leadership he or she requires will change and evolve from the autocratic to the free rein. When employees are new to a job or task, autocratic supervision is appropriate. When they gain experience, employees become more able to contribute and participate in those decisions affecting them and the work. Finally, experienced old-timers and professionals need a free rein to function most effectively.

8 **Discuss the three challenges facing leaders.**

The first challenge has to do with the traditional way of running an organization—few leaders, many followers and a hierarchy of decision makers. Today's fast-moving markets and business climates call for a much more rapid response to challenges and opportunities. This response cannot take place without empowered individuals at every layer and in every function and process. As companies downsize and outsource, fewer people are left to do the work; and that work is becoming increasingly more technical and demanding.

The second challenge is one of gaining a rapid-response capability. Time is the enemy in most situations. Competitors and markets do not remain static. Customers must be accommodated and their demands met. Empowering employees through open-book management, training, authority sharing, and selective hiring is the key. This allows the frontline to respond rapidly to both challenges and opportunities.

The third challenge leaders face is to make tough, unpleasant decisions; they must often bite the bullet and sublimate their egos. Leaders must have the courage to do what is right in line with the company's core values and their personal moral and ethical codes. When taking these difficult actions, they must obey the law. To do otherwise is to put the future of the organization and its members at risk.

KEY TERMS

autocratic style   **407**

contingency model   **412**

emotional intelligence (EI)   **418**

free-rein style   **409**

gamification   **414**

influence   **396**

leadership   **396**

Leadership Grid®   **410**

leadership style   **406**

life-cycle theory   **415**

participative style   **408**

path–goal theory   **413**

REVIEW QUESTIONS

1. In what ways do a person's traits and skills give them influence over others?

2. How are management and leadership similar? Different?

3. What are the five sources of influence over others in organizations?

4. Do you think it is better to lead through positive or negative motivational means? Why? What are the advantages and disadvantages of each approach?

5. What set of circumstances can you give that would require a leader to use an autocratic style? A participative one? A free-rein style?

6. Under what circumstances should a leader be task centered? People centered? Use a blend of both approaches?

7. What are the basic components of Fiedler's contingency model of leadership? How do they affect a leader's choice to focus on task or people?

8. What does the path–goal theory of leadership tell a leader to do?

9. What does the life-cycle theory of leadership say about the use of the three styles of decision making?

10. What are the three challenges facing leaders today? How can leaders deal with each?

DISCUSSION QUESTIONS FOR CRITICAL THINKING

1. Who is currently a leader to you, and why is he or she a leader?

2. Can a manager be a leader by simply relying on his or her positional or formal authority? Why or why not?

3. Is it essential for a manager to have a "moral compass?" Why or why not?

4. Emotional intelligence (EI) in the workplace is a skill through which employees treat emotions as valuable information in determining what to do in a situation. For example, an employee has come up with a great idea that will save the company thousands of dollars, but knows her manager tends to be irritable and short-tempered in the morning. Having emotional intelligence means that the employee will first recognize and consider this emotional fact about her manager. Despite the fact that this idea can save the company money—and her own excitement— she will regulate her own emotions, curb her enthusiasm and wait until the afternoon to approach her manager. Describe another example of an employee and manager using EI in the workplace.

Social Media Management Exercises

Groupon

Groupon is a group-buying model that combines social media and coupon marketing. It sells coupons to local businesses and takes a commission on the sale. Groupon offers a daily deal, but the coupons are valid only if a certain number of people buy them. So, deal seekers encourage their friends to buy the coupons, usually through Facebook or Twitter.

Shoppers buying the coupons hope to get deep discounts at stores and events. Businesses buying the coupons hope to get new customers. But to be profitable, the new customers need to buy products and services in addition to the discounted item. Furthermore, they need to become repeat customers.

- Price sensitivity and the ability to keep customers buying are drivers of future business success. However, obtaining employee buy-in is the most important factor influencing a Groupon promotion's success. Employees might be concerned that the company is charging too little for the product or service. Their behavior can make the Groupon offer succeed or fail. How might an onslaught of bargain hunters affect employees' hours and wages?

- What steps can managers deciding to try Groupon take to influence employees to create a positive experience for customers? How can managers keep their employees content?

See: *www.groupon.com*.

Experiential Learning

The End of Olds

"Oldsmobile is the only American automobile more than 100 years old" (Wright). Yet, on December 12, 2000, General Motors's CEO Rick Wagoner announced that the Oldsmobile Division would be phased out over several years. "It is the oldest automotive brand in America with a history that is rich with innovation and success stories, including dozens of legendary cars, and over the years it was one of the jewels in the General Motors crown," he said (Oldsmobile News). "Oldsmobile's demise has been a matter of speculation since the early 1990s when its annual sales plummeted" (Miller). Long branded as an "old man's car" and a "Buick clone," the Oldsmobile was rumored in the automotive press to be headed down the road taken by retired auto brand names Packard, Hudson, and Nash.

In 1992, John Rock became Oldsmobile's new chief executive officer. He was previously head of GMC trucks. Given a sense of urgency by the press reports, Rock swung into action. Within one month he had assembled the Olds dealers at the Oldsmobile design center. He showed them the new models that were in the pipeline and asked for their help in creating a strategy to revitalize the Olds Division. After several meetings and changes in the mix of members at each, a consensus was reached. "In January 1993, we went to GM's North American Automotive Operations with that plan, to throw out old brands and create new ones," says Rock (Mateja).

Another goal in Rock's strategy was to become more "Saturn-like." He moved the division toward, "value pricing—offering a particular car with certain options at a specific discounted price," and getting that price without "haggling" with customers. Much of Rock's strategy rested on the success of emerging product lines: Aurora, Bravada, Ciera, Achieva, and a totally redone Cutlass. By that time, Rock hoped to reach the final goal in his plan: his retirement to the wilds of Montana.

This strategy did bring in younger buyers, but not in the numbers that Oldsmobile had hoped. "Despite attempts to resurrect Olds with a new lineup and aggressive retail incentives, it sold only 265,878 vehicles during the first 11 months of 2000, putting it on pace for its worst sales year since 1952," (Miller). Oldsmobile production ended with the 2004 models. It is interesting to note that in 2003, auto auction company Kruse International named the 1972 Oldsmobile Cutlass W-30 4-4-2 convertible muscle car one of the most collectible American cars (Valdes-Dapena).

Questions

1. What kind of leadership style did Rock use with his division's dealers? What kind of leadership style did Rock's boss probably use with him? Was it appropriate?

2. Which leadership traits did Rock exhibit? Which skills?

3. Which of Yukl's leadership behaviors did Rock exhibit?

4. How did Rock's planned retirement help him to make some tough decisions?

Sources: Peter Valdes-Dapena, "Dead at 106: Oldsmobile," *CNN/Money*, April 29, 2004, *http://money.cnn.com/2004/04/28/pf/autos/olds_dead*; John Richards, "End of Olds Leaves Dealers in Limbo," *The Detroit News*, August 24, 2001, *http://www.bizjournals.com/pittsburgh/stories/2001/08/27/story6.html*; Joe Miller, "It's the End of the Road for Olds," *The Detroit News*, December 12, 2000; Richard A. Wright, "Oldsmobile Was America's Oldest Surviving Nameplate," *The Detroit News*, November 6, 2000; Jim Mateja, "Scary Wakeup Calls Worked for Olds," *Chicago Tribune*, July 10, 1995, sec. 4, p. 5; Oldsmobile News, "GM to Restructure Oldsmobile Division," *http://www.oldsmobile.com*.

Chapter 13

Team Management

LEARNING OBJECTIVES

After studying this chapter, you should be able to:

1 Discuss the nature of teams and the characteristics of effective teams

2 Identify the types of teams that organizations use

3 Discuss potential uses of teams

4 Use decision-making authority as a characteristic by which to distinguish team type

5 Identify and discuss steps in establishing teams

6 Identify and discuss the roles of team members and team leaders

7 Describe the four stages of team development

8 Discuss team cohesiveness and team norms and their relationship to team performance

9 Evaluate the benefits and costs of teams

10 Discuss the positive and negative aspects of conflict in an organization

11 Identify the sources of conflict in an organization

12 Describe a manager's role in conflict management and potential strategies to manage conflict

Management in Action

Team Dynamics

Teams allow companies to increase productivity, quality and profitability. They share values, information, best practices and make collective decisions. The team helps each member do a better job. Yet, not all teams function efficiently. They face conflict. But, they can renew themselves and learn skills of interaction.

For each of the following statements, circle the number that indicates your level of agreement. Rate your agreement as it is, not what you think it should be. Objectivity will enable you to determine your management skill strengths and weaknesses.

	Almost Always	Often	Sometimes	Rarely	Almost Never
I initiate ideas.	5	4	3	2	1
I summarize others' ideas.	5	4	3	2	1
I avoid unnecessary conflict.	5	4	3	2	1
I clarify and elaborate on discussion.	5	4	3	2	1
I ensure that people are heard.	5	4	3	2	1
I seek consensus.	5	4	3	2	1
I note tension and interest levels in a group.	5	4	3	2	1
I note when the group avoids a topic.	5	4	3	2	1
I can sense individuals' feelings.	5	4	3	2	1
I encourage others.	5	4	3	2	1

Compute your score by adding the circled numbers. The highest score is 50; the lowest score is 10. A higher score implies you are more likely to enjoy teamwork. A lower score implies a lesser degree of readiness, but it can be increased. Reading and studying this chapter will help you improve your understanding of teams.

INTRODUCTION

A not-so-quiet revolution is taking place in American business. At companies such as Google, Apple, Levi Strauss, Pixar, Microsoft, and General Electric, teams are emerging as an organizational force. Scores of service companies, such as FedEx and IDS, have boosted productivity as much as 40 percent by adopting self-managed work teams; Boeing used teams to cut the number of engineering hang-ups on its 777 passenger jet by more than half.[1] Companies realize the team approach can ignite superior performance. Teams in all their various forms—self-managed work teams, task forces and project teams—are changing organizational structures, the way work is approached, the role of managers, and the involvement of workers.[2]

Notes University of Southern California's Edward Lawler, "Teams are the Ferrari of work design. They're high performance, but high maintenance and expensive."[3]

With Professor Lawler's comments in mind, we will discuss how to maximize the potential of teams in this chapter. We will examine types of teams, how teams are created and managed, and their benefits and costs. We will also see how to keep teams functioning effectively through the management of conflict.

NATURE OF TEAMS

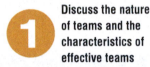

Discuss the nature of teams and the characteristics of effective teams

Teams Defined

In an organization, a **team** is a group of two or more people who interact regularly and coordinate their work to accomplish a common objective.[4] Three points characterize a team:

team
A group of two or more people who interact regularly and coordinate their work to accomplish a common objective

1   At least two people must be involved. The ultimate size of the group can vary, depending on the nature of the assignment.

2   The members must interact regularly and coordinate their work. People who are in the same department but do not interact regularly are not a team; nor are people who have lunch together every day but never actually coordinate their work.

3   Members of a team must share a common objective. Regardless of the objective—ensuring service quality, designing a new product or reducing costs—each member works toward a common, shared objective.

Characteristics of Effective Teams

Teams can and do function throughout organizations. Their effectiveness relates directly to how well managers engineer team structure and how team members behave. For example, Boeing's teams share technical and operational information across international borders, time zones and cultural differences. As Edgar Schein reported, the characteristics of effective teams include the following:

- Team members are committed to and involved in clear, shared goals.

- All team members feel free to express themselves and participate in discussions and decisions. Each member is valued and heard.

- Members trust each other. In discussions, they openly disagree without fear of negative consequences.

- When needs for leadership arise, any member feels free to volunteer. Team leadership varies with the situation.

- Decisions are made by consensus. All team members support final decisions.
- As problems occur, the team focuses on causes, not symptoms. Likewise, when members develop solutions, they direct them at the causes of the problem.
- Team members are flexible in terms of work processes and problem solving. They search for new ways of acting.
- Team members change and grow. All members encourage and support growth.[5]

Identify the types of teams that organizations use

formal team

A team created by managers to function as part of the organizational structure

vertical team

A team composed of a manager and subordinates

horizontal team

A team composed of employees from different departments

task force

A horizontal team composed of employees from different departments designed to accomplish a limited number of objectives and existing only until it has met the objectives

cross-functional team

A team with an undefined life span designed to bring together the knowledge of various functional areas to work on solutions to operational problems

committee

A horizontal team—either ad hoc or permanent—designed to focus on one objective; members represent functional areas of expertise

TYPES OF TEAMS

Many different types of teams are emerging in business organizations. These are **formal teams** created by management as a functioning part of the organizational structure. They are not informal, nor are they created by social interaction. (For a discussion of informal groups, see Chapter 7.) In terms of origin, not function, we can identify two forms of teams: vertical teams and horizontal teams.

Vertical Teams A **vertical team**—sometimes called a command team or a functional team—is composed of a manager and his or her subordinates in the formal chain of command. A vertical team may include as many as three or four levels of management. Examples include the human resources department at Citibank, the "wing team" at Boeing, and "skunkworks" at Lockheed Martin. Each fits the definition of team: two or more people interacting and coordinating their work for the purpose of achieving a common shared objective. The marketing department illustrated in Figure 13.1 is a vertical team, as are the finance, production and engineering departments.

Horizontal Teams A **horizontal team** is made up of members drawn from different departments in an organization.[6] In most cases, such a team is created to address a specific task or objective. The team may disband after the objective is achieved. Three common kinds of horizontal teams are task forces, cross-functional teams and committees.

A **task force** is designed to accomplish a limited number of objectives or tasks, and it is composed of employees from different departments. A task force exists only until it meets its objectives. Master Industries, an injection-molding company in Ohio, formed a task force to implement a smoke-free policy in the workplace within 18 months. When this objective was attained, the task force disbanded.[7]

A **cross-functional team** harnesses the knowledge of people from various functional areas to solve problems. Like task forces, cross-functional teams focus on objectives, but they have a continuous life. At Sequins International, a New York-based manufacturer of sequins, two cross-functional teams—one for product satisfaction, the other for customer support—have been created. Composed of representatives from manpower, machines, methods and material, they pursue their ongoing goal to improve product satisfaction or customer service.[8] Figure 13.1 includes a cross-functional product design team.

A **committee** might be ad hoc (set up to do a job and then disbanded) or standing (permanent). The work of a standing committee—handling grievances, for instance—is ongoing. Committee representation may be chosen by functional area to reflect department views. Individuals are not necessarily chosen for specific technical ability, as members of a task force are. Thus, to ensure participation from all areas, a budget committee may have a representative from each of the major functional areas.[9]

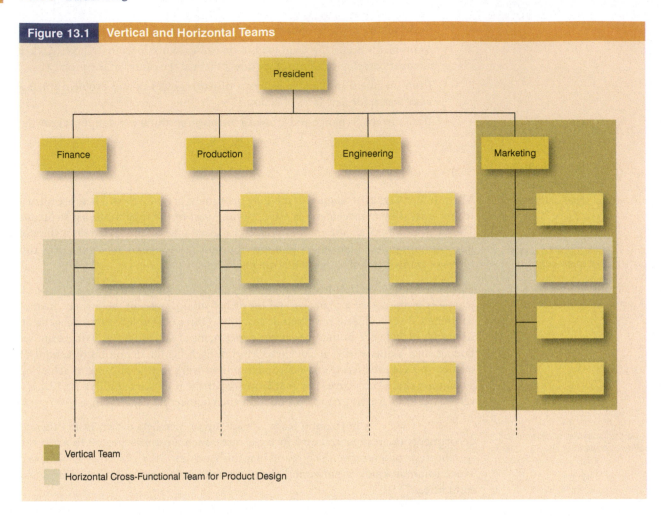

Figure 13.1   Vertical and Horizontal Teams

Vertical Team

Horizontal Cross-Functional Team for Product Design

Philosophical Issues of Team Management

Given the current trend toward the team approach in American business—and reflecting on Professor Lawler's words earlier in the chapter—many managers are asking, "What can teams do?" and "How do they function within the organization?"

HOW TO USE TEAMS

The purpose of a team is to accomplish one or more objectives. A team provides a vehicle for combining skills, securing commitment and involvement, and sharing expertise and opinions in pursuit of a specific objective. The objective could be to improve quality, design a product, solve a problem or carry out departmental work. Although managers may choose from unlimited team options, as Figure 13.2 shows, there are five main categories of teams: product development teams, project teams, quality teams, process teams and work teams.

Product Development Teams Whether they are task forces or cross-functional teams, **product development teams** are organized to create new products. At Berrios

③ Discuss potential uses of teams

product development team
A team organized to create new products

Figure 13.2   Potential Uses of Teams

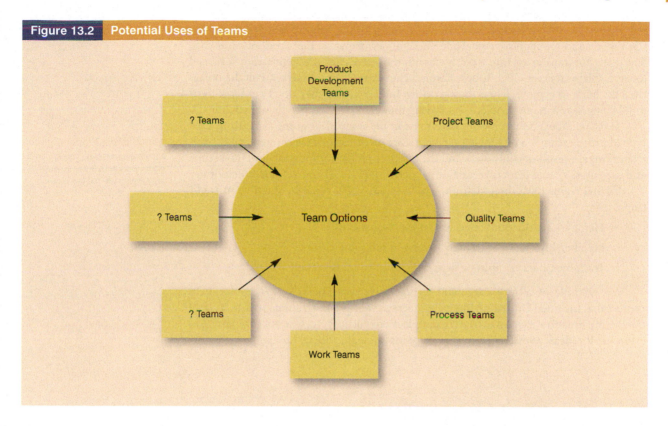

Manufacturing Company, CEO Willis Berrios created teams that combined people from different areas of expertise with the objective of smoothly bringing a new product to market. The teams included representatives from quality control, engineering, production, systems design, marketing and manufacturing. One of the first times IBM used a product development team, the ThinkPad 701 C laptop PC, code-named Butterfly, was created. It became the first on-time product from the PC group in years. The Butterfly, with two keyboard halves that came together on a single plane, was designed in one year. In the old system, product developers, working independently, took years to build a prototype. For example, it took six years for an earlier IBM innovation—an eraser like pointing device for portables—to hit the market.[10]

Project Teams Instead of focusing on development of a single product, managers often assemble **project teams** (sometimes called problem-solving teams) to complete a specific task in an organization. Project teams flourish at Xerox, Apple, Texas Instruments and Google. At Boeing, teams of engineers and operations specialists move in to work out operating problems in systems and apply their creativity to develop strategic delivery systems.[11]

Sometimes, to address an important project, teams operate outside the scope of the organizational structure. Although part of the formal organization, such teams maintain their own reporting structures. In these cases, members perceive their team as an independent and separate entity with plenty of, "corporate breathing room."[12] For example, when Chrysler creates a new model or revamps an old model, it forms a self-contained multidisciplinary project team from engineering, design, manufactur-

project team
A team organized to complete a specific task in the organization

ing, marketing and finance. Senior managers act with the team to sketch a vision for the vehicle and set aggressive goals: for design, performance, fuel economy and cost. The goals are transferred into a contract with the team, after which the team is turned loose. Explains former CEO Robert Eaton, "The contract simply sets out all the objectives we hope to achieve. Then they go away and do it, and they don't get back to us unless they have a major problem. And so far, they aren't having any major problems."[13]

Team members do not always have to be in the same place at the same time. One type of project team is a **virtual team** where team members primarily interact electronically. This is a result of computers and the Internet, global competition and travel time and expenses. Virtual teams are part of the networked world and use it to collaborate.

Virtual teams have three defining characteristics that separate them from traditional teams:

- Members are distributed across multiple locations.
- Membership can be extremely diverse in skills and culture.
- Team members can join or depart the team in midstream.[14]

An example of a very successful virtual team was Boeing's 777 development project that included United Airline's engineers as well as a horizontal cross-section of the Boeing organization. An extreme example is crowdsourcing, where a company asks everyone for ideas, as discussed in this chapter's Managing Social Media.

virtual team
A team where members primarily interact electronically because they are physically separated (by time and/or space)

Managing Social Media

Crowdsourcing

Outsourcing or moving jobs to another location, such as China or India has become common. But what about asking everyone on the Internet—the crowd—to help? *Crowdsourcing* is outsourcing a job by asking everyone who can work remotely through the Internet to apply. Karim R. Lakhani, an assistant professor at Harvard Business School, calls what most people refer to as crowdsourcing "broadcast search." "A problem statement is broadcast along with associated incentives, and people with expertise apply their talent to solving the problem."

Social media sites support user-generated content, which means any user can contribute information. Companies pose questions or problems, and users can expand on the content. For example, generally for research purposes, a company can ask customers to form a consumer panel and share their point of view about the company's products, services and concepts. Furthermore, users can rate products and services. For example, Amazon allows users to rate products with a five-star scale, comment on those products, review sellers, read comments from others and compare prices. Social media users can vote for a product, concept or idea. LEGO

has a website (*https://ideas.lego.com*) where fans can submit ideas for a LEGO set. Honda crowdsourced its, "Live Every Litre" campaign to promote the CR-Z hybrid car (Advertising Age). Companies evaluate information from the crowd and use it for continuous improvement.

➤ In his book, *The Wisdom of Crowds*, James Surowiecki claims, "Under the right circumstances, groups are remarkably intelligent, and are often smarter than the smartest people in them." When do you think that large groups of people could make better choices than smart and knowledgeable individuals?

Source: Advertising Age, "Honda Crowdsources a Movie," July 29, 2010, *http://adage.com/article/mediaworks-idea-of-the-week/honda-crowdsources-a-movie/145175*; Dan Woods, "The Myth of Crowdsourcing," *Forbes*, September 29, 2009, *http://www.forbes.com/2009/09/28/crowdsourcing-enterprise-innovation-technology-cio-network-jargonspy.html*.

Quality Teams As we have emphasized throughout the text, quality and quality assurance have become driving forces in U.S. industry. Many firms have established quality improvement teams that monitor and ensure quality. An early quality assurance tool was the *quality circle*. As discussed in Appendix A, a quality circle is a group of volunteers from the same or related work areas who meet regularly to identify the quality issues facing the company or department and offer suggestions for improvement. Other organizations have developed **quality assurance teams**, whose mission it is to guarantee the quality of services and products by contacting customers and working with vendors. For example, AT&T Global Information Solutions assembled customer service teams consisting of seven to 10 employees in the United States and abroad. They were given team training with customer participation. The teams numbered several hundred, in 110 countries, and were made up of representatives throughout the organization. Once the training was completed, members stayed in contact with the customer through regularly scheduled meetings and customer calls. Says Des Randall, former vice president of the Global Sales Program for AT&T Global Information Systems,

> In the past you may have had sales and marketing people working together with specific customers, but what we are talking about here are representatives from throughout the corporation focused on individual customers. This transformation represents a total restructuring of how a corporation does business. Customer-focused teams have access to local and global resources in order to speed decisions, increase our responsiveness, and provide world class solutions.[15]

Process Teams The stimulus provided by companies who have reengineered has led to process teams. A **process team** groups members who perform the organization's major processes into teams. A process team not only performs the processes but also refines them. Most organizations like Siemens AG, the subject of this chapter's Global Applications feature, developed process teams as they restructured from a functional organization design. The process teams remove departmental barriers and emphasize coordination. For example, Olin Industries transformed 14 functional departments into eight process teams with names like *fulfillment, new products* and *sources*. Similarly, Zeneca Agricultural Products' (now known as Syngenta) former CEO, Bob Wood, took apart every business process from product development to order fulfillment to create a dozen process teams structured to satisfy the customer.[16]

Work Teams When a company creates a small, multi-skilled team that does all the tasks previously performed by the individual members of a functional department or departments, the group is known as a **work team**. Work team members assume responsibility for the function or tasks, sharing skills and complementing each other. After adopting work teams, Frito-Lay's plant in Lubbock, Texas logged double-digit cost cuts and saw its quality jump from the bottom 20 to the top six of Frito's U.S. factories. The 11-member work teams are responsible for everything from product processing (potatoes for the potato chip team, for example) to equipment maintenance, to team scheduling. The team even interviews potential employees for the team. To help them devise ways to produce and ship products more efficiently, teammates receive weekly reports on cost, quality and service performance.[17]

quality assurance team
A team created to guarantee the quality of services and products, contact customers, and work with vendors

process team
A team that groups members who perform and refine the organization's major processes

work team
A team composed of multi-skilled workers that does all the tasks previously done by individual members in a functional department or departments

Reshaping Siemens

Step inside the new Siemens AG. After nearly a decade of hit-or-miss efforts to speed product development, Siemens, a gigantic German electrical and engineering conglomerate, has finally shed its plodding perfectionism and bureaucracy. Gone are the endless meetings, the aimless research, and the fear of taking risks. Now, a new generation of managers is fostering cooperation across the company; setting up new organizational structures, creating teams to develop products and attack new markets, thriving on accountability. The new emphasis is on revving up innovation and pleasing the customer.

Siemens is an international company, built around German engineering values. Former CEO Klaus Kleinfeld believes that global managers must think internationally, but act locally. He said, "In today's world, knowledge travels faster than ever before, so if you are talking about a sustainable competitive advantage, probably the only one is the quality of the people you have and the way they interact as a team."

➡ Kleinfeld's leadership mantra is, "Nobody's perfect, but a team can be." What do you think he means?

Sources: Knowledge at Wharton, "Siemens CEO Klaus Kleinfeld, Nobody's Perfect, But a Team Can Be," April 19, 2006, *http://knowledge.wharton.upenn.edu/article.cfm?articleid=1447*; Siemens, *http://www.siemens.com*.

HOW MUCH INDEPENDENCE TO GIVE TEAMS

④ Use decision-making authority as a characteristic by which to distinguish team type

How much authority and operating freedom should teams have? The continuum in Figure 13.3 shows the independence that various types of teams have in day-to-day operations.

Teams Closely Controlled by Management Teams holding the least authority for decision making are committees, task forces and quality circles. Although some task forces may make decisions within a normally defined charge, most operating committees and task forces are not decision-making bodies; they make recommendations to management. Quality circles, with greater latitude in defining quality, still have little authority. Like other closely controlled teams, quality circles make recommendations to management. They usually work in a setting in which the circle facilitator is either a manager or a trained worker–facilitator, and they rely on management to implement their recommendations.[18]

Teams with Moderate Independence Cross-functional, project and product development teams have more decision-making authority than closely controlled teams. Although empowered to make many decisions about the work at hand, management

Figure 13.3   Continuum of Autonomy

Controlled by Management   Independent

| Committees | Task Forces | Quality Circles | Cross-Functional Teams | Project Teams | Product Development Teams | Executive Teams, Self-Managed Work Teams |

Low ◄———————————— Day-to-Day Decision-Making Independence ————————————► High appoints the leaders of moderately independent teams. Therefore, the leaders of these teams tend to make decisions that support management. In addition, management controls budgetary decisions as well as team membership.[19]

Independent Work Teams Self-managed, or self-directed work teams and executive teams are independent. Each controls day-to-day decision making.

self-managed work team
A team, fully responsible for its own work, that sets goals, creates its own schedules, prepares its own budgets, and coordinates its work with other departments

A **self-managed work team** assumes complete responsibility for its work. The team manages itself, sets goals, takes responsibility for the quality of the output, creates its own schedules, reviews its own performance as a group, prepares its own budgets, and coordinates its work with that done by the company's other departments or divisions. These teams plan, control and improve operations independent of formal management supervision.[20]

Self-managed teams are used anywhere in an organization where work units exist— in production, customer service, engineering or design, for example. If a company has created process teams, they too may be self-managed. Companies using self-management teams report that team membership gives workers control over their jobs and a bigger stake in the company, resulting in the blossoming of creativity.[21] For example, at Taco Bell managers discarded an outmoded command-and-control management style that kept a tight rein on employees. Managers replaced it with team-managed units in which frontline crews run the day-to-day operations without supervision. Taco Bell top managers report an increased sense of ownership and responsibility for customer service and overall unit performance.[22]

executive team
A team consisting of two or more people to do the job traditionally held by one upper-level manager

In the executive suites at Nordstrom, managers decided that the jobs of chair and president were too complex for one person to handle. As a result, these responsibilities were put into the hands of **executive teams**. At Seattle-based Nordstrom, three Nordstrom brothers shared the chair and four managers shared the president's position. In the case of the chairpersons, the decisions were made by committee, but were generally limited to the control of strategic direction. Day-to-day management was left to the four presidents. "Like the co-chairmen, the presidents have ample debate, they say, and resolve most disagreements by focusing on what would be best for the customer.... [We] leave our egos at the doorstop." Each of the co-presidents concentrated on his or her own specialty area and acted with great autonomy.[23]

⑤ Identify and discuss steps in establishing teams

ESTABLISHMENT OF TEAM ORGANIZATION

Team management represents a fundamental change from conventional ways of doing business, thinking and managing. Consequently, the decision to adopt team management requires a philosophical commitment by top executives and careful, systematic implementation. The task of setting up work teams among employees must begin at the top.[24]

Process of Team Building

Successful team building requires a fresh assessment of the organization's basics. Figure 13.4 lists the steps involved.[25] The paragraphs that follow will describe each step in turn.

Assessing Feasibility

Will the team approach work? For the organization new to teams, a feasibility study should be the starting point. The study should be a thorough, penetrating review of mission, resources (especially personnel), and current and

Figure 13.4	**Steps in the Process of Team Building**

Step 1 **Assessing feasibility.** Will team building work? How long will it take? Is there a commitment to teams?

Step 2 **Identifying priorities.** What are the critical needs of the organization? Where can teams make an impact?

Step 3 **Defining mission and objectives.** What is the organization trying to achieve? How can teams help attain those goals?

Step 4 **Uncovering and eliminating barriers to team building.** What lack of skills, cultural peculiarities and process specifics might limit teams?

Step 5 **Starting with small teams.** Where can the team approach begin? Which priorities will most benefit from teams?

Step 6 **Planning for training needs.** What training or guidance is needed to make teams effective?

Step 7 **Planning to empower.** Can managers let go? Are they willing to let people make mistakes?

Step 8 **Planning for feedback and development time.** What type and frequency of feedback is needed? Can management be patient?

projected circumstances. It should provide reasonable estimates of how long it might take to institute teams and what kind of commitment is required.

Identifying Priorities An assessment of concerns by order of urgency should reveal the points where teams may be effective. The concerns could include customer needs, production processes and capacity, and delivery systems. This step should eliminate the most common trouble with teams. According to USC's Edward Lawler, most companies rush out and form the wrong kind of team for the wrong job.[26]

Defining Mission and Objectives Before an organization begins to build teams, managers should take care that the company's mission and objectives are solid, well defined, and accepted throughout the organization.

Uncovering and Eliminating Barriers to Team Building Three kinds of barriers impede teams: subject matter barriers, process barriers and cultural barriers.

1 *Subject matter barriers* arise when employees and managers are not sufficiently knowledgeable or technically proficient. Without adequate expertise, teams fail.

2 *Process barriers* stem from unwieldy procedural approaches that limit teams' ability to do their work. Cumbersome approval processes and communication channels that follow the chain of command are incompatible with effective team operation.

3 *Cultural barriers* are ways of thinking that run counter to the team approach. Especially in long-established firms, powerful departments are sometimes unwilling to relinquish authority or to change cherished habits.

Such barriers must be identified and overcome; any one of these can stop teams cold.

Starting with Small Teams Begin team projects and planning in a pocket of the company—one of the clear priority areas. A sound idea is to begin by creating a design team that represents a cross section of the company. The purpose of the team is not to design a product, but to create other teams.

Planning for Training Needs At the outset, top or middle managers should offer their unreserved help and guidance to teams as those groups refine their objectives and boundaries (as Google's top managers do with project teams when they are in their formative stages). Team members will probably need training in planning, the effective use of meetings, and team dynamics. Members of cross-functional teams will need skills training. Recognizing this, Randall Stephenson, AT&T's chairman and chief executive began "Vision 2020," a corporate education program for all employees. By 2020, Stephenson envisions that AT&T will become, "a computing company that manages all sorts of digital things: phones, satellite, television and huge volumes of data, all sorted through software managed in the cloud." In an interview, he said, "There is a need to retool yourself, and you should not expect to stop. People who do not spend five to 10 hours a week in online learning will obsolete themselves with the technology"[27] The curriculum includes online and in-class topics from digital networking and data science to problem solving.

Planning to Empower Executives and other managers must empower workers when creating teams. Senior people need to step back and let the team members make decisions, including making mistakes and failing. Empowering involves giving team members the opportunities to fail as well as to succeed.

Planning for Feedback and Development Time Teams require feedback. Eventually, teams develop their own feedback mechanisms. Initially, however, it is vital that the team builders provide one. Simultaneously, in the team environment, individuals must have ample opportunity to grow and develop. Managers must be patient.

Launching teams often raises unfamiliar issues and procedures. The process can be intimidating as well as confusing. Companies that are beginning a team program can smooth the process by using consultants who specialize in team building. Skilled and experienced consultants can design a process, assist the organization in the implementation, train workers and managers in new roles and in new ways of thinking, and identify potential barriers. Even with this assistance, however, team building takes time and patience. As management guru Peter Drucker noted, "You can't rush teams. It takes five years just to learn to build a team and decide what kind you want." The team system requires massive changes of habits:

- Individuals who used to compete against each other for recognition, raises and resources will have to learn to collaborate with each other.

- Workers who used to be paid for their individual efforts will be rewarded based on their own efforts plus the efforts of coworkers.

- Supervisors who used to be directive in their style will have to become facilitative, coaching workers instead of giving orders.[28]

Team-Building Considerations

Once top managers have decided to create teams and have prepared a comprehensive blueprint of the team-building process, they must make decisions about the details of specific teams. They must make decisions about team size, member roles and team leadership, for example.

Team Size As previously noted, it is best to begin a team program with small teams—that is, teams having fewer than 12 members. Small teams tend to reach consensus more readily than do large teams. In addition, small teams allow more opportunity for interaction and self-expression, and they tend not to break into subgroups. Small size allows members to use their diverse skills to cross train and solve problems aggressively.

If possible, small teams should be maintained after the start-up phase. As teams become larger, team members have more difficulty interacting, becoming a cohesive unit and communicating. In large teams, subgroups often form with their own agendas, and conflict occurs more readily than it does in small teams.[29] Nathan Myhrvold, Microsoft's former chief technology officer, echoes this point. "Although the temptation is there to throw bodies at a project, eight people is right for our teams." Myhrvold observes that as teams get larger, employees must spend more time communicating what's already inside their heads and less time actually applying knowledge to accomplish their work. The productivity of each employee diminishes quickly.[30]

MEMBER ROLES

6 Identify and discuss the roles of team members and team leaders

As GB Tech (the subject of this chapter's Valuing Diversity and Inclusion feature) knows, effective teams display balance. To achieve balance teams require people with diverse technical abilities and those with complementing interpersonal skills. Some members play task-oriented roles and others meet team needs for encouragement and harmony.[31] Glenn Parker reported that the typical team includes roles for task specialists and social specialists. Roles for task specialists include the following:

- *Contributor,* a data-driven person who supplies needed information and pushes for high team performance standards.
- *Challenger,* a team player who constantly questions the goals, methods and even the ethics of the team.
- *Initiator,* the person who proposes new solutions, new methods and new systems for team problems.

Roles for the social specialists include the following:

- *Collaborator,* the "big picture" person who urges the team to stay with its vision and to achieve it.
- *Communicator,* the person who listens well, facilitates well and humanizes the work of the team.
- *Cheerleader,* the person on the team who encourages and praises individual and team efforts.
- *Compromiser,* the team member who will shift opinions to maintain harmony.[32]

Having individuals in a team who can perform two or more of these roles is quite possible—even desirable. Regardless, the objective is to achieve balance. For sustained effectiveness, each team's task environments and interpersonal environments must sustain and energize members.

Team Leadership A key consideration in effective teams is team leadership. In self-managed teams, the team members provide leadership. For example, at W. L. Gore & Associates, famous for Gore-Tex waterproof fabric, the leader evolves from within the team. The leader is not appointed; he or she achieves the position by assuming leadership, which must be approved in a consensus reached through discussion—not a vote.[33]

Team leaders appointed by management require a special set of skills. The role must be filled by someone with values oriented toward teamwork and cooperation. Effective team leaders create a noncompetitive atmosphere, renew trust, think reasonably, share leadership, encourage members to assume as much responsibility as they can handle, and positively reinforce even the slightest contributions. At the same time, team leaders need to keep their teams focused on results.[34]

Experience Counts

GB Tech Inc., a Houston-based information systems company, needed help in writing bid proposals for subcontracts from the National Aeronautics and Space Administration (NASA). GB Tech managers believed the solution was to team company staff with experienced retirees. The retirees would bring much needed technical expertise to the job of completing the complex paperwork. The experienced retirees, who used to work for aerospace corporations, could also help enhance the reputation of GB Tech, a relative newcomer. As Gale Burkett, the company's chairman and CEO, noted, "We were concerned about whether we would be accepted because we were still a fairly new company."

The company began advertising for candidates in several high-tech disciplines. Respondents were carefully screened for technical as well as team skills. Ten retired technical team members were eventually hired. Each functioned effectively within teams as an internal consultant.

GB Tech, in turn, has prospered from the experience diversity brought. The company's revenues have grown. Chairman, CEO, and President Gale E. Burkett attributed much of that growth to the efforts and advice of the retirees.

➡ **Why do you think some companies underestimate the value of older workers when balancing their teams?**

Sources: GB Tech, *http://www.gbtech.com*; Houston Chronicle Survey, "Largest Minority-Owned Businesses," *Houston Chronicle*, May 19, 2001; Laura M. Litvan, "Casting a Wider Employment Net," *Nation's Business*, December 1994, 49–51.

As an effective team leader for a data storage system team on Northrop Grumman's B-2 bomber project, Eric Doremus embodies these abilities. The first time he met with the 40 members of the B-2 bomber team, he admitted he would not be much help with technical problems. "My most important task was not trying to figure out everybody's job. It was to help this team feel as if they owned the project by getting them whatever information, financial or otherwise, they needed. I knew that if we could charge up the hill together, we would be successful." Doremus was right. His team shaped the first prototype of the data storage unit in two years and delivered a fully functional unit in less than three.[35] Doremus and other successful team leaders provide these tips:

- Don't be afraid to admit ignorance.
- Know when to intervene.
- Learn to truly share power.
- Worry about what you take on, not what you give up.
- Get used to learning the job.

Charlie Pellerin, former director of astrophysics for NASA, led the team that built the Hubble Space Telescope. A flawed mirror rendered the telescope useless and the failure was blamed on leadership. Ultimately, Pellerin's repair strategy fixed the Hubble and he received NASA's Outstanding Leadership Medal. This chapter's Quality Management feature discusses how he teaches technical employees to transform underperforming groups into highly performing teams.

Management of Team Processes

Once teams are in place, managers need to address special concerns regarding the management of internal team processes. The specific processes, which relate to the changing dynamics resulting from the team structure, include the stages of team development, team cohesiveness, team norms and team personality.

Quality Management

NASA Teambuilding

How could a leadership failure render the work of the best technical minds in the world useless? It happened to Charlie Pellerin. He was the leader of the failed Hubble Space Telescope NASA team. Then, his work helped to fix the Hubble. Pellerin started 4-D Systems to improve team, leadership and individual performance. He wrote the book, *How NASA Builds Teams*.

The 4-D System (Four-Dimensional Organizing System) represents the four most important dimensions of teamwork identified by Pellerin: cultivating, visioning, including and directing (4-D Systems). Eight behaviors, two per dimension, enhance leadership effectiveness and team performance. These behaviors significantly improve the collaborative process. The eight behaviors are listed below (Hall).

- Express authentic appreciation.
- Address shared interests.
- Appropriately include others.
- Keep all your agreements.
- Express reality-based optimism.
- 100 percent commitment.
- Avoid blaming and complaining.
- Clarify roles, accountability and delegated authority.

The 4-D System helped Ball Aerospace & Technologies Corporation boost profits 40 percent in Bill Townsend's division. Townsend said,

You would think that all it takes to build successful project teams is to get a bunch of sharp, well-motivated, self-starting, creative people together. Unfortunately, it doesn't happen that way. You need people who can work together without feeling threatened by equally creative people, people who can work together with people who think differently than themselves, and people who can work together without feeling the need to withhold information to maintain a position of power within the team (Hall).

➡ **Charlie Pellerin says, "Appreciation has to be shown habitually, authentically, proportionately, specifically and promptly." What do you think this would look like in real life?**

Sources: 4-D Systems, *www.4-DSystems.com*; Cheryl Hall, "Harnessing the Power of Real Team Building," *The Dallas Morning News* (September 15, 2010) 1D, 5D.

STAGES OF TEAM DEVELOPMENT

When a team is created, its members do not come together instantly; rather, the team goes through distinct stages.[36] Figure 13.5 shows the four stages of development: forming, storming, norming and performing.

Forming During the **forming stage**, individual members become acquainted. Members test behaviors to determine which are acceptable and which are unacceptable to individuals in the group. This stage is marked by a high degree of uncertainty. As a result, the individuals accept the power and authority of both formal and informal leaders. An important task for the team leader in this stage is to provide sufficient time and a suitable atmosphere for team members to get to know each other.

Storming In the **storming stage**, disagreement and conflict occur. Individual personalities emerge and team members assert their opinions. Disagreements could arise over priorities, immediate goals or methods. Coalitions or subgroups could emerge as a means to resolve disagreements. The team is not yet unified; some unsuccessful teams never get beyond this stage. The team leader's role during this stage is to openly encourage the necessary interaction. With sound leadership, the group can work through its disagreements and enter the next stage.

7 Describe the four stages of team development

forming stage
The phase of team development in which team members are becoming acquainted

storming stage
The phase of team development characterized by disagreement and conflict as individual roles and personalities emerge

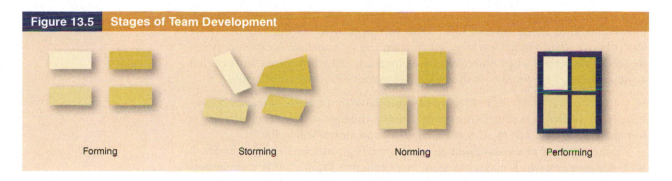

Figure 13.5   Stages of Team Development

Forming   Storming   Norming   Performing

norming stage
The phase of team development in which disagreement and conflict have been re-solved and team members enjoy unity and focus

Norming As the pattern in Figure 13.5 suggests, the team comes together in the **norming stage**. With disagreements and conflicts resolved, the team achieves unity, consensus about who holds the power, and an understanding of the roles that members will play. The team is now focused; it has oneness—a sense of team cohesion. The team leader builds on this newfound unity and helps to clarify the team's values and norms.

performing stage
The phase of team development in which team members progress toward team objectives, handle problems, coordinate work, and confront each other if necessary

Performing In the **performing stage**, the team begins to function and moves toward accomplishing its objectives. Having accepted the oneness achieved during the norming stage, team members interact well with each other. They deal with problems, coordinate work and confront each other if necessary. During this stage, the team leader's role is to provide and maintain the balance between various members' requirements.

Ellen Lord, a team leader at Davidson Interior (a division of Textron), found that it takes a good team leader to help teams through the stages. According to Lord, team leaders, "must have patience and presence of mind to act like a parent, teacher and referee all at once." When forming her product development team, Lord carefully screened workers before inviting them to join; but this careful selection did not ease the team's forming process. "We put all the people in one room and they had to work with each other. The people from different functions didn't know each other, they couldn't ask favors and infighting was pretty intense." The storming stage brought even more intensity and conflict. Team members sometimes got into fights. "A neatnik sitting next to a slob lost his cool. People were emotional about what kind of coffee was brewing in the pot. The manufacturing types thought the engineering members were focused on trivia and bluntly let them know."[37]

Eventually, according to Lord, the team came together; it reached the norming stage. The team members realized that all of them were doers who had a depth of knowledge they could apply. The team then began to perform; and perform it did. Lord's product development team created a high-tech coating that makes plastic for cars look exactly like chrome, but it won't rust, scratch or crack.

 Discuss team cohesiveness and team norms and their relationship to team performance

TEAM COHESIVENESS

An important dimension of team dynamics is cohesiveness. As discussed in Chapter 7, cohesiveness, or cohesion, is the extent to which members are attracted to the team and motivated to remain together. In a highly cohesive team, members are committed to team activities, pull together to accomplish the activities, are happy with the success of the team, and are committed to staying in the team. In contrast, members of less cohesive teams are not team focused, are less concerned about team objectives, and are more ready to leave the team.

Factors Determining Team Cohesiveness Teams with few members, frequent interaction, clear objectives and identifiable success tend to be cohesive. Teams are less cohesive when groups are large, when team size or members' location prevents frequent interaction, when objectives are ambiguous, and when team efforts do not achieve success.[38] Figure 13.6 illustrates the factors that determine cohesiveness.

Results of Team Cohesiveness Figure 13.6 also shows the outcome of team cohesiveness. High cohesiveness contributes to effectiveness and high morale. If cohesiveness is low, the team is less likely to achieve its objectives and morale will be low.[39]

Cohesiveness and success build on each other. High cohesiveness contributes to high achievement, which makes the team more cohesive. Knowing this, team leaders should foster cohesiveness by establishing clear direction, provide for frequent interaction (in regard to work and non-work topics) and design small groups.

Team Norms

As discussed in Chapter 7, a team norm is a standard of behavior that all team members accept. Norms are the ground rules, or guidelines that tell team members what they

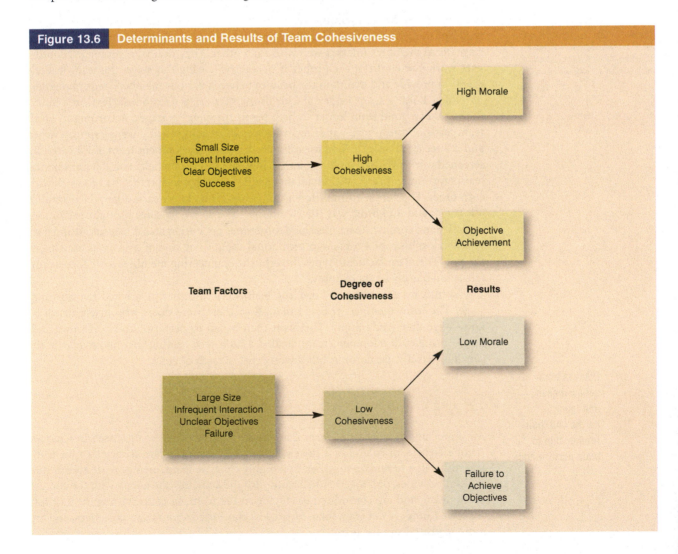

| Figure 13.6 | Determinants and Results of Team Cohesiveness |

can or cannot do under certain circumstances. They provide boundaries of acceptable behavior. Individuals conform to these norms.

The team itself sets team norms. Through an informal process, the key values, role expectations and performance expectations emerge as norms. At Lockheed Martin, team members developed a set of values and expectations. The teams believed in open communication and collaborative problem solving. These norms set the ground rules and were vital to the success of the teams.

A key norm for teams is one that identifies the acceptable level of performance—high, low or moderate. Together with team cohesiveness, this norm is a critical determinant of team productivity. As Figure 13.7 shows, productivity is highest when the team is highly cohesive and has a high performance norm (quadrant A). Moderate productivity occurs when cohesiveness is low, because team members are less committed to performance norms (quadrant B). Low-to-moderate productivity occurs when cohesiveness is low and the performance norm is low (quadrant C). The lowest productivity occurs when the team members are highly cohesive in their commitment not to perform (quadrant D).

Team Personality

A team's personality is closely related to its norms.[40] A personality for a team results from team members' cohesiveness and norms, the pressures they face, their experiences and their successes and failures. The team can be enthusiastic, energetic and cooperative—or just the reverse. A team leader must monitor the personality of the team,

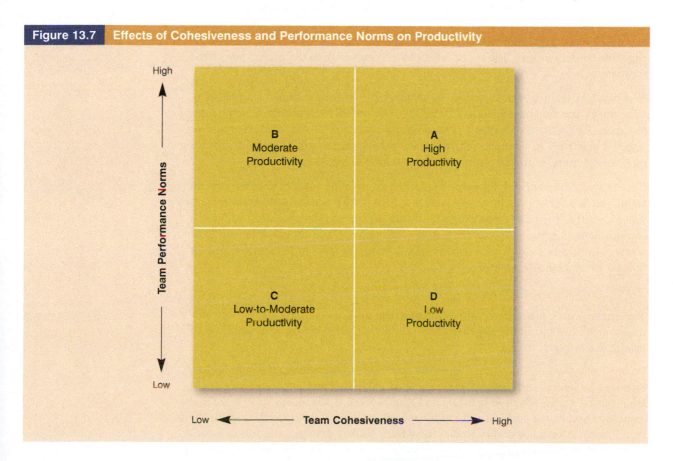

Figure 13.7   **Effects of Cohesiveness and Performance Norms on Productivity**

Team Performance Norms (High / Low)

B
Moderate
Productivity

A
High
Productivity

C
Low-to-Moderate
Productivity

D
Low
Productivity

Team Cohesiveness (Low ← → High)

identify its strengths and weaknesses and then supply the leadership to remedy weaknesses and build on strengths.

MEASUREMENTS OF TEAM EFFECTIVENESS

9 Evaluate the benefits and costs of teams

The decision to create teams, like every management decision, generates benefits and costs. Team effectiveness is measured by weighing these benefits and costs.

Benefits of Teams

If sound processes and techniques underlie team building and management, an organization can harness the benefits of a team. These benefits include synergy, increased skills and knowledge, flexibility, and commitment.

Synergy A team of employees working together develops synergy; it produces more and has more creativity and energy than do the same number of individuals working alone. Working in the team environment provides camaraderie and sharing that is often absent in normal structures. When using productivity as a measure of synergy, we find that increases ranging from 30 to 50 percent are not uncommon, especially in manufacturing and services.[41] Chrysler and IBM reported significant improvement in product development cycles using teams; moreover, as Sequins International and Published Images can attest, customer service significantly improves.

Increased Skill and Knowledge In a team, members' skills and knowledge increase. This increase is due, in part, to training. In addition to formal training, when individuals are exposed to jobs other than their own, they naturally pick up skills and knowledge from other workers. The result is their increasing worth to themselves and to the company.

Flexibility As team workers become more adaptable in their attitudes and capacity to perform, the organization gains flexibility. The broader knowledge base of team members allows them to adjust to changes in work demands and work flow and to respond positively to emergencies. Moreover, the enhanced skill of individual team members permits improved response to organizational demands.

Commitment In an era highlighted by employee demotivation and lack of commitment, teams provide the opportunity for workers to "own" their work. As more companies move toward self-managed work teams and empowerment, employee satisfaction and commitment increase. At Goodyear, former CEO Stanley Gault proudly boasted, "The teams at Goodyear are now telling the boss how to run things—and I must say, I'm not doing a half-bad job because of it."[42]

Costs of Teams

The major costs associated with implementing a team concept include power-realignment costs, training expenses, lost productivity, free-riding costs and loss of productive workers.

Power-Realignment Costs Implementing a team-centered approach results in loss of power by lower- and middle-level managers. The power in the organization shifts from central management to the team and team worker. If adjustment is difficult and resistance occurs, the cost in time and money can be high. This situation is especially true if former managers who become new team leaders embrace the job in words only. J.D. Bryant of Texas Instruments knows because that's what he did. Said Bryant,

"I didn't buy into teams.... I never let the operators do any scheduling or any ordering of parts because that was mine. I figured as long as I had that, I had a job."[43]

Team-Training Costs Employees most likely will need retraining to be able to function in teams. The financial costs associated with the retraining fall into two areas: costs for technical cross training and costs for training individuals to function as part of a team. Of the two, the technical component is usually easier to accomplish. Training in team dynamics is often hampered by the fact that many employees do not know they need it. Recall from Chapter 7 some of the potential pitfalls associated with group decision making: groupthink, excessive compromise, lost time and lack of individual accountability. Team members need to be trained to avoid these problems.

Lost Productivity Developing teams takes time, and time spent in team development is lost to production. The time spent selecting and retraining team members also lowers output of the product or service. In addition, team members need time to adjust to their new environments and roles. They will not reach peak performance overnight.

free rider
A person who receives the benefit of team membership but does not do a proportionate share of work

Free-Riding Costs A **free rider** is a team member who receives the benefits of team membership but does not do a proportionate share of the work. Free riding occurs because not all people are equally committed to the team goals or exert the same amount of effort.[44] Compounding the problem is the dilemma associated with team compensation, the subject of this chapter's Ethical Management feature. Free riders can be compensated for others' work.

Ethical Management

The Paycheck Counts

As more companies embrace teams, team concepts and empowerment, the rules of work are evolving. Managers are no longer just managers; they have become facilitators. Employees are transformed from being directed workers into being full-fledged decision-making partners.

The roles of managers and employees are being defined in the new work environment, but one area lacks consistency: team compensation. Companies are struggling with creating programs that measure performances accurately.

A pay for performance (PFP or P4P) program pays employees for meeting certain performance measures for quality and efficiency. At a manufacturing facility, accurate performance measures are easier to determine—output, quality and safety, for example. But for service companies, figuring performance can be tough. Many companies make customer satisfaction a key component of their incentive plan. Enterprise Rent-A-Car uses its Enterprise Service Quality index (ESQi) as the basis for goals. ESQi is the percentage of customers who check the top box in a survey, indicating they were completely satisfied with their rental.

Bonus systems must be developed. For service companies, a key component in surveys is measuring customer approval; but customers can be fickle, and their attitudes can be highly subjective. As a result, work teams might question the measures. Employees may begin to wonder, "I don't know how fair that is. You can work very hard and a customer may not like what you do or the way you do it." Employees might also think, "I want to be paid for what I do, not what someone thinks I do."

➡ Is it ethical to base team compensation on a subjective performance criterion? Why or why not?

➡ Should a company convert to a team structure if an appropriate compensation system has not been created?

➡ If you were a team member, what would be your response in this situation?

Source: Rob Markey, "The Dangers of Linking Pay to Customer Feedback," *Harvard Business Review*, September 8, 2011, https://hbr.org/2011/09/the-dangers-of-linking-pay-to

Loss of Productive Workers When companies move to a team system, some workers will not fit in. They do not want to think about their jobs, and they do not want increased responsibility. These workers might be forced out or resign voluntarily. Either way, the organization will lose skilled employees.[45]

TEAM AND INDIVIDUAL CONFLICT

Whether a manager is working with teams or individuals, conflict inevitably occurs. Whenever people work together, the potential for conflict exists. **Conflict** is disagreement between two or more organizational members or teams.[46] Conflict occurs because people do not always agree—on goals, issues, perceptions, and the like—and because people inevitably compete.

conflict
A disagreement between two or more organizational members or teams

Views of Conflict

What does a manager do when conflict arises? The answer depends on the manager's views and beliefs about conflict.[47] Figure 13.8 shows three basic philosophical approaches to conflict.

Traditional View The manager who views conflict as unnecessary and harmful to an organization fears conflict and eliminates all evidence of it. Such a manager holds the traditional view of conflict. If conflict does occur, the manager perceives it as a personal failure.

Behavioral View The behaviorist recognizes that conflict frequently occurs because of human nature, the need to allocate resources and organizational life. A manager who holds the behavioral view expects conflict. He or she believes that, on occasion, conflict can produce positive results. In general, however, a manager with a behavioral view believes conflict is usually harmful. With this philosophical foundation, the manager's reaction to conflict is to resolve conflict or eliminate it as soon as it occurs.

Interactionist View A more current philosophy, the interactionist view, holds that conflict is not only inevitable but also necessary for organizational health. Furthermore,

Figure 13.8	Philosophical Approaches to Conflict
BELIEFS	**REACTIONS**
TRADITIONAL VIEW	
• Conflict is unnecessary. • Conflict is to be feared. • Conflict is harmful. • Conflict is a personal failure.	• Immediately stop conflict. • Remove all evidence of conflict, including people.
BEHAVIORAL VIEW	
• Conflict occurs frequently in organizations. • Conflict is to be expected. • Conflict can be positive but is more likely harmful.	• Immediately move to resolve or eliminate conflict.
INTERACTIONIST VIEW	
• Conflict is inevitable in organizations. • Conflict is necessary for organizational health. • Conflict is neither inherently good nor bad.	• Manage conflict to maximize the positive. • Manage conflict to minimize the negative.

this view maintains that conflict can be good or bad, depending on how it is managed. A manager with an interactionist view attempts to harness conflict to maximize its positive potential for organizational growth and to minimize its negative effects.

At Facebook, Chief Executive Mark Zuckerberg is the chief conflict resolver. When team members disagree, they turn to Zuckerberg. He won't arbitrate the conflict because he expects the members to arrive at their own resolution. Jared Morgenstern, a product manager, explains that Zuckerberg expects members to share their perspective. Morgenstern says that team members "can effectively challenge Zuck and change his mind on things. Those are the people he ends up reaching out to."[48]

10 Discuss the positive and negative aspects of conflict in an organization

dysfunctional conflict
Conflict that limits the organization's ability to achieve its objectives

functional conflict
Conflict that supports the objectives of the organization

11 Identify the sources of conflict in an organization

POSITIVE AND NEGATIVE ASPECTS OF CONFLICT

A manager with an interactionist philosophy is able to identify the positive and negative aspects of conflict. The manager sees **dysfunctional conflict** as that which limits the organization's ability to achieve its objectives. **Functional conflict**, however, can support the objectives of the organization, especially when performance is low. People can be motivated to improve performance by competition—a form of conflict—if they think their approach is better than someone else's.[49]

Sources of Conflict

Competition is but one of many sources of conflict. Others include differences in objectives, values, attitudes and perceptions; disagreements about role requirements, work activities and individual approaches; and breakdowns in communication.

Competition Competition can take the form of two individuals trying to outperform each other. Competition can also erupt over a struggle for limited resources. The manager of each work unit depends on the allocation of money, personnel, equipment, materials and physical facilities to accomplish his or her objectives. Some managers inevitably receive fewer resources than others. This can lead not only to a lack of cooperation but to open conflict as well.

Conflict can also arise from competition for rewards associated with performance. Managed correctly, such conflict generates positive results.

Differences in Objectives Individual employees' objectives may differ from those of the organization. An individual may aim to advance within an organization over a three-year period, whereas the organization may have a tradition of seasoning an employee over a longer period. There may be conflict in this situation.

Individuals might have conflict with each other. For example, at Rainbow Printing, the two owners do not see eye to eye. "We just don't agree on what direction the company should take and how it should be run." In addition, each interferes with the other's work.[50]

Departments within the organization may also develop conflicting objectives. For example, if the production department focuses its energies on manufacturing a product at the lowest possible cost and the sales department wishes to promote high quality, conflict may arise.

Differences in Values, Attitudes, and Perceptions The value systems and perceptions of each individual differ from those of others. These differences can lead to conflict. For instance, an employee may place a high value on time with family. A manager may request frequent overtime or late hours, not understanding the employee's need for family time. An obvious value-system conflict arises.

Groups as well as individuals can have conflicting values, attitudes and perceptions. Upper-level managers may perceive reports and procedures as valuable control devices designed to provide information. Line workers may view such paperwork as needless drudgery.

Disagreements about Role Requirements When employees begin working in teams, their roles must change. Suppose, for example, an employee who has received numerous rewards for individual performance must now play the unaccustomed role of team player. Conflict is likely to arise between the team and the individual.

Line and staff employees may find their new roles uncomfortable at first. In team interaction of line and staff personnel, the line manager may expect the staff person to give advice, be supportive of the organization and be action oriented. The staff person may see himself or herself as one who provides answers, not advice. The staff person may be analytical (and sometimes critical) of the organization, and he or she may be reflective in reviewing potential alternatives. In such a case, conflict between the line and staff employees is almost certain.

Disagreements about Work Activities Conflict between individuals and groups can arise over the quantity of work assigned or the relationship among the work units. In the first situation, the cause of conflict can be resentment because one group or individual believes the work load is inequitable.

Conflict over the relationships of work groups can take two forms. One group or individual may depend on another to complete work before starting its own. If the work is late or is of poor quality, conflict can result. The other conflict situation arises when two work groups or individuals are purposely placed in competition with each other.

Disagreements about Individual Approaches People exhibit diverse styles and approaches in dealing with others and with situations. One person may be reflective, speaking little until ready and then speaking wisely. Another person may be combative, often taking an argumentative approach, giving immediate responses with little thought and pressuring for agreement.

Breakdowns in Communication Communication is seldom perfect, and imperfect communication may result in misperception and misunderstanding. Sometimes a communication breakdown is inadvertent. Because the receiver is not listening actively, the receiver might simply misunderstand the sender. The result can be a disagreement about goals, roles or intentions. Sometimes information is withheld intentionally, for personal gain or to embarrass a colleague.

STRATEGIES FOR MANAGING CONFLICT

A manager must recognize potential sources of conflict and be prepared to manage it. A viable strategy for conflict management begins with an analysis of the conflict situation and then moves to the development of strategy options.

Analysis of the Conflict Situation

By answering three key questions, managers can analyze a conflict situation.

1   *Who is in conflict?* The conflict may be between individuals, between individuals and teams or between departments.

Describe a manager's role in conflict management and potential strategies to manage conflict

2 *What is the source of conflict?* The conflict may arise from competition, personal differences or organizational roles. Answering this question requires trying to view each situation through the eyes of the parties involved.

3 *What is the level of conflict?* The situation might be at a stage where the manager must deal with it immediately; or the conflict may be at a moderate level of intensity. If the goals of the work group are threatened or sabotage is occurring, the manager must take action immediately. If individuals or groups are simply in disagreement, a less immediate response is required.

Development of a Strategy

When the situation requires action, what options are available? A manager can consider seven possibilities: avoidance, smoothing, compromise, collaboration, confrontation, appeals to superordinate objectives and decisions by a third party.

avoidance
A conflict strategy in which a manager ignores the conflict situation

Avoidance Sometimes **avoidance** is the best solution. The manager can withdraw or ignore the conflict, letting the participants resolve it themselves. Avoidance is best when the conflict is trivial. The manager should use it simply because he or she does not want to deal with the problem. Letting the parties disagree may be the best course if disagreement results in no consequences.

smoothing
A conflict strategy in which the manager diplomatically acknowledges that conflict exists but downplays its importance

Smoothing When using the option called **smoothing**, a manager diplomatically acknowledges conflict but downplays its importance. If there are no real issues to resolve, the approach may succeed in calming the parties. If there are real issues, however, this option will not work.

compromise
A conflict strategy in which each party gives up something

Compromise With **compromise**, each party is required to give up something in order to get something. Each party moves to find a middle ground. Compromise can be effective when the parties in conflict are about equal in power, when major values are not involved, when a temporary solution to a complex issue is desirable, or if time pressures force a quick resolution.

collaboration
A conflict strategy in which the manager focuses on mutual problem solving by both parties

Collaboration In attempting **collaboration**, the manager promotes mutual problem solving by both parties. Each party seeks to satisfy his or her interests by openly discussing the issues, understanding differences and developing a full range of alternatives. From this, the outcome sought is consensus—mutual agreement—about the best alternative.

confrontation
A conflict strategy that forces parties to verbalize their positions and area of disagreement

Confrontation If **confrontation** is used, the conflicting parties are forced to verbalize their positions and disagreements. Although this approach can produce stress, it can also be effective. The goal is to identify a reason to favor one solution or another and thus resolve the conflict. Many times, however, confrontation ends in hurt feelings and no resolution.

superordinate objective
An objective that overshadows personal interests, to which a manager can appeal as a strategy for resolving conflict

Appeals to Superordinate Objectives Sometimes a manager can identify superordinate objectives that will allow the disputing parties to rise above their conflict. A **superordinate objective** is a goal that overshadows each party's individual interest. As an example, suppose individual work groups are vying for budget allocations in the face of an organizational downturn. If the two parties agree that the reductions are in the best interest of the organization, each will move beyond the conflict.

Decisions by a Third Party At times, the manager may turn to a third party and ask him or her to resolve a conflict. The third party can be another supervisor, an upper-level manager, or someone from the human resource department. If the conflict is between two subordinates, the manager might be the third party.

Perhaps of all the conflict strategy options, collaboration, an appeal to super-ordinate objectives, and decisions by a third party are the most difficult to visualize. Applications of these strategies played a significant role in the successful redesign of the Ford Taurus by Team Taurus. Richard Landraff, project team leader, was given a clear mandate. The new Taurus was to be the first American car that truly matched the quality and engineering of Japanese rivals—specifically the Honda Accord and Toyota Camry. Landraff had to harness the creative energies of Team Taurus's 700 engineers, designers, marketers, accountants, factory-floor workers, and suppliers.[51] For example, Landraff did the following:

- *He encouraged the designers in charge of the interior and exterior of the Taurus to collaborate rather than compete.* The two, sitting side by side, constantly exchanged drawings and critiqued each other's work. As a result, the new Taurus avoids the mix-and-match dissonance of many American cars.

- *He forced designers and manufacturing engineers to focus on a superordinate objective when quality issues kept bumping up against costs.* The designers argued that each side of the Taurus body should be fashioned from a single piece of steel rather than from two panels welded together. The engineers countered that costs were prohibitive and resisted simply because this idea was differ-ent. Landraff brought the conflicting parties together, restated the Team Taurus objective and pointed to a banner that read, "Beat Accord." The issue was resolved—the body would be fashioned from one piece of steel.

- *He appealed to a third party when cost issues conflicted with manufacturing performance.* Manufacturing engineers lobbied for a new, $90 million stamping press that would replace six body presses from the 1950s and result in much higher quality. With Ford in the thick of a cost-cutting frenzy brought on by slumping car sales, finance managers argued against the purchase. Landraff took the conflict to then-Ford Chairman, Alexander Trotman. After a lengthy debate, Trotman surprised everyone by approving the purchase. "The quality argument was so persuasive that we all agreed we had to do it," he said.

Conflict Stimulation

At times, a manager might wish to increase the level of conflict and competition in a work situation. The circumstances in which a manager might wish to stimulate conflict are these:

- When team members exhibit and accept minimal performance.
- When people appear to be afraid to do anything other than the norm.
- When team members passively accept events or behavior that should motivate action.

Stephen Robbins reported that managers can choose among five strategies to stimulate conflict:[52]

1 *Bring in an outsider.* A person from outside the organization or team—some-one who does not have the same background, attitudes or values—may serve to establish the desired characteristics. Chapter 8 noted how GE and IBM relied on CEOs from outside the organization to stimulate the environment.

2 *Change the rules.* In some instances, a manager may choose to either involve people who are not ordinarily included or exclude those who are usually involved. This alteration stimulates the work environment. For example, a manager who is attempting to open up the environment may ask an informal leader to attend management-only meetings as a full participant. The result may be that both workers and manager gain new knowledge and change their actions.

3 *Change the organization.* Another approach is to realign work groups and departments. A change in reporting relationships and the composition of work teams can allow individuals to have new experiences with people and perceptions. When a company names a new CEO, either from inside or outside the company, one of the first actions the new CEO often takes to stimulate the environment is to realign work groups.

4 *Change managers.* Inserting a manager into a work group that can benefit from his or her style of leadership can be an appropriate response. The practice of rotating managers of work teams on a regular schedule can also stimulate groups.

5 *Encourage competition.* Managers can encourage competition between groups or individuals by offering bonuses, travel, time off or certificates of merit to employees who perform best.

Edgar Schein reported that the manager who chooses to encourage competition may reap one of the following benefits:[53]

- An increase in cohesion within the competitive group.
- An increased focus on task accomplishment.
- An increase in organization and efficiency.

If he or she doesn't manage the situation correctly, the competition can produce negative consequences:

- Communication between competitors can decrease or cease to exist.
- The competition may be perceived as an enemy.
- Open hostility may develop between competitors.
- One competitor can sabotage the efforts of another.

The emphasis on competition at Spectrum Associates produced all these negative consequences. The founders' strategy for the small software service company is designed to, "make sure no one gets comfortable."[54] Spectrum is organized into competitive business groups. The groups compete for customers by presenting proposals to Founders Tony Baudanza and John Nugent. "Whoever comes up with the best proposal and best quote wins," is a practice that gives competitors the license to poach. The competition exacts a toll. As one manager states, "If you put four, five or six Type-A personalities with an entrepreneurial bent in the same tank, they can end up killing each other." Not quite, but the group managers have withheld information from each other and have negotiated behind the scenes to gain advantage.

Chapter Summary

1 **Discuss the nature of teams and the characteristics of effective teams.**

For a group to be considered a team, at least two people must be involved, the members must interact regularly and coordinate their work, and members must share a common objective.

Effective teams have the following characteristics:

- Team members are committed to and involved in clear, shared goals.
- All team members feel free to express themselves and participate in discussions and decisions.
- Members trust each other.
- When needs for leadership arise, any member feels free to volunteer.
- Decisions are made by consensus.
- As problems occur, the team focuses on causes, not symptoms.
- Team members are flexible in terms of work processes and problem solving.
- Team members change and grow.

2 **Identify the types of teams that organizations use.**

The two basic types of teams are vertical teams and horizontal teams. A vertical team is composed of a manager and his or her subordinates in the formal chain of command. A horizontal team is made up of members drawn from different departments in the organization.

3 **Distinguish potential uses of teams.**

Although managers may choose from unlimited team options, five main categories of teams are common:

- Product development teams are organized to create new products.
- Project teams are designed to complete a specific task in an organization.
- Quality teams focus on quality products and services. Quality circles identify quality issues facing the company or department and offer suggestions for improvement. Quality assurance teams guarantee the quality of service and products by contacting customers and working with vendors.

- Process teams group members who perform the organization's major processes. The team not only performs the processes but also refines them.
- Work teams perform all the tasks previously performed by the individual members of a functional department or departments.

4 **Use decision-making authority as a characteristic by which to distinguish team type.**

Teams may be characterized as teams closely controlled by management, teams that have moderate independence and independent work teams.

- Teams closely controlled by management include committees, task forces and quality circles.
- Teams that have moderate independence include cross-functional teams, project teams and product development teams.
- Independent work teams include self-directed work teams and executive work teams.

5 **Identify and discuss steps in establishing teams.**

There are eight steps in building teams:

1 *Assessing feasibility.* A feasibility study should help determine if the team approach will work as well as how long it will take to initiate teams and the type of commitment it will require.

2 *Identifying priorities.* An assessment should determine the critical needs of the organization and where teams can make an impact.

3 *Defining mission and objectives.* Before an organization begins to build teams, managers should determine that the company's mission and objectives are solid, well defined and accepted throughout the organization.

4 *Uncovering and eliminating barriers to team building.* Three kinds of barriers impede teams: subject matter barriers, process barriers and cultural barriers. Such barriers must be identified and overcome.

5 *Starting with small teams.* Begin team projects and planning in a pocket of the company.

6 *Planning for training needs.* Team members will probably need training in planning, the effective use of meetings and team dynamics.

7 *Planning to empower.* Executives and other managers must empower workers when creating teams. Top managers need to step back and let team members make decisions, including making mistakes and failing.

8 *Planning for feedback and development time.* Teams require feedback. Initially team builders should provide a mechanism to provide feedback.

6 Identify and discuss the roles of team members and team leaders.

Effective teams display balance. Balance requires some people to play task-oriented roles and others to play social roles. Task specialists include the contributor, challenger and initiator. Social specialists include the collaborator, communicator, cheerleader and compromiser.

A key consideration in effective teams is team leadership. In self-managed teams, leadership is provided by team members. Team leaders appointed by management focus on teamwork, cooperation and results. Effective team leaders create a noncompetitive atmosphere, renew trust, think reasonably, share leadership, encourage members to assume as much responsibility as they can handle, and positively reinforce even the slightest contributions.

7 Describe the four stages of team development.

The four stages of team development are:

- *Forming.* During the forming stage, individual members become acquainted. Members test behaviors to determine which are acceptable and which are unacceptable.

- *Storming.* In the storming stage, disagreement and conflict occur. Individual personalities emerge and team members assert their opinions. Disagreements may arise over priorities, goals or methods.

- *Norming.* In the norming stage, the team comes together. With disagreements and conflicts resolved, the team achieves unity, consensus about who holds power and an understanding of the roles members will play.

- *Performing.* In the performing stage, the team begins to function and moves toward accomplishing its objectives.

8 Discuss team cohesiveness and team norms and their relationship to team performance.

Cohesiveness is the extent to which members are attracted to the team and motivated to remain together. Teams with few members, frequent interaction, clear objectives, and identifiable success tend to be cohesive. High cohesiveness contributes to effectiveness and high morale.

A team norm is a standard of behavior that all team members accept. Norms are guidelines that tell members what they can or cannot do under certain circumstances. Team norms are set by the team itself.

A key norm for teams is one that identifies the acceptable level of performance—high, low or moderate. Together with team cohesiveness, this norm is a critical determinant of team productivity. Productivity is highest when the team is highly cohesive and has a high performance norm. The lowest productivity occurs when the team members are highly cohesive in their commitment not to perform.

9 Evaluate the benefits and costs of teams.

The benefits of teams include synergy, increased skills and knowledge, flexibility and commitment. The costs of teams include power-realignment costs, team-training costs, lost productivity, free-riding costs and loss of productive workers.

10 Discuss the positive and negative aspects of conflict in an organization.

Dysfunctional (negative) conflict limits the organization's ability to achieve its objectives. Functional (positive) conflict can support the objectives of the organization.

11 Identify the sources of conflict in an organization.

The sources of conflict include competition, differences in objectives, values, attitudes and perceptions; disagreements about role requirements, work activities and individual approaches; and breakdowns in communication.

12 Describe a manager's role in conflict management and potential strategies to manage conflict.

A manager's role in conflict management begins with an analysis of the conflict situation and then moves to the development of strategy options. By answering the following three key questions, managers can analyze a conflict situation: (1) Who is in conflict? (2)

What is the source of conflict? And (3) What is the level of conflict?

The potential strategies to manage conflict include:

- *Avoidance.* This strategy calls for a manager to withdraw or ignore the conflict, letting the participants resolve it themselves.

- *Smoothing.* When using this option, a manager diplomatically acknowledges conflict but downplays its importance.

- *Compromise.* With compromise, each party is required to give up something in order to get something.

- *Collaboration.* In attempting collaboration, the manager promotes mutual problem solving by both parties.

- *Confrontation.* If confrontation is used, the conflicting parties are forced to verbalize their positions and disagreements.

- *Appeals to superordinate objectives.* When managers identify goals that overshadow each party's individual interests, they appeal to superordinate objectives.

- *Decisions by a third party.* At times, the manager may turn to a third party and ask him or her to resolve a conflict.

KEY TERMS

avoidance 449	forming stage 440	quality assurance team 433
collaboration 449	free rider 445	self-managed work team 435
committee 429	functional conflict 447	smoothing 449
compromise 449	Holacracy 456	storming stage 440
conflict 446	horizontal team 429	superordinate objective 449
confrontation 449	norming stage 441	task force 429
cross-functional team 429	performing stage 441	team 428
dysfunctional conflict 447	process team 433	vertical team 429
executive team 435	product development team 430	virtual team 432
formal team 429	project team 431	work team 433

REVIEW QUESTIONS

1. What elements are needed for a group to be considered a team? What are the characteristics of effective teams?

2. What are vertical teams? What three types of teams are considered horizontal teams?

3. What is the purpose of a project team? How does it differ from a work team?

4. In terms of authority for day-to-day decisions, what is the difference between a self-managed work team and a product development team?

5. What are the eight steps involved in the process of establishing teams?

6. What two major kinds of roles do team members play within a team? What is the importance of each role?

7. What are the four stages of team development? What occurs in each stage?

8. What is team cohesiveness? What factors contribute to high team cohesiveness?

9. What are the benefits associated with teams?

10. What are the positive and negative effects of conflict in an organization?

11. What are four potential sources of conflict in an organization? Explain each.

12. What strategies are available for conflict management? Explain each.

DISCUSSION QUESTIONS FOR CRITICAL THINKING

1. In what situations do you think individuals, operating independently, outperform teams in an organization? Why?

2. In your work experience have you ever been a member of a vertical team? A committee? A task force? A work team? How did your experience differ in each type of team?

3. If you were a member of a student project team and one member was not doing his or her share, which conflict management strategy would you adopt? Why?

4. When you are a member of a team at work or school, do you adopt a task specialist or social specialist role? In your opinion, which role is more important to the team's success? Why?

Social Media Management Exercises

What Kind of Team Member Are You?

- Identify the online social networks you are a member of at the present time.

- Select one group you have listed in #1 and answer the following questions.

  a. What is the size of the group?

  b. Who are the members of the group?

  c. What is the purpose of the group?

  d. What do you contribute to the group?

  e. What can you do to increase the effectiveness of this group?

Experiential Learning

Who Needs Managers?

Zappos, acquired by Amazon in 2009, is an innovative online shoe and clothing retailer known for its corporate culture with an emphasis on employees, referred to as Zapponians. CEO Tony Hsieh founded Zappos in 1999 and is an advocate of happiness and the company's 10 core values:

1. Deliver WOW Through Service

2. Embrace and Drive Change

3. Create Fun and A Little Weirdness

4. Be Adventurous, Creative, and Open-Minded

5. Pursue Growth and Learning

6. Build Open and Honest Relationships with Communication

7. Build a Positive Team and Family Spirit

8. Do More With Less

9. Be Passionate and Determined

10. Be Humble

Eight years in a row, Zappos was on Fortune's annual list of the, "100 Best Companies to Work For," and few Zapponians quit, until lately.

The company decided to adopt Holacracy and replace managers with an overlapping network of self-managed teams. *Holacracy.org* defines **Holacracy** as a, "new way of running an organization that removes power from a management hierarchy and distributes it across clear roles, which can then be executed autonomously, without a micromanaging boss." Zappos did not make the Fortune 100 Best Companies. "Two questions that generated particularly dismal results: Do employees think management has "a clear view of where the organization is going and how to get there"? And do managers "avoid playing favorites"?" (Reingold).

Questions

1. Why do you think that 14 % of Zappo employees left within weeks of the company introducing holacracy?

2. What recommendations to help the transition to self-managed teams would you make to CEO Tony Hsieh?

Sources: Zappos.com, About Zappos; Jennifer Reingold, "How a Radical Shift Left Zappos Reeling," *Fortune, http://fortune.com/zappos-tony-hsieh-holacracy.*

Holacracy
Is a new way of running an organization that removes power from a management hierarchy and distributes it across clear roles, which can then be executed autonomously without a micromanaging boss

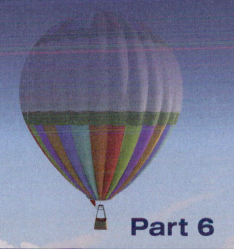

Part 6

Controlling

Chapter 14

Information Management Systems

LEARNING OBJECTIVES

After studying this chapter, you should be able to:

1 Describe the seven characteristics of useful information

2 Describe the three functions of an effective information system (IS)

3 Describe the five guidelines for establishing an information system (IS)

4 Describe the basic functions of a computerized information system (CIS)

5 Describe the two basic data-processing modes

6 Discuss the various methods used for linking computer systems

7 Explain the purposes of decision support systems (DSSs)

8 Discuss the four challenges that must be met by managers of an information system

Management in Action

Computer Literacy

Information is essential to every business. Getting data quickly and turning it into accurate information can give a business a competitive edge, because managers can use it to make good decisions faster than the competition. The quickest way to gather and process data is to use computers and high speed networks. They help businesses manage information, which is traveling faster and being shared by more individuals than ever before.

Since computers and the Internet are basic to every business, managers must be computer literate. They need to know how to use computers efficiently. The ability to learn new computer programs easily gives the manager a competitive edge. Also, managers need to be able to use the Internet and business networks to find, organize, evaluate and analyze information.

For each of the following statements, circle the number which indicates your level of agreement. Rate your agreement as it is, not what you think it should be. Objectivity will enable you to determine your management skill strengths and weaknesses.

	Almost Always	Often	Sometimes	Rarely	Almost Never
I can create letters using a word processing program.	5	4	3	2	1
I can correct errors in a document.	5	4	3	2	1
I can read an e-mail message and compose and send a reply with an attachment.	5	4	3	2	1
I can create supporting visual aids for a presentation.	5	4	3	2	1
I troubleshoot computer problems by checking electrical connections and using computer support materials.	5	4	3	2	1
I access, utilize, and research resources daily through the Internet.	5	4	3	2	1
I can install and use a new software program.	5	4	3	2	1
I access and utilize the Help function.	5	4	3	2	1
I can explain the difference between a document and a program.	5	4	3	2	1
I learn new software programs easily.	5	4	3	2	1

Compute your score by adding the circled numbers. The highest score is 50; the lowest score is 10. A higher score implies you are more likely to be computer literate. A lower score implies a lesser degree of readiness, but it can be increased. Reading and studying this chapter will help you improve your understanding of managing information.

INTRODUCTION

Managers continually make decisions that affect and are within the framework of their organization's mission, vision, core values, policies, ethical standards and culture. As leaders, they implement change and guarantee customer satisfaction by setting goals, monitoring progress toward them, and creating and maintaining effective and efficient workers and work environments. To do all this successfully, they must have support from a variety of sources.

This chapter examines **information technologies (IT)**—the means for implementing business strategy, creating and handling intellectual capital, and facilitating communication—as they relate to an **information system (IS)**. Information management can be done manually, we all do this to some degree, but organizations rely on computers, which are much faster, more accurate and have more advanced capabilities than humans. Taking advantage of developments in technology and methodology to increase the level of decision support, the concept of an information system was introduced in the mid-1960s. An information system enables an organization to effectively and efficiently share intellectual capital, and create and maintain a working environment in which employees can exploit it. Managers, "must ensure that all employees have access to information…. In the information age, a company's survival depends on its ability to capture intelligence, transform it into usable knowledge, embed it as organizational learning, and diffuse it rapidly throughout the company."[1]

INFORMATION AND THE MANAGER

Data are unprocessed facts and figures that—until they are gathered, sorted, summarized, processed and distributed to those who need them—are of little value. Data include such things as sales figures, costs, inventory items and quantities, customer complaints, social media, and government statistics on the performance of the economy. The vast amount of data available today to managers and organizations is referred to as "big data."

The importance of big data doesn't revolve around how much data you have, but what you do with it. You can take data from any source and analyze it to find answers that enable 1) cost reductions, 2) time reductions, 3) new product development and optimized offerings, and 4) smart decision making. When you combine big data with high-powered analytics, you can accomplish business-related tasks such as:

- Determining root causes of failures, issues and defects in near-real time.
- Generating coupons at the point of sale based on the customer's buying habits.
- Recalculating entire risk portfolios in minutes.
- Detecting fraudulent behavior before it affects your organization.[2]

Analytic methods used for big data include linear regression, logistic regression, text analytics, clustering, visualization, and optimization. Some real world companies that have combined data with analytics to improve business include eHarmony, IBM (Watson), Capital One, Urban Outfitters and TMobile.[3] Another great example is Moneyball, and the impact of big data on the business of baseball.[4]

Information results from processing data through information technologies. The result must have value and be useful to decision makers everywhere in an organization. "To have value, information must be linked to other information. Only then does it

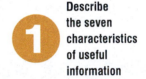

Describe the seven characteristics of useful information

become a source of knowledge and the basis of organizational learning."[5] For example, Tuesday's total sales figures become more valuable to a store manager when they are broken down by salesperson, department and inventory item. To be useful, information must have value and be understandable, reliable, relevant, complete, concise, timely and cost-effective. These characteristics are described in Figure 14.1. Examples of information include quarterly sales projections, annual budgets, and daily sales summaries by inventory item and an organization's primary financial statements. Along with its people, any organization's most vital resource is information.

For example, Boeing's global partners use technology to collaborate in real time on the 737 commercial jet. "The Next-Generation 737 has about 400,000 parts per airplane that are built by more than 325 suppliers in 30 countries, including the United States, Canada, China, France and South Korea. There are U.S. suppliers to the 737 program in 41 U.S. states and Puerto Rico."

"Boeing's suppliers around the world are valued partners to the 737 program," said Kent Fisher, Boeing Commercial Airplanes vice president and general manager of Supplier Management. "The success of the 737 shows what is possible when we partner with the world's best aerospace companies. Our long-term competitiveness in the marketplace depends on a continued focus on quality, reliability and affordability."[6]

Today, more than ever before, speed is the key to productivity and competitiveness. Adopting **digital** technologies—converting from atoms to bits—is giving companies a competitive edge. We discuss going digital in more detail later in this chapter.

Managers require a wide variety of information, depending on their positions. Functional information—about marketing, production, finance and personnel—is

digital

Data expressed as a string of 0s and 1s and transmitted or stored with electronic technology, usually computers and the Internet

Figure 14.1	Characteristics of Useful Information

- **Understandable information** is in suitable (correct) form and uses appropriate terms and symbols that the receiver will know and interpret properly. When jargon, abbreviations, shorthand notations and acronyms are used, the person receiving the information must be able to decode them.

- **Reliable information** is accurate, consistent with fact, actual and verifiable. The sources of the information, and the people who gather and process it, must be trustworthy. Reliable information will be as free from filtering and rephrasing as possible. Sales figures that have not been adjusted for returns and refunds are not reliable. Stating the value of a company's assets without showing the claims against them by others inaccurately portrays the real financial situation.

- **Relevant information** pertains to a manager's area of responsibility and is essential for the manager to have. Information about maintenance costs of the company's truck fleet, for example, is needed by only a few managers. Irrelevant information can waste a manager's time.

- **Complete information** contains all the facts that a manager needs to make decisions and solve problems. Nothing vital is left out. Managers with incomplete information are handicapped. Although information cannot always be complete, every reasonable effort should be made to obtain whatever information is missing.

- **Concise information** omits material that is extraneous. Just enough—no more, no less—is received by those in need. Giving managers a 200-page computer printout to wade through wastes their time. Summaries of key information, leaving out the details and supporting documents, may be all that is needed. Whenever appropriate, information should be displayed using visual devices, such as charts, graphs and tables. A standard used in the legal profession offers a sensible guideline: include only that which is necessary and sufficient.

- **Timely information** comes to managers when they need it. Premature information can become obsolete or be forgotten by the time it is actually needed. Information arriving after the time of need is likewise useless. Timeliness is one reason why so many managers rely on computers; they help managers monitor events as they happen and obtain the real-time information and instant feedback necessary for spotting trends and reacting promptly to circumstances and events.

- **Cost-effective information** is gathered, processed and disseminated at a reasonable cost. A weekly, detailed survey of all a company's customers might delight the sales manager, at least until the survey costs were matched against revenues. A scientifically conducted periodic survey of consumers is likely to yield comparable results at more a acceptable cost.

needed by both line and staff managers. Information gathered or generated by staff personnel—legal, public relations, computer services or research and development—may be useful to some line managers as well. Production managers need timely information about inventories, schedules, materials and labor costs and the maintenance and serviceability of machines and equipment. Supervisors in marketing need sales figures (by stores, departments and products), order-processing times, inventory levels, delivery schedules and market-research findings. Finance and accounting managers need financial statements, payroll figures, accounts-receivable and accounts-payable numbers, asset valuations, budgets and cost data. Regardless of the information needed, an organization's management system must provide it effectively and efficiently to those in need. Says one authority succinctly, "Information provides the substance for coordinating every aspect of the management process."[7]

Top-level managers need information on economic conditions, competitors, legal and political developments, technological innovations, customers' needs for and acceptance of the company's products and services and progress of operational units toward the organization's goals. Middle managers need information on their particular divisions' operations, including sales, costs, production output, personnel employed and budget status. The primary difference between what is needed at the top and what is required in the middle lies in the source of information. Much of what top management requires comes from external sources. Most of what middle managers require comes from internal sources—observations, meetings and reports.

Lower-level managers and autonomous teams need information and feedback about daily, weekly and monthly activities. The sales manager needs to know how the salespeople are spending their time and the results they generate. Production people need to know the figures on waste, quality, productivity gains, units produced and schedules met or missed. Human resources may require daily and weekly figures on safety, attendance, new hires, interviews conducted and job openings. With today's emphasis on empowering workers and staying close to the customer and supplier, feedback from these sources is essential for quick responses to the manager's needs as well as the organization's.

Flowcharting, the topic of this chapter's Quality Management, is a method to promote sharing information about improving processes.

Besides ensuring that information is useful, managers, "must build a network through which all members of the organization can exchange information, develop ideas and support one another. To do so, they must nurture the horizontal information flows."[8] In other words, managers must practice open-book management. This form of management is essential if an organization's intellectual capital is to deliver its maximum potential.

As the need for new information grows and as the organization evolves, so too must the ways in which the organization gathers, processes, stores and disseminates information. The information system must be continually updated to provide what is needed.

Management Information Systems

An information system (IS) exists to serve all employees, and all employees must have input into their organization's IS if the system is to function properly. This means that workers should be able to effectively access and use the IS and its outputs. A **management information system (MIS)** is a subsystem within an organization's IS. It is designed to serve the specific information needs of all decision makers—managers

management information system (MIS)
A formal collection of processes that provides managers with suitable quality information to allow them to make decisions, solve problems, and carry out their functions and operations effectively and efficiently

Flowcharting

Everyone in the organization, from presidents to teams to line workers, can use flowcharting to improve their work. Preparing a flowchart or a graphic representation of a work process is the first step towards understanding the opportunities that exist for improvements in productivity. Comparing the actual flowchart to the desired flowchart can identify causes of problems and suggest improvement possibilities. Opportunities for improvement include removing bottlenecks, reducing cycle time and reducing errors.

The inputs, steps and outputs of a process are depicted by a flow diagram with a set of standard flowcharting symbols. Some of the most commonly used symbols in flowcharting are depicted below. *Note:* These symbols are Shapes—available as inserts in Microsoft Word.

Start or *End* is depicted by an oval.

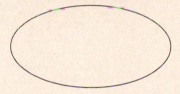

Process step is depicted by a rectangle.

Two-way decision is depicted by a diamond. Decisions include yes/no and true/false.

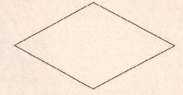

Document or paperwork required by the process is depicted by this figure.

Path and direction of flow is depicted by *arrows*.

➡ **Identify a process you would like to improve. Use the symbols above to flowchart the process. Which steps add value? Which steps do not add value? How much time is being used? Are there redundancies? What improvements can be made to this process?**

as well as empowered individuals and teams. It is a formal collection of processes that provides managers with the quality of information they need to make decisions, solve problems, implement changes, and create effective and efficient working environments.

Computers and the Internet make the process of gathering intelligence easier. Yet many managers can't always get everything they need by using just one application from one MIS. Instead of going to one central system to retrieve information, it is more common to have to go to many places to get needed information. Too much data are coming into most organizations from too many directions. Hundreds of electronic sources flow into companies separately.

Figure 14.2 depicts information flows after a product is ordered on the Internet. After accepting the payment and processing the order, a product is shipped. Dotted lines represent intangible digital (or electronic) goods, such as music, games, and books. Solid lines represent tangible physical products.

Figure 14.2   Information Flow

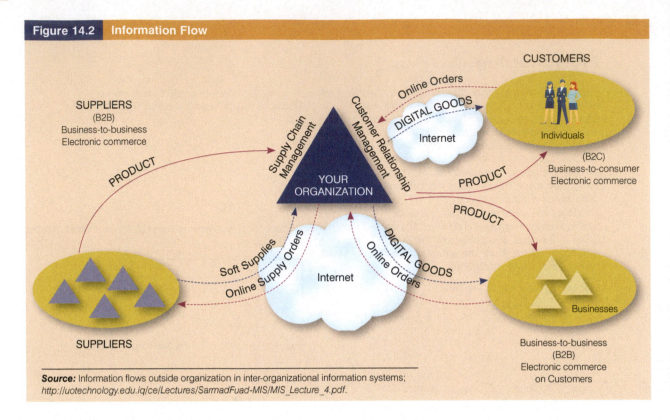

Source: Information flows outside organization in inter-organizational information systems; http://uotechnology.edu.iq/ce/Lectures/SarmadFuad-MIS/MIS_Lecture_4.pdf.

Information provided to managers through their MIS helps them control operations and properly use their resources. Information systems offer input to monitor ongoing operations as well as measure the results of these operations. Information helps to highlight actual and potential problems by keeping managers in touch with current conditions and trends. Information also gives managers the data they will need to create, and help their MIS create, forecasts and both strategic and operational plans. See Figure 14.3 for an example of a simplified MIS.

FUNCTIONS OF AN EFFECTIVE INFORMATION SYSTEM (IS)

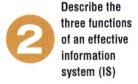 Describe the three functions of an effective information system (IS)

ISs and MISs must be designed with their users' needs in mind. In addition to linking individuals and their subsystems, they must link an organization to all external customers, partners and suppliers. Besides creating and providing valuable and useful information, an IS and an MIS should perform three functions:

1   *Assist organizations and their members in achieving their objectives.* Information systems should augment, enable and facilitate, but not interfere with processes and operations.

2   *Facilitate information access.* Ideally, people in need of information should be able to obtain it directly—that is, in person or with the assistance of appropriate technologies. When access in this manner is not possible, appropriate support personnel should provide the access.

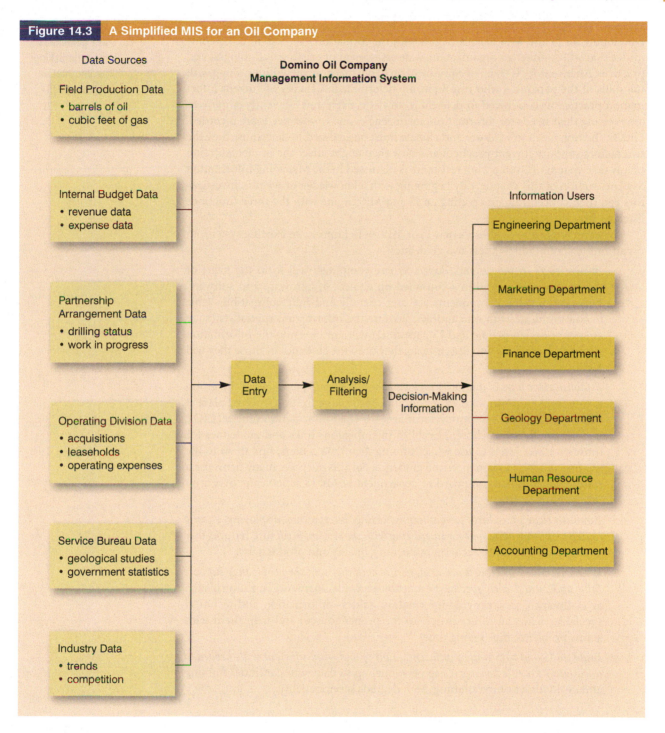

Figure 14.3   A Simplified MIS for an Oil Company

Data Sources

Domino Oil Company
Management Information System

Field Production Data
• barrels of oil
• cubic feet of gas

Internal Budget Data
• revenue data
• expense data

Partnership Arrangement Data
• drilling status
• work in progress

Operating Division Data
• acquisitions
• leaseholds
• operating expenses

Service Bureau Data
• geological studies
• government statistics

Industry Data
• trends
• competition

Data Entry → Analysis/ Filtering → Decision-Making Information

Information Users

Engineering Department

Marketing Department

Finance Department

Geology Department

Human Resource Department

Accounting Department

3 *Facilitate information flow.* The proper quantity and quality of information must flow in the fastest, most direct way to those who need it, when they need it.

Guidelines for Developing an Information System (IS)

Developing an IS and MIS usually begins with the formation of a task force or committee that will conduct an organization-wide assessment of existing technologies and practices. An inventory is taken of equipment on hand; machine capabilities, along with the skills of the personnel who run them, are determined. A survey of current information practices is conducted to determine how effectively and efficiently employees are meeting their needs for information. Inefficiencies and unmet needs are recorded. Finally, the organization's culture and climate must be analyzed to determine how the two factors support current practices and how they might affect the implementation of any new systems. (Overcoming resistance is discussed in the Managing Information Systems section of this chapter.) By beginning with a knowledge of *what is,* investigators can then concentrate on creating an IS and MIS in line with the three functions listed earlier.

Whether seeking to establish a new IS or MIS, or to improve an existing system, an organization should follow these five guidelines:

- *Involve users in the system's design.* Where computers will form the heart of the system, users should be consulted on choices of hardware and software. Make certain that components are user-friendly and fully compatible—able to communicate with one another. Because the information specialists (such as system-design people and IS personnel) will not be using the information they help to prepare and disseminate, they need the guidance of those they will serve.

- *Establish clear lines of authority and leadership for the IS personnel.* If the group is to operate a centralized IS serving the entire organization's needs, place it under the control of a top-level manager—a chief information officer (CIO). If decentralization is chosen, establish unambiguous links and guidelines for those on lower levels to use while running their data centers; link them to the top for control, coordination and guidance. For this purpose, many firms use a standing committee composed of department heads, IS supervisors or a mixture of both.

- *Establish clear procedures for gathering, sorting, interpreting, displaying, storing and distributing data, and for interacting with the system.* Structure reduces fear and helps to guarantee security, uniformity, quality and productivity.

- *Where technical specialists are used, ensure both they and the people they support fully understand each specialist's function and role.* Many organizations, such as Hallmark Cards, provide information guides—information and technical specialists who can direct people to the proper sources and help them with access problems, thus saving time.

- *Build an IS and MIS staff of sufficient quantity and with sufficient skills needed to adequately provide services.* Keep personnel up to date with continual training and avoid under or overstaffing; both degrade service quality.

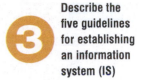

3 Describe the five guidelines for establishing an information system (IS)

COMPUTERIZED INFORMATION SYSTEMS

It is difficult to imagine how a company in any industry of any size can effectively operate without the benefits of information technology. When electronically linked to customers, suppliers and partners, businesses can conduct operations at anytime,

4 Describe the basic functions of a computerized information system (CIS)

anywhere. The improvements in speed, accuracy and cost of operations made possible by computers and their software are just too great for any company to do without.

A **computerized information system (CIS)** is an IS built on computers and their related hardware (peripherals) and software. Computers began as an engineering tool and later as a means of storing data. Today they are essential to business. Software for word processing and spreadsheets has changed the way business is conducted.

Here is a brief timeline of business applications for which the computer was used.

1960s—Computers were used by banks to automate check processing, with Electronic Recording Machine Accounting (ERMA).

1970s and 1980s—Computers were used to send and receive purchase orders, invoices and shipping notifications electronically via Electronic Data Interchange (EDI), a standard for compiling and transmitting information between computers, often over private communications networks called value-added networks (VANs). However, the expenses related to installation and maintenance of VANs put electronic communication out of the reach of many small and medium-sized businesses.

1980s—The computer enabled engineers, designers and technicians to access and work on design specifications, engineering drawings and technical documentation via internal corporate communications networks—computer-aided design (CAD), computer-aided engineering (CAE) and computer-aided manufacturing (CAM).

1990s—The Internet made electronic commerce affordable to even the smallest home office. Companies of all sizes began communicating with one another electronically, through the public Internet, intranets (networks for company use only) or extranets (a company and its business partners) and private value-added networks.

2000s—The **Internet of Things (IoTs)** with sensors and actuators connected by networks to computing systems, communicate without human interaction using Internet protocol (IP) connectivity. For example, information technology and operations technology converge at a retail location. "This requires the sophisticated integration of data across many sources: real-time location data (the shopper's whereabouts in a store), links to data from sensors in the building; customer-relationship-management data, including the shopper's online-browsing history; and data from tags in the items on display, telling the customer to enter a specific aisle, where he or she could use an instant coupon sent to a phone to buy an item previously viewed online"[9]

Computerized information systems may be centralized or decentralized. After a brief explanation of each, we examine computer operations.

The centralized CIS is under top management's direction and control, usually through the office of a chief information officer (CIO). This CIS serves to

assist other units of the organization to function in a more effective and efficient manner. Unless the information systems area also sells computing services to external users, it will not produce an end product or generate external revenue. Hence, it is of the utmost importance that managers within the information systems area understand the operations of their client departments and the company as a whole.[10]

A CIS functioning both at the top and at other management levels the organization is said to be decentralized. Each unit of a decentralized CIS is called a **data center**

---

computerized information system (CIS)
An MIS built on computer hardware and software to collect and process data and store and disseminate the resulting information

Internet of Things (IoT)
A phrase first used by Kevin Ashton, "to describe the network connecting objects in the physical world to the Internet."

data center
A unit of a decentralized CIS that operates to serve its unit's members with their own sets of hardware, software, and specialists (machine operators and programmers)

and operates to serve its unit's members by providing them with their own sets of hardware, software and specialists (machine operators and programmers).

Decentralized CISs result in **end-user computing**: the use of information technology (IT) by people who are free from control by top management. Examples of technologies used to operate an efficient office include voice mail, e-mail, word processing and desk-top publishing. When they are connected by a network, they form an **office automation system (OAS)**. Although end-user computing can stimulate innovative problem solving and decision making, it does present managers with collateral problems.

The first problem concerns control. Efforts must be made to coordinate multiple end-users' computing efforts in order to avoid duplication of work and consequent waste. Top management and other units must be encouraged to share useful approaches with one another and keep one another informed of projects and processes.

A second problem concerns possible duplication of expensive software and hardware. Planners must ensure that such components are fully compatible—able to efficiently share and exchange data through suitable interfaces and networks.

The third problem lies in the challenge of obtaining orderly, authorized access to both the organization's systems and to its **database**—a collection of data arranged for ease and speed of retrieval. In today's business environment, employees and customers want immediate access to information. So, successful websites have databases, which involve the exchange and sorting of information. As long as users have a web browser and an internet connection, they can access data via the internet. A database might simply be a list of names and addresses to which are added all the facts the organization thinks might be relevant for communicating better with its customers. Another database might be the catalog of products offered. Databases help organizations to explore and answer questions. Users interact directly with the database to retrieve information.

Much of the selling on Amazon.com is based on the effective use of database technology. For example, repeat Amazon customers are greeted by name and are given personalized book and product recommendations. The technology is called *collaborative filtering*. It looks at the customer's past purchases and compares them with other customers in aggregate. It makes a reasonably insightful guess as to what other things might interest the customer.

Databases rank among some organizations' most valuable assets: loss or impairment may shut down the enterprise cold. Imagine American Express or the New York Stock Exchange or Verizon with their computers down. A lack of trained users or inadequate controls over access and scheduling renders systems and components vulnerable to damage or compromise.

Databases may be created internally, by outsiders, or both. Accessing outside databases can be useful but expensive. Because external users are commonly billed by the amount of time they are in contact with a commercial data source, one of a firm's database users may be able to acquire information and then share it with others within the organization, thus avoiding duplication in time and billing. Also, external users may subscribe to a service. An example of an outside database is LexisNexis, a provider of information to professionals in the legal, risk management, corporate, government, law enforcement, accounting and academic markets.

The remainder of this chapter concentrates on management information systems that are at least partially computerized and thereby qualify as fully or partially computerized information systems.

end-user computing
The use of information technology (IT) by people who are not controlled and directed by top management

office automation system (OAS)
A collection of technologies to operate offices efficiently

database
A collection of computerized data arranged for ease and speed of retrieval; sometimes called a data bank

Computer Operations

Computer hardware consists of input devices, a control unit, a central processing unit (CPU), storage devices and output devices. A computer system also includes software—the programs that give the hardware the instructions for processing and storing data. Computer software encompasses two fundamental classes of programs: operating systems and application programs. An **operating system** comprises, "an extensive and complex set of programs that manages the operation of a computer and the application [programs] that run on it."[11] In other words, it is the collection of computer programs that controls how the computer works.

Computer manufacturers design their computers to run on one or more operating systems. The PC was introduced by IBM in 1981 and revolutionized communication. It was built over an Intel processor (8088) and fitted to Microsoft's operating system MS-DOS. The great majority of the IBM-compatible PCs used a graphical user interface based on Microsoft's Windows. Apple Macintosh computers employ a different operating architecture altogether, and large IBM machines (mainframes and minicomputers) run on MVS, DOS/VSE and Linux operating systems.

Application programs are software programs designed to execute specific sets of tasks, such as word processing, graphic design, accounting and finance, production operations and marketing, personnel and inventory control and many more. Some are specially designed (and programmed) in-house, whereas others may be purchased commercially from a vast array of options. Among well-known, off-the-shelf programs are Adobe Photoshop, Quicken and Microsoft Office (Word, Excel, PowerPoint, Access and Outlook). Mobile Internet usage is increasing, and *apps* are software programs that can be downloaded to a computer or a mobile device. This chapter's Managing Social Media discusses the importance of mobile sites.

Custom-developed application programs include many of Boeing's design and engineering packages, Norfolk Southern's computer-aided reporting system and the SABRE travel systems and solutions. System designers first consider the software that will meet the company's needs and then select equipment that can run that software. Care must be taken to ensure user groups and units within the company can use all equipment and software interchangeably. In the case of the SABRE systems, outside users, such as travel agents must be able to access it as well.

operating system
An extensive and complex set of instructions that manages the operation of a computer and the application programs that run on it

application program
A computer program designed to execute specific sets of tasks such as word processing

5 Describe the two basic data-processing modes

DATA-PROCESSING MODES

Two data-processing modes are commonly used in the business setting: batch processing and transactional processing. In **batch processing**, data are collected over time and entered into data banks according to prescribed policies and procedures. For example, a clerk may collect orders from outside salespeople and enter them into the order database at the end of each week. Thus, if a manager needs to make a request of the system, he or she must wait until the batch has been processed.

In general, routine business activities or transactions are recorded events, and when a computer-based information system keeps track of these transactions, it is referred to as a **transaction processing system (TPS)**. In **transactional processing**, data are received about a company's ongoing operations and entered into data banks as each transaction occurs. In order to accomplish the intended utility of transactional processing, certain kinds of information must be entered into the system in real time, or as close to real time as possible. Without such immediacy, these data would

batch processing
A computer procedure in which data are collected over time and entered into databases according to prescribed policies and procedures

transaction processing system (TPS)
A computer-based information system of a company's routine business activities

transactional processing
A computer procedure in which data are received about a company's ongoing operations and entered into data banks as each transaction occurs

Mobile Devices

For the first time in March 2015, the number of mobile-only adult internet users exceeded the number of desktop-only internet users (ComScore). According to Mary Meeker, Morgan Stanley analyst, the world is currently in the midst of the fifth major technology cycle of the past half a century. The previous four were the mainframe era of the 1950s and 60s, the mini-computer era of the 1970s, the PC era of the 1980s and the desktop Internet era that began in the 90s. The current cycle is the era of the mobile Internet.

Smartphone adoption has greatly increased mobile Internet usage. As a result of this trend, many companies develop mobile applications, commonly called *apps*. Mobile sites can reach across all smartphones and non-smartphones, as well as carriers. Apps, which offer various services and can be downloaded to a mobile device, are used for games, social media, music, and services like ordering food and making airline reservations.

Most people don't spend as much time on mobile as they do browsing the Internet. "They want to get what they're looking for and move on," (Marketing News). Furthermore, users want, "a tool that allows them to do things on the go in real time," (Marketing News). They want their apps to be convenient and easy to use and share. An example of this is Domino's Pizza app, where a customer can order a pizza while waiting for a stoplight. They can order pizza from a Ford car, over a Samsung smart TV, from a smartwatch, via a text message, or through an emoji sent to the Domino's Twitter account.

➡ **Work anytime from any location with data accessible from the cloud. What else would the ideal mobile site need for work team use?**

Sources: Jonathan Maze, "How Domino's Became a Tech Company," March 28, 2016, *http://nrn.com/technology/how-dominos-became-tech-company*; ComScore, "Number of Mobile-only Internet Users Now Exceeds Desktop-only in the U.S.," April 28, 2015, *https://www.comscore.com/Insights/Blog/Number-of-Mobile-Only-Internet-Users-Now-Exceeds-Desktop-Only-in-the-U.S.*; "Value Will Make Your App Stand Above the Crowd," *Marketing News*, March 15, 2011, p. 13. *The Mobile Internet Report* by Morgan Stanley Global Technology & Telecom Research analysts, December 15, 2009, *http://www.morganstanley.com/institutional/techresearch/mobile_internet_report122009.html*.

be unavailable to users and managers when needed. Bank automated-teller machines (ATMs) record transactions in the computer's memory as they occur; travel agents book reservations directly into the database. Most CISs are built around transactional processing to yield the best results.

LINKING COMPUTER SYSTEMS

6 Discuss the various methods used for linking computer systems

In an ideal world, all companies and their employees would have identical and up-to-date computers and software and be able to communicate with one another effortlessly. The reality, however, is that companies, as well as their customers, suppliers and partners, use a great variety of information technologies, each with differing capabilities and operating standards.

How, then, do you get hundreds of computers, made by dozens of manufacturers, operating on scores of different networks, and using many different software programs to communicate with one another? The answer lies in making them compatible through the use of middleware—software that creates compatibility links between similar networks, software programs and their computers. In banking, for example, "middleware lets each computer—at a credit reporting agency or at a branch—continue operating independently yet, without reprogramming, cooperate intimately with the others."[12]

The electronic linking of two or more computers is called **networking**. Such linkage—supported by servers, bridges, PBXs, gateways and modems—allows com-

networking
The electronic linking of two or more computers

puters to communicate directly—for example, by e-mail and file sharing—through cables, wires, microwaves, cellular or radio networks or fiber optics.

A network is a group of interconnected computers, including the hardware and software used to connect them. Local area networks (LANs) link computers throughout a facility, allowing for the transmission of data at about 10 million bits (megabits) per second; they can be linked through the use of a bridge. Wide area networks (WANs) link computers and their LANs to those at remote locations, including computers linked to the Internet—a worldwide network of computers linked by phone lines. Most businesses use WANs to link their remote operations and to connect them to the operations of their customers, partners and suppliers.

The Internet is an open network of computers providing a worldwide means of information exchange and communication. The Internet allows people who are often significantly removed from each other in time, space, thought and emotion to connect with others and to be contacted by others, almost anywhere and anytime. Voice, video and data signals can be carried simultaneously over one phone line. A modem links the line, through a gateway, to a computer and its LAN.

The Internet exists wherever devices communicate over publicly accessible networks that use a protocol called TCP/IP (Transmission Control Protocol/Internet Protocol). *Protocol* refers to the rules and standards for transferring information between computers. Some of the most common TCP/IP protocols are SMTP for e-mail, NNTP for Usenet news groups, FTP for file transfer and DNS for servers exchanging directions with each other. TCP/IPs are also widely used to build private networks, called intranets that may or may not be accessible via the Internet.

Metcalfe's Law explains the viral growth of the Internet. It says that as more and more people connect to a system, the network of contacts gains value, enticing even more people in … and so on. As this text has so often pointed out, "The biggest payoff from networking comes when companies use it to do better by their customers [and suppliers]."[13] For example, at a hotel website, Internet users link directly to a reservations database. Actual reservations can be made by credit card; various security devices protect users. See this chapter's Ethical Management feature concerning security and privacy issues.

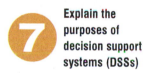

7 Explain the purposes of decision support systems (DSSs)

CIS MANAGEMENT TOOLS

Effective managers use every available asset to accomplish their jobs. Few assets rival the computer for sheer utility in helping managers plan, organize, staff, lead and control. Among the great strengths of computer technology is the ability to automate the data processing that underlies a sound MIS. The power and flexibility of most computer systems is limited only by the imagination of their users. However, it's important to remember, as the editors of a respected management handbook caution their readers, "Computers do not have the feelings, perceptions, or flexibility of the human mind."[14]

Decision Support Systems To harness the immense quantities of data now accessible to managers, imaginative thinkers have devised a specialized variant of a CIS, the decision support system (DSS). In general, the MIS produces a standard report according to a schedule. A report might provide a summary or a consolidated picture of detailed data, such as totals or charts and graphs. Another type of report might show an exception or conditions that need management attention.

Staying Close to Customers Can Get You Too Close

In an effort to get and stay close to their customers, companies are moving deeper into what is called *database marketing*—collecting all the information available about customers into a central database and using that information to drive targeted marketing efforts, such as product development and advertising messages. After all, the more companies know about you and your needs, the better they can help you meet them. Many companies require a customized approach. Off-the-shelf won't do. For this reason and others, many companies routinely practice open-book management with their suppliers and partners.

When you shop by mail, in person or on the Internet, you distribute a lot of personal information to others—your name, address, phone number, e-mail address, credit card numbers and so on. In addition, you provide data that can be used for future sales efforts when smart, aggressive salespeople ask you specific marketing-driven questions. Customer feedback of all kinds is sought and used to help improve operations, products and services. Companies store this information in their databases and often share it with other merchants. Your state's department of motor vehicles might sell your driver's license information. Credit bureaus specialize in selling your credit history.

➡ What privacy issues are raised here?

➡ What safeguards do you want businesses with information about you to exercise?

➡ What laws are you aware of that deal with protecting your privacy?

Source: U.S. Federal Trade Commission, Privacy and Security, *https://www.ftc.gov/tips-advice/business-center/privacy-and-security*.

Innovative visual displays of data give the viewer insight, which helps them learn more. It is easier for most managers to learn from pictures than from long lists of numbers. Furthermore, users can direct their own interactive experience with the data.

Unlike with an MIS, a decision maker can interact directly with the **decision support system (DSS)**, which adds speed and flexibility to the decision-making process. This interactive software-based system joins the manager's experience, judgment and intuition with the computer's data access, display and analytic capabilities. Decision makers can access databases to produce nonstandard reports that can be used on a problem-to-problem basis. Internal data sources might include the company's data about customers, ordering patterns and inventory levels. External data sources might include customer demographic data, mailing lists and census data compiled by the federal government. Managers can analyze, manipulate, format, display and output data in different ways.

The DSS provides a modeling function to help interpret the information retrieved. Each DSS is developed and adapted to support a firm's own decision problems. DSS programs are available off the shelf or may be tailored in-house. With such a system, a marketing manager may ask the computer, "What happens to sales if we lower prices by 10 percent?" The system will manipulate the model and stored data, then present likely outcomes: production volume, sales, inventories, revenues and costs.

Specialized end-user decision support programs include the **expert system**, software that stores the knowledge of a group of authorities for access by non-experts faced with the need to make topic-related decisions.[15] To build such a system, information specialists study an expert's way of analyzing an issue or solving a problem; then they write a program that simulates the expert's methods and techniques.

Expert systems are a kind of **artificial intelligence (AI)**—the capability of computers to learn, sense, and think for themselves. Other branches of AI include voice-recognition systems, speech synthesis programs, computer vision programs and

decision support system (DSS)
A specialized variant of a CIS; an analytic model that joins a manager's experience, judgment, and intuition with the computer's data access, display, and calculation processes; allows managers to interact with linked programs and databases via the keyboard

expert system
A specialized end-user decision support program that stores the knowledge of a group of authorities for access by non-experts faced with the need to make topic-related decisions

artificial intelligence (AI)
The ability of a machine to perform those activities that are normally thought to require intelligence; giving machines the capability to learn, sense, and think for themselves

neural networks. According to Purdue University engineering and computer technology professor Ray Eberts, "A neural network is a computer program modeled after the brain that can learn to perform tasks and make decisions based on past examples or experience."[16] Basic variations of expert systems using neural networks currently help diagnose and analyze medical, legal and mechanical problems for doctors, lawyers and garage mechanics.

knowledge management (KM)
The merging of a company's human and technical knowledge assets

The term **knowledge management (KM)** describes an integrated approach to identifying, capturing, evaluating, retrieving, and sharing a company's intellectual capital and technical knowledge assets. KM was introduced in Chapter 3. Knowledge management software, or expertise-profiling engines, can be purchased or developed by a company. In order to find solutions for hard-to-fix problems, Xerox came up with Eureka, an online knowledge-sharing system designed to help its service engineers with time-consuming and tough-to-tackle repair problems. Ray Everett, a field engineer for Xerox in the early 1990s and then program manager for Eureka, says that the impact was both powerful and immediate. "You went from not knowing how to fix something to being able to get the answer instantly. Even better, you could share any solutions you found with your peers around the globe within a day, as opposed to the several weeks it used to take."[17] See Figure 14.4 for a diagram of Xerox's Eureka.

It should be emphasized that a DSS is an analytical support system, not a maker of decisions.[18] As two experts observe, "a DSS allows the manager to examine more thoroughly a problem and experiment with many different solutions. This tends to give the manager more confidence in the decision. But, due to the multitude of possibilities to explore, it usually does not make the decision process any quicker."[19]

Figure 14.4   Knowledge Management at Xerox

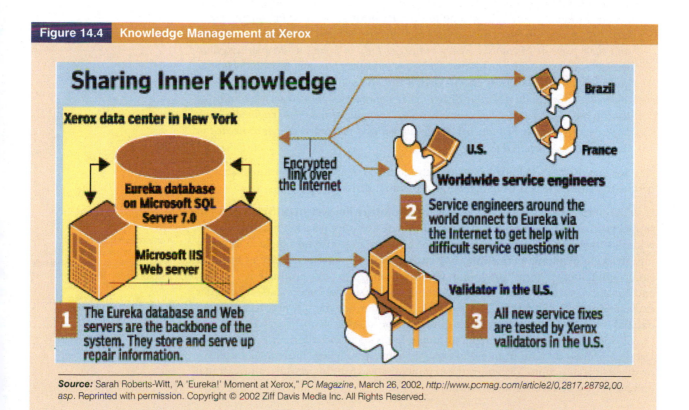

General Mills utilizes a DSS by making appropriate data available to autonomous factory teams so that they can make their own decisions:

At some beverage plants, for example, four shifts of 20-person teams are informed of marketing plans and production costs. "They have at their fingertips all the data that would normally be held by management," said Daryl D. David, a human resources director. The self-managed teams do everything from scheduling production to rejecting products not up to quality standards, and they receive bonuses based on plant performance. Some 60 percent of General Mills' plants have been converted to such high-performance work systems. The approach has produced significant gains in productivity, and the company is now moving to spread it to all operations.[20]

Yet another variant decision support system is the **group decision support system**, or **GDSS**. The GDSS allows a group focusing on a problem, like a product or process design team, to interact with one another and exchange information, data and ideas. GDSSs are used in brainstorming and problem-solving sessions and to facilitate conferencing of all kinds. For example, a group of participants, working anonymously from terminals in their offices or in remote locations, may interact in real time under the direction of a moderator, as ideas and questions are presented. A GDSS requires networking and collaboration software programs.

group decision support system (GDSS)
A variant decision support system that allows groups focusing on a problem to interact with one another and to exchange information, data, and ideas

For collaboration software to be used most effectively, a company culture that values and rewards teams and has a horizontal process focus must exist. Boeing demonstrates this kind of company culture:

Boeing maintains 10 multimedia rooms at the Everett complex for the use of collaboration teams, said John La Porta, a Boeing team leader. "They are open 365 days a year, 24 hours a day." He goes on to say. "It's always daytime somewhere." On a recent afternoon, meetings were underway between one group of engineers at Boeing and their peers at Mitsubishi Heavy Industries Ltd., in Japan, while another group worked with teams at Japan's Kawasaki Heavy Industries Ltd. and Australia's Hawker de Havilland, a Boeing subsidiary. A visualization application developed by Boeing allows the teams to do real-time design reviews of complex geometry without any lag time as the models load. "The tone is cordial, it's engineers talking to engineers," says La Porta. Meetings are conducted in English, with sidebar conversations as needed in native languages around the world.[21]

See this chapter's Valuing Diversity feature for a look at how networking can contribute to getting the best from diverse groups and individuals.

Executive Information Systems An **executive information system (EIS)** is a decision support system (DSS) custom designed to facilitate executive decision making. An EIS is known as an *executive support system (ESS)*. Typical executive uses include forecasting; strategic planning; performing risk and cost–benefit analyses; running business game simulations; linear programming; monitoring quality, productivity, ethics, and social responsibility efforts; and tracking critical success factors and stakeholder expectations.[22] EISs and DSSs, "are particularly useful when they are able to access the databases used by other organizational information systems as well."[23]

executive information system (EIS)
A decision support system custom designed to facilitate executive decision making; may include forecasting, strategic planning, and other elements

A sophisticated EIS can integrate many levels of information and abstraction. Users may draw on data from a division, department, function, individual employee or discrete transaction. Moreover, the exponentially expanding resources of external databases may be accessed electronically.

Collaboration and Diversity

Although communication in the business setting can be difficult for almost anyone, ethnic minorities face particular challenges. Individuals from certain cultural and ethnic backgrounds are reluctant to voice their true opinions to others, face-to-face, particularly their elders. They have been taught that conflict of any kind is undesirable, and to defer to people older than they are. Of course, there are individuals, no matter what their cultural background, who experience embarrassment when asked to speak in front of others. And there are those who are never asked for their opinions or are ignored when they offer them. Information technology in the form of collaboration software can help people overcome such problems by concealing the identity of both contributors and their contributions. Microsoft SharePoint is an example of collaboration software. It facilitates sharing and managing documents across a distributed system so all users can view the same information. The reports published should help users make better decisions.

The beauty of interacting with others electronically is that face-to-face communications are not necessary. The exception, of course, is web conferencing, in which, for example, a CEO delivers a live video and audio talk to worldwide office locations. Web conferencing options might include the ability to share PowerPoint slides, direct private messages between participants, list attendees, conduct polls, share files and applications, archive sessions and piggyback voice and video over the connection.

The experiences of the many companies that use collaboration software prove that most employees will express themselves more candidly when using it. Contributions can be made without fear of receiving negative feedback or contradicting others. People can step out of their cultures, knowing their contributions will be considered and recorded. One's concern about "saving face" and deferring to elders is effectively eliminated, since no one really knows who contributed what. Contributions must stand or fall on their own merits; thus, many will receive more serious consideration than they otherwise might.

➡ It is far easier to make a suggestion to your supervisor and colleagues via collaboration software than it is to do so in a pressure-filled meeting room. What are the business benefits of collaboration software?

As mentioned in Chapter 2, a business may be referred to as an *enterprise*. The business could be large or small, but most of the time, *enterprise* refers to a large organization with a lot of information to manage. An **enterprise resource planning (ERP) system** uses a common database to integrate information from multiple areas of the enterprise, such as human resources, accounting and manufacturing.[24] This allows decision makers at any level to access the information they need.

enterprise resource planning (ERP) system
A broad-based software system that integrates multiple data sources and ties together the various processes of an enterprise to enable information to flow more smoothly

Empowerment involves sharing information with teams and individuals, as well as managers, enabling them to make decisions. See Figure 14.5 for a depiction of data input, information systems, users and information output.

Discuss the four challenges that must be met by managers of an information system

MANAGING INFORMATION SYSTEMS

To manage an IS effectively, an organization must confront four basic challenges: overcome resistance to the new and different, enable employees to use the system, decide what operations to keep and what to outsource, and evaluate the results of the system's operations. Many companies, after merging, face the task of enabling their inherited employees to use a more advanced CIS. As a result, a company may outsource some initial training until a base of newcomers becomes technically proficient. These newcomers can then train others.

Overcoming Resistance
Getting people to use their IS or MIS effectively can be difficult. Thomas H. Davenport, a professor and consultant, believes this is so because managers, "glorify information

Figure 14.5 **Information Systems and Users**

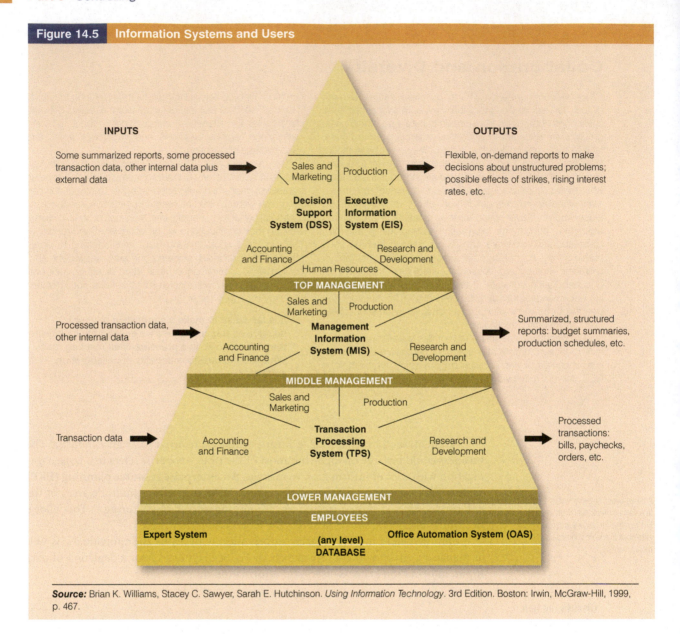

INPUTS

Some summarized reports, some processed transaction data, other internal data plus external data

OUTPUTS

Flexible, on-demand reports to make decisions about unstructured problems; possible effects of strikes, rising interest rates, etc.

Sales and Marketing | Production

Decision Support System (DSS) | **Executive Information System (EIS)**

Accounting and Finance | Research and Development

Human Resources

TOP MANAGEMENT

Sales and Marketing | Production

Management Information System (MIS)

Accounting and Finance | Research and Development

MIDDLE MANAGEMENT

Processed transaction data, other internal data

Summarized, structured reports: budget summaries, production schedules, etc.

Sales and Marketing | Production

Transaction Processing System (TPS)

Accounting and Finance | Research and Development

Transaction data

Processed transactions: bills, paychecks, orders, etc.

LOWER MANAGEMENT

EMPLOYEES

Expert System | (any level) | **Office Automation System (OAS)**

DATABASE

Source: Brian K. Williams, Stacey C. Sawyer, Sarah E. Hutchinson. *Using Information Technology.* 3rd Edition. Boston: Irwin, McGraw-Hill, 1999, p. 467.

technology and ignore human psychology."[25] They build elaborate IT systems and then wonder why people don't use them properly. What's missing is a concern for the organization's culture and, "how people in organizations actually go about acquiring, sharing and making use of information." Davenport further said that "research conducted since the mid-1960s shows that most managers don't rely on computer-based information to make decisions."[26]

Former Electronic Data Systems' Director of Client/Server Technical Services adds another dimension: "The problem is not with the technology, but with the corporate processes. Companies must fundamentally change the way they do business, and that's hard."[27] For example, a company with a traditional functional organization and vertical command structure will find it difficult to change the ways in which information is gathered and shared. Such structures impede the flow of and access to information; these structures have too many levels and filters for swift dissemination and use of vital facts and figures.

People fear change and often become irrational when faced with machines, technology and terminology they do not understand. Just as many customers are intimidated and annoyed by an organization's voice-mail system, employees react in similar fashion to technology that complicates or eliminates their established routines. Information technologies encourage and depend on information sharing. But all too often people have learned that information is a precious commodity and needs to be protected, especially when there are rewards attached to its generation and use. "Changing a company's information culture requires altering the basic behaviors, attitudes, values, management expectations and incentives that relate to information."[28]

Chapter 8 discussed culture and change in detail, but a few words are in order here about training employees before making changes. First, for change to be effective, those who will have to implement the change should be involved in the making of decisions. Second, people need to be kept informed and forewarned about impending changes and given time to adequately prepare for them through either training or development programs. Additional information on this issue appears later in this chapter.

Enabling Users

A study funded by the U.S. Department of Labor and conducted by a consulting firm and two universities, "indicates that using information technology to improve business practices brings the biggest benefits to the corporate bottom line when workers are well-trained."[29] What this chapter has already stated about overcoming resistance applies here as well. Once those who will be served by an IS and its IT have participated in building the systems, they must be adequately trained to use its technology and support services.

Support personnel need constant training. FedEx, the air freight company, knows this and takes its IS training seriously. Training focuses on three specific areas: technology, business training and "personal process enabling" skills, all of which can be developed through core business courses as well as through FedEx's proprietary business classes. Course work specific to the development of FedEx's personal process–enabling skills includes project management, leadership training and creative thinking. In addition to staying current in technologies, IS employees at FedEx must know what their customers know and need in order to serve them effectively.

Outsourcing

Massachusetts-based Computer Sciences Corporation conducted the Critical Issues Survey of senior IT managers, from 1988 to 2001. The survey tracked the strategic and technical issues businesses confront as they adapt to the evolution of information technology. Over the years, the responses to "why outsource" remained constant: to reduce costs and improve services.[30]

Among the giants that furnish outsourcing services are Dell, Computer Sciences Corporation, AT&T, IBM and Unisys. These companies, and their smaller counterparts specialize in providing the latest technologies, usually at lower cost to all kinds of IT/IS services; thus, they offer their clients greater control and efficiency.

For many companies, the decision to outsource IT/IS operations, in part or in total, is made by asking a simple question: "Does the particular IT operation provide a strategic advantage or is it a commodity that does not differentiate us from our competitors?"[31] Commodities are outsourced when more efficient providers are found; other operations are kept in house. But research suggests that such measures should be secondary; a, "company's overarching objective should be to maximize flexibility and control so that it can pursue different options as it learns more or as its circumstances change."[32]

Geoffrey Moore, the chairman and founder of the Chasm Group and a venture partner at Mohr Davidow Ventures differentiates between outsourcing core and context operations:

> *Whatever differentiates you, whatever gives you competitive advantage, is core. Everything else is context. Context still has to be done, because your customers, the government, or your own employees require it, and, moreover, it has to be done well. But it won't give you competitive advantage even if you did it brilliantly. Worse, you can do damage to that advantage if you do it badly. Because context activities have a downside but no upside, companies should do everything they can to insource core and outsource context.*[33]

Before outsourcing an IT/IS operation, a company must know what its operations are and what IT/IS needs exist for each. It must then analyze how efficiently and effectively these needs are being met. If improvements are called for, it must then ask who is best able to provide them—in-house or outside personnel? If the answer is outsiders, is it absolutely the case that in-house staff cannot be effectively upgraded to provide the service? If not, under what terms and conditions will service be provided by an outsider, and what consequences could result if the provider fails to offer adequate support? Can we afford to live with those consequences? One key to outsourcing is to retain some measure of control and flexibility over the outside provider and the service it provides. Another is to recognize that all these situations and the answers to them will continually change. Constant auditing of IT/IS operations is, therefore, a necessity. See this chapter's Global Applications feature for BP's approach to IT outsourcing.

Evaluating Results

Because information technology changes so swiftly, many companies consider their desktops and laptops to be expendable equipment, with a usable life of around two to three years, and they replace them nearly as often. Auditing by both insiders and outsiders—outside users being customers and consultants—will bring to light just what should and should not be happening with both MIS and CIS operations. First, users of the system must evaluate it; they are the ones who know whether their needs are being met. Second, the CIO and information technology managers must perform audits as well. Their primary focus is on meeting needs effectively and efficiently—within or below their budgets. Their audits should include a periodic analysis of IT policies and the costs connected with delivering MIS/CIS services. They should also conduct an annual inventory of all personnel and equipment to determine needs and capabilities. An example is a Total Cost of Ownership (TCO) Lifecycle model for assessing costs and associated operational processes. The model reveals IT operational costs by evaluating the people, processes and technology involved, and it provides a method for reducing those costs.

IT Outsourcing at BP

Information Technology outsourcing at BP has become a case study for managers to better oversee their outsourcing. British Petroleum Exploration (BPX) is a division of BP plc. the holding company of one of the world's largest petroleum and petrochemical groups. In 1993, BPX made the decision to stop focusing on *supporting* business operations and start focusing on *performing* them. The result was the outsourcing of all IT operations and a reduction in IT personnel of nearly 1,150 people.

After some experimenting with managing multiple service providers and investigating companies using a single-provider approach, the company formulated an *outsourcing vision*. It looked for firms that knew their markets and capabilities, and were dedicated to innovation, customer service, and cost containment. The company created a list of six possible service providers by carefully screening 65. The six were asked to create alliances that would meet BPX's cost objectives and IT/IS needs. Three managed to do so to BPX's satisfaction and were hired, under initial two-year contracts, to work together to provide, "a single seamless service to [its] 42 businesses around the globe."

One contractor is the primary provider and coordinates the services of the others. The contractors outsource and manage whatever services they cannot themselves provide. The company's IT department, in turn, manages the primary contractor. Business units may contract with IT suppliers for customized services. British Petroleum Exploration has the right to audit suppliers, and it evaluates each every year. Periodically, the suppliers are benchmarked against others in the industry. Suppliers who reduce their costs below BPX's targets keep one-half of the funds saved.

➡ Outsourcing, moving inside activities to outside providers, is a tool that gives a company the ability to improve operations while cutting costs. How can outsourcing be cost-effective when you can no longer exercise direct control over the providers?

➡ Insourcing is a decision a company might make to bring its activities back under its control. Research *insourcing* and explain why a company, such as BP, might decide to insource rather than outsource.

Source: John Cross, "IT Outsourcing: British Petroleum's Competitive Approach," *Harvard Business Review*, May–June 1995, pp. 94–102.

Chapter Summary

1 Describe the seven characteristics of useful information.

To be useful to decision makers, information must have value—be linked to other information—and must be

- *Understandable:* presented in a suitable form, using appropriate terms and symbols that a receiver will know and interpret properly
- *Reliable:* accurate, consistent with fact, actual and verifiable
- *Relevant:* pertains to a decision maker's area of responsibility, and is essential
- *Complete:* containing all the facts that a person or group of people needs to make decisions and solve problems
- *Concise:* just enough, omitting material that is not needed
- *Timely:* available when needed, in real time when possible
- *Cost-effective:* created and disseminated at a reasonable cost; this characteristic relates to most of the others as well

2 Describe the three functions of an effective information system (IS).

- Assisting organizations and their members in achieving their objectives
- Facilitating information access through people and technology
- Facilitating information flow by using the fastest, most direct way to disseminate and share information

3 Describe the five guidelines for establishing an information system (IS).

- Involve users in the system's design.
- Establish clear lines of authority and leadership for IS personnel.
- Establish clear procedures for gathering, sorting, interpreting, displaying, storing, and distributing data, and for interacting with the system.

- Where technical specialists are used, ensure that both they and the people they support fully understand each specialist's function and role.
- Build an IS staff of sufficient quality and quantity and with sufficient skills needed to adequately provide services.

4 Describe the basic functions of a computerized information system (CIS).

- *Computer operations:* Runs the system; involves starting jobs, mounting the proper input and output volumes, and responding to problem conditions
- *System programming:* Installs and maintains the operating system and associated system software
- *Data entry:* Enters data in machine-readable form
- *Application program development:* Writes new application systems
- *Application program maintenance:* Corrects and updates existing application systems
- *Data management:* Assures data security, access, integrity and usability
- *Communications management:* Configures and maintains the network
- *End-user computing:* Helps and educates users

5 Describe the two bsiec data-processing modes.

The two most common modes are batch processing and transactional processing. In the first, data are collected over time and entered into data banks according to prescribed policy and procedures. In the second, data are received about a company's ongoing operations and entered into data banks as each transaction occurs. The two cases presented in this chapter are about companies using transactional processing.

6 Discuss the various methods used for linking computer systems.

Networking and middleware allow for computers to communicate with one another. Networks use servers, bridges, PBXs, gateways and modems. Cables, wires, microwaves, cellular and radio networks and fiber optics allow for transmissions. Local and wide area networks (LANs and WANs) link computers internally as well as inside computers with those outside an organization. Most businesses can use their local telephone lines to simultaneously transmit voice, video and data.

7 Explain the purposes of decision support systems (DSSs).

Decision support systems are analytical models that join the manager's experience, judgment and intuition with the computer's data access, display and calculation strengths. They may be off-the-shelf or tailored for in-house use. DaimlerChrysler's new manufacturing software is tailored to meet its needs. The French company that developed it is now tailoring it for use by other manufacturers.

Expert systems are a kind of artificial intelligence and are specialized end-user decision support programs. Software stores the knowledge of a group of authorities for use by non-experts faced with the need to make topic-related decisions.

Group decision support systems allow groups focusing on a problem to collaborate with one another and exchange information, data and ideas.

8 Discuss the four challenges that must be met by managers of an information system.

To manage an IS effectively, an organization must confront four challenges: overcoming resistance to change, enabling employees to use the system, deciding which operations to keep and which to outsource; periodically evaluating the system's effectiveness and efficiency. The first and second challenges are usually dealt with through training and development programs and by involving users in the design of the system and the choice of its equipment. The third is made after carefully considering in-house capabilities and efficiencies; operations and functions that can be performed better by outsiders are usually outsourced. The fourth challenge is a basic element of control. All operations need periodic review by both insiders and outsiders. Just as conditions change, so too will the ways in which IS functions and ITs are dealt with.

KEY TERMS

application program   469

artificial intelligence (AI)   472

batch processing   469

computerized information system (CIS)   467

data   460

data center   467

database   468

decision support system (DSS)   472

digital   461

end-user computing   468

enterprise resource planning (ERP) system   475

executive information system (EIS)   474

expert system   472

group decision support system (GDSS)   474

information   460

information system (IS)   460

information technology (IT)   460

Internet of Things (IoT)   467

knowledge management (KM)   473

management information system (MIS)   462

networking   470

office automation system (OAS)   468

operating system   469

transaction processing system (TPS)   469

transactional processing   469

REVIEW QUESTIONS

1. What makes information valuable to decision makers? What makes it useful?

2. How should an organization and its strategic business units go about establishing their information systems?

3. How can an organization decide on the effectiveness of its information systems?

4. What basic functions must any CIS perform for its users?

5. What data-processing modes would you prescribe for each of the following? (a) handling airline reservations, (b) handling total sales by department for each day of operations, (c) measuring the quality of cookies coming off an assembly line.

6. How do local area networks (LANs) operate? Wide area networks (WANs)? Why do most companies usually require both?

7. What is a decision support system (DSS)? What kinds exist?

8. How does a company decide whether an IS or IT function should be outsourced? Whether the IS or IT is operating effectively? Whether people are using them to their best advantage?

DISCUSSION QUESTIONS FOR CRITICAL THINKING

1. You are the chief information officer for a neighborhood bank that has just been absorbed into a larger bank. Each institution has different hardware and software. What must you do in order for your IS to properly network with the parent's?

2. You have been asked to build and lead a committee to evaluate your company's ISs and ITs. How would you go about selecting members for your committee? What issues should you deal with at your first meeting?

3. How do information needs differ at the various levels of management? Why should all of management's computers be networked to both insiders (intranet) and outsiders (Internet)?

4. In the Digital Age, a dominant role is played by information. In *Wired* magazine (March 1998), Peter Drucker described it this way: "Economic theory is still based on the scarcity axiom, which doesn't apply to information. When I sell you a phone, I no longer have it. When I sell information to you, I have more information by the very fact that you have it and I know you have it." Explain Drucker's statement. What are the implications for managers?

Apply What You Know

Social Media Management Exercises

Communities for Collaboration

In order to align internal communications around new forms of communication, Deloitte created D Street, an enterprise social network and integrated it with the employee DeloitteNet portal.

The business case for developing D Street had six major drivers (Romeo):

- To connect people across functions

- To enable collaboration on ideas and projects
- To build communities of practice and interest
- To enhance knowledge of one another
- To empower people with a personal branding page
- To personalize the talent experience and make our really large organization feel smaller

Each D Street employee profile contains (Bingham):

- Each person's geography, tenure, contact information, function and industry
- Affiliations, certifications and specializations
- Resume, links to publications and a blog
- Participation in Deloitte programs and affinity groups
- Personal interests and lists of favorites
- Colleagues with links to their profile
- Colleagues in common with the profile owner
- Education, certifications and prior employment
- A wall for visitors to write comments, questions and messages on
- Restaurant and other local recommendations for visitors

Employees can personalize their profiles with pictures, and they can link to their Facebook and LinkedIn profiles. If they have written something for the company's knowledge management system, it is included.

➡ List at least five types of connections you would search if you worked for Deloitte.

➡ How does the ability to share yourself professionally and personally enable collaboration at work?

Sources: Tony Bingham and Marcia Conner, *The New Social Learning: A Guide to Transforming Organizations Through Social Media*, Berett-Koehler, 2010, p. 36; Patricia Romeo – D Street Leader at Deloitte, "Building participation by enabling virtual communities across the organization," *Management Innovation eXchange*, December 7, 2010, *http://www.managementexchange.com/story/building-participation-enabling-virtual-communities-across-organization*.

Experiential Learning

Distribution at VF Corporation

VF Corporation is a global leader apparel company in jeans, intimate apparel, knits, work clothes, casual clothes and swimwear. It has its own branded retail stores and sells its wares to such retail giants as Walmart, JCPenney and Federated Department Stores. Along with its stable of brands— Lee, Wrangler, Riders, Rustler, Vanity Fair, Vassarette, Bestform, Lily of France, Nautica, John Varvatos, JanSport, Eastpak, The North Face, Vans, Reef, Napapijri, Kipling, Lee Sport and Red Kap—VF is adding to its rivals' envy because of its state-of-the-art, computer-driven distribution system. Its, "Retail Floor Space Management process enables VF to determine the optimal product mix for individual stores, replenish goods rapidly and efficiently, and keep the right products in stock with minimal inventory. Higher sales on less inventory is a winning formula for success in today's retail environment," (VFC, Letter to Stockholders).

The system depends on networking with the stores being supplied. Networked stores send data gathered through their ISs to VF, which then uses the data to determine stock levels and create an order for restock, all automatically. In-stock merchandise is shipped immediately; when merchandise is not available, VF automatically creates an order for itself and ships within one week.

Customers love the VF system. It helps them avoid overstocking and leads to faster inventory turns, which saves them money: networked dealers can invest less in inventory and have fewer clearance sales. VF is happy, too.

The system has helped the company increase income and sales (VFC, Investor Relations).

While its competitors, like Levi Strauss are struggling to catch up with VF's restocking system, VF is building its system to track groups of goods, such as jeans of various sizes, styles and colors, to find sales patterns that can help retailers forecast ideal supply levels.

Furthermore, VF states on their website, "commerce is our fastest growing direct-to-consumer channel. We actively harvest data across our e-commerce sites and transform the information into a "digital playbook" that evolves and guides us on what to do next. While no tool can predict the future of digital, the playbook enables us to leverage shopping and behavior insights across brands to better understand changes in consumer preferences and then act quickly.

Questions

1. What major advantages does VF Corporation have over its competition?

2. Will such a distribution system work as well for lesser-known brands made by smaller companies? Why or why not?

3. What data must be shared by retailers with VF to make the system work? How do you suppose the retailers gather these data?

Sources: VF Corporation, Annual Report, Overview and FAQ, *http://www.vfc.com*; *http://www.vfc.com/powerful-platforms/direct-to-consumer#digital-connections*.

Chapter 15

Control: Purpose, Process, and Techniques

LEARNING OBJECTIVES

After studying this chapter, you should be able to:

1 Describe the relationship between controlling and the other four functions of management

2 List and describe the four steps in the control process

3 Describe the nature and importance of feedforward, concurrent, and feedback controls

4 Describe the importance of a control system

5 Explain the characteristics of effective controls and the steps managers can take to make controls more effective

6 Describe the content of the three primary financial statements and how managers use them

7 Explain ratio analysis and four types of ratios used by managers

8 Describe the five types of financial responsibility centers and their relationships to budgeting

9 Describe the four approaches to creating budgets

10 Explain the two major types of budgets used in businesses

11 Describe the five major marketing control techniques used in businesses

12 Describe the six major human resource control techniques used in businesses

Management in Action

Life Balance

Many employees think their managers or their company should instill a culture of work-life balance. Others have difficulty finding balance in their lives because they don't have control over their work. They are fearful about the changes happening in their community and find it challenging to juggle the demands of life. Greater enjoyment can be brought to life when people focus on the things that they can control. When people want more time for pursuits other than work or school, like family, friends or exercise, they need to take matters into their own hands and set their own life-friendly practices.

For each of the following statements, circle the number that indicates your level of agreement. Rate your agreement as it is, not what you think it should be. Objectivity will enable you to determine your management skill strengths and weaknesses.

	Almost Always	Often	Sometimes	Rarely	Almost Never
I resolve conflicts appropriately.	5	4	3	2	1
I solicit feedback on my personal behavior.	5	4	3	2	1
I accept help willingly.	5	4	3	2	1
I eat a well-balanced diet.	5	4	3	2	1
I get 8 hours of sleep each night.	5	4	3	2	1
I use positive self-talk for personal motivation.	5	4	3	2	1
I express my anger appropriately.	5	4	3	2	1
I take time for myself each day.	5	4	3	2	1
I manage my time effectively by setting priorities.	5	4	3	2	1
I take responsibility when I make a mistake.	5	4	3	2	1

Compute your score by adding the circled numbers. The highest score is 50; the lowest score is 10. A higher score implies you are more likely to feel in control when faced with trying situations. A lower score implies a lesser degree of readiness, but it can be increased. Reading and studying this chapter will help you improve your understanding of control.

INTRODUCTION

Because controlling is a management function that applies to all of the other functions, this book tackles it last. Without some way to monitor the execution of plans, managers would not know whether their work was effective or efficient. People and processes must be monitored to prevent, or detect and correct unacceptable differences between managers' expectations and actual results.

In its most basic form, **controlling** is the management function in which managers set and communicate performance standards for people, processes and devices. A **standard** is any guideline or benchmark established as the basis for the measurement of capacity, quantity, content, value, cost, quality or performance. Whether quantitative or qualitative, standards must be precise, explicit, and formal statements of the expected result. Once those who must abide by standards understand and can apply them, standards serve as mechanisms to prevent, or identify and correct unacceptable deviations from plans. Standards may be applied to people and processes before, during and after work is performed.

Controlling is about managing risks. In many companies these programs are formulated by and make use of a high-level management position, **risk manager**. This person must monitor people and processes and help transform functional managers (such as those who oversee finance) into advisers and consultants, enabling them to teach others how to deal with the risks that haunt their areas of expertise. Later in this chapter, important **control techniques**—devices designed to measure and monitor specific aspects about the performances of an organization, its people, and its processes are examined. Within these techniques are characteristics of feedforward, concurrent and feedback controlling. As we present each technique, consider how it helps managers set and achieve goals and at which management level each technique is most useful.

Keep in mind that control techniques depend on the proper interpretation and understanding of both the quantitative and qualitative information they generate by those in charge of various activities and processes. Thus the type, design and number of control techniques will vary with each level of management and with each manager and operation. However, control techniques must be integrated into a system to promote maximum effectiveness and efficiency. For example, Harrah's measures marketing performance with a variety of techniques that include sales volume, repeat customers, profits and levels of customer satisfaction. Top management uses the results to provide performance data that show results.

CONTROLLING AND THE OTHER MANAGEMENT FUNCTIONS

As Lester Bittel noted, "Controlling is the function that brings the management cycle full circle. It is the steering mechanism that links all the preceding functions of organizing, staffing and [leading] to the goals of planning."[1] The planning process determines the goals and objectives that eventually become the foundation of controls. As the first function, planning is at the heart of all the others. The strategic goals and plans made at the top level in an organization are derived from the organization's purpose and

controlling
The process through which standards for the performance of people and processes are set, communicated, and applied

standard
Any established rule or basis of comparison used to measure capacity, quantity, content, value, cost, or performance

risk manager
A high-level person in charge of planning for and overseeing efforts to control the management of all the risks an organization faces

control technique
Device designed to measure and monitor specific aspects about the performances of an organization, its people, and its processes

Describe the relationship between controlling and the other four functions of management

mission. From these plans flow the objectives to be achieved by successively lower levels of management.

As these plans and goals are developed, managers must establish controls to monitor progress toward them. The feedback from these controls should tell managers how each level of the organization—indeed, each individual—is progressing toward the relevant goals and objectives. The feedback may indicate progress is proceeding as planned. If progress falls short of the plan, however, the feedback should indicate that managers need to change the plan.[2] Let's examine how controlling affects and is affected by the other four management functions. *Planning and controlling.* A company cannot act responsibly when making its needed changes without adequate feedback from customers and its managers. Both sources helped to provide the company with the data it needs to decide which services should be emphasized and which can be modified or eliminated without compromising service quality. In addition, a company may examine every operation; it calculates costs and tries to bring them into line with the new standards set to guarantee efficiency and growth. The company needs plans to eliminate the superfluous employees. Those remaining need to be taught the new and modified procedures, thus necessitating the creation of training programs. Managers must design controls to make certain all of the changes take place effectively and efficiently. Once properly positioned financially, the company is ready to continue planning its customer loyalty efforts.

- *Organizing and controlling.* The CEO creates his own top-management team to help him reorganize and reevaluate all of the company's operations. Top management must delegate authority and define reporting relationships. The decision to centralize information technology and marketing activities results in bringing the customer loyalty strategy to fruition.

- *Staffing and controlling.* The reorganization of an area, such as marketing, causes most companies to make many personnel changes, including replacing industry veterans with customer-relationship-management specialists. Along with replacing the industry veterans, the company has to equip people to handle change efforts. It has to create teams to analyze customers and decide what to do in each area under scrutiny. The company has to combine numerous duties and reassign them to people and teams, necessitating a reevaluation of compensation levels. The company also has to staff and execute additional training efforts so that both new employees and employees with new duties can be taught the standards that would govern their behaviors and outputs.

- *Leading and controlling.* New leadership may also be required in the marketing area because of its reorganization. Leadership changes involve persuading managers to improve their customer service. In short, each organizational unit affected by changes undergoes some kind of leadership change. Leadership needs to handle the change efforts and conduct the required training to develop and enforce new standards and controls for both people and processes.

In addition to its relationship to the other four functions, controlling meets a very practical need. Organizations have limited resources. The successful acquisition and use of these resources determine a firm's survival. No person or organization should expend resources to achieve a goal without arranging to monitor the use of these resources.

CONTROL PROCESS

List and describe the four steps in the control process

We are now ready to examine the four steps of the **control process**. As Figure 15.1 shows, the steps are (1) establishing performance standards, (2) measuring performance, (3) comparing measured performance to established standards, and (4) taking corrective action.

control process
A four-step process that consists of establishing performance standards, measuring performance, comparing measured performance to established standards, and taking corrective action

Establishing Performance Standards

As you know, a *standard* is a quantitative or qualitative measuring device designed to monitor people, money, capital goods or processes. The exact nature of a standard depends on several factors:

- *Who* designs, works with, and receives the output from controls.
- *What* is being monitored.
- *Where* monitoring efforts will take place (location and functional area).
- *When* controls will be used (before, during, or after operations).

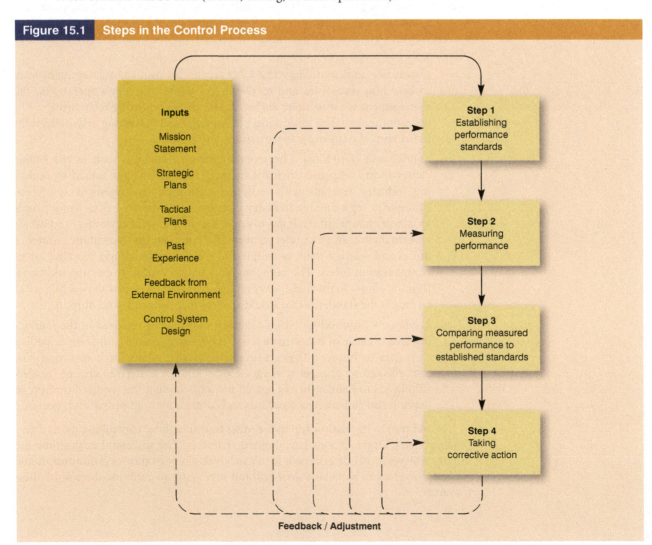

Figure 15.1 | **Steps in the Control Process**

- *How* monitoring will be used.

- *What resources* are available to expend on the controls.

Standards and the controls they are part of usually focus on measuring and monitoring productivity (cost control through effective resource management) and quality (internal and external customer/user satisfaction). Thomas Barry, of the American Society for Quality, stresses the importance of measurement and standards:

> *Measurement is the springboard to involvement, allowing the organization to initiate corrective action, set priorities, and evaluate progress. Standards and measures should reflect customer requirements and expectations. Each employee must be a partner in achieving quality goals. Teamwork involves managers, supervisors, and employees in improving service delivery, solving systemic problems, and correcting errors in all parts of work processes.*[3]

All standards and their controls must be continually reexamined to ensure they are still required and operating effectively and efficiently. Also, efforts to improve quality and productivity must not interfere with each other and must enhance profitability.

Productivity *Productivity* is the amount of output achieved from the use of a given amount of inputs. Productivity can be measured quantitatively and qualitatively. Examples of quantitative measures include the number of customers served per hour and the total units produced per machine hour of operation. Qualitative measures incorporate such factors as customer/user feedback—feedback about how well a product or service meets their needs or how a service provider treats them. Most companies use both measures.

Quality Concern for *quality,* that is, customer satisfaction, begins with the standards and methods used to recruit, hire, train, evaluate and reward employees. Concern for quality must exist within every person and process. It must be a core value within an organization's culture and within the cultures of its suppliers and partners.

To control quality, companies create standards and quality assurance (QA) systems—a validation process to ensure measurement accuracy and standardization, focusing on constant incremental quality improvement (*kaizen*) measurements and results. At times, QA is promoted by such reengineering approaches as empowered individuals and teams, stretch goals and process redesign. Harrah's employs both approaches.

Six Sigma is a process quality goal. It is a highly disciplined process that helps companies focus on developing and delivering near-perfect products and services. The statistical goal is to operate with only 3.4 defects per million transactions. Motorola and other industrial companies developed the quality management method in an effort to cut costs, build revenues and eliminate manufacturing errors. General Electric and Bank of America applied it to financial services. "One of Motorola's most significant contributions was to change the discussion of quality from one where quality levels were measured in percentages (parts per hundred) to a discussion of parts per million or even parts per billion. Motorola correctly pointed out that modern technology was so complex that old ideas about acceptable quality levels were no longer acceptable."[4]

Six Sigma
A highly disciplined process that helps companies focus on developing and delivering near-perfect products and services

Measuring Performance

After standards are established, managers must measure actual performance to determine variation from standard. The mechanisms for this purpose can be extremely sensitive, particularly in high-tech environments. Building modern airliners, for example, requires extraordinarily refined measurement and control systems. Along with visual inspections, technicians induce electric current in the metal surfaces to create magnetic fields. Any distortion in the fields indicates a problem.[5]

Computers are important as tools for measuring performance. They monitor people and operations as they occur, and they store data to be used later. Retail stores use computerized scanning equipment that simultaneously accesses prices and tallies sales and then tracks inventory by department, vendor, and branch store. The computerized scanning systems can also track the sales personnel, recording transactions and salesclerk activity. The displays and reports these systems produce often show current standards and actual performance measurements. Computerized systems of all kinds give managers the up-to-the-minute information they need to make sound decisions.

Comparing Measured Performance to Established Standards

The next step in the control process is to compare actual performance to the standards set for that performance. If deviations from the standards exist, the evaluator must decide whether they are significant—whether they require corrective action. If so, the evaluator must determine what is causing the variance.

To understand variance in regard to manufacturing, consider an operation that mills a billet of titanium into a complex shape to be used as an engine part. The established tolerance, or standard of variance for the part is plus or minus one-thousandth of an inch from the specified dimensions. Periodically throughout the milling process, the machinist measures the part to be sure it remains within tolerance. Any part milled beyond the tolerance must be rejected, in which case a search for the cause of the unacceptable variance begins.

The source of a deviation may lie beyond the employee who first discovers it. (See this chapter's Ethical Management feature for a look at how top managers' greed led to Enron's demise.) Suppliers may have shipped faulty materials. Previous operators may have been poorly trained, dishonest about results, or misinformed about applicable standards. If equipment is in poor condition, it may be incapable of producing output that meets the standards—no matter how hard the operator tries. Determining the cause of substandard performance involves going beyond an examination of task performance, however. It involves examining the standards being applied and the accuracy of the measurement and comparison processes. As Lester Bittel and Jackson Ramsey explain, the control may be too loose or too tight:

> If control is too loose, a deviation between actual and planned performance may result in poor coordination among organizational subunits and the failure to respond in time to unforeseen problems or opportunities. Loose control may also reduce some of the incentives for managers to meet their plans. On the other hand, tighter control generally calls for additional data collection, information processing, and management reporting. The cost and inconvenience of the "red tape" associated with tight control is likely to be resented by the persons being controlled. Tight control may restrict the ability of lower-level managers to exercise imagination and initiative in response to changed conditions.[6]

In today's productivity- and quality-centered environment, workers and managers are often empowered to evaluate their own work for quality, productivity and cost improvements. Individuals and groups throughout organizations are being given the responsibility to control their own behaviors and operations. By putting the authority to make decisions in the hands of those who are best equipped to carry them out, employees can respond almost instantly to substandard performance.

Enron Loses Customer Trust

In order to earn customers' trust and respect their privacy, managers must value honesty and integrity. "In corporate America, it is the chief executive who sets the tone for character. The CEO establishes a corporate culture that will either foster character or create trouble. In the recent spate of downfalls, CEOs' biggest failure has been their inability to demonstrate and nurture character" (Kansas).

Enron's CEO was greedy. A Senate report stated that, "Enron's former chief executive officer, Kenneth Lay, used his credit line to withdraw $77 million in cash from the company in one year, replaced the cash with company stock, and never mentioned his borrowings or stock sales to the board or the public," (U.S. Senate).

Enron undermined customers' trust. When customers found out that, "Enron kept hundreds of millions of dollars in debt off the company's books in partnerships, which were paying millions of dollars in fees to the Enron executives who ran them," (Oldham), customers stopped doing business with the company.

Enron, the United States' seventh-largest company in revenue in 2000, was established in 1985, after federal deregulation of natural gas pipelines. The gas pipeline company evolved into a high technology trading business. EnronOnline, the first web-based global commodity-trading site was launched in November 1999. "Enron prospered on the Net not so much because it had good technology— though the proprietary EnronOnline platform was considered leading-edge—but because online customers trusted the company to meet its price and delivery promises," (Preston).

The company became one of the world's dominant energy firms by reshaping the way natural gas and electricity were bought and sold. "Enron adopted an identity as a trader and market maker in everything from high-speed Internet access to wholesale power. But this online trading platform is virtually worthless if customers aren't willing to use it," (Oldham).

Customers lost confidence in Enron. "Executives made repeated public assurances that Enron's finances and business operations were healthy, only to have those statements refuted by subsequent revelations," (Emshwiller and Smith). The company filed for bankruptcy protection from creditors in one of the largest such filings in history. Kenneth Lay was convicted of conspiracy and fraud in a Houston courtroom on May 25, 2006. He died July 5, 2006.

➡️ **Enron's stated core values were respect, integrity, communication and excellence. Why do you think these values could not overcome individual and collective greed?**

Sources: Enron, http://www.enron.com; John Emshwiller and Rebecca Smith, *24 Days: How Two Wall Street Journal Reporters Uncovered the Lies That Destroyed Faith in Corporate America*, HarperBusiness, August 5, 2003; Dave Kansas, "A Restoration of Character Should Top the Reform List," *The Wall Street Journal*, July 2, 2002; Charlene Oldham, "Enron's Fall Promises a Legal Mess," *Dallas Morning News*, December 5, 2001, 1D; Robert Preston, "The Internet Didn't Kill Enron," *InternetWeek.com*, November 30, 2001; U.S. Senate, Senate Report: The Role of the Board of Directors in Enron's Collapse, July 8, 2002; Bill Thomas, "The Rise and Fall of the Enron Empire," *Today's CPA*, v. 28, no. 2, Spring 2002.

Taking Corrective Action

When an employee determines the cause, or causes, of a significant deviation from a standard, he or she must take corrective action to avoid repetition of the problem or defect. Policies and procedures may prescribe the actions. Such guidelines help shorten the time needed to react to deviations.

Policies and procedures cannot be employed in all instances, however. In some cases, pressures and controls imposed from outside an organization dictate the nature of corrective action. Some corrective actions are automatic. Just as a thermostat can activate a heating or cooling system automatically, assembly operations with computer-guided equipment can sense deviations and take corrective actions without the need for human involvement. Managers must not overlook automatic controls when searching for the causes of substandard performance. Even automatic controls can malfunction on occasion.

Some corrective actions call for exceptions to prescribed modes of behavior. To retain the goodwill of a valued customer, for example, a manager may authorize an exception to the firm's refund policy. Some hotel and restaurant chains empower customer-service employees to, "do whatever it takes" to guarantee customer satisfaction. If managers direct employees to do whatever it takes, the employees must be allowed to use their discretion and judgment. The employees will face problems for which no guidelines exist—problems that will demand unique and creative solutions. Procedures, rules and policies should not be substitutes for good judgment and employee initiative. This chapter's Valuing Diversity feature points out a problem for mature workers.

Valuing Diversity and Inclusion

Reliable Mature Workers

Age discrimination is a problem for mature workers. The Age Discrimination in Employment Act protects employees over the age of 40 from discrimination based on age. Most of those in this group plan to work at least part time after the age of 65 (National Council on Aging).

"The concept of retirement is changing rapidly. As people live longer and in good health, retirement is becoming a more active life stage, with more people looking for the opportunity to combine work and leisure. Many workers have retired the notion of fully retiring at age 60 or 65," (Transamerica Center for Retirement Studies).

According to the U.S. Equal Employment Opportunity Commission (EEOC), there's been a rise in the number of age-discrimination complaints filed. Between 1997 and 2007, approximately 16,000 to 19,000 were filed. But since 2008, the number of complaints has averaged 20,000 to over 24,000 a year.

The numbers prove a harsh new reality (Lommel).

As the economy slows, older workers are feeling more than their share of the pain. Perceived as less productive than younger employees and earning relatively high salaries, these workers are often targeted for termination or denied promotion.. Rightly or wrongly, they think that gray hair and experience mean that 50-plusers are reluctant to try new ways of doing their work or to tackle the relentless stream of new technology. In other words, "older" means the proverbial old dogs, unwilling or unable to learn new tricks that will help employers deal with the hurly burly of the modern workplace that is cutthroat and unforgiving.

In reality, mature workers have more experience than younger workers. In a study conducted by AARP, the majority of employers agreed that older workers tend to be more reliable and have higher levels of commitment to the organization than younger workers (Hewitt). The National Council on Aging reports that extensive research shows no relationship between age and on-the-job performance.

➡ **Traditionalists (born 1922-45), Baby Boomers (born 1946-64), Generation X (born 1965-80) and Millennials (born 1981-2000) are all in the workforce. How can the knowledge and skills be transferred among these different age groups?**

➡ **How long do you think you will want to work after you turn 50? Develop a vision of how you want to see yourself at work in your 50s, 60s and 70s.**

Sources: Transamerica Center for Retirement Studies, January 28, 2016, *https://www.transamericacenter.org/docs/default-source/global-survey-2015/tcrs2016_pr_the_new_flexible_retirement_press_release.pdf*; Aon Hewitt, "A Business Case for Workers 50+: A Look at the Value of Experience 2015," April 2015, *http://www.aarp.org/research/topics/economics/info-2015/business-case-older-workers.html*; Jane M. Lommel, Ph.D., "The New Definition of 'Older' and the New Dilemmas in the Workplace for the Older Worker," *NewWork News*, September 2001; National Council on Aging, *http://www.ncoa.org*; EEOC, "Age Discrimination in Employment Act (includes concurrent charges with Title VII, ADA and EPA) FY 1997–FY 2015," *http://www.eeoc.gov/eeoc/statistics/enforcement/adea.cfm.*

Describe the nature and importance of feedforward, concurrent, and feedback controls

TYPES OF CONTROLS AND CONTROL SYSTEMS

In this section we begin by discussing three types of controls: feedforward controls, concurrent controls and feedback controls. Each focuses on a different point of a process—before the process begins, during the process and after it ceases. Most experts agree that controls, "are most economic and effective when applied selectively at the crucial points most likely to determine the success or failure of an operation or activity."[7] A restaurant must focus on controlling the quality, preparation and presentation of its ingredients. All these control points are critical to the restaurant's safe and effective operation. Poor ingredients will yield a bad meal, as will poorly cooked food. Poor customer service will alienate diners. Figure 15.2 shows how the three types of controls apply to restaurant operations.

Feedforward Controls

feedforward control

A control that prevents defects and deviations from standards

Controls that focus on operations before they begin are called **feedforward controls**. (These are sometimes called preliminary, screening or prevention controls.) Feedforward controls are intended to prevent defects and deviations from standards. Locks on doors and bars on windows, safety equipment and guidelines, employee-selection procedures, employee-training programs and budgets are all feedforward controls. When a manufacturer works closely with its suppliers to ensure the suppliers deliver goods and services that meet standards, the manufacturer is implementing a feedforward control. A maintenance procedure that keeps equipment in top-notch shape is also a feedforward control. McAfee and Norton AntiVirus computer software are examples of feedforward control. The software, which can detect and remove known viruses from computers, is continually updated.

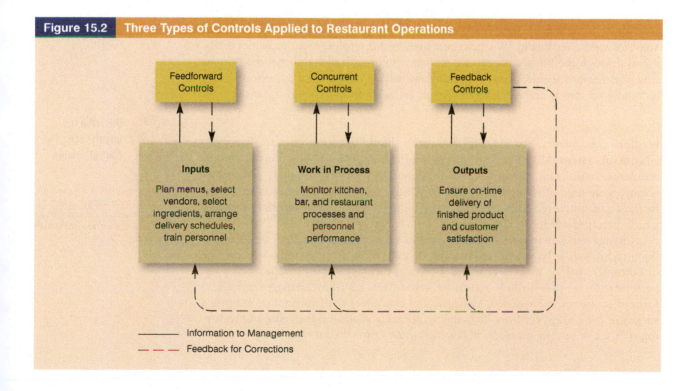

Figure 15.2   **Three Types of Controls Applied to Restaurant Operations**

Concurrent Controls

Controls that apply to processes as they are happening are called **concurrent controls** or steering controls. Consider word processing software, which allows a writer to change a document before storing or printing it. The software provides concurrent control. A word processor's spelling checker also provides concurrent control.

Some concurrent controls are designed to provide readouts or audible warnings. Most photocopiers and computer printers, for example, have display panels that alert their users to malfunctions during operation. Many of the devices on the dashboard of an automobile are concurrent controls. The odometer keeps track of miles traveled; the speedometer tracks the speed of the vehicle. Various warning lights alert the driver to impending or actual problems, such as a low fuel or oil level and problems with the brakes or computerized systems. The steering wheel is a concurrent control that allows a driver to make adjustments in the course of the vehicle. If you try to exit a newly built automobile without turning off the headlights, a warning device, perhaps even a gently scolding electronic voice may concurrently control you.

The most important concurrent control in any undertaking is often the skilled and experienced operator, whose eyes, ears and "feel" for the operation give timely warnings that things are not as they should be. Recognizing the importance of experienced employees as control mechanisms, many companies are enhancing workers' power to influence operations.

Feedback Controls

Controls that focus on the results of operations are called **feedback controls**. They are after-the-fact, or *post-performance,* controls. They are called feedback controls because the information they provide is fed back into the process or to the controller, who must then make any necessary adjustments. "On a larger scale, however, measurements and comparisons made after an operation has been concluded (post-performance) serve to guide future planning, goals, inputs and process designs."[8] At the end of the year, for example, a manager should carefully review the budget control report. Which accounts were overdrawn? Which accounts retained a surplus? Were priorities established through the budget proper and in line with organizational demands? Why or why not? Lessons learned from historical information can be used to perform every task more effectively and efficiently. Everyone can learn from past performance.

Control Systems

Feedforward, concurrent and feedback controls should be viewed as part of an overall **control system**. Able managers integrate suitable control combinations to enforce standards, make sure elements function smoothly with one another, and ensure resources are used effectively and efficiently. Today companies are emphasizing feedforward and concurrent controls. They are avoiding dependence on feedback controls, which often provide information when it is too late to avoid losses.

Change agent managers institute a rigorous overall control system by using the three techniques of control. Feedforward, or prevention controls include surveying of customers before making changes. A company's emphasis on feedback, or post-performance controls include return on investment, cash-flow management and a form of economic value added. Managers and employees at all corporate levels use a variety of concurrent controls, including scrutinizing processes, analyzing and rectifying errors, and putting measures in place to ensure errors do not reoccur.

Describe the importance of a control system

Explain the characteristics of effective controls and the steps managers can take to make controls more effective

critical control point
An area of operation that directly affects the survival of a firm and the success of its most essential activities

CHARACTERISTICS OF EFFECTIVE CONTROLS

Controls at every level focus on inputs, processes, and outputs; but what characteristics make controls effective? Effective controls are focused on critical points and integrated into the corporate culture. They are timely and accepted by those who use them or abide by them. In addition, effective controls are economically feasible, accurate and comprehensible.

Focus on Critical Points

Critical control points are all the operations that directly affect the survival of an organization and the success of its most essential activities. Critical control points exist in many areas of business activity—production, sales, customer service and finance, for example. Controls should focus on those points at which failures cannot be tolerated and where time and money costs are greatest.

The objective is to apply controls to the essential aspects of a business, not the peripheral ones. Having a salesperson report on all the activities undertaken during a long sales trip would be one method of control. The resulting report would probably obscure the important issues, however, and the task of writing it would burden the salesperson. A simple report of actual sales calls and sales revenues would be far more relevant and effective.

A focus on gaining control over costs is an area critical to a company's success. Toshiba eliminates some costs and reduces others through careful analysis and comprehensive actions, such as realigning itself around a few core areas and spinning non-essential business units into joint ventures.

Integration

Controls exhibit integration when the corporate culture supports and enforces them and when they work in harmony, not at cross-purposes. When controls and the need for them are consonant with the organization's values, the controls will be effective. Coordinated controls do not impede work; they function harmoniously to give people what they need to make informed judgments.

Risk management means more than rules. It requires reforming the company's culture and instilling in individuals the commitment to customer service and the desire to act ethically and responsibly in all their undertakings.

When managers and employees trust each other, and workers at all levels believe the controls are necessary, employees can be relied on to implement the controls. When everyone accepts the organization's mission and culture, the corporate climate nourishes self-discipline and commitment. Work teams are self-policing and share values that are consistent with those of the organization. As workers enter these supportive environments, managers and coworkers take care to ensure the newcomers "buy into" the culture.[9]

Acceptability

People must agree that controls are necessary, that the particular kinds of controls in use are appropriate, and the controls will not negatively impact individuals or their efforts to achieve personal goals. Controls that appear to be arbitrary, subjective or an invasion of privacy will not elicit the support of those they affect. Likewise, controls that are redundant (except when necessary for health and safety) or too restrictive will go unsupported. In fact, such controls will stimulate covert and overt opposition. Too many or too few controls, as well as those that are confusing, create stress and resistance. Frustration, fear and loss of motivation and initiative can result.

Through *flextime,* a motivational technique introduced in Chapter 9, employees gain more control over how and when they work. Although more than 40 percent of U.S. employers offer some kind of flexible work schedules, their employees perceive that a request for such an accommodation may put their careers and job security at risk. In many cases when employees seek such changes, their bosses view them as being in some kind of trouble, putting their private lives ahead of their working ones, or asking for "special" treatment at an inconvenient time. To prevent such biases from sabotaging efforts to accommodate its employees, WFD Consulting, "does not ask the reason for the request, so the request is easier to approve or deny strictly on business grounds."[10] The decision is made on the basis of how the new work arrangement being requested, "will benefit the company." Thus acceptance of the program by all parties is enhanced.

Timeliness

Controls must ensure that information reaches those who need it when they need it; only then can a meaningful response follow. One reason for setting deadlines is to ensure information flows promptly. If deadlines are treated casually or unrealistically (if the manager always wants things yesterday), people will soon come to ignore them. In such a case, deadlines are totally ineffective as controls.

Economic Feasibility

The costs of a control system must be weighed against its benefits. If the resources expended on the controls do not return an equal or greater value, the controls are better left unimplemented. Suppose a costly security system is composed of highly trained personnel, sophisticated electronic surveillance equipment, and fingerprint scanning. Such a system is suitable for valuable capital equipment and facilities, but not for ensuring the security of the office supply cabinet.

Sometimes controls are necessarily costly and redundant. Jet aircraft, nuclear power plant and hospital operating and intensive care facilities need redundant, or backup systems so a potentially life-threatening failure of the primary system can be overcome. Redundant and expensive controls are often required to prevent problems that, if they occur, would mean irrecoverable loss or irreparable damage far more costly than the controls.

Accuracy

Information is useful if it is accurate. Accuracy relates particularly to concurrent controls used to diagnose deviations from standards. Controls that offer inaccurate assessments feed decision makers the wrong input, which causes them to give inappropriate responses. When a project manager reports that production is two weeks behind schedule because of poor team attendance, her boss begins an investigation. It turns out that, though several people have been absent, they were not key to production. The delay was actually caused by the failure to properly plan the flow of work and set meaningful deadlines.

Comprehensibility

The more complex a control becomes, the more likely it is to create confusion. The simpler the control, the easier it will be to communicate and apply. Anyone who has struggled with assembly instructions for a hobby kit knows firsthand how rare well-written instructions are. Controls in the form of instructions are often complex because more than one person created, implemented and interpreted them. Complexity can also result when the people creating the controls lose sight of the purposes of the controls.

Too many controls can lead to confusion. (The notion that if one control is good, two must be better, is common but incorrect.) Refinements in reporting procedures often lead to the proliferation of controls. The result can be a profusion of data that sidetracks control efforts.

Computers are reducing complexity and confusion in many environments. Bar codes attached to inventory items and to materials moving along an assembly line simplify the process of tracking. Radio frequency identification technology (RFID) is used to track goods as they move from suppliers to warehouses to distribution centers to stores. The use of RFID in casinos is depicted in Figure 15.3. Some computer software allows voice commands—even commands in a foreign language—to activate or access processes. Machines that use symbols rather than words further overcome language barriers. Telematic services that use computer and electronic technology to learn about driving habits and preferences can make life easier when road conditions and traffic information are shared. All these innovations to enhance communication and reduce confusion help keep control efforts simple.

Figure 15.3	RFID in Casinos

GUEST #413
AMOUNT LOST: $500

RFID-tagged chips keep track of bets and prevent patrons from cheating.

A **central computer system** tracks each bettor's behavior, including the total amount gambled and how each hand was played.

Antennas embedded in the table receive signals from the RFID chips.

An **optical shoe** reads cards as they're dealt so the system knows which hands prompted the highest bets.

Source: Adapted from Rebecca Jarvis, "Casinos Bet Big on RFID," *Business 2.0*, April 2005, 26.

CONTROL MONITORING

Controls are effective as long as they do what they are intended to do, do not generate opposition, and do not result in costs greater than the benefits they provide. Changing circumstances require organizations to monitor controls to ensure they remain effective.

Monitoring Organizational Impacts

Managers need to know the impacts of controls. Controls can generate support or antagonism. Involving employees in the design of controls can help ensure support. Controls that employees believe are equitable seldom encounter resistance. When monitoring the impact of controls, managers can use the following techniques:

- *Before-and-after comparisons.* This approach assesses the organization's environment before and after implementation of the control and notes differences that have occurred. If defects were 10 per 100 before the control and then dropped to 1 per 1000 after the control was implemented, the organization should obviously retain the control and keep working on reducing the defects.

- *Surveys of employees affected by the controls.* A manager who wants to determine the impact of a control should collect relevant data at several points in time. Multiple surveys will not only reveal perceptions, but also show when the perceptions were formed. Positive feedback indicates that controls are accepted and integrated. Negative feedback requires that the causes of resistance be determined. Factors other than controls may affect perceptions. The manager must take care to consider all the changes that have taken place between measurements.

- *Controlled experiments.* To form a sound assessment of the effect of a change, scientific practice requires a survey of the changed group as well as of a group that works without the change. The unchanged group is called the control group. Both groups are studied to determine significant differences in their results, norms, values, perceptions and behaviors. The technique of the controlled experiment isolates those effects that can be specifically linked to the change.

Updating Controls

Controls are designed to deal with specific people, processes and circumstances. When any of these variables change, managers need to reevaluate the controls. Figure 15.4 presents a list of changes that usually call for a reexamination of an organization's controls.

People tend to get comfortable with the way things are. Once controls are introduced, implemented and yield results, people become complacent; the controls become a part of daily routine. A continual repetition of the past, however, means lost opportunities and delays in implementing needed changes. By simply relying on controls and systems that are in place, managers fail to make full use of the preventive nature of the controlling process. The instant company changes occur or are planned, managers should begin to determine if present controls will be adequate and applicable to the new situation. Invariably, changes are needed to the controlling effort as well. Controls themselves need to be controlled!

Figure 15.4	Typical Changes that Require Reexamination of Controls

CHANGES TO MISSION

- What is the present purpose of the organization?
- Was the recent change planned?
- If not, how much of the change was driven by controls and the control system?
- Are the changes good? How will current plans affect the mission?
- Should the mission be changed again? If so, how?
- How will changes to the mission affect controls and the control system?

STRUCTURAL CHANGES

- Have the changes altered the organization's ability to meet its goals?
- What roles did controls and the control system play in making these changes come about?
- Have efforts at controlling affected the organization's span of control, chain of command, degree of decentralization and job definitions? If so, have the effects been positive or negative?
- Are the controls worth any difficulties they have created?
- Have structural changes made changes to controls or the control system necessary?

CHANGES IN DECISION MAKING

- Did the control system alter the information flow required for decision making?
- Is there more decentralized decision making now than in the recent past?
- Is the quality of decisions being made today equal to that of the past?
- Is the management information system adequate?
- What roles have controls played in any of these issues?
- Do changes in decision making require changes in controls, the control process or the control system?

CHANGES IN HUMAN RELATIONS

- Do people enjoy working in the organization?
- Is there an unacceptable level of waste?
- Are high costs or frequent disciplinary actions, tardiness or absenteeism related to personnel actions?
- Have quality and productivity been affected?
- Have there been changes to group norms and cultures?
- Has the interaction between managers and their subordinates improved or worsened?
- Are controls or control systems contributing factors to improvements or declines?
- Are changes needed in either the controls or the control system?

TECHNOLOGICAL CHANGES

- What is the effect of recent technological change on controls and the control system?
- Are any changes in technology being planned?
- What will be their impacts on controls and the control process?
- Are the controls, control process, and control system using the latest beneficial technology? Should they be?
- Are the costs of using the latest technology worth its adoption?

Subsystem Controls

An organization needs an overall control system, as do its subsystems. A firm's strategic plan guides the creation of its overall control system; the plans of subsystems (most often functional areas or processes) do the same at or throughout their levels.

The functional subsystems that require integrated and flexible control techniques are finance, marketing, operations (production), human resources, management information systems and other management support activities. Among the management support subsystems are legal services, public relations and centralized computer services. This chapter examines several control techniques used by finance, marketing, and human resource managers (see Figure 15.5). (Control techniques for operations managers are discussed in Appendix B; Chapter 14 addressed techniques appropriate for those in charge of information management systems.)

Finance Controls

Finance managers need to gather as well as generate information about all aspects of the organization's operations to determine its current and future ability to meet its financial obligations. Based on the organization's strategic plan, financial managers measure and monitor ongoing operations and prepare their estimates and forecasts for future sources and uses of funds. All organizational operations affect and are affected by the work of financial managers; thus, close working relationships are necessary between them and all other managers. The organization must measure and monitor all processes to properly assess their financial impacts. It must gather, analyze and disseminate the financial data generated in a timely manner. It must also establish and enforce standards in the form of limits on spending in each unit, department and in the organization as a whole.

Figure 15.5	**Control Techniques for Common Functional Areas of a Business**

FINANCIAL CONTROL TECHNIQUES

• Plans	• Financial responsibility centers	• Ratio analysis	• Audits
• Financial statements	• Financial ratios	• Budgets	

MARKETING CONTROL TECHNIQUES

• Plans	• Test-marketing	• Sales quotas	• Budgets
• Market research	• Marketing ratios	• Stockage models	• Audits

OPERATIONS CONTROL TECHNIQUES

• Plans	• Cost centers	• Inventory reordering and delivery systems	• Budgets
• Quality assurance	• Material requirements planning	• Maintenance scheduling	• Audits
• Productivity indexes	• Production scheduling and routing	• Inspection and sampling	

HUMAN RESOURCE CONTROL TECHNIQUES

• Plans	• Human asset valuation	• Attitude surveys	• Budgets
• Statistical analysis	• Performance appraisals	• Training and development programs	• Audits

MANAGEMENT INFORMATION SYSTEMS CONTROL TECHNIQUES

• Prototype and pilot testing	• Decision support systems	• Expert systems	• Budgets
• Security systems	• Networks	• Software programs	• Audits

Marketing Controls

As with finance, the organization's strategic plan dictates in part the plans of marketing managers. Like finance managers, marketing managers must work closely with others—finance and operations in particular—in designing, pricing, promoting and distributing products and services. They must gather research on the composition and location of potential as well as current customers. They must determine product and service features and performance characteristics that meet or exceed customer expectations, but they must build these in at a price consumers are willing to pay and in line with allocated funds. Projected sales will determine, in part, production scheduling. Harrah's knows its market and the number of gamers it reaches. "Our approach is different. We stimulate demand by knowing our customers."[11]

Human Resource Controls

Although Chapter 9 discussed staffing functions and their various controls, a brief summary of the major human resource control techniques is in order here. The organization's strategic plan tells HR managers whether staffing requirements will increase or decrease over the short and long term. Managers need plans to acquire or reduce personnel. They must continually review existing jobs to keep the job descriptions and specifications up to date. Plans for expansion or decisions to reorganize anywhere in the organization may create new jobs and activities. Human Resources must establish and conduct training and development programs to teach the new and different procedures and prepare people for job changes. Managers must also periodically review each employee's morale and performance, as well as the climate and culture, to determine what, if anything, needs changing.

We now turn our attention to specific functional control techniques used to some extent by every business. We begin with the area of financial controls, examining, in turn, financial statements, ratio analysis, responsibility centers and audits. Following these, we examine budget, marketing and human resource control techniques.

Describe the content of the three primary financial statements and how managers use them

FINANCIAL CONTROLS

Financial resources are central to management. Without control over adequate funds, an organization cannot survive. Each financial activity requires specific, relevant control techniques. Some types of organizations (banks, for instance, or the Internal Revenue Service) require unique and elaborate fiscal controls. The controls such organizations use are unlike those of manufacturers and retailers. This chapter will examine control techniques common to all types of businesses.

Financial Statements

Nearly all organizations use two primary financial statements, the balance sheet and the income statement. The **balance sheet** identifies the assets of an organization—what it owns and the nature of the ownership—at a fixed point in time. The **income statement** presents the difference between an organization's income and its expenses to determine whether the enterprise operated at a profit or a loss over a specified period of time. Each provides a measure of feedback and concurrent control over financial and related activities. Both are used to prepare budgets and other kinds of plans and controls and to monitor the organization's financial health.

balance sheet

A listing of the assets of a business and the owners' and outsiders' interests in them. The equation that describes the content of a balance sheet is Assets = Liabilities + Stockholders' equity

income statement

A report that presents the difference between an organization's income and expenses to determine whether the firm operated at a profit or a loss over a specified period

Balance Sheet Figure 15.6 presents the balance sheet for one full year—or fiscal year—of operations for the Excel Corporation, a hypothetical medical supply company. (Like a calendar year, a fiscal year contains 365 days; however, it can begin at whatever time an organization dictates. The fiscal year for the U.S. government, for example, runs from October 1 to September 30.) The balance sheet presents three categories of financial data—assets, liabilities and stockholders' equity—as they exist on a specific date. The word *balance* in the term "balance sheet" derives from the fact that the total assets must equal (balance) the sum of liabilities and stockholders' equity. Thus, the equation that describes a balance sheet is;

Assets = Liabilities + Stockholders' Equity

Figure 15.6	**Balance Sheet of the Excel Corporation**

EXCEL CORPORATION
Balance Sheet
December 31, 20xx—

ASSETS			
Current Assets			
Cash	$ 17,280		
Accounts Receivable	84,280		
Inventory	41,540		
Prepaid Expenses	12,368		
Total Current Assets		$155,468	
Fixed Assets			
Building (Net)	$ 33,430		
Furniture and Fixtures (Net)	13,950		
Land	14,000		
Total Fixed Assets		61,380	
Total Assets			$216,848
LIABILITIES			
Current Liabilities			
Notes Payable	$ 10,000		
Trade Accounts Payable	41,288		
Salaries Payable	400		
Taxes Payable	14,000		
Total Current Liabilities		$ 65,688	
Long-Term Liabilities			
Mortgage Payable	$ 8,000		
Bonds Payable	3,280		
Total Long-Term Liabilities		11,280	
Total Liabilities		$ 76,968	
STOCKHOLDERS' EQUITY			
Common Stock (1000 shares at $100 par value)	$100,000		
Retained Earnings	39,880		
Total Stockholders' Equity		139,880	
Total Liabilities and Stockholders' Equity			$216,848

Assets are the resources owned by a business. They usually fall into one of two categories—current or fixed. Current assets are cash, or items that are normally converted into cash, within one year from the date of the balance sheet. Fixed assets are assets not intended for sale or conversion to cash. Fixed assets include land, buildings and the equipment used to conduct the activities of the business.

Liabilities are what a company owes—its current and long-term debts. Current liabilities are debts due and payable within one year of the date of the balance sheet. Long-term liabilities are those due after one year from the date of the balance sheet. Included as liabilities are the claims by outsiders (creditors) on the assets of a business.

The difference between the value of an organization's assets and its liabilities equals the owners' interests in the assets of the business—their equity. Since stockholders own a corporation, its equity is called *stockholders' equity*. In a sole proprietorship or partnership, the equity portion of the balance sheet is usually called *owner's equity*. To illustrate, assume a sole proprietor buys a delivery truck that costs $10,000. The proprietor puts down $3000 in cash for the truck and arranges to borrow the remaining $7000. The business owner now possesses an asset worth $10,000 but has also incurred a liability, or debt, of $7000. The difference between the truck's value and the debt created to purchase it is $3000—the amount of the proprietor's money that was used to purchase the truck. The proprietor's equity is $3000.

Even as the balance sheet is being prepared, of course, changes occur that alter the mix of assets, liabilities and equity. The utility of the balance sheet lies in the fact that it allows analysts to make comparisons from year to year and identify trends. In addition, the balance sheet yields information used to calculate various measures of the company's financial health and of its management effectiveness. We will discuss some of these measures later in this chapter.

Income Statement Figure 15.7 presents the Excel Corporation's income statement, which summarizes the firm's accumulated income and expenses for a one-year period. The content of an income statement, like the content of a balance sheet, can be expressed as an equation. The equation that describes an income statement is

Income – Expenses = Profit or Loss

Managers use income statements as tools for reviewing the expenses and revenue of a business on an ongoing basis. They can prepare these tools to reflect any necessary time frame—a day, a week, a month and so on. An income statement includes seven important categories:

1. *Net sales* or the revenue from sales minus returns and allowances.

2. *Cost of goods sold* or the costs connected with making or acquiring goods that the organization has sold.

3. *Gross profit* or the measure of operating profits (obtained by subtracting the cost of goods sold from net sales).

4. *Operating expenses* or overhead expenses (such as rent, advertising, utilities, insurance and compensation paid to personnel not engaged in producing goods) that reduce gross profit.

5. *Net income (or loss) before taxes*, or the profit or loss of the business (obtained by subtracting operating expenses from gross profit).

6. *Taxes* or the percentage of net income paid to governments.

7. *Net income* or the profit left after paying taxes (the literal "bottom line").

Figure 15.7   Income Statement of the Excel Corporation

EXCEL CORPORATION
Income Statement
Year Ended December 31, 20xx—

REVENUE

Sales	$778,918	
(Less Returns and Allowances)	(14,872)	
Net Sales		$764,046

COST OF GOODS SOLD

Beginning Inventory, January 1	$ 37,258	
Plus Net Purchases	593,674	
Goods Available for Sale	$630,932	
(Less Ending Inventory, December 31)	(41,540)	
Cost of Goods Sold		589,392
Gross Profit on Sales		$174,654

OPERATING EXPENSES

Selling Expenses	$ 69,916	
General and Administrative	45,100	
Research and Development	9,970	
Total Operating Expenses		(124,986)
Net Income before Taxes		$ 49,668
(Less Federal and State Income Taxes)		(18,315)
Net Income		$ 31,353

Like a balance sheet, an income statement yields information needed to track the health of the organization it describes. The major purpose of the income statement is to measure trends in costs and income, noting growth or decline in each category.

Sources and Uses of Funds Statement A summary of the cash flowing into an organization and how it is used over a fixed period is called its **sources and uses of funds statement**. Sometimes called a cash flow statement, this document tracks a company's cash receipts (from sales revenue and asset disposal, for example) and payments (for such items as reducing accounts payable and interest on debt). Financial managers use it as a control technique to measure net increases or decreases in cash over a period and to spot cash flow trends through comparisons to previous cash flow statements. A sources and uses of funds statement for Excel Corporation is shown in Figure 15.8.

Using financial data generated from Excel's activities throughout one year, we can construct the statement in Figure 15.8. Note that cash flow is divided into three main groupings: operating, investment and financing activities. Numbers shown in parentheses represent uses of funds—that is, decreases to cash receipts because of dollars invested or dollars used to pay debts. All other numbers are sources of funds. The sources and uses of funds statement shows a net increase of $18,353 for the one-year period covered by its balance sheet and income statement. It also shows that Excel had the cash needed to acquire new inventory and fixed assets and to reduce accounts payable, notes payable and long-term debt.

sources and uses of funds statement
A summary of the cash flowing into an organization and how it is used over a fixed period of time. This statement is often called a cash flow statement

Figure 15.8	Sources and Uses of Funds for the Excel Corporation

EXCEL CORPORATION
Sources and Uses of Funds Statement
December 31, 20xx—

CASH FLOW FROM OPERATING ACTIVITIES

Net Income after Tax	$ 31,353	
Decrease in Accounts Receivable	5,400	
Increase in Inventory	(6,200)	
Decrease in Accounts Payable	(2,550)	
Cash Provided by Operations		$28,003

CASH FLOW FROM INVESTMENT ACTIVITIES

Increase in Gross Fixed Assets	$ (4,300)	
Cash Used for Investments		(4,300)

CASH FLOW FROM FINANCING ACTIVITIES

Decrease in Notes Payable	$ (3,200)	
Decrease in Long-Term Debt	(2,150)	
Cash Used for Financing		(5,350)
Net Increase in Cash		$18,353

Explain ratio analysis and four types of ratios used by managers

financial ratio

The relationship of two critical figures from financial statements—expressed in terms of a ratio, decimal, or percentage—that helps managers measure a company's financial health and its progress toward goals

FINANCIAL RATIO ANALYSIS

A ratio expresses the relationship between numbers. The fraction 1/2 is a ratio. Ratios can be used to express the relationship between numbers in several ways: in words (as in "one to two" or "one part of two parts"), as a percentage (50%), or as a decimal (0.5).

A **financial ratio** involves selecting two critical figures from a financial statement and expressing their relationship as a ratio or percentage. Financial ratios help accountants and others measure a company's progress toward goals and assess its financial health. On the surface a firm may appear to be sound, its balance sheet reflecting impressive assets. But if the ratio of current assets to current liabilities is poor (less than 2 to 1), the company may have difficulty raising enough cash to meet short-term debts. Ratios can be involved in one of two types of comparisons. First, this year's ratio can be compared with the same kind of ratio for a past year. Or, a ratio describing one company can be compared with the same kind of ratio that describes a competitor.

Figure 15.9 lists frequently used ratios, describing how they are calculated and for what purposes they are used. This chapter will focus on four of the most common types: liquidity, profitability, debt and activity ratios.

Liquidity Ratios To measure the ability of a firm to raise enough cash to meet short-term debts, managers use liquidity ratios. To derive the most common liquidity ratio—the current ratio—the manager simply divides the figure for current assets by the figure for current liabilities (both figures are available on the company's balance sheet). To calculate the current ratio for the Excel Corporation by using the balance sheet shown in Figure 15.6, divide total current assets ($155,468) by total current liabilities

Figure 15.9	Commonly Used Financial Ratios	

Ratio	Obtained by	Purpose
Current assets to current liabilities	Dividing current assets by current liabilities	To determine a firm's ability to pay its current liabilities, short-term liabilities
Net profits to net sales	Dividing net profits after taxes by net sales	To measure the short-run profitability of the business
Net profits to tangible	Dividing net profits after taxes by tangible net worth (the difference between tangible assets and total liabilities)	To measure profitability over a relatively net worth long period
Net profits to net	Dividing net profits after taxes by net working capital (operating capital on hand)	To measure the ability of a business to working capital carry inventory and accounts receivable and to finance day-to-day operations
Net sales to tangible net worth	Dividing net sales by the firm's tangible net worth	To measure the relative turnover of investment capital
Net sales to net working	Dividing net sales by net working capital	To measure how well a company uses its capital working capital to produce sales
Collection period (receivables to credit sales)	First, dividing annual net sales by 365 to determine daily credit sales; then, dividing notes and accounts receivable by average daily credit sales	To analyze the collectability of receivables
Net sales to inventory	Dividing annual net sales by the value of the firm's merchandise inventory as carried on the balance sheet	To provide a yardstick for comparing the firm's stock-to-sales position with that of other companies or with industry averages
Fixed assets to tangible	Dividing fixed assets (the depreciated book value of such items as buildings, machinery, furniture, physical equipment, and land) by the firm's tangible net worth	To show what proportion of a firm's net worth tangible net worth consists of fixed assets (Generally, this ratio should not exceed 100% for a manufacturer and 75% for a wholesaler or retailer.)
Current liabilities to tangible net worth	Dividing current liabilities by the firm's tangible net worth	To measure the degree of indebtedness of the firm (Generally, a business is in financial trouble when this ratio exceeds 80%.)
Total liabilities to tangible net worth	Dividing current plus long-term liabilities by tangible net worth	To determine the financial soundness of the business (When this ratio exceeds 100%, the equity of the firm's creditors in the business exceeds that of the owners.)
Inventory to net working capital	Dividing merchandise inventory by net working capital	To determine whether a business has too much or too little working capital tied up in inventory (Generally, this ratio should not exceed 80%.)
Current liabilities to inventory	Dividing current liabilities by inventory	To determine whether a business has too little or too much current debt in relationship to its inventory (If current debt is excessive, the firm may have to dispose of inventory quickly, at unfavorable prices, to meet its obligations.)
Funded liabilities to working capital	Dividing funded liabilities (long-term obligations, such as mortgages, bonds, serial notes, and other liabilities that will not mature for at least one year) by net working capital	To determine whether the firm's long-term indebtedness is in proper proportion to its net working capital (Generally, this ratio should not exceed 100%.)

Source: Adapted from *1970 Key Business Ratios*. New York: Dun & Bradstreet, 1971. Reprinted by permission of The Dun & Bradstreet Corporation.

($65,688). The result is 2.37 to 1. This ratio means that Excel possesses $2.37 in cash (liquid assets) for each dollar incurred in current debt. Because most experts consider any ratio higher than 2 to 1 to be adequate, Excel may be considered fiscally healthy. Ratios lower than 2 to 1 indicate a company is overburdened with short-term debt.

Profitability Ratios Managers use profitability ratios to study a company's profits from several perspectives. To determine profits generated from sales, divide net profits after taxes by net sales. To calculate the profit generated from the owner's investment, divide net profits after taxes by tangible net worth. Using Excel's income statement, the company's profit ratio on sales ($31,353 in profit divided by $764,046 in net sales) is 0.041, which translates to 4.1 percent profit. In other words, the owners of Excel kept $4.10 for every $100 in sales their firm generated. To determine the adequacy of this ratio, Excel managers may compare it with the profitability ratios of competitors. During a recessionary period in which competitors are losing money, a 4.1 percent return on sales is probably more than adequate.

Debt Ratios A debt ratio expresses an organization's capacity to meet its debts. To calculate a debt ratio, divide total liabilities by net worth (total stockholders' equity). In terms of the Excel Corporation, this means dividing $76,968 by $139,880 to yield a ratio of 0.55, or 55 percent. This result means that Excel is financed by 55 percent debt. If the industry average is 65 percent, Excel should be able to borrow additional funds on the commercial market. But if the industry average is considerably below this level, borrowing may be difficult. Any banker that Excel approaches for a loan might think Excel was overly dependent on other people's money. Of course, when deciding to approve a loan, creditors consider other factors besides ratios—including the company's management and competitiveness.

Activity Ratios Activity ratios reveal a company's performance by shedding light on key internal areas. If managers wish to assess inventory levels, for example, several different activity ratios are helpful: inventory to net working capital, current liabilities to inventory and average inventory levels to total sales. These relationships indicate whether inventory levels are too high in relation to sales and whether too much money is tied up in inventories. When inventories are high, managers are often tempted to make hasty sales that yield a less-than-normal profit.

Activity ratios can monitor many important activities. The manager wishing to know how quickly orders are being processed, for example, can select a week and divide the number of orders filled by the number of orders received. By recording ratios for particular activities over extended time periods, the manager can spot trends and plan needed changes.

Describe the five types of financial responsibility centers and their relationships to budgeting

financial responsibility center
An organizational unit that contributes to an organization's costs, revenues, investments, or profits

FINANCIAL RESPONSIBILITY CENTERS

All management control relies on responsibility accounting, a simple idea: Each manager is responsible for a part of the company's total activity. A manager's unit and its related activities should contribute to the enterprise. A unit's contributions could be vital services, revenues or the manufacturing of a product. A **financial responsibility center** is any organizational unit that contributes costs, revenues, investments or profits. The unit manager who accepts the obligation to achieve certain goals is responsible for reporting progress toward them. The author of a respected planning handbook summarized the notion of fiscal control and responsibility this way:

> *Internal financial reports should follow management's lines of responsibility. Careful evaluation is necessary to determine whether present financial reports track the results that are controllable by the individual held responsible for them. Reasonable assurance should exist that reported information is reliable, that transactions are recorded appropriately, and corporate assets are safeguarded.*[12]

Figure 15.10 defines the principal financial responsibility centers in large businesses. Each manager's organizational unit within a firm's fiscal structure functions as a financial responsibility center. For each center, top managers must specify the specific financial objective and then decide how to measure progress toward it. Because each manager contributes to unit as well as companywide cost control and profitability, selection of each objective is important. Profit, for instance, should be used as a measure of financial responsibility only when profit increases as the direct result of actions for which the manager is responsible.[13]

Figure 15.10 indicates that the sales manager who manages a revenue center is responsible for profits generated by sales, not by cost reductions. Similarly, the production manager who leads a cost center is responsible for costs, not revenue. Only the manager of a production division, who is responsible for both revenues and costs, can be held accountable for the unit's generated profits. Identifying responsibility centers, then, focuses managers' energies on controlling those factors actually within their scope of influence.

Figure 15.10	Principal Financial Responsibility Centers

- **Standard cost centers.** A production department in a factory is an example of a standard cost center. In a standard cost center, the standard quantities of direct labor and materials required for each unit of output are specified. The supervisor's objective is to minimize the variance between actual costs and standard costs. In addition, he or she is usually responsible for a flexible overhead expense budget that is used, once again, to minimize the variance between budgeted and actual costs.

- **Revenue centers.** A sales department in which the manager does not have authority to lower prices to increase volume is an example of a revenue center. The re-sources at the manager's disposal are rejected in the expense budget. The sales manager's objective is to spend no more than the budgeted amount and produce the maximum amount of sales revenue.

- **Discretionary expense centers.** Most administrative departments are discretionary expense centers. There is no practical way to establish the relationship be-tween inputs and outputs in a legal department or information processing department, for example. Managers can only use their best judgment to set budgets. The department manager's objective is to spend the budgeted amount to produce the best (though still unmeasurable) quality of service possible.

- **Profit centers.** A profit center is a unit, such as a product division, in which the manager is responsible for achieving the best combination of costs and revenues. The objective is to maximize the bottom line, the profit that results from the manager's decisions. A great many variations on this theme can be achieved by defining "profit" as only those elements of cost and revenue for which the manager is responsible. Thus, a sales manager who is allowed to set prices may be responsible for gross profit (actual revenue less standard direct manufacturing costs). Profit for the marketing manager of a product line, on the other hand, might reject deductions for budgeted factory overhead and actual sales-promotion expenses.

- **Investment centers.** An investment center is a unit in which the manager is responsible for the magnitude of assets employed. The manager makes trade-offs between current profits and investments to increase future profits. To help them-selves appraise the desirability of new investments, many managers of investment centers think of their objective as maximizing return on investment or residual in-come (profit after a charge for the use of capital).

Financial Audits

Financial information is only as good as the data and interpretation on which it is based. **Audits** are formal investigations conducted to determine whether financial data, records, reports and statements are correct and consistent according to existing laws and the policies, rules and procedures of the organization. Insiders or outsiders may conduct audits.

audit
A formal investigation conducted to determine whether records and the data on which they are based are correct and conform to policies, rules, procedures, and laws

Internal Audits Most companies maintain controls to determine whether people are handling corporate financial activities according to policy and procedural, legal and ethical guidelines. A superior's regular appraisal of a subordinate's functions is a kind of internal audit. Most accounting systems incorporate controls to guarantee adherence to procedures, as do regular reviews by teams of internal auditors. Internal audits are meant to keep problems in house, and they are likely to be conducted by people who know operations well. Those who conduct internal audits may lack objectivity, however, and they may also lack the power to penetrate cover-ups.

External Audits The annual external audit is an American business tradition. An independent public accounting firm conducts an external audit. Such firms are staffed with certified public accountants (CPAs) who provide expert accounting and management services. Federal regulations require publicly traded companies to conduct certified external audits each year. The managers of many nonpublic companies choose to have their companies undergo external audits. The presumed objectivity of the audit enhances the organization's credibility with stockholders, creditors, investors and key insiders, and such audits often uncover important information.

A certified external audit includes thorough inspection and analysis of policies, procedures and records, and such tests as the auditors believe may be applicable to the situation. When all the parameters are satisfied, the audit team manager certifies that the financial data presented in the firm's financial reports are in keeping with generally accepted accounting practices and procedures and government regulations.

Budget Controls

The primary financial control used to manage operating organizations is a budget. As both a plan and feedforward control, a **budget** provides estimates (projections) of revenues and expenses for a given period of time. A budget serves as the standard for measuring the firm's performance, because it allows managers to compare actual revenues and expenses to projections.

budget
A plan and control for the receipt and spending of income over a fixed period

When forecasted revenue is insufficient to support projected spending (expenditures), revenue must be increased or supplemented by borrowing or the use of savings (reserves). The alternative is to reduce expenditures. Conversely, if expenditures rise more quickly than the revenue needed to support them, spending must be reduced to avoid the need to borrow or to deplete reserves.

Budgets serve managers in four important ways:

1 They expedite allocation and coordination of resources for programs and projects.

2 They operate as powerful monitoring systems when supplemented with periodic budget updates.

3 They provide rigorous control guidelines for managers by setting limits on expenditures.

4 They facilitate evaluation of individual and department performance.

Budget status reports allow managers to make timely activity adjustments. Figure 15.11 presents a sample budget status report. It includes the approved budget for certain items and actual expenditures for the first two quarters. Note that spending for international telephone calls (line 5) is 25 percent over budget at the end of the second quarter. The manager of this department must take timely corrective action to avoid a shortfall during the last quarter.

BUDGET DEVELOPMENT PROCESS

9 Describe the four approaches to creating budgets

Budgeting requires (1) setting goals, (2) planning and scheduling to reach the goals, (3) identifying and pricing resources, (4) locating needed funds and (5) adjusting goals, plans, and resources to match actual fund availability. Some organizations involve all their people in these tasks. Others involve managers only. Either way, budgets must be prepared and adhered to at each level and in each unit of an organization.

Budget preparers can follow one or more of the four standardized approaches: (1) top-down, (2) bottom-up, (3) zero-based or (4) flexible budgeting. Following a standardized approach helps ensure consistency in the process.

Top-Down Budgeting In top-down budgeting, senior managers prepare budgets and distribute them to lower levels, with or without input from below. Managers who use this method may plan and control without cooperation and knowledge of their subordinates. These managers may miss or neglect significant information about opportunities and risks—information that others could provide and that should be assessed during budget building.

Figure 15.11	**Sample Budget Status Report**					
LINE NO.	CATEGORY	APPROVED BUDGET JANUARY 1	BUDGET REPORT APRIL 1		BUDGET REPORT JULY 1	
		Actual	Actual	% Used	Actual	% Used
	Salary Expense					
1	Professional	$160,000	$40,000	25%	$80,000	50%
2	Administrative	60,000	15,000	25%	30,000	50%
3	Clerical Support	32,000	8,000	25%	16,000	50%
	Total Salary Expenses	$252,000	$63,000	25%	$126,000	50%
	Operating Expense					
4	Basic Telephone Service	$ 2,000	$ 500	25%	$ 1,000	50%
5	International Telephone Service	2,000	1,000	50%	1,500	75%
6	Insurance	8,000	2,000	25%	4,000	50%
7	Utilities	12,000	4,000	33%	9,000	75%
8	Printing	9,000	1,500	17%	3,000	33%
9	Copying	15,000	3,000	20%	6,000	40%
10	Software	15,000	10,000	67%	10,000	67%
11	Office Supplies	5,000	1,000	20%	2,000	40%
	Total Operating Expense	$ 68,000	$23,000	34%	$ 36,500	54%
	Total Salary and Operating Expenses	$320,000	$86,000	27%	$162,500	51%

Bottom-Up Budgeting Sometimes called *grassroots budgeting,* the bottom-up system taps the knowledge and experiences of all organization members. The men and women closest to the planned activities contribute to building the budget that affects them. In harmonious dialogue, participants come to understand one another's priorities, limits, perspectives and goals. They negotiate the inevitable compromises. (Few departments get all the resources their managers would like.) As input moves up the hierarchy, various views are consolidated to create an inclusive framework. A compelling advantage of this process is that it earns support for the budget from the people who will be governed by it.

Many companies today are decentralizing, forming autonomous units and divisions. Corporate headquarters provide overall guidance and goals, but the divisions set their own priorities and run their own operations. They also construct their own budgets, partly because downsized organizations no longer maintain the large staffs required for top-down budgeting.

Zero-Based Budgeting In some companies, budget preparers begin their job by looking at last year's budget and building on the numbers it contained. The preparers factor in relevant recent experience, and a new budget emerges. Some managers simply increase last year's numbers by some percentage, on the assumption that what went before should continue. Such budgeting does not force managers to examine their operations and explore more efficient ways of doing things. Zero-based budgeting eliminates such complacency by requiring preparers to launch each new budget from a clean sheet of paper (or, more likely, a blank computer spreadsheet). The head of each financial responsibility center must justify every dollar requested in light of the coming year's strategic plans and goals, not simply explain changes from previous years.

Zero-based budgeting requires managers to list their goals for the fiscal period and then identify the people and other resources they need to achieve the goals. They must also list the costs of all resources. The managers choose priorities and create alternatives for accomplishing the unit's objectives as part of its contribution to the overall strategic plan. In discussions with higher-level managers, requests and plans from each unit are studied in light of the overall availability of resources and the organization's strategic objectives. Once agreement about resource allocation is reached, the budget is created. The key to zero-based budgeting is that the process is repeated for each fiscal period.

Flexible Budgeting All approaches to budget building can utilize flexible budgeting, in which set levels of expense are correlated with specified output levels. The expense levels permit managers to judge whether expenses are acceptable at a given level of output. Managers can then adjust expenses accordingly.[14]

Flexible budgeting sets "meet or beat" standards with which expenditures can be compared. Incentives should be provided to managers at every level to meet and beat budget targets. Unit expenses within budgeted amounts are usually permitted. Managers who exceed guidelines must present compelling reasons or face curbs on their spending.

Sam Walton used flexible budgeting to build his Walmart empire:

> *I tried to operate on a two percent general office expense structure. In other words, two percent of sales should have been enough to carry our buying office, our general office expense, my salary, Bud's salary—and after we started adding district managers or any other officers—their salaries too. Believe it or not, we haven't changed that basic formula from five stores to 2,000 stores. In fact, we are actually operating at a far lower percentage today in office overhead than we did 30 years ago.[15]*

Rumor has it that when asked how he arrived at his two percent rule, Walton admitted that he just, "pulled it out of the air." Walmart's success is due in no small measure to its founder's obsession with controlling costs.

OPERATING BUDGETS

10   Explain the two major types of budgets used in businesses

Operating budgets are financial plans and controls for each financial responsibility center's revenues, expenses, and profits.

operating budget
A financial plan and control for each financial responsibility center's revenues, expenses, and profits

Revenue Budgets The organization as a whole, as well as each revenue center, uses revenue budgets, which forecast total revenues from all anticipated sources over a given time. Sears may forecast its revenues by store, line of merchandise and region. States and cities forecast revenues from various taxes and fees—license and permit fees, sales tax and property tax, for example.

Expense Budgets Like revenue budgets, expense budgets are developed for each cost center and the whole organization. Expense budgets refer to several standard categories of costs.

Fixed costs are facility-related expenses that an organization incurs regardless of the amount of activity in any function. Fixed costs include rent, real estate taxes, insurance premiums, wages and salaries of administrative and support personnel, interest payments and payments on long- and short-term debts.

Variable costs relate directly to operations and vary with revenue and production levels. The cost of utilities (typically, telephone, electricity, gas or heating oil, waste disposal and water) is a variable cost. Other variable costs include the costs of raw materials and supplies, wages and salaries paid to people engaged in production and marketing and advertising expenses.

Mixed costs are costs that contain fixed and variable elements. For example, suppose a janitor maintains office and factory buildings. Part of the janitor's salary will be allocated to administration as a fixed cost and part will be allocated to production as a variable cost. Travel expenses are sometimes mixed costs. The travel expenses of administrators may be fixed expenses, whereas those of sales and production people may be variable expenses.

Profit Budgets Profit budgets simply merge revenue and expense budgets to calculate derived profit for the organization and each profit center. IBM operates product and service profit centers, as do most large retailers. Commercial bank profit centers are established according to the types of loans they grant—real estate, consumer or commercial, for example. Profit budgets are useful in gauging manager performance. In whatever the business, where profits fail to reach projected levels, the responsible manager must increase profits or risk losing his or her line, department or division.

Financial Budgets

Financial budgets detail how each financial responsibility center will manage its cash and capital expenditures. Financial budgets include cash budgets and capital expenditures budgets.

financial budget
The details of how a financial responsibility center will manage its cash and capital expenditures

Cash Budgets Often called *cash flow budgets,* cash budgets project the amount of cash that will flow into and out of an organization and its subsystems during a fixed period. Line items include cash left over from the previous period, cash revenue from sales and monies secured through borrowing. A cash budget also accounts for outlays—cash payments for all resources, including borrowed funds. Cash flow budgets project time frames during which managers expect expenses to outstrip revenues. Such periods call for a dip into investments or for the securing of loans. Any excess cash on hand during any period can be invested, thus yielding additional revenue.

Capital Expenditures Budgets Managers use capital expenditures budgets to project the short- and long-term funding needed to acquire capital goods. Capital goods include machinery, office equipment, buildings, vehicles, computers and other expensive assets that will take more than one year to pay for.

Only sound coordination of capital goods expenditures with ongoing expenses sustain operations. When sufficient funding cannot be found from the cash budget or from borrowing, managers may lease needed capital items. Raising capital can be an exercise in creativity. Aircraft maker Boeing helps both small airlines and small countries raise the capital they need to purchase airliners by giving marketing assistance to its would-be customers. Boeing representatives actively solicit U.S. buyers for the products or services its customers offer, and the representatives bring the sellers and buyers together.

Describe the five major marketing control techniques used in businesses

MARKETING CONTROLS

Under the marketing umbrella are product design, packaging, pricing, sales, distribution and customer service. Among the control techniques marketing managers use to prevent problems and monitor operations, this chapter will examine market research, test-marketing, marketing ratios, sales quotas, and stockage.

Marketing Research

marketing research

A feedforward control technique that consists of gathering and analyzing geographic, demographic, and psychographic data to help planners decide what potential and current customers want and need

Marketing research is a feedforward control technique. It consists of gathering and analyzing geographic, demographic and psychographic data. The analysis helps planners decide what potential and current customers want and need so that the planners can design products and services to meet those needs.[16] Market researchers gather information from varied public and private sources. These sources include published materials; personal, telephone and Internet surveys; direct-mail questionnaires; and focus groups.

Market research draws on data developed by professionals in academic, government and commercial settings. Demographic data refer to a person's age, gender, marital status, education, occupation and income. Geographic data describe where people live by region, neighborhood or type of housing. Psychographic data relate to cultural origin, religion, political philosophy and personal interests. Researchers study needs, wants and the buying habits and motives of different population segments. Possessing such knowledge about current and potential customers allows managers to tailor products, advertising, sales and distribution systems to individuals and groups. See this chapter's Managing Social Media for a table of social metrics used by companies to track social media to gauge consumer sentiment.

Market research has generated many product innovations and identified discrete target markets. Imaginative research led pet food companies to formulate dog and cat food to appeal to owners with pets of different ages. Where Henry Ford once offered only a single standard model in a single hue: "any color so long as it's black," market research has spawned a dizzying array of vehicles—from Rolls-Royce limousines and zippy Fiat Spider convertibles to SUVs of every description, all with an array of options.

Metrics for Social Media

Relevant Metrics for Social Media Applications Organized by Key Social Media Objectives

This table organizes the various social metrics for social media by classifying them according to the social media applications and social media performance objectives. While it is not exhaustive, it should give marketers a useful starting point for measuring the effectiveness of social media efforts because all of the metrics listed are easily measured.

SOCIAL MEDIA APPLICATION	BRAND AWARENESS	BRAND ENGAGEMENT	WORD OF MOUTH
Blogs	• number of unique visits • number of return visits • number of times bookmarked search ranking	• number of members • number of RSS feed subscribers • number of comments • amount of user-generated content • average length of time on site • number of responses to polls, contests, surveys	• number of references to blog in other media (online/offline) • number of reblogs • number of times badge displayed on other sites • number of "likes"
Microblogging (e.g., Twitter)	• number of tweets about the brand • valence of tweets +/– • number of followers	• number of followers • number of @replies	• number of tweets
Concretion (e.g., NIKEiD)	• number of visits	• number of creation attempts	• number of references to project in other media (online/offline)
Social Bookmarking (e.g., StumbleUpon)	• number of tags	• number of followers	• number of additional taggers
Forums and Discussion Boards (e.g., Google Groups)	• number of page views • number of visits • valence of posted content +/–	• number of relevant topics/threads • number of individual replies • number of sign-ups	• incoming links • citations in other sites • tagging in social bookmarking • offline references to the forum or its members • in private communities: number of pieces of content (photos, discussions, videos); chatter pointing to the community outside of its gates • number of "likes"
Product Reviews (e.g., Amazon)	• number of reviews posted • valence of reviews • number and valence of other users' responses to reviews (+/–) • number of wish list adds • number of times product included in users' lists (i.e., Listmania! on Amazon.com)	• length of reviews • relevance of reviews • valence of other users' ratings of reviews (i.e., how many found particular review helpful) • number of wish list adds • overall number of reviewer rating scorers entered • average reviewer rating score	• number of reviews posted • valence of reviews • number and valence of other users' responses to reviews (+/–) • number of references to reviews in other sites • number of visits to review site page • number of times product included in users' lists (i.e., Listmania! on Amazon.com)
Social Networks (e.g., Bebo, Facebook, LinkedIn)	• number of members/fans • number of installs of applications • number of impressions • number of bookmarks • number of reviews/ratings (+/–)	• number of comments • number of active users • number of "likes" on friends' feeds • number of user-generated items (photos, threads, replies) • usage metrics of applications/ widgets • impressions-to-interactions ratio • rate of activity (how often members personalize profiles, bios, links, etc.)	• frequency of appearance in timeline of friends • number of posts on wall • number of reposts/shares • number of responses to friend referral invites

continues

SOCIAL MEDIA APPLICATION	BRAND AWARENESS	BRAND ENGAGEMENT	WORD OF MOUTH
Video and Photosharing (e.g., Flickr, YouTube)	• number of views of video/photo • valence of video/photo ratings (+/−)	• number of replies • number of page views • number of comments • number of subscribers	• number of embeddings • number of incoming links • number of references in mock-ups or derived work • number of times republished in other social media and offline • number of "likes"

➡ Traditionally, managers have known more or have had better access to information than those being managed. If employees have the same or better access to information (through social media), how does that affect management?

Source: Donna L. Hoffman and Marek Fodor, "Can You Measure the ROI of Your Social Media Marketing?" *MIT Sloan Management Review,* October 1, 2010. *http://sloanreview.mit.edu/the-magazine/2010-fall/52105/can-you-measure-the-roi-of-your-social-media-marketing/.*

Test-Marketing

Suppose a new product or service has been conceived and a prototype developed. Planners may decide to *test-market* the new item—that is, introduce it to a limited market on a small scale to assess its acceptance. McDonald's launches new menu items on a limited basis through careful test-marketing. First, candidate states, cities and towns are chosen. Next, advertising and in-store displays promote the new offerings. Then, customers who try the new product are asked for their opinions.

3M Corporation began test-marketing for Post-it® Notes in house. The program began with the distribution of custom-made packets of the product to managers throughout the home office. Also, the CEO sent samples of Post-it® Notes to other CEOs of Fortune 500 companies. Soon, demand outstripped 3M's capacity to supply the product; then marketing took over. This product now contributes millions of dollars to 3M sales each year.

One disadvantage of extensive test-marketing is that it can tip a company's hand to competitors. A smaller version of the practice has become popular for companies in highly competitive industries. These firms enlist small groups of users, or potential users and restrict their sampling of options. Working closely with users in a controlled environment, marketing and production people assess the marketability of a new product and make decisions on the basis of the users' feedback, however limited. Managers at Panasonic, Motorola and Sony favor this method. Honda managers consider dealers and customers to be the company's most reliable source of marketing information.

No matter which test-marketing methods are employed, planners analyze the results of testing to determine whether the company should proceed with manufacturing and distribution, and whether modifications to the new product or service are needed. Test-marketing limits the risks a company faces when introducing something new, and it increases the new item's prospects for success.

Marketing Ratios

As heads of financial responsibility centers who are responsible for profitability, marketing managers must track and control their costs. Along with supervising the sales force and reviewing income statements, marketing managers regularly calculate various ratios to monitor ongoing operations and determine needs for improvement. There are several frequently used measures: ratio of profit to sales; costs of selling to gross profit; sales calls to orders generated, and profitability of each order; and changes in sales volume to price changes. Marketing managers also calculate the ratio of bad debts to total credit granted, and sales volume to production capacity, for the entire organization and its individual product lines. Two other common measures are market share and order turnaround time.

In many industries, total market share ranks as the critical standard of success. Market share performance often shapes a marketing manager's decision making. General Motors is propelled by market share and makes decisions on brands based on market share. The automaker decided to discontinue the oldest U.S. auto brand, Oldsmobile, because of poor sales.

Foreign companies may aim to dominate the U.S. market, sometimes at little or no profit. This strategy can lead to charges of *dumping*—selling goods in an external market at less than the cost of manufacture or less than fair market value at home. Global trade negotiators wrestle with the topic in tariff negotiations. The focus on total market share has paid off in consumer electronics, an area in which large Japanese firms have all but eliminated U.S. manufacturing.

Sales Quotas

In many organizations each salesperson operates with a sales quota—a minimum dollar amount of sales within a specific time period to justify his or her salary. Many salespeople work on a commission-only basis, earning money in direct proportion to and as a fixed percentage of the value of the goods or services they sell. If commissioned salespeople make no sales, they get no pay. Commissions and quotas stimulate salespeople to meet or exceed specific quantity goals, but commissions can also lead to abuses. Overly aggressive salespeople may harass customers or sell them things they cannot afford or do not want. But managers usually favor quotas. Quotas ensure that professionals try their best and feed the ambition of those who want to succeed and advance.

Stockage

The level of inventory for any item is called *stockage*. Stockage is important to business success. You cannot sell what you do not have, and you cannot produce when components are not on hand. In addition, maintaining inventories is expensive, as Figure 15.12 shows. Money tied up in inventories is unavailable for other uses. Retailers and manufacturers must track their inventories to ensure they do not run out of needed items. They must reduce the number of slow-moving items or eliminate the items altogether. Retailers quickly learn to devote most of their best display areas to the items that yield the largest profits, either individually or by volume. By tracking stockage levels, managers can determine normal usage rates, and therefore set efficient reorder points and maintain minimum levels.

Today, large retailers and manufacturers endeavor to keep as little stock as possible. Many now rely on **just-in-time** (**JIT**) inventory control—that is, they require their suppliers to deliver inventory just in time to meet production or sales demands. Walmart, Kmart, and Sears maintain computer links that allow their suppliers to track sales of the items they produce and to ship items as needed to prevent stores from running out. On the manufacturing floor, JIT systems forward items to each production stage as necessary. The notification to move materials along comes from operator signals or

just-in-time (JIT)
An inventory control system in which materials are purchased only as needed to meet actual customer demand. JIT production is a system in which units are produced only as needed to meet actual customer demand.

Figure 15.12	Costs of Maintaining Inventories

1 Costs of producing or acquiring inventory items
2 Costs of loss to obsolescence, damage or theft
3 Freight charges
4 Security costs (guards, alarm systems, insurance)
5 Storage costs (buildings and maintenance)
6 Administrative expenses (wages and salaries of those who run storage facilities, keep track of inventory and inspect and move inventory)
7 Costs of computerized inventory control system
8 Costs of maintenance and operation of storage equipment
9 Costs connected with procurement and inspection of and payment for inventory items

computerized inventory control processes. See this chapter's Quality Management for more information on JIT.

In 1966, Sam Walton realized that to grow, he would have to add computerized merchandise controls. "Walmart went on to become the icon of just-in-time inventory control and sophisticated logistics—the ultimate user of information as a competitive advantage. Today, Walmart's computer database is second only to the Pentagon's in capacity, and though he is rarely remembered that way, Walton may have been the first true information-age CEO."[17]

Describe the six major human resource control techniques used in businesses

HUMAN RESOURCE CONTROLS

Human resource managers employ diverse control techniques. Among the most frequently used are statistical analysis, human asset valuation, training and development, performance appraisals, attitude surveys, and management audits. Each is intended to provide information about the productivity of the workforce and the quality and quantity of individual and group performance.

Statistical Analysis

Companies need to gather and store data about the composition of their workforce, compliance with equal opportunity guidelines, employee turnover and absenteeism and effectiveness of recruiting and compensation efforts. Companies need data about managerial and individual effectiveness, levels of job satisfaction and motivation and employee safety and health. Many companies create databases containing facts about employee skills, training levels, evaluations, formal education and job experiences. Such information facilitates recruiting, promotion and other employment decisions. Although data in all these categories are important, this section will focus on two standard measures: turnover and absenteeism. (Workforce composition and safety will be discussed in relation to management audits.)

Turnover The number of employees who leave an organization during a specific period of time is known as employee *turnover*. Some turnover occurs through attrition—retirement, resignation, illness and death. Some turnover is seasonal and planned—farm laborers are hired to harvest a crop, and many salesclerks are hired only for the holiday shopping rush. Some turnover results from economic conditions

JIT

A common saying among managers is, "You can't manage what you can't measure." Inventory can be measured, thus managed or controlled. An important rule for just-in-time (JIT) production is to produce something when the customer orders it. Thus, inventory of products without an order is a waste. Lean manufacturing means eliminating wastes by identifying opportunities to improve total system efficiency in the manufacturing effort. Inventory is any supply in excess of a one-piece flow through the manufacturing process. (Ideally, parts are manufactured one at a time and move throughout the production process as a single unit.)

Causes of excess inventory include:

- Misconception that this protects the company from inefficiencies and unexpected problems
- Product complexity
- Unleveled scheduling
- Poor market forecast
- Unbalanced workload
- Misunderstood communications
- Reward system
- Unreliable shipments by suppliers

The objective is to produce only the quantity ordered by the customer. "Production leveling or *heijunka* means distributing the production volume and mix evenly over time. For example, instead of assembling all the type A products in the morning and all the type B products in the afternoon, we would alternate small batches of A and B," (Dennis, p. 83). Produce the right product in the right quantity at the right time.

JIT production follows a few simple rules (Dennis, p. 69):

1 Don't produce something unless the customer has ordered it.

2 Level demand so that work may proceed smoothly throughout the plant.

3 Link all processes to customer demand through simple visual tools or *kanbans*.

4 Maximize the flexibility of people and machinery.

➥ **Just-in-time is an important component of quality management. Companies use production and purchasing strategies to reduce the time between the beginning of the production process and shipment to the customer. However, the actual implementation of these strategies may prove difficult. World events, such as the 2011 earthquake and tsunami in Japan lead to uncertain supply sources. In 2011, virtually every car maker in the world ordered some parts from Japan. After the earthquake, automakers could not get Japanese parts. As a result, they canceled overtime, cut shifts or closed plants. Prepare a production scenario, and list at least two other situations which could interrupt production. Suggest how producers can keep the global production system working as best as possible to adapt to the circumstances.**

Source: Pascal Dennis, *Lean Production Simplified*, 2nd Edition, Productivity Press, 2007.

and competitors' actions that decrease a firm's sales and its ability to support its workforce. Resulting layoffs may be permanent or temporary. Substantial turnover results from bad management. In many cases, people lost to turnover must be replaced, and replacing people is costly. It is normally in a company's best interest to retain its most valuable employees for as long as possible.

The rate of turnover often serves as a measure of an organization's internal environment—its morale, stress, and managerial skill levels. Each organization, and each subsystem needs to determine its acceptable turnover, or an acceptable number of people who must be replaced compared to the total workforce. To determine an acceptable ratio, most companies study their own past and the experiences of other companies in their industries. Some businesses, such as the fast food and hospitality industries, experience unusually high turnover rates. Managers must analyze the causes of turnover carefully and determine which among them are signs of trouble. Then managers must act to eliminate those causes.

Absenteeism *Absenteeism* is the percentage of an organization's employees who are not at work on any given day. All organizations must maintain a realistic standard for absenteeism—say, five percent. As with turnover, managers must assess the causes for absences and judge their validity. Many companies find that 90 percent of their absenteeism is caused by less than 10 percent of their work force members. At any given time, absenteeism that exceeds the standard may or may not be a sign of trouble. Circumstances such as a widespread flu outbreak or a natural disaster that prevents people from getting to work may temporarily and legitimately raise absenteeism. Many managers try to prevent absenteeism by encouraging 100 percent attendance; they offer financial rewards and set realistic and equitable attendance policies.

Human Asset Valuation

Various monitoring devices help managers assess the value of each employee to a company. One approach focuses on accounting. Another projects the long-range potential (promotability) of each person. **Human asset accounting** tracks the money spent to recruit, hire, train and develop employees. This type of accounting treats each person as an asset, not an expense. Expenditures for the development of human assets are considered investments, not unlike the investments made to build an office or factory building. Managers who use human asset accounting realize that each person represents a sizable investment of company resources, and these managers tend to be committed to retaining good people. Many managers with this view keep balance sheets that list employees as assets. (These balance sheets are not for tax purposes.) When someone leaves, the corresponding investment is deducted from the total, showing a net loss of assets.

> **human asset accounting**
> Treating employees as assets, not expenses, by recording money spent on people as increases in the value of those assets

In an approach less common than human asset accounting, managers attempt to assign a dollar value to each employee's contribution to company profits. Such calculations are not easy to make. They consist of creating general categories of employees and assigning dollar amounts to each category on a percentage basis. Arbitrary as such an approach may be, it does attempt to focus attention on people as resources, not simply expenses.

Training and Development (T&D)

As Chapter 9 (on staffing) has indicated, training and development (T&D) imparts knowledge, skills and attitudes necessary for successful job performance. The standards necessary for effective and efficient operations must be taught and then enforced, usually by those closest to these standards. T&D is a control technique concerned with preventing problems from arising and dealing with them quickly when they do. T&D gets people ready for changes before those changes arrive. The subject matter or areas of training become the standards by which employees are appraised, rewarded or punished.

Performance Appraisals

Perhaps the most important control device employed by human resource managers is the use of a regularly scheduled legal, objective and equitable appraisal system. The focus of such a system must be on comparing employee performance to established standards, and then sharing the results with each individual. Appraisal standards are feedforward control devices; the appraisals themselves are concurrent and feedback devices.

Domino's Pizza uses a computer test to gauge employees' effectiveness and alertness before they are allowed to take on their duties. When drivers are hired, they are given a hand-eye coordination test. The results are recorded as that person's standard for acceptable performance. On reporting to work each day, the driver takes the same machine-based test. The results (answers and reaction times) are compared to those for their first test. The driver who fails to meet those standards may be assigned to alternative duties, or asked to leave, for the day. The point is to keep people away from potentially dangerous and difficult-to-operate equipment when they are not in top form.

Attitude Surveys

An *attitude survey* shows how employees feel about their employer. It can highlight what is going right in the workplace and where problems exist. Top managers usually hire an outside consulting firm to conduct such a survey. The fact that outside surveys are objective and can be answered anonymously encourages employees to respond to them.

Attitude surveys ask questions about key processes, units and personnel in an organization, and they can be tailored to the specific unit being evaluated. Questions should help companies pinpoint areas of dissatisfaction and gather suggestions about how to improve people, procedures and policies. Sample questions are, "How well does your boss respond to your requests for assistance?" and "What are the sources of stress for you on your job?"

After the answers are collected and analyzed, the results are given to management. For the best outcome, the results should be shared (with nothing held back) with all employees. Data gathered from the surveys—facts about employee gender, marital status, age, and job categories—become useful for determining which programs or changes are best for which group.

Management Audits

The Occupational Safety and Health Administration (OSHA) and the Equal Employment Opportunity Commission (EEOC) require regular recording, reporting and disclosure of statistics about employment. Both agencies set national standards and procedures for the workplace. In many cases, managers must also comply with state regulations about employment.

To ensure regulations are being followed, managers should conduct regularly scheduled management audits, or compliance audits. In addition, they must continually track and record statistics about safety, health and compliance with equal employment opportunity guidelines. Violations of government employment regulations are punishable by significant sanctions.

COMPUTERS AND CONTROL

One of the major revolutions in the control function has been the application of computers to nearly every business process. More than two-thirds of employees now work to some degree with a computer as part of their daily routines, and all employees are affected by computer use.

The most important contribution that computers have made to the control process is data. Computers can provide data more quickly, cheaply and accurately than can traditional means. Computers facilitate communications throughout and among

Vietnam Controls Bird Flu

Vietnam was one of the first countries in the world to contain bird flu, the disease that has killed more than half of the nearly 200 people infected and frightened millions, since it appeared in Southeast Asia. Avian influenza occurs naturally among birds. A subtype of the virus, H5N1, can infect people who come into direct or close contact with infected birds or contaminated surfaces. According to the Centers for Disease Control, "If [the] H5N1 virus were to gain the capacity to spread easily from person to person, an influenza pandemic [worldwide outbreak of disease] could begin," (CDC).

Vietnam accomplished this by educating its citizens, vaccinating millions of birds, slaughtering millions of chickens and ducks and by being honest with the World Health Organization (WHO). Small farmers, raising chickens and ducks in their backyards make up most of Vietnam's poultry industry. Slaughtering and vaccinating birds are recommended to slow the virus. Farmers want their chickens and ducks to be immunized. Furthermore, they are disinfecting their farms every week.

The WHO has a Global Outbreak Alert and Response Network of public health specialists who stand ready to help contain outbreaks around the world. After the WHO met with Vietnamese health officials, an international team of epidemiologists and pathologists was convened, including the Vietnamese ministry of health. The international team and the ministry of health review the situation daily and set up new measures as appropriate. "No infected bird has been found at Ha Vy in its four years," said its manager, Le Xuan Viet (Silberner).

➡ **What elements linked to controlling and control techniques can you see in the case of bird flu?**

Sources: Joanne Silberner, "How Vietnam Mastered Infectious Disease Control," November 5, 2015, *http://www.pbs.org/wgbh/nova/ next/body/one-health-vietnam*; Centers for Disease Control, *http://www.cdc.gov*.

organizations and their members, placing data in the hands of anyone who needs it. Moreover, they can do so in real time.

Control needs served by computers include data collection; data analysis, reduction and reporting; statistical analysis; process control; test and inspection; and systems design. The activities of data analysis, reduction and reporting can be programmed to occur automatically as the data are collected or to occur on command. Decision rules can be employed in the program that will automatically signal the onset of a problem for which corrective action can be taken. The collection, utilization and dissemination of control information is best accomplished when the information is incorporated into a management information system (MIS), which maintains relationships with other activities, such as inventory control, purchasing, design, marketing, accounting and production control. This chapter's Global Applications feature presents the World Health Organization (WHO) centers linking and collaborating via the Internet through a searchable database.

Chapter Summary

1 **Describe the relationship between controlling and the other four functions of management.**

Planning is part of every function. Management must create standards to govern people and operations. To prevent, or identify and correct deviations from standards, management must design controls. Managers must also teach people what controls are supposed to do and how to use them effectively and efficiently.

Organizing is affected by controls known as the principles of organizing. Different levels within any company require different controls and standards. As organizations change their structures, they must eliminate, modify or create standards and controls to accommodate the changes.

Staffing and controlling are linked because people create controls and must be taught to use them correctly. Changes in job descriptions usually mean shifts in directives and the controlling process. Alterations in personnel through such actions as downsizing, promotions, and transfers mean changes to controlling efforts as well.

Leading is linked to controlling because leaders at every level must be capable of labeling critical control points, gathering needed information, creating and modifying their controls, and overseeing those who are responsible for controlling activities.

2 **List and describe the four steps in the control process.**

1 *Establishing performance standards.* Organizations create standards to help measure and monitor both productivity and quality efforts. People and processes are governed by qualitative and quantitative standards. An organization uses these standards to teach, train and evaluate; they function as the link between planning and controlling.

2 *Measuring performance.* An organization measures actual performances of people and processes to ascertain if they are functioning according to plans and expectations. Performance can be measured (diagnosed) as it takes place (in real time) or after it has taken place. Either way, what is happening must be monitored.

3 *Comparing measured performance to established standards.* This step asks the question: Is "what is" the same or better than the, "what should be?" If the answer is yes, things are going well. If the answer is no, corrective action is usually called for.

4 *Taking corrective action.* When significant deviations from established standards occur, the organization must determine the cause by identifying the nature and scope of the problem. Deviations may be caused by internal or external factors and may or may not be within the power of a controller to control. Solutions are often prescribed by procedures and policies. Some corrective actions are automatic, but even automatic controls can malfunction on occasion.

3 **Describe the nature and importance of feedforward, concurrent, and feedback controls.**

Feedforward controls are preventive in nature. They are created to screen out possible causes of problems. Procedures and training can be preventive as well as remedial. Concurrent controls monitor ongoing operations as they occur in real time, allowing for instant reactions and the spotting of trends. Feedback controls are after-action controls. Inspecting output after an operation has been performed and soliciting customer feedback are examples of after-action control. All three types of controls are important to managers and their organizations. When designed and used properly, they can prevent, or identify and correct deviations from established standards.

4 **Describe the importance of a control system.**

For an organization to achieve the maximum benefit from its controls, it must design all controls so they operate in harmony with one another, with no overlap or duplication of effort. A control system is composed of subsystems operating in integrated and cooperative ways. Productivity control, for example, must not impede the goal achievement of quality control. Controls operating in harmony will lead to increases in profitability.

5 **Explain the characteristics of effective controls and the steps managers can take to make controls more effective.**

- *Focus on critical control points.* Present in all operations, they are the most vital points at which a failure cannot be tolerated or at which the costs in time and money are the greatest. All three types of controls are needed to monitor and measure cash flow, probably the most important, or critical area in any organization.

- *Integration.* Controls are supported by the organization's culture and work in harmony with one another in a control system approach. Controls are coordinated and do not impede operations.

- *Acceptability.* Those who must apply, interpret and react to controls recognize their importance, accept them and do not resist effective use of them. Unless people are willing to enforce and live by the controls in their environments, the controls will not be effective or efficient.

- *Timeliness.* Measurements provided through controls reach the proper decision makers at the time they are needed. Only then can managers properly respond to the information provided. Deadlines are a means to guarantee timeliness in control efforts.

- *Economic feasibility.* Control costs must be measured against the benefits they provide. When benefits outweigh, in a substantial way, the costs incurred, economic feasibility exists.

- *Accuracy.* Accuracy exists when controls provide a precise enough view of what they were set up to measure. In some instances, a ballpark view is sufficient; however, most efforts to control people and processes require exactness and precise measures.

- *Comprehensibility.* A control is comprehensible when people understand everything they need to in relation to that control. The simpler, the better; as controls pile on top of controls, or become too high-tech for their users, they lose comprehensibility.

An organization must continually monitor and re-evaluate controls to see if they are still needed and are operating effectively and efficiently. Managers can use before-and-after comparisons to judge continued effectiveness. They can survey employees affected by controls to guarantee employees accept and comprehend the controls. Managers can also conduct controlled experiments (for example, when judging the effects of new medications) to determine whether the controls are doing what they are designed to do. When controls need to be dropped, redesigned or created, those affected must be enlisted to help fashion them.

6 **Describe the content of the three primary financial statements and how managers use them.**
The three statements are the balance sheet, income statement, and sources and uses of funds statement. The first lists the assets of an organization and points out who owns them and to what extent—the proprietors, partners, stockholders (equity) or creditors (liabilities). It is a snapshot of a company's situation at a given moment in time. The income statement lists income from all sources and the amount of money actually paid out during the time period covered by the statement. It is a historical summary. The sources and uses of funds statement is a summary for a given time of the flow of cash into and out of an organization. All statements help financial managers make comparisons, spot trends and forecast future financial activities.

7 **Explain ratio analysis and four types of ratios used by managers.**
Ratio analysis takes key figures and compares them to others. The purpose of ratio calculations and comparisons is to gauge the financial health of the organization and its ability to meet its obligations. Liquidity ratios measure the ability of a firm to raise enough cash to meet its near-term debts. Profitability ratios are used to study a company's profits after taxes. They answer such questions as, "What is the return on capital invested?," and, "What departments, products and services return the best profits?" Debt ratios express an organization's capacity to meet its liabilities or debts. Activity ratios help measure and monitor all internal activity areas, such as inventory turnover, sales per department and personnel costs related to human resource activities.

8 **Describe the five types of financial responsibility centers and their relationships to budgeting.**

- *Standard cost centers* are production units that have standard, or prescribed, quantities of direct labor and materials required for each unit of output. The unit supervisor's job is to minimize the variance between the actual costs in labor and materials and the standard costs. In addition, unit supervisors usually have to create and live within a budget for nonproduction-related expenses.

- *Revenue centers* generate income for an organization, but their managers, while charged with maximizing revenues, do not have the authority to adjust prices for goods or services sold to the firm's customers. Each center has a budget and must spend within its limits while conducting its activities. Center managers may or may not participate in the preparation of the budget.

- *Discretionary expense centers* are usually administrative service providers, such as staff departments. These centers and their managers exist to serve all organization personnel with their particular expertise. These centers must prepare their own budgets, usually on the basis of past performance experiences, and do their best to live within them.

- *Profit centers* generate revenues but also have the authority to manipulate pricing and offer other incentives to customers. Managers seek to obtain the best possible combination of costs and revenues. Such centers also prepare budgets and must live within their limits.

- *Investment centers* put a firm's cash to work in various ways, including short- and long-term financial instruments. The managers of such centers must struggle to maintain an appropriate balance among the firm's assets, given its immediate and future needs. The goal is to maximize the return on invested capital through the manipulation of a firm's assets. Each center prepares its budget in light of previous experience and is charged to do its best to live within it.

9 **Describe the four approaches to creating budgets.**

- *Top-down budgeting* is a budgeting approach in which senior managers prepare, with or without input from below, budgets for the entire organization and its various subsystems. This approach is most often used in not-for-profit and government organizations. Such systems usually depend on large support staffs or expense centers.

- *Bottom-up budgeting* taps into the knowledge and experience of subsystem managers and relies on them to create efficient budgets, which, when consolidated as the budgets move to the top, will govern the firm's fiscal period. This system is based on compromise and trade-offs; priorities become the driving force.

- *Zero-based budgeting* is an approach in which managers start the budgeting process by making no assumptions and by disregarding past practices. Every dollar requested is justified in light of the coming time period, not based on last year's experiences. Starting with unit goals and priorities for each, managers calculate the minimum they believe will be required to achieve those goals. In defending their requests to the higher-ups, managers must be willing to compromise in accordance with available resources.

- *Flexible budgeting* may be used with the previous approaches to budgeting. It utilizes standard costs that can be correlated to specified output levels. The manager projects output for a unit and calculates expected expenses by using standard costs assigned to each output activity. The manager's job is to meet or beat the standards set for operations. Exceeding budgeted cost is permitted only under exceptional circumstances.

10 **Explain the two major types of budgets used in businesses.**

- *Operating budgets* are financial plans and control techniques for each financial responsibility center's revenues, expenses and profits. They include revenue budgets and expense budgets. Revenue budgets are forecasts and projections of the amount of income expected from all sources over a given period. Expense budgets project the outflow of dollars for a given period.

- *Financial budgets* detail how each financial responsibility center will manage its cash and capital expenditures. Thus, a cash budget and a capital expenditures budget are called for. Cash budgets are also known as cash flow budgets. They predict the amount of money from all sources that will flow into and out of an organization over a fixed period. In this way they are similar to their feedback control counterpart, the sources and uses of funds statement. This document, however, represents financial reality, rather than a projection.

11 **Describe the five major marketing control techniques used in businesses.**

- *Marketing research* is a feedforward technique. It consists of gathering and analyzing geographic, demographic and psychographic data. After being interpreted, these data become information needed to tailor products and services to specific market segments.

- *Test-marketing* is the introduction of new products and services to a specific identifiable population group to determine their marketability. The effects of various marketing activities, such as sales promotion and advertising, can also be gauged through test-marketing. By limiting what a company does to a small enough audience, test marketers can effectively measure and analyze the audience's reactions.

- *Marketing ratios* are used to measure, monitor and project activities and trends. Frequently used ratios are profit to sales, changes in sales volume to price changes, costs of selling to gross profits and sales calls to orders generated.

- *Sales quotas* are specified revenue targets, for a given time period, to be achieved by sales activities and personnel. They are often the basis for salespeople's compensation. A minimum sales volume must be met each pay period to justify the salesperson's salary or draw. Sales in excess of quota may be rewarded with bonuses or commissions in addition to salary.

- *Stockage,* or inventory levels must be measured and monitored. Too much inventory represents waste and cash unavailable for other uses. Also, inventories must be safeguarded, housed, insured, handled and counted. All these activities are expenses that may be excessive or unnecessary if inventories are better managed.

12 **Describe the six major human resource control techniques used in businesses.**

- *Statistical analysis* helps HR managers determine and control costs. By collecting and analyzing various data on such things as employee absenteeism, turnover, safety and performance, HR managers can measure and improve the effectiveness and efficiency of the company's operations.

- *Human asset valuation* is a control technique that views people as assets, not as expenses. Money spent on recruiting, hiring, training, developing and rewarding people is considered an investment in them. Therefore, their worth to an organization increases steadily over time, and their departure represents a considerable loss to the company. The emphasis shifts from arbitrarily laying off and downsizing burdensome liabilities to retaining valuable assets.

- *Training and development* represent a considerable expenditure for most companies, and those dollars need to be spent wisely. The best way to adjust to change and prevent problems is through training. People are given the knowledge, skills and attitudes needed to perform to standards. The subject matter or areas of training also become the basis for appraising people. They will be expected to exhibit the skills they were taught.

- *Performance appraisals* monitor and measure how people carry out their duties. How well they do so is the basis for either rewards or punishments. Appraisals help measure the effectiveness of all human resource activities. They are both feedback and concurrent controls.

- *Attitude surveys* show how employees feel about their employer. Attitude surveys ask questions about key processes, units and personnel in an organization, and they can be tailored to the specific unit being evaluated. After the answers are collected and analyzed, the results are given to management. In turn, the results can highlight what is going right in the workplace and where problems exist.

- *Management audits* are performed to ensure regulations (OSHA, EEOC) and policies (ethics) are being followed. These compliance audits provide management with data to determine how well the company is meeting established standards.

KEY TERMS

audit **509**

balance sheet **501**

budget **509**

concurrent control **494**

control process **488**

control system **494**

control technique **486**

controlling **486**

critical control point **495**

feedback control **494**

feedforward control **493**

financial budget **512**

financial ratio **505**

financial responsibility center **507**

human asset accounting **519**

income statement **501**

just in time (JIT) **518**

marketing research **513**

operating budget **512**

risk manager **486**

Six Sigma **489**

sources and uses of funds statement **504**

standard **486**

REVIEW QUESTIONS

1. How is planning related to controlling? In what ways is controlling part of the other management functions?

2. What happens first in the control process? How are its Steps 1 and 3 related? What will happen in the process if no deviations from established standards are discovered?

3. Can organizations function without controls? Explain.

4. Why must controls be integrated into a coherent system to work most effectively?

5. To be effective, what characteristics should feedforward, concurrent and feedback controls have?

6. What can managers do on a regular basis to increase the effectiveness of the controls they are using?

7. What does a balance sheet tell managers? An income statement? A sources and uses of funds statement?

8. What do the four primary financial ratios measure? Why is ratio analysis used by managers?

9. What is a standard cost center? A revenue center? A discretionary expense center? A profit center? An investment center? How do all five centers enter into the budget process?

10. How does top-down budgeting work? Bottom-up budgeting? Zero-based budgeting? Flexible budgeting? What are operating budgets? Financial budgets?

11. What are the five major marketing control techniques? How does each serve the needs of marketing managers?

12. What are the six major human resource control techniques? How does each serve the needs of human resource managers?

DISCUSSION QUESTIONS FOR CRITICAL THINKING

1. What kind of controls do you use regularly? What areas of your life seem to be, "out of control?" What can you do to bring them into control?

2. What are the critical control points in the effective and efficient operation of a motel? A fast-food restaurant?

3. You are the chief financial officer for a coffee shop. How will this year's balance sheet, income statement and sources and uses of funds statement help you budget for next year's operations?

4. You are the owner and manager of a neighborhood restaurant. Your chef has created what she calls, "a delicious, fat-free cheesecake that can be made with a variety of fresh fruit toppings." She wants to add her creation to the menu. Before approving the new menu item, what do you think you should do?

5. You have just received the following in a memo from your boss:

   As the above numbers point out, your division ranks below average on the basis of the most recent statistics for our industry. Your employee turnover is twice the normal rate and your absenteeism has risen by 50 percent since one year ago. Finally, your department's recent injuries have been the primary cause of a 15 percent increase in our workers' compensation insurance premiums.

   What control devices do you think were used to reach these conclusions? Are these increases related to one another? If so, in what ways?

Apply What You Know

Social Media Management Exercises

Social Bookmarking

Do you have favorites or bookmarks on your Internet browser? Does it need organizing? If so, you can use tags, words to describe your bookmark. Tagging is a method of categorizing online content with associated keywords, allowing you to create connections between data.

What if you aren't on your computer? Can you remember all of your favorite websites? Most of us want one list of favorite websites. Delicious is a social book-marking service that lets you save your favorite websites online and add tags to categorize them. The social networking aspect of Delicious allows you to share your bookmarks and see what others are bookmarking.

Explore Delicious by clicking on "About"; searching for bookmarks and tags; clicking on bookmarks and tags. How could a Delicious account help managers? Prepare a list of 10 bookmarks with tags that could help a manager. *http://www.delicious.com/*

Experiential Learning

Toshiba Adopts Six Sigma

After decades of leading the world in productivity, Japan's giant companies began to lose momentum in the late 1990s. Cost-consciousness, recession and fierce competition had taken hold. Toshiba had needed a makeover for years. Taizo Nishimuro, then-director and chairman of the board, was faced with the challenge of getting control of the company without reducing quality.

"If we do not change, the final destination is the collapse of the company," he told management and employees (Guth). He proposed that Toshiba adopt the Six Sigma method of measuring performance. "Six Sigma was devised by U.S. firm Motorola Inc. to slash the rate of inferior goods produced to less than three or four in a million" (Industry Search). Some managers at Toshiba argued that Six Sigma was a, "U.S. version of Japanese quality control."

Gradually, managers began to believe Nishimuro's warning. "In March 1998, Toshiba reported an 89 percent plunge in net income for the fiscal year," (Guth). Efforts at gaining control began by the reexamination of everything. The relative performances of Toshiba's businesses were assessed. After careful analysis of each business, some were kept and others were modified or eliminated. Toshiba's most valuable sectors included information and Internet services, semiconductors, electronic components and information technology goods.

In late 1998, all upper-management personnel began training in Six Sigma methodology, with a directive for all employees to apply Six Sigma to their everyday job functions. Toshiba cut costs and boosted productivity and profits by introducing Six Sigma into its culture. (Industry Search).

Toshiba also helped its suppliers get control. David Tronnes, vice president of manufacturing (Toner Products Division), explained the Partners Plus program: "The Partners Plus program is a re-engineering initiative launched between Toshiba and 19 suppliers responsible for 80 percent of the Toner Division's annual purchases." Teams from Toshiba make on-site partner visits and recommend improvements.

"The recommendations for change (proposals that can effectively be implemented for mutual benefit) can originate from either Toshiba or its partners. A partner's assessment committee determines the feasibility of a recommendation, assigns in-house responsibility and begins the investigation process. The recommendations are evaluated and either approved or denied by Toshiba and its appropriate partner" (Tronnes). Recommendations include attention to or improvements in the following areas: cost, quality and delivery; lead-time parameters; productivity and design system improvements; materials handling and sourcing as a factor in purchasing; business practices; logistics and transportation; accounting practices; and electronic data interchanges and electronic commerce. Tronnes reports that Partners Plus has led to a direct bottom-line improvement.

Questions

1. What caused the general lack of control at Toshiba and who do you think was primarily responsible for it?

2. What kinds of controls did the new Toshiba institute?

3. What characteristics of effective controls did the new Toshiba have? What controls did the company lack?

Sources: 2013 Toshiba America Business Solutions, Inc., "We guarantee no one matches our guarantee," *http://business.toshiba.com/media/downloads/about/TQC_Brochure.pdf*; David Tronnes, "Case Study: Toshiba Division Substantially Improves Its Bottom Line Through an Aggressive Supply Chain Management Program," *Manufacturing & Technology News*, 2001, *http://www.manufacturingnews.com/news/editorials/tronnes.html*; Rob Guth, "Restructuring a Behemoth: How Mr. Nishimuro Reinvented Toshiba," *Wall Street Journal*, December 27, 2000; "Quality Control Plan Hoped to Save Toshiba 130 Billion Yen in FY 2000," *Industry Search*, July 11, 2000; Toshiba, *http://www.toshiba.com*.

Appendices

Appendix A

Quality Management

LEARNING OBJECTIVES

After studying this chapter, you should be able to:

1 Discuss how customers influence the quality of goods and services

2 Explain why quality must be cost-effective

3 Relate quality, productivity, and profitability to one another

4 Determine the commitments required to improve quality and productivity at the following organizational levels: top, middle, and bottom

5 Describe the external commitments required to improve an organization's quality and productivity

Management in Action

Productivity

Productivity is a relative measure of the quantity of output per time spent. Thus, the most productive people accomplish more in less time than others. They are life-long learners and know where to find information when needed. In like manner, the most productive managers are efficient, getting the most from organizational resources, whether people or products.

Results come from "doing it smarter." For each of the following statements, circle the appropriate corresponding number in the columns below. Rate your agreement as it is, not what you think it should be. Objectivity will enable you to determine your management skill strengths and weaknesses.

	Almost Always	Often	Sometimes	Rarely	Almost Never
It is easy for me to speak my mind.	5	4	3	2	1
I am comfortable talking about problems and disagreements.	5	4	3	2	1
I share information about what works, as well as what doesn't.	5	4	3	2	1
I am interested in new ways of doing things.	5	4	3	2	1
I am open to alternative ways of doing things.	5	4	3	2	1
I acknowledge my limitations with respect to knowledge, information or expertise.	5	4	3	2	1
I invest time in self-improvement.	5	4	3	2	1
I spend time reflecting.	5	4	3	2	1
I value education and training.	5	4	3	2	1
I listen carefully, without interrupting.	5	4	3	2	1

Add up the numbers you circled. Your total score will be between 10 and 50. The higher your score, the more likely you are to be productive in the workplace. A lower score implies a lesser degree of readiness, but it can be increased. Reading and studying this chapter will help you to improve your understanding of productivity.

➡ A productive person is a learner. How do you know you are learning? How do you know you are doing things correctly? How does that benefit an organization?

INTRODUCTION

From the beginning of mass production in America, producing quantity and controlling costs were the major concerns. In early factories a large number of unskilled laborers performed narrowly defined tasks, producing goods composed of interchangeable parts for mass markets under the supervision of engineers. Workers were taught their tasks and were expected to perform them exactly; they were not asked for their opinions or suggestions. Because the demand for goods in most industries exceeded supply until the late 1920s, nearly everything produced could be sold.

By the early 1900s, inspection and inspectors were standard fixtures in most industrial plants. Inspectors were charged with the duty of weeding out defective parts before the products were shipped to customers.[1] Often, operations were not inspected until they were out of control and producing defective outputs. Until the early 1970s, quality was defined in most companies as the production of goods and services without defects and was primarily the concern of production engineers. "In its early days quality control was a dimension of cost control, with the emphasis on eliminating waste."[2]

The primary difference between today's managers and their counterparts of the past is their definition of quality and the recognition that quality and efficiency are primary concerns affecting every operation and employee, not just those involved with production. Quality is now defined as the ability of a product or service to meet or exceed customer expectations and needs. Consider Toyota Motor Corporation. The Japanese company's management recognizes that the product must be satisfying in terms of quality, design and price to its customers. "Production is based on demand—pull, not pushing it out into the market. Processes are based on doing things just-in-time. If there is demand for a product, then it is made. Products aren't made in an anticipatory mode. That would be a form of waste. Of muda."[3] At Toyota, concern for quality begins with the customer.

Also, the definition of a customer has been expanded to include those inside organizations. Attention to meeting customers' needs now begins with the inception of a new product, service and process. It is linked to how effectively and efficiently each person and process functions. The table that follows compares manufacturing models of the past with those of today.

MANUFACTURING MODELS	
Mass Production 1920	**Quality Production 1980**
Standardized product focused on volume not quality	Focus on internal/external customer
Management makes decisions	Employees work in teams
Training for limited skills	Extensive, continuous training
Little discretion; simplified tasks	Some discretion; team accountability
Quality is inspected	Quality built in

1
Discuss how customers influence the quality of goods and services

QUALITY, PRODUCTIVITY, AND PROFITABILITY

Joseph M. Juran, a pioneer thinker on and advocate for quality, advises companies to focus on "product performance [which generates] product satisfaction"[4] and to produce products and services free of deficiencies that create external and internal customer dissatisfaction. Performance can mean the ability of a machine to deliver flawless output, the capability of a department or team to fill an order quickly and without errors, or the handling characteristics of an automobile. Deficiencies cause users and customers to reject or complain about products and services.

For example, when internal customers' (employees') needs for information are not met, their ability to perform may be adversely affected. They may waste time and other resources while they search for what they need. In turn, they may provide inadequate inputs to their internal customers. External customers often compare the performance characteristics of competing products as one step in their buying decisions. "A product may have no deficiencies and yet be unsalable because some competing product has better product performance."[5] Figure A.1 shows that product design should begin with consumer research.

Figure A.1 Hypothetical Customer Satisfaction Model

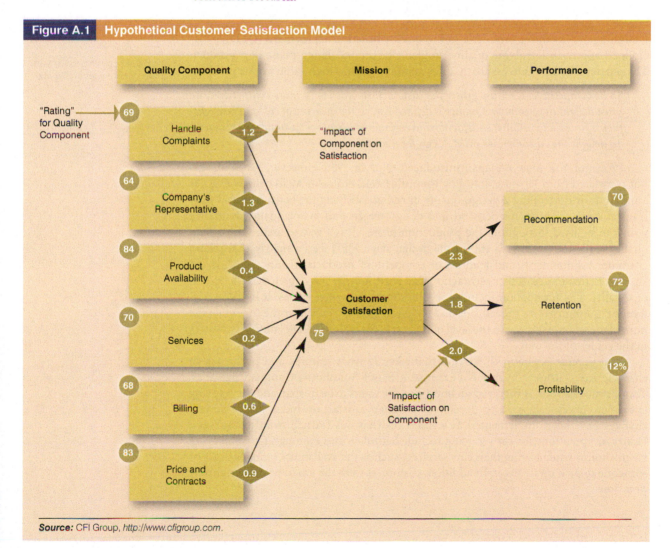

Source: CFI Group, http://www.cfigroup.com.

Quality features originate with an organization's internal and external designers, producers, users, and customers. Features and characteristics are those aspects of the product, service, process or project that lead to satisfaction or dissatisfaction. Satisfaction depends on the users' or customers' perceptions that a product or service will meet or exceed their needs or expectations.

The American Customer Satisfaction Index (ACSI) is a national economic indicator of satisfaction with the quality of products and services available to U.S. household consumers. It was introduced in 1994, and since that date, scores for one or two sectors of the U.S. economy have been updated each quarter. The index is produced by asking customers of specific companies to rate their overall satisfaction, which is then compared to their expectations. Customer satisfaction and financial returns can be correlated. In general, firms with the top ACSI scores generate greater shareholder wealth than firms with the lower scores. Professor Claes Fornell, key ACSI faculty member at the University of Michigan, said, "If accounting were to incorporate customer satisfaction as an asset on the balance sheet, we would have a better understanding of the relationship between a company's current condition and its future capacity to produce wealth."[6]

Quality Function Deployment

Designing quality into a product is key to **quality function deployment (QFD)**, a disciplined approach to solving quality problems before the design phase of a product. The purpose of QFD is to assure that the customer obtains high value from a product.

> To be competitive, we must satisfy the customer. In order to be more competitive, we must delight the customer. Quality is defined here as the measure of customer delightment. Note that customer satisfaction is a region on the scale of customer delightment. To delight the customer, we must design for quality.[7]

Professor Yoji Akao of Japan introduced QFD in 1966. However, his book was not translated from Japanese into English until 1994.[8] Professor Akao defines QFD as a method for developing a design quality aimed at satisfying the consumer and then translating the consumer's demand into design targets and major quality assurance points to be used throughout the production phase.[9] It is a way to assure the design quality while the product is still in the design stage. QFD uses a matrix that relates customer requirements and features of competitors' products to functional design characteristics and customer satisfaction. In Figure A.2, QFD is depicted as the House of Quality. The foundation includes specifications and target values. It lists the customer requirements on the left side and technical requirements near the top while the important relationships with the level of importance are shown in Relationship Matrix in the center of the tool.

The process begins with surveys that identify what features and performance characteristics customers value. For example, at Sewell Automotive Company in Dallas, Texas, each customer is surveyed on how he or she wants to be treated, and the ongoing customer surveys are used to develop a customer satisfaction index (CSI). Several changes have been implemented as a result of what was learned from the surveys. Hours of operations for car servicing include Saturdays and evenings. Customers are given choices while having their cars serviced, such as the availability of loaner cars or someone to pick up their car. In addition, customers want the job to be done right the first time.

quality function deployment (QFD)

A disciplined approach to solving quality problems before the design phase of a product

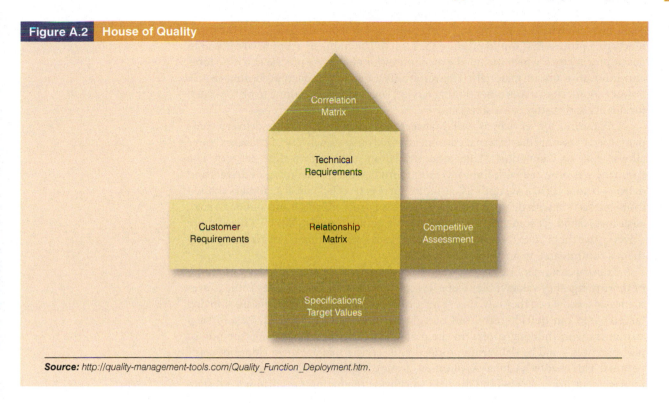

Figure A.2 House of Quality

Source: http://quality-management-tools.com/Quality_Function_Deployment.htm.

benchmark

The product to meet or beat in terms of design, manufacture, performance and service

In QFD, if a competing product already exists, a sample is purchased and disassembled to determine its particular characteristics. The best of the competing products becomes a **benchmark**—the product to meet or beat in terms of design, manufacture, performance and service. "Benchmarking is an improvement process in which a company measures its performance against that of best-in-class companies, determines how those companies achieved their performance levels, and uses the information to improve its own performance. The subjects that can be benchmarked include strategies, operations, processes and procedures."[10]

A benchmark for the Sewell Automotive Company is Disney World. In the chapter "Selling Should Be Theater" of his book with Paul B. Brown, *Customers for Life: How to Turn That One-Time Buyer into a Lifelong Customer,* Carl Sewell says:

> *I love Disney World.… [It's] the image we keep in mind when we're thinking about how our stores should look. We make sure the grass is always cut. I picked out every tree and bush. And we make sure the buildings are freshly painted.… (We even bought a street sweeper so that we'd be able to clean the roads in front of our dealerships.) Why devote all this attention to the grounds? Because we're setting a tone.… And it tells people what our values are; it's in keeping with the kind of customer we want to attract.*[11]

Toyota used QFD to design and build the Lexus LS 400, the first Lexus to be developed. In the initial stages of product design, Toyota purchased competing cars from Mercedes, Jaguar, and BMW. Toyota engineers tested the cars rigorously, disassembled them and studied the parts. The engineers were convinced that Toyota could match or exceed 11 performance goals, including goals relating to weight, fuel economy, aerodynamics and noise. Toyota continued to refine the design and the manufacturing process that would produce the LS 400. The company spent $500 million in development costs, which included expenditures for new, more precise machine tools and innovative use of materials. The result was a quality product; according to J.D. Power & Associates, a consumer polling service, Lexus models continue to be top-rated for quality and customer satisfaction.

QFD works for services as well. Managers at UPS, a large package-delivery company, used to assume that external customers prized on-time delivery of packages above all else. Like its competitors, UPS concentrated on providing on-time delivery. The company was obsessed with time and motion studies, exact scheduling of drivers and delivery before 10:30 A.M., until its customer surveys revealed that "Customers wanted more interaction with drivers…. If drivers were less [rushed] and more willing to chat, customers could get some practical advice on shipping."[12] As a result, UPS hired more drivers, gave them 30 extra minutes per day to visit with customers, and began paying them a commission on any leads that created sales.

External customers' needs and wants keep changing. "Customers today want more of those things they value. If they value low cost, they want it lower. If they value convenience or speed when they buy, they want it easier and faster."[13] Customers are "moving targets" who can quickly travel out of sight. Organizations cannot attract and keep customers with thinking rooted in the past—by failing to think outside the box of past practices—and by delivering products and services that are mere clones of competitors'. This chapter's Global Applications feature highlights "The Toyota Way"—the management principles behind Toyota's worldwide reputation for customer satisfaction and quality.

Consultants and authors Michael Treacy and Fred Wiersema believe that the companies that please their customers best commit to one or a combination of three long-term value disciplines: (1) operational excellence; (2) product leadership; and (3) customer intimacy.[14] PetSmart and Walmart exemplify the first. They provide low prices, inviting environments and unique and dependable service. Rubbermaid (a maker of household products), Nike (the athletic shoes maker) and 3M (the maker of office and consumer products) demonstrate the second discipline. All three thrive on generating vast numbers of cutting-edge products annually that truly delight their users.

An example of the third discipline is Enterprise Rent-A-Car Company. Such a company tailors its offerings to meet customers' needs at reasonable costs. "They are adept at giving the customer more than he or she expects. By constantly upgrading offerings, customer-intimate companies stay ahead of customers' rising expectations—expectations that, by the way, they themselves create."[15]

Total Quality Management   Robert Costello, an engineer and former GM executive, was the undersecretary of defense for acquisitions when he built on the work of Deming, Juran, Crosby and others to create **total quality management (TQM)** for the Department of Defense. The department's TQM Master Plan defined TQM as

> *a strategy for continuously improving performance at every level, and in all areas of responsibility. It combines fundamental management techniques, existing improvement efforts and specialized technical tools under a disciplined structure focused on continuously improving all processes. Improved performance is directed at satisfying such broad goals as cost, quality, schedule and mission need and suitability. Increasing user satisfaction is the overriding objective.*

The Toyota Way

In the United States and globally, Toyota expands without acquisitions. Toyota sets up assembly plants without local partners. It teaches the locals how to build Toyotas.

Jeffrey K. Liker, professor of Industrial and Operations Engineering at the University of Michigan, is author of *The Toyota Way: 14 Management Principles from the World's Greatest Manufacturer*, (McGraw-Hill). It is the first book for a general audience explaining the management principles used by Toyota. In the book, Professor Liker discusses these principles:

Management Principles From the World's Greatest Manufacturer

1 Base your management decisions on a long-term philosophy, even at the expense of short-term goals.
2 Create continuous process flow to bring problems to the surface.
3 Use "pull" systems to avoid overproduction.
4 Level out the workload (*heijunka*). (Work like the tortoise, not the hare.)
5 Build a culture of stopping to fix problems, to get quality right the first time.
6 Standardized tasks are the foundation for continuous improvement and employee empowerment.
7 Use visual control so that no problems are hidden.
8 Use only reliable, thoroughly tested technology that serves your people and processes.
9 Grow leaders who thoroughly understand the work, live the philosophy and teach it to others.
10 Develop exceptional people and teams who follow your company's philosophies.
11 Respect your extended network of partners and suppliers by challenging them and helping them to improve.
12 Go and see for yourself to thoroughly understand the situation (*Genchi Genbutsu*).
13 Make decisions slowly by consensus, thoroughly considering all options; implement decisions rapidly.
14 Become a learning organization through relentless reflection (*hansei*) and continuous improvement (*kaizen*).

➡ **Toyota's formula for success rests in its corporate philosophy and its ability to hire individuals who embody that philosophy. Toyota hires employees early in their careers before they are exposed to another company's culture. The first step in the hiring process for prospective managers is to view a video about Toyota's culture. How does this practice ensure employees will learn the Toyota Way?**

➡ **Why do you think Toyota describes prospective employees as open and flexible with a willingness and a desire to learn the Toyota Way?**

Figure A.3 is the seven-step model the Department of Defense developed to illustrate TQM. In step 1, the organization establishes the TQM environment. Step 2 defines the mission for each component or subsystem of the organization. Step 3 requires the setting of performance improvement opportunities; it establishes the strategic planning process. In step 4, managers or managers and their subordinates define improvement projects and plans for action. In step 5, the projects are implemented through use of the appropriate tools and techniques. (You will read more about implementation later in this chapter.) Step 6 is the evaluation phase, in which results—cycle times, costs, efficiency, and innovation—are evaluated. Step 7 mandates feedback so that processes can be continuously improved.

TQM Principles TQM is also known by and practiced under several other labels. At not-for-profit colleges, universities and hospitals, it is known as *continuous quality improvement,* or CQI; at 3M, it is known as *managing total quality;* at Xerox, the large office equipment maker, it is called *leadership through quality.* In Japanese companies, it is called *total quality control (TQC).* The Toyota Production System is referred to as *lean manufacturing, lean production* or *lean.* No matter what the name is, its concepts and principles are the same by and large:[16]

- Quality improvements create productivity gains.
- Quality is defined as conformance to requirements that satisfy user needs.

Figure A.3   **The Seven-Step TQM Model**

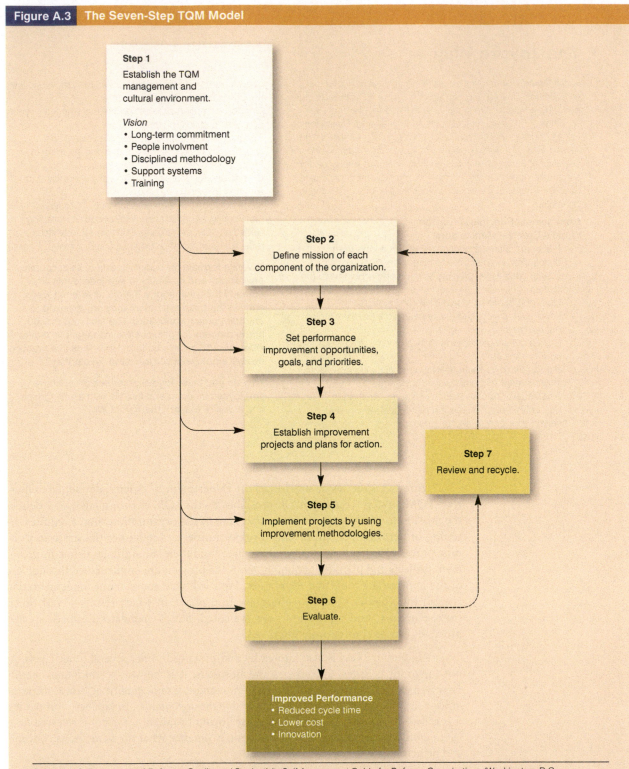

Step 1

Establish the TQM management and cultural environment.

Vision
- Long-term commitment
- People involvment
- Disciplined methodology
- Support systems
- Training

Step 2
Define mission of each component of the organization.

Step 3
Set performance improvement opportunities, goals, and priorities.

Step 4
Establish improvement projects and plans for action.

Step 7
Review and recycle.

Step 5
Implement projects by using improvement methodologies.

Step 6
Evaluate.

Improved Performance
- Reduced cycle time
- Lower cost
- Innovation

Source: U.S. Department of Defense, *Quality and Productivity Self-Assessment Guide for Defense Organizations* (Washington, D.C. Department of Defense, 1990).

- Quality is measured by continual process and product improvement as well as user satisfaction.
- Quality is determined by product design and achieved by effective process controls.
- Process-control techniques are used to prevent defects.
- Quality is part of every function in all phases of the product life cycle.
- Management is responsible for quality.
- Relationships with suppliers are formed for the long term and are quality oriented.

As Thomas J. Barry wrote, "TQM/TQC is a journey, not a destination. It is a systematic, strategic process for organizational excellence."[17]

Explain why quality must be cost-effective

COST-EFFECTIVE QUALITY

As the previous chapters indicate, meeting and exceeding customers' needs and expectations should be a primary aim of any organization. Companies that exceed customer needs both effectively and efficiently will succeed in their markets and surpass their rivals. But organizations and their people must "make sure that the quality they offer is the quality their customers want…. Quality that means little to customers doesn't produce a payoff in improved sales, profits or market share. It's wasted effort and expense."[18] Satisfying customers while focusing on the bottom line helps to guarantee that companies will not price products and services out of their markets.

Money spent on quality leads to efficiencies if it saves an organization from having to spend a relatively greater amount on repairing defects. "The cost of quality is the cost of avoiding nonconformance [to company and customer] standards and failure. Maintaining quality helps you avoid compounding costs you would incur from the deviation of not doing the right thing the first time."[19] When quality is viewed as conformance to standards, then lack of quality means a conformance failure has occurred.

Philip B. Crosby, manager, author and consultant, wrote, "Quality improvement is built on getting everyone to do it right the first time (DIRFT). But the key to DIRFT is getting requirements clearly understood and then not putting things in people's way."[20] Crosby identified the cost of poor quality as, basically, inefficiency or "the expense of doing things wrong. It is the scrap, rework, service after service, warranty, inspection, tests and similar activities made necessary by nonconformance problems."[21]

At Xerox Corporation, managers take three measurements to determine the cost of quality. They compute the cost of conformance, the cost of nonconformance, and the cost of lost opportunities.[22] Conformance requires continual measurement of work outputs against known customer requirements. Nonconformance costs are those connected with not meeting customer needs and time lost by having to go back and do things over. Lost opportunities are customers and profits lost due to lack of quality.

Productivity

productivity
The relationship between the amount of input needed to produce a given amount of output and the output itself; usually expressed as a ratio

Productivity, in its most common form, is the relationship between the amount of input needed to produce a given amount of output and the output itself. Productivity is usually expressed as the ratio of inputs to outputs.

Output (inputs produced)/Input (hours of human labor, machining time, or dollars invested) = Productivity Index (PI)

Such a ratio is a measure of efficiency that can be used to make comparisons and identify trends.

Productivity can be improved by increasing the amount of output generated by a fixed amount of input, or reducing the amount of input required to generate a fixed amount of output, or a combination of both approaches. Through both *kaizen* (gradual) and reengineering (revolutionary) approaches, processes and their related activities can be made more efficient or eliminated.

Efforts to improve productivity must improve product and process quality, and vice versa. Automating work makes workers more productive, resulting in faster, better and less expensive products and services. Jobs with relatively clear-cut, predictable activities like production or clerical positions are easier to automate than those of knowledge workers like managers, salespeople and scientists. To increase the productivity of knowledge workers, companies can create communities of practice (CoP), more commonly referred to as learning communities, the topic of this chapter's Managing Social Media.

The money saved through increased productivity can be allocated to further improve organizational operations. Improving productivity in an organization paves the way for improvements in its employees' standards of living and quality of life. This chapter's Quality Management feature discusses adding value to a product.

Quality Management

Value Added

The basis for any business activity is exchange, the process by which two or more parties give something of value to each other to satisfy each party's perceived needs. This "something of value" for the business is the product and for the customer is the money spent on the product.

During the production process, raw materials are physically transformed to the finished product. *Value* refers to the activities the customer is willing to pay for. Thus, *value added* is any activity that increases the market form or function of the product. *Non-value added* is any activity that does not add market form or function or is not necessary. The *value stream* is all of the processes required to get the product from production to the customer.

A fundamental exercise in the development of the value stream is to compare value-added and non-value added practices. If a production practice does not create value, it is wasteful and should be eliminated or minimized. Non-value activity should be redirected into value-added activity. The production team focuses on value stream efficiency, making the production process more "lean." This results in quality at the source; production cost declines as quality improves.

The following is a list of questions the production team might ask to determine if a process is a *non-value-added* activity.

1 Is this activity necessary?
2 Can this activity be simplified?
3 Does this part or material add value to the product?
4 Could a cheaper part or material be used?
5 Could standard parts be substituted for nonstandard parts?
6 Can two or more parts be replaced by a single part for a lower cost?

➡ **Sherwin-Williams revolutionized the paint can with the Twist and Pour paint package, which requires no tools to open or close. It is a space-efficient, square-shaped plastic container with twist-off lid, comfortable side handle, and easy pouring spout. Users have a new way to mix, brush and store paint. What are some other real-world value-added product examples?**

Learning Communities

Managers have discovered that forming learning communities improves their productivity. Members of the community are practitioners sharing their competence, learning from each other, and benefiting from one another's advice.

One of the best known, early examples of CoP (communities of practice) is one formed by the copy machine repair technicians at Xerox Corporation. Through networking and sharing their experiences, particularly the problems they encountered and the solutions they devised, a core group of these technicians proved extremely effective in improving the efficiency and effectiveness of efforts to diagnose and repair Xerox customers' copy machines. The impact on customer satisfaction and the business value to Xerox was invaluable. Yet, for the most part, this was a voluntary, informal gathering and sharing of expertise, not a "corporate program" (however, once the company realized the value of the knowledge being created by this CoP, steps were taken to support and enhance the efforts of the group). *(Fred Nichols,* Communities of Practice An Overview, *2003, http://www.nickols.us/CoPOverview.pdf)*

Today, social networking tools allow members to locate the right people, engage in discussions, share information and learn together. Geographic distances and differences in time zones are no longer barriers to collaboration.

The learning community shares their practices, which may include case studies, methods of problem solving and other activities shown in the table that follows. These, along with the contact and biographical information of members, become the knowledge base for the members to search.

Examples of Learning Community Activities

Problem solving	"Can we work on this design and brainstorm some ideas; I'm stuck."
Requests for information	"Where can I find the code to connect to the server?"
Seeking experience	"Has anyone dealt with a customer in this situation?"
Reusing assets	"I have a proposal for a local area network I wrote for a client last year. I can send it to you, and you can easily tweak it for this new client."
Coordination and synergy	"Can we combine our purchases of solvent to achieve bulk discounts?"
Discussing developments	"What do you think of the new system? Does it really help?"
Documentation projects	"We have faced this problem five times now. Let us write it down once and for all."
Visits	"Can we come and see your program? We need to establish one in our company."
Mapping knowledge and identifying gaps	"Who knows what, and what are we missing? What other groups should we connect with?"

➡ **Which social networking tools—blogs, wikis, Facebook, LinkedIn, Twitter, YouTube, etc.—do you think is best suited for learning communities' interactions? Explain your answer.**

Source: Etienne and Beverly Wenger-Trayner, "Communities of practice a brief introduction; April 15, 2015, *http://wenger-trayner.com/introduction-to-communities-of-practice/.*

QUALITY–PRODUCTIVITY–PROFITABILITY LINK

3 Relate quality, productivity, and profitability to one another

Profitability results when income received by a firm exceeds the cost of paying its bills. The profitability of a firm depends on its ability to efficiently produce goods and services that please its customers. "No matter how high the quality, if the product is overpriced it cannot gain customer satisfaction."[23]

W. Edwards Deming believed companies that focused on improving quality would accrue fundamental benefits. Such companies decrease costs by reducing mistakes and waste, reducing the need to rework parts and improving productivity. Improving quality, said Deming, can also help companies capture markets, ensure their future and provide more jobs. To Deming, improving quality caused a chain reaction of benefits: "Continual reduction in mistakes, continual improvement of quality, mean lower and lower costs. Less rework in manufacturing. Less waste—less waste of materials, machine time, tools, human effort."[24] Figure A.4 provides a visual representation of Deming's chain reaction.

U.S. automakers have improved their quality, but still have not caught up with the Japanese automakers.

Figure A.4   Deming's Chain Reaction: The Quality-Productivity-Profitability Link

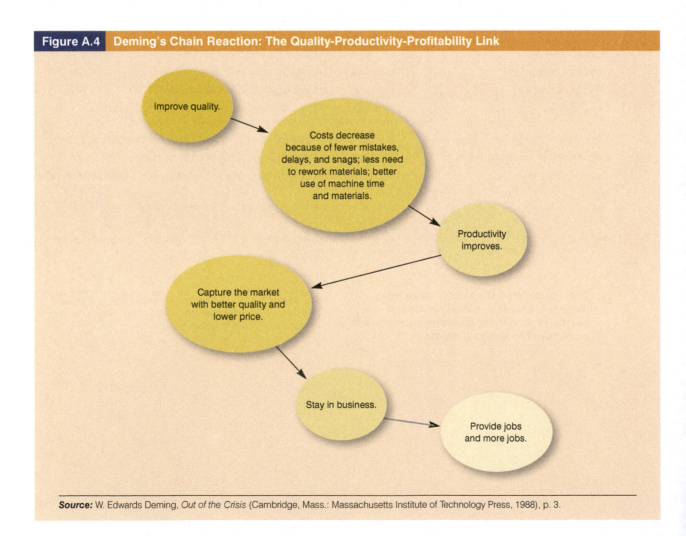

Source: W. Edwards Deming, *Out of the Crisis* (Cambridge, Mass.: Massachusetts Institute of Technology Press, 1988), p. 3.

This lingering gap prefigures a continuing slide in market share, but now another dimension may be of greater concern to the Big Three: over the past few years, consumers have changed their ideas about what defines quality—a shift that is making the uphill climb for U.S. automakers even more steep. Though buying decisions once emphasized quality defined as minimizing the number of defects in a car, consumers are now focusing more on maximizing the appeal of a handful of core product attributes—for example, whether the car is fun to drive, well designed, or stylish.[25]

Thus the definition of quality for the consumer is evolving to include intangible attributes such as design. Today, products must have high quality and their designs must appeal to the consumer. Since design attributes are intangible, they are much harder to measure than defects.

Improving Quality and Productivity

To produce significant, ongoing quality and productivity gains requires a 100 percent commitment from everyone involved. Raytheon, the subject of this chapter's Ethical Management, is committed to providing quality to its customers while maintaining ethics and integrity. As many organizations have discovered, efforts to improve have failed for two main reasons—the changes were neither companywide nor committed, and they were too dependent on too few people. As Patrick Townsend and Joan Gebhardt, writers who address quality issues, observed:

Partial understanding of and involvement in quality can produce only partial success or total failure. The only chance for a quality process to truly succeed is for a company to simultaneously attack all the issues: Leadership, participation and measurement.[26]

The same can be said as well for the pursuit of productivity gains.

Commitment to productivity and quality improvements means changes in employee thinking, methods and approaches to the identification and solution of problems. These modifications mean changes to widely held attitudes, beliefs, values, philosophies and habits of interacting. For example, an undated publication by Motorola, *The New Truths of Quality,* lists "old truths" and "new truths." The old truth said: "To err is human." The new truth says: "Perfection—total customer satisfaction—is the standard." And companies have discovered a new truth for productivity as well: "Never be satisfied with efficiency improvements."

Joseph Juran cautions that moving toward improvement means change; change breeds resistance and fear. The existing, usually diverse ways of doing things in an organization provide support and social networks. "Any proposed changes are a potential threat to the stability of the pattern and thereby a potential threat to the well-being of the members."[27] Juran's list of rules to minimize resistance to change within an organization include these seven:

1 Provide participation.
2 Provide enough time.
3 Keep proposals free of excess baggage.
4 Work with the recognized leadership.
5 Treat people with dignity.
6 Take the other person's point of view.
7 Look at the alternatives.

ASQ (American Society for Quality) Code of Ethics

Fundamental Principles

ASQ requires its members and certification holders to conduct themselves ethically by:

1 Being honest and impartial in serving the public, their employers, customers and clients.

2 Striving to increase the competence and prestige of the quality profession

3 Using their knowledge and skill for the enhancement of human welfare.

Members and certification holders are required to observe the tenets set forth below:

Relations with the Public

Article 1 – Hold paramount the safety, health and welfare of the public in the performance of their professional duties.

Relations with Employers, Customers and Clients

Article 2 – Perform services only in their areas of competence.

Article 3 – Continue their professional development throughout their careers and provide opportunities for the professional and ethical development of others.

Article 4 – Act in a professional manner in dealings with ASQ staff and each employer, customer or client.

Article 5 – Act as faithful agents or trustees and avoid conflict of interest and the appearance of conflicts of interest.

Relations with Peers

Article 6 – Build their professional reputation on the merit of their services and not compete unfairly with others.

Article 7 – Assure that credit for the work of others is given to those to whom it is due.

➡ **Why do you think ASQ publishes a code of ethics?**

Source: *http://asq.org/about-asq/who-we-are/ethics.html.*

Business Process Reengineering (BPR) Approaches

Defined in Chapter 2, reengineering is an approach for making changes that inevitably affect quality and productivity improvements. Reengineering requires that individuals and organizations "think in terms of processes—order fulfillment, for example—that may extend across many departments, and that they organize their work accordingly.... The goal, in addition to reducing costs, must be to … respond quickly and effectively to [one's] customers."[28] But every change anywhere in a company has ripple effects, as Michael Hammer's words indicate: "A sales [representative] has to recognize that his job … is acquiring orders, and that's a process in which he is only one player—it's a process that includes the finance people, the marketing people and others."[29]

Remember that the *kaizen* approach to improvement calls for gradual but continual efforts. Reengineering calls for an ongoing questioning of the need to do everything through a continuing investigation of its why and how. The aims are to determine what no longer needs to be done, what must be done, and how to better execute those processes. Says Michael Hammer, "We have to teach everybody in the organization to be creative, out-of-the-box thinkers. They need to think creatively about how they do their work."[30] Toyota's surge in productivity indicates that its management thinks "out of the box." So, too, do the managers at 3M by encouraging all their employees to research their own ideas on company time and with company resources. Google encourages innovation by giving its engineers 20 percent of their time to develop new product or service offerings, or to provide enhancements to current offerings. Some of the results include Google news, Gmail and Google Self-Driving Car.

Reengineering changes fundamental ways in which people and their organizations handle their processes. Typical results of reengineering have been to change organizations' missions, visions, values, activities and structures. Some companies have tried to practice reengineering by blindly cutting jobs, not necessarily the work they contained. The result has been more work for fewer people and the resulting insecurity, fear and stress. James Champy says that this should not happen. "Reengineering and downsizing are not synonymous…. But the two do overlap because in most reengineering, you learn to do work with dramatically fewer people."[31]

Michael Hammer wrote the book *Beyond Reengineering* to build on his earlier work and to advance the concept of the process-centered enterprise. He explained why companies have only limited success with their process redesign efforts: "Reengineering enables a company to create greatly improved operational processes; to harness their power, however, the company itself must become a process-centered enterprise."[32]

To determine which processes have customer value and which do not, Hammer says:

> *Simply map the process end to end, including both what you do and what the customer does. Then ask yourself, 'Are there redundancies here? Is anything being done more than once? What could be eliminated without affecting the ultimate outcome? Are there things that have only indirect value and need to be minimized?'*[33]

Thus, business process reengineering is a diagnostic tool that can point to long-term opportunities, eliminating all non-value-added activities.

The remainder of this section focuses on the essential commitments and elements needed by any organization to improve its quality, productivity, and profitability. We begin with top management's role.

4a Determine the commitments required to improve quality and productivity at the top of organizations

COMMITMENTS AT THE TOP

Starting with their own commitments, managers at every level must try to obtain every employee's personal commitment to participate in both quality and productivity improvement efforts. Once gained, personal commitments are sustained as long as progress toward improvement continues. Therefore, the need exists to continually carry on the struggle. Leadership begins at the top, but, as Chapter 1 indicates, it must exist at every organizational level, in every unit, and in every team.

Ford Motor Company redesigned itself in the 1980s through the efforts of top management. In 1981 Ford's president, Donald E. Petersen, invited W. Edwards Deming to speak to Ford executives. Refusing to talk about quality as it related to automobiles, Deming insisted on talking about Ford's management philosophy and corporate culture. Deming cross-examined executives on their thinking about quality. When asked to define quality, none could. When asked about their roles in quality assurance, managers talked about administration, not what Deming had in mind: commitment from the top to facilitate quality improvement. When asked by managers why America was having trouble competing with the Japanese, Deming answered angrily, "The answer is—MANAGEMENT!"[34]

Ford was one of the first American companies to embrace Deming's teachings on quality. As Donald E. Petersen wrote, "I agree with Dr. Deming's philosophy of management, and I especially liked the emphasis he placed on the importance of people. In fact, we hired him as a consultant, and I made a point of meeting with him myself roughly once a month."[35] Early efforts at implementing TQM at Ford included teaching all employees, not just quality control inspectors, how to use statistical process control (a technique discussed later in the chapter). As Petersen observed, "When something's going wrong, 80 percent of the time there's something wrong with the way your production system or process is functioning."[36]

Later, Ford's TQM program dealt with removing fear from the workplace, developing trust in people, and building a supportive structure for the concept of continuous improvement. Ford executives began to ask questions: "What's our culture?" "What do we stand for?" As Petersen put it, "Dr. Deming's philosophy, expressed in his [14 points for improving quality], helped many of us zero in on some of the key concepts we wanted to express."[37] See Figure A.5 for Deming's 14 points. After their many meetings with Deming, Ford's top management rewrote their mission and values. Today, Ford is transforming itself with ONE Ford plan, shown in Figure A.6.

Figure A.5	Deming's Fourteen Points for Improving Quality

1 **Create a constancy of purpose for improvement of product and service.** Rather than to make money, the purpose of a company is to stay in business and provide jobs through innovation, research, constant improvement and maintenance.

2 **Adopt the new philosophy.** Americans are too tolerant of poor workmanship and sullen service. We need a new "religion" in which mistakes and negativism are unacceptable.

3 **Cease dependence on mass inspection.** American firms typically inspect a product as it comes off the assembly line or at major stages along the way; defective products are either thrown out or reworked. Both practices are unnecessarily expensive. In effect, a company is paying workers to make defects and then correct them. Quality comes not from inspection but from improvement of the process. With instruction, workers can be enlisted in this improvement.

4 **End the practice of awarding business on the price tag alone.** Purchasing departments customarily operate on orders to seek the lowest-priced vendor. Frequently, this leads to supplies of low quality. Instead, buyers should seek the best quality in a long-term relationship with a single supplier for any one item.

5 **Improve constantly and forever the system of production and service.** Improvement is not a one-time effort. Management is obligated to continually look for ways to reduce waste and improve quality.

6 **Institute training.** Too often, workers have learned their jobs from other workers who were never trained properly. They are forced to follow unintelligible instructions. They cannot do their jobs well because no one tells them how to do so.

7 **Institute leadership.** The job of a supervisor is not to tell people what to do nor to punish them, but to lead. Leading consists of helping people do a better job and of learning by objective methods who is in need of individual help.

8 **Drive out fear.** Many employees are afraid to ask questions or to take a position, even when they do not understand what their job is or what is right or wrong. They will continue to do things the wrong way or not do them at all. The economic losses from fear are appalling. To promote better quality and productivity, people must feel secure.

9 **Break down barriers between staff areas.** Often a company's departments or units are competing with each other or have goals that conflict. They do not work as a team so they can solve or foresee problems. Worse, one department's goals may cause trouble for another.

10 **Eliminate slogans, exhortations and targets for the workforce.** These never helped anybody do a good job. Let workers formulate their own slogans.

11 **Eliminate numerical quotas.** Quotas take into account only numbers, not quality or methods. They are usually a guarantee of inefficiency and high cost. To hold a job, a person might meet a quota at any cost, without regard to damage to the company.

12 **Remove barriers to pride of workmanship.** People are eager to do a good job and are distressed when they cannot. Too often, misguided supervisors, faulty equipment and defective materials stand in the way of good performance. These barriers must be removed.

13 **Institute a vigorous program of education and retraining.** Both management and the workforce will have to be educated in the new methods these points promote, including teamwork and statistical techniques.

14 **Take action to accomplish the transformation.** It will require a special top-management team with a plan of action to carry out the quality mission. Workers cannot do it on their own, nor can managers.

Source: Based on material in *Deming Management at Work* by Mary Walton (New York: Putnam). Copyright © 1990 Mary Walton.

Figure A.6 **ONE** FORD

ONE FORD

ONE TEAM • ONE PLAN • ONE GOAL

ONE TEAM

People working together as a lean, global enterprise for automotive leadership, as measured by:

Customer, Employee, Dealer, Investor, Supplier, Union/ Council, and Community Satisfaction

ONE PLAN

- Aggressively restructure to operate profitably at the current demand and changing model mix

- Accelerate development of new products our customers want and value

- Finance our plan and improve our balance sheet

- Work together effectively as one team

ONE GOAL

An exciting viable Ford delivering profitable growth for all

Source: http://corporate.ford.com/dynamic/metatags/article-detail/one-ford.

Managers must be willing, in James Champy's words, "to let go of control, in terms of letting other people make decisions, particularly when they affect customers. You've got to do that in order to grow."[38]

Empowered individuals and teams give enormous flexibility to organizations. Decisions are made at the lowest level possible, allowing for quick responses to users' and customers' demands. But empowered individuals and teams will get the most from their autonomy only when they represent diverse points of view, value one another, and respect each other's contributions. See this chapter's Valuing Diversity feature for a look at how Toyota's guiding principles get the most from its empowered employees.

Empowerment at Toyota

Taichi Ohno is referred to as the Father of the Toyota Production System (TPS), also known as lean manufacturing and just-in-time (JIT). "Ohno was legendary for his zeal. His commitment. His dedication to process improvement. His asking of 'why' five times" (Vasilash). The key to TPS success is empowering production associates.

Stephen Covey—author of best-selling *The 7 Habits of Highly Effective People* and cofounder of the personal organizer retailer FranklinCovey—says his favorite example of empowerment is Toyota. "Any worker can shut down that assembly line," he explains. "They think of themselves as part of a major partnership to serve transportation needs. Toyota's using the knowledge-worker model, which is why they're eating Detroit's lunch. Every employee is trained to ask the question: Why? Why aren't we doing it this way? Why do we do it that way?" (Hartman).

The following list of Toyota's guiding principles were established in 1990 and revised in 1997.

Guiding Principles at Toyota Motor Corporation

1 Honor the language and spirit of the law of every nation and undertake open and fair corporate activities to be a good corporate citizen of the world.

2 Respect the culture and customs of every nation and contribute to economic and social development through corporate activities in the communities.

3 Dedicate ourselves to providing clean and safe products and to enhancing the quality of life everywhere through all our activities.

4 Create and develop advanced technologies and provide outstanding products and services that fulfill the needs of customers worldwide.

5 Foster a corporate culture that enhances individual creativity and teamwork value, while honoring mutual trust and respect between labor and management.

6 Pursue growth in harmony with the global community through innovative management.

7 Work with business partners in research and creation to achieve stable, long-term growth and mutual benefits, while keeping ourselves open to new partnerships.

Five Main Principles of Toyoda by Sakichi Toyoda, Founder of Toyota

- Always be faithful to your duties, thereby contributing to the company and to the overall good.

- Always be studious and creative, striving to stay ahead of the times.

- Always be practical and avoid frivolousness.

- Always strive to build a homelike atmosphere at work that is warm and friendly.

- Always have respect for spiritual matters, and remember to be grateful at all times.

➡ **Most production lines are computerized with sensors that can turn them off or signal when an adjustment is needed. Why do you think Toyota wants employee involvement for quality?**

Sources: Toyota, Guiding Principles, *http://www.toyota-global.com/company/vision_philosophy/guiding_principles.html*; Mitchell Hartman, "Managing From Within," *Oregon Business*, February 200A, *http://www.mediamerica.net/obm_020A _MH.php*; Gary S. Vasilash, "Oh, What A Company!" *Automotive Design & Production*, March 200A, *http://www.autofieldguide.com/articles/030A01.html*.

COMMITMENTS AT THE MIDDLE

Commitment to improvements must involve mid-level managers, those hardest hit in downsizing and process improvements, such as reengineering efforts. Middle managers are most active in planning and coordinating quality and productivity efforts. They must make certain that any breakthroughs are shared with others to enable any benefits to be shared throughout the organization. Because most processes are horizontal, cross-functional cooperation and communication must take place. Various methods can be used to facilitate this, including rearranging work flow, reassigning tasks, having regular meetings for individuals and teams, and developing incentives and rewards for cooperation, breakthroughs (gain-sharing, for example), and teaming.

4b Determine the commitments required to improve quality and productivity at the middle of organizations

Teams Teams may exist at every level, and they all need trained leaders, members with complementary and required skills, a supportive environment and clear goals and guidelines. Teams create synergy, which makes their efforts more effective than the individual efforts of the team's members would be. Middle managers use three specific types of empowered teams to improve organization-wide quality and productivity: teams focusing on improving quality, processes and projects.

A **quality improvement team** is usually a group of people from all the functional areas of a company. The group meets regularly to assess progress toward goals, identify and solve common problems and cooperate in planning for the future. The purpose of such a team is to facilitate operations by providing the support needed and enhancing coordination efforts. Team leaders should enjoy quick and easy access to top managers so that management strategies can be adjusted to meet changing conditions. Members "should represent the company to the outside world, schedule the education program [to bring quality improvement to internal operations] and create company-wide events [to highlight the importance and successes of efforts at quality improvement]."[39] Large corporations may have several quality improvement teams, one for each operation or operational area. Small companies may have just one.

A **process improvement team** is made up of members who are involved with a process—getting the payroll out, making a part or sorting the mail, for example. Team members meet to analyze how they can improve the process. They focus on measuring the effectiveness and efficiency of each step, reducing cycle times and identifying and correcting causes for variations in the quality of inputs and outputs.

A **project improvement team** is usually composed of a group of people involved in the same project—installing a new computer system or creating a new product, for example. Members of the team determine how to make the project better. Project improvement teams usually include those who are or will be customers or consumers of the project's output. These users may be insiders or outsiders.

Investigations by all three types of teams may lead to contact with outsiders, especially if they are the source of a problem or its possible solution. Customers and suppliers are two of the likely groups of outsiders.

Audits The U.S. Army has an old saying: "Don't expect if you don't inspect!" Usually a duty of middle managers, audits monitor progress—or lack of it—toward goals. A **quality audit** determines if customer requirements are being met. If they are not, the auditors discover why not. A quality audit can focus on a particular product, process or project. A team of insiders or outsiders—a consultant or quality improvement team— can perform the audit.

A **quality control audit** asks two basic questions: How are we doing? and What are the problems? It focuses on "the way ... the factory builds quality into a given product, control of subcontracting, the manner in which customer complaints are handled and the methods of implementing quality assurance at each step of production, starting from ... new product development."[40]

Measurements Efforts to improve quality and productivity include various statistical measurements and scientific methods during both audits and the monitoring of ongoing operations. As early as the 1930s, Bell Laboratories was using what is now called **statistical quality control (SQC)** and **statistical process control (SPC)**. SQC is the use of statistical tools and methods to determine the quality of a product or service. SPC is the use of SQC to establish boundaries that determine if a process is in control (predictable) or out of control (unpredictable).[41] Figure A.7 shows one of these tools—a control chart used to regularly monitor a process that yields frequent

---

quality improvement team
Usually a group of people from all the functional areas of a company who meet regularly to assess progress toward goals, identify and solve common problems and cooperate in planning for the future

process improvement team
A team, made up of members who are involved with a process, who meets to analyze how they can improve the process

project improvement team
A team, usually composed of a group of people involved in the same project, that determines how to make the project better

quality audit
Determines if customer requirements are being met

quality control audit
A check of quality control efforts that asks two questions: How are we doing? and What are the problems?

statistical quality control (SQC) and statistical process control (SPC)
SQC is the use of statistical tools and methods to determine the quality of a product or service. SPC is the use of SQC to establish boundaries that determine if a process is in control (predictable) or out of control (unpredictable)

Figure A.7   Control Chart Used to Monitor Performance of a Process

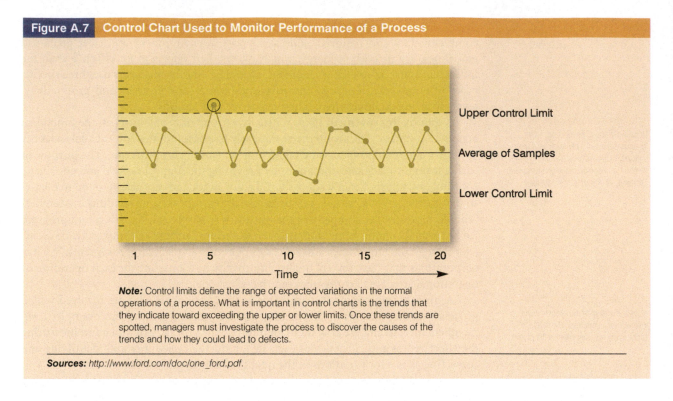

Note: Control limits define the range of expected variations in the normal operations of a process. What is important in control charts is the trends that they indicate toward exceeding the upper or lower limits. Once these trends are spotted, managers must investigate the process to discover the causes of the trends and how they could lead to defects.

Sources: http://www.ford.com/doc/one_ford.pdf.

outputs. Operations are considered to be in control as long as their outputs fall safely between the upper and lower control limits established for them. Cost accounting uses various types of tools and methods to similarly track and analyze expenses connected to all operations.

COMMITMENTS AT THE BOTTOM

Determine the commitments required to improve quality and productivity at the bottom of organizations

Empowered workers, individually and in teams, feel a dedication and obligation to continually work for improvements, especially when they share in the gains that result. Through process and product teams (cross-functional groupings), they combine talents and energies to identify and solve problems. Such teams may be permanent or temporary. A permanent team is usually in charge of an ongoing process like customer billing or customer service. A **quality circle** is a temporary team. Consisting primarily of workers who share a problem, the team meets regularly until the problem is solved. Members of a circle are usually volunteers who agree to use their knowledge and experience to eliminate barriers to both quality and productivity.

quality circle
A temporary team, consisting primarily of workers who share a problem, who meets regularly until the problem is solved

In the final analysis, company efforts to raise quality and productivity depend on committed workers and associates, who do not waste time, steal from their employers, withhold efforts, use forbidden substances on the job, nor resist needed change. Management's best efforts and millions of dollars cannot overcome such barriers. People are both the causes of and the cures for most of a company's productivity and quality problems.

Describe the external commitments required to improve an organization's quality and productivity

EXTERNAL COMMITMENTS

Various groups outside an organization have direct and indirect bearing on both the quality of its product or service and the productivity of the organization. Companies must continually interact with their customers and various partners. Customers exert by far the greatest influence. Whether an organization has individual consumers or industrial users as its customers, it must develop learning relationships—continuing connections to meet their needs and gain their loyalty.[42]

Most companies rely on input from valued customers through surveys, e-mails, toll-free customer service phone numbers, regular sales force interactions, and their involvement in the evaluations of those who serve them and of those who propose new products or services. Fred Reicheld's research shows that, in most industries, there is a strong correlation between a company's growth rate and the percentage of its customers who are "promoters"—that is, those who say they are extremely likely to recommend the product or company to a friend or colleague.[43] These examples of maintaining customer contact help producers keep their best customers and acquire new ones.

Businesses must deliver exceptional customer experiences to keep their customers. The number one purchaser influencer is word-of-mouth, and customer experience is the number one reason consumers recommend other firms. Many consumers switch to a competitive brand solely because of the better customer experience reputation of that competitive brand.

Today, customer experience is not just based on personal experience. It is based on what friends, networks and reviewers online say about products and companies. With the advent of social networks, one person's ability to tell lots of friends about a customer experience has been greatly magnified.

Toyota and dozens of other companies with hundreds of outside sources of supply must maintain close relationships with their suppliers to guarantee timely arrival of merchandise so as to avoid running out of stock. Factories, retailers and wholesalers routinely link their operations to those of their suppliers.

Partnerships with vendors and suppliers are based on openness and mutual trust. Information flows freely between the partners. Today, companies are turning increasingly to outside sources for vital materials and services. The primary reason for outsourcing is that others can do what you need done better, faster, cheaper and with better quality and greater efficiency. Companies are also concentrating on partnering with fewer but more reliable sources for what they need. Both buyer and seller, however, must have the same commitment to quality of output and efficiency of operation for the partnership to last.

In addition to audits of their own operations, companies that outsource need to continually check on their outsiders' operations. Do they know their costs? Do we know them? Are their costs out of line or in check? Are they working on cost reduction? Can we help them to reduce costs? Companies work with their suppliers to reduce costs and regularly renegotiate contracts on the basis of the savings generated.

Additional Internal and External Influences on Quality and Productivity

Systems have a number of internal components or subsystems. (Recall Chapter 2's discussion of the systems school of management thought.) Changes in any one of these can impact one or more of the others. In like manner, significant changes that occur outside a system may impact the system and its subsystems. Carl Sewell applies the works of Deming and Taguchi to his auto dealerships. For example, in his book *Customers for Life: How to Turn That One-Time Buyer into a Lifelong Customer,* the second commandment on Carl Sewell's list is, "Systems, not smiles. Saying please and thank you doesn't ensure you'll do the job right the first time, every time. Only systems guarantee you that."[44] In addition to the concepts already discussed in this chapter, we must briefly consider several internal elements and external forces and their possible impacts on quality and productivity.

Internal Influences

Nonhuman resources and how they are processed are the primary concerns under the heading of internal influences. These essential resources include information, facilities, machinery and equipment, materials and supplies and finances. Each has a direct bearing on profitability, productivity and the quality of outputs.

Information about both internal and external events must be continually gathered, generated and put to good use by all members of an organization. Knowing the state of things through such mechanisms as audits and regular progress reports keeps people informed and well prepared to plan, organize, staff, lead and control quality and productivity improvement efforts.

Facilities and information are united through **research and development (R&D)** projects, which uncover information useful to create a variety of new materials, processes and products. They represent a sizable investment of time and money that helps to guarantee an organization's future through a steady stream of customer-pleasing goods and services. Companies can practice R&D in research centers or by unleashing the creativity of individuals through empowerment and open-book management approaches.

research and development (R&D)
Projects that uncover information useful to create a variety of new materials, processes, and products

At 3M, R&D is part of every employee's job. The company encourages each person to become a product champion—to spend part of every working day attempting to create something new and different. The best ideas (those promising the greatest opportunity for financial returns) are given top priority and brought to market as quickly and efficiently as possible.

Machinery and equipment are used in R&D and manufacturing operations. The more efficient the tools and methods, the more quality and productivity will benefit. World-class manufacturing has the following characteristics:

- Direct links to customers and suppliers
- Flexible production lines capable of not only handling large or small runs of specialized products, but also, within minutes, of being reconfigured to produce another product
- Short cycle times
- Horizontal product, project and process teams
- Just-in-time delivery of vital materials
- Cleanliness
- Empowered teams and individuals performing many varied tasks
- Intense focus on efforts to improve quality and productivity at every level and throughout every process

In addition, manufacturing facilities are becoming showrooms for outsiders and laboratories for insiders.

Materials and supplies represent the inputs needed for any process. The quality of outputs is directly related to the quality of inputs. Poor-quality materials and supplies used anywhere in a process can cause defects. These, in turn, affect productivity. Careful coordination through regular interactions with suppliers is vital to satisfying internal needs and external customers.

Finally, quality and productivity affect the financial health of organizations and vice versa. Cost-effective quality pleases and attracts customers and generates income. The more inefficient the producer, the less competitive its products and services.

External Influences

Constantly changing external influences on quality and productivity include the economic, legal/political, sociocultural, natural and technological conditions existing in an organization's domestic and foreign markets. The actions of a business's competitors and the demands of its owners are additional influences.

The levels of prices in any economy affect businesses' plans and internal operations. Falling prices for needed raw materials can translate into lower production costs and higher profits. The reverse is true as well. Rising interest rates can cause a company to postpone borrowing and making the improvements those funds could generate.

Laws can make a company's products more expensive to produce or more difficult to sell. Federal antipollution and safety laws are but two examples. Both have increased production and administrative expenses for many firms; the extra costs are often passed along to the consumers of these products and services in the form of higher prices.

Sociocultural elements influence product quality because products must contain different features, in line with the requirements of different ethnic groups. McDonald's is one of several fast-food chains that adjusts its menu to different locations and customer preferences. As menu offerings change, so too will some of a company's processes and costs.

Natural forces can make things cheaper or more expensive. Locating manufacturing and distribution facilities close to inexpensive sources of raw materials can greatly reduce a producer's costs. Chicago, with its relatively cheap and plentiful supply of fresh water, is a case in point. And, as many of the residents and owners of businesses on the island of St. Thomas can attest, hurricanes can make living in the Virgin Islands and other hurricane-prone areas more expensive.

Technology affects productivity and quality through its proper application. For instance, programmable robots can perform many operations more quickly and efficiently than people. Fewer defects will usually result. Once the robots are purchased, they can be reprogrammed to meet the demands of different but similar applications.

A company may have to become more efficient to exceed the increased efficiency of a competitor. Outsourcing and downsizing are generally responses to the need of their practitioners to stay efficient and profitable by passing work to those who are more efficient at performing it. A company must continually strive to stay ahead of its competition through innovation and research and development.

Business owners demand a reasonable return on their investments and a share of their companies' profits. Money distributed to owners, however, is not available for other uses, such as improving output quality and productivity or making the investments in training and equipment that will help to guarantee the future of their businesses.

How all these factors influence managers, their organizations, and decision making in additional ways—beyond their influences on quality and productivity—is the concern of this Appendix.

Review What You've Learned

Appendix Summary

1 **Discuss how customers influence the quality of goods and services.**

Customers evaluate goods and services by comparing the quality features and costs of the goods and services against their requirements. Defects cause customers to reject goods and services or complain about them. Customer requirements must be determined and considered in the design phase of product development (QFD). The appropriate features and dimensions can then be designed into goods and services. Often some tailoring is needed to meet specific user requirements. Since customer/user needs and requirements keep changing, so too must products and services. Producers need to stay ahead of customer expectations if the next generation of products and services is to succeed in the market. A product may be defect free but still lose out to others who offer more or different features that better fit the customers' expectations.

2 **Explain why quality must be cost-effective.**

Quality is cost-effective when providers of goods and services deliver the level of quality that satisfies their customers at a reasonable price—one that yields profits as well as customer approval. Delivering quality that isn't desired results in waste and lost revenues. Efforts to produce quality should also lead to efficiency improvements. If they do not, too much is being spent to deliver quality, or the standards being met are too demanding. If efficiency improvements are met, costs are reduced, and profits increase accordingly.

3 **Relate quality, productivity, and profitability to one another.**

According to Crosby, Juran, Deming and others, quality must promote efficiency, and vice versa. If they do not promote one another, something is wrong. If quality improves, costs decrease; as costs decrease, productivity improves; customers are kept and gained, additional sales take place, company profits increase and more jobs can be provided.

4 **Determine the commitments required to improve quality and productivity at the following organizational levels: top, middle, and bottom.**

4a **Top organizational level:** Top management must sense the need for change, create a vision of it, enlist support for it and drive the movement to bring change about. Top management must articulate the company's core values, determine the approaches—*kaizen* or reengineering—it wishes to authorize, and commit the entire organization and all its members to the continual journey toward quality and productivity improvements. To get everyone's commitment, top management must use the tools of open-book management and empowerment.

4b **Middle organizational level:** Mid-level managers usually have the primary monitoring duties and oversee most of a company's projects and functions. They are responsible for creating teams, training their people to function properly in teams and providing the support both individuals and teams require. They are more responsible than managers at other levels for implementing and encouraging open-book management and empowerment initiatives.

4c **Bottom organizational level:** Without committed employees at every level, something less than success will result. People are the key. To achieve the best results, their knowledge, experience, skills, ideas and energy must be given willingly. When workers are truly empowered and can share in the gains they help create, they usually are motivated to give their best. To be effective, all employees and their teams must have relationships built on mutual respect and trust.

5 **Describe the external commitments required to improve an organization's quality and productivity.**

A commitment to partners is of great importance. True partners have no secrets. They interact continually and keep working to improve their relationships. A learning relationship must be developed and maintained between companies and their suppliers and customers. Gaining feedback from partners and helping customers to solve their particular problems is a learning experience that can lead to both quality and productivity improvements.

KEY TERMS

benchmark   **535**

process improvement team   **549**

productivity   **539**

project improvement team   **549**

quality audit   **549**

quality circle   **550**

quality control audit   **549**

quality function deployment (QFD)   **534**

quality improvement team   **549**

research and development (R&D)   **552**

statistical process control (SPC)   **549**

statistical quality control (SQC)   **549**

total quality management (TQM)   **536**

REVIEW QUESTIONS

1. What influence over the quality of a product or service do customers really have?

2. How can a company make the quality of its goods and services cost-effective?

3. Why must efforts to improve quality lead to improvements in both productivity and profits?

4. What must top management commit to if it wants its organization to improve its productivity and quality and, therefore, its profits?

5. How do middle managers contribute to their organizations' efforts to improve both quality and productivity?

6. In what ways do workers affect productivity and quality? In what way do they affect the efforts to improve both?

7. What external commitments affect quality and productivity improvement efforts?

DISCUSSION QUESTIONS FOR CRITICAL THINKING

1. Think of a time when a company exceeded your needs and expectations. Share your experience. What advantages does the company in your example give customers that others do not?

2. How can a company's suppliers affect its quality and productivity? Its profits?

3. A common approach within many companies today is to outsource any activity that can be done better, cheaper and faster by an outsider. What changes does this practice create for the outsourcer and those receiving the work?

4. What does this sentence mean to you? "The effort to improve quality is a continual journey." Can the same be said for improving productivity? Why or why not?

5. Some people believe that we should "forget about quality, it's an old-fashioned idea; concentrate instead on innovation." What is your viewpoint? Is quality now a commodity?

Apply What You Know

Social Media Management Exercises

"The Matrix of Web 2.0" shown here has examples of social media tools used in government.

Choose a company. Visit its website. Develop "The Matrix of Social Media Tools" for the company.

Matrix of Web 2.0 Technology and Government

TECHNOLOGY	SIMPLE DESCRIPTION	EXAMPLE USES	APPLICABILITY TO OPEN GOVERNMENT
Blogs	Journal or diary with social collaboration (comments)	USA.gov's Government Blog Library Webcontent.gov advice GovGab.gov	Govt info to new audiences. Puts human face on govt using informal tone. Opens public conversations. Surface issues & solve them.
Wikis	Collaborative authoring & editing	GSA Collab Environment Core.gov MAX NASA US Courts Intellipedia PTO Diplopedia PeaceCorps Utah Politicopia	Workgroup or public collaboration for project management, knowledge sharing, public input. Contributions to 3rd party sites, e.g., Wikipedia.
Video Sharing (and Multimedia)	Videos, images, & audio libraries (YouTube, AOLVideo, YahooVideo, tubemogul, heyspread…)	USA.gov Multimedia library NOAA YouTube Channel NASA YouTube Channel Coast Guard YouTube Channel CA YouTube Channel VA YouTube Channel Americorps contest Tobacco Free Florida contest	Public outreach, education, training, other communication for "connected" and on-line audiences. How-to videos & audios to improve service and achieve mission.
Photo-Sharing	Photo libraries	USA.gov fed/state photo libraries USGS gallery w Flickr API LoC gallery w Flickr API EPA contest	Cost savings potential. New audiences. Awareness.
Podcasting	Multimedia content syndicated out for use on iPod TM, Mp3 players & computers	White House NASA USA.gov federal podcast library Webcontent.gov Peacecorps Census daily podcasts	More ways to get message out. Build trust with conversational voice. Use for updates, live govt deliberations, emergencies, how-to messages.

TECHNOLOGY	SIMPLE DESCRIPTION	EXAMPLE USES	APPLICABILITY TO OPEN GOVERNMENT

Virtual Worlds	Simulations of environments & people (Webkinz, Club Penguin, Neopets, Stardoll, Whyville, Second Life, Active Worlds, Kaneva, ProtoSphere, Entropia Universe, uWorld)	NASA
		NOAA
		CDC in SL & Whyville,VA
		Natl Guard
		Energy
		DoD
		National Defense Univ
		    Federal Consortium
		    for Virtual Worlds
		Real Life Govt in 2nd Life
		    Google group
			Public outreach & other communication for kids and niche Internet audiences. Virtual Town Halls, Education, Training. Ability to bring people together worldwide for meetings, lectures, etc.

Social Networking Sites	Connecting people globally	EPA Facebook group NASA Colab USAgov Facebook page USAgov MySpace page USAgov on Linkedin	Intranet use to cross internal stovepipes. Cross government coordination. Public communities. Viral impact. Knowledge mgmt. Recruitment. Event announcements.
Syndicated Web Feeds	Automated notifications of frequently updated content (think RSS)	USA.gov Federal RSS Library NOAAWatch	Do more with RSS, XML/web feeds. Expand reach. Pull content together across government. Authoritative source. Reduce duplication.
Mashups	Combine content from multiple sources for an integrated experience	USA Search USGS NASA EPA Virtual Earth Google Earth Google maps	Lots of potential. Improved govt reach, service, usefulness, and functionality. Integrate external data. Get licenses, stay vendor neutral. Make content available to others who create mashups.

Widgets, Gadgets, Pipes	Small applications & code in web pages or for desktop use	FBI widgets
		Veterans Affairs
		Census Population Clock
		    Desktop widget
		NASA Planet Discoveries
		    Desktop widget
			Increase awareness, use and usefulness of .gov sites, information and service. Bring content to the user's home page (iGoogle, netvibes, etc.).

Social Bookmark & News (Sharing, Tagging) Sites	Ways of sharing content with others	USA.gov NASA Govt blogs Digg Delicious Technorati AddThis	Increase the popularity and use of .gov pages, information, and services. Viral marketing.
Micro-blogging. Presence Networks	Form of blogging which allows brief (Instant Message size) text updates	Twitter Jaiku Cromple Pownce NASA Edge USA.gov GovGab Univ of Mich	Seek input. Broadcast msgs: emergencies, news, announcemts. Real time reporting. Recruiting.

July 18, 2008 Bev Godwin, USA.gov and Web Best Practices, GSA Office of Citizen Services.

Source: http://www.usa.gov/webcontent/documents/Web_Technology_Matrix.pdf.

Appendix B

Operations Management

LEARNING OBJECTIVES

After studying this chapter, you should be able to:

1 Discuss the nature and importance of operations strategy and operations management

2 Discuss the nature and importance of product and service design planning

3 Describe the four main strategies for facilities layout

4 Discuss the nature of process and technology planning

5 Explain the factors in facilities location planning and capacity planning

6 Describe the role of operations control in achieving quality and productivity

7 Discuss the purpose of design controls

8 Discuss the importance of managing and controlling materials purchasing

9 Explain how EOQ, MRP, MRPII, and JIT differ

10 Discuss the importance and methods of schedule controls

11 Describe the importance and methods of product control

INTRODUCTION

Many companies involved in the competitive world of business refine and restructure their technology to gain the upper hand in the marketplace. The companies making these changes have discovered that strategic success is directly related to the efficiency and responsiveness of their production operations.[1] In turn, these companies are going on the offensive by using their operations management strategy as a competitive weapon to change the way they develop superior products and services.

Innovative managers don't just manage people; they also manage the technical resources and processes associated with the production of goods and services. This chapter is devoted to a discussion of the processes, decisions and systems involved in manufacturing and service operations. After defining operations management, this appendix will discuss how companies plan operations. The second part of the appendix will discuss operations control.

Discuss the nature and importance of operations strategy and operations management

1

operations strategy
The element of the strategic plan that defines the role, capabilities and expectations of operations

operations management
The managerial activities directed toward the processes that convert resources into products and services

NATURE OF OPERATIONS MANAGEMENT

Operations Strategy and Operations Management Defined

Operations strategy is the part of a strategic plan that defines the role, capabilities and expectations of operations. **Operations management** consists of the managerial activities and techniques used to convert resources (such as raw materials and labor) into products and services.[2] The terms *production* and *operations* are commonly applied to manufacturing operations. Remember, however, that operations management applies to all organizations, not just manufacturers.

Every organization produces something. Some companies, such as Caterpillar and Nike, produce physical goods. Others, such as Sheraton Hotels, American Airlines and the University of Michigan, produce services. Except for the fact that a service business does not produce a physical product to be placed in inventory, organizations that produce goods and services have similar operational problems:

- Each is concerned with converting resources into something saleable.
- Each must acquire materials or supplies to achieve that conversion.
- Each must schedule the process of conversion.
- Each must control processes and ensure quality.

With these similarities in mind, examine Figure B.1, which illustrates the flow of operations. Notice that every organization takes inputs and transforms them into outputs, either products or services.

Importance of Operations Management

The heart of an organization is its production of goods or services to sell. Some managers have discovered that their success is directly related to the effectiveness of their operations strategy and operations system. In addition, managers now realize that when developing strategic plans, they must include a component that consists of an operations strategy. Without an effective operations strategy and operations management, few organizations would survive.[3]

No matter the company, the goal is to squeeze the bottom line for more profits. Managers cannot increase profits if operations management is left out of strategic planning or if the goal of operations is simply to keep pace with the industry. Operations

Figure B.1	Flow of Operations

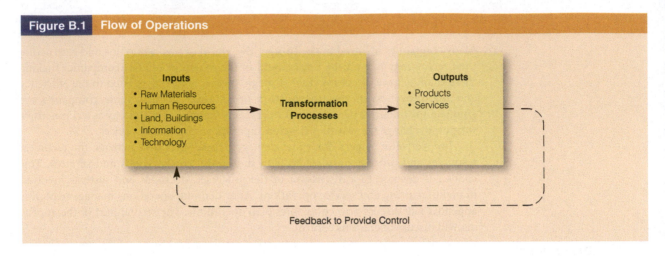

Feedback to Provide Control

management must be viewed as a competitive weapon to be used with marketing and finance. In this capacity the process of strategic management often leads to new strategic concepts.[4] The results can be lower prices or better quality, performance or responsiveness to consumer demand. When operations management receives proper emphasis, marketing and financial strategies are not the only tools of competition.[5]

Figure B.2 illustrates the pervasive role that operations management plays in an organization. Note that operations management embraces product, facilities and process design, implementation structure and control processes. In all areas of operations management, the focus is on improving productivity and quality.

OPERATIONS PLANNING

Discuss the nature and importance of product and service design planning

The starting point of any undertaking is planning. In the case of an organization's operations, the planning stage involves decisions about product or service design, facilities layout, production processes and technology, facilities location and capacity planning.

Product or Service Design Planning

Historically, product and service design has not been acknowledged as part of operations management. Managers have discovered, however, that the goals of operations management (competitiveness, response time and production efficiency) are well served by two design concepts called *design for manufacturability and assembly (DFM/A)* and *design for disassembly (DfD)*. These concepts involve designing products for effective performance while considering how they will be manufactured, assembled and disassembled.

Design for Manufacturability and Assembly In the past, design engineers designed products with a complete lack of thought—some would even say with disdain—for product manufacture and assembly. Design engineers handed finished designs to manufacturing engineers. More often than not, the products the designs specified could not be assembled easily, and they had to be inspected for quality during production. The design-centered approach also led to products that contained a greater number of parts than necessary. "The main point of DFM/A is to discover problems long before the design gets to that stage."[6]

Figure B.2   Role of Operations Strategy and Operations Management

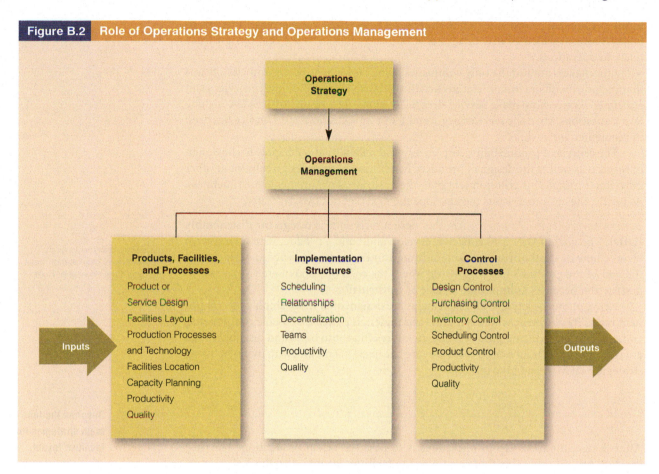

design for manufacturability and assembly (DFM/A)

Considering, during the design stage, how products will be manufactured and assembled

Design for manufacturability and assembly (DFM/A) calls for design teams consisting of designers, manufacturers and assemblers. Because these specialists all have a say in product design, actual production of the product becomes more efficient. General Motors (GM) has transformed its operations management by incorporating DFM/A. Not only have the number of parts per car been reduced, but vehicles are easier to assemble. A strategic initiative, as a result of DFM/A, is its use of common parts and the same engineering and manufacturing processes regardless of where the product is manufactured or sold. As one GM manager observed

We now have a much more effective functional execution of car building. It makes engineering more effective. It makes materials management more effective and the assembly center more effective. That is because we are using the total technical voice of the division plus the knowledge of outside suppliers.[7]

DFM/A product design involves four criteria: producibility, cost, quality and reliability. *Producibility* is the degree to which the product or service can be manufactured for the customer within the organization's operational capacity. The criterion of *cost* includes the costs of labor, materials, design, overhead and transportation. *Quality,* in the eyes of the producer, is the excellence of the product or service. In the eyes of the consumer, *quality* is the serviceability and value gained by purchasing the product. *Reliability* is the degree to which customers can count on the product or service to fulfill its intended purpose. Figure B.3 summarizes the eight *possible* major benefits of DFM/A against which all new designs are evaluated at GM. (Notice that the last three relate to operations.)

Automakers are not the only companies using DFM/A. At FedEx and UPS, teams that include members from materials handling, transportation, computer services and customer service now make service design decisions. The results of DFM/A include fewer questions when the services begin and fewer modifications after service has been implemented for a while.[8]

The criteria of producibility, cost, quality and reliability should apply to the design of services as well as the design of products. In addition, service design calls for another criterion: timing. This criterion relates to the customer's requirements for timeliness. At FedEx, the customer wants the envelope the next day, not two days later.

Design for Disassembly (DfD) Another design technique is **design for disassembly (DfD)**. The goal of DfD is to conceive, develop and build a product with a long-term view of how its components can be refurbished and reused—or disposed of safely—at the end of the product's life.[9] In a world where the costs of disposal are rising, ease of destruction becomes as important as ease of construction.

Xerox photocopiers and Kodak cameras are designed for disassembly and component reuse. By designing with fewer parts and materials as well as reusable components, companies are producing products that are more efficient to build and distribute than are conventionally built ones. This is the case because DfD meshes with manufacturing strategies: DFM/A and total quality.

design for disassembly (DfD)
Considering, during the design stage, how products will be refurbished, reused or disposed of at the end of the product's life cycle

FACILITIES LAYOUT

3 Describe the four main strategies for facilities layout

After design, the next step in operations is to plan the actual production. This step involves, among other things, determining the **facilities layout**—the physical arrangement of equipment at the manufacturing site and how the work will flow. There are four main types of layouts from which to choose: process, product, cellular, and fixed position. Figure B.4 illustrates these four options.

facilities layout
The element of operations planning concerned with the physical arrangement of equipment and work flow

Figure B.3	Major Benefits of the DFM/A Approach, Against Which GM Evaluates New Designs
Quality	Excellence of the car, including serviceability
Reliability	The degree to which the car fulfills its intended purpose
Durability	The degree to which the car withstands performance demands
Mass	The total weight of the car
Safety	The degree to which the car increases the protection of occupants
Manufacturability	The degree to which the car can be manufactured and assembled within existing operational capacity
Time to market	The time from product design until the car is ready for sale to the consumer
Total cost	The total amount of materials, labor, transportation, design and overhaul expenses associated with the design

Figure B.4 Four Options of Facilities Layout

(a) Process Layout

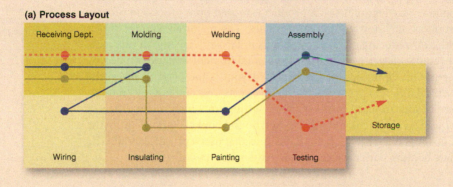

-------- Product A   ———— Product B   ———— Product V

(b) Product Layout

(c) Cellular Layout

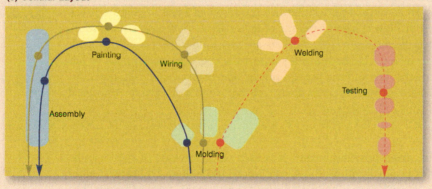

(d) Fixed-Position Layout

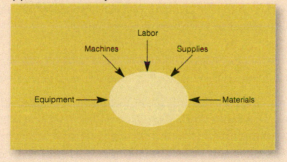

Process Layout

In a **process layout**, all the equipment or machines that perform a similar task or function are located together (see Figure B.4a). A product is moved from process to process as needed—all products may not require all processes. The major advantage of this layout is its potential for reducing costs. Because all similar work is done in one area, the process layout requires fewer people and pieces of equipment than does a decentralized arrangement. One limitation of the process layout is the need to move the product through several different processes. Each move costs time and money. In manufacturing, process layouts are used in print shops, settings in which many different products (such as business cards, color brochures and bound books) do not require the same processes. A hospital is a service-oriented business that uses a process layout. The layout is appropriate because patients receive many different types of services.

process layout
A facilities layout option in which all the equipment or machines that perform a similar task are placed together

Product Layout

In a **product layout**, machines and tasks are arranged according to the progressive steps by which the product is made (see Figure B.4b). This layout is efficient when the business produces large volumes of identical products. Car manufacturing on an assembly line is the best-known example of a product layout. Other examples include computer manufacturing and appliance assembly. A hospital might use a product layout when doctors are undertaking a large-scale vaccination effort, for example. In this case many patients are moved through a line, each receiving the same treatment.

product layout
A facilities layout option in which the machines and tasks are arranged according to the progressive steps by which the product is made

Cellular Layout

The **cellular layout** combines some of the characteristics of process and product layouts. In a cellular arrangement, all the equipment required for a sequence of operations on the same product is placed together in a group called a *cell* (see Figure B.4c). The cellular groupings allow efficient handling of materials and inventory. In addition, the cellular layout facilitates teamwork; workers are physically close enough to work together to solve problems.[10] U-shaped cells support the operator checking his or her own work by placing the start and end process side by side. In service settings, the cellular layout is used where many workers, as teams, see to the needs of a group. A hospital ward is an example of a cellular layout.

cellular layout
A facilities layout option in which equipment required for a sequence of operations on the same product is grouped into cells

Fixed-Position Layout

Figure B.4d shows a **fixed-position layout**. It is used when, because of size or bulk, the product remains in one location. Tools, equipment and human skills are brought to the product. Organizations that build planes and ships use this form of layout. The fixed-position approach is sound for bulky products and custom-ordered goods, but not for high-volume manufacturing. This type of layout is used in a hospital operating room, where a number of specialists gather to work on a single patient.

fixed-position layout
A facilities layout option in which the product stays in one place and the equipment, tools and human skills are brought to it

PRODUCTION PROCESSES AND TECHNOLOGY

4 Discuss the nature of process and technology planning

The challenge facing operations managers is to identify the proper blend of people and technology to use in transforming inputs into finished products and services. For any given production task, several conversion methods are available—some labor intensive, others equipment intensive. The nature of the product and the objectives and resources of the organization are critical factors in choosing one method over another.

The growing trend today is toward the use of more sophisticated technology in manufacturing. This type of manufacturing, associated with the "factory of the future," relies increasingly on equipment that works almost unaided by employees.

The technologies most responsible for revolutionizing manufacturing processes include robotics, CAD/CAM, flexible manufacturing systems, computer- integrated manufacturing, soft manufacturing systems and agile manufacturing.

Robotics

robotics
The use of programmed machines to handle production

The use of programmed machines to handle production constitutes **robotics**. The machines, or robots, are constructed to do the work of employees. They weld, deliver materials and parts, load and unload and more. Robots provide greater precision than do humans; therefore, they enhance quality. The disadvantages of robots include capital expenditures, maintenance costs and malfunctions.

The International Federation of Robotics (IFR) reports that about 1,500,000 industrial robots are in operation.[11] Once the province of giant corporations like Apple Inc. and Caterpillar, robots are taking their place in the manufacturing operations of far smaller companies.

CAD/CAM

computer-aided design (CAD)
A design technique that uses a computer monitor to display and manipulate proposed designs for the purpose of evaluating them

computer-aided manufacturing (CAM)
A technology in which computers coordinate people, information and processes to produce quality products efficiently

Among the most widely adopted technologies in manufacturing are **computer-aided design (CAD)** and **computer-aided manufacturing (CAM)**. CAD allows engineers and designers to develop new products by using a computer monitor to display and manipulate three-dimensional drawings. The assistance of the computer helped cut some engineers' design time in half. In addition, the CAD system allows the engineer to visualize the effects of any design change. Using CAD, the design engineers at Chrysler can call up on the computer screen a semitransparent view of a car door being worked on, operate the latch and run the windows up and down to check how they work, experiment with lighter materials by adjusting the underlying equations, and use the same data to direct machinery to make prototypes of the parts.

CAM involves the use of computers to guide and control manufacturing processes. The computer is programmed to direct a piece of equipment to perform a certain action, such as drilling holes or pouring steel. Compared with human control, computer control results in less waste, lower costs, higher quality and improved safety.

Flexible Manufacturing Systems

flexible manufacturing system (FMS)
A technology in which an automated production line is coordinated by computers and can produce more than one product

A **flexible manufacturing system (FMS)** is an automated production line. Computers coordinate the machinery. The automated line controls assembly, welding, tightening and adjusting. In addition, an FMS allows rapid adjustment of the assembly process, so the production line can produce more than one model. For example, General Motors (GM) was able to mass produce four different car models when it installed an FMS at its Lordstown, Ohio, plant.

An FMS automates the entire production line by controlling and providing instructions to all the machines. The greatest advantage of an FMS is that through computer instructions, a single manufacturing line can be adapted to produce different products. (The adaptability of an FMS is the characteristic that distinguishes it from CAM.) The computer instructs the machines to change parts, machine specifications and tools when a new product must be produced.

Computer-Integrated Manufacturing

Originally, computer-integrated manufacturing meant controlling machinery through a system of interconnected computers. Such a system was supposed to make human labor unnecessary. Today, however, **computer-integrated manufacturing (CIM)** is a computerized system that orchestrates people, information and processes to produce quality outputs efficiently. For example, CIM systems can handle business functions such as order entry, cost accounting, customer billing, employee time records and payroll. Thus, the scope of CIM technology is more comprehensive and includes all activities that are concerned with production.

computer-integrated manufacturing (CIM)
Using computers to guide and control manufacturing processes

Soft Manufacturing Systems

Soft manufacturing systems were designed as an answer to the struggle of businesses to respond to the demand for customized products. A **soft manufacturing system (SMS)** relies on computer software to continuously control and adjust the manufacturing processes. Rather than mammoth installations like FMS or CIM, a soft manufacturing system groups machines into smaller, more manageable cells and spreads computers literally around the plants.

soft manufacturing system (SMS)
A manufacturing system that relies on computer software to continuously control and adjust the manufacturing processes

Soft manufacturing systems bring unheard-of agility to the factory. Companies can customize products in quantities of one, while churning them out at mass production speeds. SMS blurs the boundaries of the traditional factory by bringing production closer to the customer.

Agile Manufacturing

"**Agile manufacturing** is a conceptual framework for more efficient manufacturing, which is now resulting in mass customization…. The basic idea (in mass customization) is to get the right product to the right person, at the right time…. This high-quality yet flexible way of producing goods involves both the manufacturer and the customer."[12] The customized goods are made as fast and as cheaply as mass-produced products.

agile manufacturing
A manufacturing system incorporating ultra-flexible production facilities; computer technology; alliances among suppliers, producers, and customers; and direct sales data to customize goods at the speed of mass production

> *Agile manufacturing includes modularization and virtual manufacturing. Modularization involves building products from components chosen by customers. GE sells railroad car 'components' in a choice of color combinations. Virtual manufacturing means a company doesn't do all its own manufacturing, but outsources some or all the work to subcontractors. Most car companies adhere to the virtual manufacturing model, allowing them to focus on services like product design and marketing. "Car companies have become auto assemblers, as opposed to auto manufacturers," Goldman says. . . . U.S. manufacturers are feeling pressure to reduce their current production cycle of about six weeks to one week or less.*[13]

Computers and the Delivery of Services

Computers and the Internet have revolutionized delivery as well as manufacturing. The widespread access to information that computers and the Internet provide has allowed businesses to improve the quality of customer service. "Thanks to global networks and telecommunication capabilities, businesses can deal with customers and suppliers on an individual basis."[14] For example, computerized point-of-sale terminals constantly update inventory records; the up-to-date records facilitate rapid response to customers' needs. At Schneider National, a major trucking firm, data sent from computers in the cabs of trucks allow dispatchers to monitor the load status and location of each rig. Dispatchers know which trucks are in the vicinity of a customer and when each will be empty. Computers and the Internet also enhance the ability to track orders. At UPS and FedEx, computerized monitoring of shipments has allowed both companies to improve delivery time and quality of service.

5

Explain the factors in facilities location planning and capacity planning

FACILITIES LOCATION

In considering the placement of facilities, managers must ask two important questions: Should the firm have one or two large plants, or several smaller ones? Where should the facilities be located?

The decision about the number of plants depends on the company's long-range objectives and distribution strategies, financial resources and equipment costs. The choice regarding location depends on a number of factors: the location of the market where the product will be sold, availability of labor skills, labor costs, proximity to suppliers, tax rates, construction expenses, utility rates and quality of life for employees.[15] To make the decision, the company must undertake a cost-benefit analysis. When TRW chooses among two or more potential locations, it analyzes the costs of land, transportation, relocation, construction, zoning and taxation. Then planners examine perceived benefits—proximity to customers, quality of work life for employees and labor supply.[16] Finally, they divide total benefits by total costs for each potential location.

CAPACITY PLANNING

capacity planning
An element of operations management that determines an organization's capability to produce the number of products or services necessary to meet demand

A critical element in operations management is **capacity planning**—determining an organization's capability to produce the products or services necessary to meet demand. Capacity planning is essentially a matter of trying to convert sales forecasts into production capabilities. Decisions about capacity should be made carefully. Too little capacity means that the organization cannot match demand and that it will lose customers. The reverse—excess capacity—results in facilities and equipment that sit idle while incurring costs.

To increase capacity, companies have a number of options. They can build new facilities, create additional shifts and hire new staff, pay present staff overtime, subcontract work to outside firms or refit existing plants. If a company has to decrease capacity, its options include laying off workers, reducing the hours of operation and closing facilities.

Capacity is a dynamic variable in operations management. It changes from month to month as well as year to year. Producers attempt to plan capacity to avoid boom-and-bust cycles of plant expansion followed by layoffs and the reduction of operations. The key determinant in capacity planning is the demand for goods and services. (As discussed in Chapter 4, managers can determine demand by using forecasting techniques.) If a company is operating with stable demand, managers should provide plant capacity equal to the monthly demand. Suppose, however, those seasonal fluctuations, uncertain economic conditions or other factors result in unstable demand. In this situation, managers should build a small plant to meet normal demand and add extra shifts or subcontract work during peak periods.[17]

MANAGEMENT OF OPERATIONS

Once managers have made the strategic planning decisions about design, layout, process and technology, location and capacity, the operations management team needs to develop specific plans for the overall production activities. This involves aggregate planning, master scheduling, and structuring for operations.

Aggregate Plan

Aggregate planning involves planning production activities and the resources needed to achieve them. It draws the "road map" for operating activities for a period of time up to one year.

Aggregate planning begins with consideration of the demand forecast for products or services and study of the capacity of the operations. By examining demand and capacity, the operations management team sets production rates, inventory levels, materials requirements and labor needs. The result of this process is a general operating (aggregate) plan. For a restaurant, such a plan would show the total number of customers to be served but not the specific meals each would consume. For a facility that makes cooking ranges, the plan would show the total number of ranges to be produced but not the color of each one. Details come later. When completed, the aggregate plan serves as the basis for the master schedule.[18]

aggregate planning
An element of operations management that involves the planning of production activities and the resources needed to achieve them

Master Schedule

The **master schedule**, derived from the aggregate plan, specifies the quantity and type of each item to be produced and how, when, and where it should be produced.[19] Figure B.5 illustrates the development of a master schedule from an aggregate plan. Materials requirements are derived from the master schedule, and the schedule affects inventory levels. These two points will be discussed later in this chapter.

master schedule
An element of operations management that specifies the quantity and type of each item to be produced and how, when and where it should be produced

Structure for Implementing Production

One more element of operations remains to be planned: the structure for implementing production. In this regard, the operations management team must decide how to organize the department, what type of employees are needed and how they should be trained, whether and how to incorporate teams, the authority of relationships and the extent of decentralization. The operations management team must address each one of these concepts (which were discussed in earlier chapters) in the context of operations. The desired result is an integrated, flexible organization structure that can respond to changes in the aggregate plan.

CONTROLS FOR QUALITY AND PRODUCTIVITY

6 Describe the role of operations control in achieving quality and productivity

As discussed in Appendix A, the driving forces in today's organizations are productivity and quality—or quality and productivity. The order is irrelevant; the two cannot be separated.

Traditionally, managers viewed productivity in terms of greater output. They did not give much thought to whether the units of output were usable or not. Enlightened managers now realize that productivity is related to saleable, high-quality units of output, whether the outputs are products or services.

The costs associated with poor productivity relate to quality. These include the costs of scrap, repair and downtime. Such costs are directly observable during pro-

Figure B.5   Development of a Master Schedule from an Aggregate Plan

Aggregate Plan (Units per Month)

	January	February	March	April	May
Electric Ranges	1,000	1,250	1,200	1,300	1,200
Gas Ranges	750	800	700	1,000	1,000
Total	1,750	2,050	1,900	2,300	2,300

Master Schedule for Electric Ranges (Units per Week)

	January				February			
	1	2	3	4	5	6	7	8
3,600	100	100	50	50	100	100	50	100
3,665	100	100	50	100	100	50	100	100
3,670	100	50	100	100	150	150	150	100

January Total   1,000   February Total   1,250

Note: Another master schedule will be developed for the gas ranges

duction. Quality is also related to costs incurred before manufacturing begins. These expenses include the cost of incoming materials, purchasing and inventory.[20]

All these factors fall within the purview of operations management. To achieve high quality and productivity, managers use a number of operational controls. These include control of design, materials, inventory, scheduling and products.

7 Discuss the purpose of design controls

design control
An area of operations control that involves incorporating reliability, functionality and serviceability into product design

DESIGN CONTROL

The team approach to product design, discussed earlier in the chapter, provides an opportunity for designers to insert quality and performance controls before a product is produced. **Design control** focuses on creating new products engineered for reliability, functionality and serviceability.

For example, the characteristics of materials to be used in manufacturing can be examined to ensure up front that they meet production standards. This orchestrated process should ensure a well-functioning final product. In creating the Ford Taurus, Team Taurus included triple rubber seals and insert doors in the car's design plans. Both innovations were in response to customer complaints. As a result, the Taurus's doors fit together and the interior was quieter.[21]

The team approach can be expanded to integrate marketing research specialists who can provide the connection between consumer needs and production capabilities; or the team may work directly with the consumer. Regardless of the approach, the team can then incorporate quality, as defined by the consumer, at the design stage.

MATERIALS CONTROL: PURCHASING

An integral component of an operations management control system, materials control is achieved through effective purchasing. **Purchasing** is the acquisition of needed goods and services. The goal of the purchasing agent is to acquire them at optimal costs from competent and reliable sources. What an organization produces depends on the inputs—the materials and supplies. Therefore, purchasing is critical for the following reasons:

- If the materials are not on hand, nothing can be produced.
- If the right quantity of materials is not available, the organization cannot meet demand.
- If the materials are of inferior quality, producing quality products is difficult or costly.

The goal of purchasing control is to ensure the availability and acceptable quality of material while balancing costs. Maintaining relationships with reliable sources is one strategy to achieve this goal. The advent of total quality management (see Appendix A) has shifted the emphasis of materials purchasing control. Traditionally, controls focused on—in order of emphasis—quantity, time and quality specifications. Now, quality has the same priority as quantity.

Managers are initiating two practices to reflect this change. First, they are building long-term relationships with suppliers. This creates a partner for the producer and a sure source of sales for the supplier. The practice of building long-term relationships contrasts starkly with the traditional practice of pitting vendors against one another. The traditional practice was a short-term approach that often led to financial savings and quality reductions.

Supplier relationship management (SRM) software enables companies and their suppliers to collaborate on sourcing and procurement for supply management. SRM applications take advantage of the capabilities of Internet technologies to provide direct, personalized communications from businesses to their suppliers. Partners are given visibility into customer demand early enough to respond to changes and synchronize internal operations to support the change.

Buyer and seller relationships are being transformed by the Internet. The world is increasingly interconnected 24 hours a day, 7 days a week. The Web has made it easier for companies to form partnerships. Competition is giving way to **co-opetition** as business entities find themselves as each other's customers, suppliers and partners. Automating the procurement process helps "manufacturers carry less inventory, reduce time to market, and eliminate costly paperwork."[22]

The second practice is the shifting of responsibility for quality to suppliers. Contracts are developed based on materials and equipment being pre-inspected and guaranteed to have minimum defects.

Outsourcing In addition to the quality movement, purchasing has been influenced by management decisions to focus on core competencies. Rather than manufacturing or assembling component parts, companies like GM, Cisco and General Mills are outsourcing. Companies that employ **outsourcing** as a strategy contract with suppliers to perform functions in lieu of performing the functions themselves. Outsourcing for some companies may include marketing, accounting or shipping; but in manu-

8 Discuss the importance of managing and controlling materials purchasing

purchasing
The acquisition of goods and services at optimal costs from competent and reliable sources

supplier relationship management (SRM)
An information system that quantifies and manages relationships with suppliers; SRM involves consolidating and classifying procurement data to provide an understanding of supplier relationships and developing procurement strategies

co-opetition
A word coined by Ray Noorda, Founder of the networking software company Novell, meaning that businesses have to compete and cooperate at the same time

outsourcing
A purchasing strategy in which a company contracts with a supplier to perform functions in lieu of the company

facturing, outsourcing encompasses suppliers who design, engineer, manufacture or integrate parts—or perform all these activities.

Paying someone else to handle all or part of a company's operations can reduce costs and avoid headaches. Outsourcing can be a successful option if managers take the following steps to minimize risk and maintain control:[23]

- Do not outsource functions critical to the company's operation. The idea is to protect the core business from delays or problems with the outside source.

- Minimize cost fluctuations by outsourcing only functions whose costs do not vary much from month to month. This way, outsourcing expenses are predictable.

- Be wary of extremely low fees. They may have been set low to get the business, then will increase dramatically next year.

- Share the risk with the vendor. Make fees contingent on meeting deadlines. Include this in the contract.

- Find out if the vendor has a heavy commitment to one large company, which signals the vendor's priorities.

- Have a backup plan that includes a list of other vendors.

- Stipulate, by contract, that all data pertaining to the business is owned by the company, not the vendor.

Outsourcing thrives in the fluid, fast-changing world of computers. Many big companies don't manufacture anything. Dell concentrates on marketing. They buy circuit boards, disc drives and other modules—designed specifically for them from outside manufacturers—and assemble the computers in their own warehouses.[24] Planning and execution functions are driven by demand in real time, rather than companies building products to a forecast of future demand. Instead of outsourcing like other computer manufacturers, Dell manufactures computers (after the orders have been placed).

Inventory Control

inventory
The goods an organization keeps on hand

The goods an organization keeps on hand are called **inventory**. Inventory control is critical to operations management because inventory represents a major investment. The aim is to get the parts in and out of the factory as fast as possible. Many of the machines used for manufacturing can communicate with one another electronically, which gives manufacturers real-time data about their inventories.

Most organizations have three types of inventory: raw materials, work-in-process and finished goods. Each type is associated with a different stage of the production process, as Figure B.6 shows.

raw materials inventory
Inventory consisting of the raw materials, parts and supplies used as inputs to production

The **raw materials inventory** includes the materials, parts and supplies an organization uses as inputs to production. The raw materials for a Hewlett Packard Enterprise (HP Inc.) laser printer include the printer engine, the circuit boards and the power supply. At a Wendy's fast-food restaurant, the inventory includes meat patties, buns, tomatoes and lettuce. Raw materials inventory is the least expensive type of inventory because the organization has not yet invested any labor in it. Nevertheless, an excessive raw materials inventory ties up cash unnecessarily.

work-in-process inventory
Inventory consisting of materials and parts that have begun moving through the production process but are not yet assembled into a completed product

Work-in-process inventory consists of the materials and parts that have begun moving through the production process but are not yet a completed product. At HP Inc., the toner and drum assembly and the shell of a laser printer are work-in-process

---

Figure B.6 **Three Types of Inventory**

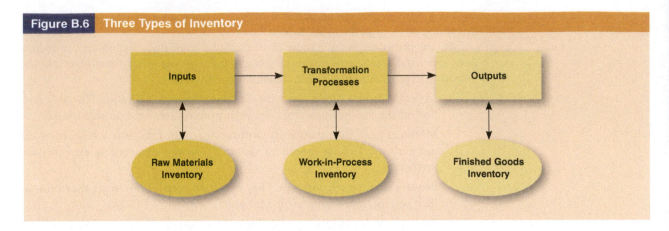

---

inventory. Because labor has been expended to produce work-in-process inventory, this type of inventory represents a greater investment than raw materials inventory.

The **finished goods inventory** consists of the products that have completed the entire production process but have not yet been sold. Assembled and boxed HP Inc. printers, for example, stored in a warehouse before shipping are finished goods inventory. This inventory, of course, represents the greatest investment of all three types.

Importance of Inventory Control At one time, managers prided themselves on maintaining large inventories. Inventories were regarded as measures of wealth. Today, managers realize that a large inventory can indicate wasted resources. Money not tied up in inventory can be used elsewhere. The goal of inventory control is to sustain the proper flow of materials while maintaining adequate inventory levels and minimum costs.

Many companies let customers use the web to cut the ordering time for parts. "When you let customers order on the web with speed, you have to be able to manufacture and deliver the product with speed."[25]

> *Improvements in manufacturing have shortened production time and allowed manufacturers to respond quickly to signs of slackening demand. In fact, in its recent decision to cut its discount rate by half a percentage point, the Federal Reserve suggested the rapid slowdown in manufacturing was the result of 'new technologies' appearing to have accelerated the response of production and demand to high inventories. New technologies for **supply-chain management** and flexible manufacturing imply that businesses can perceive imbalances in inventories at a very early stage—virtually in real time. Quicker production means manufacturers need to keep less inventory on hand.*[26]

Traditionally, organizations have four specific techniques for inventory management. They are: economic order quantity, materials requirement planning, manufacturing resource planning and just-in-time inventory systems.

finished goods inventory
Inventory consisting of products that have not been sold

supply-chain management
Includes managing supply and demand, sourcing raw materials and parts, manufacturing and assembly, warehousing and inventory tracking, order entry and order management, distribution across all channels and delivery to the customer

Explain how EOQ, MRP, MRPII, and JIT differ

economic order quantity (EOQ)
An inventory technique that helps managers determine how much material to order by minimizing the total of ordering costs and holding costs based on the organization's usage rate

ECONOMIC ORDER QUANTITY

The **economic order quantity (EOQ)** is the order quantity that minimizes ordering and holding costs based on the rate of inventory use. Ordering costs are the costs of placing the order. Ordering costs include, for example, the costs of postage, receiving and inspections. Holding costs are the costs of keeping the inventory on hand. These expenses include the costs of storage space, financing and taxes.[27]

The EOQ may be derived by calculation. The formula for EOQ is

$$\sqrt{\frac{2 \times D \times C}{H}}$$

where D represents demand, or annual usage rate; C represents ordering costs; and H represents holding costs.

Suppose the manager of a small shop that manufactures valves needs to order one inch valve gaskets. A review of records indicates that ordering costs for the gaskets amount to $20, the annual holding cost is $12 and the annual demand for the gasket is 1,815. The formula to calculate the EOQ in this case is:

$$\sqrt{\frac{2 \times 1,815 \times \$20}{\$12}} = 77.8$$

The best order quantity, then, is 78.

The next question facing the manager is when to order. This is determined by calculating the **reorder point (ROP)**. The formula for ROP is:

$$\frac{D}{Time} \times \text{Lead Time}$$

Assuming that gaskets can be delivered five days after the order is placed, the manager determines the ROP by using the following calculation:

$$\frac{1,815}{365} \times 5 = 24.86 \text{ (or 25)}$$

This formula tells the manager that, because the time to receive new orders is five days, at least 25 gaskets should be in inventory at all times. Any time the number of gaskets drops to 25, a new order for 78 gaskets should be placed.

EOQ forces managers to evaluate usage rates, ordering costs and holding costs. The major disadvantage of EOQ is that it focuses on optimal order quantity while ignoring quality. Another disadvantage of EOQ is that it does not take into account supplier performance.

reorder point (ROP)
The most economical point at which an inventory item should be reordered

materials requirement planning (MRP)
A production planning and inventory system that uses forecasts of customer orders to schedule the exact amount of materials needed for production

MATERIALS REQUIREMENT PLANNING

EOQ is useful so long as each inventory item, as in the valve example, is independent of others. When demand for one inventory item depends on other inventory items, however, EOQ is no longer applicable. Such is the case for the Boeing Company, for example. To produce one hundred 747 aircraft, each of which includes some 3,000,000 parts, Boeing must have a vast number of discrete components on hand. One technique for managing such an inventory is **materials requirement planning (MRP)**.

This production planning and inventory system uses forecasts of customer orders to schedule the exact amount of materials needed to support the manufacture of the desired number of products.

An MRP program begins with a master schedule of planned production. (Recall that a master schedule uses sales forecasts to determine the quantities of finished goods required in a specific time period.) The next step is to use a computer to analyze product design and determine all the parts and supplies needed to manufacture the finished product. This information is then merged with existing inventory records. The quantities of each item on hand are identified, and usage rates are calculated. Then the system can determine ordering times and quantities. In essence, MRP incorporates EOQ, perpetual inventory control, and statistics to provide a comprehensive system for purchasing materials and scheduling various production activities to meet projected customer orders.[28]

MRP results in purchasing on time and according to actual needs. In most cases, MRP means a reduction in inventory and fewer production stops due to lack of stock. The changes save money. The major limitation associated with MRP is the extensive organizational commitment it requires. To use MRP properly, an organization must develop adequate support systems and skilled personnel. The system cannot be implemented in a piecemeal fashion.

MRP solved Boeing's inventory problems. The system that preceded MRP at Boeing was designed to keep track of the several million parts that went into each plane, rather than following the development of the plane itself. The system worked when Boeing was building 10,000 identical planes, but it became a major problem when each airline wanted its planes to be slightly different. Moreover, the list of parts produced by engineering for a given airplane was configured differently from the list put together by manufacturing, customer service or other Boeing operations. So the parts list had to be broken down, converted and recomputed as many as thirteen times during the construction of a single plane.

Instead of treating most airplane parts as unique, Boeing's MRP system groups them into three categories, depending on how frequently they are used. Boeing also assembled a complete parts list that every division can use without modification or tabbing. In place of defining a plane by the parts that go into it, Boeing defines the parts by the plane they are in.[29]

MANUFACTURING RESOURCE PLANNING

Even more sophisticated than MRP is **manufacturing resource planning (MRPII)**. MRP is used to manage inventory; MRPII, on the other hand, is a comprehensive planning system. It emphasizes planning and controlling all of a firm's resources—its finances, capital and marketing strategies—as well as production and materials management.[30] MRPII creates a model of the overall business, allowing top managers to control production scheduling, cash flow, human resources, capacity, inventory, purchasing and distribution. Because of its comprehensiveness, MRPII can be used effectively for strategic planning.

manufacturing resource planning (MRPII)
A comprehensive planning system that controls the total resources of a firm

The value of MRPII lies in its comprehensiveness. It is a strategic management system that links the entire organization. Because it is very expensive to implement, only large companies can afford to use it. In addition, it must be custom designed for the user, which involves a major commitment of the organization's time and human resources.

JUST-IN-TIME INVENTORY SYSTEMS

Another technique for inventory control is designed to reduce inventory by coordinating supply deliveries with production. **Lean manufacturing** or manufacturing without waste requires inventory reduction. This technique, called the just-in-time (JIT) inventory system, originated in Japan and was discussed in Chapter 15. The JIT concept is sometimes referred to as the *kanban system, the stockless system* or *zero-inventory system*.

With the JIT approach, suppliers deliver exact quantities of materials directly to manufacturers, as the manufacturers need them. There is no buffer of "safety" inventory. There is no warehousing or in-process handling. The benefits managers expect to receive from JIT include reduced inventory and setup time, better workflow, shorter manufacturing time and less consumption of space. They often reap unexpected benefits, however. When a company changes to a JIT system, managers are often able to identify problems that were masked by inventory reserves, slack schedules and devices that workers developed to keep up the required flow.[31]

A JIT system depends on reliable suppliers who must meet strict delivery schedules. When the system works, it works well. At Behlen Manufacturing Company, within two years from adopting a just-in-time inventory system, inventory costs were down $10 million, work flow improved, and delivery time for finished goods improved 20 percent.[32] But when the supplier has troubles, the result is production stoppages.

10 Discuss the importance and methods of schedule controls

SCHEDULING CONTROL

Another important element of operations control is schedule control—techniques for scheduling operations and tracking production. There are two basic scheduling techniques: Gantt charts and network scheduling.

Gantt Charts

Henry L. Gantt, an early pioneer in scientific management, was the first to devise a reliable method for reserving machine time for jobs in production. The method promotes the orderly flow of work from one process to the next, with a minimum of lost time or delays. His method involved a tool called a **Gantt chart**. As you can see by examining Figure B.7, a Gantt chart tracks a project from beginning to end, comparing the time estimates for the steps involved with the actual time they require and adjusting the starting and ending times of steps if necessary.

Figure B.7 shows a Gantt chart for a manufacturing department. The processes it tracks are machining, assembling and shipping. To aid the production manager in monitoring the progress of each process and making any required adjustments, the chart presents two sets of information: (1) the planned time for each task, represented by the area enclosed in brackets; and (2) the actual completion time, represented by a solid bar within each set of brackets. The length of the line indicates how much of the task is complete.

Gantt charts work best for scheduling and tracking sequential events, the completion times of which will determine the total time for an entire project. Gantt charts are not appropriate for highly complex projects requiring many different kinds of sequential operations that begin or run simultaneously.

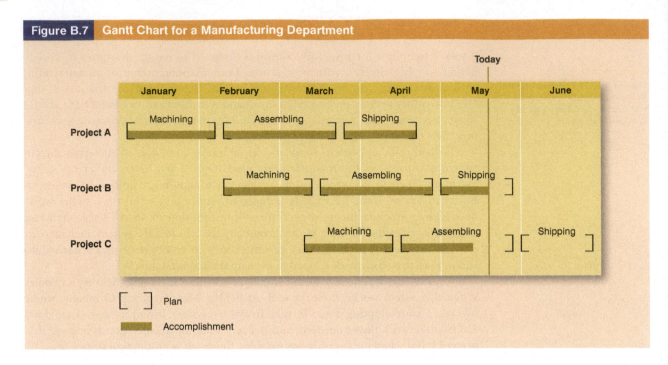

Figure B.7   Gantt Chart for a Manufacturing Department

Network Scheduling

Managers use **network scheduling** to schedule and track projects in which the events or activities are interrelated. This technique for scheduling and controlling uses events and activities that have time estimates assigned to them. Figure B.8 presents a network diagram. Events, represented by circles, indicate the starting point of some production operation, such as delivery of materials. Activities, or processes, are represented by lines with arrows. The lines indicate the time required to complete the event.

The network diagram in Figure B.8 shows the schedule for a project that involves 15 events and 18 activities. Event Number 1 marks the start of Activities A and B. The notation "A.10" means that Activity A is scheduled for ten days. Event Number 2 marks the end of Activity A and the beginning of Activity C, which is scheduled to take 2 days. To construct this network, the managers had to list each activity, estimate the time for each and identify the immediate predecessors for each activity. Note that an activity cannot be started until its predecessor has been completed. Note, too, that some activities can take place simultaneously.

The **program evaluation and review technique (PERT)**, an adaptation of network scheduling, assigns four time estimates to activities: optimistic, most likely, pessimistic and expected. The expected time (the amount of time the manager thinks the activity will actually take) is based on a probability analysis of the other three time estimates.

The PERT method, originally devised at Lockheed Corporation for planning complex aerospace development projects, provides managers with a graphic view of the details of the project from initiation to completion. It functions as a control device by helping the manager spot trouble areas and see when a project is falling behind schedule. The manager can take corrective action before the delay becomes critical.

One benefit of a PERT network is that it helps managers identify the **critical path**—the longest possible path or least direct route from the beginning to the end of a network diagram. Given current time estimates the critical path shows the longest

network scheduling
A scheduling technique used to track projects in which events or activities are interrelated and have time estimates assigned to them

program evaluation and review technique (PERT)
A network scheduling technique for planning and charting the progress of a complex project in terms of the time it is expected to take—an estimate that is derived from probability analysis

critical path
The longest sequence of events and activities in a network production schedule or the longest time a job could take

Figure B.8	Network Diagram Showing How to Replace a Pipeline

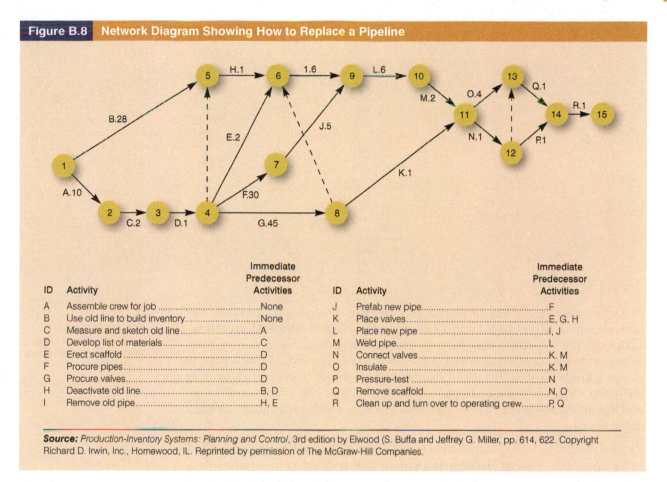

			Immediate Predecessor				Immediate Predecessor
ID	Activity		Activities	ID	Activity		Activities
A	Assemble crew for job		None	J	Prefab new pipe		F
B	Use old line to build inventory		None	K	Place valves		E, G, H
C	Measure and sketch old line		A	L	Place new pipe		I, J
D	Develop list of materials		C	M	Weld pipe		L
E	Erect scaffold		D	N	Connect valves		K, M
F	Procure pipes		D	O	Insulate		K, M
G	Procure valves		D	P	Pressure-test		N
H	Deactivate old line		B, D	Q	Remove scaffold		N, O
I	Remove old pipe		H, E	R	Clean up and turn over to operating crew		P, Q

Source: *Production-Inventory Systems: Planning and Control*, 3rd edition by Elwood (S. Buffa and Jeffrey G. Miller, pp. 614, 622. Copyright Richard D. Irwin, Inc., Homewood, IL. Reprinted by permission of The McGraw-Hill Companies.

time a job could take. Figure B.9 shows the calculations that define the critical path for the pipeline project introduced in Figure B.8. The critical path represents the earliest possible completion time for the project—65 days—assuming that the worst combination of events occurs.

Awareness of the critical path equips a manager with the ability to really control a project. For example, a delay in the completion of Activity B by 1 day will not affect the total project's completion time. If, however, Activity G takes 47 days instead of 45, the entire project will be 2 days off schedule, unless the manager takes some corrective action. By maneuvering to ensure that the length of the critical path does not increase, the manager can maintain effective control of the project.

Describe the importance and methods of product control

product control
A component of operations control that reduces the probability and costs of poor quality and unreliable products by implementing controls from purchasing to end use

PRODUCT CONTROL

At one time, the entire concept of operations control focused on inspection of the physical product. With the advent of TQM, inspection was placed in a new perspective, as only one part of controlling. Now, **product control** encompasses controls from purchasing to end use. It involves reducing the probability and costs of poor quality and unreliable products. Product controls focus on inspection and testing techniques.

Figure B.9	Calculation of the Critical Path

ACTIVITY	TIME IN DAYS
A	10
C	2
D	1
G	45
K	1
O	4
Q	1
R	1
Critical Path =	65 Days

Acceptance Sampling Any inspection of a representative group of products that takes place prior to the beginning of a new phase of production constitutes **acceptance sampling**. The inspection may occur prior to the receipt of raw materials, when subassemblies are completed, after critical processes of manufacturing and prior to shipping finished goods. The data from the sample are used to evaluate all items in the group. Organizations use acceptance sampling to make cost-effective evaluations on large numbers of items. The evaluations determine whether they accept or reject entire batches.

Detailed Inspections and Tests Rather than a sampling approach to product control, some operations conduct **detailed inspections and tests** on every finished item. Medicines, for example, are tested this way. The goal of the technique is to identify all parts not meeting standards. The inspection or test may consist of an examination of attributes or variables. The inspection and classification of items as acceptable or unacceptable is called **attribute inspection**. Potato chips and nail polish are evaluated this way. An inspector compares the items against a standard and rates their quality as acceptable or unacceptable. In comparison, **variable inspection** involves taking a measurement to determine how much an item varies from standards. Any item that measures within the range is accepted, and those outside are rejected. For example, Ross/Flex might test a valve to see whether a valve would hold between 300 and 350 pounds of pressure per square inch. If it did not, the valve would not meet tolerance standards.

Process Control Sampling With **process control sampling** the purpose is to detect variations in production processes. The technique involves periodic tests to uncover problems with equipment, worn tools, bad parts or personnel. When managers know about problems, they can correct them. For example, a process control procedure at Frito-Lay would be able to detect if a bagging machine was out of adjustment because it was filling 32-ounce bags with only 16 ounces of potato chips. Managers could then stop the process and adjust the machine.

acceptance sampling
A product control technique involving a representative group of products before a new stage of production

detailed inspections and tests
A product control technique in which every finished item receives an examination or performance test

attribute inspection
A product control technique that compares items against a standard and rates their quality as acceptable or unacceptable

variable inspection
A product control technique that involves taking measurements to determine how much an item varies from standards and, therefore, whether it will be accepted or rejected

process control sampling
A product control technique designed to detect variations in production processes

qualification testing
A product control technique in which products are tested for performance on the basis of reliability and safety

Qualification Testing In **qualification testing**, a sample product is checked for performance on the basis of reliability and safety. New car models are driven hundreds of thousands of miles so engineers can test the overall car and its components. Thousands of golf balls are hit by automated golf clubs so that engineers can check on the quality of the balls and the reliability of their flight. The goal of qualification testing is to ensure that a product, as a class, performs as it should. The purpose of detailed testing is to ensure that each version of the product meets established standards.

Review What You've Learned

Appendix Summary

1 **Discuss the nature and importance of operations strategy and operations management.**

Operations strategy is the part of a strategic plan that defines the role, capabilities and expectations of operations. Operations management consists of the managerial activities and techniques used to convert resources into products and services. Without an effective operations strategy and operations management, few organizations would survive. Together they are viewed as a competitive weapon to be used with marketing and finance. When this is the case, the results can be lower prices or better quality, performance or responsiveness to consumer demand.

2 **Discuss the nature and importance of product and service design planning.**

In the past, engineers designed products with a complete lack of thought for product manufacture and assembly. The products could not be assembled easily, contained more parts than necessary and had to be inspected for quality during production. Adopting a concept called design for manufacturability and assembly (DFM/A) can reduce the problems. DFM/A calls for design by teams consisting of designers, manufacturers and assemblers. Because these specialists have a say in product design, actual production of the product becomes more efficient. Design for disassembly (DfD) is another design concept. Its goal is to close the production loop—that is, to conceive, develop and build a product with a long-term view of how its components can be refurbished and reused at the end of the product's life cycle.

3 **Describe the four main strategies for facilities layout.**

The four main strategies for facilities layout are:

- *Process layout.* In a process layout all the equipment and machines that perform a similar task or function are located together. A product is moved from process to process as needed.
- *Product layout.* In a product layout the machines and tasks are arranged according to the progressive steps by which the product is made.
- *Cellular layout.* The cellular layout combines the characteristics of process and product layouts. In a cellular arrangement all the equipment required for a sequence of operations on the same product is placed together in a group called a cell.
- *Fixed-position layout.* A fixed-position layout is used when, because of bulk or size, the product remains in one location. Tools, equipment and human skills are brought to the product.

4 **Discuss the nature of process and technology planning.**

The challenge facing operations managers is to identify the proper blend of people and technology to use in transforming inputs into finished products or services. For any given production task, several conversion methods are available—some labor intensive, others equipment intensive. The nature of the product and the objectives and resources of the organization are critical factors in choosing one method over another. The growing trend today is toward the use of more sophisticated technology in manufacturing. The technology responsible for revolutionizing manufacturing processes includes robotics, CAD/CAM, flexible manufacturing systems, computer integrated manufacturing, soft manufacturing systems and agile manufacturing.

5 **Explain the factors in facilities location planning and capacity planning.**

In considering the location of facilities, managers must ask two important questions: Should the firm have one or two large plants or several smaller ones? Where should the facilities be located? The decision on the number of plants will depend on the company's long-range objectives and distribution strategies, financial resources and equipment costs. The choice of location depends on the location of the market where the product will be sold, availability of labor skills, labor costs, proximity to suppliers, tax rates, construction expenses, utility rates and quality of life for the employees. Capacity planning is a matter of trying to convert sales forecasts into production facilities. Too little capacity means that the organization cannot match demand and that it will lose customers. The reverse results in facilities and equipment sitting idle while incurring costs.

6 **Describe the role of operations control in achieving quality and productivity.**

The costs associated with poor productivity relate to quality. These include the costs of scrap, repair and downtime. Such costs are directly observable during production. Quality is also related to costs incurred before manufacturing begins. These expenses include the cost of incoming materials, purchasing and inventory. All of these factors fall within the purview of operations management. To achieve high quality and productivity, managers can use a number of operations controls. These include control of design, materials, inventory, scheduling and products.

7 **Discuss the purpose of design controls.**

Design control focuses on creating new products engineered for reliability, functionality and serviceability.

8 **Discuss the importance of managing and controlling materials purchasing.**

What an organization produces depends on the inputs—the materials and supplies. Therefore purchasing is critical for the following reasons:

- If the materials are not on hand, nothing can be produced.
- If the right quantity of materials is not available, demand cannot be met.
- If the materials are of inferior quality, producing quality products is difficult or costly.

The goal of purchasing control is to ensure the availability and acceptable quality of material while balancing costs.

9 **Explain how EOQ, MRP, MRPII, and JIT differ.**

- *EOQ.* The economic order quantity (EOQ) is the order quantity that minimizes ordering and building costs based on the rate of inventory use. EOQ is useful as long as each inventory item is independent of others.
- *MRP.* When the demand for one inventory item depends on other inventory items, materials requirement planning (MRP) is applicable. This production planning and inventory system uses forecasts of customer orders to schedule the exact amount of materials needed to support the manufacture of the desired number of products.

- *MRPII.* Even more sophisticated than MRP is manufacturing resource planning (MRPII). MRP is used to manage inventory; MRPII is a comprehensive planning system. It emphasizes planning and controlling all of a firm's resources—its finances, capital and marketing strategies as well as its production and materials management. MRPII creates a model of the overall business, allowing top managers to control production scheduling, cash flow, human resources, capacity, inventory, purchasing and distribution.

- *JIT.* The just-in-time inventory system is designed to reduce inventory by coordinating supply deliveries with production. With the JIT approach, suppliers deliver exact quantities of materials directly to manufacturers as the manufacturers need them. There is no buffer of "safety" inventory or in-process handling.

10 **Discuss the importance and methods of schedule controls.**

Schedule controls are techniques for scheduling operations and tracking production. There are two basic scheduling techniques: Gantt charts and network scheduling.

- A Gantt chart tracks a project from beginning to end, comparing the time estimates for the steps involved with the actual time they require and adjusting the starting and ending times of steps if necessary. Gantt charts work best for scheduling and tracking sequential events. Gantt charts are not appropriate for highly complex operations requiring many different kinds of sequential operations that begin or run simultaneously.

- Network scheduling is used to schedule and track projects in which events or activities are interrelated. This technique uses events and activities that have time estimates assigned to them. An adaptation of network scheduling is program evaluation and review technique (PERT). PERT assigns four time estimates to activities: optimistic, most likely, pessimistic and expected. The expected time is based on probability analysis of the other three time estimates. One benefit of a PERT network is that it helps managers identify the critical path—the longest path or least direct route from beginning to the end of a network diagram. The critical path equips a manager with the ability to really control a project. By maneuvering to ensure that the length of the critical path does not increase, the manager can gain effective control of the project.

11 Describe the importance and methods of product control.

Product control encompasses controls from purchasing to end use. It involves reducing the probability and cost of poor quality and unreliable products. There are four methods of product controls.

- *Acceptance sampling.* Any inspection of a representative group of products that takes place prior to the beginning of a new phase of production constitutes acceptance sampling. Organizations use acceptance sampling to make cost-effective evaluations of large numbers of items. The evaluations determine whether they accept or reject entire batches.

- *Detailed inspections and tests.* Rather than a sampling approach, some operations conduct detailed inspections and tests on every finished item. The inspections may consist of an examination of attributes or variables.

- *Process control sampling.* With process control sampling, the purpose is to detect variations in production processes. The technique involves periodic tests to uncover problems with equipment, worn tools, bad parts or personnel.

- *Qualification testing.* In qualification testing, a sample product is checked for performance on the basis of reliability and safety. The goal of qualification testing is to ensure that a product, as a class, performs as it should.

KEY TERMS

acceptance sampling   578

aggregate planning   568

agile manufacturing   566

attribute inspection   578

capacity planning   567

cellular layout   564

computer-aided design (CAD)   565

computer-aided manufacturing (CAM)   565

computer-integrated manufacturing (CIM)   566

co-opetition   570

critical path   576

design control   569

design for disassembly (DfD)   562

design for manufacturability and assembly (DFM/A)   561

detailed inspections and tests   578

economic order quantity (EOQ)   573

facilities layout   562

finished goods inventory   572

fixed-position layout   564

flexible manufacturing system (FMS)   565

Gantt chart   575

inventory   571

Lean manufacturing   575

manufacturing resource planning (MRPII)   574

master schedule   568

materials requirement planning (MRP)   573

network scheduling   576

operations management   559

operations strategy   559

outsourcing   570

process control sampling   578

process layout   564

product control   577

product layout   564

program evaluation and review technique (PERT)   576

purchasing   570

qualification testing   579

raw materials inventory   571

reorder point (ROP)   573

robotics   565

soft manufacturing system (SMS)   566

supplier relationship management (SRM)   570

supply-chain management   572

variable inspection   578

work-in-process inventory   571

REVIEW QUESTIONS

1. What is operations management? Why is operations strategy important?

2. Why is design for manufacturability and assembly important in terms of overall operations management?

3. When should a process layout be used? Why?

4. What benefits can CAD or CAM technology provide for a manufacturer?

5. What factors should managers consider when selecting a facility location? What is the role of a cost-benefit analysis in the decision?

6. What is the role of operations control in achieving quality and productivity?

7. What is the purpose of design controls?

8. Why is it important for an organization to control materials purchasing?

9. How do EOQ and JIT systems control inventory?

10. What is the purpose of a Gantt chart? What is the purpose of PERT scheduling?

11. What is the difference between acceptance sampling and process control sampling?

DISCUSSION QUESTIONS FOR CRITICAL THINKING

1. Are operations management and operations strategy most closely related to corporate-level, business-level or functional-level strategy? Why? In what way?

2. You have been asked by the owner of a local jewelry store to identify a possible location for a second store. How would you proceed? How would you help the store owner determine the new store's capacity?

3. Of the three types of inventory, which of these is most likely to be affected by the just-in-time inventory system? Why?

4. If you were the manager of a donut shop, what product control would be the most critical? What would be the least critical? Why?

Appendix C

International Management

LEARNING OBJECTIVES

After studying this chapter, you should be able to:

1   Explain the primary reasons why businesses become international

2   Describe the characteristics of multinational corporations

3   Discuss the political, legal, economic, sociocultural, and technological elements of the international environment

4   Describe the major strategies for going international

5   Explain the phases a company goes through when moving from domestic operations to a multinational structure

6   Discuss the major staffing concerns for an international corporation

7   Describe the major concerns relating to leading a cross-cultural workforce

8   Discuss the major concerns relating to controlling an international corporation

INTRODUCTION

American businesses are part of a global economy regardless of how large or small they are. Most U.S. businesses have discovered that significant portions of their inputs come from other nations. Today, companies need the flexibility to acquire needed inputs from sources offering the highest quality, greatest dependability and lowest cost, whether located overseas or down the street.

As probably never before in our nation's history, managers must pay attention to what is going on in economies around the globe. The world is changing more rapidly every day, and the changes are monumental. After communism lost its hold in the Soviet Union, many of its former satellite republics became independent nations and opened their borders to foreign investment and international trade. Soon after East Germany merged with West Germany, the republic of Czechoslovakia split into two nations. Twenty-seven European Communities (EC) formed an economic union referred to as the European Union (EU) and created a common currency (the euro) and banking system. EU citizens carry one passport. China opened its doors to foreign investment and is investing in the United States. Great Britain and countries in Central and South America are moving steadily away from socialist economies with the privatization of many government-owned operations. (The sale of Telmex, Mexico's telephone company, to private investors is but one example.) These events and others discussed throughout this text mean vast economic challenges to and opportunities for both businesses and individual consumers around the world.

Companies in every country need the freedom and flexibility to act quickly in anticipation of or in reaction to changes taking place around the world. Each day the values of countries' currencies fluctuate, offering advantages and disadvantages. As the value of the dollar falls against a foreign currency, U.S. goods and services become cheaper and more appealing to the citizens in that country. As the value of the U.S. dollar rises against that of another country's currency, that country's products and services become more appealing to U.S. consumers and companies.

1 Explain the primary reasons why businesses become international

WHY BUSINESSES BECOME INTERNATIONAL

Companies see expansion into new foreign markets as a primary strategy for survival, as well as for boosting sales and profits. McDonald's is America's best-known global food-service retailer. It expands through various means from building company-owned outlets to licensing and partnership agreements. McDonald's is but one U.S. company that has found domestic sales slowing due to saturated domestic markets, thus leaving it little choice about how to increase earnings. Apple is another U.S. company that is pursuing overseas markets to overcome disappointing domestic sales growth. For fiscal fourth-quarter 2015, Apple reported that international sales accounted for 62 percent of the quarter's revenue.[1]

In general, companies go international for two basic sets of reasons or motives: proactive and reactive. Proactive motives include the search for new customers, new markets, increased market share, increased return on investments, needed raw materials and other resources, tax advantages, lower costs and economies of scale. This last reason, economies of scale, encourages companies to find foreign partners to share the costs connected with building factories, conducting research and expanding one's sales and presence in additional markets. The drive to reduce costs has led to setting up operations in countries with lower wages and fewer restrictions on business.

Reactive motives include the desire to escape from trade barriers and other government regulations, to better serve a customer or group of customers (many Japanese auto parts suppliers, for instance, have moved to the United States to be near the Japanese companies they supply) and to remain competitive. Fear of potential trade restrictions has led U.S. automakers to expand their presence in Europe, Asia and Latin America and has led Japanese and German automakers and their suppliers to build plants in the United States. Nearly every major foreign producer of automobiles has established subsidiaries in the United States to escape actual or potential American trade restrictions. One example is Mercedes-Benz, with its manufacturing operations in Alabama, mentioned in Chapter 4's Global Applications.

The desire to escape government regulation is not limited to automobile manufacturers. Hundreds of U.S. companies have established their own foreign subsidiaries. Likewise, Japan's largest cosmetics maker, the Shiseido Company, entered U.S. and European markets in response to government actions. Shiseido had long enjoyed a comfortable dominance of Japan's cosmetics market. Lax antitrust enforcement let it keep retail prices high, while import regulations insulated it from cheap foreign products. But since mid-1995, Japan has clamped down on Shiseido's business practices and deregulated cosmetics imports. Shiseido acquired a number of foreign acquisitions to wean itself from the Japanese market. Shiseido's overseas sales by region include the Americas and Europe, as well as Asia/Oceania.[2]

THE MULTINATIONAL CORPORATION

Describe the characteristics of multinational corporations

Many firms around the world, large and small, have become involved in international business over the past decade. The managers of these businesses conduct international trade and are engaged in **international management**—managing resources (people, information, funds, inventories and technologies) across national boundaries and adapting management principles and functions to the demands of foreign competition and environments.

These international companies can do business in foreign countries in several ways. Some simply maintain sales offices in other lands; others only buy materials from companies in other countries. Those companies with *operating facilities*, not just sales offices, in one or more foreign countries are classified as **multinational corporations**.[3]

In general, there are two kinds of multinational companies: those that market their product lines in relatively unaltered states throughout the world (standardization), and those that modify their products and services along with the marketing of them to appeal to specific groups of consumers in specific geographical areas (customization). Products that illustrate the first group are sporting goods, soft drinks, cigarettes, chemicals, oil products, liquors, and certain types of clothing—Lee Jeans, for example. Both Pepsi and Wrigley's chewing gum are sold around the world with only their packaging, promotion and labeling altered to suit foreign requirements. Examples of customization include computer software programmed to work in foreign languages; cars manufactured to meet a country's safety, pollution and drivers' preferences (right-hand drive, for example); fast-food menus altered to cater to cultural tastes; and cosmetics formulated to complement the skin tones and coloring of different populations. McDonald's, for example, adjusts its menus and food services to suit the tastes of foreign customers (black currant shakes in Poland, salads with shrimp in Germany, veggie burgers in Switzerland).

international management

The process of managing resources (people, information, funds, inventories and technologies) across national boundaries and adapting management principles and functions to the demands of foreign competition and environments

multinational corporation

A company with operating facilities, not just sales offices, in one or more foreign countries; where management favors a global market and strategy and sees the world as its market

Customization is often the best strategy to adopt. Companies that attempt to sell the same product to different nationalities soon discover that there will be problems. Some classic examples follow. "Germans, for example, demand a product that's gentle on lakes and rivers and will pay a premium for it. Spaniards want cheaper products that get shirts white and soft. And Greeks want smaller packages that allow them to hold down the cost of each store visit."[4] Whirlpool Corporation has discovered in its European experience that "not only are kitchen appliances different from one country to another, but consumers also react differently to advertising messages from one country to the next."[5]

Characteristics of Multinationals

Even though multinationals around the world differ in sales volumes, profits, markets serviced and the number of their subsidiaries, they do share some common traits. One common trait is the creation of foreign affiliates, which may be wholly owned by the multinational or jointly held with one or more partners from foreign countries. The multinational company maintains control by having the right to approve the foreign affiliate's plans. McDonald's and Whirlpool are examples of multinationals with affiliates in foreign countries.

Another common characteristic of multinationals is that their management operates with a global vision and strategy—viewing the world as their market. Top managers coordinate long-range plans and usually allow the foreign affiliates to work with great autonomy, leaving the day-to-day management decisions to those closest to the problems in foreign markets. Affiliates' operations are integrated and controls are exercised through management reports; frequent meetings and communications between headquarters staff and those in the affiliates; and the setting of objectives both alone and with headquarters' inputs. Foreign affiliates become the training grounds for company managers as well as the sources for them. Johnson & Johnson provides managers of its far-flung empire with autonomy. Its top management believes "the people closest to the action have the best view." As former CEO Ralph Larsen explains, "Decentralization is at the heart of Johnson & Johnson. With decentralization you get tremendous speed at the local level."[6]

A third characteristic is the tendency of multinationals to choose certain types of business activities. Most multinationals are engaged in manufacturing. The rest tend to cluster around the petroleum industry, banking, agriculture, and public utilities.[7]

Also shared by multinationals is the tendency to locate affiliates in the developed countries of the world—EU nations, Canada, South Korea, Taiwan, Japan, and the United States. Less-developed countries (LDCs) tend to be seen as sources for raw materials and cheap labor, and as markets for fairly inexpensive consumer products that can be mass-produced to standardized designs. Many operations in China exemplify this latter category. A fifth characteristic is the adoption of one of three basic strategies regarding staffing. The first is to decide to adopt a *high skills strategy,* in which the company exports products, not jobs. The second is to *dumb down jobs* and shift the work to cheap-labor countries. This has been the choice for the majority of companies around the world. The third strategy is to mix the preceding two strategies.

3

Discuss the political, legal, economic, sociocultural, and technological elements of the international environment

INTERNATIONAL ENVIRONMENT

The environment in which managers in an international company function is far more complex than its domestic management settings. The key task for top management in a multinational company is to develop and maintain an in-depth understanding of the environments of every country in which it has operations, affiliates, suppliers and customers. Environments monitored include political, legal, economic, sociocultural, and technological. Each environment is constantly undergoing change. Figure C.1 summarizes the components of each environment. The discussion that follows focuses on the key issues of each.

Figure C.1	Components of the International Environment

POLITICAL ENVIRONMENT	
Form of government	Social unrest
Political ideology	Political strife and insurgency
Stability of government	Governmental attitude toward foreign firms
Strength of opposition parties	Foreign policy and groups

LEGAL ENVIRONMENT	
Legal tradition	Patent and trademark laws
Effectiveness of legal system	Laws affecting business firms
Treaties with foreign nations	

ECONOMIC ENVIRONMENT	
Level of economic development	Membership in regional economic blocks (EU, ASEAN, NAFTA)
Population	
Gross domestic product	Monetary and fiscal policies
Per-capita income	Nature of competition
Literacy level	Currency convertibility
Social infrastructure	Inflation
Natural resources	Taxation system
Climate	Interest rates
	Wage and salary levels

SOCIOCULTURAL ENVIRONMENT	
Customs, norms, values, and beliefs	Social institutions
Languages	Status symbols
Attitudes	Religions
Motivations	Demographics and psychographics

TECHNOLOGICAL ENVIRONMENT	
State-of-the-art in various industries	CAD, CAM and CIM
Research and development	Host countries' levels of acceptance and utilization
Recent innovations	Presence of educated workforce in host countries
Robotics	Potential partners around the globe

Source: Adapted from *International Dimensions of Management*, 4th edition, by Phatak. Copyright © 1995. Reprinted with permission of South-Western, a part of Cengage Learning, *www.cengage.com/permissions*.

Political Environment

Political environments can foster or hinder economic development and investment by native and foreign investors and businesses. The political philosophy and type of economic philosophy held by a nation's leaders can give rise to laws that promote domestic commerce and raise barriers to trade with the outside world. The stability of a government and its support by the people will affect decisions to seek commercial opportunities or to avoid investments in a nation. "As the fast-food industry's super-power, McDonald's is a global symbol of Western pop culture, Yankee know-how and American corporate cunning. But prominence on the world stage can be a lightning rod for trouble, and the company is often exposed to outbursts of anti-American sentiment and a myriad of political grievances."[8]

Various groups of citizens with vested interests—farmers, manufacturers, distributors and political parties—can create civil protests and promote protectionist legislation to safeguard their particular interests. Japanese farmers pressured their government successfully for years to keep foreign agricultural commodities such as rice out of the country. They didn't want competition because they could sell their domestic rice for six times the price of California rice.[9]

When the Tokyo discount liquor store chain, Kawachiya Shuhan Co., imported sake—the traditional Japanese rice wine—made in California with California rice, the chain was able to sell the wine cheaper than the Japanese product. The company soon encountered resistance from Japanese brewers. The president of the chain, Yukio Higuchi, said that "all five U.S. brewers, which are affiliates of Japanese sake makers and wholesalers, refused to supply his stores—or any Japanese liquor store—with the U.S.-made sake." Higuchi suspected "liquor makers, fearing that the cheaper sake would threaten the high prices of Japanese sake, joined forces against him."[10]

Prior to its 2002 bankruptcy, Enron Corporation suffered a huge blow to its global ambitions with the cancellation of a $2.9 billion power project by the Maharashtra (India) state government. Enron found itself in the middle of a power struggle between the Bharatiya Janata party (BJP) and the ruling Congress party. Long in search of a way to counter the Congress party, the BJP formed a coalition with the Shiv Sena party. After its actions crushed Enron, BJP President L. K. Advani, delivered a nationalistic message. The party "has no objection to foreign investment as long as it doesn't compromise the nation's economic sovereignty."[11]

Legal Environment

Each country has its own unique set of laws that have an impact on commerce. Laws designed to protect the rights of individuals and labor unions differ as well. Just as managers working in America need to be certain that their actions will not violate any of the many laws bearing on commerce, so, too, must international managers in each host country.

Some countries erect trade barriers, such as quotas, tariffs and embargoes. A **quota** limits the import of a product to a specified amount per year. The Japanese automakers agreed to restrict their imports into America and the EU nations to a specific number of cars each year for several years.

Tariffs are taxes placed on goods in order to make them more expensive and less competitive. Under the North American Free Trade Agreement (NAFTA) between Mexico, Canada and the United States, Mexican tariffs on imported agricultural commodities were phased out over a period of years. Under the terms of the treaty, all non-tariff barriers to agricultural trade between the United States and Mexico were eliminated beginning January 1, 2008.[12]

quota
A government regulation that limits the import of a product to a specified amount per year

tariff
A tax placed on imported goods to make them more expensive and thus less competitive in order to protect domestic producers

Embargoes keep a product out of a country for a time or entirely. The United States has had a long standing embargo against Cuba, hoping to improve human rights in that country. The embargo took effect soon after Fidel Castro came into power in 1959. The trade embargo still exists, but economic and travel restrictions have been eased.

embargoes
Government regulations enacted to keep a product out of a country for a time or entirely

Economic Environment

When companies analyze their options for going multinational, they must consider factors such as the stability of a country's currency, its infrastructure, its availability of needed raw materials and supplies, its levels of inflation and taxes, its citizens' levels of income, its closeness to customers and its climate.

Sociocultural Environment

The sociocultural environment for the international manager includes such concerns as a people's traditions, languages, customs, values, religion and levels of education. To accomplish the company's objectives, the international manager works daily in the cultures of different nations and regions, which differ from his or her own culture.

Understanding the host country's people and their values (and how to respond to them) has helped Amway expand its overseas operation. Before American managers go abroad, it is imperative that they understand the cultures of countries in which they must operate and how those cultures compare to America's. To gain this understanding, the manager must first understand what makes American culture what it is. Figure C.2 shows five dimensions of American society.

Figure C.2	Five Characteristics of American Culture Pertaining to Business
Individualism	The attitude of independence of people who feel that a large degree of freedom in the conduct of their personal life constitutes their individualism. The effects of individualism can be seen in self-expression and individual accomplishment. This value may not be shared in other cultures.
Informality	Informality has two components. First, American culture does not place a great deal of importance on tradition, ceremony or social rules. Second, the "style" in American culture is to be direct and not waste time in the conduct of meetings and conversation. Neither of these values may be significant when conducting business in Latin America or the Middle East.
Materialism	There are two elements in American materialism. First, there is a tendency to attach status to physical objects—certain types of cars or designer clothing, for example. Second, because of vast natural resources, Americans are inclined to buy objects and then discard them while they still have a functional value. Both of these behaviors, if exhibited in other societies, may create problems for the international manager.
Change	Although viewed as part of American culture, change is also perceived as something an individual can influence. That one person can bring about significant change is a fundamental tenet of American culture. In other societies, this same cultural value might not exist. Change is seen as inevitable but as a phenomenon that occurs naturally—a part of the overall evolution of people and their world. Change is accepted; it is predetermined. There is no deliberate attempt to influence it or bring it about.
Time orientation	Time in American culture is seen as a scarce and precious resource. As a result, there is an emphasis on the efficient use of time. This belief dictates the practices of setting deadlines and of making and keeping appointments. But in other societies, time is often viewed as an unlimited and never-ending resource. This attitude explains why people in some cultures tend to be quite casual about keeping appointments or meeting deadlines.

Source: From *International Dimensions of Management*, 4th edition, by Phatak. Copyright © 1995. Reprinted with permission of South-Western, a part of Cengage Learning, *www.cengage.com/permissions*.

After analyzing American culture, the international manager must evaluate the cultures in the countries and regions where he or she will be doing business. One suggested approach is to use the following five dimensions:

1   *Material culture.* The international manager needs to evaluate the technology and the technological know-how for producing goods in a country, the manner in which the country makes use of these abilities, and the resulting economic benefits to the society.

2   *Social institutions.* The international manager needs to analyze the influence on individuals of social institutions—schools, family, social class, religions, and political parties. These strongly affect individuals' work ethics and their abilities and willingness to work in groups.

3   *Humans and the universe.* The values and beliefs of people in other cultures may be influenced greatly by religion, customs, and superstitions. The international manager needs to understand that these elements are an integral part of the culture.

4   *Aesthetics.* This dimension is composed of the art, folklore, myths, music, drama, and native traditions in a culture. These factors can be important in interpreting the symbolic meanings of artistic expressions and various kinds of communications, such as gestures and visual representations. Failure to interpret these signals as the natives do is bound to cause problems.

5   *Languages.* The most difficult dimension for the international manager is languages and their various dialects. Not only does the manager need to speak the language of the host country, an international manager must also understand the interpretations and nuances of the languages as their words have more than dictionary meanings. This dimension logically extends to understanding which groups within a society are at odds with one another and which traditionally get along.[13]

Technological Environment

This environment contains the innovations that are rapidly occurring in all types of technologies, from robotics to smart phones. In the global environment, American technology companies are forging strategic alliances with Swiss, Japanese, German, Chinese and Indian rivals at an unprecedented rate in an effort to survive and remain competitive in the global marketplace. The name of the game is to achieve world-class product development and delivery. The goal is to deliver—not necessarily build—the highest-quality products and bring them to market in the shortest possible time.

Unless companies want to go it alone with all the expenses in money, time and bricks and mortar that such a decision carries with it, they must join forces with others to quicken the pace and to cut the costs connected with this goal. Sony and Samsung created a joint venture to develop and manufacture LCD (liquid crystal display) panels. They are vying with other LCD panel manufacturers such as LG.Philips LCD, a joint venture between Royal Philips Electronics of the Netherlands and Korea's LG Electronics.[14] The LCD can be used in just about every product requiring a visual display. As its price came down and its size increased, LCD televisions surpassed worldwide sales of cathode ray tube (CRT) televisions.

Regardless of the kind of business a company is in, it must choose partners and locations that have what it lacks. The best equipment and state-of-the-art technology will be wasted unless those chosen to employ it in manufacturing have the know-how and the willingness to learn how to use it properly.

PLANNING AND THE INTERNATIONAL MANAGER

4 Describe the major strategies for going international

Regardless of whether a manager is planning for domestic or international operations, forecasts for the future depend on assumptions. Planning on an international level involves the same planning elements that we discussed earlier in this text: assessing the environment, developing assumptions, and then forecasting based on those assumptions. Although the process is the same, planning in an international company will be more difficult because many more variables and environments must be considered.

Choosing Strategies

There are basically four ways to get involved in overseas trade. When deciding to "go international," a company may consider any combination of the following strategies:

1. Export your product or service.
2. License others to act on your behalf (such as sales agents, franchisees or users of your processes and patents).
3. Enter into joint ventures (partnerships) for mutual benefit to produce, to market or to do both.
4. Build or purchase facilities outside your home country to conduct your business on your own.

Most companies begin by exporting their goods through foreign distributorships that can successfully place the products on dealer shelves or in consumers' hands. Before deciding on one or another course, however, a company must choose a target market.

In 1987, Recreational Equipment Incorporated (REI), a Seattle-based consumer co-op, successfully used the first strategy. REI began to find unsolicited cash flowing from Japanese consumers looking for the company's lines of sporting goods. It got the message and began offering its catalog (printed in English and with prices in dollars) "through ads in Japanese outdoor publications." By 1991, it had quadrupled its sales to the Japanese market and had 10,000 Japanese members.[15] Today, in addition to ordering by catalog, Japanese members can order online. Japanese direct sales are supported by an REI customer service desk in Tokyo.

Coca-Cola Company of Atlanta used the second strategy to expand into Central and Eastern Europe. It invested more than $1 billion with its licensed affiliates to achieve the expansion. Harley-Davidson is using strategy number three. It has formed several partnerships around the world to market its motorcycles and its line of sportswear. McDonald's uses licensing, partnerships and stand-alone operations in its international

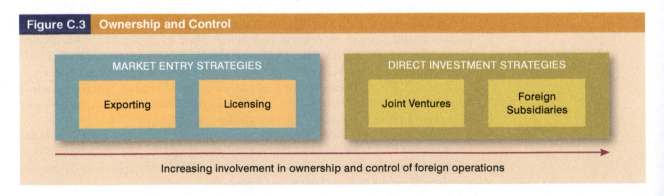

Figure C.3   Ownership and Control

MARKET ENTRY STRATEGIES — Exporting | Licensing

DIRECT INVESTMENT STRATEGIES — Joint Ventures | Foreign Subsidiaries

Increasing involvement in ownership and control of foreign operations

operations. London-based Ebookers Plc, a travel agency, is using strategy number four to outsource call center jobs and the workers who perform them to India.[16]

Assessing the External Variables

In an international company, the managers must assess and monitor the changes in the five environments of the countries in which the company has operations to determine the presence of threats and opportunities. They must determine how these independent external environments will have an impact on and influence each other, and how these impacts and influences will affect the company's internal environment—the areas for which individual managers are responsible and over which they have control. They must then choose goals and strategies and create programs to bring them to reality. In developing plans, the international manager is monitoring and assessing a set of unique external issues and problem areas, including the following seven:

1. *Political instability and risk.* Changes in both governments and their policies can and do affect commerce, company plans and strategies, and the ability to conduct trade within and outside of the host country's borders.

2. *Currency instability.* Changes in the exchange rates of currencies mean changes in the ways in which companies conduct their operations. Large sums are at stake because a company's earnings are in local currencies and must be spent around the globe as well as within the borders of a host country. Large multinationals are dealing with millions of dollars, yen, euros and pounds daily.

3. *Competition from national governments.* State-owned or controlled companies and industries often operate with sizable government assistance and subsidies and are often not expected or required to earn profits. This policy places any international competitor at a great disadvantage. It gives the host country monopoly powers to use for or against both domestic and foreign competitors.

4. *Pressures from national governments.* Companies have been and can be accused of sending unsafe or environmentally unsound technologies and products to a host country, exporting technology and jobs, and interfering with domestic industries. It is important for corporations, like individuals, to be good citizens.

5. *Nationalism.* In developing countries and developed nations, national pride creates political ideologies that can inhibit commerce, especially from foreign-owned operations. From such ideologies can come trade restrictions, local ownership restrictions, and limits on how much money can be exported.

6. *Patent and trademark protection.* Some countries will offer no protection, and anyone's property is fair game. Others offer limited protection to foreign-owned enterprises. Some countries and industries are known for their piracy of ideas and technology.

7. *Intense competition.* Lucrative markets will always exhibit intense competition from both the domestic and foreign sectors. Companies should expect competition in the best markets and most profitable product areas to increase.[17]

A factor that will continue to expand competition is the quality of a company's products or services. In this regard, a set of quality standards is rapidly becoming the passport for success in the international marketplace. The standards were created in the late 1980s by the International Organization for Standardization. The set of technical standards, known collectively as **ISO 9000**, was designed to offer a uniform way of determining whether manufacturing plants and service organizations implement and document sound quality procedures.

ISO 9000
The set of five technical standards, known collectively as ISO 9000, designed to offer a uniform way of determining whether manufacturing and service organizations implement and document sound quality procedures

To register, a company must undergo an audit of its manufacturing and customer service processes, covering everything from how it designs, produces and installs its goods to how it inspects, packages, and markets them. More than 160 countries, including the United States and those in the European Union (EU), have endorsed the standards.

As we can see from these variables, planning in the international marketplace is extremely complicated and surrounded by many issues and uncertainties. The consequences of inadequately assessing the variables will usually mean failures in such things as timing, selection of strategies and financial decisions. The effectiveness of the assessment efforts depends on whether a company can decide how to (1) apportion responsibility for gathering and analyzing information between line and staff managers and between in-house personnel and outside consultants, (2) build credibility and effectiveness into the analysis so that the organization takes it seriously, and (3) bring an understanding of the importance of analysis into corporate operations, particularly capital budgeting and long-term planning.[18]

Assessments lead to forecasts, which managers then use to construct their plans. The aim of all the efforts at assessing, interpreting, forecasting, creating goals, strategies and tactics is to create a unity within management of the multinational and to be a decent corporate citizen in the host countries. Corporate strategy determines how the organization will deploy its resources in order to achieve its objectives. It will become the framework for the formulation of strategies in the affiliates around the world. Figure C.4 highlights the major areas in which global corporate objectives are needed and the areas toward which strategies are directed.

Figure C.4	Areas to be Addressed by the Objectives of a Multinational Manager

PROFITABILITY
- Level of profits
- Return on asset, investment equity, sales
- Annual profit growth
- Annual earnings per share growth

FINANCE
- Financing of foreign affiliates—retained earnings or local borrowing
- Taxation—minimizing tax burden globally
- Optimum capital structure
- Foreign exchange management—minimizing losses from foreign fluctuations

PERSONNEL
- Development of managers with global orientation
- Management development of host-country nationals

MARKETING
- Total sales volume
- Market share—worldwide, region, country
- Growth in sales volume and growth in market share
- Integration of host-country markets for marketing efficiency and effectiveness

TECHNOLOGY
- Type of technology to be transferred abroad—new or old generation
- Adaptation of technology to local needs and circumstances

RESEARCH AND DEVELOPMENT
- Innovation of patentable products
- Innovation of patentable production technology
- Geographic dispersion of research and development laboratories

PRODUCTION
- Economies of scale via international production integration
- Quality and cost control
- Introduction of cost-efficient production methods

HOST GOVERNMENT RELATIONS
- Adapting affiliate plans to host-government developmental plans
- Adherence to local laws, customs and ethical standards

ENVIRONMENT
- Harmony with the physical and biological environment
- Adherence to local environmental legislation

Source: From *International Dimensions of Management*, 4th edition, by Phatak. Copyright © 1995. Reprinted with permission of South-Western, a part of Cengage Learning, *www.cengage.com/permissions*.

ORGANIZING AND THE INTERNATIONAL MANAGER

Companies develop organizational structures to achieve objectives. As the objectives of the organizations change, so too will their organizations. As companies extend their operations to host countries, their internal organization structures must evolve. The structures a firm chooses at any time in its evolution depend on the extent of the operations of these companies abroad, their locations and contributions to the parent company, and the degree of experience and competence possessed by both the parent and host-country managers. The structure chosen must be able to cope with sociocultural, political, legal and economic differences between the host-country and parent-country operations. The structure developed to simply market a product overseas will have to change when the company moves to actually produce the product overseas. A decision about the degree of decentralization must be made and continually reexamined as time and operations unfold.

When a firm attempts to establish an international organization, it must address traditional issues, including the following:

- Achieving operational efficiencies
- Creating flexibility to respond to national and global changes
- Allowing units to share information and technology quickly
- Coordinating activities from various cultures
- Responding swiftly to changes in consumer needs and demands
- Differentiating operations by function, product, customers or geography
- Developing management teams with common goals and shared visions

Although the organization structure utilized by a company depends on its objectives, the typical evolution for a company becoming multinational takes it through three phases: pre-international division phase, international division phase and global structure phase.[19] A major point to note as we trace the evolution of these phases is that in a domestic company, a two-dimensional structure—functional and product or functional and territorial—is often used to meet objectives. In the international arena, a three-dimensional structure is eventually required. It combines functional, product and territorial patterns to provide the functional expertise, product and technical know-how, and host-country knowledge for a company.[20]

Pre-International Division Phase

Companies with a unique product, a product that incorporates the latest technology, a superior product (in features, performance or price), or a totally new product should consider themselves ready for entry into the international arena. For many companies, the first strategy used to introduce the product to a new nation or nations of consumers is to find a way to export the product. The result is typically the addition of an export manager to the marketing department. Companies with a broad line of products—such as a chemical company—might establish an export manager who reports directly to the CEO and works in a staff capacity with the individual product divisions to coordinate production and marketing. The export manager will establish the methods chosen for foreign distribution and marketing—whether to place parent company employees in a host country or to work through agents (importers, distributors or retailers) already established there. Figure C.5 shows the addition of the export manager to an established domestic management structure.

International Division Phase

In time, pressures might mount from host-country laws, trade restrictions and competition, placing the company at a cost disadvantage. In such an event, the company often decides to defend and to expand its foreign market position by establishing marketing or production operations in one or more host countries. Figure C.6 shows the establishment of an **international division**, with its head reporting directly to the CEO.

The international division structure works well for companies in the early stages of international involvement. These firms typically have certain characteristics: "limited product diversity, comparatively small sales (compared to domestic and export sales) generated by foreign subsidiaries, limited geographic diversity, and few executives with international expertise."[21]

In the early stages, companies often practice centralization to keep a tight control over the establishment and staffing of the international facilities. In time, decentralization begins, giving those closest to the problems and opportunities the authority they

international division
A parent company's corporate unit, commonly a marketing or production operation, located in a host country offshore from the parent headquarters and whose head reports directly to the CEO

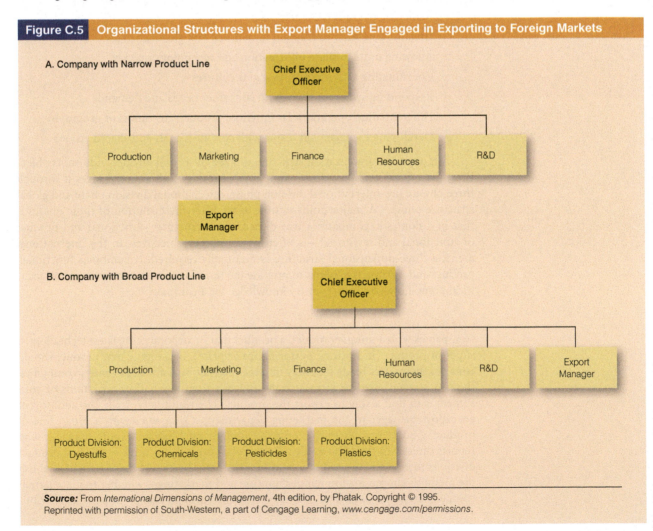

Figure C.5   Organizational Structures with Export Manager Engaged in Exporting to Foreign Markets

A. Company with Narrow Product Line

B. Company with Broad Product Line

Source: From *International Dimensions of Management*, 4th edition, by Phatak. Copyright © 1995. Reprinted with permission of South-Western, a part of Cengage Learning, www.cengage.com/permissions.

Figure C.6   International Division of a Company in the Early Stages of Global Involvement

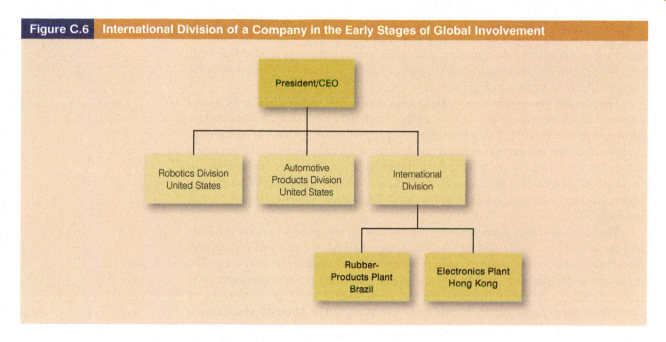

need to respond quickly to customer, political and economic demands and challenges. As those on site gain expertise, they pass it on for future planning purposes and become trainers for those who will follow them in current or future overseas ventures. Many managers will pass through the international divisions on their way to regional and corporate headquarters jobs.

Global Structure Phase

As the international operations gain success, top management makes a greater commitment to them and begins to view the company in a global perspective. Most companies, as is the case with McDonald's, find that as their international operations expand, a greater percentage of revenues and profits begin to flow from them. With its international division, the company finds itself better able to serve many more markets than it could without them. It becomes nearly immune from most trade restrictions and is closer to its customers. It usually finds itself with an ever-increasing number of foreign nationals on its payrolls and running its operations, both in foreign markets and in the firm's various headquarters. The company's culture begins to change as these forces for change are absorbed and take power.

According to the research conducted by *Business International*, a company is ready to move away from an international division phase when it meets the following criteria:

- The international market is as important to it as the domestic market.
- Senior officials in the company have both foreign and domestic experience.
- International sales represent 25 to 35 percent of total sales.
- The technology used in the domestic division has far outstripped that of the international division.[22]

global structure
The arrangement of an organization's management decision making to efficiently and effectively operate in a multinational context; form may contain functional, product and geographic features based on worldwide product or area units

The shift to a **global structure** means a change in the ways in which decision making will take place. Typically, decisions that previously were made by separate and autonomous divisions will, after the shift, be made at the corporate headquarters for the total enterprise. Corporate decisions now need a total-company perspective. The final structure will contain functional, product and geographic features and may be based on worldwide product groups, worldwide area groups or a mixture of these two. Each group becomes a profit center, with command and control passing from the president/CEO to a group vice president.

The product group structure works best for diverse and widely dispersed product lines and for those with relatively high levels of technology or research and development operations. Figure C.7 illustrates product group structure. Johnson & Johnson has capitalized on the product group structure by organizing its more than 250 operating companies that manufacture and market thousands of branded health care products in hundreds of categories in 60 countries into four worldwide customer product groups: pharmaceutical products, medical devices and diagnostics, biologics and consumer products.[23]

The regional or area approach works best with a narrow group of similar products and those that are closely tied to local consumer markets. Oil companies, specialty food manufacturers and rubber products companies tend to adopt this structure. The functions of the international division are carried out by the regional managers, who report directly to the parent headquarters (see Figure C.8). Mobil Corporation was an example of the regional approach structure when it aligned its 11 business groups, or strategic business units (SBUs), into three categories:

1 North American businesses, comprising exploration, production, refining, and marketing

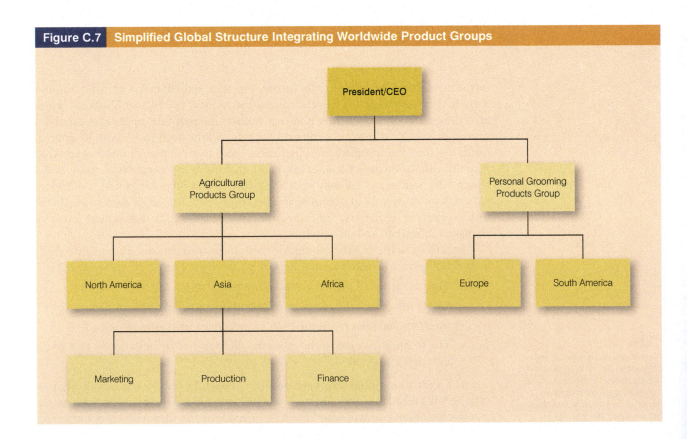

Figure C.7   **Simplified Global Structure Integrating Worldwide Product Groups**

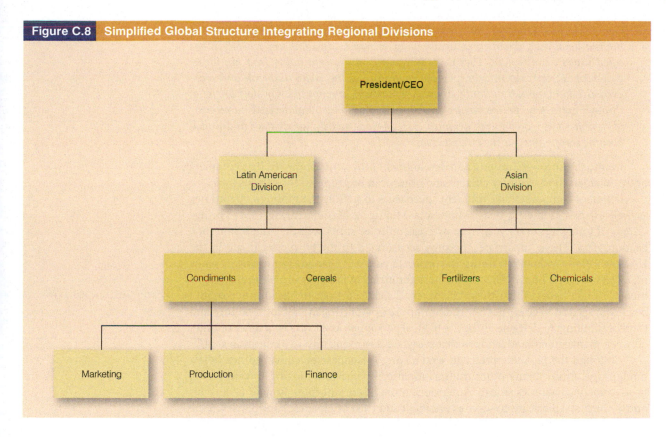

Figure C.8   Simplified Global Structure Integrating Regional Divisions

2 Integrated regional businesses, combining Mobil's exploration, production, refining and marketing in four areas: Africa and the Middle East, Asia-Pacific, Europe, and South America

3 Worldwide businesses that consist of chemicals, liquefied gas, and independent power projects; new exploration and production ventures; and supply trading and transportation[24]

Discuss the major staffing concerns for an international operation

STAFFING AND THE INTERNATIONAL MANAGER

The role of the staffing function in an organization is to identify and acquire qualified human resources to ensure the success of the organization. In an international company, staffing becomes far more complex because the search for talent knows no national boundaries.

Staffing Problems and Solutions

Finding qualified persons to fill jobs in host countries can be difficult, especially when a company attempts to find qualified managerial and technical people in developing or less-developed countries. In the initial stages of expansion into overseas markets, positions in host-country operations may have to be filled from those already on board in domestic operations. But, this is not always an adequate approach.

Companies face a tougher time these days persuading U.S. managers to accept certain international assignments and, occasionally, to travel abroad. A key reason: intensified jitters about safety. They're an outgrowth of the continuing Iraq hostilities, post-Sept. 11 terrorist attacks, possible resurgence of the SARS outbreak and more executive kidnappings in South America. Employers attempt to allay staff anxieties through extra pay, pre-departure security briefings, and computerized monitoring of trouble spots—along with armored cars, 24-hour guards, attack dogs and walled housing compounds for the riskiest areas.[25]

Eventually, through training and development programs conducted by a company or by outsiders, host-country citizens and others can be groomed for various jobs.

Different companies take different approaches to staffing their foreign operations, as well as their domestic ones. Minnesota Mining & Manufacturing (3M) "brings dozens of foreigners every year from overseas units for stints at its St. Paul, Minnesota, headquarters. These 'inpatriates' become accustomed to the business climate in the U.S. and receive valuable training in corporate culture."[26] Honda, by contrast, sends managers from its home office to the host countries. While they are on these assignments, Honda believes that these "managers dispatched from the head office should be encouraged to become part of the community by understanding local culture and ways of thinking; to delegate authority to local personnel; and to create a sense of unity between management and labor so that everyone is working toward a common goal."[27]

Although the Japanese prefer to send a core of Japanese executives to head their foreign operations, many other multinational companies are moving toward giving host-country citizens, especially Americans, more important roles. Ronald G. Shaw is one of the first Americans to serve as president and CEO of Japanese subsidiaries in the United States. "He was elected to the board of directors of the parent company, Pilot Corporation, becoming one of only six Americans ever elevated to the board of any publicly held Japanese company. The following year he was promoted to chief executive officer of Pilot Pen Corporation of America, making him one of a select number of Americans to serve as CEO of a Japanese company based in the United States."[28]

George Varga, the former manager of GE's lighting manufacturing plant in Hungary, is an example of an ideal international manager. He is a veteran of overseas assignments. A native of Hungary, he left as a teenager and has worked in the United States, Spain, Holland, Switzerland and Mexico. He speaks six languages and has Western know-how in marketing and financial management. While he was at GE Hungary one of his first decisions was to replace half the Hungarian managers with seasoned GE executives (his managers averaged over eighteen years of service). "We didn't want the young tigers. We needed people with sensitivity to perform a cultural marriage. We had the ideal team to sell our ideas to the Hungarians."[29]

Whereas Ronald Shaw is an American in a Japanese company and George Varga is an expatriate Hungarian who returned home, many foreign nationals have risen through the ranks to head up the headquarters staffs of American multinationals. Current Chairperson and CEO of Pepsi, Indra Krishnamurthy Nooyi is an India-born, naturalized American. Past CEOs of Coca-Cola include E. Neville Isdell, an Irish citizen, and Douglas Daft, an Australian citizen. Before becoming U.S. Secretary of Commerce, Carlos Miguel Gutierrez, was Chairman of the Board and CEO of the Kellogg Company. He was born in Cuba and began his career in Mexico City. Alain J. P. Belda was born in French Morocco, became a Brazilian citizen, and worked for Alcoa in Brazil before becoming Chairman of the Board and CEO of Alcoa. Fred Hassan, Chairman of the Board and CEO of Schering-Plough Corporation, was born in Pakistan.

For managers who would like to duplicate the success of Noovi, Shaw, Varga, Isdell and others, David Smith, managing director at Accenture, has sound advice: "A broad global outlook, including understanding nuances in other cultures and a willingness to relocate, is key for landing top positions. Two otherwise identical applicants would have to prove they know how international markets differ from domestic ones, and show that they know how to manage expectations to team members in other countries."[30] Professor James G. Clawson, University of Virginia, reinforces Smith's advice by noting that certain skills are needed to be a global business leader: overseas experience, deep self-awareness, sensitivity to cultural diversity, humility, lifelong curiosity, cautious honesty, global strategic thinking, patient impatience, well-spoken, good negotiator, and presence.[31]

Compensation

Compensating host-country personnel in line with parent-company practices seldom works. Traditions, legally mandated pay scales and benefits, differing tax rates and levels of inflation, differing standards of living, the relative values of currencies, and host-country competitors all combine to make compensation a difficult issue. The U.S. custom of rewarding individuals and groups on the basis of short-term performances and rewarding managers for their departments' or divisions' successes must be tempered with the contributions they make to the whole enterprise and the kinds of barriers they have had to overcome. Some cultures shun group compensation plans; others live by them. Some countries have strong unions (Germany, for example); others have none. In addition, factors such as the value of seniority, the cost of living in a host country (Singapore is one of the highest), and the level of status a manager has as perceived by peers must be considered, and compensation plans must be adjusted accordingly.

Perks for managers and salespeople working abroad—things provided in addition to voluntary and legally mandated benefits—include the following: In Belgium, as elsewhere in Western Europe, a car and a cellular phone along with a discretionary expense account; in Japan, a company car for executives; in Great Britain, company cars equipped with telephones; in South Korea, pickup by a car pool, graduating to a company car and driver, and a generous expense account; in Hungary, a company car for managers and salespeople and payment in hard (Western) currency. By law, every country in the European Union has four weeks of paid vacation.

7

Describe the major concerns relating to leading a cross-cultural workforce

LEADING AND THE INTERNATIONAL MANAGER

People are not the same around the world. They have different languages, cultures, traditions and attitudes that affect the ways in which they work, how they want to be approached, and how they approach others. These differences make directing foreign nationals a challenge for the international manager. Managers who are not natives of the countries in which they manage need to pay particular attention to the ways they communicate and interact with foreign nationals. What should be kept in mind throughout this section is that most nations today are blends of nationalities. Their workforces reflect cross-cultural influences just as the American workforce does. Most European nations are hosts to many peoples from around the world—Turks, Arabs and Asians—as well as other Europeans. Many Asians, particularly Koreans, work in Japan. Blending of populations can be expected to continue as European, Asian, and Latin

American countries continue to attract foreign labor and as multinational businesses expand their operations to more and more nations.

The key for organizations "going international" is to recognize and value the contributions that diversity will bring to the organization. Companies that will be successful in the decades to come will continue to change their definition of diversity as they evolve.

Employee Attitudes

John E. Rehfeld has worked in an executive capacity for two major Japanese companies in the United States. He points out two differences between traditional U.S. and Japanese management attitudes. First, when something goes wrong in a Japanese company, the emphasis is on solving problems, not placing blame. Japanese managers want to know what went wrong and how to fix it. Second, when Japanese managers set a goal and achieve it, they keep going and don't wait for praise. "The Japanese simply are not interested only in absolute results; they are equally interested in the process and in how you can do it better next time…. [T]hey not only plan something and do it but also stop to see the result to determine how it could be done better."[32]

When GE took over the management of the Tungsram works in Hungary, it found 18,000 workers—about as many as it had in the rest of its lighting division in the United States, which generated seven times the sales volume. "In the West the solution would be huge layoffs. But the Hungarians' deep fear of joblessness [prompted] GE to take a more modest approach." It chose to reduce worker ranks by early retirements and normal attrition. Hungarians are also used to being paid in cash and few have checking accounts. GE chose to continue to keep stuffing pay envelopes with cash.[33]

At Ahlstrom Fakop (now Foster Wheeler Energy Fakop), a boiler manufacturing facility in Poland that had 400 employees, the same attitude about job security proved a key to turning the company around. Conventional business wisdom in the West believes an effective way to motivate workers is through incentive pay. But, the incentive pay failed to revive low employee morale; so the company responded by offering to maintain staffing at current levels if sales targets were met. The result: an increase in sales and morale. Turned inside out by the transition to a market economy, the employees were more concerned with keeping their jobs than getting a bonus.[34]

Communication Problems

An international manager may be presented with a number of communication dilemmas. Not only words, but body language as well differs from one culture to another. For example, it is considered an insult by Arabs to cross your feet or legs or to show the bottoms of your shoes to them. In Spain, the "okay" sign using the thumb and the forefinger is considered to be a vulgar gesture. Seating yourself at a formal meeting before those of a higher rank are seated is acceptable in American businesses, but it is viewed as disrespectful in many other cultures.

Money might even cause communication problems. The parent company might wish to transact business in English and in dollars, but it will have to adjust to Japanese, Korean, German, Chinese, Indian and other languages and currencies. Also, a manager at headquarters may be Swiss and speak German and meet with host-country managers who are Italian, German, American and Chinese or mixtures of several nationalities. One solution used by some companies is to have all company correspondence and conversations among managers take place in one language—usually English or French in American and Western European companies and Japanese in Japanese companies.

Relying on translators can be tricky. Host-country nationals might pretend to lack understanding when it is in their interest to do so. Also, many words in one language have no direct translation into others.

Even though English is becoming more and more the language of international business, and most educated people around the world must learn it, host-country managers must have a firm grounding in their host country's language. There just is no good substitute for language fluency when it comes to directing the host-country's workforce, dealing with in-country unions and government officials, keeping abreast of local commercial and political affairs, and negotiating with suppliers and customers from several nations. Some companies give language instruction to their managers before placing them in foreign countries.

As a final word on communications, consider the messages sent by the choice of a gift for a foreign colleague or business associate. This is an area with many potential problems. The choice of a gift can cause embarrassment or trouble for the gift giver if a country's customs and traditions are not understood. Figure C.9 outlines a few rules for giving gifts to foreign associates.

Cross-Cultural Management

cross-cultural management
An emerging discipline focused on improving work in organizations with employee and client populations from several cultures

Culture has been defined earlier in this text as a societal group's shared beliefs, traditions, customs, behaviors and values. **Cross-cultural management** "studies the behavior of people in organizations around the world and trains people to work in organizations with employee and client populations from several cultures." It describes and compares organizational behavior within and across countries and cultures and

Figure C.9	Tips on How to Avoid Common Pitfalls of Gift Giving Among Foreign Associates

- Don't rely on your own taste.
- Don't bring a gift to an Arab man's wife; in fact, don't ask about her at all. Bringing gifts for the children is, however, acceptable.
- In Arab countries, don't admire an object openly. The owner might feel obligated to give it to you.
- Do not bring liquor to an Arab home. For many Arabs, alcohol is forbidden by religious law.
- Don't try to out-give the Japanese. It causes great embarrassment and obligates them to reciprocate even if they cannot afford it.
- Do not insist that your Japanese counterpart open the gift in your presence. This is not their custom and can easily cause embarrassment on the part of the recipient.
- As a courtesy, hold your gift with two hands when presenting it to a Japanese businessperson, but do not make a big thing of the presentation.
- Be careful when selecting colors or deciding on the number of items. The color purple is inappropriate in Latin America because it is associated with Lent.

- Avoid giving knives and handkerchiefs in Latin America. Knives suggest the cutting off of the relationship, and handkerchiefs imply that you wish the recipient hardship. To offset the bad luck, the recipient must offer you money.
- Logos should be unobtrusive.
- In Germany, red roses imply that you are in love with the recipient. Perfume is too personal a gift for business relationships.
- In the People's Republic of China, expensive presents are not acceptable and cause great embarrassment. Give a collective gift from your company to theirs.
- In China, a banquet is acceptable, but you will insult your hosts if you give a more lavish banquet than the one given you.
- A clock is a symbol of bad luck in China.
- The most important rule is to investigate first. After all, no one laughs at gift games. True, it is the thought that counts: the thought you give to understanding the culture and the taste of the people with whom you plan to negotiate.

"seeks to understand and improve the interaction of coworkers, clients, suppliers and alliance partners from different countries and cultures."[35]

Managers of global enterprises interact regularly with people of differing backgrounds, educational systems, business training and personal perspectives and biases. "Diversity exists both within and among cultures; but within a single culture, certain behaviors are favored and others repressed. The norm for a society is the most common and generally most acceptable pattern of values, attitudes and behavior."[36] We have mentioned a few of these in our discussion of communication differences. In this section, we look briefly at what can be said collectively about the norms that international managers must recognize and with which they must cope.

Individualism Versus Collectivism In general, Americans and citizens of many Western countries like to think and act as individuals, preferring to gain their personal identities through personal achievements and individual efforts. Many societies, such as Japan and several Latin American countries, however, are more group oriented. From an early age, children are taught to work in groups and to obtain a large portion of their personal identity through group membership and efforts. Working with teams, especially those that need to be empowered and autonomous, may not be so easy in cultures that foster individualism.

Doing Versus Being A doing orientation is an action orientation. Western culture fosters this orientation; citizens like to be rewarded for individual actions and behaviors. "Managers in doing-oriented cultures motivate employees with promotions, raises, bonuses and other forms of public recognition."[37] By contrast, a being orientation "finds people, events, and ideas flowing spontaneously; the people stress release, indulgence of existing desires, and working for the moment ... they will not work strictly for future rewards."[38]

Asian cultures foster the being orientation. Individual performance rewards are not popular. Employers are often viewed as surrogate parents and usually offer job security and collective benefits to encourage a family atmosphere and long-term commitments from employees. Progression in such companies is methodical, slow and through the ranks, with few if any shortcuts or fast-track careers.

Value of and Focus on Time Some cultures value time more than others. To many people in the Middle East, time is not considered a precious commodity. Many people see work as a means to support life, not as a reason for living. Some cultures promote precise timetables and deadlines; others see precise deadlines and the need to meet them as relatively unimportant. Some cultures emphasize planning for the long term; others focus on the present or the past and the following of traditions.

Masculinity Versus Femininity Geert Hofstede defines masculinity as the extent to which the dominant values in a society emphasize assertiveness and the acquisition of money and things, while not emphasizing concern for people. He defines femininity as the extent to which the dominant values in society emphasize relationships among people, concern for others, and the overall quality of life.[39] Hofstede sees the Scandinavian countries as feminine; he sees Mexico, Japan and much of Western Europe as masculine. Societies with feminine cultures "tend to create high-tax environments, extra money often fails to strongly motivate employees.... Conversely, masculine societies tend to develop into lower-tax environments in which extra money or other visible signs of success effectively reward achievement (Mexico, for example)."[40]

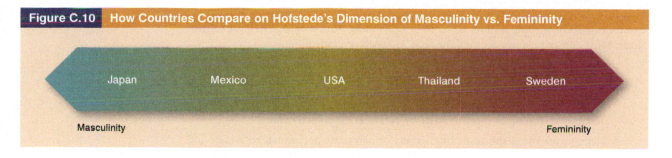

Figure C.10 **How Countries Compare on Hofstede's Dimension of Masculinity vs. Femininity**

Japan   Mexico   USA   Thailand   Sweden

Masculinity   Femininity

Once these values, attitudes and behaviors are identified, training can be developed. Training programs typically deal with such areas as understanding cultures, language training, managing one's family life in the host country and career development.[41] A company's network of experienced **expatriates**—home country nationals with overseas experience—can help the newcomers settle in overseas.

When employees return to their home bases from foreign assignments, the training is not necessarily over. They often require programs to help them adjust. For example, the purposes of a repatriation program might include reversing the effects of any culture shock for both expatriates and their families, helping them adjust to their new home assignment, and facilitating the sharing of their knowledge and experiences.

expatriates
Home-country nationals with overseas experience

8 Discuss the major concerns relating to controlling an international corporation

CONTROLLING AND THE INTERNATIONAL MANAGER

The management function of control involves setting standards, measuring performances, applying standards to performances, and taking corrective actions as needed. These fundamentals do not change with multinational operations, but some of the specifics about controlling do. We look next at control characteristics and problems for international managers.

Characteristics of Controls

Multinationals use a variety of controls to monitor and to adjust the performances of their foreign affiliates. These controls fall into two groups: direct and indirect controls. Direct controls include the use of such devices as periodic meetings, visits by the home office top-management teams to foreign operations, and the staffing of the foreign affiliates by home-country nationals. Meetings are often held using the internet, satellite communications linkups, and by teleconferencing between both foreign affiliates and the company's top management. Periodically, host-country managers are called to headquarters to give first-hand reports on strategic progress. Such is the case with McDonald's international managers.

Indirect controls include the various kinds of reports sent daily, weekly, or monthly. The main criteria used to measure performances are the costs being experienced, the return on invested capital, the market share held by an affiliate, and the profits earned by each affiliate by product line and areas of operations. In the same family of reports are whole arrays of budgetary and financial controls that are imposed by both local and corporate headquarters managers.

Control Problems

International controlling is made difficult by everything from language to legal restrictions. Most companies rely on the following methods of controlling:

1 Regular reporting procedures and communications between affiliates and their headquarters

2 Progress reports toward goals established with local input by strategic planners

3 Regular screening of reported data by area and functional experts

4 Regular on-site inspections by a variety of corporate personnel, both staff and line

A final note on controlling human resources abroad. In many countries, bonuses, pensions, holidays and vacation days are legally required and considered by many employees to be their right. Particularly powerful unions exist in many parts of the world, and their demands restrict management's freedom to operate. Many countries have laws requiring that money be paid regularly into funds to provide for employee separations and terminations. Also, it can be expensive to fire or lay off a manager in many countries that have steep severance pay costs.

Review What You've Learned

Appendix Summary

1 Explain the primary reasons why businesses become international.

Companies go international for two basic sets of reasons or motives: proactive and reactive.

- Proactive motives include the search for new customers, new markets, increased market share, increased return on investments, needed raw materials and other resources, tax advantages, lower costs and economies of scale.

- Reactive motives include the desire to escape from trade barriers and other government regulations, to better serve a customer or group of customers and to remain competitive.

2 Describe the characteristics of multinational corporations.

Multinational corporations are companies with operating facilities, not just sales offices, in one or more foreign countries. In general, there are two kinds of multinational companies: those that market their product lines in relatively unaltered states throughout the world (standardization), and those that modify their products and services along with the marketing of them to appeal to specific groups of consumers in specific geographic areas (customization).

Even though multinationals around the world differ in sales volumes, profits, markets serviced, and the number of their subsidiaries, they do share some common characteristics. These include

- Creating foreign affiliates, which may be wholly owned by the multinational or jointly held with one or more partners from foreign countries
- Viewing the world as the market
- Choosing specific types of business activities (manufacturing, petroleum, banking, agriculture, public utilities)
- Locating affiliates in the developed countries of the world
- Adopting one of three basic strategies regarding staffing: (1) a high skills strategy in which the company exports products, not jobs; (2) a strategy to "dumb down jobs" and shift the work to cheap labor countries; and (3) a strategy to mix the preceding two strategies

3 Discuss the political, legal, economic, sociocultural, and technological elements of the international environment.

The five environments of the international manager are:

- *Political environment:* This environment can foster or hinder economic development and investment by native and foreign investors and businesses. The political philosophy and type of economic philosophy held by a nation's leaders can give rise to laws that promote domestic commerce and raise barriers to trade with the outside world. The stability of the government and its support by the people will affect decisions to seek commercial opportunities or to avoid investments in a nation.

- *Legal environment:* Each country has its own unique set of laws that have an impact on commerce. Laws designed to protect the rights of individuals and labor unions differ as well. In addition, some countries erect trade barriers, such as quotas, tariffs, and embargoes. International managers must be aware of these legal constraints.

- *Economic environment:* When companies analyze their options for going multinational they must consider such factors as the stability of a country's currency, its infrastructure, its availability of needed raw materials and supplies, levels of inflation and taxes, citizens' level of income, closeness to customers and climate.

- *Sociocultural environment:* This environment includes such concerns as a people's traditions, languages, customs, values, religion and levels of education. The international manager can analyze the cultures in countries following these dimensions: material culture, social institutions, humans and the universe, aesthetics and languages.

- *Technological environment:* This environment contains all the innovations that are rapidly occurring in all types of technologies. Regardless of what kind of a business a company is in, it must choose partners and locations that have what it lacks.

4 Describe the major strategies for going international.

There are basically four ways to get involved in overseas trade:

1 Export your product or service.

2 License others to act on your behalf (as sales agents, franchisees or users of your processes or patents).

3 Enter into joint ventures (partnerships) for mutual benefit to produce, to market or to do both.

4 Build or purchase facilities outside your home country to conduct business on your own.

5 Explain the phases a company goes through when moving from domestic operations to a multinational structure.

The evolution of a company becoming multinational takes it through three phases: pre-international division phase, international division phase, and global structure phase.

- *Pre-international division phase:* The first strategy used to introduce the product to a new nation is to find a way to export it. The result is typically the addition of an export manager to the marketing department. The export manager will establish the methods for foreign distribution and marketing—whether to place parent-company employees in a host country or to work through agents (importers, distributors or retailers).

- *International division phase:* Pressures from host-country laws, trade restrictions and competition may place the company at a cost disadvantage. In response, the company establishes marketing or production operations in one or more countries. This international division reports directly to the CEO.

- *Global structure phase:* As the international operations gain success, top management makes a greater commitment to them and begins to see the company in a global perspective. Decisions that previously were made by separate and autonomous divisions need a total-company perspective. The final structure will contain functional, product and geographic features and may be based on worldwide product groups, worldwide area groups or a mixture of these two.

6 **Discuss the major staffing concerns for an international corporation.**

One major staffing concern for an international corporation involves finding qualified persons to fill jobs in host countries, especially finding qualified managerial and technical people in developing or less-developed countries. A second concern relates to compensating host-country personnel. Traditions, legally mandated pay scales and benefits, differing tax rates and levels of inflation, differing standards of living, the relative values of currencies and host-country competitors all combine to make compensation a difficult issue.

7 **Describe the major concerns relating to leading a cross-cultural workforce.**

The major concerns relating to leading a cross-cultural workforce are employee attitudes, communication problems and cultural norms.

- *Employee attitudes:* Attitudes about work are different throughout the world. For example, when something goes wrong in a Japanese company, the emphasis is on solving problems, not placing the blame. Japanese managers want to know what went wrong and how to fix it. Second, when Japanese managers set a goal and achieve it, they keep going and don't wait for praise. Also, in both Hungary and Poland job security are prime motivators.

- *Communication problems:* An international manager may be presented with a number of communication dilemmas. Both words and body language differ from one culture to another. The decision on what language to use (English, French, Japanese) in a meeting can present problems.

- *Cultural norms:* The norm for a society is the most common and generally most acceptable pattern of values, attitudes and behavior. International managers must recognize and cope with the following norms: individualism versus collectivism, doing versus being, value of and focus on time and masculinity versus femininity.

8 **Discuss the major concerns relating to controlling an international corporation.**

Controlling is made difficult by everything from language to legal restrictions. As a result, most companies rely on the following:

1 Regular reporting procedures and communications between affiliates and their headquarters

2 Progress reports toward goals established with local input by strategic planners

3 Regular screening of reported data by area and functional experts

4 Regular on-site inspections by a variety of corporate personnel

An additional concern focuses on controlling human resources abroad. In many countries, bonuses, pensions, holidays and vacation days are legally required and considered by many employees to be their right. Particularly powerful unions exist in many parts of the world, and their demands restrict management's freedom to operate. Many countries have laws requiring that money be paid regularly into funds to provide for employee separations and terminations. Also, it can be quite expensive to fire or lay off a manager in many countries.

KEY TERMS

REVIEW QUESTIONS

1. What are two reasons why a company becomes international?

2. What are the major characteristics of the multinational company?

3. What are the major components of each of the following international environments: political, legal, economic, sociocultural and technological?

4. What are the major strategies for going international?

5. What are the three organizational phases that a company passes through in going multinational?

6. What are two concerns faced when attempting to staff international affiliates?

7. What are three problems connected with directing a cross-cultural workforce?

8. What are the major control problems for a multinational corporation?

DISCUSSION QUESTIONS FOR CRITICAL THINKING

1. You are the CEO of a rapidly growing restaurant and have plans to go international in the very near future. What steps would you take to enter the international marketplace? How would you organize your company? Why?

2. Which of the four strategies for going international require the greatest commitment by management? Why? What factors should be considered when selecting a strategy? Which is the most important?

3. An organization that is seeking to expand into international operations needs to monitor several environments. What aspect of each environment has changed or will change the way in which businesses select and train managers?

4. How might the cultural norms of individualism/collectivism and masculinity/femininity affect the management process and organizational design in an international company?

Appendix D

Succeeding in Your Organization

LEARNING OBJECTIVES

After studying this chapter, you should be able to:

1 Discuss the nature of careers

2 Describe what is meant by having a career perspective

3 Describe the changes that have occurred in the career environment

4 Identify and describe the four stages of career development

5 Identify and discuss the five steps for career planning

6 Discuss how a manager can understand his or her organization and why it is important to do so

7 Identify and describe the abilities and actions that organizations value in managers

8 Discuss the strategies associated with career advancement

9 Discuss the organizational dilemmas experienced when personal and organizational interests are in conflict

INTRODUCTION

Successful managers achieve success in two areas: job and career. They are knowledge-able and get results. Successful managers develop their own career plans by focusing on the key elements: planning, preparation and understanding the workings of organizations.

New managers need support. They need ongoing professional development. They need a sense of belonging, of common cause, and the knowledge that over time they will make a difference not only in the lives of individual employees they manage, but in their organizations. The need for this support is the focus of career development and the mentoring process.

Mentoring is not a new idea. People have always sought the wisdom and counsel of those with more experience. In Homer's epic poem, *The Odyssey,* a wise old sea captain named Mentor gives Odysseus's son, Telemachus, guidance in coping with his father's long absence. Mentor teaches Telemachus the values he will need to rule Ithaca.

Not all companies have a formal mentoring program, pairing younger managers with older managers to help the younger ones excel. Yet, each employee can develop his or her career by finding a mentor. Lindsey Pollak, a career expert and author of *Becoming the Boss: New Rules for the Next Generation of Leaders,* recommends having several different mentors and thinking of them as your board of advisors.[1] Not all mentors need to be older. Mentors may be your peers or even younger employees.[2]

This chapter is about being successful in career management. First, the chapter will examine the nature of careers and then discuss the elements of career planning. The remainder of the chapter will examine career management and some associated dilemmas.

1 Discuss the nature of careers

job
A specific position a person holds in an organization

career
The series of jobs a person holds over a lifetime and the person's attitude toward the involvement in those job experiences; includes a long-term perspective, a sequence of positions, and a psychological involvement

MANAGING TO SUCCESS

Nature of Careers

Minnesota State Colleges and Universities career and education resource, Iseek, puts the matter succinctly. "Think of it this way: If life were a video game, a job would be just one level. Having a career means that you are committed to playing the game to get better over time and advance to higher levels."[3] For some people, work is a **job**—a specific position they hold in an organization. They take pride in it and do well; but a job does not take on a long-term perspective nor imply that the person doing it extends himself or herself beyond its requirements.

A **career** on the other hand, is the sequence of jobs a person holds over a life-time and the person's attitude toward his or her involvement in those jobs. A career is a person's entire life in a work setting or settings. Because it encompasses a lifetime, a career reflects a long-term perspective and includes a series of jobs.[4] A career also denotes involvement. People who have careers are so psychologically involved in their work that they extend themselves beyond its requirements.

2 Describe what is meant by having a career perspective

career perspective
A proactive strategy that involves a global view of career progress or growth over time

CAREER PERSPECTIVE

Adopting a career perspective can increase an individual's probability of success in his or her career. A **career perspective**, as illustrated in Figure D.1, is a proactive strategy that involves a global view of career progress or growth over time. It requires a person

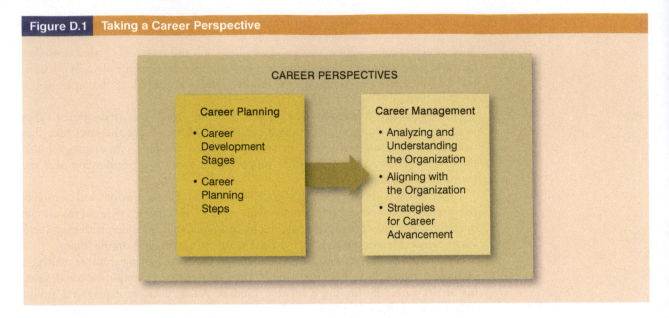

to adopt a broad vision that includes all the elements involved in a successful career: objectives, timetables, career stages, skills improvement, organizational politics, power, stress, and values. Adopting such a broad vision can be accomplished through *career planning*, which emphasizes the activities involved in making career decisions, and *career management*, which emphasizes the activities and behaviors involved in career advancement.

NEW CAREER ENVIRONMENT

Describe the changes that have occurred in the career environment

As a prerequisite for career planning, a manager must understand the new career environment. In recent years, many facets of careers have radically changed. "As a result of globalization, outsourcing, contracting, downsizing, recession, and even natural disaster, *job security* can seem like a thing of the past."[5] Employees can no longer expect to work for one employer and then retire with a pension. According to Arne Kalleberg, author of *Good Jobs, Bad Jobs,* "the psychological contract between employers and employees in which stability and security were exchanged for loyalty and hard work" has been severed.[6] Individuals are in charge of their careers.

The economy and industries are changing so rapidly that no company can really know what it will be doing one or more years in the future. The emphasis now is on gaining a competitive edge. Downsizing, restructuring, empowering, telecommuting, employee leasing, teaming, decentralizing, outsourcing, and business process reengineering are all changing the complexion of work and the workplace. All these efforts bring sudden and often painful changes to a company's employees and careers. Business process reengineering has eliminated many of the old "career pathways." The middle-manager staircase is gone in most organizations. Businesses have redrawn their boundaries as they focus on core competencies and outsource noncore work. As a result, work follows a contractor–subcontractor model, not one of vertical integration. Project-based (versus position-based) work, long the norm in industries like construction and many professional services, has become the new normal.

For the career manager, the message is clear. The rules indeed have changed. Now instead of security, seek opportunity. Instead of position, chart your contribution. Careers will be defined less by companies ("I work for IBM") and more by profession ("I am a professional manager"). Harvard Business School Professor John Kotter has taken a new look at success in this dynamic environment. In his book *The New Rules*, Kotter identifies seven rules for career success:

1. *Do not rely on convention.* Career paths that were winners for most of the twentieth century are often no longer providing much success.

2. *Keep your eyes on globalization and its consequences.* With competition and opportunity arising all over the world, success comes to the alert and agile.

3. Move toward the small and entrepreneurial organization and away from the big and bureaucratic.

4. *Do not just manage; now you must also lead.* Managers cope with change; leaders cause it and make the competition cope.

5. *Never stop trying to grow.* Lifelong learning is increasingly necessary for success.

6. *Increase your competitive drive.* Driven people reap the greatest rewards.

7. *Wheel and deal if you can.* Take chances and seek opportunities.[7]

The new environment, with its new rules, makes it even more important to plan and monitor a career.

Career Planning

One of the most important principles about careers is that you alone are responsible for your career. Although you may be fortunate to work for organizations and managers who help you develop your career and help you advance, the hard fact is that you cannot sit back and wait for that to happen. Employees must take charge of their careers. It is simply not enough to work hard and be good at work. Those people who plan their careers greatly improve the chance of long-term success.

career planning
The process of developing a realistic view about how individuals want their careers to proceed and then taking steps to ensure they follow that course

Career planning is the process of developing a realistic view about how one wants one's career to proceed and then making plans to ensure it follows that course. The process includes a series of activities to help make informed decisions: performing a self-assessment, identifying opportunities, matching skills to career-related activities, developing objectives and timetables, and evaluating progress. The process is important because it links personal needs and skills with career goals and opportunities.

Planning one's career is a successful process because it is systematic. Such planning involves linking long-term and short-term objectives, developing personal capabilities en route, and performing a focused analysis of progress. It is not, however, a one-time process. Career planning is ongoing and must be updated continually.

Identify and describe the four stages of career development

STAGES OF CAREER DEVELOPMENT

To understand how to plan a career, it is helpful to view how careers unfold. Most careers go through four distinct stages, each dealing with different issues and tasks.[8] Figure D.2 illustrates these four stages, and Figure D.3 lists the tasks for each stage.

Stage 1: Exploration and Trial This first stage usually occurs between the ages of 15 and 25. For most people, it begins with the decision to become serious about employment after having concentrated on education. This stage is a learning process because

| Figure D.2 | Four Stages of Career Development |

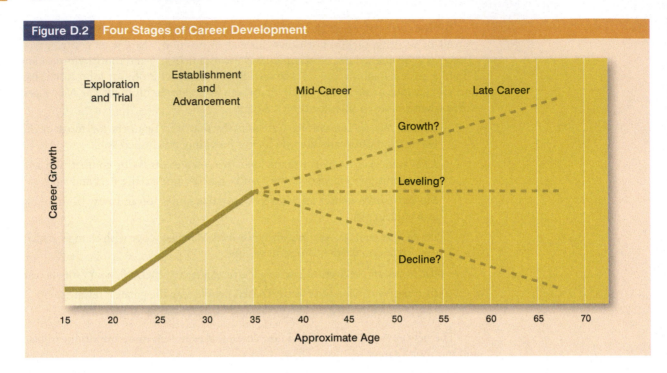

| Figure D.3 | Characteristics of the Four Stages of Career Development |

STAGE	TASK NEEDS
Exploration and Trial	• Varied job activities • Self-exploration
Establishment and Advancement	• Job challenge • Developing competence in a specialty area • Developing creativity and innovation • Rotating into a new area after three to five years
Mid-Career	• Technical updating • Developing skills in training and coaching others (younger employees) • Rotating into a new job requiring new skills • Developing broader view of work and role in the organization
Late Career	• Shifting from power role to one of consultation and guidance • Identifying and developing successors • Beginning activities outside the organization • Planning for retirement

Source: D. T. Hall and M. A. Morgan, "Career Development and Planning," *Contemporary Problems in Personnel,* revised edition. W. C. Hammer and Frank L. Schmidt, editors (Chicago: St. Clair Press), 1977.

it includes many firsts—the first job interview, first part-time job, and first full-time job—and introduces the individual to the challenges associated with working. People in this stage face the issue of staying with an organization or moving to a job with another company.

Stage 2: Establishment and Advancement In this second stage—normally occurring between the ages of 25 and 35—people are involved in their first "real job." They experience success as well as frustrations and receive promotions and transfers. In this period, most people take stock and begin to develop a career strategy—they begin to identify a field of specialization and weigh long-term success. For many, this stage includes new specialties and offers for new jobs outside the organization.

Stage 3: Mid-Career The mid-career stage most often occurs between the ages of 35 and 50. Most people don't face their first career dilemma until they reach this stage. In the modern-day organization, a career may take one of three possible directions at this point: growth, leveling, or decline.

If the direction is growth, the person is valued by the organization and is receiving promotions and increased responsibility. Career growth is the direct result of a strategy focused on enhancing skills and continual learning.

If the career levels off, the individual may receive transfers but not promotions. The person may be secure, but with no growth in sight, he or she should consider the option of developing a second career.

If the career is in decline, the person is seen as surplus in the eyes of the organization; he or she feels insecure and has a growing sense of failure. Tactically, such a person should try to move to a different company. Switching careers can pay off, both in money and satisfaction.

Obviously, the mid-career stage is critical. In today's business environment, companies have little patience or tolerance for individuals who allow their skills and careers to level or decline. Being proactive and committed to continuous improvement is important.

Stage 4: Late Career The late career stage—occurring between the ages of 50 and retirement—is marked by a peak in prestige for those who experienced growth in the prior stage. Their value to the organization lies in their judgment and experience and their ability to share this knowledge with others. Such managers become reliable trainers of the next generation of managers. Normally, plans are made to slow down, develop outside interests, and prepare for retirement.

5 Identify and discuss the five steps for career planning

STEPS IN CAREER PLANNING

A person should use the career planning model continuously in his or her employment life. Regardless of whether a person is on the outside looking in—just beginning a career—or trying to advance within an organization, the same steps apply.[9] Figure D.4 illustrates the steps in career planning.

Step 1: Self-Assessment Performing a realistic self-assessment is the first step to career planning. A thorough data-gathering process includes evaluating your values, interests, skills, abilities, experience, likes, and dislikes. This step requires a clear and objective view of what you believe is important (values), what makes you happy at work, and what rewards you expect. Figure D.5 provides an assessment checklist that a person can use to identify skills and values.

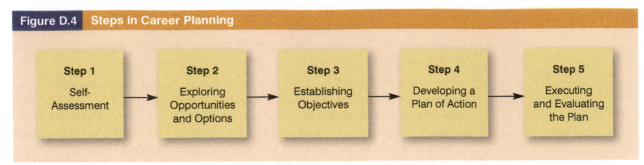

Figure D.4 | **Steps in Career Planning**

Step 1 Self-Assessment → **Step 2** Exploring Opportunities and Options → **Step 3** Establishing Objectives → **Step 4** Developing a Plan of Action → **Step 5** Executing and Evaluating the Plan

Figure D.5 | **Assessment Checklist for Identifying Skills and Values**

WHAT DO I DO WELL?

☐ Organizing
☐ Handling details
☐ Making things
☐ Researching
☐ Creating
☐ Reasoning / logic
☐ Writing
☐ Drawing / painting
☐ My five most important abilities are:

☐ Computing / mathematics
☐ Dealing with others
☐ Innovating
☐ Making decisions
☐ Teaching others
☐ Supervising
☐ Dressing well
☐ Persuading

☐ Communicating
☐ Dealing with criticism
☐ Coordinating activities
☐ Developing new skills
☐ Other (specify)_____
_____
_____

_____
_____
_____
_____
_____

WHAT IS IMPORTANT TO ME?

☐ Helping others
☐ Working along
☐ Working with others
☐ Making decisions
☐ Chance for advancement
☐ Monetary reward
☐ Physical challenge
☐ Power and authority
☐ My five most important abilities are:

☐ Improving society
☐ Competition
☐ Fast pace
☐ Gaining knowledge
☐ Creativity
☐ Change and variety
☐ Security
☐ Recognition

☐ Excitement
☐ Independence
☐ Responsibility
☐ Intellectual challenge
☐ Other (specify)_____
_____
_____

_____
_____
_____
_____
_____
_____

Source: W. Richard Plunkett, *Supervision,* 6/e, 1992, p. 39. © 1992 by Prentice Hall, Inc.
Reprinted by permission of Pearson Education, Inc., Upper Saddle River, NJ.

At the beginning of a career, this step involves identifying initial skills and interests. For an aspiring manager in today's business environment, being independent, flexible, and a team player are points against which to benchmark. The person who likes to learn, is flexible and adaptable meets the prescription for the future. Figure D.6 outlines 10 attributes that organizations look for in filling management positions.

As a career progresses, a person should continue to undertake self-assessments to ensure he or she has retained his or her focus and to see what additional skills and training are needed. Avoiding obsolescence is essential. **Obsolescence** exists when a person is no longer capable of performing up to job standards or management's expectations.[10] A person can become obsolete in attitudes, knowledge, skills, and abilities. Obsolescence in any of these areas marks a person as a potential candidate for the scrap heap. Such a person may become too costly to maintain. Figure D.7 provides a short quiz a person can continue to use to identify areas of obsolescence.

For managers, personal obsolescence can happen quite suddenly. Reengineering that shifts a company from vertical layers of management to cross-functional teams can render an individual's performance inadequate or unnecessary. If a company decides to outsource, positions are eliminated. When a manager refuses to learn new technology, he or she is left standing at the train station. Avoiding obsolescence is critical in career management. Later in the chapter we will discuss strategies for avoiding obsolescence.

obsolescence

A state or condition that exists when a person is no longer capable of performing up to job standards or to management's expectations

---

Figure D.6	Ten Attributes That Organizations Look For in Applicants for Management Positions

1 **Oral communication skills:** Effective expression in individual or group situations (includes gestures and nonverbal communication).

2 **Oral presentation skills:** Effective expression when presenting ideas or tasks to an individual or group when given time for presentation (includes gestures and nonverbal communication).

3 **Written communication skills:** Clear expression of ideas in writing and in correct grammatical form.

4 **Job motivation:** The extent to which activities and responsibilities available in the job correspond with activities and responsibilities that result in personal satisfaction.

5 **Initiative:** Active attempts to influence events to achieve goals; self-starting rather than passive acceptance; taking action to achieve goals beyond those called for; instigating change.

6 **Leadership:** Utilizing appropriate interpersonal styles and methods in guiding individuals (subordinates, peers, superiors) or groups toward task accomplishment.

7 **Planning and organization:** Establishing a course of action for self and/or others to accomplish a specific goal; planning proper assignments of personnel and appropriate allocation of resources.

8 **Analysis:** Relating and comparing data from different sources, identifying issues, securing relevant information, and identifying relationships.

9 **Judgment:** Developing alternative courses of action and making decisions that are based on logical assumptions and reflect factual information.

10 **Management control:** Establishing procedures to monitor and/or regulate processes, tasks, or the responsibilities of subordinates; taking action to monitor the results of delegated assignments or projects.

Source: William C. Byham, "Starting an Assessment Center," *Personnel Administrator* (February 1980). Reprinted with the permission of *HR Magazine*, published by The Society for Human Resource Management, Alexandria, VA.

Figure D.7	Twenty Questions to Help Assess the Degree of Personal Obsolescence

ATTITUDES

1 Is my mind free from anxiety over personal matters while I work?

2 Do I believe in myself—my knowledge, skills, and abilities—and in my associates?

3 Am I open and receptive to advice and suggestions, regardless of their sources?

4 Do I look for the pluses before looking for the minuses?

5 Am I more concerned with the cause of management's action than with its effect?

KNOWLEDGE

1 Am I curious—do I still seek the why behind actions and events?

2 Do I read something and learn something new every day?

3 Do I question the old and the routine?

4 Do I converse regularly with my subordinates, peers, and superiors?

5 Have I a definite program for increasing my knowledge?

SKILLS

1 Is what I am able to do still needed?

2 In light of recent trends and developments in my company and industry, will my skills be required one year from now?

3 Do I practice my skills regularly?

4 Do I regularly observe how others perform their skills?

5 Have I a concrete program for acquiring new skills?

ABILITIES

1 Do my subordinates, peers, and superiors consider me competent?

2 Do I consistently look for a better way of doing things?

3 Am I willing to take calculated risks?

4 Do I keep morally and physically fit?

5 Have I a specific program for improving my performance?

Source: W. Richard Plunkett, *Supervision*, 7th ed., 1995, p. 40. © 1995 by Prentice Hall, Inc. Reprinted by permission of Pearson Education, Inc., Upper Saddle River, NJ.

Step 2: Exploring Opportunities and Options The second step in career planning requires examining the opportunities that exist in the industry and within a company. At the beginning of a career, this step involves determining the following:

- What are the future prospects for the industry?
- What career opportunities exist in the industry?
- What jobs are available?
- What jobs relate to a career path?

For a person in mid-career, the emphasis shifts to evaluating options both inside and outside the organization:

- What are the future prospects for the company?
- What positions will open up in the company?
- What skills does the company value?
- What training and development are available?
- Who is being promoted?
- When are they being promoted?
- What is the job market?

In the new business environment, which emphasizes flatter organization structures and team orientation, this step becomes even more critical. The answers to many of the questions—what opportunities exist, what jobs are important to the company, what positions will open up in a company, who is being promoted—evolve on a day-to-day basis. For the career planner the implications are clear: research thoroughly, build in flexibility, constantly evaluate, and update.

Remember, times have changed. It takes more personal energy and vigilance to see signs of career trouble and to identify opportunities. Warnings are subtler; many are available to only the person, not the boss or colleagues. Warning signs include the following:[11]

- *Are you learning?* If you can't say what you've learned in the past six months or what you expect to learn in the next, beware. Says Harvard's John Kotter, "When there is nothing you can learn where you are, you've got to move on even if they give you promotions."

- *If your job was open, would you get it?* Benchmark your skills regularly. Said Betsy Collard, program director at the Career Action Center, "Look at the want ads and see what they are looking for in your field."

- *What would you do if your job disappeared tomorrow?* The answer to the question identifies marketable skills. More and more people have to sell themselves inside the company.

Step 3: Establishing Objectives Once the opportunities are identified, the career planner has to make short-and long-term decisions. The key is to make the long-term decisions first and then derive the short-term decisions from them. Traditionally, according to Professor Sal Davita, "The two issues of paramount importance once were: what position do you want to hold the day you retire, and in what industry do you want to make a career?" The decision on the industry is still critical for a few reasons. First, an individual's abilities and interests are more or less suited to work in different industries. Second, industries vary in their future prospects.[12] The decision on the final position is not as relevant as it once was because many career paths will not exist in the future. Instead, according to management consultant Michael Hammer, the second objective is for, "you to think of yourself as self-employed—think of yourself as a business. Then, the next decision is to define the business's product or service: the area of expertise. This leads directly to a crucial, career-defining choice: specialist or generalist?"[13] The answer means the person concentrates on one area of expertise or instead develops a broad range of skills.

Opinions on the best decision vary. The conventional wisdom is that generalists are better off. The basic idea of a "portfolio" approach to your professional life is to think of your work not as a single, stable activity, with a name like «marketing manager» or «web developer,» but as the set of interests, passions, and activities that underlies and animates your role. What if instead of identifying with a job description, you began to see this whole mass of things you do as a portfolio of skills and abilities?[14] Adds headhunter Gary Knisely, "Never narrow your options. To the extent that technical expertise narrows your market, you've made a bad career decision. Companies may love you at the moment, but if you've got that good of a crystal ball, get out of a job and into investing."[15] Betting your career on a specialty is like putting all your money in one stock.

On the other hand, says David Hatch, a human resources vice president at PepsiCo, "It's a little dangerous to be esoteric, but companies treat specialists very well—as the scarce resource they are—compared to people who are more interchangeable." For example, the Big 4 accounting firms (EY, Deloitte, KPMG, and PwC) have structured development programs for partner track associates. The structure might have three levels, such as leader, director, and partner. This makes it more motivating for a specialist to stay with the company.

Once these long-term objectives are established, other decisions follow:

- Which functional or specialty area of the organization needs to be learned?
- What jobs and experiences will lead to the ultimate objective?
- What skills are needed to attain the objective?
- What people and other resources are necessary to achieve the objectives?
- What work assignments will be valuable?

Step 4: Developing a Plan of Action This step provides the detailed map to accomplish the objectives. It requires thinking through specifically how to acquire the skills—whether the career planner needs formal education or whether he or she can learn the skills by seeking a special project. The plan should include establishing specific time-tables for completing training, reaching a new job level, and gaining new exposure in a company. This stage also identifies potential barriers and resources to work around the barriers.

Step 5: Executing and Evaluating the Plan Once the plan is in place, it must be put into action. In this step, the career planner takes charge of his or her career, rather than waiting for things to happen. The second part of this step is to follow up and evaluate progress on the plan. As the environment changes, adjusting the plan may become necessary. The evaluation also needs to consider individual growth, career progress, and new assignments—those items that were targeted by objectives and developed in the action plan. This execution phase—career management—is the next topic of discussion.

Before we move on to the topic of career management, however, let us look at Beth Randolph, who provides us with an excellent example of how the steps in career planning unfold. Randolph, a self-motivated achiever, put herself through two-year Hocking College by working in a call center facility operated by Choice Hotels. "I was a sponge," says Randolph, who managed the center when her boss was away. "I love travel. I absolutely love the hospitality industry." Randolph had found her industry and the start of her career.

After graduation, Randolph worked as a travel agent. Then Choice, which operates Quality Inns and Comfort Inns, called to say the company planned to open a large reservation center in North Dakota: and would she like to manage it? She hurriedly moved to Minot and built a business from scratch. She interviewed most job candidates, trained the supervisors, and negotiated contracts for office equipment, cleaning supplies, and even food for the kitchen.

Randolph overcame early fears of supervising people older than herself. She built a cohesive team and received recognition from top management. Building on success, Randolph told Don Brockway, Choice's vice president of reservation operations, "I'm ready to be more creative and solve problems on a higher level." In response, Brockway chose Randolph over three older candidates to oversee Choice's rapidly expanding reservations system across Europe. "This was a huge decision," said Brockway, "she's a fireball who always gets the job done." Beth Randolph is in charge of her own career.[16]

Discuss how a manager can understand his or her organization and why it is important to do so

career management
The planning, activities, and behaviors involved in executing a career

CAREER MANAGEMENT

The key to success is to be self-reliant: to take charge and actively manage your career. **Career management** involves three elements—understanding the organization, aligning yourself with the organization, and implementing career-enhancing strategies.

Analyzing and Understanding the Organization

As noted in Chapter 8, all organizations are unique. Each develops its own methods, values, rewards; each makes clear what it accepts and does not tolerate. Before a person can develop strategies for career growth, he or she must know the company—what abilities it values, what actions it rewards, how it compensates achievers. He or she must both accept the organization's way and be accepted by it. This critical phase has been identified by organizational psychologist Edgar H. Schein as the organizational socialization process.

organizational socialization
A process through which new members of an organization gain exposure to its values, norms, policies, and procedures

Organizational Socialization Regardless of whether it is a new employee's first or fifth company, he or she undergoes **organizational socialization**. In this process new members of an organization gain exposure to its values, norms, policies, and procedures. At the same time, they discover who wields power, what restrictions there are on behavior, and how to succeed and survive.

Figure D.8 presents Schein's model for the process through which an employee becomes an accepted and conforming member of the organization. In Phase I, a job seeker forms impressions and expectations of the company. Phase II is the period of adjustment in which the new employee matches individual needs to those of the organization. Phase III marks the mutual acceptance of employee and organization. Not all employees survive these last two phases; faced with conflicts and compromises too great to overcome, employees who cannot adjust and conform may quit voluntarily or be asked to leave.[17]

psychological contract
The unspoken contract that marks the end product of the organizational socialization process and defines what people are expected to give to the organization and what they can expect to receive

At the end of Phase III, the employee and the organization enter into a **psychological contract**, an unspoken agreement defining what people are expected to give the organization and what they can expect to receive in return. Formed in the mind of the employee, it is based on experiences, promises, and personal observations of how the organization operates. The terms of the contract are the result of the interaction between the employee and boss, the employee and coworkers, and the employee's first-hand experience with the organization's efforts to enforce the rules and behaviors it considers essential. A sense of fairness or equity must exist between employee and employer—each must believe the other is doing his or her part and giving in proportion to what he or she expects to receive.

The psychological contract today is often far different from one in the past. "In the days of the Organization Man, job security, raises, and promotions were exchanged for hard work, loyalty, and a job-first philosophy."[18] In the new employer–employee contract, "you are responsible for your own career; we, your employer, will help provide you the experience and training to keep you marketable, but not necessarily a job forever."[19] In practice, this contract is best represented by the sentiments of William Paine, bond salesman at Gruntal & Company: "I'm very loyal. I'll remain loyal if they supply me phones, a computer, execution, and inventory. I owe them integrity and production."[20]

Figure D.8	Schein's Model of the Phases of Organizational Socialization

PHASE I — ENTRY

- Occupational choice
- Occupational image
- Anticipatory socialization to occupation
- Entry into labor market

PHASE II — SOCIALIZATION

- Accepting the reality of the human organization
- Dealing with resistance to change
- Learning how to work: coping with too much or too little organization and too much or too little job definition
- Dealing with the boss and deciphering the reward system—learning how to get ahead
- Locating one's place in the organization and developing an identity

PHASE III — MUTUAL ACCEPTANCE: THE PSYCHOLOGICAL CONTRACT

Organizational acceptance

- Positive performance appraisal
- Pay increase
- New job
- Sharing organizational secrets
- Initiation rites
- Promotion

Individual acceptance

- Continued participation in organization
- Acceptable job performance
- High job satisfaction

Source: Edgar H. Schein, *Career Dynamics*, © 1978 by Addison-Wesley Publishing Company, Inc. Reprinted by permission of Pearson Education, Inc., Upper Saddle River, NJ.

DETERMINING WHAT IS VALUED AND REWARDED

Identify and describe the abilities and actions that organizations value in managers

Organizational socialization provides the employee with the opportunity to identify and focus on what the organization values and rewards—what abilities are associated with advancement and what actions are seen as valuable. Although it is critical to identify the abilities that a specific organization values, a survey of major organizations and leading CEOs identified a number of abilities that are associated with career success in a broad spectrum of companies:[21]

- *Communications skills.* The ability to communicate one-to-one, in groups, and in writing.

- *Interpersonal skills.* The ability to work with others, relating well to people at all levels of the organization, understanding how others feel, and establishing networks.

- *Competence.* The ability to produce quality work, get results, be accountable, know the field, perform consistently, and upgrade skills.

- *Conceptual skills.* The ability to focus on the big picture and understand all the interlocking pieces.

- *Decision skills.* The ability to handle more and more complex problems.

- *Flexibility.* The ability to adjust to rapid change, new variables, and new environments.

Interviews conducted at Fortune 500 companies revealed that the actions most likely to be valued and rewarded in today's organization include the following:[22]

- *Hard work.* Working hard means being willing to accept more responsibility, being committed, and being dedicated. It also involves working more hours than the standard workweek and producing high-quality work.

- *Risk taking.* This action includes a willingness to move into unfamiliar areas of the business, take on new assignments, and accept increases in responsibility.

- *Making contributions.* Making contributions involves focusing on the critical parts of a job—quality and innovation. It also involves looking at the company's objectives and seeing how the current position fits in and how it affects the bottom line.

- *Being a team player.* Being a team player means being dedicated to making the organization run more effectively rather than focusing on just a job or a department. It involves a person being able to step back and align his or her objectives with those of others, rather than trying to dominate or isolate.

In commenting on the team player, Professor Leonard Greenlaugh notes, "The action today is all about connectedness, about forming effective teams, and building strategic alliances." Robert L. Smith, of the executive search firm that bears his name, agrees:

> In the past a lot of people looked for what I would call the equivalent of the singles tennis pro, the individual who could move mountains and catch bullets in his teeth. In the market today, not only is that no longer desired, it's shunned. We're looking for the team player because in today's environment an executive can't get the job done without support from everyone else.[23]

Assessment and Alignment

After individuals have identified the abilities and actions that are valued and rewarded by the organization, they need to assess both of these and possibly make a mid-course correction. Their actions and abilities must align with those the organization values. To assist this process, the individual must ask the following questions:

- How do my skills match those the organization values?
- Am I capable of the actions necessary?
- What other preparation—education or training—do I need?

Becoming committed to continuous evaluation and skill building is equally important for the employee.

Discuss the strategies associated with career advancement

STRATEGIES FOR CAREER ADVANCEMENT

Knowing and understanding the organization provide the basis on which to develop and implement strategies for career advancement. As shown in Figure D.9, these strategies focus on committing to lifelong learning, creating visibility, developing mentor relationships, developing networks, understanding power and politics, working with the boss, and managing stress.

Figure D.9   Strategies for Career Advancement

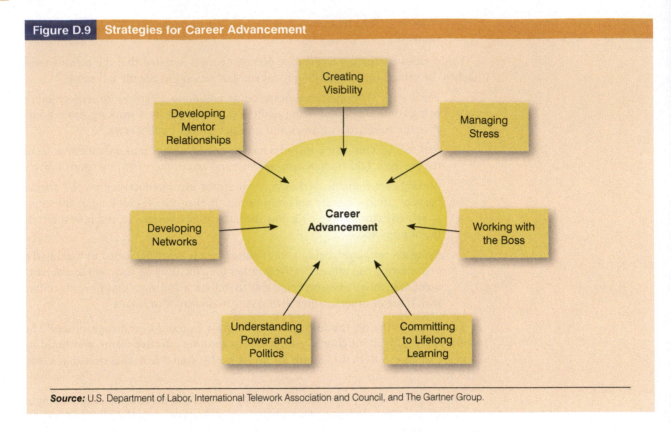

Source: U.S. Department of Labor, International Telework Association and Council, and The Gartner Group.

Committing to Lifelong Learning

"I've got people who report to me who need to learn how to type, because if they can't get on the Internet, they're going to be obsolete," states former Raychem CEO Robert Saldich. The key to avoiding obsolescence—and creating a successful career—is a commitment to lifelong learning. Just as corporations are changing, managers must accept the fact that multiple career changes will become increasingly common. One university president told incoming freshmen that as many as 85 percent of the jobs that would be available in the next 20 years have not been thought of yet. He also predicted that the students should expect to have four to five career—not job—changes during their working life.[24]

What this situation clearly indicates is the need for constant preparation, for learning new technology, and for packaging new skills. To avoid obsolescence (and to resolve the generalist/specialist dilemma discussed earlier), Walter Kiechel advises that you have to be both a generalist and a specialist. "From the very first day on the job, managers have to bring some special expertise to the party. In the new economy, managers will have to add content." Even as a manager you have to add value. "And as managers of technical teams, they will need to understand the different technologies and disciplines to be able to mediate among them."[25]

To upgrade skills and balance the generalist-specialist scale, former Dean John Rau of Indiana University's School of Business has this advice:

> [Focus] along each of three dimensions. On what [is called] traditional content: the classic choices are functions like marketing or finance, but because more companies

are thinking of their businesses as processes, perhaps some focus on that—distribution, say, or customer acquisition. Then overlay a concentration on a particular industry or sector—publishing for instance, or health care. Finally, you will of course need process skills—team leadership, team membership, the ability to communicate. [26]

Futurist Thomas Frey writes the following skills will be highly prized in the future.[27]

14 Hot New Skills

1. *Transitionists* – Those who can help make a transition.

2. *Expansionists* – A talent for adapting along with a growing environment.

3. *Maximizers* – An ability to maximize processes, situations, and opportunities.

4. *Optimizers* – The skill and persistence to tweak variables until it produces better results.

5. *Inflectionists* – Finding critical inflection points in a system will become a much-prized skill.

6. *Dismantlers* – Every industry will eventually end, and this requires talented people who know how to scale things back in an orderly fashion.

7. *Feedback Loopers* – Those who can devise the best possible feedback loops.

8. *Backlashers* – Every new technology will have its detractors, and each backlash will require a response.

9. *Last Milers* – Technologies commonly reach a point of diminishing returns as they attempt to extend their full capacity to the end user. People with the ability to mastermind these solutions will be in hot demand.

10. *Contexualists* – In between the application and the big picture lays the operational context for every new technology.

11. *Ethicists* – There will be an ever-growing demand for people who can ask the tough question and standards to apply moral decency to some increasingly complex situations.

12. *Philosophers* – With companies in a constant battle over "my-brain-is-bigger-than-your-brain," it becomes the overarching philosophy that wins the day.

13. *Theorists* – Every new product, service, and industry begins with a theory.

14. *Legacists* – Those who are passionate and skilled with leaving a legacy.

Creating Visibility

Of course, one way to create visibility on the job is to perform effectively. People who do a good job get noticed. Unfortunately, performance evaluations and recommendations for promotion may involve a substantial degree of subjectivity. Make sure to come into contact with others outside of your department in the organization.

Organizational visibility is the spotlighting and highlighting of a person's abilities, talents, and contributions for those people in the organization who influence promotion and advancement. In addition to the subjective nature of evaluation, many individuals perform jobs that have low visibility—they work in remote locations or have limited contact outside a department. For your talent to be recognized and rewarded, you must be observed. Not all companies support employees by giving them jobs with visibility. Most people must seek visibility on their own.

organizational visibility
A strategy for career advancement that involves the highlighting of a person's abilities, talents, and contributions for those people in the organization who influence promotions and advancements

Documenting Contributions Making others—your immediate supervisor and upper-level managers—aware of your accomplishments is often necessary. Therefore, an approach to gaining visibility is to document contributions. One method is to follow the example of a technician at the Battelle Memorial Institute who told Gene Dalton of the Novations Group that, "he made sure he could give anyone who asked a two-minute summary of what he did, why it mattered, and what he accomplished." Another approach is to identify accomplishments through progress reports to the boss.

Documentation is especially important for teleworkers or **telecommuters**. Remote workers can choose to live away from large cities, with all their noise, pollution, and traffic. They work on computers from their homes, offices, or in their cars, and send the work to their employers over the Internet.

Telework can provide employees with more personal balance between their professional and personal life. It is important that employees be trained to telework, mentored by current teleworkers, and given guidelines for setting up alternative offices. On any given project when employees require any given expertise, they have the opportunity to work seamlessly and electronically with whoever in the world is best at that particular activity.

Volunteering for Visibility Another approach to obtaining visibility is to volunteer for projects, task forces, and other high-profile assignments.[28] These assignments not only highlight talents and abilities, but also provide young executives with developmental opportunities. To reach general management responsibilities, individuals should, preferably, spend time in two of the major functions of an organization. Getting that range of experience can be accelerated through volunteering.[29]

Not every task force, project, or extra assignment should be targeted for volunteering. Rather, for career spotlighting, the decision to volunteer should come after you consider the following points:

- What new experience or knowledge can be gained?
- What will the impact be on your immediate boss and the boss's success?
- What will the impact be on the organization?
- What will the exposure be to multilevel management?

Sponsorship Yet another approach for gaining visibility is to find a **sponsor**—a person who will actively promote a subordinate's talents and look out for his or her organizational welfare. A sponsor is someone in the organization who is at least one position higher than the immediate boss, is successful, and who has a promising future.

Developing Mentor Relationships

Another key strategy for career advancement is to find a mentor. Whereas a sponsor actively promotes the abilities of and seeks opportunities for a protégé, a **mentor** is a skilled employee who acts as a guide, teacher, counselor, and coach. A mentor takes a less-experienced person under his or her wing and helps that person navigate the organization. A mentor should be someone who is successful and well thought of in the organization.[30]

For individuals working in companies without formal mentoring programs, Joyce Lain Kennedy offers the following advice:

- *At your own company, find a leader to learn from.* Ask a supervisor if you can assist or 'shadow' one with interesting projects. Or choose a hero and directly communicate your appreciation of that individual's work and talents; start

telecommuting
The partial or total substitution of telecommunications technology (such as computers, mobile phones, fax machines, and the Internet) for the trip to and from the primary workplace. Simply put, it's moving the work to the workers, instead of the workers to work

telework
Remote work in which corporate employees work outside the office at least two days a week

sponsor
An individual in the organization who will promote a person's talents and look out for his or her organizational welfare

mentor
A senior employee who acts as guide, teacher, counselor, and coach for a less-experienced person in the organization

informally and, if you're receiving the help you need, propose a regular mentor-ship—perhaps an interactive meeting at lunchtime every two weeks—to take stock of your progress.

- *At your own company and in your professional community, discover multiple mentors, each of whom excels in a different area where you need growth.* Florence Stone identifies examples: market knowledge, researching capability, writing skills, organizational talent, and technical knowledge.
- *Internet savvy?* Look online for mentors in your field.
- *Ask at your college alumni office, women's group, or minority organization.* The right headhunter can be a treasure.[31]

Developing Networks

networking
A strategy for career advancement that involves building long-term, two-way interaction based on shared ideas, personal relationships, and common experiences

Some managers still view networking as a short-term activity leading to a specific goal like a new job or a career change. Today, however, **networking** is viewed as a long-term, two-way interaction, based on shared ideas, personal relationships, and common experiences. Successful networking for the 21st century means assembling a focused, highly select group of advisers who can help assess situations, refine strategies, make decisions, and define management style.

In today's business climate, downsizing and flattened corporate hierarchies have resulted in managers with significantly less career security. At the same time, managers often face intense pressure to make decisions and perform successfully. A network can help managers perform better in their current assignments and manage their careers more successfully.

Stephanie Sammons teaches executives how to build personal digital influence using LinkedIn, the world's largest online professional network. For your profile on LinkedIn, she recommends choosing a professional picture; writing in first person to share the part of your story that fits the professional person you want to convey; and making connections by bringing people together.

To build a strategic network and choose connections, she suggests asking the following questions.

- Do they live and work in your community?
- Did they go to the same school as you?
- Do they work in the same industry?
- Did you work together before?[32]

Understanding Power and Politics

organizational politics
The unwritten rules of work life and informal methods of gaining power and advantage

In an ideal world, everybody would receive raises, promotions, and a fair share of desirable and undesirable assignments—based on merit. But in real life, many of these decisions are decided by **organizational politics**—the strategies of work life and informal methods to achieve power. The politics of any organization result from the interaction between those in positions of influence and those seeking influence. These interactions are evidenced by power being acquired, transferred, and exercised on others.

The term *politics* offends many people—organizational veterans and novices alike—because it connotes deceit and deception. But engaging in politics is simply a matter of seeking an advantage. As noted management consultant and author Tom Peters notes, "If you want to escape organizational politics—forget it. Politics is life. Politics involves investing in a relationship—investing time, energy, and emotions."[33]

Although this sentiment has probably always been true, in today's fiercely competitive corporate environment, rife with justifiable insecurity and radically shifting power bases, it is even more important. Now a person will need every bit of political moxie that he or she can muster. According to Dorry Hollander in *Managerial Reality*, "the newly restructured organizations … are competitive playing fields without referees, cluttered with confusing ambiguities, and competing factions…. It's hard for most of us to know what's expected anymore. All this calls for greater ability to read between the lines…. If you don't activate your political horse sense, you might as well park your career in a time capsule."[34]

Identifying the Power Structure Knowing politics is a way of life, the first strategy is to identify the power structure in the organization. Doing so means examining both the formal organizational structure and the workings of the informal organization. In this process you determine the following:

- Who are the people on whom the leaders of the organizations rely?
- What skills and knowledge do these people provide?
- Are you able to supply the same skills and knowledge?
- Could these people help you as sponsors or mentors?

Once you identify the key people, the next step is to acquire power.

Acquiring Power From a career management viewpoint, people obtain power—the ability to influence—in four ways:

1 *Developing expertise in areas critical to the company.* Knowledge and reputation in a specific area can provide the opportunity to participate in projects and lend advice. In today's marketplace, expertise is valued in quality control, understanding consumer preferences, making teams successful, and working with ailing organizations to cure problems.[35]

2 *Developing a network of contacts.* As previously discussed, by developing a network, you can acquire information, you can gather support for new ideas, and you can make expertise for solving problems available. Being a lone wolf will not get you ahead in organizational politics.

3 *Acquiring line responsibility.* The position a person holds in an organization automatically carries certain power. But line managers—those whose work is tied directly to the primary purpose of the organization—have more power than staff groups.

4 *Solving others' problems.* Career advancement is associated with positive support from as many areas as possible. A good way to acquire power and support is to help someone else—a colleague, someone in another department, or a superior—by solving his or her problems. The result will be positive.

Working with the Boss

A major strategy in career management involves learning to work with the boss. A career can be extinguished by not developing a positive alliance with a superior.[36]

Understanding the Boss To work with the boss, you must spend time determining and understanding your boss's priorities, objectives, and negative "hot buttons." The valued subordinate is one who understands that his or her job is to relieve the boss's pressure, not add to it.

Making the Boss Successful The second element of working with the boss is to add to his or her success. After identifying the boss's objectives and priorities, you should develop a set of sub-objectives that support the accomplishment of these major objectives. Doing so will keep the objectives aligned, which is not only a good strategy for career advancement, but sound management.

Supporting versus Bucking the Boss No boss–subordinate relationship is ideal. An expectation in any working relationship is that there will not always be agreement, operations won't always run smoothly, and problems will inevitably surface. In such situations, the subordinate can take several approaches:

- *Provide solutions rather than register complaints.* Identifying a problem is only the first step. The people who advance are those who develop an array of alternative solutions to problems.

- *Practice constructive disagreement rather than rebellion.* This is disagreement focused on a problem—not on a person—with the aim of identifying weaknesses and solutions. Once the discussion is over—win or lose—the job gets done. In contrast, rebellion says, "my way only." Rebellion also means the disagreement doesn't end with the discussion—it will continue in other places with other people.

- *Support the decision.* Once the boss makes a decision, the subordinate should carry it out with the intention of making it work. Ignoring the decision or sabotaging it by not implementing it effectively will not endear the subordinate to the manager. In situations in which the decision may counter the organization's goals or be ethically questionable, the subordinate may need to take the issue to someone other than the boss. In such a situation, having a mentor can be valuable.

Managing Stress

Another cornerstone of career management is stress management. A rapid pace, conflicting deadlines, and multiple events characterize a manager's job. In addition, all managers have responsibility for planning, organizing, and controlling the actions of their departments; and the amount of this responsibility increases as the manager moves up in an organization. Given these realities, stress is obviously a part of the job.

Nature of Stress

stress
The physiological and psychological reaction of the body as a result of demands made on it

Stress is the physiological and psychological reaction of the body as a result of demands made on it.[37] The demands may be emotional (role conflict, fear of unemployment, sexual harassment) or environmental (noise, a lack of privacy, or improper ventilation).

People experiencing stress perceive, through their body's reactions, that the stressful situation is demanding beyond their ability to cope. People experience stress when they aren't finished with a project and the deadline looms, or when they are trying to solve a customer's problem but cannot reach a key decision maker.

Positive and Negative Stress Although stress is always discussed in a negative context, not all stress is negative. Moderate stress is a normal part of a manager's work. A deadline—determined three months earlier—to submit the year's budget forecast for approval causes stress as the date approaches. As shown in Figure D.10, a moderate amount of stress has a positive effect on performance, as it provides motivation.

Extreme levels of stress, on the other hand, are negative and contribute to performance decline. As shown in Figure D.10, if the periods of high stress are extended over

Figure D.10	Manager's Stress Level and Performance

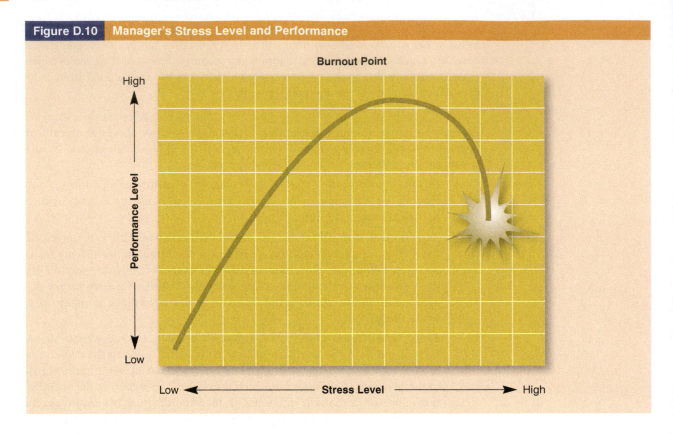

a long period of time the result can be **burnout**—a state of emotional exhaustion as a result of overexposure to stress.[38]

The many possible causes of negative stress for managers are summarized in Figure D.11. For career managers the most critical include the following:

- Incongruence of values between the manager and the company
- Downsizing or layoffs that threaten security or long-range plans
- Limited opportunities for advancement
- Role ambiguity
- Incompatibility with the immediate supervisor's leadership style

In addition, George Gendron reports that in today's organization one of the major causes of stress for managers is the growing complexity of business.[39] There really is no simple business anymore. Thanks to technological change, the globalization of markets, and the rise of government regulation, even the smallest businesses have become enormously complicated. As complexity increases, so have the time and energy required to manage a company's internal functions.

This situation, in turn, has enormous consequences for managers. They are forced to focus more narrowly on their specific parts of the business process. As a result, "they feel isolated, insecure, and unsure—or [they may even question] whether they are contributing to the well-being of the business as a whole. Increased stress is the result."[40]

Although the manager may be stressed by these situations, it is important to remember he or she may, in turn, be the source of stress for others by causing these

burnout
A state of emotional exhaustion as a result of overexposure to stress

Figure D.11	Causes of Negative Stress for Managers

- Downsizing or other threats to security
- Limited opportunities for advancement
- Role ambiguity
- Interpersonal conflict
- Limited decision-making responsibility
- Incompatibility with immediate supervisor's leadership style
- Incongruence of values between the manager and the company
- Boredom or underutilization
- Take-home work and erratic work schedule
- Constant change
- Task or work overload
- Unrealistic deadlines
- Sexual harassment
- Physical environment: noise, lighting, privacy, and climate

situations. When employees develop the following perceptions, managers are the source of stress:

- Uncertainty about the specific responsibilities of the job
- Inability to make decisions or have decisions made when needed
- Unrealistic deadlines
- Lack of control over the things that affect the person in the work environment
- Work overload

The last point, work overload, is the primary cause of employee stress in the work setting. In a survey conducted by Harris Research, more than half of the respondents claim they have too few staff or their level of activity and responsibility has increased. In commenting on the situation, Catherine Romano states, "corporate anorexia resulting from management downsizing and restructuring seems to be producing significant numbers of overworked, and overstressed employees."[41] The situation is such that one third of the respondents would not choose the same career again if they had the chance. Management has caused this situation and must address it if stress is to be managed.

Symptoms of Stress What are the signs that might indicate an excessive stress level? Common symptoms include anxiety, increased blood pressure, headache, backache, fatigue, insomnia, depression, irritability, muscular tightness, and inattention. What these signs don't indicate is the degree of wear and tear on the individual—emotionally and physically. The hidden effects can cost the organization through loss of productivity, absenteeism, and health care expenses. Excessive stress can also cost the individual his or her health and future.

Three types of strategies available for managing stress relate to the manager's own stress, that of employees, or organization wide stress management programs. A manager's own strategy involves developing a balanced approach to life that includes plenty of rest, good eating habits, exercise, and anticipating personal stressors. The other key to combating stress is to identify personal stressors. Not all people react the same way to a situation. Knowing what causes stress allows a person to develop preventive maintenance. A manager must also learn to delegate, to disagree constructively with the boss, and to try consciously to limit the hours of work.[42] Managers help themselves by learning to say no to workloads that are unacceptable and unrealistic.

Managers have an obligation to monitor employees and the work environment for signs of stress. A manager can minimize employees' stress by providing clear and current job descriptions and expectations, initiating timely and relevant feedback, facilitating employees' control over their own jobs, recognizing employee contributions, and encouraging work and personal support groups.[43]

Many companies have chosen to institute formalized stress management programs. These programs might use a combination of exercise, smoking cessation, hypertension screening and control, relaxation, and nutrition counseling. Other organizations have provided the following to help manage employees' stress:

- Facilities for physical exercise, ranging from jogging tracks to full gyms with instructors and organized classes
- Quiet rooms for meditating and reading
- On-site and off-site clinical psychologists or counselors
- Courses focusing on stress reduction and coping techniques[44]

ORGANIZATIONAL DILEMMAS

Discuss the organizational dilemmas experienced when personal and organizational interests are in conflict

Within career planning and management, an individual is often confronted with organizational dilemmas. The four dilemmas involve value conflicts, loyalty demands, decisions on advancement, and concerns for independence.

Conflicts Between Personal and Organizational Values

To have a successful career, a person's value system needs to fit that of the organization. Figure D.12 shows how the values of America's workforce have changed over time. Despite socialization, there are times when a person's values do come in conflict with the organization's, resulting in dissatisfaction.[45]

To minimize this possibility, managers need to do periodic self-analyses to determine their personal values and to select an organization that ensures a match. In addition, they should constantly analyze the demands of the organization against their values to monitor any conflict. But even when individuals are vigilant, the organization may evolve and its values may change. Or individuals may not have completely analyzed the value system and a conflict can occur.[46] For example, a job that initially required minimal travel now requires the manager to be out of town for two weeks each month. This change creates a conflict in the manager's values of home and family. Of course, each individual will resolve this situation differently. Some will accept the development, thriving on the travel or hoping the situation will change again shortly; others will switch jobs, feeling that the new demands are unacceptable.

In other instances, when the values conflict touches on ethical or illegal practices, managers may opt to inform their bosses, the media, or government agencies. As discussed in Chapter 6, these managers are referred to as *whistle-blowers*.[47] Because circumstances do change, managers must be ready to consult their own values—and goals—in developing a response to those changes.

Figure D.12   The Emerging Workforce Has Different Values

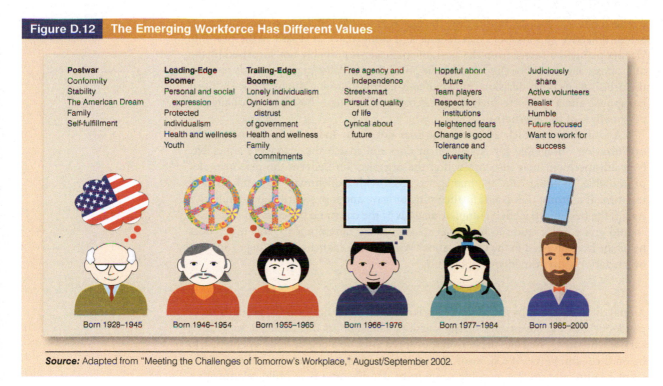

Postwar
Conformity
Stability
The American Dream
Family
Self-fulfillment

Leading-Edge Boomer
Personal and social
  expression
Protected
  individualism
Health and wellness
Youth

Trailing-Edge Boomer
Lonely individualism
Cynicism and
  distrust
of government
Health and wellness
Family
  commitments

Free agency and
  independence
Street-smart
Pursuit of quality
  of life
Cynical about
  future

Hopeful about
  future
Team players
Respect for
  institutions
Heightened fears
Change is good
Tolerance and
  diversity

Judiciously
  share
Active volunteers
Realist
Humble
Future focused
Want to work for
  success

Born 1928–1945   Born 1946–1954   Born 1955–1965   Born 1966–1976   Born 1977–1984   Born 1985–2000

Source: Adapted from "Meeting the Challenges of Tomorrow's Workplace," August/September 2002.

Loyalty Demands

A dilemma intimately related to a person's value system is the question of loyalty. Often, early in a career, loyalty demands are made on a person by the immediate supervisor, who may convey messages such as, "Don't make me look bad, protect me," or "Trust me, tell me about...."

Both of these messages are requests for loyalty. In both cases, the subordinate faces a dilemma. The first loyalty demand—don't make me look bad, protect me—may not seem so unusual. Employees should naturally try to make the boss look good by doing excellent work. Likewise, protecting the boss by keeping him or her informed—no surprises—is a sound practice. But these demands go beyond that; they may involve covering up for weak performance or holding back information that would place a superior in a bad light. In such situations, the subordinate needs to acknowledge what is happening and not be drawn into that behavior. A demand for loyalty—trust me, tell me about ...—potentially places the subordinate in the position of being an informant on someone or of violating a confidence. The superior has gained information but at the same time has caused the subordinate to compromise his or her values. Such a demand for loyalty should be recognized for what it is and avoided.

Advancement Decisions

Another set of dilemmas is met in regard to advancement. They fall into two categories: (1) whether to take a position when it is offered, and (2) what to do when advancement does not occur.

Taking a new job offer may be problematic if it requires a person to move, uproot a family, or relocate to an undesirable location. The situation may be complicated as well by a spouse's career. The offer may come at a time when the manager believes he or she is not really ready. In this case, the manager should talk to his or her mentor to get an objective appraisal of current skills and competence in regard to the new job. Having planned a career from the start, the manager is probably not surprised by the offer; he or she should be prepared for the possibility. Still, the manager needs to make the decision, and that decision can come only after a thorough discussion with his or her spouse and a complete analysis of the costs and benefits—both professionally and personally—of the alternatives.

A situation in which advancement does not occur may simply mean that the organization's timetable for advancement does not match the manager's timetable. Non-advancement may also mean that the organization believes the person is not promotable. In either case, the manager is faced with a dilemma—stay and possibly lose time if a promotion is not forthcoming or leave and lose security and familiarity. Again, the best approach is a complete analysis of the costs and benefits. The manager should give consideration to his or her stage in career development. How much does he or she have invested in the organization? What are the chances of moving to another organization with immediate opportunity?

Independence and Sponsorship

A final dilemma faced by individuals is striking the balance between the need for independence and the advantages of sponsorship. The support of a sponsor sometimes carries a negative price tag; the person sponsored gives up a degree of independence to be on the team. Worse, if a sponsor is fired, the person who was sponsored may suffer similar consequences.[48] A possible solution to the dilemma is to build relationships with many individuals and groups in the organization.

Review What You've Learned

Appendix Summary

1 Discuss the nature of careers.

A career comprises the series of jobs a person holds over a lifetime and the person's attitude toward involvement in these job experiences. It includes a long-term perspective, a sequence of positions, and psychological involvement.

2 Describe what is meant by having a career perspective.

A career perspective is a proactive strategy that takes a global view of career progress or growth over time as it develops. It requires a person to adopt a broad vision that includes all the elements involved in a successful career—objectives, timetables, career stages, skills improvement, organizational politics, power, stress, and values.

3 **Describe the changes that have occurred in the career environment.**

A person can no longer be guaranteed a career with one organization. Gone are the days of lifetime employment and paternalism. Instead, the individual can expect to have many jobs and careers in a lifetime. The person must be self-reliant, constantly update and upgrade skills, seek opportunity rather than security, and chart contributions.

4 **Identify and describe the four stages of career development.**

A person's career normally evolves through four stages: exploration and trial, establishment and advancement, mid-career, and late career.

- *Exploration and trial.* This first stage usually occurs between the ages of 15 and 25. It begins with the decision to become serious about employment; this stage is a learning process.

- *Establishment and advancement.* In this stage, normally between ages 25 and 35, people are involved in their first real job. This is the stage when most people take stock and begin to develop a career strategy.

- *Mid-career.* The mid-career stage most often occurs between the ages of 35 and 50. There are three possible directions a career may take at this point: growth, leveling, or decline.

- *Late career.* The late career stage—between the ages of 50 and retirement—is marked by a peak prestige for those who experienced growth in the prior stage. These people become trainers for the next generation of managers. In addition, plans are made to slow down, develop outside interests, and prepare for retirement.

5 **Identify and discuss the five steps for career planning.**

Career planning involves five steps: self-assessment, exploring opportunities and options, establishing objectives, developing a plan of action, and executing and evaluating the plan.

- *Self-assessment.* Performing a realistic self-assessment involves gathering and analyzing data on your values, interests, skills, abilities, experiences, likes, and dislikes. This step is not only critical for an aspiring manager but should be done on a continuous basis to avoid obsolescence.

- *Exploring opportunities and options.* This step requires examining the opportunities that exist in the industry and a company.

- *Establishing objectives.* Once the opportunities are identified, the career planner has to make short- and long-term decisions. The first decision involves selecting an industry. The next major decision is to choose between being a specialist or generalist. Once that decision is made, other decisions involve identifying needed skills, resources, assignments, training, and experiences that will help accomplish the objectives.

- *Developing a plan of action.* This step provides the detailed map to accomplish the objectives. The plan should include establishing specific timetables for training, reaching a new job level, and gaining new exposure in a company. This stage also identifies potential barriers and the resources to work around the barriers.

- *Executing and evaluating the plan.* Once the plan is in place, it must be put into action. This is a matter of taking charge of your career, rather than waiting for things to happen. The second part of this action is to follow up and evaluate progress. You may need to adjust the plan as the environment changes and there is individual growth, career progress, and new assignments.

6 **Discuss how a manager can understand his or her organization and why it is important to do so.**

All organizations are unique. Each develops its own methods, values, rewards; each makes clear what it accepts and does not tolerate. Before a person can develop strategies for career growth, he or she must know the company—what abilities it values, what actions it rewards, how it compensates its achievers; he or she must both accept the organization and be accepted by it.

The process by which this mutual acceptance is accomplished is known as organizational socialization. In this process, new members of an organization gain exposure to its values, norms, policies, and procedures. At the same time, they discover who wields power, what restrictions there are on behavior, and how to succeed and survive. Eventually, through this process an employee either becomes an accepted and conforming member of the organization or leaves the organization.

7 Identify and describe the abilities and actions that organizations value in managers.

The abilities that organizations value in managers include communication, interpersonal, conceptual, and decision skills; competence; and flexibility. Organizations also value individuals who make contributions, take risks, work hard, and are team players.

8 Discuss the strategies associated with career advancement.

To advance in an organization, an individual must develop and implement strategies that focus on committing to lifelong learning, creating visibility, developing mentor relationships, developing networks, understanding power and politics, working with the boss, and managing stress.

- Committing to lifelong learning is the key to avoiding obsolescence. Managers must reengineer themselves through constant preparation, learning new technology, and packaging new skills.

- Creating organizational visibility involves the spotlighting and highlighting of a person's abilities, talents, and contributions for those in the organization who influence promotion and advancement. Organizational visibility can be obtained by documenting contributions, volunteering, and finding a sponsor.

- By developing a mentor relationship, a person has available a senior employee who acts as a guide, teacher, counselor, and coach. The mentor helps the person navigate the organization.

- Developing a network involves assembling a focused, highly select group of advisers. These advisers help assess situations, refine strategies, make decisions, and refine management style.

- Understanding power and politics is necessary for career success. Organizational politics are the unwritten rules of work life and informal methods of gaining power and influence. Individuals need to not only understand politics but also become adept at it. The first strategy is to identify the power structure; the next is to acquire power.

- Working with the boss is a major strategy in career management. Three elements of the strategy involve understanding the boss, making the boss successful, and supporting the boss.

- Managing stress is another cornerstone of career management. Stress, the physiological and psychological reaction of the body as a result of demands made on it, is a part of all managers' jobs. Managers must learn the causes and symptoms of stress as well as strategies for managing it.

9 Discuss the organizational dilemmas experienced when personal and organizational interests are in conflict.

There are four organizational dilemmas experienced when personal and organizational interests are in conflict. The four dilemmas involve value conflicts, loyalty demands, decisions on advancement, and concerns for independence.

- *Conflicts between personal and organizational values.* There are times when a person's values come in conflict with the organization, resulting in dissatisfaction. When this situation occurs, some will accept the development hoping the situation will change shortly; others may switch jobs, feeling that the new demands are unacceptable. In other instances in which the values conflict touches on ethics or illegality, managers may opt to become whistle-blowers and inform their bosses, the media, or government agencies.

- *Loyalty demands.* Often loyalty demands are made on a person by the immediate supervisor. Requests for loyalty take the form of, "Don't make me look bad, protect me," or, "Trust me, tell me about…." Each creates a dilemma for the manager.

- *Advancement decisions.* These dilemmas fall into two categories: (1) whether to take a position when it is offered, and (2) what to do when advancement does not occur.

- *Independence and sponsorship.* Many individuals face a dilemma caused by trying to strike a balance between the need for independence and the advantages of sponsorship.

KEY TERMS

burnout 630

career 611

career management 621

career perspective 611

career planning 613

job 611

mentor 626

networking 627

obsolescence 617

organizational politics 627

organizational socialization 621

organizational visibility 625

psychological contract 621

sponsor 626

stress 629

telecommuting 626

telework 626

REVIEW QUESTIONS

1. What is the difference between a job and a career?

2. What is meant by the statement "A manager should have a career perspective"?

3. What changes have occurred in the career environment? How do the changes affect career planning and management?

4. What are the four stages of career development?

5. What are the five steps involved in career planning?

6. Why is it important for a manager to understand his or her organization?

7. What abilities do organizations typically value in managers seeking advancement?

8. What is the importance of organizational visibility? How can it be achieved?

9. How does a decision on advancement present an organizational dilemma?

DISCUSSION QUESTIONS FOR CRITICAL THINKING

1. What satisfaction might come from having a career rather than a job?

2. Although you are responsible for your career, what obligation does the organization have for a plateaued employee whose skills have become obsolescent?

3. What career-planning steps have you taken? What additional steps will you take based on educational progress or career progress?

4. Which two of the strategies suggested for career advancement are the most valuable to you? Why?

References

Chapter 1

1 Drucker, Peter F. *Management Challenges for the 21st Century.* HarperCollins, 1999, Chapter 1.

2 Johnson, Mike. "Drucker Speaks His Mind." *American Management Association* (October 1995), 10–14.

3 See note 2.

4 Erez, M., and P. C. Earley. *Culture, Self-Identity and Work.* New York: Oxford University Press, 1993.

5 Schultz, David P. "Top 100 Retailers." *STORES.org.* NRF Enterprises Inc, July 2010. Web. 21 July 2010. <*http://www.stores.org/stores-magazine-july-2010/top-100-retailers*>.

6 Sherman, Stratford. "How Tomorrow's Best Leaders Are Learning Their Stuff." *Fortune* (November 27, 1995), 90–93, 96, 100.

7 Johnson, Ross, and William O. Winchell. *Management and Quality.* Milwaukee: ASQC Press, 1989.

8 Kroski, Ellyssa. "The Hype and the Hullabaloo of Web 2.0." *InfoTangle* (1/31/06). < *http://infotangle.blogsome.com/2006/01/13/the-hype-and-the-hullabaloo-of-web-20*>

9 Bennis, Warren. "The Leadership Advantage." *Leader to Leader* (12 Spring 1999), 18–23. <*http://drucker.org/leaderbooks/L2L/spring99/bennis.html*>.

10 Huey, John. "The New Post-Heroic Leadership." *Fortune* (February 21, 1994), 42–44, 48, 50.

11 See note 10.

12 See note 9.

13 Dunfee, Thomas W. "Employee Ethical Attitudes and Business Firm Productivity." *The Wharton Annual.* University of Pennsylvania, Pergamon Press, 1984, 76.

14 Cox, Danny, with John Hoover. *Leadership When the Heat's On.* New York: McGraw-Hill, 1992, 23.

15 Fagiano, David. "Coping with the Global Village." *Management Review* (May 1995), 5.

16 Hammonds, Keith H. "The New Face of Global Competition." *Fast Company* (January 2003), Issue 67, 90. <*http://www.fastcompany.com/online/67/newface.html*>.

17 Woodruff, David. "Talk About Life in the Fast Lane." *BusinessWeek* (October 17, 1994), 155–166.

18 Huy, Quy Nguyen. "In Praise of Middle Managers." *Harvard Business Review* (September 2001).

19 Solomon, Melissa. "Middle Managers: Developing the Right Skill Sets." *Computerworld* (May 13, 2002).<*http://www.computerworld.com/careertopics/careers/story/0,10801,71064,00.html?nlid=AM*>.

20 Wendorf, Nancy. "Dinosaurs and Middle Managers: Evolution for Global Survival." APICS International Conference Proceedings 1998, 282–289.

21 See note 20.

22 See note 19.

23 Plunkett, W. Richard. *Supervision: Diversity and Teams in the Workplace.* Englewood Cliffs, N.J.: Prentice-Hall, 1996.

24 Harari, Oren. "The Missing Link in Performance." *Management Review* (March 1995), 21.

25 Katz, Robert L. "Skills of an Effective Administrator." *Harvard Business Review* (September–October 1974), 90–102.

26 See note 24.

27 See note 16.

28 *American Management Association,* 2001 Managerial Skills And Competencies Survey.

29 Mercado, Gus. "CEO Profile: Herb Kelleher." *Business Horizons* (December–January–February 1995), 42–44, 46–47, 65.

30 Longenecker, Clinton O., and Dennis A. Gioia. "Ten Myths of Managing Managers." *Sloan Management Review,* vol. 33, no. 1, 1991, 81–90.

31 Charan, Ram, and Geoffrey Colvin. "Why CEOs Fail." *Fortune* (June 21, 1999).

32 "Rude Awakenings Come Early." *Chicago Tribune* (November 20, 1995), sec. 4, 3.

Chapter 2

1 Haigh, Christopher, ed. *The Cambridge Historical Encyclopedia of Great Britain and Ireland.* Cambridge, England: Cambridge University Press, 1990, 269.

2 Merrill, Harwood F., ed. *Classics in Management,* rev. ed. New York: American Management Association, 1970, 10, 56, 188.

3 Bartlett, Christopher A., and Sumantra Ghoshal. "Changing the Role of Top Management: Beyond Systems to People." *Harvard Business Review* (May–June 1995), 134.

4 See note 2.

5 Matteson, Michael T., and John M. Ivancevich, eds. *Management Classics,* 3d ed. Santa Monica, Calif., Business Publications, 1986, 18, 156, 232, 280.

6 See note 5.

7 See note 5.

8 See note 2.

9 Mayo, Elton. *The Human Problems of an Industrial Civilization.* New York: Macmillan, 1933.

10 McGregor, Douglas. The Human Side of Enterprise. New York: McGraw-Hill, 1960, 33–48.

11 Griffith, Victoria. "Emergent Leadership: Bringing Free-Market Risks and Rewards to Commands-and-Control Corporations." *Strategy & Business* (Fourth Quarter, 1998), 3.

12 Campbell, Jeremy. *Grammatical Man: Information, Entropy, Language, and Life.* New York: Simon & Schuster, 1982, 15–31.

13 Bittel, Lester R., and Jackson E. Ramsey, eds. *Handbook for Professional Managers.* New York: McGraw-Hill, 1985, 634.

14 See note 13.

1 Gonsalves, Antone. "Supply-Chain Systems Help P&G Meet Aggressive Financial Goals." *Internet Week* (January 31, 2003).

2 Hammer, Michael, and James Champy. *Reengineering the Corporation.* New York: HarperBusiness, 1993, 32–33.

3 See note 16.

4 Davenport, Thomas H. "The Fad That Forgot People." *Fast Company* (October 1995), 70. <*http://www.fastcompany.com/online/01/reengin.html*>.

5 Sethi, Arjun, and Olivier Aries. "The End of Outsourcing (As We Know It)." *Bloomberg Business Week* (August 10, 2010). <*http://www.businessweek.com/technology/content/aug2010/tc20100810_440259.htm*>

Chapter 3

1 Senge, P. M. "The Laws of the Fifth Discipline." *The Fifth Discipline.* New York: Currency Doubleday, 1994, 57–67.

2 Bertalanffy, L. von. "The Theory of Open Systems in Physics and Biology." *Science,* 111 (January 13, 1950), 23–29.

3 Churchman, W. *The Systems Approach.* New York: Delacorte Press, 1968.

4 Labich, Kenneth. "Why Companies Fail." *Fortune* (November 14, 1994), 52–54, 58, 60, 64, 68.

5 Yates, Ronald E. "Intellectual Capital a Downsizing Casualty." *Chicago Tribune* (June 4, 1995), sec. 7, p. 2.

6 Pinchot & Company, Bainbridge Island, "Bill of Rights," http://www.pinchot.com

7 Loeb, Marshall. "Ten Commandments for Managing Creative People." *Fortune* (January 16, 1995), 135–136.

8 Senge, P. M. "The Leader's New Work." *Executive Excellence* 11 (11), 1994, 8–9.

9 Gensler. "2008 Workplace Survey United States." <http://www.gensler.com/uploads/documents/2008_Gensler_Workplace_Survey_US_09_30_2009.pdf>

10 Maxon, Terry. "Area economy soared with D/FW." *The Dallas Morning News* (August 15, 2010), 15A.

11 Manyika, James M., Roger P. Roberts and Kara L. Sprague. "Eight business technology trends to watch." McKinsey on Business Technology (Fall 2008). <http://www.mckinsey.com/clientservice/bto/pointofview/pdf/eight_business_technology_trends_watch.pdf>

12 A.T. Kearney. "Creating value through strategic supply management." (2004 Assessment of Excellence in Procurement). http://www.atkearney.com/index.php/Publications/creating-value-through-strategic-supply-management.html

13 Bridget van Kralingen, "IBM Transformation, From Survival to Success." Forbes, July 7, 2010. http://www.forbes.com/2010/07/07/ibm-transformation-lessons-leadership-managing-change.html

14 Bureau of Labor Statistics, Message from the Secretary of Labor, *Report on the American Workforce 2001*, http://www.bls.gov/opub/rtaw/message.htm

15 Bureau of Labor Statistics. "2008–2018 Employment Projections." (December 10, 2009). < http://www.bls.gov/news.release/ecopro.nr0.htm>.

16 Smart, Tim. "A Lot of the Weaknesses Carbide Had Are Behind It." *BusinessWeek* (January 23, 1995), 83–84.

17 U.S. Office of Management and Budget (OMB). "2010 Report to Congress on the Costs and Benefits of Federal Regulations and Unfunded Mandates on State, Local, and Tribal Entities." <http://www.whitehouse.gov/sites/default/files/omb/legislative/reports/2010_Benefit_Cost_Report.pdf >.

18 "Disney Surrenders, Won't Build Theme Park Near Civil War Site." Chicago Tribune (September 29, 1994).

19 Bittel, Lester R. *The McGraw-Hill 36-Hour Management Course.* New York: McGraw-Hill, 1989, 31–34, 179, 184–185.

Chapter 4

1 Lorange, P. *Strategic Planning and Control.* Cambridge, Mass.: Blackwell, 1993.

2 Drucker, Peter F. *The Practice of Management.* New York: Harper & Row, 1954, 49–61, 65–83.

3 Ward, John, and Craig Aronoff. "Passion and Its Place in Business." *Nation's Business* (March 1995), 50–51.

4 Tully, Shawn. "Why to Go for Stretch Targets." *Fortune* (November 14, 1994), 145.

5 Collins, James C., and Jerry Porras. *Built to Last.* New York: HarperCollins, 1994, 91–114.

6 Confino, Jo. "PepsiCo's 'big hairy audacious goals'." *Guardian News* (May 26, 2010), http://www.guardian.co.uk/sustainable-business/pepsico-background-sustainability-programme

7 See note 2.

8 See note 2.

9 Mangelsdorf, Martha E. "Plan of Attack." *Inc* (January 1996), 41–44.

10 Hill, Charles W. L., and Gareth R. Jones. *Strategic Management: An Analytical Approach.* Boston: Houghton Mifflin, 1989.

11 Treacy, Michael, and Fred Wiersema. "How Market Leaders Keep Their Edge." *Fortune* (February 6, 1995), 88–89.

12 Daft, Richard L. *Management,* 3d ed. Homewood, Ill.: Dryden Press, 1994, 220.

13 Garvin, David. "Leveraging Processes for Strategic Advantage." *Harvard Business Review* (September–October 1995), 77–90.

14 See note 13.

15 See note 13.

16 Miller, Robert. "Cashing In at Southwest." *Dallas Morning News* (May 3, 1995), 3D.

17 Loeb, Marshall. "Where Leaders Come From." *Fortune* (September 19, 1994), 241.

18 Galbraith, Jay R., and Robert Kazanjian. *Strategy Implementation: Structure, Systems, and Process,* 2d ed. St. Paul, MN.: West, 1986.

19 Yang, Dori Jones. "The Starbucks Enterprise Shifts into Warp Speed." *BusinessWeek* (October 24, 1994), 76, 78–79.

20 See note 20.

21 Gupta, Anil K., and V. Govindarajan. "Business Unit Strategy, Managerial Characteristics, and Business Unit Effectiveness at Strategy Implementation." *Academy of Management Journal* 29 (March 1984), 25–41.

22 Miles, Raymond E., and Charles E. Snow. *Organizational Strategy, Structure, and Process.* New York: McGraw-Hill, 1978.

23 Porter, Michael E. *Competitive Strategy: Techniques for Analyzing Industries and Competitors.* New York: Free Press, 1980, 36–46.

24 See note 24.

25 Lohr, Steve. "Apple and I.B.M. Aren't All That Different." *The New York Times.* November 7, 2010. BU4 http://www.statista.com/statistics/274821/ibms-expenditure-on-research-and-development-since-2005/

chapter 5

1 Holt, David H. *Management: Principles and Practices,* 2d ed. Englewood Cliffs, N.J.: Prentice-Hall, 1990, 100.

2 Howard, Ronald A. "Decision Analysis: Practice and Promise." *Management Science* 34 (1988), 679–695.

3 Netflix, Inc. "How it Works", March 2016, <http://www.netflix.com>.

4 Ecommerce, Tech Target, March 2016, http://searchcio.techtarget.com/definition/e-commerce.

5 RJ Metrics "2015 Ecommerce Benchmark Report", https://rjmetrics.com/resources/reports/2015-ecommerce-growth-benchmark/

6 Amazon Investor Relations, February 2016, http://phx.corporate-ir.net/phoenix.zhtml?c=97664&p=irol-irhome

7 Simon, Herbert A. *The New Science of Management.* Englewood Cliffs, N.J.: Prentice-Hall, 1977, 47.

8 Bazerman, Max H. *Judgment in Managerial Decision Making.* New York: Wiley, 1986, 42.

9 Drucker, Peter F. *The Practice of Management.* New York: Harper & Row, 1954, 351.

10 Peters, Tom. "Time-Obsessed Competition." *Management Review* (September 1990), 17–18.

11 Kepner, C., and B. Tregoe. *The Rational Manager.* New York: McGraw-Hill, 1965.

12 Etzioni, Amitai. "Humble Decision-making." *Harvard Business Review* (July–August 1989), 122–126.

13 Eilon, Samuel. "Structuring Unstructured Decisions." *Management Science* 33 (1987), 121–123.

14 Rousell, Philip A. "Cutting Down the Guess Work in R & D," *Harvard Business Review* (September–October 1983), 154–157.

15 Vroom, Victor H., and Phillip Yetton. "A New Look at Managerial Decision-making." *Organizational Dynamics* (Spring 1973), 67.

16 Maier, Norman R.F. *Problem-Solving Discussions and Conferences.* New York: McGraw-Hill, 1963.

17 See note 15.

18 Whyte, Glenn. "Decision Failures: Why They Occur and How to Prevent Them." *Academy of Management Executive* 5, no. 3 (1991), 23–31.

19 Wire Reports, "Faster than a speeding merger." *The Dallas Morning News*, May 10, 2010. 4D.

20 Steel, Charles R. "The Starbucks Enterprise Shifts into Warp Speed." *BusinessWeek* (October 24, 1994), 76.

21 Starbucks. "Company Profile." *http://www.starbucks.com/business/international-stores*, 2016.

22 Etorre, Barbara. "Breaking the Glass—or Just Window Dressing." *Management Review* (March 1992), 16.

23 Stewart, Thomas A. "Mapping Corporate Brainpower." *Fortune* (October 30, 1995), 209–211.

24 Ettling, Jennifer T., and Arthur G. Jago. "Participation Under Conditions of Conflict: More on the Vroom-Yetton Model." *Journal of Management Studies* 25 (1988) 73–83.

25 Grover, Edward L. "Group Decision-making: Approaches to Problem Solving," *Small Business Reports* (July 1988), 30–33.

26 Briggins, Angela. "Win-Win Initiatives for Women." *Management Review* (June 1995), 6.

27 Fox, William M. "The Improved Nominal Group Technique." *Journal of Management Development* (August 1989), 20–27.

28 Shermach, Kelly. "Sheraton Adds Staff, Laptops to Improve Satisfaction." *Marketing News* (April 24, 1995), 14.

29 Whyte, Glenn. "Groupthink Reconsidered." *Academy of Management Review* 14 (1989), 40–56.

30 Helm, Leslie. "Playing to Win." *Dallas Morning News* (October 22, 1994), 1F.

31 Ireland, R. Duane, Michael A. Hill, and J. Clifton Williams. "Self-Confidence and Decisiveness: Prerequisites for Effective Management in the 1990s." *Business Horizons* (January–February 1992), 36–42.

Chapter 6

1 Davidson, Daniel D., et. al. *Business Law, Principles and Cases,* 9e Southwestern Publishing, 2003.

2 Solomon, Robert C., and Kristine R. Hanson. *It's Good Business.* New York: Athenaeum, 1985, xiii–xiv, 20–21, 46–49, 146–148.

3 "Social Media Research Raises Privacy and Ethics Issues." USA Today, March 12, 2014

4 Dunfee, Thomas W. "Employee Ethical Attitudes and Business Firm Productivity." *The Wharton Annual.* University of Pennsylvania: Pergamon Press, 1984, 76.

5 Walker Information. "The Walker Loyalty Report for Loyalty in the Workplace." (September 2007). <*http://walkerinfo.com/pics/wlr/Employee_ExecSumm_07.pdf*>

6 Cox, Danny, with John Hoover. *Leadership When the Heat's On.* New York: McGraw-Hill, 1992, 23.

7 Henderson, Verne E. *What's Ethical in Business?* New York: McGraw-Hill, 1992, 62, 74–75, 202, 205.

8 Levitt, Arthur. *Take On the Street: What Wall Street and Corporate America Don't Want You to Know.* New York: Pantheon Books, 2002.

9 Frost, Peter J., Vance F. Mitchell, and Walter R. Nord. *Managerial Reality: Balancing Technique, Practice, and Values.* New York: HarperCollins, 1995, 307–309.

10 Gellerman, Saul W. *Motivation in the Real World.* New York: Dutton, 1992, 265, 266–267, 269–271, 273–274.

11 Paine, Lynn Sharp. "Managing for Organizational Integrity." *Harvard Business Review* (March–April 1994), 106–117.

12 See note 7.

13 See note 11.

14 See note 10.

15 See note 2.

16 Bushnell, Davis. "Scandals Revive Focus on Ethics." *Boston Sunday Globe* (June 23, 2002).

17 Human Resources Management: Ideas & Trends in Personnel 273. "The best ethics training goes beyond legal compliance by giving people skills needed to make value-based decisions," an interview with Dr. Peter Madsen. Chicago: Commerce Clearing House, (April 15, 1992), 60.

18 Byrne, John A. "Businesses Are Signing Up for Ethics 101." *BusinessWeek* (February 15, 1988), 56–57.

19 See note 17.

20 See note 7.

21 Ethics & Compliance Officer Association. "ECOA Values." <*http://www.theecoa.org/imis15/ECOAPublic/ABOUT_THE_ECOA/Mission__Vision__and_Values/ECOAPublic/AboutContent/Mission_and_Vision.aspx?hkey=d11443d2-fbab-4e78-8dfe-84bd99e3aa3a*>.

22 Voss, Don. "Dilbert™ Goes Corporate... or How to Navigate the Thorny Thickets of Corporate America without Selling Your Soul." <*http://www.stc.org/confproceed/1999/PDFs/060.PDF*>

23 Alsop, Ronald J. *The 18 Immutable Laws of Corporate Reputation.* New York, NY: Free Press, 2004, 67

24 Barrett, Jennifer. "An Ethical Dilemma." *Newsweek* (February 19, 2003). <*http://www.newsweek.com/2003/02/18/an-ethical-dilemma.html*>.

25 See note 1.

26 See note 17.

27 Barry, Vincent. *Moral Issues in Business,* 3d ed. Belmont, Calif.: Wadsworth, 1986, 5, 9–10, 156.

28 Grennan, John. "Ethics and the Bottom Line." *Saint Mary's Magazine* (Winter 2010). <*http://www.stmarys-ca.edu/news-and-events/saint-marys magazine/2010/winter/features/05.html*>

29 Jacobs, Deborah L. "Stiff New Penalties: Companies Can Be Fined For Workers' Misdeeds." *Your Company* (Winter 1992), 12.

30 See note 10.

31 Stahl, Stephanie. "IT Takes the Lead in Enforcing Ethics." *InformationWeek* Newsletter (February 23, 2001). <*http://www.informationweek.com/magazine*>.

32 Gellerman, Saul W. "Why 'Good' Managers Make Bad Ethical Choices." *Harvard Business Review* (July–August 1986), 88–89.

33 See note 10.

34 See note 2.

35 See note 10.

36 Blanchard, Kenneth, and Norman Vincent Peale. *The Power of Ethical Management.* New York: Morrow, 1988, 27.

37 Davis, Keith. "Five Propositions for Social Responsibility." *Business Horizons* 18, no. 3 (June 1975). Adapted from article reprinted in Barry, 1986, 156.

38 Buchholz, Rogene A. *Fundamental Concepts and Problems in Business Ethics.* Englewood Cliffs, N.J.: Prentice-Hall, 1989, 5.

39 Watson, Charles E. *Managing with Integrity, Insights from America's CEOs.* New York: Praeger, 1991, 321.

40 Haas, Robert D. Acceptance speech, Lawrence A. Wein Prize in Corporate Social Responsibility, Columbia University, New York, November 19, 1984: as recorded in Watson, 1991, 321–322.

41 Harris Interactive Inc. "Annual Reputation Quotient (RQ)." <http://www.harrisinteractive.com/Products/ReputationQuotient.aspx>.

42 See note 1.

43 GreenBiz.com, "U.S. Oil and Gas Companies Bow to Shareholders on Climate." (March 21, 2005). <http://www.greenbiz.com/news/news_third.cfm?NewsID=27816>.

44 National Philanthropic Trust, The Charitable Giving Report for 2014. <http://www.nptrust.org/philanthropic-resources/charitable-giving-statistics/>

45 Schwartz, Nelson, and Tim Smart. "Giving—and Getting Something Back." *BusinessWeek* (August 28, 1995), 81.

46 General Electric. "GE Foundation – Developing Futures™ in Education." <http://www.ge.com/foundation/developing_futures_in_education/index.jsp>.

47 Hirschman, Carolyn. "Protected Behaviors at the State Level." *HR Magazine* (February 2003). <http://www.shrm.org/Publications/hrmagazine/EditorialContent/Pages/0203hirschmana.aspx>.

48 Nolo. "Consumer Protection Laws." <http://www.nolo.com/legal-encyclopedia/article-29641.html>.

49 Willcocks, Leslie P., and Sara Cullen. "The Outsourcing Enterprise: The Power of Relationships." Logica in association with Warwick Business School (November 24, 2005). <http://www.logica.co.uk>.

50 Ryan, Nancy. "McDonald's Update for Special Menus." *Chicago Tribune* (March 12, 1992), sec. 3, 3.

51 Hunt, Christopher B., and Ellen R. Auster. "Proactive Environmental Management: Avoiding the Toxic Trap." *The Best of MIT's Sloan Management Review* (Winter 1990), 7–18.

52 Buehler, Vernon M., and Y. K. Shetty. "Managerial Response to Social Responsibility Challenge." *Academy of Management Journal* (March 1976), 69.

Chapter 7

1 Child, John. *Organization: A Guide to Problems and Practices,* 2d ed. London: Harper & Row, 1984.

2 *Reuters.* "GE doubles down on restructuring to offset slow growth," January 22, 2016. <http://www.reuters.com/article/us-general-electric-results-idUSKCN0V01DQ>

3 *Newsweek.* "Lay off the Layoffs." (February 5, 2010). <http://www.newsweek.com/2010/02/04/lay-off-the-layoffs.html>

4 Lawrence, Paul R., and Jay W. Lorsch. *Organization and Environment.* Homewood, Ill.: Irwin, 1967.

5 Daft, Richard L. *Management,* 12 ed. Cengage Learning, 2016.

6 Smith, Adam. *The Wealth of Nations.* New York: Modern Library, 1937.

7 Miner, Anne S. "Idiosyncratic Jobs in Formal Organizations." *Administrative Science Quarterly* (September 1987), 327–351.

8 Twomey, Daniel, Frederick C. Scherer, and Walter S. Hunt. "Configuration of a Functional Department: A Study of Contextual and Structural Variables." *Journal of Organizational Behavior,* vol. 9 (1988), 61–75.

9 Drucker, Peter. "Management's New Paradigms." *Forbes* (October 5, 1998). <http://www.forbes.com/forbes/98/1005/6207152a.htm>.

10 See note 9.

11 Moskal, Brian S. "The Buck Doesn't Stop Here." *Industry Week* (July 15, 1992), 29–30.

12 O'Reilly, Brian. "Johnson & Johnson Is on a Roll." *Fortune* (December 26, 1994), 190.

13 Fayol, Henri. *General and Industrial Management.* London: Pitman, 1949.

14 See note 9.

15 Kent, Carolyn. "The Technical and Administrative Staff of the Future." *Work Teams Newsletter,* Center for the Study of Work Teams, The University of North Texas (Summer 1997).

16 Hammonds, Keith H. "Rethinking Work." *BusinessWeek* (October 17, 1994), 87.

17 Ayers-Williams, Roz. "Mastering the Fine Art of Delegation." *Black Enterprise* (April 1992), 91–93.

18 Hellman, Paul. "Delegating Is Easy, Deputizing a Posse Is Tough." *Management Review,* (June 1992), 58.

19 Davis, Ralph C. *Fundamentals of Top Management.* New York: Harper & Row, 1951.

20 Urwick, Lyndall F. *Scientific Principles and Organization.* New York: American Management Association, 1938.

21 Van Fleet, David. "Span of Management Research and Issues." *Academy of Management Journal* (September 1983), 546–552.

22 Kountz, Harold, and Cyril O'Donnel. *Management.* New York: McGraw-Hill, 1976, 375.

23 Spertus, Philip. "It's Easy to Fool the Boss." *Management Review* (May 1992), 28.

24 Jacob, Raul. "How One Red Hot Retailer Wins Customer Loyalty." *Fortune* (July 10, 1995), 77–80.

25 John Newstrom. *Human Behavior at Work: Organizational Behavior,* 14th ed. New York: McGraw-Hill, 2014.

26 See note 25.

27 See note 25.

28 Harmon, Theo, and William B. Scott. *Management in the Modern Organization.* Boston: Houghton Mifflin, 1970, 452.

29 See note 25.

30 See note 25.

Chapter 8

1 Robbins, Stephen P. *Management,* 13th ed. Pearson Education Upper Saddle River NJ, 2015.

2 Jacob, Rahul. "The Struggle to Create an Organization for the 21st Century." *Fortune* (April 3, 1995), 92.

3 Burns, Tom, and G. M. Stalker. *The Management of Innovation.* London: Taristock, 1961.

4 See note 1.

5 Simnacher, Joe. "Boardroom Rumblings." *Dallas Morning News* (April 8, 1992), 18–20.

6 Miles, Raymond E., and Charles C. Snow. *Organizational Strategy, Structure, and Process.* Stanford University Press, Stanford CA, March 2003.

7 Porter, Michael E. *Competitive Strategy.* New York: Free Press, 1980, 36–46.

8 Lawrence, Paul R., and Jay W. Lorsch. *Organization and Environment, Managing Differentiation and Integration HBS Classics, 1986.*

9 Astley, W. Graham. "Organization Size and Bureaucratic Structure." *Organization Studies* 6 (1985), 201–228.

10 Quinn, Robert E., and Kim Cameron. "Organizational Life Cycles and Shifting Criteria of Effectiveness: Some Preliminary Evidence." *Management Science* 29 (1983), 33–51.

11 Burns, Lawton R. "Matrix Management in Hospitals: Testing Theories of Matrix Structure and Development." *Administrative Science Quarterly* 34 (1989), 349–368.

12 Koloday, Harvey F. "Managing Effectively in a Matrix," HBR August 10, 2012

13 Miles, Raymond E. "Adapting to Technology and Competition: A New Industrial Relation System for the 21st Century." *California Management Review* (Winter 1989), 9–28.

14 Rammrath, Herbert G. "Globalization Isn't for Whiners." *The Wall Street Journal* (April 6, 1992), C27.

15 Freiberg, Kevin and Jackie. "Southwest Can Find Another Pilot." *The Wall Street Journal* (March 26, 2001).

16 Peters, Thomas J., and Robert H. Waterman, Jr. *In Search of Excellence: Lessons from America's Best-Run Companies.* New York: Harper & Row, 1982, 173.

17 Kotter, John P. *Organizational Dynamics: Diagnosis and Intervention* 1978. Prentice Hall Organizational Development Series.

18 Mars Incorporated. "The Five Principles." <*http://www.mars.com/global/about+us/the+five+principles*>.

19 Spector, Robert, and Patrick D. McCarthy. *The Nordstrom Way to Customer Service Excellence: The Handbook For Becoming the "Nordstrom" of Your Industry* Paperback—March 5, 2012 Robert Spector (Author), Patrick D. McCarthy (Author hold copyright now)

20 Henkel Consumer Adhesives, Inc. "Culture." <*http://www.henkelna.com/about-henkel-corporate-culture-9099.htm*>.

21 Collins, James C. "Building Companies to Last." *Inc* (January 1995), 83-85.

22 Collins, James C., and Jerry I. Porras. *Built to Last.* New York: Harper Business Essentials, 1994, 3, 117–118, 132, 134.

23 Kotter, John P., and James Heskett. *Corporate Culture and Performance.* New York: Free Press, 1992, 11.

24 See note 23.

25 Dubrin, Andrew J. *Fundamentals of Organizational Behavior 4e.* Southwestern Publishing, Cincinnati OH, 2006.

26 Hammer, Michael, and James Champy. *Reengineering the Corporation.* New York: HarperBusiness, 1993, 32–33.

27 Manganelli, Raymond, and Mark Klein. "Your Engineering Toolkit." *Management Review* (August 1994), 26–30.

28 Tichy, Noel M., and Stratford Sherman. *Control Your Destiny or Someone Else Will.*
New York: Doubleday Currency, 1993, 245–246.

29 Greiner, Larry. "Evolution and Revolution as Organizations Grow." *Harvard Business Review* (July–August 1972), 55–64.

30 Barnes, Louis B. "Managing the Paradox of Organizational Trust." *Harvard Business Review* (March–April 1981), 107–118.

31 Argyris, Chris, and Don Schon. *Organizational Learning: A Theory of Action Perspective.* Reading, Mass.: Addison-Wesley, 1978.

32 Fisher, Anne B. "Making Change Stick." *Fortune* (April 17, 1995), 122–131.

33 Davis Wiki. "Square Tomato." <*http://daviswiki.org/square_tomato*>.

34 Lewin, Kurt. "Frontiers in Group Dynamics: Concept, Method, and Reality in Social Science." *Human Relations* (1947), 5–41.

35 Burton, Gene E. "Organizational Development—A Systematic Process." *Management World* (March 1976).

Chapter 9

1 Nulty, Peter. "Serial Entrepreneur: Tips from a Man Who Started 28 Businesses." *Fortune* (July 10, 1995), 182.

2 Brown, Tom. "Manage with a Conscience." *Industry Week* (January 9, 1995), 20–22, 25.

3 Fraser, Jill. "Tis Better to Give and Receive." *Inc* (February 1995), 84–86, 88, 90.

4 Source: *http://www.shrm.org/about/foundation/products/pages/onboardingepg.aspx#sthash.okIZVukB.dpuf*

5 Future of Work Symposium, December 10, 2015, *http://www.dol.gov/featured/fow/factsheet.pdf*. U.S. Senate. Subcommittee on Labor of the Committee on Labor and Public Welfare. Equal Employment Opportunity Act of 1972 (March 1972), 3.

6 E. Jackson, Schuler, Randall R. *Managing Human Resources*, 11th ed. New York: Cengage, 2012.

7 Job Accommodation Network. "Workplace Accommodations: Low Cost, High Impact" (09/01/15) *https://askjan.org/media/lowcosthighimpact.html*

8 Bravo, Ellen, and Ellen Cassedy. *The Updated and Expanded 9 to 5 Guide to Combating Sexual Harassment.* 9 to 5 Working Women Education Fund; Rev Exp edition (August 1, 1999).

9 See note 8.

10 U.S. Department of Labor. Office of the Secretary. "Trends and Challenges for Work in the 21st Century." <*http://www.*
dol.gov/oasam/programs/history/herman/reports/futurework/report.htm*>.

11 See note 10.

12 See note 10.

13 Report on the Glass Ceiling Initiative. U. S. Department of Labor, 1991. *http://digitalcommons.ilr.cornell.edu/glassceiling*

14 Catalyst. "Cracking the Glass Ceiling, 2000 Edition," *http://www.catalyst.org/publication/68/cracking-the-glass-ceiling-strategies-for-success*; "Women in Male-Dominated Industries and Occupations" October 20, 2015 *http://www.catalyst.org/knowledge/women-male-dominated-industries-and-occupations*.

15 DDI Global Leadership Forecast 2014-2015 <*http://www.ddiworld.com/glf2014*>

16 Stodghill, Ron. "Managing AIDS." *BusinessWeek* (February 1, 1993), 48–52.

17 U.S. Department of Health and Human Services, SAMHSA, Office of Applied Studies. "Drugs in the Workplace: A Summary of Research and Survey Findings." (Last updated: October 13, 2005) <*http://www.whitehousedrugpolicy.gov/prevent/workplace/research.html*>.

18 See note 17.

19 Hoerr, John, et al. "Privacy." *BusinessWeek* (March 28, 1988), 61, 65.

20 Bureau of Labor Statistics. "Union Members Summary." (January 21, 2011), <*http://www.bls.gov/news.release/union2.nr0.htm*>.

21 Klimas, Molly. "How to Recruit a Smart Team." *Nation's Business* (May 1995), 26–27.

22 Equal Employment Opportunity Commission. "Uniform Guidelines on Employee Selection Procedures." <*http://www.uniformguidelines.com*>.

23 Kleiman, Carol. "From Genetics to Honesty, Firms Expand Employee Tests, Screening." *Chicago Tribune* (February 9, 1992), sec. 8, p. 1.

24 Armour, Stephanie. "Worker Background Checks Raise Privacy Concerns." *USA Today* (May 21, 2002). *http://www.ides.illinois.gov/Pages/default.aspx*

25 Whitaker, Aja, "Employee Screening Rises While Hiring Remains Slow." *Tampa Bay Business Journal* (January 18, 2002). <*http://tampabay.bizjournals.com/tampabay/stories/2002/01/21/focus2.html*>.

26 Fenn, Donna, ed. "Check My References—Please!" *Inc* (April 1995), 111.

27 ASTD. "Training for the Next Economy"—ASTD's Latest "State of the Industry" Report. <*http://www.astd.org*>.

28 U.S. Department of Labor. Bureau of Labor Statistics. "Report on the American Workforce"—Message from the Secretary of Labor, 2001. <*http://www.bls.gov/opub/rtaw/message.htm*>.

29 Hammonds, Keith H., Kevin Kelly, and Karen Thurston. "The New World of Work." *BusinessWeek* (October 17, 1994), 76–77, 80–81, 84–87.

30 Bulkeley, William M. "Computer Use by Illiterates Grows at Work." *The Wall Street Journal* (June 9, 1992), B1.

31 Mohrman, Allan, Jr., Susan Resnick-West, and E. E. Lawler III. *Designing Performance Appraisal Systems: Aligning Appraisals and Organizational Realities.* San Francisco: Jossey-Bass, 1989.

32 Beck, Joan. "Matching the Workplace to the Work Force." *Chicago Tribune* (March 9, 1992), sec. 1, 15.

33 Steinert-Threlkeld, Tom. "Computer Revenge a Growing Threat." *Chicago Tribune* (March 9, 1992), sec. 4, 3.

34 Society of Human Resource Management. *Study of Retention Practices.* <*http://www.shrm.org*>.

35 Bennett, Amanda. "Executive Pay: A Little Pain and a Lot to Gain." *The Wall Street Journal* (April 22, 1992), R1.

Chapter 10

1 Walton, Sam, with John Huey. *Sam Walton: Made in America.* New York: Doubleday, 1992, 247–248.

2 Taylor, Paul and Wendy Wang. "The Fading Glory of the Television and Telephone." Pew Research Center, August 19, 2010, <*http://pewsocialtrends.org/2010/08/19/the-fading-glory-of-the-television-and-telephone*>

3 Mintzberg, Henry. *The Nature of Managerial Work.* New York: Harper & Row, 1973.

4 Deutschman, Alan. "The CEO's Secret of Managing Time." *Fortune* (June 1, 1992), 136, 140, 144, 146.

5 See note 4.

6 Sprout, Alison L. "Reality Boost." *Fortune* (March 21, 1994), 93.

7 Plunkett, Lorne C., and Robert Fournier. *Participative Management.* New York: Wiley, 1991, 123–124, 126–127.

8 Dumaine, Brian. "The Trouble with Teams." *Fortune* (September 5, 1994), 92.

9 See note 8.

10 See note 7.

11 Sayles, Leonard R., and George Strauss. *Human Behavior in Organizations.*

Englewood Cliffs, N.J.: Prentice-Hall, 1966, 93–94, 238–246.

12 Spragins, Ellen E. "An Employee Newsletter with Zing." *Inc* (April 1992), 121.

13 Peters, Tom. "Steps to Turn Workers into Business People." *Chicago Tribune* (November 25, 1991), sec. 4, 4.

14 Fisher, Anne B. "CEOs Think That Morale Is Dandy." *Fortune* (November 18, 1991), 83–84.

15 Denove, Chris and James Power. *Satisfaction How Every Great Company Listens to the Voice of the Customer.* Portfolio Hardcover, 2006, Foreword xi.

16 Mateja, Jim. "J. D. Power Speaks; Chrysler Listens." *Chicago Tribune* (August 21, 1994), sec. 4, 7.

17 See note 16.

18 Davis, Keith. *Human Behavior at Work: Organizational Behavior.* New York: McGraw-Hill, 1989.

19 "Meeting the Challenges of Tomorrow's Workplace," *Chief Executive* (August/September 2002). <*http://www.chiefexecutive.net*>.

20 Edelman Press Release, 2011 Trust Barometer, <*http://www.edelman.com/trust/2011*>. 2016 trust barometer <*http://www.edelman.com/insights/intellectual-property/2016-edelman-trust-barometer/*>. Quote from Executive Summary http://www.edelman.com/insights/intellectual-property/2016-edelman-trust-barometer/executive-summary/.

21 Bustin, Greg. "Honesty: Still the Best Policy." *Bustin & Co.* (February 2005). <*http://www.bustin.com*>.

22 Huber, Janean. "The Big Picture: Learning from Big Business." *Entrepreneur* (June 1992), 186–187.

23 Kenney, Charles C. *Riding the Runaway Horse.* New York: Little, Brown, 1992.

24 Gabarro, John J. "Retrospective Commentary." *Harvard Business Review* (November–December 1991), 108.

Chapter 11

1 Straub, Joseph T., and Raymond Attner. *Introduction to Business,* 5th ed. Boston: PWS-KENT, 1994, 182. *http://www.mckinsey.com/global-themes/leadership/when-to-change-how-you-lead* 2015

2 Case, John. "Collective Effort." *Inc* (January 1992), 32–43.

3 "SAS ranks No.1 on the FORTUNE '2011 100 Best Companies to Work For' list," *http://www.sas.com/news/fortune2011.html*

4 Steers, Richard M., and Lyman W. Porter, eds. *Motivation and Work Behavior,* 4th ed. New York: McGraw-Hill, 1987, 3–4.

5 Collins, James C., and Jerry I. Porras. *Built to Last.* New York: HarperBusiness, 1993, 156–158.

6 John W. Newstrom. *Human Behavior at Work: Organizational Behavior,* 14th ed. New York: McGraw-Hill, 2014.

7 Daft, Richard L. *Management,* 3d ed. Fort Worth, Tex.: Dryden Press, 1994, 515–521. 12e, 2015

8 Maslow, Abraham H. "A Theory of Human Motivation." *Psychological Review* 50 (1943), 370–396.

9 See note 8.

10 Krizan, William G. "Award of Excellence." *Engineering News-Record* (April 17, 2000).

11 See note 8.

12 Trimble, Vance H. *Sam Walton: The Inside Story of America's Richest Man.* New York: Signet, 1992, 109.

13 Herzberg, Frederick. "One More Time: How Do You Motivate Employees?" *Business Classics: Fifteen Key Concepts for Management Success.* Cambridge, Mass.: Harvard Business Review, 1975, 16–17.

14 See note 13.

15 Hyatt, Joshua. "Real-World Re-Engineering." *Inc* (April 1995), 40–53.

16 See note 10.

17 Julie Weber, "How Southwest Airlines Hires Such Motivated People," Harvard Business Review, December 2, 2015, *https://hbr.org/2015/12/how-southwest-airlines-hires-such-dedicated-people.*

18 McClelland, David C. *The Achieving Society.* New York: Van Nostrand Reinhold, 1971.

19 McClelland, David C., and David Burnham. "Power Is the Great Motivator." *Harvard Business Review* (March–April 1976), 100–110.

20 See note 15.

21 Alderfer, Clayton. *Existence, Relatedness, and Growth: Human Needs in Organizational Settings.* New York: Free Press, 1972.

22 Case, John. "The Open-Book Revolution." *Inc* (June 1995), 26–40.

23 Vroom, Victor H. *Work and Motivation.* New York: Wiley, 1964.

24 See note 23.

25 Porter, Lawrence W., and Edward E. Lawler. *Managerial Attitudes and Performance.* Homewood, Ill.: Irwin, 1968.

26 Schuler, Randall S. *Personnel and Human Resource Management,* 3d ed. St. Paul, Minn.: West, 1987, 41–43.

27 Gleckman, Howard. "Bonus Pay: Buzzword or Bonanza." *BusinessWeek* (November 14, 1994), 62–64.

28 Skinner, B. F. *Contingencies of Reinforcement.* New York: Appleton-Century-Crofts, 1969.

29 Tarpy, R. M. *Basic Principles of Learning.* Glenview, Ill.: Scott Foresman, 1974, 71–79.

30 Hamner, W. C. "Reinforcement Theory and Contingency Management in Organizational Settings." *Organizational Behavior and Management: A Contingency Approach.* H. L. Tosi and W. C. Hamner, eds. New York: Wiley, 1974, 86–112.

31 See note 22.

32 Adams, J. Stacy. "Toward an Understanding of Equity." *Journal of Abnormal and Social Psychology* (November 1963), 422–436.

33 Goodman, Paul S., and Abraham Friedman. "An Examination of Adam's Theory of Inequity." *Administrative Science Quarterly* (December 1971), 271–288.

34 Robbins, Stephen P. *Organizational Behavior: Concepts, Controversies, and Applications,* 5th ed. Englewood Cliffs, N.J.: Prentice-Hall, 1991, 209.

35 See note 10.

36 Stewart, Thomas A. "How to Lead a Revolution." *Fortune* (November 28, 1994), 48–61.

37 See note 10.

38 McGregor, Douglas. *The Human Side of Enterprise.* New York: McGraw-Hill, 1960, 23–27.

39 Argyris, Chris. *Personality and Organization.* New York: Harper & Bros., 1957.

40 CBS News *60 Minutes.* "Working the Good Life." (April 20, 2003). <*http://www.cbsnews.com/stories/2003/04/18/60minutes/main550102.shtml*>.

41 Single, John L. "The Power of Expectations: Productivity and the Self-Fulfilling Prophecy." *Management World* (November, 1980), 19, 37–38.

42 See note 12.

43 American Management Association (AMA). "Leading the Four Generations at Work." (January 23, 2007) <*http://www.amanet.org/training/articles/Leading-the-Four-Generations-at-Work.aspx*>

44 Oliver, Joyce Ann. "Mattel Chief Followed Her Vision." *Marketing News* (March 16, 1992), 15.

45 See note 37.

46 Hall, Cheryl. "The Brinker Touch." *Dallas Morning News* (March 3, 1992), 23H.

47 Schlossberg, Howard. "Internal Marketing Helps Companies Understand Culturally Diverse Markets." *Marketing News* (January 21, 1991), 7, 9.

48 Files, Jennifer. "Incentive for Everyone." *Dallas Morning News* (July 25, 1992), 1D, 4D.

49 Etorre, Barbara. "Breaking the Glass—or Just Window Dressing." *Management Review* (March 1992), 17.

50 Fleming, Peter C. "Empowerment Strengthens the Rock." *Management Review* (March 1992), 34–37.

51 Peters, Tom. "Time-Obsessed Competition." *Management Review* (September 1990), 18.

52 Barrier, Michael. "Re-Engineering Revisited." *Nation's Business* (May 19, 1995), 36.

53 See note 22.

54 See note 2.

55 Van Fleet, David D. *Contemporary Management,* 2d ed. Boston: Houghton Mifflin, 1991, 371.

56 See note 27.

57 See note 13.

58 See note 22.

59 Winters, Terry E., and Donald L. Murfin. "Venture Capital Investing for Corporate Development Objectives." *Journal of Business Venturing* (Summer 1988), 207.

60 Kuratko, Donald F., and Richard M. Hodgetts. *Entrepreneurship: A Contemporary Approach.* Chicago: Dryden Press, 1989.

61 Pinchot, Gifford. *Entrepreneuring.* New York: Harper & Row, 1985.

62 See note 5.

63 Executive Management Forum. "Job Sharing Is Family Friendly." *Management Review* (April 1995), 2.

64 Austin, Nancy K. "How Managers Manage Flexibility." *Management Review* (August 1994), 19–20.

Chapter 12

1 Meyers, William. "Conscience in a Cup of Coffee." *USNews.com* (October 31, 2005). <*http://www.usnews.com/usnews/news/articles/051031/31schultz.htm*>.

2 Kleiman, Carol. *The 100 Best Jobs for the 1990s and Beyond.* Chicago: Dearborn Financial Publishing, 1992.

3 Kiechell, Walter, III. "The Leader As Servant." *Fortune* (May 4, 1992), 121–122.

4 See note 3.

5 Yukl, Gary A. *Leadership in Organizations.* Englewood Cliffs, N.J.: Prentice-Hall, 1981, 70, 121–125.

6 Peace, William H. "The Hard Work of Being a Soft Manager." *Harvard Business Review* (November–December 1991), 40–47.

7 "Managing People." *Inc* (October 1992), 33.

8 See note 5.

9 Nulty, Peter. "How to Live by Your Wits." *Fortune* (April 20, 1992), 119.

10 Holly Lebowitz Rossi, "7 Core Values Statement that Inspire," March 13, 2015, *http://fortune.com/2015/03/13/company-slogans/*

11 Kotter, John P., and James L. Heskett. *Corporate Culture and Performance.* New York: Free Press, 1992, 94–96.

12 See note 11.

13 Kotter, John P. "Leading Change: Why Transformation Efforts Fail." *Harvard Business Review* (March–April 1995), 59–67.

14 See note 13.

15 Fisher, Anne B. "Making Change Stick." *Fortune* (April 17, 1995), 121–122, 124, 128–131.

16 See note 15.

17 Jargon, Julie. "Coffee Break: Starbucks Chief on Prices, McDonald's Rivalry." *The Wall Street Journal* (March 7, 2011), <*http://online.wsj.com/article/SB10001424052748704076804576180313111969984.html*>

18 Davis, Keith, and John Newstrom. *Human Behavior at Work: Organizational Behavior,* 8th ed. New York: McGraw-Hill, 1989, 213, 215.

19 See note 18.

20 Keller, Robert, and Andrew Szilagyi. "A Longitudinal Study of Leader Reward Behavior, Subordinate Expectations, and Satisfaction." *Personnel Psychology* (Spring 1978), 119–129.

21 See note 7.

22 Likert, Rensis. *The Human Organization.* New York: McGraw-Hill, 1976.

23 See note 22.

24 Likert, Rensis. "From Production- and Employee-Centeredness to Systems 1–4." *Journal of Management* 5 (1979), 147–156.

25 Schriesheim, C. A., and B. J. Bird. "Contributions of the Ohio State Studies to the Field of Leadership." *Journal of Management* 5 (1979), 135–145.

26 See note 25.

27 Fiedler, Fred E. "The Contingency Model—New Directions for Leadership

Utilization." *Journal of Contemporary Business* 3, no. 4 (Autumn 1974), 65–80.

28 House, Robert J., and Terrence R. Mitchell. "Path–Goal Theory of Leadership." *Journal of Contemporary Business* 3, no. 4 (Autumn 1974), 81–97.

29 House, Robert J. "A Path–Goal Theory of Leader Effectiveness." *Administrative Science Quarterly* 16 (1971), 321–338.

30 See note 28.

31 See note 28.

32 Gartner redefines gamification, (*http://blogs.gartner.com/brian_burke/2014/04/04/gartner-redefines-gamification*).

33 Cooper, Helen. "Carpet Firm Sets Up an In-House School to Stay Competitive." *The Wall Street Journal* (October 5, 1992), A1, A5.

34 See note 33.

35 Hersey, Paul, and Kenneth H. Blanchard. *Management of Organizational Behavior,* 4th ed. Englewood Cliffs, N.J.: Prentice-Hall, 1982.

36 Erdman, Andrew. "Staying Ahead of 800 Competitors." *Fortune* (June 1, 1992), 111.

37 Boyett, Joseph H., and Henry P. Conn. *Workplace 2000.* New York: Plume, 1991, 330–331.

38 See note 37.

39 Walton, Sam, with John Huey. *Sam Walton: Made in America.* New York: Doubleday, 1992, 169.

40 Goleman, Daniel. *Emotional Intelligence: Why It Can Matter More Than IQ.* Bantom, 1995.

41 Goleman, Daniel. *Working with Emotional Intelligence.* Bantom, 1998.

42 See note 41, p. 41.

43 See note 41, p. 42.

44 Goleman, Daniel. Richard Boyatzis and Annie McKee. *Primal Leadership: Realizing the Power of Emotional Intelligence.* Harvard Business Press, 2002.

45 Henkoff, Ronald. "Finding, Training, & Keeping the Best Service Workers." *Fortune* (October 3, 1994), 110–111, 114, 116, 118, 120, 122.

46 See note 45.

47 Giuliani, Rudolph. *Leadership.* Miramax, 2002.

48 Losee, Stephanie. "Revolution from Within." *Fortune* (June 1, 1992), 112.

49 Wharton School of the University of Pennsylvania. "How Pepsi Got Its Fizz Back." (October 22, 2003). <*http://knowledge.wharton.upenn.edu/index.cfm?fa=viewArticle&ID=865*>.

Chapter 13

1 Dumaine, Brian. "The Trouble with Teams." *Fortune* (September 5, 1994), 86–92.

2 Cox, Allan. "The Homework Behind Teamwork." *Industry Week* (January 7, 1992), 21.

3 Lawler III, Edward E. *Organizing for High Performance: Employee Involvement, TQM, Reengineering, and Knowledge Management in the Fortune 1000.* Jossey-Bass, 2001.

4 Larson, Carl E., and Frank M. J. LaFasto. *TeamWork.* Newbury Park, Calif.: Sage, 1989.

5 Schein, Edgar. *Process Consultation.* Reading, Mass.: Addison-Wesley, 1969, 42–43.

6 Owens, Thomas. "Business Teams." *Small Business Report* (January 1989), 50–58.

7 McKee, Bradford. "Turn Your Workers into a Team." *Nation's Business* (July 1992), 36.

8 Etorre, Barbara. "Retooling People and Processes." *Management Review* (June 1995), 19–23.

9 Dumaine, Brian. "Unleash Workers and Cut Costs." *Fortune* (May 18, 1992), 88.

10 Sager, Ida. "The Butterfly: From a Little Girl's Building Blocks." *BusinessWeek* (July 24, 1995), 72.

11 See note 1.

12 Daft, Richard L. *Management,* 3d ed. Fort Worth, Tex.: Dryden Press, 1994, 585.

13 Gunn, Eileen P. "Empowerment That Pays Off." *Fortune* (March 20, 1995), 145–146.

14 Fisher, Kimball, and Mareen D. Fisher. *The Distributed Mind: Achieving High Performance through the Collective Intelligence of Knowledge Work Teams.* AMACOM, 1997.

15 Executive Management Forum. "Customer-Focused Teams (CFTeams) on The Start." *Management Review* (September 1994), 2.

16 Stewart, Thomas A. "How to Lead a Revolution." *Fortune* (September 28, 1994), 48–61.

17 Zellner, Wendy. "Team Player: No More 'Same-ol-Same ol'." *BusinessWeek* (October 17, 1994), 95–96.

18 Reynolds, Larry. "Quality Circles." *Management Review* (January 1992), 53–54.

19 Greenwald, John. "Is Mr. Nice Guy Back." *TIME* (January 27, 1992), 42–44.

20 Byham, William C. "Self-Directed Work Team Magic." *Boardroom Reports* (June 15, 1992), 1–8.

21 Case, John. "Collective Effort." *Inc* (January 1992), 35.

22 Executive Management Forum. "Teaming a Cornerstone at Reengineered Taco Bell." *Management Review* (December 1994), 2.

23 Yang, Dori Jones. "Nordstrom's Gang of Four." *BusinessWeek* (June 15, 1992), 122–123.

24 Brown, Tom. "Want to Be a Real Team." *Industry Week* (July 20, 1992), 17.

25 See note 7.

26 See note 1.

27 Wire Reports, "At AT&T, Adapt or Go Away," The Dallas Morning News, (February, 16, 2016), p. 1A and 7A.

28 Executive Management Forum. "The Facts of Life about Teambuilding." *Management Review* (February 1995), 4.

29 Shaw, M. E. *Group Dynamics,* 3d ed. New York: McGraw-Hill, 1985.

30 Deutschman, Alan. "The Managing Wisdom of High-Tech Superstars." *Fortune* (October 17, 1994), 200.

31 Prince, George. "Recognizing Genuine Teamwork." *Supervisory Management* (April 1989), 25–36.

32 Parker, Glenn. *Team Players and Teamwork.* San Francisco: Jossey-Bass, 1990.

33 Huey, John. "The New Post-Heroic Leadership." *Fortune* (February 21, 1994), 48.

34 See note 28.

35 Caminiti, Susan. "What Team Leaders Need to Know." *Fortune* (February 20, 1995), 93–100.

36 Tuckman, B. W. "Developmental Sequence in Small Groups." *Psychological Bulletin* 63 (1965), 384–389.

37 See note 1.

38 See note 29.

39 Cartright, Dorwin, and Alvin Zandler. *Group Dynamics: Research and Theory,* 3d ed. New York: Harper & Row, 1968.

40 Uris, Auren. *Techniques of Leadership.* New York: McGraw-Hill, 1964, 58.

41 See note 28.

42 See note 19.

43 See note 35.

44 Albanese, Robert, and David D. Van Fleet. "Rational Behavior in Groups: The Free-Riding Tendency." *Academy of Management Review* 10 (1985), 244–255.

45 Verespej, Michael A. "When Workers Get New Roles." *Industry Week* (February 3, 1992), 11.

46 Stoner, James A. F. *Management,* 3d ed. Englewood Cliffs, N.J.: Prentice-Hall, 1986, 85.

47 Thomas, Kenneth W. "Conflict and Conflict Management." *Handbook of Industrial and Organizational Psychology,* Marvin Donnette, ed. Chicago: Rand McNally, 1976, 889–935.

48 Ferenstein, Greg. "In a Cutthroat World, Some Web Giants Thrive by Cooperating." *The Washington Post* (February 19, 2011), <*http://www.washingtonpost. com/wp-dyn/content/article/2011/02/19/ AR2011021902888.html*>.

49 See note old 46.

50 Singer, Merv, and Susan Lazar. "Who's in Charge Here?" *Nation's Business* (January 1995), 37.

51 Kerwin, Kathleen, Edith Updike, and Keith Naughton. "The Shape of a New Machine." *BusinessWeek* (July 24, 1995), 60–66.

52 Robbins, Stephen. *Managing Organizational Conflict,* 3d ed. Englewood Cliffs, N.J.: Prentice-Hall, 1986, 321.

53 Schein, Edgar H. *Organizational Psychology.* Englewood Cliffs, N.J.: Prentice-Hall, 1970.

54 Murphy, Anne. "The Enemy Within." *Inc* (March 1994), 58–69.

Chapter 14

1 Bartlett, Christopher A., and Sumantra Ghoshal. "Changing the Role of Top Management: Beyond Systems to People." *Harvard Business Review* (May–June 1995), 132–142.

2 SAS, "What is Big Data?" *http://www.sas. com/en_us/insights/big-data/what-is-big-data.html*

3 "4 Big Companies Using Big Data Successfully" Smart Data Collective, *July 14, 2015 http://www.smartdatacollective. com/jessoaks11/330428/4-big-companies-using-big-data-successfully*

4 "Beyond Moneyball; How Big Data is Changing Baseball", SportTechie, November 11, 2014. *http://www. sporttechie.com/2014/11/11/beyond-moneyball-how-big-data-is-changing-baseball/*

5 See note 1.

6 Cone, Edward. "Boeing: New Jet, New Way of Doing Business." *CIO Insight* (March 6, 2006), <*http://www.cioinsight.com/ article2/ 0,1540,1938894,00.asp*>. "Boeing Celebrates Global Supplier Partners on Delivery of 7,500th 737," March 26, 2013, *http://boeing.mediaroom.com/2013-03-26-Boeing-Celebrates-Global-Supplier-Partners-on-Delivery-of-7-500th-737.*

7 Bittel, Lester R. *The McGraw-Hill 36-Hour Management Course.* New York: McGraw-Hill, 1989, 229.

8 See note 1.

9 Bughin, Jacques Michael Chui, and James Manyika, "An Executive's Guide to the Internet of Things," August 2015, *http:// www.mckinsey.com/business-functions/ business-technology/our-insights/ an-executives-guide-to-the-internet-of-things*).

10 Mensching, James R., and Dennis A. Adams. *Managing an Information System.* Englewood Cliffs, N.J.: Prentice-Hall, 1991.

11 Keen, Peter G. W. *Every Manager's Guide to Information Technology: A Glossary of Key Terms and Concepts for Today's Business Leader.* Boston: Harvard Business School Press 1991, 156–157.

12 Verity, John W. "Cyber-Networks Need a Lot of Spackle." *BusinessWeek* (June 26, 1995), 92–93.

13 Arnst, Catherine. "The Networked Corporation." *BusinessWeek* (June 26, 1995), 86–89.

14 Virga, Patricia H., ed. *The NMA Handbook for Managers, Englewood Cliffs NJ Prentice Hall, 1987.*

15 See note 10. (Mensching)

16 Kleiman, Carol. "Top Executives Are Different from Other Bosses." *Chicago Tribune* (August 9, 1995), sec. 6, p. 5.

17 Roberts-Witt, Sarah. "A 'Eureka!' Moment at Xerox." *PC Magazine* (March 26, 2002). <*http://www.pcmag.com/ article2/0,2817,28792,00.asp*>.

18 Bittel, Lester R., and Jackson E. Ramsey, eds. *Handbook for Professional Managers.* New York: McGraw-Hill, 1985, 220, 222.

19 See note 10. (Mensching)

20 Byrne, John, "Management's New Gurus." *BusinessWeek* (August 31, 1992), 50.

21 See note 6.

22 Crockett, Fess. "Revitalizing Executive Information Systems." *Sloan Management Review* (Summer 1992), 41.

23 See note 18.

24 Evans, Alan, Kendall Martin, Mary Anne Poatsy. *Technology in Action.* Upper Saddle River, New Jersey: Pearson, 2011, 541.

25 Davenport, Thomas H. "Saving IT's Soul: Human-Centered Information Management." *Harvard Business Review* (March–April 1994), 119–131.

26 See note 25.

27 See note 13.

28 See note 24.

29 McGee, Marianne K., ed. "Show Workers the Way to Go." *InformationWeek* (June 26, 1995), 124.

30 Computer Sciences Corporation. "Critical Issues of Information Systems Management: A Look Back," *CSC World* (December 2002–February 2003).

31 Lacity, Mary C., Leslie P. Willcocks, and David F. Feeny. "IT Outsourcing: Maximize Flexibility and Control." *Harvard Business Review* (May–June 1995), 84–93.

32 See note 30. CSC reference

33 Computer Sciences Corporation. "Geoffrey Moore on the Age of Outsourcing." *CSC World* (December 2002–February 2003).

Chapter 15

1 Bittel, Lester R. *The McGraw-Hill 36-Hour Management Course.* New York: McGraw-Hill, 1989, 179, 184–185.

2 Odiorne, George, Heinz Weihrich, and Jack Mendelson. *Executive Skills: A Management by Objectives Approach.* Dubuque, Iowa: Brown, 1980, 26–28.

3 Barry, Thomas J. *Management Excellence Through Quality.* Milwaukee: ASQC Press, 1991, 5–6.

4 Hardy, Quentin. "The Killer Ad Machine." *Forbes Global* (December 11, 2000).

5 "This Inspector Gets Under a Plane's Skin." *BusinessWeek* (November 18, 1991), 69.

6 Bittel, Lester R., and Jackson E. Ramsey, eds. *Handbook for Professional Managers.* New York: McGraw-Hill, 1985, 194, 196.

7 See note 1.

8 See note 1.

9 Walton, Richard E. "From Control to Commitment in the Workplace." *Harvard Business Review* (March–April 1985), 76–84.

10 Bianchi, Alessandra. "The Strictly Business Flextime Request Form." *Inc* (May 1995), 79.

11 Levinson, Meridith. "Harrah's Entertainment – Jackpot! Using IT to Manage Customer Information," *CIO Magazine* (February 1, 2001), <*http:// www.cio.com/article/29547/HARRAH_S_ ENTERTAINMENT_Jackpot_Using_IT_ to_Manage_Customer_Information*>.

12 Dudick, Thomas S., ed. *Handbook of Business Planning and Budgeting.* New York: Van Nostrand Reinhold, 1983, 22, 74.

13 Vancil, Richard F. "What Kind of Management Control Do You Need?"

Harvard Business Review on Management. New York: Harper & Row, 1975, 481.

14 Heyel, Carl, ed. *The Encyclopedia of Management,* 3d ed. New York: Van Nostrand Reinhold, 1982, 328.

15 Walton, Sam, with John Huey. *Sam Walton: Made in America.* New York: Doubleday, 1992, 231.

16 Bittel, Lester R., and Jackson E. Ramsey, eds. *Handbook for Professional Managers.* New York: McGraw-Hill, 1985, 550.

17 Huey, John. "Discounting Dynamo Sam Walton." *TIME,* (December 7, 1998).

Appendix A

1 Hart, Christopher W. L., and Christopher E. Bogan. *The Baldrige: What It Is, How It's Won, How to Use It to Improve Quality in Your Company.* New York: McGraw-Hill, 1992, A, 8, 77, 96, 128–130.

2 Shewhart, Walter A. *Statistical Method from the Viewpoint of Quality Control.* Washington, D.C.: Graduate School of the Department of Agriculture, 1939, 2–4.

3 Vasilash, Gary S. "Oh, What A Company!" *Automotive Design & Production* (March 200A). <*http://www.autofieldguide.com/ articles/030A01.html*>

4 Juran, Joseph M., and A. Blanton Godfrey, eds. *Juran's Quality Handbook,* Ath ed. McGraw-Hill Book Company 1999.

5 See note 4.

6 Fornell, Claes. "No Pullback in ACSI: Many Companies Improve Customer Relationships." *The American Customer Satisfaction Index* (August 20, 2003). <*http://www.theacsi.org/index. php?option=com_content&task=view &id=91&Itemid=107*>.

7 Dean, Edwin B. *Design for Quality from the Perspective of Competitive Advantage.* NASA Langley Research Center, 1998.

8 Mizuno, Shigeru, and Yoji Akao, eds. *QFD: The Customer-Driven Approach to Quality Planning and Development.* Tokyo: Asian Productivity Organization.

9 Akao, Yoji, ed. *Quality Function Deployment.* Productivity Press, 1990.

10 ASQ "American Society for Quality." Glossary of Terms. <*http://www.asq.org/ glossary/b.html*>.

11 Sewell, Carl, and Paul B. Brown. *Customers for Life: How to Turn That One-Time Buyer into a Lifelong Customer.* Pocket Books, 1998.

12 Greising, David. "Quality: How to Make It Pay." *BusinessWeek* (August 8, 1994), A4–A9.

13 Treacy, Michael, and Fred Wiersema. *The Discipline of Market Leaders: Choose Your Customers, Narrow Your Focus, Dominate Your Market.* Perseus Press, 1997.

14 See note 13.

15 See note 13.

16 Hunt, Daniel V. *Quality in America: How to Implement a Competitive Quality Program.* Irwin Professional Publishers, 199A.

17 Barry, Thomas J. *Management Excellence Through Quality.* Milwaukee: ASQC Press, 1991, ix, 3, 7, 19.

18 See note 12.

19 See note 17.

20 Crosby, Philip B. *Quality Without Tears.* New York: Plume, 1984, A9–63, 99–100, 106–107.

21 Crosby, Philip B. *Quality Is Free: The Art of Making Quality Certain.* New York: Mentor, New American Library, 1979.

22 Hunt, Daniel V. *Quality in America.* Homewood, Ill.: Business One Irwin, 1992, 23, 43, 64–76, 268–269, 286.

23 Ishikawa, Kaoru, *What is Total Quality Control?* Englewood Cliffs NJ, Prentice Hall, 1985, 44-45, 98, 125-128, 186.

24 AAAWalton, Mary. *The Deming Management Method at Work.* New York: Perigee, 1986, 19–20, 2A–26, 72.

25 Ganguli, Niladri, T.V. Kumaresh, and Aurobind Satpathy. "Detroit's New Quality Gap." *The McKinsey Quarterly,* 2003, 1.

26 Townsend, Patrick L., and Joan E. Gebhardt. *Quality in Action.* New York: Wiley, 1992, 17.

27 See note 4.

28 Barrier, Michael. "Re-engineering Revisited." *Nation's Business* (May 199A), 36.

29 "The 'Discoverer' of Reengineering Pounds His Critics, But Michael Hammer Still Has a Few Details to Nail Down." *Performance* (March 199A), 2A–28.

30 See note 29.

31 Longworth, R. C. "Downsizing Craze Turns Out to Be Profitless Folly." *Chicago Tribune* (April 23, 199A), sec. 4, 1, 4.

32 Hammer, Michael. *Beyond Reengineering: How the Processed-Centered Organization is Changing Our Work and Our Lives.* New York: HarperCollins, 1997.

33 Hammer, Michael, and Francis J. Quinn. "Q & A: Reengineering the Supply Chain: An Interview With Michael Hammer." *Supply Chain Management Review* (April 1, 1999).<*http:// www. manufacturing.net/ scm/index.asp?layout= articleWebzine&articleid=CA1AA060*>.

34 Collins, James. *Built to Last: Successful Habits of Visionary Companies.* New York: HarperCollins, 1994.

35 Gabor, Andrea. *The Man Who Discovered Quality.* New York: Penguin, 1990, 47–48, 126–127.

36 Petersen, Donald E., and John Hillkirk. *A Better Idea: Redefining the Way Americans Work.* Boston: Houghton Mifflin, 1991, 6–11.

37 See note 36.

38 Vaghefi, M. Reza. "Creating Sustainable Competitive Advantage: The Toyota Philosophy and Its Effects." *Financial Times* (September A, 2002). <*http://sysdoc. doors.ch/TOYOTA/toyotaphilosohy.pdf* >.

39 See note 28.

40 See note 20.

41 See note 23.

42 Richman, Louis S. "The New Work Force Builds Itself." *Fortune* (June 27, 1994), 68–70, 74, 76.

43 Reicheld, Fred. "The One Number You Need to Grow" *Harvard Business Review,* Dec 1, 2003.

44 See note 11.

Appendix B

1 Morley, Brad. "Management's Competitive Weapon." *Industry Week* (May 18, 1992), 44.

2 Adam, Everett E., Jr., and Ronald J. Ebert. *Production and Operations Management,* 4th ed. Englewood Cliffs, N.J.: Prentice-Hall, 1989.

3 Adam, Everett E., Jr., and Paul M. Swamidass. "Assessing Operations Management from a Strategic Objective." *Journal of Management* (June 1989), 181–204.

4 Hayes, R. H., and S. C. Wheelright. *Restoring Our Competitive Edge: Competing Through Manufacturing.* New York: Wiley, 1984.

5 Hill, T. *Manufacturing Strategy: The Strategic Management of the Manufacturing Function.* London: Macmillan, 1985.

6 Greco, Joe. "Design for Manufacturability and Assembly." *Cadence* (March 2000).

7 Taylor, Alex. "The Auto Industry Meets the New Economy." *Fortune* (September 5, 1994), 52–60.

8 Brown, Tom. "Managing for Quality." *Industry Week* (July 20, 1992), 28.

9 Bylinsky, Gene. "Manufacturing for Reuse." *Fortune* (February 6, 1995), 102–112.

10 Daft, Richard L. *Management,* 3d ed. Fort Worth, Tex.: Dryden Press, 1994, 723, 730–731.

11 IFR Statistical Department, *World Robotics* (August 2009). *http://www.ifr.org/industrial-robots/statistics/*

12 Emigh, Jaqueline. "Agile Manufacturing." *Computerworld* (August 30, 1999).

13 See note 12.

14 See note 12.

15 Straub, Joseph, and Raymond Attner. *Introduction to Business,* 5th ed. Boston: PWS-KENT, 1994, 241–244.

16 Robbins, John. "TRW Relocation on the Horizon." *Dallas Morning News* (February 14, 1992), C1.

17 Williams, Frederick P. *Production/Operations Management.* Boston: Houghton Mifflin, 1990, 32.

18 See note 17.

19 Robbins, Stephen P. *Management,* 4th ed. Englewood Cliffs, N.J.: Prentice-Hall, 1994, 638.

20 Holt, David. *Management: Principles and Practices,* 2d ed. Englewood Cliffs, N.J.: Prentice-Hall, 1991, 550.

21 Kerwin, Kathleen, Edith Updike, and Keith Naughton. "The Shape of a New Machine." *BusinessWeek* (July 24, 1995), 60–66.

22 Leon, Mark. "Putting the direct procurement pieces together." *InfoWorld* (April 6, 2001).

23 Snyder, Gary T. "Avoiding the Pitfalls of Outsourcing." *Nation's Business* (May 1995), 12.

24 Tully, Shawn. "You'll Never Guess Who Really Makes …" *Fortune* (October 3, 1994), 124–128.

25 Liesman, Steve. "High-Tech Devices Speed Manufacturing, and May Play Larger Role in Economy." *The Wall Street Journal* (February 15, 2001). *<http://interactive.wsj.com/articles/SB982187508898449347.htm>*.

26 See note 25.

27 See note 10.

28 Taylor, Alex. "Boeing: Sleeping in Seattle." *Fortune* (August 7, 1995), 97–98.

29 Migliorelli, Marcia, and Robert T. Swan. "MRP and Aggregate Planning—A Problem Solution." *Production and Inventory Management Journal* 29, No. 2 (1988), 42–44.

30 Marenghi, Catherine. "Stanley Hammers on Quality." *Computerworld* (February 6, 1992), 62.

31 Greco, Susan. "The Decade-Long Overnight Success." *Inc* (December 1994), 73–79.

32 Daniel, Mel. "Statistical Software Rings in Quality." *Computerworld* (January 6, 1992), 64.

Appendix C

1 Apple Press Info, *http://www.apple.com/pr/library/2015/10/27Apple-Reports-Record-Fourth-Quarter-Results.html*

2 "Shiseido Annual Report." Shiseido Co. Ltd. *<http://www.shiseido.co.jp>*.

3 Baker, Stephen. "Along the Border, Free Trade Is Becoming a Fact of Life." *BusinessWeek* (June 18, 1992), 41.

4 Morris, Betsy. "The Brand's the Thing." *Fortune* (May 4, 1996), 84.

5 Nelson, Mark M. "Whirlpool Gives Pan-European Approach a Spin." *The Wall Street Journal* (April 23, 1992), B1.

6 O'Reilly, Brian. "Johnson & Johnson Is on a Roll." *Fortune* (December 21, 1994), 178–192.

7 Heyel, Carl, ed. *The Encyclopedia of Management,* 3d ed. New York: Van Nostrand Reinhold, 1982, 495.

8 Block, Robert. "How Big Mac Kept From Becoming a Serb Archenemy." *The Wall Street Journal* (September 3, 1999), B1.

9 Ono, Umiko. "Japanese Liquor Dealer Imports Sake Made in United States, Igniting a Controversy." *The Wall Street Journal* (February 28, 1992), D3.

10 See note 9.

11 Moshavi, Sharon. "India's Pols May Be Turning Against Foreign Business." *BusinessWeek* (August 21, 1995), 44.

12 USDA Foreign Agricultural Service (FAS), The North American Free Trade Agreement (NAFTA). *<http://www.fas.usda.gov/itp/Policy/NAFTA/nafta.asp>*.

13 Phatak, Arvind, International Dimensions of Management, Boston PWS Kent, 1992.

14 Frauenheim, Ed. "Sony, Samsung complete LCD plant." *ZDNet News* (July 15, 2004). *<http://news.cnet.com/Sony,-Samsung-complete-LCD-plant/2100-1041_3-5271407.html>*.

15 "Co-Op Hits the Jackpot in Japan." *Chicago Tribune* (June 21, 1992), sec. 7, 8C.

16 Delaney, Kevin J. "Outsourcing Jobs—and Workers—to India." *The Wall Street Journal* (October 13, 2003), B1–B2.

17 See note 13.

18 See note 13.

19 See note 13.

20 See note 13.

21 See note 13.

22 *Business International,* 1970.

23 Johnson & Johnson. "Our Company: Fast Facts." *<http://www.jnj.com/our_company/fast_facts/history.htm>*.

24 Davidson, Dale. "Mobil Realigns Operations into 11 Business Groups." *Dallas Morning News* (June 4, 1996), 7D.

25 Lublin, Joann S. "Sending Employees Abroad Becomes Tougher Than Ever." *The Wall Street Journal* (November 7, 2003).

26 "3M Tries to Scotch Inpatriate Problems." *The Wall Street Journal* (June 16, 1992), B1.

27 Sigiura, Hideo. "How Honda Localizes Its Global Strategy." *Sloan Management Review* (Fall 1990), 78.

28 Shaw, Ron, and Richard Krevolin. *Pilot Your Life.* Prentice Hall, 2001.

29 Tully, Shawn. "GE in Hungary: Let There Be Light." *Fortune* (October 22, 1992), 37.

30 Middleton, Diana. "Schools Set Global Track, for Students and Programs." *The Wall Street Journal* (April 8, 2011),-

31 James G. Clawson, "11 Characteristics of a Global Leader," January 16, 2014, *https://ideas.darden.virginia.edu/2014/01/11-key-characteristics-of-a-global-business-leader*

32 Rehfeld, John. "What Working for a Japanese Company Taught Me." *Harvard Business Review* (November–December), 1990, 169.

33 See note 29.

34 Jacob, Raul. "Secure Jobs Trump Higher Pay." *Fortune* (March 20, 1995), 24.

35 Adler, Nancy J. *International Dimensions of Organizational Behavior.* Boston: PWS-KENT, 1991, 10–11.

36 See note 35.

37 See note 35.

38 See note 35.

39 Hofstede, Geert. "Motivation, Leadership, and Organizations: Do American Theories Apply Abroad?" *Organizational Dynamics* (Summer 1980), 42–63.

40 See note 35.

41 Sherman, Arthur, George Bohlander, and Scott Snell. *Managing Human Resources,* 10th ed. Cincinnati: South-Western, 1996, 695–706.

Appendix D

1 Lindsey Pollak, "Becoming the Boss: New Rules for the Next Generation of Leaders" Harper Collins, 2014.

2 Vreeland, Leslie. "Managing the Risks." Working Woman (April 1992), 61-63.

3 Iseek, Minnesota State Colleges and Universities career and education

resource. *https://www.iseek.org/mymncareers/advance-career*

4 Hall, Douglas T. *Career Development in Organizations.* San Francisco: Jossey-Bass, 1986.

5 Mind Tools, Living with a lack of security, *https://www.mindtools.com/pages/article/newCDV_57.htm*

6 Arne L. Kalleberg, *Good Jobs, Bad Jobs: The Rise of Polarized and Precarious Employment Systems in the United States, 19702-2000s.* New York: Russell Sage Foundation, 2011.

7 Kotter, John P. *The New Rules.* New York: Free Press, 1995.

8 Stewert, Thomas A. "Planning a Career in a World Without Managers", Fortune (March 20, 1995), 72-80.

9 Plunkett, W. Richard. *Supervision,* 7th ed. Englewood Cliffs, N.J.: Prentice Hall, 1995, 38, 44.

10 See note 9.

11 See note 8.

12 Davita, Sal. "The Two Most Important Decisions in Career Designing." *Marketing News* (July 6, 1992), 16.

13 See note 8.

14 Jeff Goins, *"Three Ways to Reinvent Your Career for the New Economy,"* Fast Company, 12/16/15. *http://www.fastcompany.com/3054652/the-future-of-work*

15 See note 8.

16 Sellers, Patricia. "Don't Call Me Slacker." *Fortune* (December 12, 1994), 182–187.

17 Schein, Edgar H. *Career Dynamics.* Reading, Mass.: Addison-Wesley, 1978.

18 Penzias, Arno. *Harmony.* New York: HarperCollins, 1995, 30.

19 Kiechel, Walter. "A Managers Career in the New Economy," Fortune (April 4, 1994), 68-72.

20 See note 8.

21 Fram, Eugene. "Today's Mercurial Career Path." *Management Review* (November 1994), 40–44.

22 See note 19.

23 Harari, Oren. "An Open Letter to Job Seekers." *Management Review* (December 1994), 38–42.

24 Unger, Paul. "Culture Shock: Tips for Transitioners", *Management Review* (June 1995) 44-47.

25 See note 19.

26 See note 19.

27 Thomas Frey, *"162 Future Jobs: Preparing for Jobs that Don't Yet Exist,"* March 21, 2014. *http://www.futuristspeaker.com*

28 Schlee, Adele. "Feeling Invisible? Here's How to Get Clout." *Working Woman* (February 1992), 36–37.

29 Fiant, Ray J. "Leadership Training for Long-Term Results." *Management Review* (July 1992), 50–53.

30 Kram, Kathy E. *Mentoring at Work: Developmental Relationships in Organizational Life.* Glenview, Ill.: Scott Foresman, 1985.

31 Kennedy, Joyce Lain. "Forgotten Art of Mentoring Can Put New Zip in Your Career." *Dallas Morning News* (February 7, 1999), sec. D, 1.

32 Stephanie Sammons, "Build Digital Influence" *http://www.stephaniesammons.com*

33 Peters, Tom. "If You Want to Escape Office Politics—Forget It." *Chicago Tribune* (July 27, 1992), sec. 4, 7.

34 Hollander, Dorry. *Managerial Reality.* New York: HarperCollins, 1995, 130.

35 See note 9.

36 Jensen, Blair. "How to Figure Out What Others Expect of You." *Computerworld* (January 20, 1992), 1.

37 Beehr, T. A., and R. S. Bhagat. *Human Stress and Cognition in Organizations: An Integrated Perspective.* New York: Wiley, 1985.

38 Freudenberger, Herbert J. *Burnout: The High Cost of High Achievement.* Garden City, N.Y.: Anchor Press, 1980, 13.

39 Gendron, George. "Working Twice As Hard for the Same Results (and How to Stop)." *Inc* (November 1994), 11.

40 See note 39.

41 Romano, Catherine. "Too Much Work Causes Stress." *Management Review* (March 1995), 6.

42 Maturi, Richard. "Stress Can Be Beaten." *Industry Week* (July 20, 1992), 23–26.

43 See note 42.

44 See note 42.

45 Davita, Sal. "Personal Values Affect Your Career Satisfaction." *Marketing News* (April 13, 1992), 16.

46 See note 45.

47 Straub, Joseph, and Raymond Attner. *Introduction to Business,* 5th ed. Belmont, Calif.: Wadsworth, 1994, 58.

48 DuBrin, Andrew. *Winning Office Politics: DuBrin's Guide for the '90s.* Englewood Cliffs, N.J.: Prentice Hall, 1990, 167.

Glossary

A

acceptance sampling A product control technique involving a representative group of products before a new stage of production

accountability The need to answer to someone for your actions; it means accepting the consequences—either credit or blame—of these actions

affirmative action A plan to give members of specific groups priority in hiring or promotion

aggregate planning An element of operations management that involves the planning of production activities and the resources needed to achieve them

agile manufacturing A manufacturing system incorporating ultra-flexible production facilities; computer technology; alliances among suppliers, producers, and customers; and direct sales data to customize goods at the speed of mass production

alternatives Potential solutions to the problem

application program A computer program designed to execute specific sets of tasks such as word processing

artificial intelligence (AI) The ability of a machine to perform those activities that are normally thought to require intelligence; giving machines the capability to learn, sense, and think for themselves

assessment center A place where candidates are screened for managerial positions, which usually involves extensive testing and hands-on exercises

attribute inspection A product control technique that compares items against a standard and rates their quality as acceptable or unacceptable

audit A formal investigation conducted to determine whether records and the data on which they are based are correct and conform to policies, rules, procedures, and laws

authority The formal and legitimate right of a manager to make decisions, give orders and allocate resources

autocratic style A leadership approach in which a manager does not share decision-making authority with subordinates

avoidance A conflict strategy in which a manager ignores the conflict situation

balance sheet A listing of the assets of a business and the owners' and outsiders' interests in them. The equation that describes the content of a balance sheet is Assets = Liabilities + Stockholders' equity

batch processing A computer procedure in which data are collected over time and entered into databases according to prescribed policies and procedures

B

behavioral school Recognized employees as individuals with concrete, human needs, as parts of work groups and as members of a larger society

benchmark The product to meet or beat in terms of design, manufacture, performance and service

benefit Legally required or voluntary compensation provided to employees in addition to their salaries or wages

boundary spanning The surveillance of outside areas and factors that can influence plans, forecasts, decisions and organizations. Sometimes called environmental scanning

boundaryless organizations Organizations not defined or limited by horizontal, vertical, or external boundaries imposed by a predetermined structure

brainstorming A group effort at generating ideas and alternatives that can help a manager solve a problem or seize an opportunity

budget A plan and control for the receipt and spending of income over a fixed period

budget A single-use plan that predicts sources and amounts of income that will be available over a fixed period of time and how those funds will be used

bureaucracies Rational organizations based on the control of knowledge

burnout A state of emotional exhaustion as a result of overexposure to stress

business ethics The rules or standards governing the conduct of persons or members of organizations in the field of commerce

business-level strategy Answers the question, "How do we compete?" It focuses on how each product line or business unit within an organization competes for customers

BYOD An acronym for a policy permitting employees to bring personally owned devices to work. Bring your own device (BYOD) may be referred to as bring your own technology (BYOT) or bring your own applications (BYOA).

C

capacity planning An element of operations management that determines an organization's capability to produce the number of products or services necessary to meet demand

career management The planning, activities, and behaviors involved in executing a career

career perspective A proactive strategy that involves a global view of career progress or growth over time

career planning The process of developing a realistic view about how individuals want their careers to proceed and then taking steps to ensure they follow that course

career The series of jobs a person holds over a lifetime and the person's attitude toward the involvement in those job experiences; includes a long-term perspective, a sequence of positions, and a psychological involvement

cellular layout A facilities layout option in which equipment required for a sequence of operations on the same product is grouped into cells

centralization A philosophy of organization and management that focuses on systematically retaining authority in the hands of higher-level managers

chain of command The unbroken line of reporting relationships from the bottom to the top of the organization

change agent A person who implements planned change

change Any alteration in the current work environment

classical administrative school Emphasized the flow of information and how organizations should operate

classical management theory A theory that focused on finding the "one best way" to perform and manage tasks

classical scientific school Focused on the manufacturing environment and getting work done on the factory floor

cloud computing A concept used in information technology (IT) to depict sharing computer resources remotely rather than storing software or data on a local server or computer. This al-lows companies to store data—such as customer contacts, inventory lists and documents—on servers owned by others and access that data via the Internet.

co-opetition A word coined by Ray Noorda, Founder of the networking software company Novell, meaning that businesses have to compete and cooperate at the same time

coercive power The power dependent on fear of the negative results that may happen if one fails to comply

cohesion A strong attachment to the group and a closeness measured by a singleness of purpose and a high degree of cooperation

collaboration A conflict strategy in which the manager focuses on mutual problem solving by both parties

collective bargaining Negotiation between a union and an employer in regard to wages, benefits, hours, rules and working conditions

committee A horizontal team—either ad hoc or permanent—designed to focus on one objective; members represent functional areas of expertise

communication The transmission of information and understanding from one person or group to another

compensation All forms of financial payments to employees. Compensation includes salaries, wages and benefits

compressed workweek A schedule that allows employees to fulfill weekly time obligations in fewer days than the traditional five-day workweek

compromise A conflict strategy in which each party gives up something

computer-aided design (CAD) A design technique that uses a computer monitor to display and manipulate proposed designs for the purpose of evaluating them

computer-aided manufacturing (CAM) A technology in which computers coordinate people, information and processes to produce quality products efficiently

computer-integrated manufacturing (CIM) Using computers to guide and control manufacturing processes

computerized information system (CIS) An MIS built on computer hardware and software to collect and process data and store and disseminate the resulting information

conceptual skills The mental capacity to conceive and manipulate ideas and abstract relationships

concurrent control A control that applies to processes as they are happening

conflict A disagreement between two or more organizational members or teams

confrontation A conflict strategy that forces parties to verbalize their positions and area of disagreement

content theories A group of motivation theories emphasizing the needs that motivate people

contingency model A leadership theory stating that a manager should focus on either tasks or employees, depending on the interaction of three variables—leader–member relations, task structure, and leader position power

contingency plan An alternative goal and course or courses of action to reach that goal if and when circumstances and assumptions change so drastically as to make an original plan unusable

contingency school A theory based on the premise that managers' preferred actions or approaches depend on the variables of the situations they face

control process A four-step process that consists of establishing performance standards, measuring performance, comparing measured performance to established standards, and taking corrective action

control system A system in which feedforward, concurrent, and feedback controls operate in harmony to ensure standards are enforced, goals are reached, and resources are used effectively and efficiently

control technique Device designed to measure and monitor specific aspects about the performances of an organization, its people, and its processes

controlling The process through which standards for the performance of people and processes are set, communicated, and applied

core values Values that should never change; "bedrock principles"

corporate-level strategy Answers the questions: "What business are we in?" and "What business should we be in?"

critical control point An area of operation that directly affects the survival of a firm and the success of its most essential activities

critical path The longest sequence of events and activities in a network production schedule or the longest time a job could take

cross-cultural management An emerging discipline focused on improving work in organizations with employee and client populations from several cultures

cross-functional team A team with an undefined life span designed to bring together the knowledge of various functional areas to work on solutions to operational problems

customer Any person or group, both inside and outside an organization, who uses or consumes outputs from an organization or its members

customer departmentalization Grouping activities and responsibilities in departments based on the needs of specific customer groups

customer relationship management (CRM) A long-term management approach to customer relations that attempts to strengthen the bond between the customer and the organization

D

data center A unit of a decentralized CIS that operates to serve its unit's members with their own sets of hardware, software, and specialists (machine operators and programmers)

data Unprocessed facts and figures

database A collection of computerized data arranged for ease and speed of retrieval; sometimes called a data bank

decentralization A philosophy of organization and management that focuses on systematically delegating authority throughout the organization to middle- and lower-level managers

decision A choice made from available alternatives

decision support system (DSS) A specialized variant of a CIS; an analytic model that joins a manager's experience, judgment, and intuition with the computer's data access, display, and calculation processes; allows managers to interact with linked programs and databases via the keyboard

decision tree A graphical representation of the actions a manager can take and how these actions relate to other events

decision making The process of identifying problems and opportunities, developing alternative solutions, choosing an alternative, and implementing it

delegation The downward transfer of formal authority from one person to another

Delphi technique Group decision making conducted by a group leader through the use of written questionnaires; it provides a structure, leads to consensus, and emphasizes equal participation

demotion A reduction in an employee's status, pay and responsibility

departmentalization The basic organizational format or departmental structure for the company

design control An area of operations control that involves incorporating reliability, functionality and serviceability into product design

design for disassembly (DfD) Considering, during the design stage, how products will be refurbished, reused or disposed of at the end of the product's life cycle

design for manufacturability and assembly (DFM/A) Considering, during the design stage, how products will be manufactured and assembled

detailed inspections and tests A product control technique in which every finished item receives an examination or performance test

development Efforts to acquire the knowledge, skills, and attitudes needed to move to a job with greater authority and responsibility

diction The choice and use of words in speech and writing

digital Data expressed as a string of 0s and 1s and transmitted or stored with electronic technology, usually computers and the Internet

directly interactive forces An organization's owners, customers, suppliers and partners, competitors, and exter-nal labor pool

discrimination Using illegal criteria when making employment decisions. Discrimination results in an adverse impact on members of protected groups

disparate impact The result of using employment criteria that have a significantly greater negative effect on some groups than on others

diversity Includes people from differing age groups, genders, ethnic and racial backgrounds, cultural and national origins and mental and physical capabilities

divisional structure An organizational design that groups departments based on organizational outputs; these divisions are self-contained strategic business units that produce a single product

downsizing Also known as rightsizing, it calls for shrinking both the size of the company and the number of employees

dysfunctional conflict Conflict that limits the organization's ability to achieve its objectives

E

economic forces Conditions in an economy that influence management decisions and the costs and availability of resources

economic order quantity (EOQ) An inventory technique that helps managers determine how much material to order by minimizing the total of ordering costs and holding costs based on the organization's usage rate

electronic commerce All forms of business transactions involving both organizations and individuals that are based upon the processing and transmission of digitized data, including text, sound and visual images

embargoes Government regulations enacted to keep a product out of a country for a time or entirely

emotional intelligence (EI) A set of competencies that distinguishes how people manage feelings, interact and communicate. Effective leaders combine mental intelligence with emotional intelligence to handle themselves and others. The four main sets of emotional competence are self-awareness, self-management, social awareness and relationship management

end-user computing The use of information technology (IT) by people who are not controlled and directed by top management

enterprise resource planning (ERP) system A broad-based software system that integrates multiple data sources and ties together the various processes of an enterprise to enable information to flow more smoothly

environmental scanning The process of collecting information about the external environment to identify and analyze trends

equal employment opportunity Legislation designed to protect individuals and groups from discrimination

equity theory A motivation theory in which comparisons of relative input-outcome ratios influence behavior choices

ERG theory A motivation theory establishing three categories of human needs: existence needs, relatedness needs and growth needs

ethical dilemma A situation that arises when all courses of action open to a decision maker are judged to be unethical

ethics The branch of philosophy concerned with what constitutes right and wrong human conduct, including values and actions, in a given set of circumstances

evolutionary change The incremental steps taken to bring about progress and change

executive information system (EIS) A decision support system custom designed to facilitate executive decision making; may include forecasting, strategic planning, and other elements

executive team A team consisting of two or more people to do the job traditionally held by one upper-level manager

expatriates Home-country nationals with overseas experience

expectancy theory A motivation theory stating that three factors influence behavior: the value of rewards, the relationship of rewards to the necessary performance, and the effort required for performance

expert power Influence due to abilities, skills, knowledge or experience

expert system A specialized end-user decision support program that stores the knowledge of a group of authorities for access by non-experts faced with the need to make topic-related decisions

external environment Includes all the forces outside an organization's borders that interact directly or indi-rectly with it

F

facilities layout The element of operations planning concerned with the physical arrangement of equipment and work flow

feedback control A control that focuses on the outputs or results of operations

feedback Information about the receiver's perception of the sender's message

feedforward control A control that prevents defects and deviations from standards

financial budget The details of how a financial responsibility center will manage its cash and capital expenditures

financial ratio The relationship of two critical figures from financial statements—expressed in terms of a ratio, decimal, or percentage—that helps managers measure a company's financial health and its progress toward goals

financial responsibility center An organizational unit that contributes to an organization's costs, revenues, investments, or profits

finished goods inventory Inventory consisting of products that have not been sold

first-line management Supervisors, team leaders, and team facilitators who oversee the work of non-management people, often called operating employees, associates, or team members

fixed-position layout A facilities layout option in which the product stays in one place and the equipment, tools and human skills are brought to it

flexible manufacturing system (FMS) A technology in which an automated production line is coordinated by computers and can produce more than one product

flextime An employment alternative allowing employees to decide, within a certain range, when to begin and end each workday

force-field analysis A technique to implement change by determining which forces drive change and which forces resist it

forecasting A planning technique used by an organization's managers to concentrate on developing predictions about the future

formal communication channels Management-designated pipelines—running up, down and across the organizational structure—used for official communication efforts

formal communication networks Electronic links between people and their equipment and between people and databases

formal organization The official organizational structure that top management conceives and builds

formal team A team created by managers to function as part of the organizational structure

forming stage The phase of team development in which team members are becoming acquainted

free rider A person who receives the benefit of team membership but does not do a proportionate share of work

free-rein style A leadership approach in which a manager shares decision-making authority with subordinates, empowering them to function without direct involvement from managers to whom they report

functional authority The authority that permits staff managers to make decisions about specific activities performed by employees within other departments

functional conflict Conflict that supports the objectives of the organization

functional definition The activities to be performed determine the type and quantity of authority necessary

functional departmentalization Creating departments on the basis of the specialized activities of the business—finance, production, marketing and human resources

functional managers Managers whose expertise lies primarily in one or another of the specialty areas

functional structure An organizational design that groups positions into departments based on similar skills, expertise and resources

functional-level strategy Focuses on the major activities of the company: human resources management, research and development, marketing, finance and production

G

game theory Attempts to predict how people or organizations will behave in competitive situations

gamification Gartner defines gamification as, "the use of game mechanics and experience design to digitally engage and motivate people to achieve their goals"

Gantt chart A scheduling and control tool that helps managers plan and control a sequence of events

geographical departmentalization Grouping activities and responsibilities according to territory

gig economy Independent contractors or self-employed people work for short-term engagements

global structure The arrangement of an organization's management decision making to efficiently and effectively operate in a multinational context; form may contain functional, product and geographic features based on worldwide product or area units

goal An outcome to be achieved or a destination to be reached over a period of time through the exercise of management functions and the expenditure of resources

goal-setting theory A motivation theory stating that behavior is influenced by goals, which tell employees what they need to do and how much effort they need to expend

grand strategy The overall framework or plan of action developed at the corporate level to achieve an organization's objectives. There are five basic grand strategies—growth, integration, diversification, retrenchment or stability

grapevine An informal communication channel

green products Those products with reduced energy and pollution connected with their manufacture and disposal

group decision support system (GDSS) A variant decision support system that allows groups focusing on a problem to interact with one another and to exchange information, data, and ideas

groupthink Group members becoming so committed to the group that they become reluctant to disagree

H

Holacracy Is a new way of running an organization that removes power from a management hierarchy and distributes it across clear roles, which can then be executed autonomously without a micromanaging boss

horizontal team A team composed of employees from different departments

human asset accounting Treating employees as assets, not expenses, by recording money spent on people as increases in the value of those assets

human resource manager or personnel manager A manager who fulfills one or more personnel, or human resource, function

human skills The abilities to interact and communicate successfully with other persons

hygiene factors Maintenance factors (such as salary, status, working conditions) that do not relate directly to a person's actual work activity, but when of low quality are the cause of unhappiness on the job

I

income statement A report that presents the difference between an organization's income and expenses to determine whether the firm operated at a profit or a loss over a specified period

independent contractors Self-employed workers hired by companies with a verbal agreement for a short term or under terms specified in a contract

indirectly interactive forces Domestic and foreign economic, legal/political, sociocultural, technological, and natu-ral forces

influence The power to sway people to one's will or views

informal communication channels The informal networks, existing outside the formal channels, which are used to transmit casual, personal and social messages at work

informal organization A network of personal and social relationships that arise spontaneously as people associate with one another in a work environment

information Data that have been deliberately selected, processed, and organized to be useful to an individual manager

information Processed data that is useful to the receiver

information system (IS) An organizational subsystem enabling an organization to effectively and efficiently share intellectual capital and create and maintain a working environment in which employees can exploit it

information technology (IT) Manual and electronic means for creating and handling intellectual capital and facilitating organizational communication

intellectual capital An organization's collective experiences, wisdom, knowledge, and expertise

interaction chart A diagram that aids in identifying the informal organization structure by spotlighting the informal interactions people have with one another

internal environment Composed of elements within an organization's borders that managers create, acquire, and utilize, including the organization's mission, vision, core values, core competencies, leadership, culture, climate, structure, and available resources

international division A parent company's corporate unit, commonly a marketing or production operation, located in a host country offshore from the parent headquarters and whose head reports directly to the CEO

international management The process of managing resources (people, information, funds, inventories and technologies) across national boundaries and adapting management principles and functions to the demands of foreign competition and environments

Internet of Things (IoT) A phrase first used by Kevin Ashton, "to describe the network connecting objects in the physical world to the Internet."

interpersonal communication Face-to-face or voice-to-voice (telephone) conversations that take place in real time and allow instant feedback

intrapreneurship Entrepreneurship within an organization, allowing employees flexibility and authority in pursuing and developing new ideas

inventory The goods an organization keeps on hand

ISO 9000 The set of five technical standards, known collectively as ISO 9000, designed to offer a uniform way of determining whether manufacturing and service organizations implement and document sound quality procedures

jargon The specialized or technical language of a trade, profession, subculture or other group

J

job A specific position a person holds in an organization

job analysis A study that determines the duties associated with a job and the human qualities needed to perform it

job depth An element of job redesign referring to the degree of discretion an employee has to alter the job

job enlargement Increasing the variety or the number of tasks in a job, not the quality or the challenge of those tasks

job enrichment Designing a job to provide more responsibility, control, feedback, and authority for decision making

job evaluation A study that determines the worth of a job in terms of its value to an organization

job redesign The application of motivational theories to the structure of work, to increase output and satisfaction

job rotation Temporarily assigning people to different jobs or tasks on a rotating basis

job scope An element of job redesign that refers to the variety of tasks incorporated into a job

job sharing A technique to provide flexibility by permitting two part-time workers to divide one full-time job

just-in-time (JIT) An inventory control system in which materials are purchased only as needed to meet actual customer demand. JIT production is a system in which units are produced only as needed to meet actual customer demand.

just-in-time inventory Delivery of raw materials or other kinds of normal inventories to correspond to production schedules, leading to the elimination of the need to warehouse items

K

kaizen A Japanese term used in business to mean incremental, continuous improvement for people, products, and processes

knowledge management (KM) The merging of a company's human and technical knowledge assets

L

Leadership Grid® Blake and Mouton's two-dimensional model for visualizing the extent to which a manager focuses on tasks, employees, or both

leadership style The perceived approaches and behaviors a manager uses to influence others

leadership The ability to get people to follow voluntarily

leadership The process of influencing individuals and groups to set and achieve goals

Lean A systematic approach to identifying and eliminating waste (non-value added activities) through continuous improvement by flowing the product at the pull of the customer in pursuit of perfection. (The MEP Lean Network)

Lean manufacturing Originally developed by Toyota, adaptations are now used around the world to reduce waste or anything that does not add value in the production stream

learning organization A process whereby groups and individuals within the organization challenge existing models of behavior and learn to rapidly and creatively adapt to a changing environment

legal/political forces The general framework of statutes enacted by legislatures; precedents established by court decisions; regulations and rulings created by various federal, state, and local regulatory agencies; and agreements between and among governments and companies from different nations

legitimate power The power possessed by managers and derived from the positions they occupy in the formal organization

life-cycle theory A view of management that asserts that a leader's behavior toward a subordinate should relate to the subordinate's maturity level. The focus on tasks and relationships should vary as the subordinate matures

limiting factors Those constraints that rule out certain alternative solutions; one common limitation is time

line authority The relationship between superior and subordinate; any manager who supervises operating employees—or other managers—has line authority

line departments The departments established to meet the major objectives of the business and directly influence the success (profitability) of a business

M

management by objectives (MBO) A technique that emphasizes collaborative setting by managers and their subordinates

management by reaction A management method that does not anticipate change but merely reacts to it

management hierarchy The top, middle and first-line levels of management

management information system (MIS) A formal collection of processes that provides managers with suitable quality information to allow them to make decisions, solve problems, and carry out their functions and operations effectively and efficiently

management One or more managers individually and collectively setting and achieving goals by exercising related functions (planning, organizing, staffing, leading and controlling) and coordinating various resources (information, materials, money and people)

management science The study of complex systems of people, money, equipment, and procedures, with the goal of understanding them and improving their effectiveness

managers People who allocate and oversee the use of resources

manufacturing resource planning (MRPII) A comprehensive planning system that controls the total resources of a firm

marketing research A feedforward control technique that consists of gathering and analyzing geographic, demographic, and psychographic data to help planners decide what potential and cur-rent customers want and need

master schedule An element of operations management that specifies the quantity and type of each item to be produced and how, when and where it should be produced

materials requirement planning (MRP) A production planning and inventory system that uses forecasts of customer orders to schedule the exact amount of materials needed for production

matrix structure An organizational design that utilizes functional and divisional chains of command simultaneously in the same part of the organization

maximize Managers want to make the perfect decisions

mechanistic structure A tight organizational structure characterized by rigidly defined tasks, formalization, many rules and regulations and centralized decision making

medium The means by which a sender transmits a message

mentor A senior employee who acts as guide, teacher, counselor, and coach for a less-experienced person in the organization

message The information the sender wants to transmit

middle management Includes managers below the rank of vice president but above the supervisory level

mission A clear, concise, written declaration of an organization's central and common purpose, its reason for existence

mission statement When a mission is formalized in writing and communicated to all organizational members

morale The attitude or feelings workers have about the organization and their total work life

morality Core values and beliefs that act as a guide (i.e., conscience) when individuals formulate courses of action

motivation factors The conditions, intrinsic to the job, that can lead to an individual's job satisfaction

motivation The result of the interaction of a person's internal needs and external influences—involving perceptions of equity, expectancy, previous conditioning, and goal setting—which determine how a person will behave

multinational corporation A company with operating facilities, not just sales offices, in one or more foreign countries; where management favors a global market and strategy and sees the world as its market

mutual trust The ability of individuals to rely on each other based their character, ability and truthfulness

N

natural forces Forces such as climate, weather, geography, and geology that affect how businesses operate and locate their operations

needs Physiological or psychological conditions in humans that act as stimuli for behavior

network scheduling A scheduling technique used to track projects in which events or activities are interrelated and have time estimates assigned to them

network structure An organizational design option in which a small central organization relies on other organizations to perform manufacturing, marketing, engineering or other critical functions on a contract basis

networking A strategy for career advancement that involves building long-term, two-way interaction based on shared ideas, personal relationships, and common experiences

networking The electronic linking of two or more computers

noise Anything in the environment of a communication that interferes with the sending and receiving of messages

nominal group technique Creating a structure to provide for equal—but independent—participation by all members

nonprogrammed decisions Decisions made in response to problems and opportunities that have unique circum-stances, unpredictable results, and important consequences for the company

nonverbal communication Images, actions and behaviors that transmit messages

norming stage The phase of team development in which disagreement and conflict have been re-solved and team members enjoy unity and focus

norms Values or attitudes that employees as a group accept as standards of behavior and that serve as a guideline of behavior and an internal control device on members

O

obsolescence A state or condition that exists when a person is no longer capable of performing up to job standards or to management's expectations

office automation system (OAS) A collection of technologies to operate offices efficiently

onboarding The process by which new hires get adjusted to the social and performance aspects of their jobs quickly and smoothly, and learn the attitudes, knowledge, skills and behaviors required to function effectively within an organization

open system A system that regularly affects and is affected by various and constantly changing forces (elements and components) outside itself

operating budget A financial plan and control for each financial responsibility center's revenues, ex-penses, and profits

operating system An extensive and complex set of instructions that manages the operation of a computer and the application programs that run on it

operational plan The first-line manager's tool for executing daily, weekly and monthly activities. Operational plans fall into two major categories: single-use and standing plans

operations management The branch of management science that applies to manufacturing or service industries

operations management The managerial activities directed toward the processes that convert resources into products and services

operations research An area of management science that commonly uses models, simulations, and games

operations strategy The element of the strategic plan that defines the role, capabilities and expectations of operations

opportunity A chance, occasion, event, or breakthrough that requires a decision to be made

organic structure A flexible, free-flowing organizational structure that has few rules and regulations and decentralizes decision making right down to the employees performing the job

organization An entity managed by one or more persons to achieve stated goals

organization chart The complete organizational structure shown visually

organizational climate An outgrowth of a corporation's culture showing how employees feel about working there

organizational culture Dynamic system of shared values, beliefs, philosophies, experiences, customs, and norms of behavior that give an organization its distinctive character

organizational design The creation of or change to an organization's structure

organizational development (OD) A process of conducting a thorough analysis of an organization's problems and then implementing long-term solutions to solve them

organizational learning the ability to integrate new ideas into an organization's established systems to produce better ways of doing things

organizational life cycle The stages an organization goes through: birth, youth, midlife and maturity, where each stage involves changes in overall structure

organizational politics The unwritten rules of work life and informal methods of gaining power and advantage

organizational socialization A process through which new members of an organization gain exposure to its values, norms, policies, and procedures

organizational visibility A strategy for career advancement that involves the highlighting of a person's abilities, talents, and contributions for those people in the organization who influence promotions and advancements

organizing The management function that establishes relationships between activity and authority

orientation Introducing new employees to the organization by explaining their duties, helping them meet their coworkers, and acclimating them to their work environment

outside-the-box thinking To adopt a new perspective and see it work; not get caught up in the old ways

outsourcing A purchasing strategy in which a company contracts with a supplier to perform functions in lieu of the company

outsourcing The use of outside resources to perform a business process, such as payroll, insurance records, health claims, or credit card applications

P

participative style A leadership approach in which a manager shares decision-making authority with subordinates

path–goal theory A view of management asserting that subordinates' behaviors and motivations are influenced by the behaviors managers exhibit toward them

payback analysis A technique that ranks alternatives according to how long each takes to pay back its initial cost

perceptions Ways in which people observe and the bases for their judgments about the stimuli they experience

performance appraisal A formal, structured comparison between employee performance and established quantity and quality standards

performing stage The phase of team development in which team members progress toward team objectives, handle problems, coordinate work, and confront each other if necessary

perk A payment or benefit received in addition to a regular wage or salary

philosophy of management A manager's attitude about work and the people who perform it, which influences the motivation approaches he or she selects

plan The end result of the planning effort—commits individuals, departments, entire organizations and the resources of each to specific courses of action for days, months and years into the future

planned change Trying to anticipate what changes will occur in both the external and internal environment and then developing a response that will maximize the organization's success

planning Preparing for tomorrow, today

policy A broad guide for organizational members to follow when dealing with important and recurring areas of decision making. They set limits and provide boundaries for decision makers

portfolio strategy Determines the mix of business units and product lines that will provide a maximum competitive advantage

power The ability to exert influence in the organization; power is personal

proactive approach A social responsibility strategy in which businesses continually look to the needs of constituents and try to find ways to meet those needs

problem The difference between the current and desired performance or situation

procedure A set of step-by-step directions for carrying out activities or tasks

process control sampling A product control technique designed to detect variations in production processes

process improvement team A team, made up of members who are involved with a process, who meets to analyze how they can improve the process

process layout A facilities layout option in which all the equipment or machines that perform a similar task are placed together

process team A team that groups members who perform and refine the organization's major processes

process theories A group of theories that explain how employees choose behaviors to meet their needs and how they determine whether their choices were successful

product control A component of operations control that reduces the probability and costs of poor quality and unreliable products by implementing controls from purchasing to end use

product departmentalization Assembling the activities of creating, producing, and marketing each product into a separate department

product development team A team organized to create new products

product layout A facilities layout option in which the machines and tasks are arranged according to the progressive steps by which the product is made

productivity The relationship between the amount of input needed to produce a given amount of output and the output itself; usually expressed as a ratio

program A single-use plan for an operation from its beginning to its end

program evaluation and review technique (PERT) A network scheduling technique for planning and charting the progress of a complex project in terms of the time it is expected to take—an estimate that is derived from probability analysis

programmed decisions Decisions that involve problems or situations that have occurred often enough that both the circumstances and solutions are predictable; made in response to recurring organizational problems

project improvement team A team, usually composed of a group of people involved in the same project, that determines how to make the project better

project team A team organized to complete a specific task in the organization

promotion A job change that results in increased status, compensation and responsibility

psychological contract The unspoken contract that marks the end product of the organizational socialization process and defines what people are expected to give to the organization and what they can expect to receive

purchasing The acquisition of goods and services at optimal costs from competent and reliable sources

Q

qualification testing A product control technique in which products are tested for performance on the basis of reliability and safety

quality assurance team A team created to guarantee the quality of services and products, contact customers, and work with vendors

quality audit Determines if customer requirements are being met

quality circle A temporary team, consisting primarily of workers who share a problem, who meets regularly until the problem is solved

quality control audit A check of quality control efforts that asks two questions: How are we doing? and What are the problems?

quality function deployment (QFD) A disciplined approach to solving quality problems before the design phase of a product

quality improvement team Usually a group of people from all the functional areas of a company who meet regularly to assess progress toward goals, identify and solve common problems and cooperate in planning for the future

quality of work life (QWL) Factors in the work environment contributing positively or negatively to workers' physical and emotional well-being and job satisfaction

quality school The essence of the quality of any output is its ability to meet the needs of the person or group

quality The features and characteristics of a product or service that allow it to satisfy requirements of those who use or consume them

quantitative school Emphasized mathematical approaches to management problems

queuing models or waiting-line models Models that help managers decide what length of waiting line or queue would be optimal

quota A government regulation that limits the import of a product to a specified amount per year

R

raw materials inventory Inventory consisting of the raw materials, parts and supplies used as inputs to production

reactive approach A social responsibility strategy in which businesses wait for demands to be made and then react to them, choosing a response by evaluating alternatives

receiver The person or group for whom a communication effort is intended

recruiting Efforts to find qualified people and encourage them to apply for positions that need to be filled

reengineering Business processes are redesigned to achieve improvements in performance

referent power The power that is based on the kind of personality or charisma an individual has and how others perceive it

reinforcement theory A motivation theory that states a supervisor's reactions and past rewards and penalties affect employees' behavior

reorder point (ROP) The most economical point at which an inventory item should be reordered

research and development (R&D) Projects that uncover information useful to create a variety of new materials, processes, and products

resistance approach A social responsibility strategy in which businesses actively fight to eliminate, delay or fend off demands being made on them

responsibility The obligation to carry out one's assigned duties to the best of one's ability

revolutionary change Bold, discontinuous advances that bring about dramatic transformations in organizational strategies and structure

reward power The power that comes from the ability to promise or grant rewards

risk manager A high-level person in charge of planning for and overseeing efforts to control the management of all the risks an organization faces

robotics The use of programmed machines to handle production

role A set of expectations for a manager's behavior

rule An ongoing, specific guide for human behavior and conduct at work. Rules are usually "do" and "do not" statements established to promote employee safety, ensure the uniform treatment of employees, and regulate civil behavior

S

sanctions Rewards or penalties used by an informal group to persuade its members to conform to its norms

Sarbanes–Oxley Act (SOX) Law requiring publicly traded companies to disclose in their financial reports any "material weaknesses" in their financial-reporting systems. The CEO and CFO must certify that those reports are accurate

satisfice To make the best decision possible with the time, resources, and information available

selection Evaluating applicants and finding those best qualified to perform a job and most likely to fit into the culture of the organization

self-managed work team A team, fully responsible for its own work, that sets goals, creates its own schedules, prepares its own budgets, and coordinates its work with other departments

semantics The study of the meanings of words

sender The person or group who initiates the communication process

separation The voluntary or involuntary departure of employees from a company

sexual harassment Unwelcome verbal or physical conduct of a sexual nature that implies, directly or in-directly, that sexual compliance is a condition of employment or advancement or that interferes with an employee's work performance

sharing economy The peer-to-peer rental market

simulation A model of a real activity or process

situation analysis (SWOT) A search for strengths, weaknesses, opportunities and threats

Six Sigma A highly disciplined process that helps companies focus on developing and delivering near-perfect products and services

smoothing A conflict strategy in which the manager diplomatically acknowledges that conflict exists but downplays its importance

social audit A report on the social performance of a business

social media A set of online technologies enabling a community of participants to collaborate

social responsibility The notion that, in addition to their business interests, individuals and organizations have certain obligations to protect and benefit other individuals and society and to avoid actions that could harm them

sociocultural forces The influences and contributions from diverse groups outside an organization

soft manufacturing system (SMS) A manufacturing system that relies on computer software to continuously control and adjust the manufacturing processes

sources and uses of funds statement A summary of the cash flowing into an organization and how it is used over a fixed period of time. This statement is often called a cash flow statement

span of control The number of subordinates under the direction of a manager

specialization of labor or division of labor Breaks a potentially complex job down into simpler tasks or activities

sponsor An individual in the organization who will promote a person's talents and look out for his or her organizational welfare

staff authority The authority to serve in an advisory capacity; it flows upward to the decision maker

staff departments The departments—including legal, human resources, computer services, and public relations—that provide assistance to the line departments and to each other, making money indirectly for the company through advice, service and assistance

staffing Efforts designed to attract, hire, train, develop, reward, and retain the people needed to accomplish an organization's goals and promote job satisfaction

stakeholders Groups directly or indirectly affected by the ways in which business is conducted and by the ways in which managers conduct themselves. Stakeholders include owners, employees, customers, suppliers, and society

standard Any established rule or basis of comparison used to measure capacity, quantity, con-tent, value, cost, quality, or performance

statistical quality control (SQC) and statistical process control (SPC) SQC is the use of statistical tools and methods to determine the quality of a product or service. SPC is the use of SQC to establish boundaries that determine if a process is in control (predictable) or out of control (unpredictable)

stereotypes Predetermined beliefs about a group of people

storming stage The phase of team development characterized by disagreement and conflict as individual roles and personalities emerge

strategic business units (SBUs) Autonomous businesses with their own identities but operating within the framework of one organization

strategic management A responsibility of top management, it defines the firm's position, formulates strategies and guides the execution of long-term organizational functions and processes

strategic plan Contains the answers to who, what, when, where, how and how much for achieving strategic goals—long-term, companywide goals established by top management

strategy A course of action created to achieve a long-term goal

strategy formulation The planning and decision making that goes into developing the company's strategic goals and plans, including assessing the environments, analyzing core competencies and creating goals and plans

strategy implementation The means associated with executing the strategic plan. These include creating teams, adapting new technologies, focusing on processes rather than functions, facilitating communications, offering incentives and making structural changes

stress The physiological and psychological reaction of the body as a result of demands made on it

stretch goals Goal that requires great leaps forward on such measures as product development time, return on investment, sales growth, quality improvement, and reduction of manufacturing cycle times

subculture A unit within an organization that is based on the shared values, norms and beliefs of its members

superordinate objective An objective that overshadows personal interests, to which a manager can appeal as a strategy for resolving conflict

supplier relationship management (SRM) An information system that quantifies and manages relationships with suppliers; SRM involves consolidating and classifying procurement data to provide an understanding of supplier relationships and developing procurement strategies

supply-chain management Includes managing supply and demand, sourcing raw materials and parts, manufacturing and assembly, warehousing and inventory tracking, order entry and order management, distribution across all channels and delivery to the customer

sustainable communities Healthy, livable communities effectively using resources—economic, social and environmental—to meet today's community needs while ensuring that these resources are available to meet the community's future needs.

symptom Signals that something is wrong and draws the manager's attention to finding the cause—that is, the problem

synergy The increased effectiveness that results from combined action or cooperation

system A set of interrelated parts that work together to achieve stated goals or to function according to a plan or design

systems school The theory that an organization comprises various parts (subsystems) that must per-form tasks necessary for the survival and proper functioning of the system as a whole

T

tactic A course of action designed to achieve a short-term goal—an objective

tactical plan Developed by middle managers, this plan has more details, shorter time frames, and narrower scopes than a strategic plan; it usually spans one year or less

tariff A tax placed on imported goods to make them more expensive and thus less competitive in order to protect domestic producers

task force A horizontal team composed of employees from different departments designed to accomplish a limited number of objectives and existing only until it has met the objectives

team A group of two or more people who interact regularly and coordinate their work to accomplish a common objective

team structure An organizational design that places separate functions or processes into a group according to one overall objective

technical skills The abilities to use the processes, practices, techniques and tools of the specialty area a manager supervises

technological forces The combined effects of processes, materials, knowledge, and other discoveries resulting from research and development activities

technology The knowledge, machinery, work procedures and materials that transform the inputs into outputs

technology The practical application of knowledge

telecommuting The partial or total substitution of telecommunications technology (such as computers, mobile phones, fax machines, and the Internet) for the trip to and from the primary workplace. Simply put, it's moving the work to the workers, instead of the workers to work

telework Remote work in which corporate employees work outside the office at least two days a week

test Any criterion or performance measure used as a basis for an employment decision

theory Part of an art or science that attempts to explain the relationships between and among its underlying principles

Theory X A philosophy of management with a negative perception of subordinates' potential for and attitudes toward work

Theory Y A philosophy of management with a positive perception of subordinates' potential for and attitudes toward work

three-step approach a technique of behavior modification to change attitudes in lasting ways; it consists of three phases: unfreezing, change and refreezing

top management The chief executive officer (CEO) and/or president and his, her, or their immediate subordinates, usually called vice presidents

total quality management (TQM) "A strategy for continuously improving performance at every level, and in all areas of responsibility"

training Giving employees the knowledge, skills, and attitudes needed to perform their jobs

transaction processing system (TPS) A computer-based information system of a company's routine business activities

transactional processing A computer procedure in which data are received about a company's ongoing operations and entered into data banks as each transaction occurs

transfer Moving an employee to a job with similar levels of status, compensation and responsibility

tunnel vision Having a narrow viewpoint

U

understanding The situation that exists when all senders and receivers agree about the meaning and intent of a message

unity of command The organizing principle that states that each person within an organization should take orders from and report to only one person

unity of direction The establishment of one authority figure for each designated task of the organization

V

variable inspection A product control technique that involves taking measurements to determine how much an item varies from standards and, therefore, whether it will be accepted or rejected

vertical team A team composed of a manager and subordinates

virtual team A team where members primarily interact electronically because they are physically separated (by time and/or space)

vision A clear statement as to where an organization wants to be in the future

Vroom and Yetton decision tree A series of questions that guide the manager to the appropriate option

W

whistle-blower Individual who takes action to inform bosses, the media or government agencies about unethical or illegal practices within an organization

work team A team composed of multi-skilled workers that does all the tasks previously done by individual members in a functional department or departments

work-in-process inventory Inventory consisting of materials and parts that have begun moving through the production process but are not yet assembled into a completed product

Index

Page numbers with an *"f"* indicate a figure.

COMPANY/BRAND INDEX

SUBJECT INDEX

Chapter	Management in Action	Quality Management	Managing Social Media
1	Skills for the 21st Century	The Socratic Method	Customer Relationship Managemen
2	Openness to Change	Kaizen's American Roots	The Networked Enterprise
3	Learning Style	The Scientific Method	Knowledge Management (KM)
4	Strategic Thinking	Hoshin Planning and MBO	Bring Your Own Device (BYOD)
5	Decision Making	Five Why Analysis	Breakthrough Business Models
6	Morale-Building	TQM Foundation	Social Media Ethics Terms
7	Power	Lean Defined	Monitoring Corporate Image
8	Organizational Culture	Changing Roles of Supervisors and Production Personnel	Social Media
9	Intrapreneur/Entrepreneur	Lean Factories Avoid Layoffs	Recruiting with LinkedIn
10	Communicating Skills	Communication Plan	Social Media for Communications
11	Empowerment	Changing Roles	Tech Savvy Millennials
12	Leadership	Mutual Trust	Open Leadership
13	Team Dynamics	NASA Teambuilding	Crowdsourcing
14	Computer Literacy	Flowcharting	Mobile Devices
15	Life Balance	JIT	Metrics for Social Media
Appendix A	Productivity	Value Added	Learning Communities

CPSIA information can be obtained
at www.ICGtesting.com
Printed in the USA
LVOW02*0750190716
496813LV00001B/1/P